ANNOTATED INSTRUCTOR'S EDITION **15e**

D0509189

Becoming a
MASTER STUDENT

Dave Ellis

Doug Toft
Contributing Editor

CENGAGE
Learning®

Australia • Brazil • Canada • Mexico • Singapore • Spain • United Kingdom • United States

Copyright © 2015 Cengage Learning. All Rights Reserved. May not be scanned, copied or duplicated, or posted to a publicly accessible website, in whole or in part.

CENGAGE
Learning

Becoming a Master Student, Fifteenth Edition

Ellis

Product Director: Annie Todd

Senior Product Manager: Shani Fisher

Senior Content Developer: Marita Sermolins

Associate Content Developer: Elizabeth Rice

Product Assistant: Kayla Gagne

Senior Media Developer: Amy Gibbons

Marketing Manager: Lydia LeStar

Content Project Manager: Jill Quinn

Senior Art Director: Pam Galbreath

Manufacturing Planner: Sandee Milewski

Rights Acquisition Specialist: Shalice
    Shah-Caldwell

Production Service: MPS Limited

Text and Cover Designer: Irene Morris

Cover Image:
    Open Book: © Microzoa/Stone/Getty Images;
    Graduating Students: © Robert Churchill/
    the Agency Collection/Getty Images; iPad Frame:
    © Alberto Masnovo/Fotolia

Compositor: MPS Limited

© 2015, 2013, 2011 Cengage Learning

ALL RIGHTS RESERVED. No part of this work covered by the copyright herein may be reproduced, transmitted, stored, or used in any form or by any means graphic, electronic, or mechanical, including but not limited to photocopying, recording, scanning, digitizing, taping, web distribution, information networks, or information storage and retrieval systems, except as permitted under Section 107 or 108 of the 1976 United States Copyright Act, without the prior written permission of the publisher.

For product information and technology assistance, contact us at
Cengage Learning Customer & Sales Support, 1-800-354-9706

For permission to use material from this text or product, submit all requests online at **www.cengage.com/permissions**.
Further permissions questions can be emailed to
permissionrequest@cengage.com.

Library of Congress Control Number: 2013949207
Student Edition:
ISBN-13: 978-1-285-19389-2
ISBN-10: 1-285-19389-X

Annotated Instructor's Edition:
ISBN-13: 978-1-285-43717-0
ISBN-10: 1-285-43717-9

Cengage Learning
200 First Stamford Place, 4th Floor
Stamford, CT 06902
USA

Cengage Learning is a leading provider of customized learning solutions with office locations around the globe, including Singapore, the United Kingdom, Australia, Mexico, Brazil and Japan. Locate your local office at **international.cengage.com/region**.

Cengage Learning products are represented in Canada by Nelson Education, Ltd.

For your course and learning solutions, visit **www.cengage.com**.
Purchase any of our products at your local college store or at our preferred online store **www.cengagebrain.com**.
Instructors: Please visit **login.cengage.com** and log in to access instructor-specific resources.

Printed in the United States of America
1 2 3 4 5 6 7 17 16 15 14

Copyright ©2015 Cengage Learning. All Rights Reserved. May not be scanned, copied or duplicated, or posted to a publicly accessible website, in whole or in part.

BRIEF CONTENTS

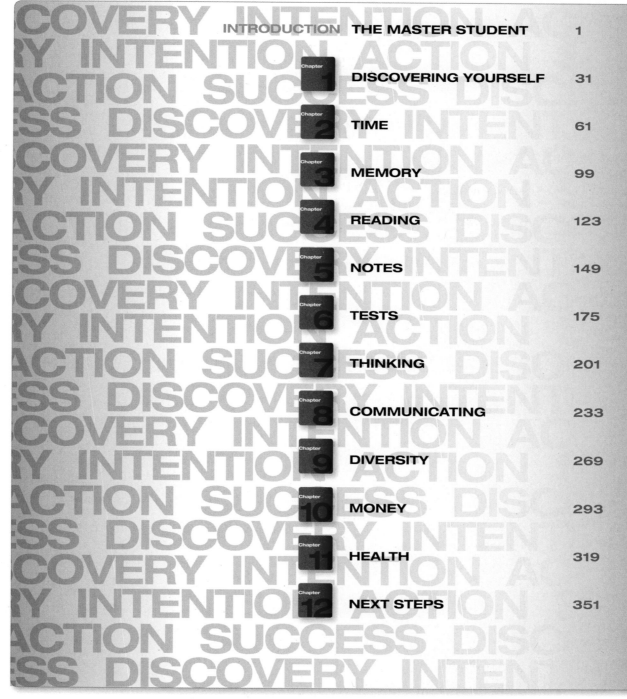

Copyright © 2015 Cengage Learning. All Rights Reserved. May not be scanned, copied or duplicated, or posted to a publicly accessible website, in whole or in part.

Copyright © 2015 Cengage Learning. All Rights Reserved. May not be scanned, copied or duplicated, or posted to a publicly accessible website, in whole or in part. / Photo Credit: Stockbyte/Getty Images. Second Photo: John Lund/Stone/Getty Images. Third Photo: Oliver Cleve/Getty Images. Fourth Photo: © Maciej Oleksy/Shutterstock.com.

CONTENTS

Introduction

THE MASTER STUDENT

What's New? Here's A Sampling ...*

New articles: "The master student process—Discovery," "The master student process—Intention," "The master student process—Action," and "Keep the process alive" clearly define the process of learning about yourself and how to commit to intentions that will yield action and changes in your life

New article: "Leading the way—Succeeding as a first-generation student"

New article: "Developing a professional work ethic"

*For a full listing of all revisions, please see page AIE-xxxiv, which lists all major chapter changes.

Chapter 1 — DISCOVERING YOURSELF

What's New? Here's A Sampling ...*

New Journal Entry 5: "Get back to the big picture about learning styles"
New article: "Six paths to more powerful thinking" prepares students to work through the Practicing Critical Thinking exercises

32	**POWER PROCESS:** Ideas are tools
33	First Step: Truth is a key to mastery
35	**Exercise 5:** Taking the first step
36	**Exercise 6:** The Discovery Wheel
40	**Skills Snapshot**
41	Learning styles: Discovering how you learn
42	*Journal Entry 3:* Prepare for the Learning Style Inventory (LSI)
42	Directions for completing the Learning Style Inventory
LSI-1	Learning Style Inventory
LSI-2	Taking the next steps
LSI-3	Scoring your inventory
LSI-5	Learning Style Graph
LSI-6	Interpreting your Learning Style Graph
LSI-7	Developing all four modes of learning
LSI-8	Balancing your preferences
43	Using your learning style profile to succeed
47	Claim your multiple intelligences
47	**Exercise 7:** Develop your multiple intelligences
50	Learning by seeing, hearing, and moving: The VAK system
53	*Journal Entry 4:* Choosing your purpose
54	*Journal Entry 5:* Get back to the big picture about learning styles
55	Six paths to more powerful thinking
57	**Practicing Critical Thinking 1**
57	Master Student Profiles
58	**Master Student Profile:** Teresa Amabile
59	**Quiz**
60	**Skills Snapshot**

Chapter 2 — TIME

What's New? Here's A Sampling ...*

New Journal Entry 6: "Discover the impact of technology on your time and attention"
New article: "Create a work flow that works" provides suggestions for how to successfully plan taking projects from start to finish
New article: "There's an app for that: Using technology for time management"

62	**POWER PROCESS:** Be here now
63	You've got the time
64	Make choices about multitasking
65	**Exercise 8:** The Time Monitor
69	*Journal Entry 6:* Discover the impact of technology on your time
70	Define your values
71	Setting and achieving goals
72	**Exercise 9:** Create a lifeline
73	**Exercise 10:** Get real with your goals
74	The ABC daily to-do list
76	Planning sets you free
78	**Exercise 11:** Master monthly calendar
81	Break it down, get it done: Using a long-term planner
84	Create a work flow that works
85	There's an app for that: Using technology for time management
86	Stop procrastination now
87	The 7-step antiprocrastination plan
88	**Practicing Critical Thinking 2**
89	25 ways to get the most out of now
91	Setting limits on screen time
94	Beyond time management: Stay focused on what matters
95	*Journal Entry 7:* Create a not-to-do list
96	**Master Student Profile:** Sampson Davis
97	**Quiz**
98	**Skills Snapshot**

*For a full listing of all revisions, please see page AIE-xxxiv, which lists all major chapter changes.

Copyright © 2015 Cengage Learning. All Rights Reserved. May not be scanned, copied or duplicated, or posted to a publicly accessible website, in whole or in part. / Photo Credit: © Andresr/Shutterstock.com. Second Photo: Fotosearch/Getty Images. Third Photo: Daniel Grill/JGI/JGI/Blend Images/Getty Images.

Copyright © 2015 Cengage Learning. All Rights Reserved. May not be scanned, copied or duplicated, or posted to a publicly accessible website, in whole or in part. / Photo Credit: DrAfter123/Vetta/Getty Images. Second Photo: Masterfile. Third Photo: Chris Pancewicz / Alamy.

Chapter 3 · MEMORY

What's New? Here's A Sampling ...*

New article: "Your memory and your brain—6 key principles" focuses on the stages of the memory process and strategies for making the most of each stage

New article: "Retool your memory" gives suggestions for how to use technology to support memory

New Master Student Profile of Sonia Sotomayor

Chapter 4 · READING

What's New? Here's A Sampling ...*

New article: "Extending Muscle Reading to Web pages and ebooks"

New sidebar: "Take Muscle Reading to work" relates Muscle Reading concepts to applicable workplace situations where reading is necessary

New Journal Entry 11: "Reflect on your online reading habits"

*For a full listing of all revisions, please see page AIE-xxxiv, which lists all major chapter changes.

Copyright © 2015 Cengage Learning. All Rights Reserved. May not be scanned, copied or duplicated, or posted to a publicly accessible website, in whole or in part. | Photo Credit: © Paula kc/Shutterstock.com. Second Photo: Yellow Dog Productions/Lifesize/Getty Images. Third Photo: © Chad McDermott/Shutterstock.com.

Chapter 5 — NOTES

What's New? Here's A Sampling ...*

New article: "Note-taking 2.0" with suggestions for how to use several of the note-taking applications available on the Web, smartphones, and tablets

New Master Student Profile of Richard Blanco

Chapter 6 — TESTS

What's New? Here's A Sampling ...*

Revised article: "What to do before the test" focuses more on study techniques for rehearsal and practice

Revised article: "Cooperative learning: Studying in groups" expands on how the important cooperative concepts apply to workplace situations

*For a full listing of all revisions, please see page AIE-xxxiv, which lists all major chapter changes.

Copyright © 2015 Cengage Learning. All Rights Reserved. May not be scanned, copied or duplicated, or posted to a publicly accessible website, in whole or in part./ Photo Credit: ©nomchaj/ShutterStock.com; Second Photo: Garry Batte/Digital Vision/Getty Images; Third Photo: Hannele Lahti/National Geographic/Getty Images; Fourth Photo: kutay tanir/E+/Getty Images; Fifth Photo: Andrew Murray/Flickr/Getty Images.

Chapter 7 **THINKING**

What's New? Here's A Sampling ...*

New Power Process: "Embrace the new" focuses on how being open to new experiences and adaptable to changes are key qualities of a master student

New Exercise 20: "Critical thinking scenarios" challenges students to put critical thinking skills into action by evaluating three scenarios likely familiar to them

New Journal Entries 16 and 17: "Use divergent thinking to brainstorm goals" and "Use convergent thinking to plan habits" help students put thinking skills to use

*For a full listing of all revisions, please see page AIE-xxxiv, which lists all major chapter changes.

What's New? Here's A Sampling ...*

Revised article: "Communicating in teams—Getting things done as a group"

New sidebar: "Using technology to collaborate" provides details for various online solutions that promote and support group work

New Master Student Profile of Salman Khan

*For a full listing of all revisions, please see page AIE-xxxiv, which lists all major chapter changes.

Copyright © 2015 Cengage Learning. All Rights Reserved. May not be scanned, copied or duplicated, or posted to a publicly accessible website, in whole or in part. / Photo Credit: Erie Pelaez/Stone+/Getty Images. Second Photo: © savageultralight/ShutterStock.com. / Third Photo: © iStockphoto.com/DNY59. Fifth Photo: © Bernhard Lang/Getty Images.

Chapter 9

DIVERSITY

Chapter 10

MONEY

What's New? Here's A Sampling ...*

New sidebar: "Prevent cyberbullying" defines cyberbullying and ways to address instances of it

Revised Practicing Critical Thinking 9: Helps students work through the levels of critical thinking by combining them and taking them in a different sequence as they think about discrimination

What's New? Here's A Sampling ...*

New article: "Use tools to tame your money" examines the ways students can use technology to track and control their budgets

Revised Practicing Critical Thinking 10

New Master Student Profile of Sara Blakely

Copyright © 2015 Cengage Learning. All Rights Reserved. May not be scanned, copied or duplicated, or posted to a publicly accessible website, in whole or in part. / Photo Credit: Jeff Hunter/Getty Images. Second Photo: Brand New Images/Lifesize/Getty Images. Third Photo: © zimmytws/Shutterstock.com.

*For a full listing of all revisions, please see page AIE-xxxiv, which lists all major chapter changes.

What's New? Here's A Sampling ...*

New Journal Entry 24: "Choose your stress management strategies"

New Journal Entry 25: "Reflect on your experience with asking for help"

*For a full listing of all revisions, please see page AIE-xxxiv, which lists all major chapter changes.

Copyright © 2015 Cengage Learning. All Rights Reserved. May not be scanned, copied or duplicated, or posted to a publicly accessible website, in whole or in part. / Photo Credit: Photodisc/Fotosearch-Second-Photos © joyfull/Shutterstock. Third Photo: Masterfile. Fourth Photo: © iStockphoto.com/RLimages.

Copyright © 2015 Cengage Learning. All Rights Reserved. May not be scanned, copied or duplicated, or posted to a publicly accessible website, in whole or in part. / Photo Credit: Katie Edwards/Ikon Images/Getty Images. Second Photo: Alex Slobodkin/E+/Getty Images. Third Photo: ©iStockphoto.com/Eolla. Fourth Photo: © Santiago Cornejo/Shutterstock.com. Fifth Photo: © iStockphoto.com/Sergey Mostovoy.

Chapter 12

NEXT STEPS

What's New? Here's A Sampling ...*

New Power Process: "Persist" emphasizes that the road to graduation is often unglamorous and necessitates persistence and resilience

New Journal Entry 26: "Use the 'five Cs' to develop transferable skills" asks students to consider the categories of skills employers most look for in potential employees—creative thinking, critical thinking, communication, collaboration, and character

New article: "Taking the road to graduation" shows how reexamining academic goals and study strategies, connecting with services and others on campus, and remaining motivated can aid in persisting until graduation

*For a full listing of all revisions, please see page AIE-xxxiv, which lists all major chapter changes.

STUDENTS ARE EMBARKING ON A NEW JOURNEY IN COLLEGE—

Becoming a Master Student is here to help them

EMBRACE THE NEW

What Master Instructors are saying...

❝*Becoming a Master Student is the quintessential tool for students wishing to improve their learning skills. It's friendly, fun, and imaginative. It befriends the reader with a 'let me put my arm around you and show you the way' kind of attitude. The book lets students know that their struggles and failures are common struggles and failures. In spite of what they've done before, they can improve if they practice these suggestions.*❞

—*Laura Bazan, Central Piedmont Community College*

❝*Becoming a Master Student addresses the whole student as a person, not just as a student, to help them focus their learning for life beyond the classroom.*❞

—*Karey Pharris, Pikes Peak Community College*

❝*I have looked over other books that try to deliver what this one delivers, and none of them have the combination and presentation of materials put together as well as this one.... I still find new angles on traditional concepts that I can help students grasp more effectively. I believe the organization and presentation of ideas and concepts in this text helps me discover these new angles or perspectives on concepts and ideas.*❞

—*Anthony Lowman, Collins College*

What Master Students are saying...

❝*Becoming a Master Student is very helpful, even when you think it wouldn't be. It has many tips and examples in it that I would have never thought of before, and those tips have helped me become more confident.*❞

—*Shelby Ellis, Hinds Community College*

❝*There was not a chapter in the Becoming a Master Student book that I couldn't utilize in my own life.*❞

—*Akeem Ruhman Hall, Nashville State Community College*

❝*Becoming a Master Student is a very good experience and offers you many different techniques that will help you through school and even your life experiences. These techniques that you learn can be used every day no matter what you are doing.*❞

—*Christina Rodgers, Hinds Community College*

AIE-xv

Copyright © 2015 Cengage Learning. All Rights Reserved. May not be scanned, copied or duplicated, or posted to a publicly accessible website, in whole or in part. / Photo Credit: Thinkstock/Comstock Images/Getty Images. Second Photo: Stockbyte/Getty Images. Third Photo: © savageultralight/ShutterStock.com.

Becoming a Master Student is
EMBRACING TECHNOLOGY
with MindTap™

MindTap is a fully online, highly personalized learning experience built upon *Becoming a Master Student*. MindTap combines student learning tools—readings, multimedia, activities, and assessments—into a singular Learning Path that guides students through their course. Instructors personalize the experience by customizing authoritative Cengage Learning content and learning tools with their own content in the Learning Path via apps that integrate into the MindTap framework.

LEARNING PATH

The MindTap experience begins with the Learning Path, which lists pre-reading and post-reading resources for each unit, including a Learning Outcomes video and video-based Engagement and Reflection activities tied to master student qualities and Power Process topics. Interactive versions of the chapter activities may be accessed directly from within the reading itself. This intuitive navigator guides students to mastery of the subject matter and provides instant access to the resources they need along the way. With MindTap, you can add content to the Learning Path via apps so you can personalize your course.

APLIA

Aplia exercises are integrated directly into the Learning Path so that students can seamlessly practice chapter concepts. Engaging, interactive assignments ensure that students meet learning objectives, and automatically graded assignments offer immediate and constructive feedback. The problems and activities in Aplia for *Becoming a Master Student* teach students to develop the critical skills that they need to earn better grades, discover their potential, and chart a course for the future.

MINDTAP READER

The MindTap Reader is more than a digital version of a textbook. It is an interactive learning resource that was built from the ground up to create a digital reading experience based on how students assimilate information in an online environment. The robust functionality of the MindTap Reader allows learners to make notes, highlight text, and even find a definition right from the page.

COMPLETELY PERSONAL

Personalizing MindTap is easy! Instructors can change due dates, rename course sections, and remove activities they don't need. You can add videos, flashcards, Web links, and your own content to foster immediacy and contextual relevancy. What an advantage for capitalizing on today's teachable moments!

MINDAPPS

Each MindTap course is enriched through a comprehensive library of learning apps, called MindApps.

Copyright © 2015 Cengage Learning. All Rights Reserved. May not be scanned, copied or duplicated, or posted to a publicly accessible website, in whole or in part.

Copyright © 2015 Cengage Learning. All Rights Reserved. May not be scanned, copied or duplicated, or posted to a publicly accessible website, in whole or in part.

What Master Instructors are saying...

❝ *MindTap is the tool of the future for engaging students. With Cengage Learning, the future is here today.* ❞

—*R. Scott Domowicz, Director of Curriculum & Faculty Development, Erie Institute of Technology*

❝ *I love the mind mapping approach [used for the Learning Outcomes videos]. This is what we teach for the visual learners, and for all learners to help aid memory.* ❞

—*Annette McCreedy, Nashville State Community College*

❝ *I really like the usage of mind maps. Not only do they illustrate the subject at hand, but they reinforce the note-taking concept from Chapter 5.* ❞

—*Kanya Allen, Hopkinsville Community College*

Becoming a Master Student
EMBRACES THE NEW WITH...
TWO NEW POWER PROCESSES

The Power Process articles—short, unique motivational articles designed to emphasize academic success in terms of life skills and behaviors—appear at the beginning of each chapter to motivate students and illustrate how simple behaviors can lead to great changes and successes in academics, work, and life. Power Processes "Embrace the new" (Chapter 7) and "Persist" (Chapter 12) help motivate students to unleash their hidden potential by being open to new things that may be unfamiliar and honing their abilities to be patient and persistent.

◄ From **"Embrace the new"**: "What's new is often going to stick around anyway. You have two basic options: Resist it. Or embrace it. The former is a recipe for frustration. The latter offers a fresh possibility in every moment."

◄ From **"Persist"**: "Master students harness their critical thinking skills to cut through all the hype. They know that they are in the game for the long haul and that there are no quick fixes. They know that getting a degree is like training for a marathon. They remember that every class attended and every assignment completed is one small win on the way to a big victory."

What **Master Instructors** are saying...

❝ *This Power Process ["Persist"] reminds students that they are in it for the long haul. There are no quick fixes. But the payoff can be as big as the effort put into it. This is realistic and very encouraging.* ❞

—*Ronda Jacobs, College of Southern Maryland*

❝ *The Power Processes are my favorite feature in* Becoming a Master Student. *They can be applied to all life situations. They're great for "teachable moments" during the semester as well. I've heard students tell their classmates to "Be here now" when they were engaged in side conversations or to apply "I create it all" when they made excuses for not completing a homework assignment.* ❞

—*Debbie Warfield, Seminole Community College*

Copyright © 2015 Cengage Learning. All Rights Reserved. May not be scanned, copied or duplicated, or posted to a publicly accessible website, in whole or in part.

MASTER STUDENT
PROFILE
SONIA SOTOMAYOR

(1964–) Appointed an associate justice of the United States Supreme Court in 2009—the third woman and first Hispanic to serve in that role

When the two big boxes labeled *Encyclopaedia Britannica* arrived, it was Christmas come early. Junior and I sat on the floor surrounded by piles of books like explorers at the base of Everest. Each of the twenty-four volumes was a doorstop, the kind of book you'd expect to see in a library, never in someone's home and certainly not twenty-four of them, including a whole separate book just for the index! As I turned the densely set onionskin pages at random, I found myself wandering the world's geography, pondering molecules like daisy chains, marveling at the physiology of the eye. . . .

There was one more reason, beyond the pleasure of reading, the influence of English, and my Mother's various interventions, that I finally started to thrive at school. Mrs. Reilly, our fifth-grade teacher, unleashed my competitive spirit. She would put up a gold star on the blackboard each time a student did something really well, and I was a sucker for those gold stars! I was determined to collect as many as I could. After the first A's began

Sonia Sotomayor is willing to be uncomfortable.

You can go beyond your comfort zone by taking the initiative to approach people.

It was then, in Mrs. Reilly's class, under the allure of those gold stars, that I did something very unusual for a child, though it seemed like common sense to me at the time. I decided to approach one of the smartest girls in the class and ask her how to study. Donna Renella looked suprised, maybe even flattered. In any case, she generously divulged her technique: how, while she was reading, she underlined important facts and took notes to condense information into smaller bits that were easier to remember; how, the night before a test, she would reread the relevant chapter. Obvious things once you've learned them, but at the time deriving them on my own would have been like trying to invent the wheel.

NEW MASTER STUDENT PROFILES

Master Student Profiles in every chapter are brief articles about a real person who encompasses master student qualities. Six new Master Student Profiles introduce students to motivating, modern figures that have sharpened their master student qualities to succeed: Teresa Amabile (Chapter 1), Sonia Sotomayor (Chapter 3), Richard Blanco (Chapter 5), Irshad Manji (Chapter 7), Salman Khan (Chapter 8), Chimamanda Adichie (Chapter 9), and Sara Blakely (Chapter 10).

What Master Instructors are saying...

The profiles demonstrate how other individuals excelled and allowed themselves to become risk takers, critical/analytical thinkers, and problem solvers. Students are able to identify with the persons who are profiled.

—*Patricia Sheriff-Taylor, Jackson State University*

INTEGRATED TECHNOLOGY COVERAGE

Technology usage is highlighted throughout all the chapters, giving students a variety of suggestions to navigate the plethora of apps and Web resources that are available today. "There's an app for that—Using technology for time management" (Chapter 2), "Retool your memory" (Chapter 3), "Extending Muscle Reading to Web pages and ebooks" (Chapter 4), "Note-taking 2.0" (Chapter 5), "Using tools to tame your money life" (Chapter 10), and "Tools for lifelong learning" (Chapter 12) are all examples of how technology has been seamlessly interwoven into key study skills topics.

A RENEWED EMPHASIS ON DISCOVERY AND INTENTION JOURNAL SYSTEM

In the Introduction, the Discovery and Intention Journal System explanations have been redesigned as part of the master student process. Four new articles address the steps and outcomes of the Discovery and Intention Journal System: "The master student process—Discovery", "The master student process—Intention", "The master student process—Action", and "Keep the process alive." Also, many new journal entries have been added throughout the chapters to reinforce the importance of discovery, intention, and action. Journal entry topics include Declare your intention to change a habit (Introduction), Discover the impact of technology on your time and attention (Chapter 2), Create a not-to-do list (Chapter 2), Reflect on the care and feeding of your brain (Chapter 3), Reflect on your online reading habits (Chapter 4), Reflect on your stress management strategies (Chapter 11), and Celebrate your gains, clarify your intentions (Chapter 12).

What Master Instructors are saying...

Many students have reported in their evaluations the importance of the journal system, allowing them to reflect on what they have learned and then make a commitment to take action.

—*Debbie Warfield, Seminole Community College*

What Master Students are saying...

You will change profoundly and, even if you never apply any of the suggestions this book gives you, gain understanding about yourself that may just restore your confidence in tackling college.

—*Jonathan Steinke, Mesa Community College*

AIE-xix

Copyright © 2015 Cengage Learning. All Rights Reserved. May not be scanned, copied or duplicated, or posted to a publicly accessible website, in whole or in part.

Becoming a Master Student is *both* a

& TEXTBOOK WORKBOOK

SELF-ASSESSMENTS *GET STUDENTS* FOCUSING *ON* METACOGNITION

Discovery Wheel. The most widely recognized feature of *Becoming a Master Student*, the Discovery Wheel gets students thinking about the kind of student they are and the kind of student that they want to become. Assigned at the outset of the course, this exercise helps students assess their current strengths and weaknesses in different areas of student success. Students are reminded of this when they complete the Discovery Wheel again, at the end of the textbook, to measure their growth.

What Master Instructors are saying...

❝ *The Discovery Wheel is brilliant because it allows the students to quickly identify where they may be weak and directs them to the chapter that can assist them.* **❞**

—*Chris Douse, Indiana University–Purdue University Fort Wayne*

Exercises. Only action makes this book work. Student exercises found throughout the chapters encourage active learning and help develop critical thinking. All of the student exercises, Journal Entries, and quizzes can be completed directly in the MindTap.

Skills Snapshot. The Skills Snapshot activity ends each chapter and asks students to revisit their initial Discovery Wheel answers, link them to what they've learned about the chapter skill, and apply what they've learned to the discovery, intention, and action process.

What Master Instructors are saying...

❝ *I like assigning and collecting the Skills Snapshot exercises at the end of each chapter. When I read them I can assess the behavior changes and progress my students are making.* **❞**

—*Dean Mancina, Golden West College*

Copyright © 2015 Cengage Learning. All Rights Reserved. May not be scanned, copied or duplicated, or posted to a publicly accessible website, in whole or in part.

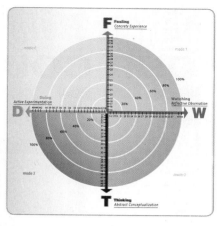

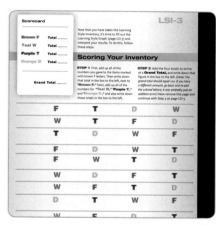

The Learning Style Inventory (LSI). People are fascinated by why they do what they do—and students are no exception. Students can take the Kolb Learning Style Inventory (LSI) in Chapter 1 to increase their self-awareness as learners. The LSI, which is printed on carbonless paper for easy scoring and is also available online, helps students make sense of what they're experiencing in college. Following the LSI, students get clear explanations of what their test results mean about how they learn. Students can opt to complete an online version of the LSI in the MindTap.

The Discovery and Intention Journal Entry system. These journal prompts ask students to explain the whys, whats, and hows of applying the chapter skills to themselves in writing, and they offer instructors a more specific and measurable form of journal writing than any other text. Students have an opportunity to reflect on their discoveries while setting a plan for action by writing their intentions.

What Master Instructors are saying...

❝Becoming a Master Student gives students the knowledge necessary in the different areas that will help them be successful in college and in life, as well as the opportunity to reflect on where they are now and where they want to be. The intention statements encourage them to take the next step.❞

—Dana Dildine, Eastern New Mexico University–Ruidoso Branch

What Master Students are saying...

❝Read this book and have it handy. It's a great resource to go to when you need a pick-me-up of where to start again.❞

—Lauren Plagens, South Plains College

Copyright © 2015 Cengage Learning. All Rights Reserved. May not be scanned, copied or duplicated, or posted to a publicly accessible website, in whole or in part.

Instructor Resources Help
KEEP YOUR COURSE
FRESH

What **Master Instructors** are saying...

❝ *We have kept using* Becoming a Master Student *because of the instructor support resources.* ❞

—*Tim Cook, Clark College*

❝ *The AIE offers a multitude of suggestions to integrate in classes. The Instructor Companion Site has everything needed to conduct a successful class including a test bank. Faculty support is incredible with* Becoming a Master Student. *Peer-to-Peer Faculty consultants are truly committed to student success and are dedicated to assist us in course implementation, planning as well as provide training opportunities both on and off campus.* ❞

—*Debbie Warfield, Seminole Community College*

MINDTAP FOR BECOMING A MASTER STUDENT

MindTap is a fully online, highly personalized learning experience built upon Cengage Learning content. MindTap combines student learning tools—readings, multimedia, activities, and assessments—into a singular Learning Path that guides students through their course. Instructors personalize the experience by customizing authoritative Cengage Learning content and learning tools with their own content in the Learning Path via apps that integrate into the MindTap framework. MindTap is more than an eBook, homework solution, digital supplement, resource center Web site, course delivery platform, or Learning Management System. It is the first in a new category—the personal learning experience. Students can complete assignments, read text materials, watch videos, and complete Aplia homework, all in one place.

INSTRUCTOR COMPANION SITE

Accessible via **login.cengage.com**, the Instructor Companion Site is a one-stop resource for new and experienced instructors. Test banks, PowerPoint presentations, and sample syllabi are all available. Also featured is the Online Course Manual, which includes guidance for developing and leading your course. The manual features lecture ideas, teaching strategies, group activity suggestions, and many other useful resources to help you streamline your course preparation.

Copyright © 2015 Cengage Learning. All Rights Reserved. May not be scanned, copied or duplicated, or posted to a publicly accessible website, in whole or in part.

DISCOVERY WHEEL (ISBN 9781285437194)

A stand-alone version of the Discovery Wheel is available so students can respond and hand in their results to you directly. Or consider using this Discovery Wheel as a handout to use in trainings or workshops with students and faculty.

COLLEGE SUCCESS PLANNER

Package *Becoming a Master Student* with this 18-month, week-at-a-glance academic planner. The College Success Planner assists students in making the best use of their time both on and off campus and includes additional reading about key learning strategies and life skills for success in college. Ask your Cengage Learning sales representative for more details.

COLLEGE SUCCESS FACTORS INDEX

Use the College Success Factors Index (CSFI) to measure and promote your student's success. Assess students at the start of your course in 10 key areas linked to college success. Identify at-risk students with early-alert reporting and support assessment results with text-specific remediation. Validate your college success program with a post-course assessment of your student's progress— and improve your institution's retention rates. For more information and a demo of CSFI, visit **www.cengage.com/success/csfi2.**

NOEL-LEVITZ COLLEGE STUDENT INVENTORY

The Retention Management System™ College Student Inventory (CSI from Noel-Levitz) is an early-alert, early-intervention program that identifies students with tendencies that contribute to dropping out of school. Cengage Learning offers you three assessment options that evaluate students on 19 different scales: Form A (194 items), Form B (100 items), or an online e-token (that provides access to either Form A, B, or C; 74 items).

THE MYERS-BRIGGS TYPE INDICATOR® (MBTI®) INSTRUMENT

MBTI is the most widely used personality inventory in history—and it is also available for packaging with *Becoming a Master Student*. Cengage Learning's exclusive partnership with CPP, publisher of the MBTI, now includes the MBTI Complete, an online version that is *complete* with interpretation. The MBTI can be used to enhance the instruction of topics such as learning styles, study skills, time management, communication skills, and conflict management. And even more resources are available for instructors to harness the power of this tool in the classroom—*16 Paths to Success* is available on the Instructor Companion Web site and includes four lesson plans for integrating the MBTI into class instruction, with accompanying PowerPoint presentations and activities. Load the MBTI Complete into your Single Sign On (SSO) dashboard **(www.cengage.com/sso)** by entering ISBN 9781111678975 in the search field or ask your Cengage Learning Consultant for a demonstration. The standard Form M self-scorable instrument is also still available for bundling with your textbook, using ISBN 0618120076.

CENGAGE LEARNING'S PEER-TO-PEER FACULTY DEVELOPMENT AND CONSULTING

Cengage Learning's Peer-to-Peer Faculty Development and Consulting team is dedicated to providing educators with proven instructional strategies and tools that lead to student success. For more than a decade, our consultants have helped faculty reach and engage first-year students by offering peer-to-peer consulting on curriculum and assessment, faculty training, and workshops. Our consultants are higher-education professionals who provide full-time support to help educators establish and maintain effective student success programs. They are available to help you to establish or improve your student success program and provide training on the implementation of our textbooks and technology. To connect with your Cengage Learning Peer-to-Peer Professional Educator visit **www.cengage.com/teamup.**

Copyright © 2015 Cengage Learning. All Rights Reserved. May not be scanned, copied or duplicated, or posted to a publicly accessible website, in whole or in part.

Acknowledgments

ADVISORY BOARD

Kanya Allen, Hopkinsville Community College

Elizabeth Fitzgerald, Kaplan University

Ronda Jacobs, College of Southern Maryland

Kimberly Koledoye, Houston Community College System

Joan Ledbetter, Georgia Highlands College

FACULTY REVIEWERS

Maria Gaylon, Jefferson Community & Technical College

Janet Griffiths, Mesalands Community College

Dale Haralson, Hinds Community College

Christina Hawkey, Arizona Western College

Loretta Holloway, Framingham State University

Juliet Laughlin, Central Piedmont Community College

Anthony Lowman, Collins College

Dean Mancina, Golden West College

Fernanda Ortiz, University of Arizona

Brian Schell, Lincoln College of Technology

Jane Speer, Alpena Community College

Jose Valdes, Institute of Business and Medical Careers

Copyright © 2015 Cengage Learning. All Rights Reserved. May not be scanned, copied or duplicated, or posted to a publicly accessible website, in whole or in part.

ANNOTATED INSTRUCTOR'S EDITION
TABLE OF CONTENTS

PART 1
RESOURCES AVAILABLE WITH *BECOMING A MASTER STUDENT*

PART 2
TEACHING WITH *BECOMING A MASTER STUDENT*

Chapter Annotations

Please note: Chapter annotations can be found on an insert that appears before the beginning of each of the main text chapters, starting with the Introduction.

Copyright © 2015 Cengage Learning. All Rights Reserved. May not be scanned, copied or duplicated, or posted to a publicly accessible website, in whole or in part.

CENGAGE brain.com

PART 1
RESOURCES AVAILABLE WITH *BECOMING A MASTER STUDENT*

LOGGING INTO *BECOMING A MASTER STUDENT* DIGITAL RESOURCES

INSTRUCTOR ACCESS

To access instructor digital resources, such as the Instructor Companion Site for *Becoming a Master Student*, follow these steps:

1. Visit **login.cengage.com.**

2. If you have not previously created a faculty account, choose the "Create a new Faculty Account," and follow the prompts.

3. If you have created a faculty account previously, log in with your e-mail address or user name and password.

4. Search for *Becoming a Master Student* to add the available additional digital resources to your bookshelf.

You will always need to return to **http://login.cengagebrain.com** and enter your e-mail address and password to sign in to access these resources. Use this space to write down your e-mail address or user name and password:

E-mail Address: _____

Password: _____

STUDENT ACCESS

Note: The log-in process for students is different from the way instructors access the resources.

To help your students navigate the log in process for the additional course materials, have them follow these steps:

1. To register a product using an access code, go to **http://cengagebrain.com**.

2. Register as a new user, or log in as an existing user if you already have an account with Cengage Learning or CengageBrain.com.
   Note: The access code is the student's password. Students will use the access code only once, when they first register their product. They will then be prompted to create a password to use each time they return to the site.

3. Follow the online prompts.

For future access, make sure students keep a record of their e-mail address, password, and course code.

To access digital resources, students will always need to return to **http://cengagebrain.com** and enter their e-mail address and password to sign in.

PROBLEMS WITH ACCESS CODES?

CONTACT CENGAGE LEARNING TECHNICAL SUPPORT:

CENGAGE Learning·

www.cengage.com/support
Phone 1-800-354-9706
Monday–Thursday
Friday

Featuring 24/7 Live Student Chat!

8:30 a.m. to 9:00 p.m. EST
8:30 a.m. to 6:00 p.m. EST

Copyright © 2015 Cengage Learning. All Rights Reserved. May not be scanned, copied or duplicated, or posted to a publicly accessible website, in whole or in part.

INSTRUCTOR COMPANION SITE
Is a One-Stop INSTRUCTOR'S RESOURCE

The Instructor Companion Site provides a one-stop teacher's resource to support your teaching of this course. Access to instructional materials, provided in electronic format, allows you to easily customize and then print, e-mail, or post materials to a Web site or course-management system. The Instructor Companion Site includes the following:

Online Course Manual. The online Course Manual serves as an invaluable reference for developing and teaching a College Success course with *Becoming a Master Student*. The Course Manual provides advice on general teaching topics such as preparing for classes, classroom management, grading, and communicating with students of various backgrounds. Specific strategies on getting the most out of various features in *Becoming a Master Student*, such as the Discovery Wheel and Learning Style Inventory are also available. Do a Course Manual reconnaissance to find ideas that you can use in your course right now.

- *Detailed Activity Guide.* Organized by chapter, this invaluable guide will help you make the most of the vast resources and additional content that accompanies *Becoming a Master Student*.
- *Sample Syllabi.* Instructors who have used *Becoming a Master Student* previously have generously shared a variety of sample syllabi showcasing the various ways a course can be structured around the textbook.
- *Best Practices.* Is your course feeling stale? Or perhaps you are new to teaching with *Becoming a Master Student* and want some tried-and-true ideas to use in your course. These Best Practices were collected as a way to simulate a free exchange of ideas among instructors. Find even more ideas for icebreakers, lecture ideas, classroom activities, and writing assignments.

PowerPoint Library. This master library of PowerPoint presentations makes it easy to find the right PowerPoint for you! In the library you will find PowerPoint slides for every chapter as well as every Power Process article covered in the book. All PowerPoint slides are downloadable and customizable to fit your needs.

- *Chapter PowerPoints:* Available for each chapter, these PowerPoints highlight the chapter's main points. Visually engaging and interactive, download these PowerPoints and customize them as you wish for your course.
- *Power Process PowerPoints:* Using the same concept as the Chapter PowerPoints these presentations cover the main points of the Power Process articles. Each chapter features group activities to practice and reinforce Power Process skills.

Master Teachers in Action videos. The Master Teachers in Action videos provide you with an inside look at how *Becoming a Master Student* is used by professors, including information on their favorite parts and how specific articles and activities from the text prepare students for achieving success. Hear from Dave Ellis himself and other instructors about what works for them when teaching the Learning Style Assessment and the Discovery Wheel.

Test Banks. These customizable, text-specific content quizzes are a great way to test student's knowledge and understanding of the text. Cengage Learning testing powered by Cognero is an online system that allows you to create tests from school, home, the coffee shop—anywhere with Internet access. With this flexibility you can deliver tests from your LMS easily, and you will have no problem accessing the multiple choice, true/false, completion, and short answer questions.

To access the Instructor Companion Site, visit **login.cengage.com** or go to page AIE-xxv to learn more about how to access electronic resources that accompany *Becoming a Master Student*. ∎

Copyright © 2015 Cengage Learning. All Rights Reserved. May not be scanned, copied or duplicated, or posted to a publicly accessible website, in whole or in part.

MASTER INSTRUCTOR RESOURCES HELP YOU REACH & TEACH

YOUR STUDENTS

YOUR COURSE

Becoming a Master Student is accompanied by various resources available to you through Cengage Learning to help make teaching your course easier. Take advantage of these valuable tools to assist you in designing your course. Remember to call your Cengage Learning sales representative or Peer-to-Peer faculty consultant if you have any questions about acquiring materials or integrating them into your course, or if you have a suggestion you would like to see implemented in the future. Other instructor resources available via the Instructor Companion Site are described on page AIE-xxvi.

Discovery Wheel (ISBN 9781285437194).
A stand-alone version of the Discovery Wheel is available so students can respond and hand in their results to you directly. Or consider using this Discovery Wheel as a handout to use in trainings or workshops with students and faculty.

College Success Planner.
Package *Becoming a Master Student* with this 12-month, week-at-a-glance academic planner. The College Success Planner assists students in making the best use of their time both on and off campus, and includes additional reading about key learning strategies and life skills for success in college. Ask your Cengage Learning sales representative for more details.

Noel-Levitz College Student Inventory.
The Retention Management System™ College Student Inventory (CSI from Noel-Levitz) is an early-alert, early-intervention program that identifies students with tendencies that contribute to dropping out of school. Cengage Learning offers you three assessment options that evaluate students on 19 different scales: Form A (194 items), Form B (100 items), or an online e-token (that provides access to either Form A, B, or C; 74 items). For more in-depth information, contact your Cengage Learning sales representative.

The Myers-Briggs Type Indicator® (MBTI®) Instrument.
MBTI is the most widely used personality inventory in history—and it is also available for packaging with *Becoming a Master Student*. The standard Form M self-scorable instrument contains 93 items that determine preferences on four scales: Extraversion-Introversion, Sensing-Intuition, Thinking-Feeling, and Judging-Perceiving. For more in-depth information, contact your Cengage Learning sales representative.

3 × 5 cards (ISBN 0395676010).
Provided at no charge to instructors who purchase *Becoming a Master Student*, 3 × 5 cards facilitate classroom participation. The text suggests a variety of uses for 3 × 5 cards. Instructors and students often report becoming obsessed with them. They find them lurking in closets, hiding under their beds, stuck on their mirrors, pinned to bulletin boards, tucked into pockets, slipped into their notes, marking their places in books, resting next to their telephones, even replacing their address and recipe books. Some instructors ask students to carry 3 × 5 cards with them for a few days and to jot down how they use their time. By doing so, students can monitor what they are doing and the amount of time they spend doing it.

Copyright © 2015 Cengage Learning. All Rights Reserved. May not be scanned, copied or duplicated, or posted to a publicly accessible website, in whole or in part.

Two-part exercise sheets (ISBN 039567896X).
Two-part exercise sheets (up to five per book ordered) provide a way to encourage students to participate in class. The final step in any classroom exercise can be for students to write Journal Entries on two-part sheets. If you collect the original, letting students keep a copy for their own use, you can read some of the student discoveries and insights anonymously to the rest of the class. Students are interested in what their peers think. Collecting two-part sheets can also be a convenient way to take attendance.

Three-part quiz sheets (ISBN 0395678978).
Students can take a more active role in learning by participating in grading their own quizzes, using three-part quiz sheets (up to 10 per book ordered). Here's how it works: Put the quiz questions on a projected screen, blackboard, or separate sheet of paper. Ask students to write their answers on the three-part sheet. After students complete the quiz, have them turn in the original white copy. Then have students look up the answers to correct and grade their own work. On the original, you can indicate the number of the text page where each answer can be found and the date of the lecture so students can refer to their notes. They then turn in one of the corrected copies and keep the other one for their own use. Students get immediate feedback, and you save time by not grading and returning individual quizzes. ◼

Could your students use an extra $1,000?

Cengage Learning College Success is proud to present three students each year with a $1,000 scholarship for tuition reimbursement. Students at post-secondary schools in the United States and Canada that offer a student success course are welcome to participate in this scholarship. To be considered, students must write an essay that answers the question "How do you define success?"

Here's one way to get your students to participate. Host a school-wide competition for students enrolled in a first-year student success or study skills course. Consider having students participate by including the competition in your syllabus as a goal-setting or writing assignment. In your local contest, ask all of your students to write an essay on the topic "How do you define success?" The essay should not exceed 750 words.

Materials to advertise the scholarship competition are available on the Instructor Companion Site. Download flyers for posting on bulletin boards around campus or for posting to online bulletin boards on your course Web site or in your course management system.

Students can send in their individual essays by filling out an entry form available at **www.cengagebrain.com.** Multiple students from the same school may enter their essays. Entries are due each year on December 15. The winners are announced the following spring. Invite your students to read the winning essays of previous entrants, available from the MindTap.

Copyright © 2015 Cengage Learning. All Rights Reserved. May not be scanned, copied or duplicated, or posted to a publicly accessible website, in whole or in part.

USE THE COLLEGE SUCCESS FACTORS INDEX

to measure and promote your students' success!

How much of a difference does your college success course make in your students' academic success? The College Success Factors Index (CSFI) is an online survey that will give you the answers you're looking for. In use by colleges and universities for over 20 years, the CSFI contains 100 self-scoring statements designed to determine the readiness of college students to successfully complete their early years in higher education. At the start of the course, it helps you assess incoming students and tailor your course topics to meet their needs. As a post-test, it allows you and your students to measure their progress. The CSFI tool is accessed online, so students can take the assessment in a lab, their home, or anywhere there's a computer.

Many factors indicate potential academic success in universities and colleges throughout the country. Most notably, grade point average in high school and aptitude scores, such as SAT or ACT scores, are used to predict success in college. However, additional factors that are often unmeasured have a very important place in the retention of students and their continuing success in higher education. For example, how a student uses his or her time or approaches the tasks assigned may be more critical to success than aptitude and previous academic records.

Moreover, factors such as involvement in activities at the college and family interest may in fact be greater success indices than previously known. The former allows student involvement with college activities, interaction with faculty, and the development of peer relationships. The latter relates to families that encourage success in college by providing encouragement, flexibility in the family calendar, and the sharing of family resources.

The CSFI is coupled with Early Alert functionality. Early Alert allows students and professional staff to identify areas that need improvement the first day of school, thereby increasing the possibility for retention. Through Early Alert, staff may offer interventions that keep students in college.

The College Success Factors Index has been developed to help measure many of the undiscovered fundamentals and factors that are critical to academic success:

 Responsibility/Control: If students do not take control over the responsibilities they assume in college, less success is possible.

Competition: The need to compete is part of our culture and thus an aspect of college and career success. For successful students, competition becomes internalized—they compete with themselves.

 Task Planning: A strong task orientation and a desire to complete a task in a planned step-by-step manner are very important to college success.

Expectations: Successful students have goals that are related to assignments, areas of study, and future careers.

Family Involvement: Family encouragement and/or participation in planning and decision making are factors in a student's success.

College Involvement: Being involved in college activities, relating to faculty, and developing strong peer relationships are important factors in retention.

 Time Management: How students maximize their time and prioritize class assignments affects their productivity and success.

Wellness: People need ways to handle their problems. Stress, anger, sleeplessness, alcohol or drug use, inadequate diet, and lack of exercise are deterrents to college success.

 Precision: To approach one's education by being exact, careful with details, and specific with assignments is a measure of success.

Persistence: To face a task with diligence, self-encouragement, and a sense of personal urgency, even when some tasks take extra effort and are repetitious, is a mark of academic success. ■

For more information, visit our Web site at www.cengage.com/success/csfi2.

AIE-xxxiii

Copyright © 2015 Cengage Learning. All Rights Reserved. May not be scanned, copied or duplicated, or posted to a publicly accessible website, in whole or in part.

PEER-TO-PEER FACULTY DEVELOPMENT & CONSULTING
Committed to Student Success

Cengage Learning's Peer-to-Peer Faculty Development & Consulting team is dedicated to providing educators with proven instructional strategies and tools that lead to student success. For the past 24 years, our team of Professional Educators has provided guidance and training through our TeamUP College Survival programs for the design and implementation of student success and first-year courses.

The Peer-to-Peer Faculty Development & Consulting team is available to assist with any stage of student success program development, including these:

- Developing student retention strategies
- Implementing student success courses
- Training faculty members
- Helping faculty engage students as active learners
- Transforming the learning environment
- Presenting conferences and workshops

OUR TEAM

Our team of Professional Educators has extensive experience in teaching and administering the first-year course and in facilitating training at national education conferences throughout the year. We provide support to help educators establish and maintain effective student success programs.

WEB SITE

Visit our Web site at **www.cengage.com/teamup** for additional resources and more information about College Survival:

- Get the latest industry information.
- Get updates on the latest technology available through Cengage Learning texts.
- Get connected to our support services.

CONFERENCES/WORKSHOPS

TeamUP College Survival conferences and workshops offer highly interactive and informative sessions designed to equip you with ideas and activities that you can apply immediately in your classroom. All educators involved in enhancing instruction and improving students' motivation and performance are encouraged to attend.

- **About our national conferences.** Our two- to three-day conferences provide informative, interactive sessions on a wide range of topics such as adult learners, learning styles, student retention, motivation, and technology. Presenters include nationally known authors, student success instructors, and Peer-to-Peer Professional Educators who offer invaluable instructional strategies based on their experience teaching the first-year course. This forum for learning and sharing with colleagues will furnish you with activities and ideas to implement immediately in your course.

- **About our on-campus workshops.** Led by Peer-to-Peer Professional Educators, our on-campus workshops are customized to the needs of instructors on a particular campus. These workshops will equip you with ideas and activities to enliven the teaching and learning experience. Ask your Cengage Learning Representative to help you set up a training at your institution.

- **Who should attend an event?** If you are an educator, new or experienced, who is dedicated to promoting student success in career schools, community colleges, or four-year colleges and universities, these events are for you! Those who will benefit from these workshops include:
  - Academic and student affairs administrators
  - Student success and freshman seminar coordinators
  - Faculty members (full-time and adjunct instructors)
  - Retention/enrollment management directors
  - Counselors and orientation directors

How can we help? Your Cengage Learning Peer-to-Peer Professional Educator can help you with ideas for introducing a topic, creating community in the classroom, designing your syllabus, and figuring out what to do in class tomorrow. All you have to do is contact us. Check the TeamUP Web site to find your Professional Educator: **www.cengage.com/teamup** ■

Copyright © 2015 Cengage Learning. All Rights Reserved. May not be scanned, copied or duplicated, or posted to a publicly accessible website, in whole or in part.

PART 2

TEACHING WITH
BECOMING A MASTER
STUDENT

Message from Master Instructor, Annette McCreedy

After years of teaching learning strategies classes for Nashville State Community College, I created a course called College Success, which incorporated all the critical elements of study skills, combined with advising and two-year college plans. This process culminates in career connections for our students. College Success allows me to function as a mentor for my students, a role in which I share knowledge and success, but also failures and challenges. I researched many textbooks, and I found that *Becoming a Master Student* provides the components we need for this three-pronged approach: study skills, academic planning, and career goals.

Be a leader. You will find that your students see you as the professional that you currently are. They need to be reminded that you too have faced challenges in your career and had to work for years to achieve the position you now hold. **Be willing to laugh.** Try to remember how you functioned as a freshman in college—a bit embarrassing for most of us! Chances are you were less secure and confident of your abilities in and out of the classroom. It's important to be mindful of where you personally have come in this journey in order to better relate to where your students are.

Be willing to change. I challenge you to evolve in your own teaching techniques. Just as with your students, growing and learning to become a master student enables you to teach new strategies. **Be willing to take risks.** This process can include some discomfort as we force ourselves outside the security that comes with old habits. **Be spontaneous.** As you begin to experiment with the many tools that *Becoming a Master Student* includes, both online and in the text, you will probably find yourself out of your comfort zone at times. If you embrace this attitude, you will be better able to model this learning by stretching beyond your comfort level. **Be "tech" savvy.** The technology included with *Becoming a Master Student* adds richness far beyond the text. You can actually bring Dave Ellis into your classroom, and students can hear him articulate his experiences and his advice, bringing them closer to the original intent of the text. You will face a learning curve as you learn not only how to manage these tools but also how to teach your students to use the technology. **Be able to organize and sort.** Make notes and remind yourself for future semesters which tools you find most helpful and how you use them in new ways.

Be willing to participate. You serve as a facilitator in your classroom. The more passionate you are about teaching this course, the more passion you will arouse from your students. **Be joyful. Be energetic.** This course changes lives. I grow as I share with my students; they teach me as I teach them. **Be hungry.** The textbook contains so many resources, allowing you the rewarding challenge of keeping the classroom setting fresh, adding and subtracting elements each semester. **Be inquisitive.** You can continue to refine your understanding of the myriad of opportunities available within the resources, but you can also customize the course elements to individual classes. **Be willing to suspend judgment.** For example, by examining the low scores of students' Discovery Wheel, I determine early in the semester which areas I need to emphasize. Also, getting ongoing feedback from students facilitates this customization. The appeal of this course, in part, is that it is not a cookie-cutter course. **Be creative.**

Embrace the important connection between the classroom and the workplace. In the annotated chapters, you will see a section called Workplace Applications, which brings the chapter skills into a workplace perspective. I stress these applications of the chapter to my students, reminding them that their motivation should not only improve their personal lives and increase personal awareness, but that these skills translate into the workplace.

Do you notice that as you walk through this process, you are also participating in your own journey toward becoming a master student? As teachers, you are also participating in your own personal journey of discovery. As you teach these concepts to your students, you are also modeling all the master student qualities, teaching and leading by example. **The lessons of this book are not just study skills, but life skills.** *Becoming a Master Student* is not just a static textbook, but a workbook that begs for use and interaction. I had a former student who expressed it this way at the close of the semester: "This book has become my friend. These pages are dog-eared with love." This course challenges you to interact with your students as a mentor, guide, and facilitator. We are not just shaping students; we are shaping responsible, hard-working people.

Your students will hear your passion in your voice and see it on your face. Enjoy the ride; enthusiasm for success is contagious! Teaching this course has become a passion and a privilege for me, and I am sure you will find this journey as personally and professionally rewarding as I have. ■

Copyright © 2015 Cengage Learning. All Rights Reserved. May not be scanned, copied or duplicated, or posted to a publicly accessible website, in whole or in part.

USING THE ANNOTATED INSTRUCTOR'S EDITION

master instructor best practice

"Inevitably I end up having a class where what I've been doing just isn't working, or I'm just looking to try something different. I always find exciting ideas to take into class by reviewing the Annotated Instructor pages."

—Terry Carles, Valencia Community College

All members of the team of consultants have extensive experience in teaching and administering the first-year course and in facilitating training sessions and conferences. Get to know your consultant today by calling 1-800-856-5727. Or visit the team online at **www.cengage.com/teamup**. Be sure to ask a consultant how you can attend a conference or workshop—for free!

GET FAMILIAR WITH THE ANNOTATED INSTRUCTOR'S EDITION

The Annotated Instructor's Edition of *Becoming a Master Student*, 15th Edition, will help guide you as you use this textbook. Whether you are a first-time user of *Becoming a Master Student* or a long-time fan, there is something here for you. In this Annotated Edition, strategies to aid your teaching are available at the front of the main text, and content-specific ideas appear prior to each chapter. All of these pages have a separate numbering system so that the textbook pages are numbered the same as the student edition of the text. This allows you to stay on the same page as your students when assigning readings and exercises.

DO A TEXTBOOK RECONNAISSANCE

Flip through the pages of this textbook right now to get the big picture of the 15th edition. Look for fresh ideas you can use to support your course objectives. The Table of Contents of this book outlines what's new and revised for each chapter in this edition. Consider creating a textbook, ebook, or Web site scavenger hunt for students so they can participate in the textbook reconnaissance too. Locate exercises, articles, or activities, and ask students to work in groups, seeing who can successfully locate the resources. Possibly offer prizes or incentives.

GET TO KNOW YOUR PEER-TO-PEER FACULTY CONSULTANT

For more than 20 years, Peer-to-Peer Faculty Consultants have provided consultation and training for the design and implementation of student success and first-year courses.

LISTEN TO YOUR PEERS

Throughout the Annotated Instructor's Edition, you will find tips from Master Instructor Annette McCreedy of Nashville State Community College, as well as various best practices from Master Instructors across the country. As you dig into the following chapters, think about what you would say if you could add your voice to theirs. Send an e-mail to **csweb.CollegeSurvival@cengage.com** to share your comments. In addition, take what you have learned back to your campus. Consider hosting workshops on your campus, inviting instructors to share their best practices and success stories.

USE THE TRANSITION GUIDE TO FIND YOUR WAY

If you have used previous editions of *Becoming a Master Student*, you may need some help finding your favorite articles and exercises. The transition guide on the Instructor Companion Site will help you navigate the changes made to the 15th edition. This transition guide is also available on page AIE-xxxiv.

MAKE THIS BOOK YOUR OWN

The length of student success courses varies, so there may be more content here than you can share during your course. If some sections of the book don't apply to your course at all, skip them. Take notes in the book signaling articles and exercises you plan to cover and how. Write down ideas for lesson plans, activities, quiz questions, guest speakers, and homework assignments. Change the exercises in the book to fit your needs. Create a new technique by combining several others. Create a technique out of thin air! Consider creating a document where you record the date and what you plan to cover in class that day, including homework to be assigned, upcoming test dates, and class announcements. You can add entries all semester, then easily monitor your progress throughout

Copyright © 2015 Cengage Learning. All Rights Reserved. May not be scanned, copied or duplicated, or posted to a publicly accessible website, in whole or in part.

the semester, noting what worked well, what didn't, and why. You can easily refer to this next semester, decreasing planning time and allowing you to document new ideas and assignments. In addition, when students ask about homework missed, you have a handy record. End your course by suggesting that students explore any unread sections of the book as one of the ways to continue their journey of student success.

MODEL THE CONCEPTS

Action makes this book work. Completing the exercises along with your students will enable you to stay involved and speak from experience when you discuss each chapter in class. The exercises and articles will help you write, touch, feel, move, see, search, ponder, speak, listen, recall, choose, commit, and create. In this way, you join your students on their road to success. Remember to explain your own personal journey of successes and challenges. You are a significant mentor and role model for your students, and it is important to remind them that you have not always been the successful, self-actualized person they see before them today!

INTEGRATE LEARNING STYLES INTO YOUR TEACHING

On the opening page of each chapter, four basic questions—*Why? What? How?* and *What if?*— guide students toward maximum learning that correlate to the Learning Style Inventory as explained in Chapter 1. By becoming aware of their preferred learning style, students will be better able to understand and practice new styles.

USE THE MATERIALS BEFORE EACH CHAPTER TO HELP YOU CREATE LESSON PLANS

There are four instructor pages before each chapter. These sections provide content-related ideas for guest speakers, lectures, activities, homework assignments, and previews/reviews to help bring the classroom alive for your students. The organization of these pages is based on the seven-part lesson plan structure described on page AIE-xli. Flip to one of the chapters and review the instructor pages now. Try to include a variety of activities that appeal to many learning styles, including short lectures, group work, hands-on activities, and textbook activities.

LINK TO THE WEB

Part of the support for you when using this textbook is an Instructor Companion Site that contains best practices, lesson plan and lecture ideas, PowerPoints, activities, handouts, videos, test questions, and more. These tools were submitted by faculty around the country who wanted to share effective strategies they have used in their class-rooms. Register now at **login.cengage.com** so that you can explore additional resources to use with your students. See page AIE-xxv for detailed instructions on how to access the available additional digital resources.

POWER PROCESSES

The Power Processes are a long-standing popular feature of *Becoming a Master Student*. These articles describe approaches to student success that are more philosophical in nature than most of the tools in the text and serve to empower students at the onset of the chapter. Review the pre-chapter instructor resources in the book or on the Instructor Companion Site for strategies to help your students make full value of these special tools.

HELP STUDENTS TAKE THIS BOOK TO WORK

Although the focus of this textbook is success in college, students can apply nearly all of the techniques in this book to any career. Students with less experience in the work-place, however, may not see how these tools apply at work. Many articles feature "Take this article to work" headings to provide information for how the skills being taught can apply to workplace situations. Ask your students to record their own experiences, and make your own set of examples to share with future classes.

MASTER STUDENT PROFILES

Becoming a Master Student has always included a brief article about a real person who encompasses master student qualities. In each new edition of the textbook, several of the stories are replaced with new ones. Read the article "Master student qualities" on page 4, and then check out the Table of Contents to discover the 12 people on the roster of master students for the 15th edition. ◼

Copyright © 2015 Cengage Learning. All Rights Reserved. May not be scanned, copied or duplicated, or posted to a publicly accessible website, in whole or in part.

A GUIDE FOR INSTRUCTORS *who have used* PREVIOUS EDITIONS OF THIS BOOK

The foundations and themes for student success in *Becoming a Master Student* have been used by millions of students. Since the first edition, students and instructors have helped shape this book by providing strategies, insights, and suggestions. As a result of its continuous evaluation and refinement, students are inspired and motivated by this book to adopt, develop, and commit to using the skills needed for success in college and throughout life. These ideas are now a part of the 15th edition.

Every word in every article has been evaluated for its helpfulness to students. Statistics have been updated; recent research has been included; and articles have been shortened or lengthened as necessary to maximize clarity of concepts and strategies. Here are some of the major changes you will see in this edition.

KEY UPDATES

- The Chapter Opener for each chapter has been given a modern visual facelift to highlight what's new in the chapter, as well as to focus students' attention on how and why the chapter is important and what students stand to gain by learning the material.

- The Skills Snapshot feature has been revised to help students understand their strengths and weaknesses relative to the chapter skill; identify new strategies to commit to using at school and in the workplace; predict possible obstacles to those strategies; and propose ways to overcome any obstacles.

- Put This Chapter to Work concepts have been integrated into relevant chapter articles, many times noted with a "Take this article to work" heading, so that students can immediately see how a chapter concept is directly related to their current and future work lives.

CHAPTER-BY-CHAPTER UPDATES

Introduction: The Master Student

- ***New articles*** "The master student process—Discovery," "The master student process—Intention,"

and "The master student process—Action" (pages 8–10) clearly define the process students will go through by using *Becoming a Master Student*—a process of learning about themselves and how to commit to intentions that will yield action and changes in their lives. Distinct guidelines for how to respond to the Journal Entries throughout the book that address discovery, intention, and action are provided.

- ***New sidebar*** "The secret of student success" (page 11) reveals to students that there are no secrets to success other than self-discovery and participation.

- ***New article*** "Keep the process alive" (page 11) further reinforces that the master student process needs to be a continual practice or else students won't reap the benefits that *Becoming a Master Student* offers.

- ***New sidebar*** "Avoid high-tech time wasters" (page 17) provides students with some general suggestions on how to use (and not use) technology to become more focused and organized.

- ***New article*** "Leading the way—Succeeding as a first-generation student" (page 20) demystifies the unique challenges first-generation students face and encourages this population to reach for success.

- ***Revised article*** "Enroll your instructor in your success" (pages 21–22) and the **revised sidebar** "Communicating with your instructor" work hand in hand to inform students how to make the most of their relationships with instructors and how to connect with their instructors by phone, e-mail, or in person.

- ***New article*** "Developing a professional work ethic" (page 23) helps students to recognize the appropriate behaviors expected of them in their college courses.

- ***Revised Exercise 4*** "Reprogram your attitude" (page 28) now includes a Step 5 where students reflect on how affirmations and visualizations are changing their behaviors.

- ***New Journal Entry 2*** "Declare your intention to change a habit" (page 30) supports the ideas presented in "Ways to change a habit."

Copyright © 2015 Cengage Learning. All Rights Reserved. May not be scanned, copied or duplicated, or posted to a publicly accessible website, in whole or in part.

Chapter 1: Discovering Yourself

- *Revised title* reflects the chapter focus of students discovering their learning capabilities and how they can use this knowledge to succeed in their courses.

- *Revised Exercise 6* "The Discovery Wheel" (page 36) has been redesigned to be more user-friendly.

- *New Journal Entry 5* "Get back to the big picture about learning styles" (page 54) encourages students to embrace metacognition and evaluate how what they've learned about themselves through the LSI, multiple intelligences, and the VAK system is interrelated and will benefit their learning.

- *New article* "Six paths to more powerful thinking" (pages 55–56) introduces students to the concepts of the six levels of thinking of Bloom's Taxonomy, so they will be prepared to work through the Practicing Critical Thinking exercises that appear in every chapter.

- *Revised Practicing Critical Thinking 1* (page 57) gives a more detailed example and assignment guidelines, so students can effectively practice at Level 2: Understanding.

- *New Master Student Profile* (page 58) of Teresa Amabile.

Chapter 2: Time

- *Revised article* "Make choices about multitasking" (page 64) has been moved closer to the beginning of the chapter, because today's students must learn how to negotiate multitasking amidst all their commitments and technology experiences.

- *New Journal Entry 6* "Discover the impact of technology on your time and attention" (page 69) helps students monitor how much time they spend online and use technology.

- *Revised article* "Define your values" (page 70) (previously in Chapter 12) now focuses on how our values guide our moment-to-moment choices and priorities.

- *Revised article* "Planning sets you free" (pages 76–77) (previously "More strategies for planning") emphasizes how advance planning can positively impact your time management.

- *Revised article* "Break it down, get it down" (pages 81–83) now includes a revised long-term planner with wider rows that are more functional for writing.

- *New article* "Create a work flow that works" (page 84) provides suggestions for how to successfully plan taking projects from start to finish.

- *New article* "There's an app for that: Using technology for time management" (page 85) directs students to the various available technologies that can simplify time management.

- *New Journal Entry 7* "Create a not-to-do list" (page 95) shows students low-value activities that can be stopped.

- *Revised Master Student Profile* (page 96) of Sampson Davis (previously in Chapter 9).

Chapter 3: Memory

- *Revised Power Process* "Love your problems" (page 100) delves into how problems serve a significant purpose: stimulating us to find worthy problems and solutions.

- *New article* "Your memory and your brain—6 key principles" (pages 101–103) focuses on how the memory process works in stages, and provides strategies for how to make the most of each stage.

- *New Journal Entry 8* "Reflect on the care and feeding of your brain" (page 103) gets students thinking about how they can better use their brains and memories.

- *Revised article* "25 memory techniques"(pages 106–111) includes an additional five techniques that are now categorized into the stages of the memory process.

- *New article* "Retool your memory" (page 116) gives suggestions for how to use technology to support memory.

- *New Master Student Profile* (page 120) of Sonia Sotomayor.

Chapter 4: Reading

- *New article* "Extending Muscle Reading to Web pages and ebooks" (pages 132–133) adapts the Muscle Reading phases to reading materials available online and on technology devices.

- *New sidebar* "Take Muscle Reading to work" (page 132) relates Muscle Reading concepts to applicable workplace situations where reading is necessary.

- *New Journal Entry 11* "Reflect on your online reading habits" (page 133) asks students to reflect on how they read Web pages and ebooks differently from printed materials.

- *Revised article* "Developing information literacy" (pages 141–144) now also covers how to generate ideas for a research topic, ask the right questions, refine key words, and utilize the "deep Web" to uncover sources.

- *Revised Practicing Critical Thinking 4* (page 145) refines the questions associated with the evaluating level of thinking and gives more detailed instruction for how to evaluate.

Chapter 5: Notes

- *Revised article* "Record: The note-taking process flows" (pages 155–159) now includes authentic, student-created note-taking examples.

- *Revised article title* "Visualize ideas with concept maps" (page 167) (previously was "Get to the bones of your book with concept maps").

- *Revised article* "Taking effective notes for online coursework" (pages 168–169) considers how managing time and tasks is key to success with online coursework.

AIE-xxxix

Copyright © 2015 Cengage Learning. All Rights Reserved. May not be scanned, copied or duplicated, or posted to a publicly accessible website, in whole or in part.

- **New article** "Note-taking 2.0" (page 170) gives students suggestions for how to use several of the note-taking applications available on the Web, smartphones, and tablets.
- **New sidebar** "Taking notes during meetings" (page 166) provides the four "A's" for how to adapt academic note taking to the workplace with the addition of attendance, agenda, agreements, and actions.
- **New Master Student Profile** (page 172) of Richard Blanco.

Chapter 6: Tests
- **Revised article title** "Think beyond the grade" (page 177) was previously titled "Disarm tests."
- **Revised article** "What to do before the test" (pages 179–180) focuses more on study techniques for rehearsal and practice.
- **Revised article** "Cooperative learning: Studying in groups" (pages 182–183) expands on how the important cooperative concepts apply to workplace situations.
- **Revised article** "Let go of test anxiety" (pages 188–189) expands on the following ideas: accepting any feelings students may be having about tests, over-preparing for tests, and how test-like situations present themselves at work.
- **Revised article title** "Studying across the curriculum" (page 194) was previously "Learning across the curriculum."
- **New article** to this chapter "Notable failures" (page 197) (previously in Chapter 3).

Chapter 7: Thinking
- **New Power Process** "Embrace the new" (page 202) focuses on how being open to new experiences and adaptable to changing experiences are key components of a master student.
- **Revised article** "A process for critical thinking" (pages 205–208) (previously titled "Becoming a critical thinker") builds on the foundation laid in Chapter 1 (see "Six paths to more powerful thinking") and asks students to take their thinking to a higher level by checking attitudes, logic, and evidence.
- **New Exercise 20** "Critical thinking scenarios" (pages 209–210) challenges students to put critical thinking skills into action by evaluating three scenarios that are likely familiar to them.
- **New Journal Entries 16 and 17** "Use divergent thinking to brainstorm goals" and "Use convergent thinking to plan habits" (page 212) help students put thinking skills to use.
- **Revised article** "Don't *fool* yourself: Fifteen common mistakes in logic" (pages 217–219) updates many of the examples of logical fallacies.

- **Revised article title** "Service-learning: Turn thinking into contribution" (pages 227–228) was previously "Service-learning: Turn thinking into action."
- **Revised Practicing Critical Thinking 7** (page 229) guides students on how to ask productive questions to help hone critical thought.
- **New Master Student Profile** (page 230) of Irshad Manji.

Chapter 8: Communicating
- **Revised article** "Communicating in teams—Getting things done as a group" (pages 243–245) (previously titled "Take your teamwork to a new level") gives guidelines for how a team can set up successful communication.
- **New sidebar** "Using technology to collaborate" (page 245) provides details for various online solutions that promote and support group work.
- **Revised article** "Staying safe on social networks" (pages 252–253) (previously titled "Mastering social networks") emphasizes the importance of privacy and discretion when communicating in social networks.
- **New sidebar** "Writing for online readers" (page 256) explains how to keep e-mail and Web site writing succinct, informative, and respectful.
- **New sidebar** "Befriend your word processor" (page 257) provides tips for making the most of common word processing software.
- **Revised Practicing Critical Thinking 8** (page 265) helps students work through the levels of critical thinking by combining them and taking them in a different sequence as they think about conflict resolution.
- **New Master Student Profile** (page 266) of Salman Khan.

Chapter 9: Diversity
- **Revised article** "Diversity is real—and valuable" (pages 272–273) expands on discrimination the GLBT community faces.
- **Revised article** "Building relationships across cultures" (pages 274–277) applies cultural competence to workplace situations students are likely to face.
- **New sidebar** "Prevent cyberbullying" (page 276) defines cyberbullying and ways to address instances of it.
- **Revised sidebar** "8 strategies for nonsexist communication" (page 283) includes one additional strategy: Consider the "singular their."
- **New sidebar** "Leaders on leadership" (page 286) provides inspiring quotes about leadership.
- **Revised Practicing Critical Thinking 9** (page 289) helps students work through the levels of critical thinking by combining them and taking them in a different sequence as they think about discrimination.
- **New Master Student Profile** (page 290) of Chimamanda Adichie.

Copyright © 2015 Cengage Learning. All Rights Reserved. May not be scanned, copied or duplicated, or posted to a publicly accessible website, in whole or in part.

Chapter 10: Money

- *Revised Journal Entry 23* "Create a new experience of money" (page 311) (previously "Start setting money goals") has a greater focus on intentions.

- *Revised article title* "Education pays off—and you can pay for it" (page 312) was previously "Education is worth it—and you can pay for it."

- *New article* "Use tools to tame your money" (page 313) examines the ways students can use technology to track and control their budgets.

- *Revised Practicing Critical Thinking 10* (page 315) challenges students to list and evaluate strategies for getting the most value from time and money spent on higher education.

- *New Master Student Profile* (page 316) of Sara Blakely.

Chapter 11: Health

- *Revised article* "Choose freedom from distress" (pages 324–327) (previously "Choose emotional health") focuses on how stress can positively and negatively impact students' lives and provides strategies for managing stress.

- *New Journal Entry 24* "Choose your stress management strategies" (page 328) helps students identify stressors, how they currently manage those stressors, and what improvements to managing their stressors they can make.

- *New Journal Entry 25* "Reflect on your experience with asking for help" (page 332) asks students to evaluate how they handled a situation where they felt overwhelmed.

Chapter 12: Next Steps

- *Revised chapter title* (previously "What's Next") highlights that students should continue applying *Becoming a Master Student* strategies in any next steps they take.

- *New Power Process* "Persist" (page 352) emphasizes that the road to graduation is often unglamorous and necessitates persistence and resilience.

- *New Journal Entry 26* "Use the 'five Cs' to develop transferable skills" (page 356–357) asks students to consider the categories of skills employers most look for in potential employees—creative thinking, critical thinking, communication, collaboration, and character.

- *New article* "Taking the road to graduation" (page 360–361) shows students how reexamining academic goals and study strategies, connecting with services and others on campus, and remaining motivated can aid in persisting until graduation.

- *New Journal Entry 27* "Whom are you bringing with you?" (page 362) helps students discover the intricate network of support available for the taking.

- *Revised article title* "Start creating your career" (pages 366–367) was previously "Create your career now."

- *New sidebar* "Another option: Don't plan your career" (page 367) offers an alternative to conventional career planning.

- *New Journal Entry 28* "Plan a career by naming names" (page 368) lets students experiment with career planning by listing.

- *Revised article title* "Start creating your résumé" (page 369) previously was "Build an irresistible résumé" and succinctly focuses on how students can begin building a résumé as a way to plan skills to develop.

- *New article* "Discover the hidden job market" (page 370) reveals tips for where and how to look for jobs.

- *Revised article title* "Develop interviewing skills" (page 371) previously was "Use job interviews to 'hire' an employer" and delivers concise interviewing strategies.

- *New Exercise 35* "Craft the story of you" (page 372) helps students prepare for interviewing.

- *Revised article title* "Persist on the path of mastery" (pages 373–374) was previously "'Use the following suggestions to continue. . .'."

- *New article* "Tools for lifelong learning" (page 375) provides suggestions for how students can continue to expand their education in all things.

- *New Journal Entry 29* "Celebrate your gains, clarify your intentions" (page 381) allows students to reflect on what they've gained from their student success course.

- *Revised Practicing Critical Thinking 12* (page 383) helps students work through the levels of critical thinking by combining them and taking them in a different sequence as they think about all the strategies they have learned in *Becoming a Master Student*.

- *Revised Master Student Profile* (page 384) of Lalita Booth (previously in Chapter 1). ■

Copyright © 2015 Cengage Learning. All Rights Reserved. May not be scanned, copied or duplicated, or posted to a publicly accessible website, in whole or in part.

Finding
THE MASTER
INSTRUCTOR
IN YOU

Teaching a student success course for the first time may seem intimidating. Most of us teach classes in our primary field of expertise, so teaching a course outside our knowledge base can be challenging on many levels. Here are a few suggestions to help you get started.

MODEL THE BEHAVIOR YOU WANT TO SEE IN YOUR STUDENTS

If you want your students to be organized, be organized in your class. If you want your students to show up on time, always be punctual yourself. This applies to the resources in the course also. For example, your students may need help understanding assignments and online resources. It is important that you spend time with these resources in advance. You may even point out to students that preparing in advance of class allows them to also have a better understanding of the assignments and materials before they come to class.

THE TEXTBOOK IS FOR YOU TOO

You can apply the strategies in this textbook to your professional and personal life. Use the same student success tools to sharpen your memory, manage your time, and improve relationships with colleagues, friends, and loved ones. Use the Table of Contents and the Index to look for strategies to help you start, stop, or change habits in your life.

In a teacher training workshop, a dedicated instructor once asked, "How can I model and teach promptness if I'm always late to class?" This was an opportunity for personal and professional growth! For us, as for our students, however, change is a choice we must choose to make.

BE INQUISITIVE

There are many resources for you to use in the process of developing lesson plans for your student success course. In addition to this Annotated Instructor's Edition, with its suggestions here and on the pages preceding each chapter, explore these additional resources to help you create and improve lesson plans and organize all aspects of your course:

- **Instructor Companion Site**—provides specific tools to use while teaching your course, including video clips, PowerPoint slides, sample syllabi, best practices, quizzes, Web links, and more. You can edit most of the downloadable files to tailor them for your course.

- **Peer-to-Peer Faculty consultants**—available by toll-free phone (1-800-856-5727) and e-mail (serviceandtraining@cengage.com), a consultant can assist you with planning, class activities, research, and implementing a course on your campus. Ask about a customized on-campus training session or how you can attend a TeamUP conference for free.

- **Faculty members on your campus**—invite a respected colleague to lunch to find out how he or she solves grading, attendance, logistic, and classroom management issues. Consider setting up a campus workshop or periodic lunch groups with others who teach the course, so you can share strengths, best practices, and solutions. This creates a support base on your own campus. We all bring different strengths to this course, and sharing with other faculty is a great way to keep your course fresh and effective.

TAKE IT ONE STEP AT A TIME

Creating the perfect course isn't likely to happen overnight. This textbook explains tools and techniques clearly so that you don't need to try to cover all of them in class. Start by identifying one or two topics in each chapter that you have personally found valuable. Look for activities or lecture ideas at the Instructor Companion Site or in this Annotated Instructor's Edition, and build your lesson plans around the topics that you want to emphasize. Use videos and guest speakers from your campus to augment your class meetings. You may want to try to record these speakers for additional use in online courses; or if the speaker is off-campus; or if your class is at a time that is inconvenient for your speaker. You can then reuse the video for future classes. Be careful to check periodically for timeliness of the material. You don't want to include an interview, for example, with the director of career counseling explaining services that are out of date! Reinforce concepts by conducting review sessions and giving weekly quizzes. For additional lesson-planning strategies, see the article "Creating engaging classes" on page xli. ■

Copyright © 2015 Cengage Learning. All Rights Reserved. May not be scanned, copied or duplicated, or posted to a publicly accessible website, in whole or in part.

Master Instructor
BEST PRACTICES

Throughout the Annotated Instructor's Edition, you will find Master Instructor Best Practices to inspire instructors to try new activities for *Becoming a Master Student* that have been successful for others across the country. Whether it's to make a new course your own or to help keep your course fresh, this sampling of Best Practices reveals innovative ways to get your students involved and invested in becoming master students! For more Best Practices, visit the Instructor Companion Site.

Explore *Becoming a Master Student* with chapter pairings (course organization)

" Exploring all of the chapters in 16 weeks presents quite a challenge. Because all of the chapters offer valuable information for college and for life, I decided to pair the chapters. Emphasis is placed on the academic chapters, but these issues are linked with life-skill chapters. Students and I are pleased with this organization for all of the aspects for success are explored in six units. The pairings are as follows:

Unit I: Introduction/Chapter 1—First Steps of a Master Student

Unit II: Chapter 2 and Chapter 10—Managing Time and Money

Unit III: Chapter 3 and Chapter 11—Success Is Mental and Physical

Unit IV: Chapter 4 and Chapter 7—Reading and Critical Thinking

Unit V: Chapter 5 and Chapter 8—Notes and Communicating

Unit VI: Chapter 6, Chapter 9, and Chapter 12—Tests, Cooperative Learning, and Diversity; So, What's Next? "

—*Paula Wimbish, Hinds Community College*

Learning (and remembering) vocabulary (accompanies chapters 3 and 4)

" With this assignment students are not only learning and improving vocabulary and reading skills but also exposing themselves to successful memory improving strategies as employed by other students.

A list of terms I create (mine has 325 terms) is distributed to the students. For homework, the students are required to learn all or part of the list. If the class meets once a week, I usually assign about 50 terms. They are told there will be a quiz where I will test them on 10 of the terms at the next class meeting. They are also told that they will have to report (orally and in writing!) on the strategy that they employed to learn the terms.

At the next class meeting, I have the students first hand in their write-ups and then report on how they learned the terms. I then tell the class that the quiz has been postponed until the next class meeting. I urge them to try memory strategies suggested by their fellow students. By doing the quiz (usually consisting of only 10 of the 50 terms that have been assigned) a week later, the students have an opportunity to try out memory strategies presented in class by their peers. "

—*Frank Baker, Golden West College*

Best listener (accompanies chapter 8)

" This activity is used as part of a unit on communication and prior to introducing the concept of Active

Copyright ©2015 Cengage Learning. All Rights Reserved. May not be scanned, copied or duplicated, or posted to a publicly accessible website, in whole or in part.

Listening. First, I ask the students to think about the person in their life whom they consider to be their "best listener." Specifically, I ask them to think about the person they go to the most often when they feel the need to talk about a problem or situation. Once they have that person in mind, I ask them to make a list of at least five behavioral characteristics that make this person a good listener. I try to avoid giving them examples, but I will ask questions to get them thinking, like "What does this person do while they are listening to you, or what specific words would you use to describe their actions and responses?" I then divide them into groups of three to four and have them share their lists. The group then has to come up with its top five behavioral characteristics of a good listener and present them to the class. When we have debriefed all of the lists, I conclude by summarizing the responses and pointing out similarities among the lists.

At this point, I begin a brief presentation on the concept and characteristics of Active Listening (such as empathy, paraphrasing, probing (asking questions), reflection, summary, verbal prompts, silence). I conclude by pointing out how many of the behaviors from their lists are considered to be a part of Active Listening. I follow this up with a quick discussion on open-ended and closed-ended questions. To illustrate the difference, we play a quick game of 20 questions. I think of an object, and in the first round the students can only ask questions that can be answered with "yes" or "no" (closed-ended questions). I give them three or four minutes to ask questions, after which I tell them the object if they haven't guessed it. In the next round, they can ask any question. It usually doesn't take very long for them to guess the second item. Usually within the first three questions, someone asks, "What is it?" I conclude by discussing the role of appropriate questions in Active Listening and good communication in general. **"**

—*Maggie Seymour, South Plains College*

The health monitor

(accompanies chapter 11)

" Mimicking the Time Monitor exercise from Chapter 2, students record all food and drink for five to seven days. At the end of the assigned period of time, students analyze their eating and drinking habits and make a plan for possible changes. After monitoring their intake of food and drink for a period of time, students then write a one- or two-page essay that answers these questions:

- What have you learned about your diet/nutrition from keeping track of everything you consumed for five days? What surprised you? What did you notice that you did not notice before?

- What things can you add to or delete from your diet to make your nutrition healthier?

- What can you promise to change about your diet now that you have completed this exercise? **"**

—*Laura Bazan, Central Piedmont Community College*

Portfolio assignment

(cumulative project)

" I have found this assignment to be one of the most rewarding, both for me as an instructor and for my students. Students apply and reflect upon the content and their experiences of **Becoming a Master Student** and the course. Students' master student portfolios must begin with a two-page reflective overview that describes the portfolio theme, the items chosen for the portfolio, and their significance. The portfolio must include application examples, such as a copy of a page from a planner to demonstrate time management skills and a page (or pages) of notes taken for this or another class, using either (or both) the Cornell or mind-map note-taking styles. The information included in the portfolio should demonstrate how students have applied master student techniques and must also address how those techniques worked for them. Have students also discuss techniques they tried but that didn't work, and tell them to explain why. Students should also answer these questions: In what areas has this class helped you to improve the most? What areas do you think you still need to work on? How do you plan to apply techniques from this class to continue to improve in those areas? This serves as their final exam, and they must present their portfolio and a brief summary of the contents of their accompanying paper. **"**

—*Jane Speer, Alpena Community College* ∎

Copyright © 2015 Cengage Learning. All Rights Reserved. May not be scanned, copied or duplicated, or posted to a publicly accessible website, in whole or in part.

CREATING ENGAGING CLASSES

USING THE SEVEN-PART COURSE MODEL IN YOUR CLASSROOM

Use the following lesson-planning model as a framework to provide more opportunities to engage students as active participants and partners in their learning process. The objective is to use varying modes of instruction to facilitate a course that accesses and maximizes each student's method of learning. Try using this seven-part course model as a weekly guideline when developing your lesson plans:

Lectures	**20 percent**
Exercises	**20 percent**
Sharing	**20 percent**
Guest speakers	**20 percent**
Evaluation Preview/review Assignment }	**20 percent**

It will not always be possible to include all parts each week and that's okay. A complete overview of this course model is available on the Instructor Companion Site. The Annotated Instructor's Edition models this structure for every chapter. Flip to the four pages before one of the chapters to see this model in action.

Using this seven-part course model can be challenging at first and may seem like more work than lecturing. Although the initial investment to create or redesign your lesson plans may be significant, by using this method, class time is spent with students. Students enjoy the variety, and class goes by much more quickly.

COLLECT HOMEWORK

Try to collect homework at the beginning of each class. If homework is late, don't necessarily count it for full credit (unless following an absence). Once you have moved into another chapter, do not accept late work, or make comments on the work, or allow the submission for a grade. This is in keeping with the workplace, where late work is typically frowned upon or unacceptable. Additional suggestions regarding collecting and grading homework assignments are available on the Instructor Companion Site.

PREVIEW

Preview the opening page of each chapter to give students an idea of the components to be found in each chapter. Survey the chapter, asking students to consider these questions before covering the material:

- What has been your experience with this topic?
- Have you experienced success or failure?
- Is this an area you would like to work on? If so, jot down personal ideas as you see strategies which you feel would be helpful.

GUEST SPEAKER

Invite guest speakers from various departments on campus. Also search YouTube for relevant videos; many schools (perhaps even your own) have already uploaded clips with representatives from several departments on campuses, like the career employment center and the library. This allows instructors who teach online, are at an off-campus site, or can't schedule a speaker for a given time to still have access to critical members of the teaching community. Consider filming any guest speakers you may have come into your classroom, and share that video with other instructors teaching the course at your institution. One of the important factors for student retention has been identified as campus involvement. Often it is difficult for online students, evening students, or off-campus

master instructor
best practice

" As a new faculty member (former administrator) I was struggling with the concept of developing an engaging class. I am the product of traditional, lecture-style classes, as my bachelor's degree is in finance. I knew that I wanted/needed to engage the students—I just didn't know how, as I had never personally experienced an engaging class! The article "Creating engaging classes" was an excellent starting point for me. The course model gave me a great guideline to start with and try to follow. It also helped to keep me on task as the semester went along and I found myself lecturing too much, as that is what I experienced as a student. "

—Leigh Smith, Lamar Institute of Technology

Copyright © 2015 Cengage Learning. All Rights Reserved. May not be scanned, copied or duplicated, or posted to a publicly accessible website, in whole or in part.

site students to feel that connectedness to the institution. By seeing the faces and hearing the voices of members of your school community, students can build this connection beyond the walls of the school.

LECTURE

Each class period consider completing a mini-lecture, utilizing your own notes and PowerPoint. PowerPoints for *Becoming a Master Student* that you can tailor to your course are also available at the Instructor Companion Site. Consider posting your PowerPoints online for students to preview before your lecture or access after the lecture, to review. To keep students engaged, make use of videos as part of your lecture.

ACTIVITY

Try to alternate types of activities you use in every class, to provide variety and keep the class exciting for both yourself and the students. This also helps to incorporate different learning styles, appealing to individual student strengths. The Instructor Companion Site has many Best Practice activities tied to *Becoming a Master Student*, content provided by advisors, consultants, and instructors. Skim them, pick a few that fit your teaching style and time constraints, and try them with your class.

SHARING

Consider including recurring group work in your classroom to emulate the workforce structure. Throughout the semester, you can create "teachable moments" if group members are absent. For example, each group member must learn how to communicate effectively and to function as a whole, just as they would on the job. Stress the fact that when projects are due, students may find some members in their group are absent. On the day when a group project is due, if only one or two students in a group attend, students may not have the materials needed, because a vital group member is absent. Each group member is responsible for the material. Give students a personal example from the workplace where there's an unprofessional outcome, and remind students that in a time when the economy suffers and jobs are at a premium, they should attempt to make themselves an invaluable part of the work community, a member who is able, in spite of unforeseen circumstances, to "save the day."

EVALUATION

Although tests are important, synthesis and application are more critical in this class; tell your students this. You can also use a portfolio approach, emphasizing product-based learning, including such items as the CSFI 2.0, the Discovery Wheel, a college or academic plan, a résumé, and a PowerPoint presentation on the student's anticipated major and/or career.

ASSIGNMENTS

Emphasize to students that assignments are not intended as busywork. Assignments are intended for self-analysis and personal and professional growth. Consider consistently assigning certain features such as the Journal Entries. Let other assignments evolve as you see needs or interests expressed in individual classes.

GAINING SUPPORT

Student success courses and first-year seminar programs help students learn to be more effective in school, thereby improving their academic performance and increasing their level of commitment. Gaining approval and support from administrators is important to the success of your course and requires preparation and communication. This backing is necessary to sustain the course long enough to establish both its effectiveness and its value. These suggestions can help you establish that base of support:

Write a statement of purpose for your course. One possibility is "The purpose of our student success course is to improve students' academic performance and increase their level of commitment to our college."

Refer to your statement of purpose often. When negotiating any aspect of your course, be sure to avoid compromises that would sabotage its purpose from either the institution's or the students' perspective. For example, it would be a mistake to settle for too few course contact hours.

Seek grassroots support. The more people who have a vested interest in your proposal, the more likely it is to be accepted. Ask for assistance from the top of the administrative hierarchy. Draw a political road map encompassing crucial factors for gaining support and identifying key individuals. Enlist the support of colleagues who trust you. Spend time with key individuals who may not support your concept but are key curriculum decision makers.

Become a retention expert on your campus. Familiarize yourself with all the data, research, and institutional studies related to student performance and retention at your school. Explore options your institution might use to improve student performance and reduce attrition. ■

Copyright © 2015 Cengage Learning. All Rights Reserved. May not be scanned, copied or duplicated, or posted to a publicly accessible website, in whole or in part.

Setting up your
SYLLABUS

Both the students and the purpose and focus of the course will be different at each school. *Becoming a Master Student* is designed to give students and instructors a variety of topics and ideas. By using this Annotated Instructor's Edition and the Instructor Companion Site, you can select material that is most appropriate both for your students and for your course purpose.

There are dozens of approaches to creating the syllabus for your student success course. It may be as brief as one page, providing only the most essential information for students, or it may be several pages long, with detailed assignments, due dates, and other information about the course. Here are some ideas to consider:

Choose what to include. In addition to the course name, class time, room, instructor name, office hours, and instructor contact information, here are some common elements that may be included in your syllabus:

- Required and optional textbook information
- Other materials you will require students to have. You should provide students with any needed online components and suggest a consistent place for them to record their username and passwords. This will save time and frustration.
- Class support Web site URL
- Assignments, with or without instructions, and due dates
- Important dates, including midterm, final exam, and last day to withdraw from classes
- Official course outline
- Agendas for each class meeting
- Learning outcomes
- Grading method
- Additional recommended readings and/or resources
- Class rules, including your policy for attendance, tardiness, late work, and plagiarism

If you're creating a syllabus for your course for the first time, a more general syllabus may be a better choice. As you progress through the course material, you may discover that some topics take more or less time than you anticipated. You will find that this varies from class to class, or semester to semester.

Organize and sequence the course topics.
The official course outline of record and the total student contact hours for your course will provide you with parameters for organizing the material you will cover during the term. Based on the length of your course, decide how much time you will spend on each topic/chapter. Consider the order in which you will present the topics. Although the text chapters are organized in a logical sequence, once you complete the Introduction and Chapter 1, each chapter has independent content, so you can teach the chapters in whatever order you prefer. Some teachers let the students prioritize the chapters by voting on each of the chapter topic names. Continue to get feedback from students. You may choose to vary the content and the delivery pace, depending on student input. It is much better to successfully cover two topics than to hurriedly cover three. You can often make up the time by altering future assignments.

Identify key dates. After you have organized and sequenced the course topics/chapters, identify key dates for you and your students. Decide when the midterm will be given, when major projects will be due, and which guest speakers you want to invite and when during the term you want them to come. As you will read in Chapter 3, it is important to prepare for the unexpected. Be flexible in your time frame when possible. For example, an invited guest speaker may find he is unavailable at the last minute.

Choose a grading method. Decide how you will weight quizzes, tests, homework, and other assignments. How many quizzes will you give? Will students be allowed to drop their lowest quiz score? Will there be an option for extra credit? Develop an objective system for grading that is applied consistently to each student.

Choose class rules. Class rules include written clarification of the boundaries you set for behavior in the classroom, instructions on the way assignments should be presented for grading, and parameters for how your students should interact with each other and with you. For example, if you are more easily contacted by course e-mail than by phone, you might want to explain this to students. Listed here are some topics you may want to address:

- Attendance
- Assignments turned in with no name
- Late assignments
- Makeup test and quiz policy
- Word-processed (versus handwritten) assignments
- Side conversations

Copyright © 2015 Cengage Learning. All Rights Reserved. May not be scanned, copied or duplicated, or posted to a publicly accessible website, in whole or in part.

- Cell phone and laptop computer use in class
- Academic honesty
- Formatting requirements for electronically transmitted assignments (.pdf, .doc, etc.). It is helpful to be thorough in your instructions. The more detail you can give, the more likely students will be successful. For example, you can't assume students will understand how to upload a document or to log onto their course. Although this is especially true in online classes, it is also true of on-ground classes. You might consider including a document with screen shots of what students will see as they log in to the course. Or you might consider including a tutorial for preparing, saving, or submitting documents.
- Logging-in frequency for online courses

Evaluate and refine. Each semester, make notes about what works and what doesn't work in your syllabus so that you can modify it for the next term. Consider asking your students at the end of the term to provide feedback as to how the syllabus could have been more helpful to them. Create your own evaluation form for your students. No later than midterm, ask questions to guide your instruction, such as these: Which methods in this course have been successful for you? Which methods have not been successful? What elements would you like to see used more in class (including such elements as group work, journals, lecture, hands-on activities)? What ideas can you suggest for making this class more effective for you? For more sample syllabi, log on to the Instructor Companion Site. ■

NSCC 1000—College Success Syllabus

Professor: Dr. Annette McCreedy

E-mail: annette@computer.net

Office: 201 Reed

Hours: By appointment (see posted door schedule) and via e-mail

Phone: (345) 555-0102

Textbook: *Becoming a Master Student at Nashville State Community College*

Course Description A course designed to empower students to reach their educational and career goals; introduces students to strategies, techniques, and self-management tools commonly recognized to lead to success. Topics include educational/career goal-setting and success strategies, campus resources, use of technology, and beginning research skills. This course is available to all students for college-level credit.

The following are the components of the course and the grade percentage assigned to each:

1. Quizzes and homework, including text, online, and other homework (20%)

2. Student Portfolio as follows (30%)
   - Login page where student will record all course codes and passwords for course
   - Discovery Wheel
   - CSFI 2.0
   - Learning Style Inventory
   - Individual health/stress management plan
   - Résumé
   - Copy of the final career PowerPoint

3. Class Participation (10%)

4. PowerPoint career project (20%)

5. Final Exam (20%)

Grading Scale	
A	90–100
B	80–89
C	70–79
D	65–69
F	Below 65
FA	(Attendance-Related Failure)

Copyright © 2015 Cengage Learning. All Rights Reserved. May not be scanned, copied or duplicated, or posted to a publicly accessible website, in whole or in part.

SELLING THIS CLASS
TO STUDENTS ON DAY 1

Copyright © 2015 Cengage Learning. All Rights Reserved. May not be scanned, copied or duplicated, or posted to a publicly accessible website, in whole or in part.

If your student success course is required, you are likely to have a number of student resisters in your class. In colleges and universities where taking such a course is an option, some students enroll because they think it looks like an "easy A" in the catalog. In either case, you can positively influence students on the first day of class so that they'll be more likely to stay and discover for themselves the value of this course. Here are seven suggestions to help build interest and commitment on Day 1.

1 **Student testimonial letters.** At the end of each semester, ask students to write a letter of advice to a future student in your course. Encourage them to include the information they would have liked to have known on the first day of class. Distribute copies of these letters to your students during the first class meeting. Because these letters consist of opinions and not always facts, it may be useful to have the students exchange letters or share key information in the letters in groups or with the class as a whole. Students believe the content in these letters from unknown peers, and many will be inspired by what they read. Master Instructor Dean Mancina puts these letters in envelopes before handing them out—the sealed envelopes add to the impact!

2 **Student guest speakers.** This idea can be used as an alternative or in conjunction with the testimonial letters above. At the end of the semester, invite students to return as guest speakers on the first day of your class the following semester. Get their e-mail addresses and/or phone numbers so that you can send them a reminder a week or two before the next term begins. Having two or three students tell their peers how valuable the course is raises the commitment level of students who are still "shopping" for classes during the first week of the term. Consider video recording these speakers. Or you may choose to save these interviews, allowing you to show these in your course's online platform. In addition, this allows you to save the most powerful speakers' thoughts for future semesters. Powerful student feedback builds buy-in from current students.

3 **Show your enthusiasm.** If you've taught this course before, you know the profound impact it can have on your students. Share that in a dramatic and enthusiastic way. Let your students know how much impact this course can have on their lives. Share some stories of the success your prior students have achieved, but don't mention names to protect your students' privacy.

4 **Ask, "What do you want?"** During the first class, ask students to write down three skills that would be so beneficial that if they could learn them, staying in this course would be "worth it." Brainstorm several skills first to prompt their thinking. Use two-part paper. Have the students pass a copy forward. Read their responses aloud, anonymously, and announce whether each skill is part of the content of this course. This activity helps personalize the course and demonstrates that the content includes material that students want to learn. It also helps to clarify what this class is *not* about, as it's doubtful your course will cover everything the students want.

5 **Talk about the text.** *Becoming a Master Student* is one of the most used college textbooks on any subject in North America. This is a proven product that works. Hold the book up and turn to key pages such as the Discovery Wheel. Tell the students this is a book they will not want to burn or sell at the end of the semester, but will keep as a reference tool for the rest of their college years . . . and beyond! You can suggest that students consider the topics in terms of their families or other important individuals in their lives. For example, when discussing learning styles, encourage students to give the assessments to their significant others. This will help explain some of the frustrations in their personal interactions. For instance, a boss who is a holistic thinker may cause frustration for a linear thinker. This student buy-in affects their personal lives, sometimes even resulting in family members or friends registering for the course in future semesters.

6 **Group discussion and anonymous questions.** Divide students into groups of four and ask them to brainstorm questions about this course that they don't know the answers to. Have the students submit their questions anonymously on 3×5 cards or in an online discussion board. Read the questions aloud and answer them. Addressing concerns students may not wish to state openly can help quell anxiety and fears that could result in students dropping the course.

7 **Tell the truth.** Be honest about both the "good news" and the "bad news." "This course is *not* an easy A! But it's also about more than you thought it was when you enrolled." ■

master instructor
best practice

❝ *On the first day, I share this thought with my students: This course can change your life. But you need to be open to taking an honest look at yourself.* ❞

—Annette McCreedy, Nashville State Community College

CLASSROOM MANAGEMENT STRATEGIES

Students can achieve maximum success in an environment that fosters creativity, critical thinking, focus, and commitment. Developing your classroom management skills can help you create that environment. There are as many approaches to effective classroom management as there are instructors. To be effective, a strategy has to fit your style. For example, if you like a structured, linear environment, set up your class to fit that style. Consider expanding your comfort zone, however, as you model flexibility. Brainstorm a list of answers to the following question: What is the optimum teaching environment for you and your students? The answer to this question may provide you with guidance in formulating strategies that will provide an environment conducive to learning. Consider asking tenured colleagues what works and what doesn't work for them. They know the culture of the students attending your institution.

After you decide what you want, make sure that you clearly communicate to your students how you conduct your class. Have a conversation with your students about this topic during the first week of class. Follow up with key aspects about your class in writing to enhance clarity. This information might be part of your syllabus or a separate handout.

Finally, implement consistently. Public institutions must be able to defend that students are not being discriminated against. No instructor wants to be accused of treating students with favoritism at any institution, public or private.

CLASS RULES TO CONSIDER

You may want to include these rules in your class syllabus.

- ***Respect—for peers, for the instructor, and for guest speakers.*** What are the minimum standards you want to set?

- ***Side conversations.*** Some side conversations in class are related to the class topic being discussed, but others may be unrelated to the topic. Seating students in groups promotes more active learning but may also facilitate more side conversations. Side conversations may distract you from your lecture. Further, when two students engage in a side conversation, not only do they miss what's actually happening in class but the students around them may also be distracted as well. You can minimize this problem if you periodically change how you group students for class work. For example, if you are forming four groups, ask students to number off and form groups, thereby breaking up

friends sitting together. For the next group assignment, start counting off from the opposite direction, again altering group structure.

- ***Absences.*** What is your policy regarding missed class meetings? How will students get the assignments, handouts, information, and class experiences they missed? Flexibility here is helpful for students, but if you're teaching many courses or are a part-time instructor, providing copies of all of your previous handouts and class summaries and taking the time to go over missed classes with students may not be realistic.

- ***Arriving late to class.*** Some instructors and students are distracted when students arrive late to class. How can late-arriving students minimize the disruption they cause? Will you still accept their homework? Does this count against students' grades? Will a set number of tardies count as an absence?

- ***Cell phones/laptops/other technologies.*** Many students have come to believe that they need to stay in touch with their family and friends even during class. If you don't want students constantly stepping out of the classroom to answer their phones, checking their e-mail, surfing the Web, or texting instead of being engaged in what's happening in class, you'll need to set parameters for the use of such devices. You should determine whether you will allow students to use technology to take notes in class. It is difficult to monitor activity, especially if students have Internet access. Temptations can be strong to surf social sites during class.

- ***Turning in assignments late.*** Will you accept assignments after they are due? If so, what are the limits to that policy, if any? Set limits early in the term. Put policies in the syllabus, and be consistent.

- ***Makeups for missed quizzes and tests.*** Can your students arrange to make up a quiz or test they miss? Consider giving quizzes at the beginning of class. This is especially effective if you do not allow makeup quizzes. You will deter tardiness by this strategy.

- ***Accommodations.*** Students should go through your campus' proper channels for obtaining accommodations. These should not be granted after the fact. In other words, after receiving a poor grade, a student may say he should have had special accommodations due to learning or physical challenges. These arrangements should be made early in the semester.

Copyright © 2015 Cengage Learning. All Rights Reserved. May not be scanned, copied or duplicated, or posted to a publicly accessible website, in whole or in part.

- *Cheating.* What is your school's policy regarding cheating?
- *Progressive discipline.* How will you handle violations of your class rules?

Some instructors provide a written list of class rules and review them during class. Other instructors create such a list with the students at the beginning of the course. Such documents can even take the form of a class contract that the instructor and students must sign.

As for discipline, first find out your college's policies and procedures regarding student discipline for cheating and disruptive classroom behavior. Your dean or another administrator may be responsible for student discipline and can give you guidance and direction that is consistent with the institution's policies. Decide ahead of time what your progressive discipline plan will be if a student violates or refuses to follow your rules. Your behavior in that situation will set an example and inform other students of the consequences of not following your rules. Depending on the specific infraction, you might start by approaching the student individually and reminding him of the rule he has broken. If he repeats the violation, you might call him out in front of the class, remind him that you have already talked to him about this, and say that the next time you will tell him to leave the class. Then follow through with his removal if he violates the rule a third time. Make sure you know your school's policy, including calling campus security for unmanageable or threatening conduct. ∎

Course Policies and Class Rules

1. Attendance at each class meeting is required. Be in class on time. Although I understand that there may be days when you may be unable to attend, there are no "excused" absences. In other words, an absence will be recorded. You are allowed four hours of absence before your grade is penalized. If you miss class, it is your responsibility to get makeup assignments and to stay current with class progress. If you are not certain how many absences you have accumulated, you can see me or e-mail me.

2. Be on time for class. Tardiness is disruptive, and you will miss vital information. Two tardies will count as one absence, Tardiness exceeding 15 minutes will be counted as an absence.

3. Side conversations are not permitted. This includes texting!

4. Turn cell phones to Off or Silent and keep them out of sight during class.

5. Laptop computers may be used in class, but students must focus at all times on College Success content.

6. Read and follow the Academic Integrity Policy in your syllabus. Ignorance of this policy is dangerous!

7. You are responsible for understanding and following the course syllabus and any other materials presented in this class. If you do not understand something, ask me *before* a due date arrives.

8. You must purchase a three-ring binder for your text, handouts, notes, and other materials.

9. My course requires online access. Do not use an e-mail address shared with others. E-mail attachments must be sent in Word, rtf, or PDF format. No other formats will be accepted.

10. If you drop this course at any time during the semester, it is your responsibility to officially process the withdrawal paperwork. Note that failure to officially withdraw will result in a failure for non-attendance (FA). This will negatively impact your GPA.

11. My class and Web site are hate-free zones. **Inappropriate, disrespectful, or disruptive behavior will not be tolerated.**

12. Achievement of Student Learning Outcomes is based on the premise that you attend all class meetings, participate actively, and complete all outside of class activities. Generally, students should expect to spend an average of two hours outside of class for every hour spent in class in most transferable college courses, including this one.

13. Students with disabilities who believe they may need accommodations should contact the Disabilities Coordinator as soon as possible. Any accommodations must be recommended by this office. You must fill out the correct paperwork and bring me a copy of the approved accommodations. All accommodations must be designated before due dates. In other words, it is not acceptable to complain about a grade after the fact, stating that you should have received accommodations. All disabilities and accommodations remain confidential.

Copyright © 2015 Cengage Learning. All Rights Reserved. May not be scanned, copied or duplicated, or posted to a publicly accessible website, in whole or in part.

TIPS FOR
TEACHING STUDENT SUCCESS ONLINE

Many of the strategies in the Annotated Instructor's Edition and on the Instructor Companion Site can be adapted for use in your online student success course. One of the most important roles of the online instructor is to ensure a high degree of interactivity and participation by managing the discussion forum. In a classroom, the instructor builds motivation in front of the students by her on-stage demeanor. Online, that role is portrayed in the projects, instructions, and guidance the instructor gives, which together promote a dynamic, interactive environment for online students. For example, when assigning text exercises such as the Discovery Wheel, instead of having students turn in the reflective responses to the exercise, have them post a Discovery/Intention Statement to the Discussion Board and respond to at least two classmates' posts.

Here are some suggestions to help you manage your online Discussion Board:

- Stagger due dates for postings and replies each week to keep the conversation moving.

- Require discussion participation, and make it part of the student's grade in the course.

- Provide expectations that must be met to receive full credit. Include a rubric with specific expectations for Discussion postings. Students often try to piggyback off other students' postings, or they may only write a few words, trying to submit the bare minimum. Your rubric could include categories such as relevance, originality, and coherence. Then give the qualities necessary for certain points or grades on the discussion, including what makes up superior, average, and poor submissions.

- Teach students to create succinct, accurate titles for the subject line of their posts.

- Don't let students use abbreviated writing; teach netiquette. Search online for netiquette standards for other schools.

Consider the following examples of online activities:

1. **Article Response.** For example, after students read the article "Don't fool yourself: 15 common mistakes in logic" (page 217), instruct them to pick one common mistake in logic and post a personal example to the Discussion Board. The second part of the assignment includes responding to classmates' posts.

master instructor
best practice

"I have my students participate in an online scavenger hunt to discover what support programs are available to them while attending this community college. Many students do not attend classes on campus so I have them search the school Web site and then post on the Discussion Board what they discover. My assignment includes several different questions regarding student resources. Each student must respond to a different question."

—Connie Marten, Online Instructor, Golden West College

2. **Weekly Journal.** The weekly journal is an avenue for students and the instructor to relate one on one. Solicit feedback from your students. Ask them how they are doing in class. Often an online class may be more difficult or time-consuming than they anticipated. In the journals, students often share frustrations with other classes, work, or not having enough time with family and friends. Direct them to a specific article in the textbook that may help, or quote something from the book in your reply.

3. **Internet Search.** Consider having students do some research on a topic. For example, use the "Building Relationships across Cultures" article (page 274). Ask each student to complete an Internet search on the phrase "cultural generalization" from the article. Finally, ask students to post their discovery statements about cultural generalization to the Discussion Board, backing up their discoveries with links to the Web sites they researched. As noted above, each student should also respond to two of these posts to keep the discussion moving. ■

AIE-lii

Copyright © 2015 Cengage Learning. All Rights Reserved. May not be scanned, copied or duplicated, or posted to a publicly accessible website, in whole or in part.

ICEBREAKERS:
SOME IDEAS FOR FIRST-DAY-OF-CLASS ACTIVITIES

Creating a sense of community in your classroom starts during your first class meeting. Icebreakers can help both you and your students create a comfortable environment that supports self-discovery and honest reflection—two processes that will help your students achieve success. Here are several possible first-day icebreakers to get you started. Refer to the Instructor Companion Site for more Best Practices related to specific chapters that can be used at any time throughout your course. It creates an atmosphere of enjoyable personal growth, and it may be a novel idea for some students. With some modification, these ideas can be included in online courses also.

Becoming a Master Student has many unique messages in the beginning of the text. These messages are helpful for instructors to remember and highlight when starting the course.

"THIS BOOK IS WORTHLESS"

Have you ever seen a book with this statement? All books are worthless unless read, so this book is useless unless students strive to adapt and adopt methods to attain personal and academic success. Students often complain about the cost of their textbooks. Yet the cost is even higher when they pay for a text but do not actively read it and implement its strategies to promote their success. Ask your students what specific steps they will take to ensure they get the most out of their investment in this textbook. Point out the following exercises as specific tasks to help them get started on this journey: The Discovery Wheel and Learning Style Inventory.

WHAT IS A MASTER STUDENT?

Student success courses are offered at colleges and universities nationwide. Students often exhibit less resistance to taking this course when they realize that their school is not the only one requiring it. The qualities of a successful student are also the qualities of successful employees. This course can help students define the characteristics that promote excellence in their studies and relationships and in preparation for the world of work. Have your students review the article "Master student qualities" in the Introduction. Divide them into groups of four, and ask them to list the qualities of people they admire (family members, celebrities, or friends). When each group has named 10 characteristics, create a combined list of 20 of these for the entire class. Ask students to rank in order the qualities that might contribute to success in school, work, and life.

Ask your students to consider these qualities of success and then write an essay entitled "How do I define success?" Submit the best essay to the Cengage Learning Student Success scholarship competition (see complete details on page AIE-xxviii).

The Discovery Wheel

The Discovery Wheel is an opportunity for students to think about the kind of student they are and the kind of student that they want to become. Its 12 sections correspond to the 12 chapters in the text. This exercise is assigned at the outset of the course to help students assess their current strengths and weaknesses in different areas of student success. Students answer a series of questions and then plot their scores on their Discovery Wheel—a graphic illustration of their skill levels. This is especially helpful for visual learners. At the end of Chapter 12 is an identical Discovery Wheel. By repeating the exercise at the completion of the course, students can trace their progress in acquiring skills and techniques that can ensure their success in school and later in life. The purpose of this exercise is to give students the opportunity to change their behavior. Completing the Discovery Wheel a second time allows students to see what behaviors they have changed on their journey to becoming a master student.

Having your students complete the Skills Snapshot that follows the second Discovery Wheel provides them with another opportunity to state how they intend to change. Encourage them to reconsider tools that they did not think they could use the first time they encountered them in the text.

Note: Student scores may be lower on the second Discovery Wheel. That's okay. Lower scores might result from increased self-awareness and honesty, valuable assets in themselves.

Copyright © 2015 Cengage Learning. All Rights Reserved. May not be scanned, copied or duplicated, or posted to a publicly accessible website, in whole or in part.

Encourage students to participate

Your student success course will benefit from class participation that motivates students to contribute and share. As you create a sense of community in your classroom, use these suggestions for increasing overall participation.

Facilitate students getting to know each other. Having students do projects in groups with non-threatening group assignments (such as "Plan participation activities," following) helps them to get to know each other. It's less intimidating to participate with people you've met than with strangers. Randomly assign students to different groups for a brief activity each week. As evidenced by the CSFI 2.0, campus involvement is a strong factor leading to college success. This becomes especially challenging in an online class. Utilize discussion boards and create groups within your class, requiring students to work together.

Plan participation activities. Divide your students into small groups (three to four students is ideal) to review articles from the textbook or assignments that may have been completed outside class. Provide some guidelines and post them (on a whiteboard, PowerPoint slide, etc.) so that all students can see them. Suggest the number of minutes that students should talk about each question you have assigned. For example, you may ask your students to do the following: "Identify the time-management strategy that was most interesting to you and describe how you plan to use it in the upcoming week (two minutes per person)."

After your students have discussed this with their group, bring the discussion back to the classroom as a whole. Create a tally to show which strategy was the most popular. Consider discussing why some of the less popular strategies are beneficial, and challenge your students to try the one they selected and then one of the less popular strategies. As the instructor, also commit to planning to practice these new strategies and collectively report back on results during the next class period. Sharing enthusiasm with students is a master instructor quality that will help to increase positive feedback and results in your course.

Call on students rather than waiting for them to volunteer. Allow all of your students to think about questions that you are asking, permitting time for reflection and contemplation. Suggest that your students who frequently get called on should first write down their answers while everyone in the class has time to think. Break the ice by selecting one of your eager students. Then select students who have not had a chance to share. Remind students that participating in class is a great way to connect with the instructor and that a student success class is a perfect classroom for practicing their public speaking skills. Challenge your students to participate in their other courses as much as they participate in this class—it's engaging!

Acknowledge uncomfortableness. Trying new techniques, changing habits, and practicing new behaviors can be uncomfortable at first. Discomfort can be a sign of personal growth. Nevertheless, these activities make up much of what a student success course is about. When describing the benefits of the course, it is wise to be honest about the challenges that students face, while expressing confidence in their ability to succeed. Ask students to write their names with their nondominant hands, to introduce themselves to one another by shaking their left hands, or to cross their arms in reverse of the way they normally do. Everyone can relate when they all feel the awkwardness of these movements. But with practice, these movements will begin to feel natural. So will participating in class.

Reinforce speaking up. Surprise a student who speaks up with "bonus points" or a coupon for a beverage in the school food service.

master instructor
best practice

"*I collect office supplies and self-improvement books throughout the year (at store sales and yard sales) to use as rewards throughout the semester, or as a special reward for a student who has shown great personal improvement in the class.*"

—*Annette McCreedy,*
Nashville State Community College

Copyright © 2015 Cengage Learning. All Rights Reserved. May not be scanned, copied or duplicated, or posted to a publicly accessible website, in whole or in part.

"WHAT DO YOU WANT?"

Research indicates that more than 60 percent of first-year college and university students are not yet sure of their career choice, even if they have declared a major. A student might choose a major because of parental pressure or the institution's policy rather than because of a passionate commitment to that field of study or career. This lack of clarity about her destination could negatively affect a student's level of dedication and involvement. She might experience a lack of desire or frustration when she encounters difficulties, because she does not sense that current distresses might result in long-term benefits.

When they are asked "What do you want?" students can begin to find answers to what they hope to accomplish in the course, in the term, and in the academic year. Consider having your students share their answers in class in small groups.

CREATE A COLLEGE SURVIVAL KIT

Divide students into groups, and ask them to brainstorm what this kit would have in it. Ask each group to report out to the class four items that have not been shared by another group.

SCAVENGER HUNT

Create a scavenger hunt list about the services at the college. This encourages students to meet their peers, become familiar with the campus layout, and learn which services are available. The winner of the scavenger hunt might be rewarded by being taken to lunch by the college president.

STUDENT SUCCESS ALUMNI

Invite former students to speak about their experiences taking the student success course and to describe specific successes they've had in college subsequent to completing this course. Also consider recording these students so you can share the videos with future students as well as college faculty and administrators. Allow these coworkers to see the personal benefits from the students—something you see every day!

CLASS AS A WORKSITE

Tell the class that you are the supervisor and they are the employees. Ask them the implications for being late, absent, attentive, and productive. Create a list of expected behaviors in the "workplace." You may periodically ask students to go back to this list, rating their own work in class or that of their groups in group projects.

PULL OBJECTS OUT OF THE BAG

Bring in bags of office supplies, allowing one bag for each group. Each student pulls one item out of the bag. Ask students to describe how they are like the object they draw. For example, a student who draws a paperclip can state that he is the one who emotionally holds his family together. Or after drawing a rubber band from the bag, she may explain that she is flexible in life.

NAMING NAMES

Have each student introduce him or herself with a unique name that describes the person. These aliases could be used throughout the term.

CHOOSE YOUR FINAL GRADE

Many students wonder on the first day about the grade they'll get at the end of the term. Provide a list of each assignment, quiz, and test in the course, as well the maximum points possible. Ask students to set a goal score for each item. Then tell them to total their scores to see their final (goal) grade. This activity generates good first-day questions about course assignments throughout the term. It also demonstrates course goal setting.

GROUP SYLLABUS QUESTIONS

Divide students into groups, and ask each group to come up with three questions about the syllabus. Respond to the entire class about each of the groups' questions. Students are generally more attentive to responses to their inquiries than to your "lecture" about the syllabus. You may also ask students to trade their list of questions with another group. Then each group would answer the questions their group received. ∎

Copyright © 2015 Cengage Learning. All Rights Reserved. May not be scanned, copied or duplicated, or posted to a publicly accessible website, in whole or in part.

Administering and interpreting
THE LEARNING STYLE INVENTORY

The Learning Style Inventory (LSI) is an important tool to help your students discover their preferred mode of learning. Some instructors have found their students feel overwhelmed when they are left on their own to take the LSI, score it, and interpret the results. Consider the following suggestions.

Begin by introducing the LSI to your students. The article "Learning styles: Discovering how you learn" (page 41) will help you set the stage. Page 42 highlights the step-by-step directions for completing the LSI, which begins on page LSI-1. Review the directions with your students. If you are assigning the LSI as homework, consider walking students through the scoring process in class first. Or ask them to hold off scoring the inventory until they're in class with you. As you explain the process to students in class, ask them to help those sitting around them. This builds classroom connections. Guide them in using the interpretive material—help your students connect it with their own experience. Doing so will pay big dividends. Not only will your students begin to understand why they make the choices they do, but they'll be better partners in the learning process.

Be sure to review the cycle of learning with your students. The examples will be easily identifiable to your students and will encourage them to put the information they have discovered about themselves into practice right away. Begin your discussion by asking students about their preferred way to learn historical information or new technology. Ask students, "Did you ever have a difficult or unpleasant subject in school? But at one point you had a teacher who explained it in a way that connected for you—you understood the material and found yourself enjoying the process? This is an indication that the teacher appealed to your preferred learning style." Beginning on page 43, the article "Using your learning style profile to succeed" will have your students participating in a Mode 4 activity. Students can use their understanding of learning styles to make choices that support their academic progress. Ask them to apply *What? Why? How?* and *What if?* questions to the LSI:

- **"Why** should I involve myself in this learning situation?" *Self-awareness control* is the ability to consciously monitor and intentionally control thinking and establish purposeful reasons for action. Asking the question *Why?* helps students regulate their thinking by establishing purposeful reasons for their actions.

- **"What** will I need to do to understand the concept?" *Critical analysis* is the ability to identify key ideas, gather necessary information, and recognize the importance of essential ideas. Asking *What?* questions helps students recognize the knowledge level of essential ideas by their order of importance.

- **"How** is this learning meaningful to me?" *Reasoned synthesis* is the ability to combine essential ideas to create meaningful applications of knowledge. Asking *How?* questions helps students utilize essential ideas and create meaningful applications of their knowledge.

- **"What if** I apply this strategy to my other courses or to my life?" *Creative transfer application* is the ability to adapt applications for different concepts and choose the most effective strategies for specific situations. Asking *What if?* questions helps students imagine alternative applications and choose the most effective strategy for the situation.

Integrating knowledge of learning styles into the curriculum can help instructors design a course that promotes success for all students. As you choose your teaching methods to address various preferences at different points in the course, you meet different students' needs. Students in your classes typically represent all four modes of learning, so some students will sometimes find a good fit with what you are doing, whereas at other times they'll need to stretch beyond their preferences. Acknowledging different learning styles allows instructors to shift their energy from lecturing to facilitating. Rather than just focusing on the transfer of knowledge, you can use feedback about your students' learning to inform your teaching. You may also find yourself challenged in new and exciting ways. Students come to realize that their interactions shape what happens in the classroom, and they become active participants in constructing their learning experience. Working together, instructors and students create an environment that promotes success.

More suggestions for creating lesson plans that support all four modes of learning are available at the Instructor Companion Site. In addition, video clips from the *Learning Style Inventory* video—an overview of the LSI and its application—are available at the Instructor Companion Site. ∎

Copyright © 2015 Cengage Learning. All Rights Reserved. May not be scanned, copied or duplicated, or posted to a publicly accessible website, in whole or in part.

TEACHING LEARNING STYLES
in your classroom

Becoming a master student includes three approaches to learning styles: the Learning Style Inventory, multiple intelligences, and the VAK (visual, auditory, and kinesthetic) system. That's a lot of information to absorb. It is important to recognize that each approach presents a valid option and is not the final word on learning styles. Encourage your students to look for ideas from any of these methods that they can put to immediate use. When they write Intention Statements, have your students keep these questions in mind: "How can I use this idea to *be* more successful in school?" "What will I *do* differently as a result of reading about learning styles?" "If I develop new learning styles, what skill will I *have* that I don't have now?"

The Learning Style Inventory (LSI). People are often fascinated by why they do what they do—and students are no exception. Others may actually avoid introspection (low intrapersonal intelligence according to Gardner's multiple intelligences theory) or may fear the results. Students may ask whether their scores are "bad." It is important to point out to students that there are no right or wrong answers or learning styles. Taking the Learning Style Inventory (LSI) in Chapter 1 gives students a chance to increase their self-awareness as learners. The LSI helps students make sense of what they're experiencing in college. You should also complete the inventory to increase your understanding of the course content and to model the course concepts.

Using learning styles to improve learning and problem-solving skills

Students can improve their ability to learn and solve problems in three ways.

First strategy: Develop supportive relationships. This is the easiest way to improve learning skills. It is important for students to recognize their own learning style strengths and build on them. At the same time, it is important to understand and value other people's different learning styles. Also, students should not assume that they have to solve problems alone. Learning power is increased by working with others. Although students might be drawn to people who have similar learning skills, they'll learn more and experience the learning cycle more fully with friends and coworkers who have different learning skills. Try grouping students with the same learning styles and asking them to determine what does and does not work for them in a classroom setting. Share group responses aloud. For other exercises, try groups that combine students with different learning styles, encouraging them to discuss these differences and how they shape their decisions and behavior. If someone has an abstract learning style, such as Mode 3, he can learn to communicate ideas more effectively by associating with those who are more concrete and people oriented, such as learners who prefer Mode 1. A person with a more reflective style can benefit from observing the risk taking and experimentation of people who are more active, such as learners who prefer Mode 4.

Second strategy: Improve the match or fit between students' learning styles and their tasks. There are a number of ways to do this. For some people, this might mean a change of career to a field where they feel more comfortable with the values and skills required of them. Most people, however, can improve the match between their learning style and their tasks by reorganizing their priorities and activities. They can concentrate on those tasks and activities that lie in their areas of learning strength and rely on other people's help in areas of learning weakness.

Third strategy: Become a flexible learner. This strategy is the most challenging, but also the most rewarding. By becoming flexible and strengthening their weakest learning skills, students will be able to cope with problems of all kinds, and they will be more adaptable in changing situations. This strategy requires more time and tolerance for mistakes and failures, but it builds confidence. Model this for your students. Discuss a time when you had to adjust to someone or some situation. Explain your thought process, and discuss the outcome. Students should develop a long-term plan. Look for improvements and payoffs over months and years. Students should find situations where they can test new skills and will not be punished for failure. Ask students to take a few minutes to brainstorm immediate opportunities to work on this skill. Then discuss answers with the whole class. This process creates student bonds and encourages critical thinking.

Copyright © 2015 Cengage Learning. All Rights Reserved. May not be scanned, copied or duplicated, or posted to a publicly accessible website, in whole or in part.

Applying the learning styles for critical thinking

Have students use the following scale to rate their confidence in their ability to utilize the four questions *Why? What? How?* and *What if?* to effectively accomplish the tasks listed below.

o Never confident   1 Rarely confident

2 Occasionally confident   3 Sometimes confident

4 Often confident   5 Almost always confident

_____ 1. You are a learner, and your biology professor only shows you how to do an experiment. Rate your confidence in your ability to answer any questions (*Why? What?* and/or *What if?*) you still have.

_____ 2. After your professor repeats the instructions for an assignment, they are still not clear to you. How confident are you that you can gain the clarity you need to successfully complete the assignment by asking yourself the four questions?

_____ 3. As you plan your schedule for the next semester, you find there are a number of English classes to choose from. How confident are you in your ability to discover which class would be best for you to take?

_____ 4. You are preparing for a test, but you have little, if any, prior background knowledge about the subject.

_____ 5. You have a problem, and you are trying to understand all the factors that have contributed to the problem so that you can solve it.

_____ 6. You are reviewing your class notes for a test, and you do not remember why a certain entry was so important for you to remember.

_____ 7. You need to choose your career and declare a major, but you are not sure what steps to take first.

_____ 8. Your car breaks down, and you are the one responsible for fixing it.

_____ 9. You are planning a party, and you have been elected to be in charge of buying the food and arranging for the entertainment.

_____ 10. You are sending out invitations to an important event, and you discover that you have more friends and family on your list than you have designated funds for, to cover food and other expenses.

Developed by Dr. David Kolb at Case Western Reserve University in Cleveland, Ohio, the LSI measures a learner's preferences for *perceiving* information (taking it in) and *processing* information (making sense of what she takes in). When these preferences are plotted on two continuums, four unique modes of learning are formed.

The first page of each chapter highlights these four modes to help students become more effective learners through an understanding of their own learning style preferences as related to the concepts found in each chapter.

Multiple intelligences. Howard Gardner of Harvard University believes that no single measure of intelligence can tell us how smart we are. Instead, Gardner identifies many types of intelligence, which are described in *Becoming a Master Student* on page 47. By applying Gardner's concepts, students can explore additional methods for achieving success in school, work, and relationships. *Becoming a Master Student* is designed to help students develop these different intelligences. Charts accompany the definitions of Gardner's multiple intelligences in the text, highlighting the characteristics of each intelligence, the learning strategies that are preferred by people with this type of intelligence, and the careers that might interest them. Have your students apply this information to their core courses. For example, a student with musical/rhythmic intelligence could write songs using lyrics based on class notes and could experiment with various kinds of background music while studying. When students begin to acknowledge and trust all of their intelligences (realizing there are no right or wrong styles or intelligences), they can understand and appreciate themselves more.

The VAK system. The VAK system is a simple and powerful technique that focuses on perception through three sense channels: seeing, or *visual* learning; hearing, or *auditory* learning; and movement, or *kinesthetic* learning. Invite your students to discover their VAK preferences by taking the informal inventory included in the text.

Strategies in the text highlight ways students can build on their current learning preferences and develop new options by utilizing their other sense channels. It is important that you teach students to take in information efficiently through their preferred learning style, but it is equally important that you teach them to study and learn information efficiently through a variety of other learning styles. Understanding these concepts is helpful in dealing effectively in personal and workplace relationships, and in understanding that others also operate through their own styles and strengths. As their instructor, you can set an example by using a mix of strategies to teach students ways to learn the largest amount of material in the least amount of time. Additional ideas for implementing variety in your teaching strategies can be found at the Instructor Companion Site. ■

Copyright ©2015 Cengage Learning. All Rights Reserved. May not be scanned, copied or duplicated, or posted to a publicly-accessible website, in whole or in part.

CRITICAL THINKING: IT'S ALL OVER THIS BOOK

Critical thinking skills are necessary on the first day of the semester, and the tools throughout the text are designed to prepare students for the more in-depth coverage provided in Chapter 7: Thinking.

A first-year experience course can help students develop higher-level thinking and learning skills through self-awareness, self-regulation, and self-instruction. *Becoming a Master Student* offers many opportunities for critical thinking, through the introduction of self-awareness tools; strategies for successful studying; and opportunities for connection with other students, faculty, and campus resources.

Self-discovery is encouraged in Chapter 1 through the Discovery Wheel, the Learning Style Inventory, and other learning styles models. The self-awareness that students gain through using these tools provides them with a foundation for honestly assessing their experiences for the rest of their lives. Introspection can be modeled and learned. By completing the Discovery Wheel again at the end of the text, students can evaluate the work they have accomplished over the semester.

Time management is a crucial skill in the classroom. The exercises in Chapter 2 help students take a first step in learning how to manage their time and set short-, medium-, and long-term goals.

As students develop effective thinking and study skills, as well as master memory, reading, note taking, and test taking, encourage them to begin to transfer these concepts to their core courses. The application of these skills requires a higher level of thinking and promotes their overall success in college.

Once students reach Chapter 7: Thinking, they have experienced the rigors of higher education and are ready to engage in *thorough thinking*. Master students use thorough thinking to select a major, choose courses for the second semester, and plan for their future. They have also actively employed decision-making skills and are ready to transition to the next step of solving problems more creatively and confidently. They exhibit a certain attitude toward success that is highlighted in the way they ask questions, make decisions, and solve problems. Critical thinking is an important aspect of upper-division courses and in the workplace. Learning these skills early makes the transition more successful.

The development of more advanced thinking skills in the early chapters helps students transition to later chapters. There they broaden their scope to consider the impact of their decisions and experiences in higher education in such areas as diversity, communication, money, health, their careers, and life beyond.

Throughout the text, students are encouraged to participate actively in developing and implementing concepts. The ideas in the text are not a list of instructions; they are tools that students can try and then decide what works best for them.

The first page of each chapter encourages students to ask questions related to the four modes of learning identified in the Learning Style Inventory in Chapter 1. These questions promote curiosity and invite students to explore and investigate new materials.

Discovery and Intention Journal Entries, which appear throughout the text, promote a form of decision making that requires students to make declarations that lead to focused action.

Exercises and Practicing Critical Thinking activities promote the application of strategies and allow students to practice problem solving. Students develop thinking techniques and chart their own course. Ask students to brainstorm specific problems they face, as they sharpen their thinking skills in a classroom setting.

The tools provided in *Becoming a Master Student* are a foundation for this success, and as the instructor, you have the ability to foster the attitudes of a critical thinker in your classroom. Ask your students *how* they will apply these skills. Advertise how these strategies work by suggesting that students ask *What if* questions: *"What if* I apply these test-taking strategies to prepare for exams in my biology course? And *what if* I do not?" ■

Copyright © 2015 Cengage Learning. All Rights Reserved. May not be scanned, copied or duplicated, or posted to a publicly accessible website, in whole or in part.

EMBRACING DIVERSITY

Research indicates that although successful students benefit from having a relationship with a caring and competent adult, they are most likely to excel if they receive positive support from a peer group. The information below will help you foster that sense of belonging and assist students of all backgrounds in sharing with each other their discoveries and insights about higher education.

Research also shows that when students interact with diverse student groups, they experience many benefits including these:

- Improved cultural understanding and tolerance
- Decreased cultural prejudice and discrimination
- Stronger connection to the campus community
- Preparation for challenges of global society
- Development of creativity and critical thinking skills

These benefits can be realized only if students extend themselves beyond both real and imagined barriers that exist.

One of the major goals of diversity awareness is to understand how each person fits into the lives and worlds of others. For some of your students, college may be their first experience with someone different from themselves. As you prepare for your course, keep in mind that some kinds of diversity can be less obvious, though just as profound, as others. To the student from rural America, a classmate from New York or Chicago might seem nearly as strange as one from Finland or Zimbabwe, and vice versa.

International students will have additional adjustment issues beyond those of the other students in your class. Keep in mind that some statements, activities, or attitudes that seem perfectly natural in our society may seem curious or even offensive to students from other countries. Familiarize yourself with cultural differences and issues that could frustrate these students.

Finding common ground can be an important learning experience in the classroom. Routinely pairing students from different backgrounds and circumstances when assigning group projects and activities can provide students with the opportunity to encounter ideas, attitudes, and experiences different from their own. Throughout the semester, schedule a variety of activities involving students in individual, partner, small-group, and whole-class settings that exercise and accentuate the similarities among your students and also celebrate the wealth of their differences.

AIE-Ix

CLASSROOM STRATEGIES

Help ensure success. You can individualize your instruction and structure your course so that students experience success. Total success in school is achieved by taking a series of small, successful steps. Set high but realistic expectations. If your course is too easy, students will lose interest. If it is too difficult, students may become discouraged. By continually evaluating students, monitoring their progress, and getting feedback from them, you can plan your classes in ways that help ensure student success. You are a valuable role model and mentor for your students as you go through this process.

Provide opportunities to talk. Invite students to speak about their perspectives. Suggest that students talk to others to share their concerns, celebrations, compliments, and complaints. Use small-group discussions and exercises. If you teach online or have a supplemental Web site for your class, use the Discussion Board for this purpose. Promote the idea of visiting with counselors and forming peer support groups. Try to find out what your students' options are, avoiding a generic "Get involved." Be as specific as possible. The suggestions for conversations and sharing at the Instructor Companion Site include many ideas for stimulating discussions.

Acknowledge and appreciate cultural differences. We can learn from each other and from exploring values that are different from our own. When we exchange ideas, we can expand our perceptions and examine our values. Use conversations, publications, and special events to recognize and celebrate diversity. Consider using YouTube, Public Radio, or other podcasts to provide viewpoints on global events.

Communicate the advantages of being bicultural. Learning new ways of speaking and behaving does not mean denying or letting go of our traditional languages or customs. Adding alternatives does not eliminate anything. Expanding our options increases our ability to operate effectively in a variety of situations and improves our chances of success.

Discuss how the school environment is similar to, and different from, students' home environments. Then discuss ways to make effective transitions back and forth from one to the other. Explore how the expectations of

Copyright © 2015 Cengage Learning. All Rights Reserved. May not be scanned, copied or duplicated, or posted to a publicly accessible website, in whole or in part.

one environment can be assets or liabilities in another. Recognize that a strength in one culture might be a disadvantage in another. Tennis rackets are great on a tennis court, but they don't work very well in a golf game. How can a student adapt so that she is successful in both environments?

Recognize different beliefs regarding time, competitiveness, and respect for authority. In some cultures, punctuality is a plus. In others, time is not measured in hours, minutes, and seconds; instead, it is measured by the movement of the sun, the changing of the seasons, and an intuitive sense of community readiness. In some cultures, competitiveness is a common incentive toward achievement. In others, it is considered antisocial and insulting. Eye contact during conversations is considered respectful in some cultures and disrespectful in others.

You can acknowledge a wide range of beliefs and, at the same time, communicate the expectations of your institution. An advantage to being bicultural is the ability to adopt behaviors that promote success in a specific environment.

Encourage exposure to different backgrounds. Encourage students to break out of old patterns and habits by associating with people from different backgrounds as well as with those whose backgrounds are similar to their own. They could choose new lab partners, form groups with people they don't know for in-class exercises, sit in new areas in the student union, or attend events that are likely to draw crowds different from those with whom they are comfortable. Invite your class to brainstorm ways to gain exposure to people with different backgrounds. Research a variety of cultural events at your campus or in your community. When students attend these events, use these experiences as a springboard for class discussion.

Survey student needs. Evaluate frequently. When you become aware that a student is struggling in a certain area, make an appointment with that student to formulate an action plan.

Individualize feedback. Students appreciate getting specific feedback about their individual performance. Students may initially share cultural concerns or issues in their writing rather than speaking up in class or even individually to you. Write sensitive, relevant comments on papers you return. If possible, always try to include at least one encouraging comment on student assignments. Some students have a strong reaction to red ink, so consider using a more neutral color when correcting papers. Send messages and comments to students through the school e-mail. Thank a student who has actively participated as he leaves the classroom.

Set clear expectations. Communicate expectations clearly. State them several times in several different ways. Use examples to illustrate both what is acceptable and

what isn't. Invite students to ask questions in class or to contact you during your office hours or via e-mail if they have any questions or concerns.

Be a mediator. You can facilitate communication between students and administrators. Pass students' complaints and compliments on to the people who are most directly involved. Ask for responses from those people, and report back to the students. Follow up on all communications until the matter is resolved. Students often drop through the cracks without follow-up. Modeling advocacy can help create self-advocacy in students.

Include other cultural experiences. Use speakers, textbooks, classroom materials, activities, and media presentations that incorporate diverse cultural experiences. Ask students, colleagues, administrators, and community members for recommendations.

Use a critical thinking approach. Ask students to decide what they think about relevant issues and, more importantly, why they think it. Then ask them to seek other views and gather evidence to support the various viewpoints. Discuss which view or views are the most reasonable. When discussing issues, you can apply the strategies outlined in the articles on critical thinking in the text to recognize any errors in thinking.

Encourage proaction. When students face uncomfortable and difficult situations, they sometimes choose avoidance. Help students consider the long-term costs of giving up. Help them see the benefits of a positive, healthy, and proactive approach. Rather than giving up, students can garner support and find or create forums to discuss and resolve their issues. Sometimes, thoughtful grouping of students in class can create a critical connection. For example, a young mother or a defiant young man can be effectively grouped with a more mature student who can provide wisdom and guidance and model critical thinking skills.

Allow personal expression. Invite students to translate material into their own words. Ask them how certain techniques, or variations of those techniques, might be applied in their own culture. For example, a gay, lesbian, or transgender student may want to "come out" to the class while sharing in groups or with the whole class. Be ready to provide leadership and support if students respond in an insensitive or inappropriate manner.

Acknowledge student expertise. Ask students to communicate course content from their unique cultural perspective. Experiencing a concept from a different cultural perspective reinforces it. Give an assignment requiring students to combine a student success strategy with some cultural event, personality, tradition, or value. For example, they could create original music and lyrics

Copyright © 2015 Cengage Learning. All Rights Reserved. May not be scanned, copied or duplicated, or posted to a publicly accessible website, in whole or in part.

or describe the role that a particular success strategy may have played in how a cultural hero changed history.

Use guest speakers. Invite guest speakers to your class who represent successful role models. Ask them to share struggles they have experienced and successes they have achieved. Be sure to include time for a question-and-answer period. For off-site, online, or evening classes, record these speakers for class use.

PERSONAL STRATEGIES

Avoid generalizations. All generalizations are suspect—even this one. Avoid tendencies to lump together all people of one race or culture. Consider speaking up when you hear generalizations being made.

Examine your own prejudices. If you have painful memories that contribute to your prejudices, judgments, and generalizations, examine them. Tell the truth about the costs and benefits of holding on to them. Look at how your history encouraged you to be prejudiced in certain ways. Talk about your prejudices, and formulate a plan to heal and grow.

Examine your assumptions about students. Where do you think your students go during their vacations? How would you expect them to spend extra money? What type of music do they enjoy? Who are their heroes? Which holidays do they celebrate? Consider how often your assumptions direct your teaching and your conversations with students. How would your teaching and your conversations be different if you assumed nothing about your students? Get to know them as individuals, and allow them to see a personal side of you as well.

Find a translator. Taking a first step by admitting that you are unfamiliar or uncomfortable with students from other cultures helps bridge the gap. Ask around to find someone who can act as a translator. In this sense, a translator is someone from the students' ethnic or cultural background who has successfully adapted to the mainstream environment. Ask students whether they are willing to have this person be present when you discuss various issues.

Increase your sensitivity to society's exclusions and inclusions. When you become aware of what to look for, you can see many examples of how one cultural or ethnic group excludes or includes others. Watch advertising and television shows. Examine the policies and notice the membership demographics of schools, businesses, neighborhoods, religious institutions, and athletic clubs. Look for subtle or hidden messages of exclusion and inclusion as well as blatant, formal structures. Expand your personal comfort zone, just as you request of your students.

Give specific feedback. Feedback promotes student success. When feedback is given with a sincere desire to promote success, it is likely to be appreciated. ■

Copyright © 2015 Cengage Learning. All Rights Reserved. May not be scanned, copied or duplicated, or posted to a publicly accessible website, in whole or in part.

INSTRUCTOR TOOLS & TIPS

Introduction | ## THE MASTER STUDENT

"Change and growth take place when a person has risked himself and dares to become involved with experimenting with his own life." —Herbert Otto

Each chapter in the Annotated Instructor Edition is preceded by pages with suggestions for instructors. These suggestions are organized using the seven-part course model on page AIE-xli.

PREVIEW

The introductory chapter, "The Master Student," is an important gateway to *Becoming a Master Student* because it sets the stage for entering the culture of higher education and connecting to new surroundings. It also explains how students should write the important Discovery and Intention Journal Entries throughout the book. Encourage your students to read "Master student qualities" the first week of class.

GUEST SPEAKER

Two or three students from your previous term's class can make great guest speakers for the first week of class. Students respond well to hearing from their peers. You might provide some guidance about the types of experiences the speakers should share. Ask them to briefly discuss why they enrolled in this course and the three most useful tools they learned in the class. Then invite students to ask the guests questions about the course. Consider taping the presentation in case no former students are available to speak next term. As many courses may be taught online or at off-campus sites, these students miss out in activities in daytime classes on the main campus. Video-taping guest speakers allows these students the ability to feel a connection to the campus. Today, cell phones or other electronic devices can easily videotape and upload to YouTube. This option will also provide closed captioning, which can help your campus be more ADA compliant. Captioning also facilitates second-language students.

LECTURE

The master student process—Discovery, intention, action (pages 8–10). The master student process allows students to begin the reflective critical thinking process they will need to grasp the concepts and develop the skills studied in this course and to transfer

master instructor
best practice

During the first class, I ask my students to preview the text, paying particular attention to the Table of Contents. I then give students my course syllabus, which lists a suggested schedule of topics for the semester. The students' first assignment is to look at the Table of Contents and rearrange the schedule of topics in a way that fits their needs. (Another way to do this is to use students' completed Discovery Wheels—see Chapter 1.) During the second class meeting, we list the topics on a flip chart and vote on the order of the chapters. Then we rearrange the syllabus according to the preferences of the students. This method helps me design the course to meet students' immediate needs. Because the course is mandatory, some of the students have negative feelings when they come to class. Allowing them input on the order of the topics sparks interest and gives them ownership of the course.

—Dr. Jennifer Hurd, TeamUP Consultant

those skills to their other classes. This simple yet powerful process is one of the foundations of the textbook. As students read the book, they are often asked to write Discovery Statements about what they are learning and Intention Statements about what they plan to do, based on the new information they are assimilating.

In addition to assigning the many Discovery and Intention Statements in the book, ask students to write statements in class after activities such as guest speakers, videos, or lectures.

AIE-i

Copyright © 2015 Cengage Learning. All Rights Reserved. May not be scanned, copied or duplicated, or posted to a publicly accessible website, in whole or in part.

Here is one formula for writing Discovery Statements:

"When I [what you experienced], I discovered that [specifically what you became aware of]."

This is a formula for Intention Statements:

"I intend to/will [specifically what action you plan to take] by [time frame or date]. My reward will be [the tangible reward you'll give yourself if you complete your intended goal]."

Sharing these aloud can also help students model the thought process for each other.

Organize for success. Encourage your students to identify a student in each class who seems responsible and dependable. Have them exchange and record e-mail addresses and phone numbers with this person. Suggest to students that if they know they won't be in class, they should contact their student "buddy" ahead of time to ask him or her to pick up extra copies of handouts, and to request to copy this person's notes. Take this opportunity to invite your students to visit you during office hours. Provide your e-mail address, phone number, and office location. You might choose to share your office schedule with your students. Students often are confused about how to read a door schedule. Although we are accustomed to terms such as *office* and *open hours*, this may be confusing to new students.

Workplace Applications: Master Student Qualities = Master Employee Qualities. Explain to students that the same master student qualities (competence, joy, creativity, etc.) they will learn in class are also the same qualities they will use as a successful employee. Knowing how to stay motivated at work makes it easier to complete even those tasks they don't like ("Motivation—I'm just not in the mood," pages 25–26). Understanding classroom civility goes a long way in managing workplace conflict ("Communicating respect in the classroom," page 24). The same way a student shows a teacher respect in the classroom (attending class, showing up for class on time, completing all assigned tasks) is the same way an employee shows respect for the job and the employer. These transferable skills, skills that can be applied regardless of work environment, are very important for workplace success.

Many of the steps in "Making the transition to higher education" (pages 15–17) can also be adapted for use in the workplace. Allowing time for transition from school to career is necessary in order to adjust and so as not to be overwhelmed by a new work experience. Employers look for workers who work well in a team, are dependable, and show initiative. Cultivating the ability to be a self-regulated learner while in college will translate to being a conscientious employee after graduation. This introduction allows you to add additional selling points

master instructor
best practice

❝ *One of the assignments in my class is a group presentation on a Power Process. Early in the term, students pick a Power Process to work on. Small groups are formed with students interested in the same one. At midterm time, presentations are given. It is one of the highlights of the term.* **❞**

—*Joe Rine, Minneapolis Community & Technical College*

for making the most out of *Becoming a Master Student*. Not only will the skills learned from this book be useful in college, but there are lifelong benefits as well.

EXERCISES/ACTIVITIES

1. **Power Process: Discover what you want (page 2).** Explain the purpose of each Power Process to your students: The Power Process will change the way they think, or change their consciousness, because it is their consciousness that determines their behavior. Ask students to consider and discuss in groups: (1) *why* this Power Process might matter to them (or to their children, family, coworkers, and the like), (2) *what* this Power Process means with regard to the transition to college, (3) *how* they will make this transition work for them, and (4) *what if* they do not make this transition now.

2. **Master student qualities (pages 4–6).** After students read this article outside class, reinforce the concept of mastery with the following team-building activity in class. Randomly assign students to groups of four, and ask each group to select five of the most important master student qualities for the classroom and also to select five of the most important qualities in the workplace. The group members must agree on the five qualities they pick and be able to justify their decision to choose them. Ask students to examine the qualities on both lists. Do the lists overlap? What does this tell them? Have each group report to the whole class on their choices.

3. **Commitment exercise (page 14).** After students have read the Introduction and completed this exercise, at the following class meeting ask them to open their books to this exercise so that they can review what they wrote. This simple exercise, which takes less than five minutes to complete, helps students confirm their commitment to this course and, indirectly, to their entire college experience. Have students write in large letters on a sheet of paper the words of the level of commitment they chose and

Copyright © 2015 Cengage Learning. All Rights Reserved. May not be scanned, copied or duplicated, or posted to a publicly accessible website, in whole or in part.

Copyright ©2015 Cengage Learning. All Rights Reserved. May not be scanned, copied or duplicated, or posted To a publicly accessible website, in whole or in part.

master instructor
best practice

" I cover classroom civility in my classes. I have found that we can't assume that students know what is expected of them in terms of what are appropriate college classroom behaviors. For many, they are the first in their family to attend college. There is a misconception among students that because they pay for classes, any behavior is acceptable in the classroom. (The customer is always right!) Many of the students are also under a great deal of stress due to the state of the economy. This also influences their behaviors. During the first week of class, we have a discussion on classroom civility, and I have them sign the student agreement. "

—Debbie Warfield, *Seminole Community College*

then sign their name at the bottom. Have them put this paper at the front of their binder so that every time they open their binder, they'll be reminded of their commitment to this textbook—and to their student success.

4. **Making the transition to higher education (pages 15–17).** Have your students choose partners and review the list of expectations in this article. Ask them to predict the two transition areas from the article that would cause them the most trouble and to discuss why. Then they should discuss some possible solutions. Collecting these from students can allow you to recognize issues early. It also allows you to keep challenges in mind when grouping students. For example, a struggling, exhausted young mother can benefit from a group assignment with a mature, more experienced parent. This can create life-changing bonds.

5. **Ways to change a habit (pages 29–30).** Challenge your students to brainstorm habits they would like to start, stop, or change. Then ask them to pick a habit that they would like to commit to change successfully over the course of the term. Using the two-part note paper available from Cengage, have them write down their habit and separate the paper. Tell the students to put one part in a self-addressed envelope and to keep the copy for themselves as a reference and reminder of their plan to change the habit. Collect the self-addressed envelopes, and mail them to the students in four months (after the course is over) as an incentive for them to keep working on their habit change.

CONVERSATION/SHARING

"Sell" this course to resistant students. Whether your course is required or not, it's likely that you have some students who are not pleased by the idea of taking your class. If you share with your class an experience that you had as a student in college, your students may feel that you are more of a partner with them in their educational explorations. Students particularly enjoy hearing stories of the mistakes you made while in college!

HOMEWORK

Textbook reconnaissance (page 3). Even though many students won't have purchased the textbook on the first day of class, hold up your copy of the book, and show them the Textbook Reconnaissance exercise. When you assign textbook reading each week, tell students that they must read the articles *and* do all of the chapter exercises, Practicing Critical Thinking exercises, and Discovery/Intention Journal Entries within the assigned pages. The thinking/writing assignments in the book help students personalize what they are reading. To encourage students to buy the textbook early in the term, you might want to assign homework early, pointing out that in college courses, grading begins early, placing students at a disadvantage if they do not come prepared. For example, you might want to count the Discovery Wheel as an early grade, especially given the fact that this should be completed as early as possible if it is to be a true gauge of accomplishment when the Discovery Wheel assignment is given again at the close of the term.

EVALUATION

Frequent quizzes ensure that students focus attention during class and keep up with the text reading assignments. Quizzes also provide students with opportunities for written reflection regarding new discoveries and intentions. Evaluation also helps you identify topics and concepts that students have not yet mastered. Questions may be based on the textbook reading assignment, guest speakers, class activities, and/or the lecture.

At your request, Cengage Learning will provide packages of three-part NCR quiz paper to facilitate quick quizzes in class. First, make up your quiz question(s). These may be multiple-choice, true/false, short-answer, or essay questions. Students answer the quiz question(s) on the white (top) sheet, simultaneously making two copies on the yellow and pink paper. When the quiz time is up, direct students to tear off the white copy and pass it forward. They can no longer change their answers, because you have the original white sheet. Then direct them to look up the correct answers in their book and grade their own quiz. Finally, have them pass the yellow copy forward for your review and so you can record their scores. Students keep the pink copy.

AIE-iii

MindTap™

EMBRACE VALUABLE RESOURCES

FOR THE INTRODUCTION

STUDENT RESOURCES: MINDTAP

- **Learning Outcomes.** Every chapter begins with an engaging video that visually outlines in a mind map format the key learning outcomes for that chapter. Students should find these short introductions not only helpful as chapter organizers but also as valuable note-taking models.

- **Engagement Activity: Master Students in Action.** In this video, students will be introduced to one of the hallmarks of *Becoming a Master Student*— the master student qualities. Students hear firsthand from other students about how they have exemplified all the master student qualities. The video should be accompanied with the article "Master student qualities" (pages 4–6).

- **MindTap Reader.** The MindTap Reader is more than a digital version of a textbook. It is an interactive, learning resource that was built from the ground up to create a digital reading experience based on how students assimilate information in an online environment. The robust functionality of the MindTap Reader allows learners to make notes, highlight text, and even find a definition right from the page.

- **Aplia Homework Assignment: Discovery.** In this assignment, students develop a mindset for self-discovery and learn how discovery and intention statements along with action plans lead to mastery by examining a student's journal entry and exploring what his most important discovery and intentions might be.

MindTap™ *Your personal learning experience—learn anywhere, anytime.*

INSTRUCTOR COMPANION SITE

- **Need some general advice about using Becoming a Master Student in your course?** The online Course Manual serves as an invaluable reference for those developing and teaching a College Success course with *Becoming a Master Student*. The Course Manual features tried-and-true best practices, a variety of lecture topics, group activities, and suggested homework assignments. The Course Manual also provides advice on general teaching issues such as preparing for classes, classroom management, grading, and communicating with students of various backgrounds, as well as specific strategies for getting the most out of various features in *Becoming a Master Student*, such as the Discovery Wheel and Learning Style Inventory. Download the Course Manual now and do a reconnaissance to find ideas that you can use in your course.

- **Looking for test banks?** Customizable, text-specific content quizzes are a great way to test students' knowledge and understanding of the text, and are available for every chapter. Powered by Cognero, the test banks can be exported in an LMS or print-friendly format. You will have no problem accessing the multiple-choice, true/false, completion, and short-answer questions.

- **Check out the new PowerPoint Library!** This master library of PowerPoint presentations makes it easy to find the right PowerPoint for you! In the library, you will find PowerPoint slides for every chapter as well as every Power Process article covered in the book. All PowerPoint slides are downloadable and customizable to fit your needs.

  Please visit login.cengage.com to log in and access the Instructor Companion Site.

Copyright © 2015 Cengage Learning. All Rights Reserved. May not be scanned, copied or duplicated, or posted to a publicly accessible website, in whole or in part.

Introduction

THE MASTER STUDENT

Why

You can ease your transition to higher education and set up a lifelong pattern of success by starting with some key strategies.

How

Take a few minutes to skim this chapter. Find three suggestions that look especially useful. Make a note to yourself or mark the pages where the strategies that you intend to use are located in the chapter.

What if ...

I could use the ideas in this book to more consistently get what I want in my life?

The master student process You can use this process to learn about any subject, change your habits, and acquire new skills. Experience it firsthand. Test the process in daily life. Then watch the results unfold. ■ 8

Developing a professional work ethic ■ 23

Master student qualities
Master students share certain qualities. These are attitudes and core values. Although they imply various strategies for learning, they ultimately go beyond what you do. Master student qualities are ways of *being* exceptional. ■ 4

Leading the way— Succeeding as a first-generation student
Entering higher education means walking into a new culture. You might feel that the ground rules have changed and that you have no idea how to fit in. This is normal. ■ 20

What is included ...

Copyright © 2015 Cengage Learning. All Rights Reserved. May not be scanned, copied or duplicated, or posted to a publicly accessible website, in whole or in part. | Photo Credit: Stockbyte/Getty Images. Second Photo: John Lund/Stone/Getty Images. Third Photo: Oliver Cleve/Getty Images. Fourth Photo: © Maciej Oleksy/Shutterstock.com.

DISCOVER
WHAT YOU WANT

Imagine a man who tries to buy a plane ticket for his next vacation with no destination in mind. He pulls out his iPad and logs in to his favorite website for trip planning. He gets a screen that prompts him for details about his destination. And he leaves all the fields blank.

"I'm not fussy," says the would-be vacationer. "I just want to get away. I'll just accept whatever the computer coughs up."

Compare this person to another traveler who books a flight to Ixtapa, Mexico, departing on Saturday, March 23, and returning Sunday, April 7—window seat, first class, and vegetarian meals.

Now, ask yourself which traveler is more likely to end up with a vacation that he'll enjoy.

The same principle applies in any area of life. Knowing where we want to go increases the probability that we will arrive at our destination. Discovering what we want makes it more likely that we'll attain it.

Okay, so the example about the traveler with no destination is far-fetched. Before you dismiss it, though, do an informal experiment: Ask three other students what they want to get out of their education. Be prepared for hemming, hawing, and vague generalities.

This is amazing, considering the stakes involved. Students routinely invest years of their lives and thousands of dollars, with only a hazy idea of their destination in life.

Now suppose that you asked someone what she wanted from her education and you got this answer: "I plan to get a degree in journalism, with double minors in earth science and Portuguese, so that I can work as a reporter covering the environment in Brazil." The details of a person's vision offer clues to their skills and sense of purpose.

Another clue is the presence of "stretch goals"—those that are big *and* achievable. A 40-year-old might spend years talking about his desire to be a professional athlete someday. Chances are, that's no longer achievable. However, setting a goal to lose 10 pounds by playing basketball at the gym three days a week is another matter. That's a stretch—a challenge. It's also doable.

Discovering what you want helps you succeed in higher education. Many students quit school simply because they are unsure about what they want from it. With well-defined goals in mind, you can look for connections between what you want and what you study. The more connections, the more likely you'll stay in school—and get what you want in every area of life.[1] ■

Tobias Titz/Getty Images

Copyright © 2015 Cengage Learning. All Rights Reserved. May not be scanned, copied or duplicated, or posted to a publicly accessible website, in whole or in part.

REWRITE
this BOOK

© maigi/Shutterstock.com

Some books should be preserved in pristine condition. This book isn't one of them.

Something happens when you get involved with a book by writing in it. *Becoming a Master Student* is about learning, and learning results when you are active. When you make notes in the margin, you can hear yourself talking with the author. When you doodle and underline, you see the author's ideas taking shape. You can even argue with the author and come up with your own theories and explanations. In all of these ways, you can become a coauthor of this book. Rewrite it to make it yours.

While you're at it, you can create symbols or codes that will help you when reviewing the text later on. You might insert a "Q" where you have questions, or put exclamation points or stars next to important ideas. You could also circle words to look up in a dictionary.

Remember, if any idea in this book doesn't work for you, you can rewrite it. Change the exercises to fit your needs. Create a new technique by combining several others. Create a technique out of thin air!

Find something you agree or disagree with and write a short note in the margin about it. Or draw a diagram. Better yet, do both. Let creativity be your guide. Have fun.

Begin rewriting now. ■

Copyright © 2015 Cengage Learning. All Rights Reserved. May not be scanned, copied or duplicated, or posted to a publicly accessible website, in whole or in part.

Interactive

Exercise 1 Textbook reconnaissance

Start becoming a master student this moment by doing a 15-minute "textbook reconnaissance." First, read this book's Table of Contents. Do it in three minutes or less. Next, look at every page in the book. Move quickly. Scan headlines. Look at pictures. Notice forms, charts, and diagrams.

Look especially for ideas you can use. When you find one, note the page number and a short description of the idea. You also can use sticky notes to flag pages that look useful. (If you're reading *Becoming a Master Student* as an ebook, you can flag pages electronically.)

_____

_____

_____

_____

_____

_____

_____

_____

_____

_____

Oliver Cleve/Getty Images

MASTER STUDENT
qualities

This book is about something that cannot be taught. It's about becoming a master student.

Mastery means attaining a level of skill that goes beyond technique. For a master, work is effortless. Struggle evaporates. The master carpenter is so familiar with her tools that they are part of her. To a master chef, utensils are old friends. Because these masters don't have to think about the details of the process, they bring more of themselves to their work.

Mastery can lead to flashy results: an incredible painting, for example, or a gem of a short story. In basketball, mastery might result in an unbelievable shot at the buzzer. For a musician, it might be the performance of a lifetime, the moment when everything comes together. You could describe the experience as "flow" or "being in the zone."

Often, the result of mastery is a sense of profound satisfaction, well-being, and timelessness. Distractions fade. Time stops. Work becomes play. After hours of patient practice, after setting clear goals and getting precise feedback, the master has learned to be fully in control.

At the same time, he lets go of control. Results happen without effort, struggle, or worry. Work seems self-propelled. The master is in control by being out of control. He lets go and allows the creative process to take over. That's why after a spectacular performance by an athlete or performer, observers often say, "He played full out—and made it look like he wasn't even trying."

Likewise, the master student is one who makes learning look easy. She works hard without seeming to make any effort. She's relaxed *and* alert, disciplined *and* spontaneous, focused *and* fun-loving.

You might say that those statements don't make sense. Actually, mastery does *not* make sense. It cannot be captured with words. It defies analysis. Mastery cannot be taught. It can only be learned and experienced.

By design, you are a learning machine. As an infant, you learned to walk. As a toddler, you learned to talk. By the time you reached age 5, you'd mastered many skills needed to thrive in the world. And you learned all these things without formal instruction, without lectures,

without books, without conscious effort, and without fear. You can rediscover that natural learner within you. Each chapter of this book is about a step you can take on this path.

Master students share certain qualities. These are attitudes and core values. Although they imply various strategies for learning, they ultimately go beyond what you do. Master student qualities are ways of *being* exceptional.

Following is a list of master student qualities. Remember that the list is not complete. It merely points in a direction. As you read, look to yourself. Put a check mark next to each quality that you've already demonstrated. Put another mark, say an exclamation point, next to each quality you want to actively work on possessing. This is not a test. It is simply a chance to celebrate what you've accomplished so far—and start thinking about what's possible for your future.

☐ **Inquisitive.** The master student is curious about everything. By posing questions, she can generate interest in the most mundane, humdrum situations. When she is bored during a biology lecture, she thinks to herself, "I always get bored when I listen to this instructor. Why is that? Maybe it's because he reminds me of my boring Uncle Ralph, who always tells those endless fishing stories. He even looks like Uncle Ralph. Amazing! Boredom is certainly interesting." Then she asks herself, "What can I do to get value out of this lecture, even though it seems boring?" And she finds an answer.

☐ **Able to focus attention.** Watch a 2-year-old at play. Pay attention to his eyes. The wide-eyed look reveals an energy and a capacity for amazement that keep his attention absolutely focused in the here and now. The master student's focused attention has a childlike quality. The world, to a child, is always new. Because the master student can focus attention, to him the world is always new too.

Copyright © 2015 Cengage Learning. All Rights Reserved. May not be scanned, copied or duplicated, or posted to a publicly accessible website, in whole or in part.

☐ **Willing to change.** The unknown does not frighten the master student. In fact, she welcomes it—even the unknown in herself. We all have pictures of who we think we are, and these pictures can be useful. But they also can prevent learning and growth. The master student embraces new ideas and new strategies for success.

☐ **Able to organize and sort.** The master student can take a large body of information and sift through it to discover relationships. He can play with information, organizing data by size, color, function, timeliness, and hundreds of other categories. He has the guts to set big goals—and the precision to plan carefully so that those goals can be achieved.

☐ **Competent.** Mastery of skills is important to the master student. When she learns mathematical formulas, she studies them until they become second nature. She practices until she knows them cold—then puts in a few extra minutes. She also is able to apply what she learns to new and different situations.

☐ **Joyful.** More often than not, the master student is seen with a smile on his face—sometimes a smile at nothing in particular other than amazement at the world and his experience of it.

☐ **Able to suspend judgment.** The master student has opinions and positions, and she is able to let go of them when appropriate. She realizes she is more than her thoughts. She can quiet her internal dialogue and listen to an opposing viewpoint. She doesn't let judgment get in the way of learning. Rather than approaching discussions with a "Prove it to me and then I'll believe it" attitude, she asks herself, "What if this is true?" and explores possibilities.

☐ **Energetic.** Notice the master student with a spring in his step, the one who is enthusiastic and involved in class. When he reads, he often sits on the very edge of his chair, and he plays with the same intensity. He is determined and persistent.

☐ **Well.** Health is important to the master student, though not necessarily in the sense of being free of illness. Rather, she values her body and treats it with respect. She tends to her emotional and spiritual health as well as her physical health.

> *If a master student takes a required class that most students consider boring, she chooses to take responsibility for her interest level. She looks for ways to link the class to one of her goals and experiment with new study techniques that will enhance her performance in any course.*

☐ **Self-aware.** The master student is willing to evaluate himself and his behavior. He regularly tells the truth about his strengths and those aspects that could be improved.

☐ **Responsible.** There is a difference between responsibility and blame, and the master student knows it well. She is willing to take responsibility for everything in her life—even for events that most people would blame on others. For example, if a master student takes a required class that most students consider boring, she chooses to take responsibility for her interest level. She looks for ways to link the class to one of her goals and experiment with new study techniques that will enhance her performance in any course.

☐ **Willing to take risks.** The master student often takes on projects with no guarantee of success. He participates in class dialogues at the risk of looking foolish. He tackles difficult subjects in term papers. He welcomes the risk of a challenging course.

☐ **Willing to participate.** Don't look for the master student on the sidelines. She's a collaborator—a team player who can be counted on. She is engaged at school, at work, and with friends and family. She is willing to make a commitment and to follow through on it.

☐ **A generalist.** The master student is interested in everything around him. In the classroom, he is fully present. Outside the classroom, he actively seeks out ways to deepen his learning—through study groups, campus events, student organizations, and team-based projects. Through such experiences, he develops a broad base of knowledge in many fields that can apply to his specialties.

☐ **Willing to accept paradox.** The word *paradox* comes from two Greek words, *para* ("beyond") and *doxen* ("opinion"). A paradox is something that is beyond opinion or, more accurately, something that might seem contradictory or absurd yet might actually have meaning. For example, the master student can be committed to managing money and reaching her financial goals. At the same time, she can be totally detached from money, knowing that her real worth is independent of how much money she has.

Copyright © 2015 Cengage Learning. All Rights Reserved. May not be scanned, copied or duplicated, or posted to a publicly accessible website, in whole or in part.

☐ **Courageous.** The master student admits his fear and fully experiences it. For example, he will approach a tough exam as an opportunity to explore feelings of anxiety and tension related to the pressure to perform. He does not deny fear; he embraces it. If he doesn't understand something or if he makes a mistake, he admits it. When he faces a challenge and bumps into his limits, he asks for help. And he's just as willing to give help as to receive it.

☐ **Self-directed.** Rewards or punishments provided by others do not motivate the master student. Her desire to learn comes from within, and her goals come from herself. She competes like a star athlete—not to defeat other people but to push herself to the next level of excellence.

☐ **Spontaneous.** The master student is truly in the here and now. He is able to respond to the moment in fresh, surprising, and unplanned ways.

☐ **Relaxed about grades.** Grades make the master student neither depressed nor euphoric. She recognizes that sometimes grades are important. At the same time, grades are not the only reason she studies. She does not measure her worth as a human being by the grades she receives.

☐ **"Tech" savvy.** A master student defines *technology* as any tool that's used to achieve a human purpose. From this point of view, computers become tools for deeper learning, higher productivity, and greater success. When faced with a task to accomplish, the master student chooses effectively from the latest options in hardware and software. He doesn't get overwhelmed with unfamiliar technology. Instead, he embraces learning about the new technology and finding ways to use it to help him succeed at the given task. He also knows when to go "offline" and fully engage with his personal community of friends, family members, classmates, instructors, and coworkers.

☐ **Intuitive.** The master student has an inner sense that cannot be explained by logic alone. She trusts her "gut instincts" as well as her mind.

☐ **Creative.** Where others see dull details and trivia, the master student sees opportunities to create. He can gather pieces of knowledge from a wide range of subjects and put them together in new ways. The master student is creative in every aspect of his life.

☐ **Willing to be uncomfortable.** The master student does not place comfort first. When discomfort is necessary to reach a goal, she is willing to experience it. She can endure personal hardships and can look at unpleasant things with detachment.

☐ **Optimistic.** The master student sees setbacks as temporary and isolated, knowing that he can choose his response to any circumstance.

☐ **Willing to laugh.** The master student might laugh at any moment, and her sense of humor includes the ability to laugh at herself. While going to school is a big investment, with high stakes, you don't have to enroll in the deferred-fun program. A master student celebrates learning, and one of the best ways of doing that is to laugh now and then.

☐ **Hungry.** Human beings begin life with a natural appetite for knowledge. In some people it soon gets dulled. The master student has tapped that hunger, and it gives him a desire to learn for the sake of learning.

☐ **Willing to work.** Once inspired, the master student is willing to follow through with sweat. She knows that genius and creativity are the result of persistence and work. When in high gear, the master student works with the intensity of a child at play.

☐ **Caring.** A master student cares about knowledge and has a passion for ideas. He also cares about people and appreciates learning from others. He collaborates on projects and thrives on teams. He flourishes in a community that values win-win outcomes, cooperation, and love. ◾

Copyright © 2015 Cengage Learning. All Rights Reserved. May not be scanned, copied or duplicated, or posted to a publicly accessible website, in whole or in part.

Exercise 2 The master student in you

The purpose of this exercise is to demonstrate to yourself that you truly are a master student. Start by remembering a time in your life when you learned something well or demonstrated mastery. This experience does not have to relate to school. It might be a time when you aced a test, played a flawless soccer game, created a work of art that won recognition, or burst forth with a blazing guitar solo. It might be a time when you spoke from your heart in a way that moved someone else. Or it might be a time when you listened deeply to another person who was in pain, comforted him, and connected with him at a level beyond words.

Step 1

Describe the details of such an experience in your life. Include the place, time, and people involved. Describe what happened and how you felt about it.

_____

_____

_____

_____

_____

_____

_____

_____

_____

_____

Step 2

Now, review the article "Master student qualities" and take a look at the master student qualities that you checked off. These are the qualities that apply to you. Give a brief example of how you demonstrated at least one of those qualities.

_____

_____

Step 3

Now think of other qualities of a master student— characteristics that were not mentioned in the article. List those qualities along with a one-sentence description of each.

_____

_____

_____

_____

_____

_____

_____

_____

Copyright © 2015 Cengage Learning. All Rights Reserved. May not be scanned, copied or duplicated, or posted to a publicly accessible website, in whole or in part.

The MASTER STUDENT PROCESS—
DISCOVERY

John Lund/Stone/Getty Images

One way to become a better student is to grit your teeth and try harder. There is a better way—the master student process. The purpose of using this process is to develop the qualities of a master student.

You can use this process to learn about any subject, change your habits, and acquire new skills. Once you start using the process in earnest, your self-awareness will deepen.

Those are large claims. If you're skeptical, that means you're already developing one quality of a master student—being inquisitive. Balance it with another quality—the ability to suspend judgment while considering a new idea.

First, get an overview of the master student process. There are three phases:
- Discovery
- Intention
- Action

As you experiment with the master student process, remember that there's nothing you need to take on faith. Experience it firsthand. Test the process in daily life. Then watch the results unfold.

GUIDELINES FOR DISCOVERY STATEMENTS

Throughout this book, you'll see Journal Entries. These are suggestions for writing that guide you through the master student process.

Some of these Journal Entries are called Discovery Statements. Their purpose is to help you gain awareness of "where you are"—your current thoughts, feelings, and behaviors. Use Discovery Statements to describe your strengths and the aspects of your life that you'd like to change. The result is a running record of how you are learning and growing.

Sometimes Discovery Statements capture an "aha!" moment—a sudden flash of insight. Perhaps a new solution to an old problem suddenly occurs to you. Maybe a life-changing insight wells up from the deepest part of your mind. Don't let such moments disappear. Capture them in Discovery Statements.

To get the most value from Discovery Statements, keep the following guidelines in mind.

- ***Record the specifics about your thoughts, feelings, and behavior.*** Thoughts include inner voices. We talk to ourselves constantly in our head. When internal chatter gets in the way, write down what you tell yourself. If this seems difficult at first, just start writing. The act of writing can trigger a flood of thoughts.

Thoughts also include mental pictures. These are especially powerful. Picturing yourself flunking a test is like a rehearsal to do just that. One way to take away the power of negative images is to describe them in detail.

Also notice how you feel when you function well. Use Discovery Statements to pinpoint exactly where and when you learn most effectively.

In addition, observe your emotions and actions, and record the facts. If you spent 90 minutes chatting online with a favorite cousin instead of reading your anatomy text, write about it. Include the details—when you did it, where you did it, and how it felt.

- ***Use discomfort as a signal.*** When you approach a hard task, such as a difficult math problem, notice your physical sensations. These might include a churning stomach, shallow breathing, and yawning. Feeling uncomfortable, bored, or tired can be a signal that you're about to do valuable work. Stick with it. Write about it. Tell yourself you can handle the discomfort just a little bit longer. You will be rewarded with a new insight.

- ***Suspend judgment.*** As you learn about yourself, be gentle. Suspend self-judgment. If you continually judge your behaviors as "bad" or "stupid," your mind will quit making discoveries rather than put up with abuse. For your own benefit, be kind to yourself.

- ***Tell the truth.*** Suspending judgment helps you tell the truth about yourself. "The truth will set you free" is a saying that endures for a reason. The closer you get to the truth, the more powerful your Discovery Statements. And if you notice that you are avoiding the truth, don't blame yourself. Just tell the truth about it. ■

Copyright © 2015 Cengage Learning. All Rights Reserved. May not be scanned, copied or duplicated, or posted to a publicly accessible website, in whole or in part.

The MASTER STUDENT PROCESS—
INTENTION

Some Journal Entries in this book are called Intention Statements. These are about your commitment to take action. Use Intention Statements to describe how you will change your thinking and behavior.

Gary Waters/Ikon Images/Getty Images

In terms of the master student process, Intention Statements and Discovery Statements are linked.

Whereas Discovery Statements promote insights, Intention Statements are blueprints for action based on those insights.

To remind you of this connection, many Journal Entries in this book are labeled as Discovery/Intention Statements.

The act of writing will focus your energy on specific tasks and help you aim at particular goals. Here are more ways to create Intention Statements that make a positive difference in your life:

- **Make intentions observable.** Rather than writing "I will work harder on my history assignments," write, "I intend to review my class notes, and I intend to make summary sheets of my reading." Then when you review your progress, you can actually tell whether you did what you intended to do.

- **Make intentions small and achievable.** Give yourself the chance to succeed. Set goals that you can meet. Break large goals into small, specific tasks that can be accomplished quickly. If you want to get an A in biology, ask yourself, *What can I do today?* You might choose to talk to three classmates about forming a study group. Make that your intention.

- **Anticipate self-sabotage.** Be aware of what you might do, consciously or unconsciously, to undermine your best intentions. If you intend to study differential equations at 9:00 p.m., notice when you sit down to watch a two-hour movie that starts at 8:00 p.m.

- **Be careful with intentions that depend on other people.** If you intend for your study group to complete an assignment by Monday, then your success depends on the students in the group. However, you can support your group's success by writing an Intention Statement about completing your part of the assignment.

- **Set timelines.** Timelines can focus your attention. For example, if you are assigned a paper to write, break the assignment into small tasks and set a precise due date for each one. For example, you might write, *I will select a topic for my paper by 9 a.m. Wednesday.*

  Timelines are especially useful when your intention is to experiment with a technique suggested in this book. The sooner you act on a new idea, the better. Plan to practice a new behavior within 24 hours after you first learn about it.

  Remember that you create timelines for your own benefit—not to feel guilty. And you can always adjust the timeline to allow for unplanned events.

- **Reward yourself.** When you carry out your intention on time, celebrate that fact. Remember that some rewards follow directly from your accomplishment. For example, one possible reward for earning your degree is getting to work in the career that you want.

  Other rewards are more immediate and related to smaller tasks. When you turn in a paper on time, you could reward yourself with a movie or a long bike ride in the park.

  In either case, rewards work best when you are willing to withhold them. If you plan to take a nap on Sunday afternoon whether or not you complete a reading assignment, then the nap is not an effective reward.

  Another way to reward yourself is to sit quietly after finishing a task and savor the feeling. One reason that success breeds success is that it feels good. ■

Copyright © 2015 Cengage Learning. All Rights Reserved. May not be scanned, copied or duplicated, or posted to a publicly accessible website, in whole or in part.

Gary Waters/Ikon Images/Getty Images

The MASTER STUDENT
PROCESS—
ACTION

Here's the deal: Life responds to what you do. The action phase of the master student process is where you jump "off the page" and into your life. This is where the magic happens.

A well-written Discovery Statement can move you to tears. A carefully crafted Intention Statement can fill you with inspiration. And if they fail to change your behavior, both kinds of Journal Entries are useless.

There's an old saying: If you do what you've always done, you'll get what you've always gotten. That seems so obvious. To get new results, be willing to experiment with new behaviors.

Successful people consistently produce the results that they want. And results follow from specific, consistent behaviors. There are some useful guidelines to keep in your back pocket as you move into action.

As you move into action, welcome discomfort, your old friend. Changing your behavior might lead to feelings of discomfort. Instead of going back to your old behaviors, befriend the yucky feelings. Taking action has a way of dissolving discomfort.

- **Discover the joy of "baby steps."** Even simple changes in behavior can produce results. If you feel like procrastinating, then tackle just one small, specific task related to your intention. Find something you can complete in five minutes or less, and do it *now*. For example, access just one website related to the topic of your next assigned paper. Spend just three minutes previewing a reading assignment. Taking tiny steps like these can move you into action with grace and ease.

- **If you're unsure about what to do, then tweak your intentions.** Make sure that your Intention Statements include specific behaviors. Describe what you'll actually *do*—the kind of physical actions that would show up on a video recording. Get your legs, arms, and mouth moving.

- **When you get stuck, tell the truth about it.** As you become a student of human behavior, you'll see

people expecting new results from old behaviors—and then wondering why they feel stuck. Don't be surprised if you discover this tendency in yourself. Just tell the truth about it, review your intentions, and take your next action.

- **Look for prompts to action throughout this book.** In addition to Journal Entries, you'll see exercises scattered throughout *Becoming a Master Student*. These are suggestions for taking specific actions based on the ideas in the text. To get the most out of this book, do the exercises.

- **Remember that it's not about self-improvement.** If you walk into a bookstore or browse an online bookseller, you might notice titles that are listed under a category called "self-improvement." *Becoming a Master Student* is not a "self-improvement" book. It's based on the idea that you already *are* a master student. All that's needed is a process to unlock what's already present within you.

Actually, this is a self-*experimenting* book. It's about defining what matters to you and choosing what to do as a result. There's nothing mysterious or "New Age" about it. Just discover what works for you. Then do it. ■

Copyright © 2015 Cengage Learning. All Rights Reserved. May not be scanned, copied or duplicated, or posted to a publicly accessible website, in whole or in part.

KEEP THE PROCESS ALIVE

The first edition of this book began with a memorable sentence: *This book is worthless*. Many students thought that this was a trick to get their attention. It wasn't.

Others thought it was "reverse psychology." It wasn't that either.

What was true of that first edition is true of this one as well: This book is worthless *if reading it is all you do*.

When you consistently move through the master student process—from discovery to intention and all the way to action—prepare for a different outcome. Practicing the process is what keeps it alive.

Think about the process as flying a plane.
Airplanes are seldom exactly on course. Human and automatic pilots are always checking an airplane's positions and making corrections. The resulting path looks like a zigzag. The plane is almost always flying in the wrong direction. Yet through constant observation and course correction, it flies in the right direction.

That's how the master student process works. Discovery Statements call for constant observation. Intention Statements call for course correction. And moving into action keeps you on course, headed in your desired direction.

By the way, straying off course is normal. Don't panic when you forget a Discovery Statement or fail to complete an intended task. Simply make the necessary corrections.

Work smarter, not harder.
Sometimes—and especially in college—learning *does* take effort. As you become a master student, you can learn many ways to get the most out of that effort.

Though the following statement might strike you as improbable, you may well discover that it's true: It can take the same amount of energy to get what you *don't* want in school as it takes to get what you *do* want. Sometimes getting what you don't want takes even more effort. An airplane burns the same amount of fuel flying away from its destination as it does flying toward it. It pays to stay on course.

Take a path to self-actualization.
Abraham Maslow is an important figure in the history of psychology. One of his most memorable discoveries is that we are meant to do more than just satisfy our basic needs for physical safety and survival. We also need to:

- Love and be loved.
- Experience accomplishment and self-esteem.
- Fully develop our unique talents.
- Go beyond self-centeredness and find fulfillment in contributing to other people.

When we are meeting this full range of needs, we are self-actualizing.[2]

Maslow's ideas are a major inspiration for this book. One goal of the master student process is to put you on a path to self-actualizing. As you gain experience with writing Discovery and Intention Statements, you'll learn to think more critically and creatively. And as you move into action, you'll learn to overcome procrastination and manage your behaviors in the midst of constantly changing moods. Each time that you increase your skill in the master student process, you move higher up the hierarchy of needs.

See the process as a lifelong adventure.
Remember that this book is big for a reason. There are far more ideas in this book than you can possibly put into action during a single term.

This is not a mistake. In fact, it is quite intentional. There are many ideas in this book because no one expects all of them to work for you. If one technique fizzles out, you have dozens more to choose from.

Consider the first word in the title of this book—*becoming*. This word implies that mastery is not an end state or final goal. Rather, mastery is a continuous process. ■

The secret of student success

Okay, we're done kidding around. It's time to reveal the secret of student success.

(Provide your own drum roll here.)

The secret is . . .

. . . *there are no secrets.*

The strategies that successful students use are well-known. You have hundreds of them at your fingertips right now, in this book.

Use those strategies. Modify them. Invent new ones. With the master student process, you become the authority on what works for you.

What makes any strategy work is discovery, intention, and action. Without them, the pages of *Becoming a Master Student* are just 2.1 pounds of expensive mulch.

Add your participation and these pages become priceless.

Copyright © 2016 Cengage Learning. All Rights Reserved. May not be scanned, copied or duplicated, or posted to a publicly accessible website, in whole or in part.

GET THE MOST FROM THIS BOOK

GET USED TO A NEW LOOK AND TONE

This book looks different from traditional textbooks. *Becoming a Master Student* presents major ideas in magazine-style articles. There are lots of lists, blurbs, one-liners, pictures, charts, graphs, illustrations, and even a joke or two.

SKIP AROUND

Feel free to use this book in several different ways. Read it straight through. Or pick it up, turn to any page, and find an idea you can use right now. You might find that this book presents similar ideas in several places. This repetition is intentional. Repetition reinforces key points. A technique that works in one area of your life might work in others as well.

USE WHAT WORKS

If there are sections of this book that don't apply to you at all, skip them—unless, of course, they are assigned. In that case, see whether you can gain value from those sections anyway. When you commit to get value from this book, even an idea that seems irrelevant or ineffective at first can turn out to be a powerful tool in the future. If it works, use it. If it doesn't, lose it.

RIP 'EM OUT

The pages of *Becoming a Master Student* are perforated because some of the information here is too important to leave in the book. You can rip out pages, then reinsert them later by sticking them into the spine of the book. A piece of tape will hold them in place.

PRACTICE CRITICAL THINKING

Practicing Critical Thinking activities appear throughout this book. Other elements of this text, including other exercises and Journal Entries, also promote critical thinking.

LEARN ABOUT LEARNING STYLES

Check out the Learning Style Inventory and related articles in Chapter 1. This material can help you discover your preferred learning styles and allow you to explore new styles. Then, throughout the rest of this book, you'll find suggestions for applying your knowledge of learning styles.

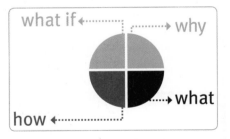

The modes of learning can be accessed by asking four basic questions: *Why? What? How?* and *What if?* You can use this four-part structure to effectively learn anything.

Copyright © 2015 Cengage Learning. All Rights Reserved. May not be scanned, copied or duplicated, or posted to a publicly accessible website, in whole or in part.

EXPERIENCE THE POWER OF THE POWER PROCESSES

A Power Process is a suggestion to shift your perspective or try on a new behavior. Look for this feature on the second page of each chapter. Users of *Becoming a Master Student* often refer to these articles as their favorite part of the book. Approach them with a sense of play and possibility. Start with an open mind, experiment with the ideas, and see what works.

READ THE SIDEBARS

Look for sidebars—short bursts of words placed between longer articles—throughout the book. These short pieces might offer insights that transform your experience of higher education.

Here's the sales pitch

The purpose of this book is to help you make a successful transition to higher education by setting up a pattern of success that will last the rest of your life. You probably won't take action and use the ideas in this book until you are convinced that you have something to gain.

Before you stiffen up and resist this sales pitch, remember that you have already bought the book. Now you can get value for your money by committing yourself to becoming a master student. Here's what's in it for you.

Get full value for your money. Your college education is one of the most expensive things you will ever buy. When you add up all the direct and indirect expenses, you might be paying $100 an hour or more to sit in class.

At the same time, you control the value you get out of your education. And that value can be considerable. The joy of learning aside, higher levels of education relate to higher lifetime income and more consistent employment.[3] It pays to be a master student.

Get suggestions from thousands of students. The ideas and techniques in this book are here not just because learning theorists, educators, and psychologists say they work. They're here because tens of thousands of students from all kinds of backgrounds use them.

Get a tested product. The previous editions of this book have proved successful for millions of students. In particular, students with successful histories have praised the techniques in this book.

Copyright © 2015 Cengage Learning. All Rights Reserved. May not be scanned, copied or duplicated, or posted to a publicly accessible website, in whole or in part.

Interactive

Journal Entry 1
Discovery Statement

Declare what you want

Review the articles that you've read so far in this chapter. Then use this Journal Entry to start experiencing the master student process—the ongoing cycle of discovery, intention, and action.

Brainstorm many possible ways to complete this sentence: *I discovered that what I want most from my education is . . .* When you're done, choose the ending that feels best to you and write it down.

I discovered that what I want most from my education is ...

_____

_____

_____

Interactive

Exercise 3 Commitment

This book is worthless unless you actively participate in its activities and exercises. One powerful way to begin taking action is to make a commitment. Conversely, if you don't make a commitment, then sustained action is unlikely. The result is a worthless book. Therefore, in the interest of saving your valuable time and energy, this exercise gives you a chance to declare your level of involvement upfront. From the options, choose the sentence that best reflects your commitment to using this book.

1. Well, I'm reading this book right now, aren't I?

2. I will skim the book and read the interesting parts.

3. I will read the book, think about it, and do the exercises that look interesting.

4. I will read the book, do some exercises, and complete some of the Journal Entries.

5. I will read the book, do some exercises and Journal Entries, and use some of the techniques.

6. I will read the book, do most of the exercises and Journal Entries, and use some of the techniques.

7. I will study this book, do most of the exercises and Journal Entries, and use some of the techniques.

8. I will study this book, do most of the exercises and Journal Entries, and experiment with many of the techniques in order to discover what works best for me.

9. I promise myself that I will create value from this course by studying this book, doing all the exercises and Journal Entries, and experimenting with most of the techniques.

10. I will use this book as if the quality of my education depended on it—doing all the exercises and Journal Entries, experimenting with most of the techniques, inventing techniques of my own, and planning to reread this book in the future.

Enter the number of the sentence that reflects your commitment level and today's date:

Commitment level _____ Date _____

If you selected commitment level 1 or 2, you probably won't create a lot of value in this class, and you might consider passing this book on to a friend. If your commitment level is 9 or 10, you are on your way to terrific success in school. If your level is somewhere in between, experiment with the techniques and learning strategies in this book. If you find that they work, consider returning to this exercise and raising your level of commitment.

Copyright © 2015 Cengage Learning. All Rights Reserved. May not be scanned, copied or duplicated, or posted to a publicly accessible website, in whole or in part.

© iStockphoto.com\istock_designer/Mahazabin Gori

Making the transition to
HIGHER EDUCATION

You share one thing in common with other students at your school: Entering higher education represents a major change in your life. You've joined a new culture with its own set of rules, both spoken and unspoken.

Whether you've just graduated from high school or have been out of the classroom for decades, you'll discover many differences between secondary and post-secondary education. The sooner you understand such differences, the sooner you can deal with them. Some examples of what you might face include the following:

- *New academic standards.* Once you enter higher education, you'll probably find yourself working harder in school than ever before. Instructors will often present more material at a faster pace. There probably will be fewer tests in higher education than in high school, and the grading might be tougher. Compared to high school, you'll have more to read, more to write, more problems to solve, and more to remember.

- *A new level of independence.* College instructors typically give less guidance about how or when to study. You may not get reminders about when assignments are due or when quizzes and tests will take place. You probably won't get study sheets before a test. And anything that's said in class or included in assigned readings might appear on an exam. Overall, you might receive less consistent feedback about how well you are doing in each of your courses. Don't let this tempt you into putting off work until the last minute. You will still be held accountable for all course work. And anything that's said in class or included in assigned readings might appear on an exam.

- *Differences in teaching styles.* Instructors at colleges, universities, and vocational schools are often steeped in their subject matter. Many did not take courses on how to teach and might not be as interesting as some of your high school teachers. And some professors might seem more focused on research than on teaching.

- *A larger playing field.* The institution you've just joined might seem immense, impersonal, and even frightening. The sheer size of the campus, the variety of courses offered, the large number of departments—all of these opportunities can add up to a confusing array of options.

- *More students and more diversity.* The school you're attending right now might enroll hundreds or thousands more students than your high school. And the range of diversity among these students might surprise you.

Decrease the unknowns. To reduce surprise, anticipate changes. Before classes begin, get a map of the school property and walk through your first day's schedule, perhaps with a classmate or friend. Visit your instructors in their offices and introduce yourself. Anything you can do to get familiar with the new routine will help. In addition, consider buying your textbooks before class begins. Scan them to get a preview of your courses.

Admit your feelings—whatever they are. School can be an intimidating experience for new students. People of diverse cultures, adult learners, commuters, and people with disabilities may feel excluded. Anyone can feel anxious, lonely, and homesick.

Those emotions are common among new students, and there's nothing wrong with them. Simply admitting the truth about how you feel—to yourself and to someone else—can help you cope. And you can almost always do something constructive in the present moment, no matter how you feel.

If your feelings about this transition make it hard for you to carry out the activities of daily life—going to class, working, studying, and relating to people—then get

Copyright © 2015 Cengage Learning. All Rights Reserved. May not be scanned, copied or duplicated, or posted to a publicly accessible website, in whole or in part.

professional help. Start with a counselor at the student health service on your campus. The mere act of seeking help can make a difference.

Allow time for transition. You don't have to master the transition to higher education right away. Give it some time. Also, plan your academic schedule with your needs for transition in mind. Balance time-intensive courses with others that don't make as many demands.

Find and use resources. A supercharger increases the air supply to an internal combustion engine. The resulting difference in power can be dramatic. You can make just as powerful a difference in your education by supercharging it with resources. In this case, your "air supply" includes student services, campus events, and extracurricular activities. Any of them can help you succeed in school. And many of them are free.

For example, visit the career planning center and financial aid office. Check out tutoring services and computer labs. Check the schedule for on-campus concerts, films, and plays. Extracurricular activities include athletics, fraternities, sororities, student newspapers, debate teams, service-learning projects, internships, student government, and political action groups, to name just a few. Check your school's website for more.

Accessing resources is especially important if you are the first person in your family to enter higher education. As a first-generation student, you are having experiences that people in your family may not understand. Talk to your relatives about your activities at school. If they ask how they can help you, give specific answers. Also, ask your instructors about programs for first-generation students on your campus.

Take the initiative in meeting new people. Of all resources, people are the most important. You can isolate yourself, study hard, and get a good education. However, doing this is not the most powerful use of your tuition money. When you establish relationships with teachers, staff members, fellow students, and employers, you can get a *great* education. Build a network of people who will personally support your success in school.

Introduce yourself to classmates and instructors. Just before or after class is a good time. Realize that most of the people in this new world of higher education are waiting to be welcomed. You can help them and help yourself at the same time. Connecting to school socially as well as academically promotes your success and your enjoyment.

Meet with your academic advisor. One person in particular—your academic advisor—can help you access resources and make the transition to higher education. Meet with this person regularly. Advisors generally know about course requirements, options for declaring majors, and the resources available at your school. Peer advisors might also be available.

When you work with an advisor, remember that you're a paying customer and have a right to be satisfied with the service you get. Don't be afraid to change advisors when that seems appropriate.

Learn the language of higher education. Terms such as *grade point average (GPA), prerequisite, accreditation, matriculation, tenure,* and *syllabus* might be new to you. Ease your transition to higher education by checking your school catalog or school website for definitions of these words and others that you don't understand. Also ask your academic advisor for clarification.

Show up for class. In higher education, teachers generally don't take attendance. Yet you'll find that attending class is essential to your success. The amount that you pay in tuition and fees makes a powerful argument for going to classes regularly and getting your money's worth. In large part, the material that you're tested on comes from events that take place in class.

Manage out-of-class time. Instructors give you the raw materials for understanding a subject while a class meets. You then take those materials, combine them, and *teach yourself* outside of class.

To allow for this process, schedule two hours of study time for each hour that you spend in class. Also, get a calendar that covers the entire academic year. With the syllabus for each of your courses in hand, note key events for the entire term—dates for tests, papers, and other projects. Getting a big picture of your course load makes it easier to get assignments done on time and prevent all-night study sessions.

> *Realize that most of the people in this new world of higher education are waiting to be welcomed. You can help them and help yourself at the same time. Connecting to school socially as well as academically promotes your success and your enjoyment.*

Copyright © 2015 Cengage Learning. All Rights Reserved. May not be scanned, copied or duplicated, or posted to a publicly accessible website, in whole or in part.

Experiment with new ways to study. You can cope with increased workloads and higher academic expectations by putting all of your study habits on the table and evaluating them. Don't assume that the learning strategies you used in the past—in high school or the workplace—will automatically transfer to your new role in higher education. Keep the habits that serve you, drop those that hold you back, and adopt new ones to promote your success. On every page of this book, you'll find helpful suggestions.

Become a self-regulated learner. Reflect on your transition to higher education. Think about what's working well, what you'd like to change, and ways to make those changes. Psychologists use the term *self-regulation* to describe this kind of thinking.[4] Self-regulated learners set goals, monitor their progress toward those goals, and change their behavior based on the results they get.

Becoming a Master Student promotes self-regulation through the ongoing cycle of discovery, intention, and action. Write Discovery Statements to monitor your behavior and evaluate the results you're currently creating in any area of your life. Write about your level of commitment to school, your satisfaction with your classes and grades, your social life, and your family's support for your education.

Based on your discoveries, write Intention Statements about your goals for this term, this year, next year, and the rest of your college career. Describe exactly what you will do to create new results in each of these time frames. Then follow through with action. In this way, you take charge of your transition to higher education, starting now. ■

Avoid high-tech time wasters

Time management is about to take on a new meaning in your life. What you do *outside* class will matter as much as—or even more than—what you do during class. To make a successful transition to higher education, start taking charge of your time and attention. The following suggestions are ways to begin.

Limit your time on social networks. Track how much time you spend each day on websites such as Facebook, Twitter, LinkedIn, Google+, and Pinterest. Focus on just one or two of them. Check them just once or twice daily, and for just a few minutes at a time. If you don't post updates every day, your friends will forgive you. Remind them that you're going to school.

Save online activity for down times. During the times of the day when your energy peaks, tackle more demanding tasks such as homework and exercising.

Start your day as a student, not a consumer. The first things that you do in the morning set the tone for the entire day. Instead of surfing the web, start off with a task that supports your success in school.

Simplify e-mail. Most e-mail programs provide an option to save messages into folders for future reference. You can manage all your e-mail with two folders. One is for messages that require follow-up action. The other is for messages to archive for future reference. Trash everything else.

Turn off notifications. You don't need to hear an alert from your digital devices whenever someone posts a Facebook update or sends you an e-mail. Savor the silence and extra space for concentration.

Copyright © 2015 Cengage Learning. All Rights Reserved. May not be scanned, copied or duplicated, or posted to a publicly accessible website, in whole or in part.

SUCCEEDING IN SCHOOL—
AT ANY AGE

Being an adult learner puts you on a strong footing. With a rich store of life experiences, you can ask meaningful questions and make connections between course work and daily life. Any abilities that you've developed to work on teams, manage projects, meet deadlines, and solve problems are assets. Many instructors will especially enjoy working with you.

Following are some suggestions for adult learners who want to ease their transition to higher education. If you're a younger student, commuting student, or community college student, look for useful ideas here as well.

Acknowledge your concerns. Adult learners might express any of the following fears:

- *I'll be the oldest person in all my classes.*
- *I've been out of the classroom too long.*
- *I'm concerned about my math, reading, and writing skills.*
- *I'm worried about making tuition payments.*
- *How will I ever make the time to study, on top of everything else I'm doing?*
- *I won't be able to keep up with all the new technology.*

Those concerns are understandable. Now consider some facts:

- College classrooms are more diverse than ever before. According to the U.S. Census Bureau, 36 percent of part-time students in our nation's colleges are age 35 and older.[5]
- Adult learners can take advantage of evening classes, weekend classes, summer classes, distance learning, and online courses. Also look for classes in off-campus locations, closer to where you work or live.
- Colleges offer financial aid for students of all ages, including scholarships, grants, and low-interest loans.
- You can meet other students and make new friends by taking part in orientation programs. Look for programs that are targeted to adult learners.
- You are now enrolled in a course that can help boost your skills at math, reading, writing, note taking, time management, and other key skills.

Stockbyte/Getty Images

Ease into it. If you're new to higher education, consider easing into it. You can choose to attend school part-time before making a full-time commitment. If you've taken college-level classes in the past, find out if any of those credits will transfer into your current program.

Plan ahead. By planning a week or month at a time, you get a bigger picture of your multiple roles as a student, an employee, and a family member. With that awareness, you can make conscious adjustments in the number of hours you devote to each domain of activity in your life. For example:

- If your responsibilities at work or home will be heavy in the near future, then register for fewer classes next term.
- Choose recreational activities carefully, focusing on those that relax you and recharge you the most.
- Don't load your schedule with classes that require unusually heavy amounts of reading or writing.

Copyright © 2015 Cengage Learning. All Rights Reserved. May not be scanned, copied or duplicated, or posted to a publicly accessible website, in whole or in part.

Delegate tasks. If you have children, delegate some of the household chores to them. Or start a meal co-op in your neighborhood. Cook dinner for yourself and someone else one night each week. In return, ask that person to furnish you with a meal on another night. A similar strategy can apply to child care and other household tasks.

Get to know other returning students. Introduce yourself to other adult learners. Being in the same classroom gives you an immediate bond. You can exchange work, home, or cell phone numbers and build a network of mutual support. Some students adopt a buddy system, pairing up with another student in each class to complete assignments and prepare for tests.

In addition, learn about student services and organizations. Many schools have a learning assistance center with workshops geared to adult learners. Sign up and attend. Meet people on campus. Personal connections are key to your success.

> Ask the key people in your life for help. Share your reason for getting a degree, and talk about what your whole family has to gain from this change in your life.

Find common ground with traditional students. Traditional and nontraditional students have many things in common. They seek to gain knowledge and skills for their chosen careers. They desire financial stability and personal fulfillment. And, like their older peers, many younger students are concerned about whether they have the skills to succeed in higher education.

Consider pooling resources with younger students. Share notes, edit one another's papers, and form study groups. Look for ways to build on one another's strengths. If you want help with using a computer for assignments, you might ask a younger student for help. In group projects and case studies, you can expand the discussion by sharing insights from your experiences.

Jamie Grill/Blend Images/Getty Images

Enlist your employer's support. Let your employer in on your educational plans. Point out how the skills you gain in the classroom will help you meet work objectives. Offer informal seminars at work to share what you're learning in school. You might find that your company reimburses its employees for some tuition costs or even grants time off to attend classes.

Get extra mileage out of your current tasks. Look for ways to relate your schoolwork to your job. For example, when you're assigned a research paper, choose a topic that relates to your current job tasks. Some schools even offer academic credit for work and life experience.

Review your subjects before you start classes. Say that you've registered for trigonometry and you haven't taken a math class since high school. Consider brushing up on the subject before classes begin. Also, talk with future instructors about ways to prepare for their classes.

"Publish" your schedule. After you plan your study and class sessions for the week, write up your schedule and post it in a place where others who live with you will see it. If you use an online calendar, print out copies to put in your school binder or on your refrigerator door, bathroom mirror, or kitchen cupboard.

Enroll family and friends in your success. School can cut into your social life. Prepare friends and family members by discussing this issue ahead of time.

You can also involve your spouse, partner, children, or close friends in your schooling. Offer to give them a tour of the campus, introduce them to your instructors and classmates, and encourage them to attend social events at school with you. Share ideas from this book, and from your other courses.

Take this process a step further, and ask the key people in your life for help. Share your reason for getting a degree, and talk about what your whole family has to gain from this change in your life. Ask them to think of ways that they can support your success in school and to commit to those actions. Make your own education a joint mission that benefits everyone. ■

Copyright © 2015 Cengage Learning. All Rights Reserved. May not be scanned, copied or duplicated, or posted to a publicly accessible website, in whole or in part.

Leading the way—
SUCCEEDING AS A FIRST-GENERATION STUDENT

American history confirms that people who are the first in their family to enter higher education can succeed. These range from the former slaves who enrolled in the country's first African-American colleges to the ex-soldiers who used the GI Bill to earn advanced degrees. From their experiences, you can take some life-changing lessons.

REMEMBER YOUR STRENGTHS

The fact you're reading this book right now is a sign of your accomplishments. You applied to school. You got admitted. You've already taken a huge step to success: You showed up.

Celebrate every one of your successes in higher education, no matter how small they seem. Every assignment you complete, every paper you turn in, and every question you answer is a measurable and meaningful step to getting a degree.

To discover more of your strengths, think creatively about facts that others might see as a barrier. Look for the hidden advantage.

Did you grow up in a family that struggled to make ends meet financially? Then you know about how to live on a tight budget.

Did you work to support your family while you were in high school? Then you know about managing your time to balance major commitments.

Did you grow up in a neighborhood with people of many races, religions, and levels of income? Then you know about how to thrive with diversity.

Put your strengths in writing. Write Discovery Statements about specific challenges you faced in the past. Describe how you coped with personal, academic, and financial problems. Then follow up with Intention Statements about ways to meet new challenges in higher education.

Also keep showing up. Go to every class, every lab session, and every study group meeting. All of these are ways to squeeze the most value from your tuition bills.

EXPECT CHANGE AND DISCOMFORT

Entering higher education means walking into a new culture. You might feel that the ground rules have changed, and that you have no idea how to fit in. This is normal.

When you walked into your first class this semester, you carried your personal hopes for the future. You also brought along the expectations of your family members. Those people might assume that you'll return home and be the same person you were last year.

The reality is that you will change while you're in school. Your attitudes, your friends, and your career goals may all shift. You might think that some of the people back home have limited ideas. In turn, they might criticize you.

Being a first-generation student in higher education is sometimes about standing between two worlds. You know that you are changing. At the same time, you feel uncertain about what the future holds.

This is also normal. Education is all about change. It can be exciting, frustrating, and frightening—all at the same time. Making mistakes and moving through disappointment is part of the process.

ASK FOR SUPPORT

You don't have to go it alone. Your tuition buys access to many services, including academic advising, career planning, tutoring, and counseling. Explore all these sources of support. Ask about specific programs for first-generation students.

The key is to ask for help right away. Do this as soon as you feel stuck in class or confused about an important relationship.

Keep a list of every person who stands behind you—relatives, friends, instructors, advisors, and more. Check in with them regularly via phone, e-mail, and personal visits. Remind yourself that you are surrounded by people who want you to succeed.

Also remember that being in school might mean that you have less time for family members and friends. You are not being selfish. By getting an education, you are gaining skills that you can use to contribute to others.

PAY IT FORWARD

You are an inspiration to your family, friends, and fellow students. In the future, people might apply to school on the strength of your example. Talk to them about what you've learned. Your words and your example can make a difference that extends far beyond your generation. ■

Copyright © 2015 Cengage Learning. All Rights Reserved. May not be scanned, copied or duplicated, or posted to a publicly accessible website, in whole or in part.

Thinkstock/Comstock Images/
Getty Images

ENROLL YOUR INSTRUCTOR
in your success

Faced with an instructor you don't like, you have two basic choices. One is to label the instructor a "dud" and let it go at that. When you make this choice, you get to endure class and complain to other students. The other option is take responsibility for your education, no matter who teaches your classes.

The word *enroll* in this headline is a play on words. Usually we think of students as the people who enroll in school. Turn this idea on its head. See whether you can enlist instructors as partners in getting what you want from higher education.

Research the instructor. When deciding what classes to take, you can look for formal and informal sources of information about instructors. One source is the school catalog. Alumni magazines or newsletters or the school newspaper might run articles on teachers. Also talk to students who have taken courses from the instructor you're researching.

Also introduce yourself to the instructor. Set up a visit during office hours, and ask about the course. This conversation can help you get the flavor of a class and the instructor's teaching style. Other clues to an instructor's style include the *types* of material he presents (ranging from theory or fact) and the *ways* that the material is presented (ranging from lectures to discussion and other in-class activities). Ask for syllabi from the instructor's past courses and take a look at the instructor's website.

Show interest in class. Students give teachers moment-by-moment feedback in class. That feedback comes through posture, eye contact, responses to questions, and participation in class discussions. If you find a class boring, recreate the instructor through a massive display of interest. Ask lots of questions. Sit up straight, make eye contact, take detailed notes. Your enthusiasm might enliven your instructor. If not, you are still creating a more enjoyable class for yourself.

Release judgments. Maybe your instructor reminds you of someone you don't like—your annoying Aunt Edna, a rude store clerk, or the fifth-grade teacher who kept you after school. Your attitudes are in your own head and beyond the instructor's control. Likewise, an instructor's

beliefs about politics, religion, or feminism are not related to teaching ability. Being aware of such things can help you let go of negative judgments.

Get to know the instructor. Meet with your instructor during office hours. Teachers who seem boring in class can be fascinating in person. Students who do well in higher education often get to know at least one instructor outside of class. In some cases, these instructors become mentors and informal advisors.

Separate liking from learning. You don't have to like an instructor to learn from her. See whether you can focus on content instead of form. *Form* is the way something is organized or presented. If you are irritated at the sound of an instructor's voice, you're focusing on form. When you put aside your concern about her voice and turn your attention to the points she's making, you're focusing on *content*.

Form your own opinion about each instructor. You might hear conflicting reports about teachers from other students. The same instructor could be described by two different students as a riveting speaker and as completely lacking in charisma. Decide for yourself what descriptions are accurate.

Seek alternatives. You might feel more comfortable with another teacher's style or method of organizing course materials. Consider changing teachers, asking another teacher for help outside class, or attending an additional section taught by a different instructor.

Avoid excuses. Instructors know them all. Most teachers can see a snow job coming before the first flake hits the ground. Accept responsibility for your own mistakes, and avoid thinking that you can fool the teacher.

Submit professional work. Prepare papers and projects as if you were submitting them to an employer. Imagine that your work will determine whether you get a promotion and raise. Instructors often grade hundreds of papers during a term. Your neat, orderly, well-organized paper can stand out and lift a teacher's spirits, ultimately helping you.

Copyright © 2015 Cengage Learning. All Rights Reserved. May not be scanned, copied or duplicated, or posted to a publicly accessible website, in whole or in part.

Accept criticism. Learn from your teachers' comments about your work. It is a teacher's job to give feedback so that you can improve. Don't take it personally, but rather work harder and better next time.

Use course evaluations. In many classes, you'll have an opportunity to evaluate the instructor. Respond honestly. Write about the aspects of the class that did not work well for you. Offer specific ideas for improvement. Also note what *did* work well. Keep it positive, remembering that you might have this instructor again for another class.

Take further steps, if appropriate. If you're in conflict with an instructor, do not try to resolve the situation during a few minutes before or after class. Instead, schedule a time during the instructor's office hours to meet with her in person. During this meeting, be specific. State the facts about the problem. Also be positive. Offer possible solutions, and state what you're willing to do to resolve the conflict.

If this meeting does not lead to a solution, then find out your school's grievance procedures. You are a consumer of education and have a right to fair treatment. ▪

Communicating with your instructor

By phone. Ask your instructors how they prefer to be contacted. If they take phone calls, leave a voice mail message that includes your first and last name, course name, section, and phone number.

By e-mail. If your instructor encourages contact via e-mail, then craft your messages with care. Start by including your name, course title, and section number in the subject line. Keep the body of your message brief and get to the point immediately.

Remember that the person who receives your e-mail is a human being whose culture, language, and humor may have different points of reference from your own. Write clearly, and keep the tone positive. Do not type in FULL CAPS, which is equivalent to shouting.

Proofread your message carefully and fix any errors. Write with full words and complete sentences. Avoid the abbreviations that you might use in a text message.

If there's a problem to solve, focus on solutions rather than blame. For example, avoid: "Why do you grade so unfairly?" Instead, write, "I'd like to understand your criteria for grading our assignments so that I can raise my scores."

Finally, remember that instructors are busy people with personal lives. Don't expect them to be online at the same time as you.

In person. Meeting with an instructor outside class can save hours of study time and help boost your grade. To get the most from these meetings:

- **Schedule a meeting time.** Ask for the instructor's office hours. These are often listed in the course syllabus and on the instructor's office door. If you need to cancel or reschedule, let your instructor know well in advance.

- **Prepare.** Bring a list of questions to ask and any materials you'll need. During the meeting, take notes on the instructor's suggestions.

- **Get the most from your meeting time.** Focus on one thing that will help you succeed in the course. For example, show the instructor your class notes to see whether you're capturing essential material. Get feedback on outlines that you've created for papers. Go over items you missed on exams. Get overall feedback on your progress.

- **Avoid questions that might offend your instructor.** A common example: "I missed class on Monday. Did we do anything important?"

- **Ask about what's next.** Talk about ways to prepare for upcoming exams. Ask whether your instructor is willing to answer further questions via e-mail or a phone call. And if the course is in a subject area that interests you, then also ask about the possibilities of declaring a major in that area and the possible careers associated with that major.

- **End with courtesy.** Stick to your scheduled meeting time. Conclude by thanking your instructor for seeing you. Most of all—relax. You're not graded on meeting with your instructor.

Copyright © 2015 Cengage Learning. All Rights Reserved. May not be scanned, copied or duplicated, or posted to a publicly accessible website, in whole or in part.

© Maciej Oleksy/Shutterstock.com

Developing a
PROFESSIONAL
WORK ETHIC

Through their behavior at school and at work, some people give the impression that they are merely warming chairs or taking up space. They perform just up to minimum requirements without much energy, enthusiasm, or commitment. Their verbal and nonverbal behavior often conveys a single message: *I'd really rather be somewhere else.*

If you want to succeed in school and open up new options for the future, then demonstrate a *professional work ethic.* You'll see those three words in many job descriptions. They're not just filler. Employers value people who stand out from the crowd and demonstrate excellence.

People with a professional work ethic use their school and work experiences for constant learning and contribution. They function as team players, and they're also willing to take the lead. They contribute ideas, and they're also willing to change their mind. They learn new tasks quickly and push through obstacles until projects are completed. These are all qualities of a master student, and you can start developing them now.

START WITH THIS QUESTION

If you were employed as a student, would you be earning your wages? If that question seems off-base, then remember one thing: You *are*, in fact, employed as a student. You are paying a big price for the privilege of getting an education. Every minute and every dollar counts. Get the most value by spending as much energy on school as you would on a well-paying job.

DEMONSTRATE INITIATIVE

When people spot a problem, there are two distinct ways for them to respond. The unprofessional response is to ignore the problem or complain about it. The professional response is to try to help solve the problem.

Demonstrating initiative means thinking carefully before making statements such as:

- *I'm not going to do that—it's not in my job description.*
- *I don't get paid enough to do that.*
- *This problem has been around for years, and it's here to stay.*
- *I'll wait until I get a promotion, then I'll think about getting involved.*

Remember that you don't need a new job title in order to become a leader. When you spot a problem, describe it an objective way—without judgment or blame. Stick to the facts about what's working and what's not working. Then offer a possible solution. Better yet, offer several solutions.

DEMONSTRATE HUMILITY

During the course of your career, you'll meet people who value prestige above all else. These people tend to be fussy about their job title and position on the company's organization chart. They typically consider certain tasks to be "beneath" them. If they think that their achievements are ignored, they take offense and look for ways to get revenge.

In contrast, people with a professional work ethic see what needs to be done and pitch in. Instead of worrying about status or recognition, they join a team and look for ways to contribute.

Humility is a word that's often misunderstood. It does not mean downplaying your strengths or being the first to take blame. The true mark of a humble person is treating everyone in a workplace—from the janitor to the chief executive officer—as an equal.

Humility also means:

- **Assuming the posture of a learner.** A professional doesn't pretend to know all the answers or speak the final words on any topic. She asks other people for their suggestions. She respects points of view that differ from her own. And she refuses to criticize an idea until she's taken the time to fully understand it.

- **Admitting mistakes.** A professional is open to coaching. He routinely asks for feedback, and he receives it without becoming defensive. If he makes an error, he quickly admits it and apologizes. He also looks for ways to make amends.

- **Giving others credit.** When a project goes well, unprofessional people try to take credit. In contrast, professional people look for ways to *give* credit. They make a habit of expressing appreciation for the contributions of other people. ■

Copyright ©2015 Cengage Learning. All Rights Reserved. May not be scanned, copied or duplicated, or posted to a publicly accessible website, in whole or in part.

COMMUNICATING RESPECT

in the classroom

This topic might seem like common sense, yet sometimes students forget the simple behaviors that create a sense of safety, mutual respect, and community.

Consider an example: A student arrives 15 minutes late to a lecture and lets the door slam behind her. She pulls a fast-food burger out of a paper bag (hear the sound of that crackling paper). Then her cell phone rings at full volume. She answers it and carries on an extended conversation while the instructor is talking.

Behaviors like these send a message to everyone in the room: "I can do anything I want, at any time. And if it prevents you from getting what you want, too bad."

In a school setting, communicating respect is called *classroom civility*. It starts with observing yourself and discovering the messages that you send with your actions as well as your words.

You will invest hundreds of hours and thousands of dollars in getting a degree. You deserve to enter classrooms that are free of disruptions, discipline problems, and bullies.

Also remember that with classroom civility, you win. When you treat instructors with respect, you're more likely to be treated that way in return. A respectful relationship with an instructor could turn into a favorable reference letter, a mentorship, a job referral, or a friendship that lasts for years after you graduate. Politeness pays.

Lack of civility boils down to a group of habits. Like any other habits, these can be changed. The following suggestions reflect common sense, and they make an uncommon difference.

Attend classes regularly. Show up for classes on time. If you know that you're going to miss a class or be late, then let your instructor know. Take the initiative to ask your instructor or another student about what you missed.

If you arrive late, do not disrupt class. Close the door quietly and take a seat. When you know that you will have to leave class early, tell your instructor before class begins, and sit near an exit. If you leave class to use the restroom or handle an emergency, do so quietly.

During class, participate fully. Take notes and join in discussions. Turn off your cell phone or any other electronic device that you don't need for class. Remember that sleeping, texting, or doing work for another class is a waste of your time and money. Instructors notice distracting activities and take them as a sign of your lack of interest and commitment. So do employers.

Before packing up your notebooks and other materials, wait until class has been dismissed. Instructors often give assignments or make a key point at the end of a class period. Be there when it happens.

Communicate respect. When you speak in class, begin by addressing your instructor as *Ms., Mrs., Mr., Dr., Professor,* or whatever the teacher prefers.

Discussions gain value when everyone gets a chance to speak. Show respect for others by not monopolizing class discussions. Refrain from side conversations and profanity. When presenting viewpoints that conflict with those of classmates or your instructor, combine the passion for your opinion with respect for the opinions of others.

Respect gets communicated in the smallest details, such as maintaining good hygiene. Avoid making distracting noises, and cover your mouth if you yawn or cough. Also avoid wearing inappropriate revealing clothing. And even if you meet your future spouse in class, refrain from public displays of affection.

If you disagree with a class requirement or grade you received, then talk to your instructor about it after class in a respectful way. In a private setting, your ideas will get more attention.

See civility as a contribution. Every class you enter has the potential to become a community of people who talk openly, listen fully, share laughter, and arrive at life-changing insights. These are master student qualities. Every time you demonstrate them, you make a contribution to your community. ■

Copyright © 2015 Cengage Learning. All Rights Reserved. May not be scanned, copied or duplicated, or posted to a publicly accessible website, in whole or in part.

Copyright © 2015 Cengage Learning. All Rights Reserved. May not be scanned, copied or duplicated, or posted to a publicly accessible website, in whole or in part.

MOTIVATION—
I'm just not in the mood

©ollyy/Shutterstock.com

In large part, this chapter is about your motivation to succeed in school. There are at least two ways to think about motivation. One is that the terms *self-discipline, willpower,* and *motivation* describe something missing in ourselves. We use these words to explain another person's success—or our own shortcomings: "If I were more motivated, I'd get more involved in school." "Of course she got an A. She has self-discipline." "If I had more willpower, I'd lose weight." It seems that certain people are born with lots of motivation, whereas others miss out on it.

A second approach to thinking about motivation is to stop assuming that motivation is mysterious, determined at birth, or hard to come by. Perhaps there's nothing missing in you. What we call motivation could be something that you already possess—the ability to do a task even when you don't feel like it. This is a habit that you can develop with practice. The following suggestions offer ways to do that.

Promise it. Motivation can come simply from being clear about your goals and acting on them. Say that you want to start a study group. You can commit yourself to inviting people and setting a time and place to meet. Promise your classmates that you'll do this, and ask them to hold you accountable. Self-discipline, willpower, motivation—none of these mysterious characteristics has to get in your way. Just make a promise and keep your word.

Befriend your discomfort. Sometimes keeping your word means doing a task you'd rather put off. The mere thought of doing laundry, reading a chapter in a statistics book, or proofreading a term paper can lead to discomfort.

In the face of such discomfort, you can procrastinate. Or you can use this barrier as a means to getting the job done.

Begin by investigating the discomfort. Notice the thoughts running through your head, and speak them out loud: "I'd rather walk on a bed of coals than do this." "This is the last thing I want to do right now."

Also observe what's happening with your body. For example, are you breathing faster or slower than usual? Are your shoulders tight? Do you feel any tension in your stomach?

Once you're in contact with your mind and body, stay with the discomfort a few minutes longer. Don't judge it as good or bad. Accepting the thoughts and body sensations robs them of power. They might still be there, but in time they can stop being a barrier for you.

Change your mind—and your body. You can also get past discomfort by planting new thoughts in your mind or changing your physical stance. For example, instead of slumping in a chair, sit up straight or stand up. You can also get physically active by taking a short walk. Notice what happens to your discomfort.

Work with your thoughts also. Replace "I can't stand this" with "I'll feel great when this is done" or "Doing this will help me get something I want."

Sweeten the task. Sometimes it's just one aspect of a task that holds you back. You can stop procrastinating merely by changing that aspect. If distaste for your physical environment keeps you from studying, you can change that environment. Reading about social psychology might seem like a yawner when you're alone in a dark corner of the house. Moving to a cheery, well-lit library can sweeten the task.

When you're done with an important task, reward yourself for a job well done. The simplest rewards—such as a walk, a hot bath, or a favorite snack—can be the most effective.

Talk about how bad it is. One way to get past negative attitudes is to take them to an extreme. When faced with an unpleasant task, launch into a no-holds-barred gripe session. Pull out all the stops: "There's no way I can start my income taxes now. This is terrible beyond words—an absolute disaster. This is a catastrophe of global proportions!" Griping taken this far can restore perspective. It shows how self-talk can turn inconveniences into crises.

Turn up the pressure. Sometimes motivation is a luxury. Pretend that the due date for your project has been moved up one month, one week, or one day. Raising the stress level slightly can spur you into action. Then the issue of motivation seems beside the point, and meeting the due date moves to the forefront.

Turn down the pressure. The mere thought of starting a huge task can induce anxiety. To get past this feeling, turn down the pressure by taking "baby steps." Divide a large project into small tasks. In 30 minutes or less, you could preview a book, create a rough outline for a paper, or solve two or three math problems. Careful planning can help you discover many such steps to make a big job doable.

Ask for support. Other people can become your allies in overcoming procrastination. For example, form a support group and declare what you intend to accomplish before each meeting. Then ask members to hold you accountable. If you want to begin exercising regularly, ask another person to walk with you three times weekly. People in support groups ranging from Alcoholics Anonymous to Weight Watchers know the power of this strategy.

Adopt a model. One strategy for succeeding at any task is to hang around the masters. Find someone you consider successful, and spend time with her. Observe this person and use her as a model for your own behavior. You can "try on" this person's actions and attitudes. Look for tools that feel right for you. This person can become a mentor for you.

Compare the payoffs to the costs. All behaviors have payoffs and costs. Even unwanted behaviors such as cramming for exams or neglecting exercise have payoffs. Cramming might give you more time that's free of commitments. Neglecting exercise can give you more time to sleep.

One way to let go of such unwanted behaviors is first to celebrate them—even embrace them. We can openly acknowledge the payoffs.

Celebration can be especially powerful when you follow it up with the next step—determining the costs. For example, skipping a reading assignment can give you time to go to the movies. However, you might be unprepared for class and have twice as much to read the following week.

Maybe there is another way to get the payoff (going to the movies) without paying the cost (skipping the reading assignment). With some thoughtful weekly planning, you might choose to give up a few hours of television and end up with enough time to read the assignment *and* go to the movies.

Comparing the costs and benefits of any behavior can fuel our motivation. We can choose new behaviors because they align with what we want most.

Do it later. At times, it's effective to save a task for later. For example, writing a résumé can wait until you've taken the time to analyze your job skills and map out your career goals. Putting it off does not show a lack of motivation—it shows planning.

When you do choose to do a task later, turn this decision into a promise. Estimate how long the task will take, and schedule a specific date and time for it on your calendar.

Heed the message. Sometimes lack of motivation carries a message that's worth heeding. An example is the student who majors in accounting but seizes every chance to be with children. His chronic reluctance to read accounting textbooks might not be a problem. Instead, it might reveal his desire to major in elementary education. His original career choice might have come from the belief that "real men don't teach kindergarten." In such cases, an apparent lack of motivation signals a deeper wisdom trying to get through. ∎

©Galina Barskaya/Shutterstock.com

Copyright © 2015 Cengage Learning. All Rights Reserved. May not be scanned, copied or duplicated, or posted to a publicly accessible website, in whole or in part.

ATTITUDES, AFFIRMATIONS, & VISUALIZATIONS

"I have a bad attitude." Some of us say this as if we were talking about having the flu. An attitude is certainly as strong as the flu, but it isn't something we have to live with forever, anymore than the flu is. You can change your attitudes through regular practice with affirmations and visualizations.

Affirm it. An affirmation is a statement describing what you want. The most effective affirmations are:

- **Present tense.** Determine what you want. Then describe yourself as if you already have it. To get what you want from your education, you could write, "I am a master student. I take full responsibility for my education. I learn with joy. I use my experiences in each course to create the life that I want."

- **Detailed.** Use brand names, people's names, and your own name. Involve all of your senses—sight, sound, smell, taste, and touch.

- **Positive.** Instead of saying, "I am not fat," say, "I am slender."

Visualize it. This technique complements affirmations. It's a favorite among athletes and performance artists.

To begin, choose what you want to improve. Then describe in writing what it would look like, sound like, and feel like to experience that improvement in your life.

If you are learning to play the piano, write down briefly what you would see, hear, and feel if you were playing skillfully. If you want to improve your relationships with your children, write down what you would see, hear, and feel if you were communicating with them successfully.

Once you have a mental picture of successful behavior, practice it in your imagination. Whenever you toss the basketball, it swishes through the net. Every time you invite someone out on a date, the person says "yes." Each test the teacher hands back to you is graded an A. Do your visualizations at least once a day. Then wait for the results to unfold in your life. ∎

Simple attitude replacements

You can use affirmations to replace a negative attitude with a positive one. There are no limitations, other than your imagination and your willingness to practice. Here are some sample affirmations. Modify them to suit your individual hopes and dreams, and then practice them.

- I have abundant energy and vitality throughout the day.
- I exercise regularly.
- I work effectively with many different kinds of people.
- I eat wisely.
- I plan my days and use time wisely.

- I have a powerful memory.
- I take tests calmly and confidently.
- I fall asleep quickly and sleep soundly.
- I have relationships that are mutually satisfying.
- I contribute to other people through my job.
- I make regular time to play and have fun.
- I focus my attention easily.
- I like myself.
- I have an income that far exceeds my expenses.
- I live my life in positive ways for the highest good of all people.

Copyright © 2015 Cengage Learning. All Rights Reserved. May not be scanned, copied or duplicated, or posted to a publicly accessible website, in whole or in part.

Interactive

Exercise 4 Reprogram your attitude

Use this exercise to change your approach to any situation.

Step 1

Pick something in your life that you would like to change. It can be related to anything—relationships, work, money, or personal skills. Describe briefly what you choose to change.

_____

_____

_____

_____

Step 2

Add more details about the change you described in Step 1. Explain how you would like the change to come about. Be outlandish. Imagine that you are about to ask your fairy godmother for a wish that you know she will grant. Be detailed in your description of your wish.

_____

_____

_____

_____

_____

_____

_____

Step 3

Use affirmations and visualizations to start yourself on the path to creating exactly what you wrote about in Step 2. Provide at least two affirmations that describe your dream wish. Also, briefly outline a visualization that you can use to picture your wish. Be specific, detailed, and positive.

_____

_____

_____

_____

Step 4

Put your new attitudes to work. Set up a schedule to practice them. Let the first time you practice be right now. Then set up at least five other times and places where you intend to practice your affirmations and visualizations.

I intend to relax and practice my affirmations and visualizations for at least five minutes on the following dates and at the time(s) and location(s) given.

	Date	Time	Location
1.			
2.			
3.			
4.			
5.			

Step 5

Attitude change takes time. End this exercise by reflecting on your progress. Ask whether your practice of affirmations and visualization is actually changing the way that you speak and behave in daily life. You might want to change your affirmations and visualizations so that they're more detailed, positive, and vivid. Write down your revised versions.

_____

_____

_____

_____

_____

_____

_____

_____

Copyright © 2015 Cengage Learning. All Rights Reserved. May not be scanned, copied or duplicated, or posted to a publicly accessible website, in whole or in part.

Ways to change a
HABIT

Consider a new way to think about the word *habit*. Imagine for a moment that many of our most troublesome problems and even our most basic traits are just habits.

The expanding waistline that your friend blames on her spouse's cooking—maybe that's just a habit called overeating.

The fit of rage that a student blames on a teacher—maybe that's just the student's habit of closing the door to new ideas.

Procrastination, stress, and money shortages might just be names that we give to collections of habits—scores of simple, small, repeated behaviors that combine to create a huge result. The same goes for health, wealth, love, and many of the other things that we want from life.

One way of thinking about success or failure is to focus on habits. Behaviors such as failing to complete reading assignments or skipping class might be habits leading to outcomes that "could not" be avoided, including dropping out of school. In the same way, behaviors such as completing assignments and attending class might lead to the outcome of getting an A.

When you confront a behavior that undermines your goals or creates a circumstance that you don't want, consider a new attitude: That behavior is just a habit. And it can be changed.

Thinking about ourselves as creatures of habit actually gives us power. Then we are not faced with the monumental task of changing our very nature. Rather, we can take on the doable job of changing our habits. One change in behavior that seems insignificant at first can have effects that ripple throughout your life.

START SMALL

Many people sabotage their success by planning changes that are too big or too hard. Avoid this mistake by starting with a small, easy change. Take what you think you

"should" do and reduce it. Then reduce it again. Whittle down the task until it's easy to start.

Draw on the "power of 1." Change one habit at a time—a behavior that you will do once each day. Instead of planning to floss all your teeth, for example, plan to floss just one. Instead of planning to walk 1 mile, plan to walk one block. Set yourself up for success by making the new habit easy to start. Instead of planning a big change in your diet, plan to eat just one extra piece of fruit each day.

Do not be deceived by the simplicity of this approach. It works for a simple reason: The hardest part of developing a new habit is simply getting started. Once you succeed with a tiny habit change, it's easier to extend the behavior. Over time, flossing one tooth can gradually and naturally extend to flossing all your teeth. Spending 1 minute on the mat can extend to 10 or 15. Walking one block can extend to 1 mile.

Learn more about the power of changing behaviors in small steps. For example, check out the 3 Tiny Habits course (tinyhabits.com) created by B. J. Fogg, a professor of psychology at Stanford University. One of his main suggestions for habit change is to make sure that your new behavior is truly tiny.

GET FEEDBACK AND SUPPORT

Getting feedback and support is a crucial step in adopting a new behavior. It is also a point at which many plans for change break down. It's easy to practice your new behavior with enthusiasm for a few days. After the initial rush of excitement, though, things can get a little tougher. You begin to find excuses for slipping back into old habits: "One more cigarette won't hurt." "I can get back to my paper tomorrow." "It's been a tough day. I deserve to skip class."

One way to get feedback is to bring other people into the picture. Ask others to remind you that you are changing your habit if they see you backsliding.

MONITOR YOUR BEHAVIOR

Jerry Seinfeld told one aspiring comedian that "the way to be a better comic was to create better jokes, and the way to create better jokes was to write every day."[6] Seinfeld also revealed his own system for creating a writing habit: He bought a big wall calendar that displayed the whole year on one page. On each day that he wrote jokes, Seinfeld marked a big red X on the appropriate day on the wall calendar. He knew that he'd established a new habit

© Jason Stitt/Shutterstock.com

© Zdorov Kirill Vladimirovich/Shutterstock.com

Copyright © 2015 Cengage Learning. All Rights Reserved. May not be scanned, copied or duplicated, or posted to a publicly accessible website, in whole or in part.

when he looked at the calendar and saw an unbroken chain of X's. You can use the same strategy to take a series of small steps that add up to a big change.

Search for habit change apps. Examples are Habit List (habitlist.com) and Way of Life (wayoflifeapp.com). Some apps allow you to create a Seinfeld-style calendar for tracking your daily behavior.

Act on your intention over and over again. If you fail or forget, let go of any self-judgment. Just keep practicing the new habit. Allow whatever time it takes to make a change. ■

Interactive

Journal Entry 2
Discovery/Intention Statement

Declare your intention to change a habit

In his book *The Power of Habit*, Charles Duhigg explains that any habit has three elements:[7]

- **Routine.** This is a behavior that we repeat, usually without thinking. Examples are taking a second helping at dinner, biting fingernails, or automatically hitting the "snooze" button when the alarm goes off in the morning.

- **Cue.** Also known as a *trigger*, this is an event that occurs right before we perform the routine. It might be an internal event, such as a change in mood. Or it could be an external event, such as seeing an advertisement that triggers food cravings.

- **Reward.** This is the payoff for the routine—usually a feeling of pleasure or a reduction in stress.

Taken together, these elements form a habit loop: You perceive a *cue* and then perform a *routine* in order to get a *reward*. Use this Journal Entry to test Duhigg's ideas for yourself.

Step 1: Identify the routine.

Describe the habit that you want to change. Refer to a specific behavior that anyone could observe—preferably a physical, visible action that you perform every day.

I discovered that the habit I want to change is . . .

_____

_____

_____

Step 2: Identify the cue.

Next, think about what takes place immediately before you perform the routine. For instance, drinking a cup of coffee (cue) might trigger the urge to eat a cookie (routine).

I discovered that the cue for the behavior I described is . . .

_____

_____

_____

Step 3: Identify the reward.

Now for the "goodie." Reflect on the reward you get from your routine. Do you gain a distraction from discomfort? A pleasant sensation in your body? A chance to socialize with friends or coworkers? Describe the details.

I discovered that my reward for this behavior is . . .

_____

_____

_____

Step 4: Choose a new routine.

Now choose a different routine that you can perform in response to the cue. The challenge is to choose a behavior that offers a reward with as few disadvantages as possible. Instead of eating a whole cookie, for example, you could break off just one small section and eat it slowly, with full attention. This would allow you to experience a familiar pleasure with a fraction of the calories. Describe your new routine.

The new routine that I intend to do is . . .

_____

_____

_____

Copyright © 2015 Cengage Learning. All Rights Reserved. May not be scanned, copied or duplicated, or posted to a publicly accessible website, in whole or in part.

INSTRUCTOR TOOLS & TIPS

Copyright © 2015 Cengage Learning. All Rights Reserved. May not be scanned, copied or duplicated, or posted to a publicly accessible website, in whole or in part.

Chapter 1

DISCOVERING YOURSELF

"In oneself lies the whole world, and if you know how to look and learn, then the door is there and the key is in your hand. Nobody on earth can give you either that key or the door to open, except yourself." —*J. Krishnamurti*

PREVIEW

Many students taking a student success course start out the semester with a high level of enthusiasm and energy, and that's good because there's a lot of meaty and important foundational material in the Introduction and in Chapters 1 and 2. If students learn the important concepts presented in these chapters, they are well on the way to achieving their educational goals. Use the visual table of contents on the chapter opener page to inspire your students, stimulate class discussion, and preview the chapter topics.

GUEST SPEAKER

Consider inviting past students back to speak to your class. Have the students discuss what they discovered about themselves during the course and using this textbook. How did what they learn about themselves prepare them for their other college courses? Did they make any changes to their learning and studying behaviors after what they learned from this chapter? Students appreciate hearing directly from peers, usually viewing the information as more authentic than when it comes from you.

If a speaker isn't available, consider using the Master Student Profile articles as guest speakers. Each chapter of this text includes a profile of a person who embodies several qualities of a master student. Invite your students to look for timeless qualities in the people they read about. Use Teresa Amabile's story to start a conversation about how important it is to celebrate the small successes students have throughout college so that they can remain motivated until graduation. Ask students to think of a person in their lives who embodies the qualities of a master student. Share these stories aloud.

LECTURE

Learning Style Inventory (pages LSI-1–LSI-8).
Being aware of learning styles is an important strategy for success because it helps students understand differences in the ways people like to perceive and process new information. Students learn about their own preferred style of learning and how this tool can help them observe and ascertain

the preferred teaching styles of their professors. Encourage students to share the instruments in this vital chapter with their significant others—friends and family. This helps create a support network for course principles, and it also can help students understand that some issues may be a result of differences in learning styles and strengths. You may even find this buy-in leads to family members and friends enrolling in the course once they see the power of the principles in action.

The Learning Style Inventory (LSI) is a unifying theme woven throughout *Becoming a Master Student*. Activities are crafted to engage students not only in the strengths of their own learning preference but in the strengths of other styles as well. Study skills do not transfer from a student success class to other courses accidentally. Explain that some individuals are not necessarily strong in the area of intrapersonal intelligence (Gardner's Multiple Intelligences) and may not be accustomed to thinking about their thinking (metacognition). But this is something that can be taught to a large extent. Even unaccustomed students can be made aware of the importance of understanding their own strengths and learning styles. It takes a talented and prepared instructor to help students build other schema and develop the confidence that is necessary to transfer new strategies to different learning settings. Teaching this might seem intimidating for first-time instructors. Remember, when you teach with *Becoming a Master Student,* you are not alone. Network with experienced college success teachers on your own campus. This saves time and can help you to avoid frustration. Your support materials include a Peer-to-Peer Faculty Development and Consulting team. Visit **www.cengage.com/teamup** today!

Additional resources to help guide you in administering the LSI and applying the Learning Styles Application are on the Instructor Companion Site.

Claim your multiple intelligences (page 47).
Howard Gardner's theory of several types of intelligence complements this chapter's discussion of different learning styles: both recognize that there are alternative ways for people to learn and assimilate knowledge. This article provides students with concepts for exploring

AIE-i

additional methods to achieve success in school, work, and relationships. Have students further explore career choices as they consider different majors or areas of focused study.

Workplace Application: The Career Center. Students are asked to make several important decisions when they enroll in college, one being selecting a career plan. This decision can be challenging and overwhelming. Encourage students to visit the career center early in their college experience and not just a few months before graduation and the beginning of the much-anticipated job search. The career services office assists students, community members, and alumni with all aspects of career exploration, including deciding on a college major or area of study, finding employment both during college and after completion, exploring internship opportunities, as well as teaching job search strategies like effective interviewing, work ethics, and quality résumé writing. Career counselors utilize a variety of resources to appeal to an individual's learning style. Many students enter college with a career path in mind, but their preferences and choices may change with time, maturity, and education. Students should be prepared to revise their career plan continually. Career planning is something students will engage in throughout their work lives. It is not a linear process, but a continuous loop where some stages overlap. The goal of the career center is to support students as they maneuver through this process. A trained career counselor is usually available to assist with employment trends and labor market research. Ask the career counselor to visit your class or take a tour of the career center during class. Most of the services, including résumé writing and career assessment, are free to students during college and even after graduation. Some career centers even assist students with transfer and graduate school application processes. Students may also be advised by trained peer counselors and advisors with similar interests and experiences.

EXERCISES/ACTIVITIES

1. **Power Process: Ideas are tools (page 32).** Each Power Process can be illustrated by a simple yet meaningful object lesson. For example, to illustrate this Power Process, bring a drinking straw, a spoon, a hammer, and a piece of chalk or a whiteboard marker to class. Ask for volunteers to help write an assignment on the board. Hand out the various "ideas/tools" for them to use to write on the board. In seconds, all of the students will realize the power of this process. Although each of these ideas is an excellent tool for the job it was designed to do, only the student with the right tool is successful at the current task.

2. **The Discovery Wheel (pages 36–39).** The Discovery Wheel is a critical tool in this course. After students complete the Discovery Wheel, ask them to identify their three lowest areas identified by the Discovery Wheel. Discuss these results in class. Did these test results surprise students? Do they agree with their results? Suggest that students notice their lowest areas. Ask students to locate at least one resource from the book or the media that they feel may be especially useful as they address these lowest areas. Share responses in class.

3. **Learning by seeing, hearing, and moving: The VAK system (pages 50–52).** Learning by seeing (visual learning), hearing (auditory learning), and moving (kinesthetic learning) allows students to perceive information through their senses. Engage your students by asking them to take the informal inventory and to continue to take steps towards self-discovery. Have your students submit Discovery Statements to highlight the new strategies they have discovered and Intention Statements to describe the new options for learning that they intend to implement. Ask students to remember a time in their education when a teacher finally presented course material in a way that "connected" for them. Suggest that students reflect on what learning style this successful teaching strategy utilized.

4. **Celebrate strengths.** Assign students to create a visual representation of their strengths and multiple intelligences. This can be in the form of a collage, concept map, or other visual elements. Ask students to focus on the highest areas on the Discovery Wheel and on their multiple intelligences and learning styles. This is an interesting exercise for students who are not visual learners! Emphasize that students do not need to be good at drawing or art to complete a visual representation. Remind them they all enjoyed cutting, coloring, and creating as children. Invite them to relax and have fun with this exercise. Share student creations in class.

CONVERSATION/SHARING

Refer students to "First Step: Truth is a key to mastery" on pages 33–34. Assure students that even though this journey may feel intimidating at first, First Steps are indeed challenging—and rewarding! As students complete the inventories in this chapter, remind them there are no right or wrong answers. But using them as opportunities to take charge makes this an exciting process. Remind students that the work will be hard but rewarding if they are willing to invest the time and energy in the process. Ask students whether they have heard about this course from former students. Share these stories aloud.

HOMEWORK

The Discovery Wheel (pages 36–39). The Discovery Wheel is an opportunity for students to take a first step in telling the truth about the kind of student they are and the kind of student they want to become. Students complete the Discovery Wheel in Chapter 1 and

Copyright © 2015 Cengage Learning. All Rights Reserved. May not be scanned, copied or duplicated, or posted to a publicly accessible website, in whole or in part.

Copyright ©2015 Cengage Learning. All Rights Reserved. May not be scanned, copied or duplicated, or posted to a publicly accessible website, in whole or in part.

master instructor
best practice

"*I make this concrete comparison which usually gets students' attention: If, during this course, you put forth the effort and attention that most of us do when purchasing a cell phone, you will be surprised at your progress in this course. How sad it is that we will often research and do the legwork required to buy a phone, but we will not make improvements in the quality of our own lives and futures! This course is a gift that you can give yourselves and your families—a new and more aware you!*"

—Annette McCreedy, Nashville State Community College

then again in Chapter 12. This enables them to measure their progress. Results from the Discovery Wheel exercises can be used in your course in a variety of ways:

- Ask students to list their intentions or commitments for improving particular skills during the term. At the end of the term, they can assess their progress in those areas by using the Discovery Wheel in Chapter 12.

- Create an assignment requiring students to contact people on campus or in the community who can assist them in enhancing particular skills. For example, the reading center or learning center can provide specific strategies for improving comprehension, word attack skills, and concentration.

- Allow the Discovery Wheel exercises to help shape course content. You can use the results to plan future lessons or to determine what students want to learn or accomplish during the course as a result of their self-assessments. You might create assignments for each component of the Discovery Wheel, asking students to complete the assignments for their three lowest areas of the Discovery Wheel. This allows students to focus on their own self-identified weak areas, without feeling like they are involved in "busy work." Suggest the following analogy: The components of your Discovery Wheel are like the components of a functioning automobile. Although the car can function even though the tires are somewhat worn, it can perform optimally when all components receive attention. Likewise, by addressing their lowest areas of the Discovery Wheel, students can improve their performance and increase their chances of college success.

- Ask students to form small groups and coach each other. Coaching could include how to capitalize on and share talents and how to strengthen areas for growth.

If you choose to do this activity, let students know your reasons for forming small groups. For many, self-assessment is personal, and sharing the results might seem risky. Ask students to take their best suggestions and implement them.

- Create a resource network. Take the titles of the sections of the Discovery Wheel (Attitude, Time, Memory, and so on) and list each title on a piece of paper. Ask students to sign their names to a particular piece of paper if they are willing to assist others in enhancing their skills in this area. Then distribute the lists to the class or post them on your course Web site.

EVALUATION
Quiz Ideas for Chapter 1
Ask students to:

- Explain the role of truth in the mastery of student success.

- Discuss discoveries they made from completing the Discovery Wheel.

- Describe their preferred learning style and the characteristics of students who like to learn using this style.

- Explain challenges in college for someone with their particular learning style, giving examples.

- Name and give examples of two multiple intelligences.

master instructor
best practice

"*To save class time for instruction and discussion, I tell my students that I am going to select only one 10-point question for the quiz. It will be one of the questions in the book quiz. I present the question and ask students to respond using the three-part quiz forms (available through your sales rep). When they are through answering the question, I remind students to write their name on the quiz before tearing off the white sheet and handing it in. Then they compare answers with the person next to them to seek insights from each other. If they did not have the answer, I tell them that if they return the pink sheet with the answers to all ten questions, I will give them 7 out of 10 points.*"

—Eldon McMurray, Utah Valley State College

MindTap™ # EMBRACE VALUABLE RESOURCES

FOR CHAPTER 1

STUDENT RESOURCES: MINDTAP

- **Engagement Activity: Master Students in Action.** This video focuses on the importance of the Discovery Wheel to the student's discovery process. This video should prepare students for completing their own Discovery Wheel; the thoughtful questions it poses encourage students to think critically about the work they'll complete as part of the Discovery Wheel exercise.

- **Aplia Homework Assignment: The Discovery Wheel.** In this assignment, students learn how to interpret Discovery Wheel results and respond by planning and taking action. By examining a student's sample Discovery Wheel results, students can identify actions that will help them identify their weakest areas.

- **Reflection Activity: How to Peel an Orange.** This Slice of Life video, created by student Will Donovan, examines the importance of finding and embracing one's own unique learning style, as personally experienced by a ceramics student.

 MindTap™ *Your personal learning experience—learn anywhere, anytime.*

master instructor
best practice

your multiple intelligence, dissected

Have students take the free multiple intelligence inventory at www.ldpride.net/ learningstyles.MI.htm. This exercise helps students identify their particular type of intelligence and shows them characteristics, possible learning strategies, and careers unique to them. Because this inventory is located on a site for individuals with disabilities, we talk about why it would be important for people with disabilities to understand how they learn the best. We discuss what it will do for them in their work environment as well as everyday life. We have many thought-provoking conversations about this topic just by accessing the site!

—*Krista Clay-Lieffring, Neosho County Community College*

INSTRUCTOR COMPANION SITE

- **Need guidance on how to teach with the Discovery Wheel and Learning Style Inventory?** The Master Teachers in Action videos provide you with an inside look at how *Becoming a Master Student* is used by professors, including information on their favorite parts, and how specific articles and activities from the text prepare students for achieving success. Hear from Dave Ellis himself and other instructors about what works for

them when teaching the Discovery Wheel and the Learning Style Inventory.

- **Looking for fresh, innovative ways to teach Chapter 1 topics?** Browse through the Course Manual to see what other Master Instructors have been successfully doing with their students.

Please visit login.cengage.com to log in and access the Instructor Companion Site.

Copyright © 2015 Cengage Learning. All Rights Reserved. May not be scanned, copied or duplicated, or posted to a publicly accessible website, in whole or in part.

Copyright © 2015 Cengage Learning. All Rights Reserved. May not be scanned, copied or duplicated, or posted to a publicly accessible website, in whole or in part. / Photo Credit: ©Andresr/Shutterstock.com. Second Photo: ©ziva7/Shutterstock.com. Third Photo: Steve Cole/PhotoDisc/Getty Images.

Chapter 1

DISCOVERING YOURSELF

Why

Success starts with telling the truth about what *is* working—and what *isn't*—in your life right now.

First Step: Truth is a key to mastery ■ 33

The Discovery Wheel ■ 36

How

Skim this chapter for three techniques that you'd like to use in school or in your personal life during the upcoming week. Make a note to yourself or mark the pages where the strategies that you intend to use are located in the chapter.

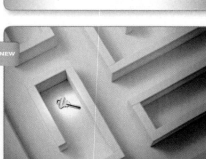

Six paths to more powerful thinking One quality of a master student is the ability to ask questions that lead to deeper learning. Learn how becoming a critical thinker means being flexible and asking a wide range of questions. ■ 55

What if ...

I could start to create new outcomes in my life by accepting the way I am right now?

What is included ...

Learning Style Inventory

To help you become more aware of learning styles, a psychologist named David Kolb developed the Learning Style Inventory (LSI). Responding to the items in the LSI can help you discover a lot about the ways you learn. You'll complete a Learning Style Graph to give you an idea of your preferred mode of learning—the kind of behaviors that feel most comfortable and familiar to you when you are learning something. ■ **LSI-1**

POWER PROCESS

IDEAS ARE TOOLS

There are many ideas in this book. When you first encounter them, don't believe any of them. Instead, think of the ideas as tools.

For example, you use a hammer for a purpose—to drive a nail. You don't try to figure out whether the hammer is "right." You just use it. If it works, you use it again. If it doesn't work, you get a different hammer.

People have plenty of room in their lives for different kinds of hammers, but they tend to limit their openness to different kinds of ideas. A new idea, at some level, is a threat to their very being—unlike a new hammer, which is simply a new hammer.

Most of us have a built-in desire to be right. Our ideas, we often think, represent ourselves.

Some ideas are worth dying for. But please note: This book does not contain any of those ideas. The ideas on these pages are strictly "hammers."

Imagine someone defending a hammer. Picture this person holding up a hammer and declaring, "I hold this hammer to be self-evident. Give me this hammer or give me death. Those other hammers are flawed. There are only two kinds of people in this world: people who believe in this hammer and people who don't."

That ridiculous picture makes a point. This book is not a manifesto. It's a toolbox, and tools are meant to be used.

If you read about a tool in this book that doesn't sound "right" or one that sounds a little goofy, remember that the ideas here are for using, not necessarily for believing. Suspend your judgment. Test the idea for yourself. If it works, use it. If it doesn't, don't use it.

Any tool—a hammer, a computer program, a study technique—is designed to do a specific job. A master mechanic carries a variety of tools because no single tool works for all jobs. If you throw a tool away because it doesn't work in one situation, you won't be able to pull it out later when it's just what you need. So if an idea doesn't work for you and you are satisfied that you gave it a fair chance, don't throw it away. File it away instead. The idea might come in handy soon.

And remember, this book is not about figuring out the "right" way. Even the "ideas are tools" approach is not "right."

It's just a tool.

Steve Cole/Photodisc/Getty Images

Copyright © 2015 Cengage Learning. All Rights Reserved. May not be scanned, copied or duplicated, or posted to a publicly accessible website, in whole or in part.

© akva/Shutterstock.com

FIRST STEP:
Truth is a key to
MASTERY

The First Step is one of the most valuable tools in this book. It magnifies the power of all the other techniques. It is a key to becoming a master student.

The First Step technique is simple: Tell the truth about who you are and what you want. End of discussion. Now, proceed to Chapter 2. Well . . . it's not *quite* that simple.

To succeed in school, tell the truth about what kind of student you are and what kind of student you want to become. Success starts with telling the truth about what *is* working—and what is *not* working—in your life right now.

An article about telling the truth might sound like pie-in-the-sky moralizing. However, there is nothing pie-in-the-sky or moralizing about a First Step. It is a practical, down-to-earth principle to use whenever you want to change your behavior.

When we acknowledge our strengths, we gain an accurate picture of what we can accomplish. When we admit that we have a problem, we are free to find a solution. Ignoring the truth, on the other hand, can lead to problems that stick around for decades.

FIRST STEPS ARE UNIVERSAL

When you see a doctor, the First Step is to tell the truth about your current symptoms. That way you can get an accurate diagnosis and effective treatment plan. This principle is universal. It works for just about any problem in any area of life.

First Steps are used by millions of people who want to turn their lives around. No technique in this book has been field-tested more often or more successfully—or under tougher circumstances.

For example, members of Alcoholics Anonymous start by telling the truth about their drinking. Their First Step is to admit that they are powerless over alcohol. That's when their lives start to change.

When people join Weight Watchers, their First Step is telling the truth about how much they currently weigh.

When people go for credit counseling, their First Step is telling the truth about how much money they earn, how much they spend, and how much they owe.

People dealing with a variety of other challenges—including troubled relationships with food, drugs, sex, and work—also start by telling the truth. They use First Steps

to change their behavior, and they do it for a reason: First Steps work.

FIRST STEPS ARE CHALLENGING—AND REWARDING

Let's be truthful: It's not easy to tell the truth about ourselves.

It's not fun to admit our weaknesses. Many of us approach a frank evaluation of ourselves about as enthusiastically as we'd greet a phone call from the bank about an overdrawn account. We might end up admitting that we're afraid of algebra, that we don't complete term papers on time, or that coming up with the money to pay for tuition is a constant challenge.

There is another way to think about self-evaluations. If we could see them as opportunities to solve problems and take charge of our lives, we might welcome them. Believe it or not, we can begin working with our list of weaknesses by celebrating them.

Consider the most accomplished, "together" people you know. If they were totally candid with you, they would talk about their mistakes and regrets as well as their rewards and recognition. The most successful people tend to be the most willing to look at their flaws.

It may seem natural to judge our own shortcomings and feel bad about them. Some people believe that such feelings are necessary to correct their errors. Others think that a healthy dose of shame can prevent the moral decay of our society.

Copyright © 2015 Cengage Learning. All Rights Reserved. May not be scanned, copied or duplicated, or posted to a publicly accessible website, in whole or in part.

Think again. In fact, consider the opposite idea: We can gain skill without feeling rotten about the past. We can change the way things *are* without having to criticize the way things *have been*. We can learn to see shame or blame as excess baggage and just set them aside.

If the whole idea of telling the truth about yourself puts a knot in your stomach, that's good. Notice the knot. It is your friend. It is a reminder that First Steps call for courage and compassion. These are qualities of a master student.

FIRST STEPS FREE US TO CHANGE

Master students get the most value from a First Step by turning their perceived shortcomings into goals. "I don't exercise enough" turns into "I will walk briskly for 30 minutes at least three times per week."

"I don't take clear notes" turns into "I will review my notes within 24 hours after class and rewrite them for clarity."

"I am in conflict with my parents" turns into "When my parents call, I will take time to understand their point of view before disagreeing with them."

"I get so nervous during the night before a big test that I find it hard to sleep" turns into "I will find ways to reduce stress during the 24 hours before a test so that I sleep better."

Another quality of master students is that they refuse to let their First Steps turn into excuses. These students avoid using the phrase "I can't" and its endless variations.

The key is to state First Steps in a way that allows for new possibilities in the future. Use language in a way that reinforces your freedom to change.

For example, "I can't succeed in math" is better stated like this: "During math courses, I tend to get confused early in the term and find it hard to ask questions. I could be more assertive in asking for help right away."

"I can't say no to my underage friends who like to drink until they get drunk" is better stated as "I have friends who drink illegally and drink too much. I want to be alcohol-free and still be friends with them."

Telling the truth about what we don't want gives us more clarity about what we *do* want. By taking a First Step, we can free up all the energy that it takes to deny our problems and avoid change. We can redirect that

energy and use it to take actions that align with our values.

FIRST STEPS INCLUDE STRENGTHS

For some of us, it's even harder to recognize our strengths than to recognize our weaknesses. Maybe we don't want to brag. Maybe we're attached to a poor self-image.

The reasons don't matter. The point is that using the First Step technique in *Becoming a Master Student* means telling the truth about our positive qualities too.

Remember that weaknesses are often strengths taken to an extreme. The student who carefully revises her writing can make significant improvements in a term paper. If she revises too much and hands in the paper late, though, her grade might suffer. Any success strategy carried too far can backfire.

FIRST STEPS ARE SPECIFIC

Whether written or verbal, the ways that we express our First Steps are more powerful when they are specific.

For example, if you want to improve your note-taking skills, you might write, "I am an awful note taker"; but it would be more effective to write, "I can't read 80 percent of the notes I took in Introduction to psychology last week, and I have no idea what was important in that class."

Be just as specific about what you plan to achieve. You might declare, "I want to take legible notes that help me predict what questions will be on the final exam."

The exercises and Journal Entries in this chapter are all about getting specific. They can help you tap resources you never knew you had. For example, do the Discovery Wheel to get a big-picture view of your personal effectiveness. And use the Learning Style Inventory, along with the articles about multiple intelligences and the VAK system, to tell the truth about how you perceive and process information.

As you use these elements of *Becoming a Master Student*, you might feel surprised at what you discover. You might even disagree with the results of an exercise. That's fine. Just tell the truth about it. Use your disagreement as a tool for further discussion and self-discovery.

This book is full of First Steps. It's just that simple. The truth has power. ■

> *Telling the truth about what we don't want gives us more clarity about what we do want. We can free up all the energy that it takes to deny our problems and avoid change. Redirect that energy and use it to take actions that align with our values.*

Copyright © 2015 Cengage Learning. All Rights Reserved. May not be scanned, copied or duplicated, or posted to a publicly accessible website, in whole or in part.

Exercise 5 Taking the First Step

The purpose of this exercise is to give you a chance to discover and acknowledge your own strengths, as well as areas for improvement. For many students, this exercise is the most difficult one in the book. To make the exercise worthwhile, do it with courage.

Some people suggest that looking at areas for improvement means focusing on personal weaknesses. They view it as a negative approach that runs counter to positive thinking. Well, perhaps. Positive thinking is a great technique. So is telling the truth, especially when we see the whole picture—the negative aspects as well as the positive ones.

If you admit that you can't add or subtract, and that's indeed the truth, then you have taken a strong, positive First Step toward learning basic math. On the other hand, if you say that you are a terrible math student, but that's not the truth, then you are programming yourself to accept unnecessary failure.

The point is to tell the truth. This exercise is similar to the Discovery Statements that appear in every chapter. The difference is that, in this case, for reasons of confidentiality, you won't write down your discoveries in the book.

You are likely to disclose some things about yourself that you wouldn't want others to read. You might even write down some truths that could get you into trouble. Do this exercise on separate sheets of paper; then hide or destroy them. Protect your privacy. To make this exercise work, follow these suggestions.

- **Be specific.** It is not effective to write, "I can improve my communication skills." Of course you can. Instead, write down precisely what you can *do* to improve your communication skills—for example, "I can spend more time really listening while the other person is talking, instead of thinking about what I'm going to say next."

- **Be self-aware.** Look beyond the classroom. What goes on outside school often has the greatest impact on your ability to be an effective student. Consider your strengths and weaknesses that you may think have nothing to do with school.

- **Be courageous.** This exercise calls for an important master student quality—courage. It is a waste of time if this exercise is done half heartedly. Be willing to take risks. You might open a door that reveals a part of yourself that you didn't want to admit was there. The power of this technique is that once you know what is there, you can do something about it.

Part 1

Time yourself, and for 10 minutes write as fast as you can, completing each of the following sentences at least 10 times with anything that comes to mind. If you get stuck, don't stop. Just write something—even if it seems crazy.

I never succeed when I . . .

I'm not very good at . . .

Something I'd like to change about myself is . . .

Part 2

When you have completed the first part of the exercise, review what you have written, crossing off things that don't make any sense. The sentences that remain suggest possible goals for becoming a master student.

Part 3

Here's the tough part. Time yourself, and for 10 minutes write as fast as you can, completing the following sentences with anything that comes to mind. As in Part 1, complete each sentence at least 10 times. Just keep writing, even if it sounds silly.

I always succeed when I . . .

I am very good at . . .

Something I like about myself is . . .

Part 4

Review what you have written, and circle the things that you can fully celebrate. This list is a good thing to keep for those times when you question your own value and worth.

Copyright © 2015 Cengage Learning. All Rights Reserved. May not be scanned, copied or duplicated, or posted to a publicly accessible website, in whole or in part.

Exercise 6 The Discovery Wheel

The Discovery Wheel gives you an in-depth opportunity to practice the master student process—the ongoing cycle of discovery, intention, and action. Like many other students, you might find the Discovery Wheel to be the most valuable exercise in this book.

This is not a test. There are no trick questions, and the answers will have meaning only for you.

Here are two suggestions to make this exercise more effective. First, think of it as the beginning of an opportunity to change. Second, lighten up. A little laughter can make self-evaluations a lot more effective.

Here's how the Discovery Wheel works. By the end of this exercise, you will have filled in a circle similar to the one on this page. The Discovery Wheel circle is a picture of how you see yourself as a student. The closer the shading comes to the outer edge of the circle, the higher the evaluation of a specific skill. In Figure 1.1, the student has rated her reading skills low and her note-taking skills high.

The terms *high* and *low* are not meant to reflect judgment. The Discovery Wheel is not a permanent picture of who you are. It is a picture of how you view your strengths and weaknesses as a student today. To begin this exercise, read the following statements and award yourself points for each one, using

the point system described here. Then add up your point total for each section, and shade the Discovery Wheel in Figure 1.2 on page 39 to the appropriate level.

5 points	This statement is always or almost always true of me.
4 points	This statement is often true of me.
3 points	This statement is true of me about half the time.
2 points	This statement is seldom true of me.
1 point	This statement is never or almost never true of me.

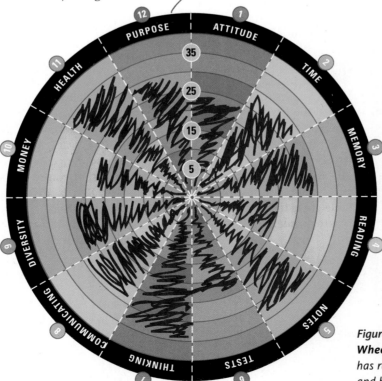

Figure 1.1 Sample Discovery Wheel. *Notice how this student has rated her reading skills low and her note-taking skills high.*

Copyright © 2005 Cengage Learning. All Rights Reserved. May not be scanned, copied or duplicated, or posted to a publicly accessible website, in whole or in part.

1 Attitude

_____ I enjoy learning.
_____ I understand and apply the concept of multiple intelligences.
_____ I connect my courses to my purpose for being in school.
_____ I make a habit of assessing my personal strengths and areas for improvement.
_____ I am satisfied with how I am progressing toward achieving my goals.
_____ I use my knowledge of learning styles to support my success in school.
_____ I am willing to consider any idea that can help me succeed in school.
_____ I regularly remind myself of the benefits I intend to get from my education.
_____ **Total Score: Attitude**

2 Time

_____ I set long-term goals and periodically review them.
_____ I set short-term goals to support my long-term goals.
_____ I write a plan for each day and each week.
_____ I assign priorities to what I choose to do each day.
_____ I plan review time so I don't have to cram before tests.
_____ I plan regular recreation time.
_____ I adjust my study time to meet the demands of individual courses.
_____ I have adequate time each day to accomplish what I plan.
_____ **Total Score: Time**

3 Memory

_____ I am confident of my ability to remember.
_____ I can remember people's names.
_____ At the end of a lecture, I can summarize what was presented.
_____ I apply techniques that enhance my memory skills.
_____ I can recall information when I'm under pressure.
_____ I remember important information clearly and easily.
_____ I can jog my memory when I have difficulty recalling.
_____ I can relate new information to what I've already learned.
_____ **Total Score: Memory**

4 Reading

_____ I preview and review reading assignments.
_____ When reading, I ask myself questions about the material.
_____ I underline or highlight important passages when reading.
_____ When I read textbooks, I am alert and awake.
_____ I relate what I read to my life.
_____ I select a reading strategy to fit the type of material I'm reading.
_____ I take effective notes when I read.
_____ When I don't understand what I'm reading, I note my questions and find answers.
_____ **Total Score: Reading**

5 Notes

_____ When I am in class, I focus my attention.
_____ I take notes in class.
_____ I know about many methods for taking notes and choose those that work best for me.
_____ I distinguish important material and note key phrases in a lecture.
_____ I copy down material that the instructor writes on the board or overhead display.
_____ I can put important concepts into my own words.
_____ My notes are valuable for review.
_____ I review class notes within 24 hours.
_____ **Total Score: Notes**

6 Tests

_____ I use techniques to manage stress related to exams.
_____ I manage my time during exams and am able to complete them.
_____ I am able to predict test questions.
_____ I adapt my test-taking strategy to the kind of test I'm taking.
_____ I understand what essay questions ask and can answer them completely and accurately.
_____ I start reviewing for tests at the beginning of the term.
_____ I continue reviewing for tests throughout the term.
_____ My sense of personal worth is independent of my test scores.
_____ **Total Score: Tests**

Copyright © 2015 Cengage Learning. All Rights Reserved. May not be scanned, copied or duplicated, or posted to a publicly accessible website, in whole or in part.

7 Thinking

_____ I have flashes of insight and think of solutions to problems at unusual times.

_____ I use brainstorming to generate solutions to a variety of problems.

_____ When I get stuck on a creative project, I use specific methods to get unstuck.

_____ I learn by thinking about ways to contribute to the lives of other people.

_____ I am willing to consider different points of view and alternative solutions.

_____ I can detect common errors in logic.

_____ I construct viewpoints by drawing on information and ideas from many sources.

_____ As I share my viewpoints with others, I am open to their feedback.

_____ **Total Score: Thinking**

8 Communicating

_____ I am honest with others about who I am, what I feel, and what I want.

_____ Other people tell me that I am a good listener.

_____ I can communicate my upset and anger without blaming others.

_____ I can make friends and create valuable relationships in a new setting.

_____ I am open to being with people I don't especially like in order to learn from them.

_____ I can effectively plan and research a large writing assignment.

_____ I create first drafts without criticizing my writing, then edit later for clarity, accuracy, and coherence.

_____ I know ways to prepare and deliver effective speeches.

_____ **Total Score: Communicating**

9 Diversity

_____ I build rewarding relationships with people from diverse backgrounds.

_____ I use critical thinking to overcome stereotypes.

_____ I point out examples of discrimination and harassment and effectively respond to them.

_____ I am constantly learning ways to thrive with diversity.

_____ I can effectively resolve conflict with people from other cultures.

_____ My writing and speaking are free of sexist expressions.

_____ I take diversity into account when assuming a leadership role.

_____ I respond effectively to changing demographics in my country and community.

_____ **Total Score: Diversity**

10 Money

_____ I am in control of my personal finances.

_____ I can access a variety of resources to finance my education.

_____ I am confident that I will have enough money to complete my education.

_____ I take on debts carefully and repay them on time.

_____ I have long-range financial goals and a plan to meet them.

_____ I make regular deposits to a savings account.

_____ I pay off the balance on credit card accounts each month.

_____ I can have fun without spending money.

_____ **Total Score: Money**

11 Health

_____ I have enough energy to study and work—and still enjoy other areas of my life.

_____ If the situation calls for it, I have enough reserve energy to put in a long day.

_____ The way I eat supports my long-term health.

_____ The way I eat is independent of my feelings of self-worth.

_____ I exercise regularly to maintain a healthful weight.

_____ My emotional health supports my ability to learn.

_____ I notice changes in my physical condition and respond effectively.

_____ I am in control of any alcohol or other drugs I put into my body.

_____ **Total Score: Health**

12 Purpose

_____ I see learning as a lifelong process.

_____ I relate school to what I plan to do for the rest of my life.

_____ I see problems and tough choices as opportunities for learning and personal growth.

_____ I use technology in a way that enriches my life and supports my success.

_____ I am developing skills that will be useful in the workplace.

_____ I take responsibility for the quality of my education—and my life.

_____ I live by a set of values that translates into daily actions.

_____ I am willing to accept challenges even when I'm not sure how to meet them.

_____ **Total Score: Purpose**

Copyright © 2015 Cengage Learning. All Rights Reserved. May not be scanned, copied or duplicated, or posted to a publicly accessible website, in whole or in part.

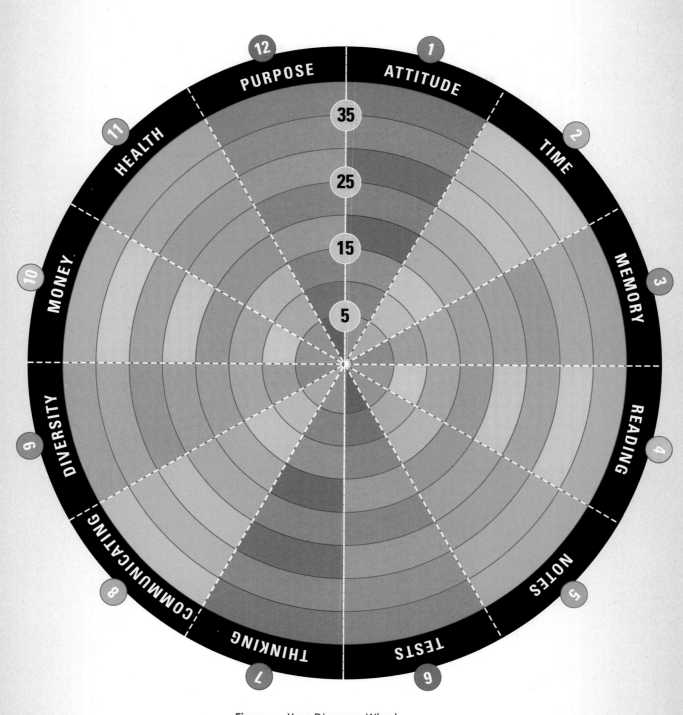

Figure 1.2 Your Discovery Wheel

Filling in your Discovery Wheel

Using the total score from each category, shade in each corresponding wedge of the Discovery Wheel in Figure 1.2. Use different colors, if you want. For example, you could use green to denote areas you want to work on. When you have finished, complete the Skills Snapshot on the next page.

Copyright © 2015 Cengage Learning. All Rights Reserved. May not be scanned, copied or duplicated, or posted to a publicly accessible website, in whole or in part.

Interactive

SKILLS SNAPSHOT

Discovery Wheel

Now that you have completed your Discovery Wheel, it's time to get a sense of its weight, shape, and balance. Can you imagine running your hands around it? If you could lift it, would it feel light or heavy? How would it sound if it rolled down a hill? Would it roll very far? Would it wobble? Make your observations without judging the wheel as good or bad. Simply be with the picture you have created.

After you have spent a few minutes studying your Discovery Wheel, complete the following sentences. Just put down whatever comes to mind. Remember, this is not a test.

Overview

This wheel is an accurate picture of my ability as a student because . . .

My self-evaluation surprises me because . . .

Strengths

One area where I show strong skills is . . .

Another area of strength is . . .

Goals

The area in which I most want to improve is . . .

It is also important for me to get better at . . .

I want to concentrate on improving these areas because . . .

To meet my goals for improvement, I intend to . . .

Copyright © 2015 Cengage Learning. All Rights Reserved. May not be scanned, copied or duplicated, or posted to a publicly accessible website, in whole or in part.

LEARNING STYLES:
Discovering how you learn

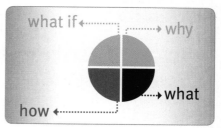

Right now, you are investing substantial amounts of time, money, and energy in your education. What you get in return for this investment depends on how well you understand the process of learning and use it to your advantage.

If you don't understand learning, you might feel bored or confused in class. Over time, frustration can mount to the point where you question the value of being in school.

Some students answer that question by dropping out of school. These students lose a chance to create the life they want. You can prevent that outcome for yourself.

Start by understanding the different ways that people create meaning from their experience and change their behavior. In other words, learn about *how* we learn.

WE LEARN BY PERCEIVING AND PROCESSING

When we learn well, says psychologist David Kolb, two things happen.[1] First, we *perceive*. That is, we notice events and "take in" new experiences.

Second, we *process*. We "deal with" experiences in a way that helps us make sense of them.

Some people especially prefer to perceive through *feeling* (also called *concrete experience*). They like to absorb information through their five senses. They learn by getting directly involved in new experiences. When solving problems, they rely on intuition as much as intellect. These people typically function well in unstructured classes that allow them to take initiative.

Other people like to perceive by *thinking* (also called *abstract conceptualization*). They take in information best when they can think about it as a subject separate from themselves. They analyze, intellectualize, and create theories. Often these people take a scientific approach to problem solving and excel in traditional classrooms.

Some people prefer to process by *watching* (also called *reflective observation*). They prefer to stand back, watch what is going on, and think about it. They consider several points of view as they attempt to make sense of things and generate many ideas about how something happens. They value patience, good judgment, and a thorough approach to learning.

Other people like to process by *doing* (also called *active experimentation*). They prefer to jump in and start doing things immediately. These people do not mind taking risks as they attempt to make sense of things; this helps them learn. They are results oriented and look for practical ways to apply what they have learned.

PERCEIVING AND PROCESSING—AN EXAMPLE

Suppose that you get a new cell phone. It has more features than any phone you've used before. You have many options for learning how to use it. For example:

- Just get your hands on the phone right away, press some buttons, and see whether you can dial a number or send a text message.
- Read the instruction manual and view help screens on the phone before you try to make a call.
- Recall experiences you've had with phones in the past and what you've learned by watching other people use their cell phones.
- Ask a friend who owns the same type of phone to coach you as you experiment with making calls and sending messages.

These actions illustrate the different approaches to learning:

- Getting your hands on the phone right away and seeing whether you can make it work is an example of learning through *feeling* (or *concrete experience*).
- Reading the manual and help screens before you use the phone is an example of learning through *thinking* (or *abstract conceptualization*).
- Recalling what you've experienced in the past is an example of learning through watching (or *reflective observation*).
- Asking a friend to coach you through a "hands-on" activity is an example of learning through *doing* (or *active experimentation*).

In summary, your learning style is the unique way that you blend thinking, feeling, watching, and doing. You tend to use this approach in learning anything. Reading the next few pages and doing the recommended activities will help you explore your learning style in more detail. ■

Copyright © 2015 Cengage Learning. All Rights Reserved. May not be scanned, copied or duplicated, or posted to a publicly accessible website, in whole or in part.

Journal Entry 3
Discovery Statement

Prepare for the Learning Style Inventory (LSI)

As a "warm-up" for the LSI, spend a minute or two thinking about times in the past when you felt successful at learning. Underline or highlight any of the following statements that describe those situations:

- I was in a highly structured setting with a lot of directions about what to do and feedback on how well I did at each step.
- I was free to learn at my own pace and in my own way.
- I learned as part of a small group.
- I learned mainly by working alone in a quiet place.
- I learned in a place where there was a lot of activity going on.
- I learned by forming pictures in my mind.
- I learned by *doing* something—moving around, touching something, or trying out a process for myself.
- I learned by talking to myself or explaining ideas to other people.
- I got the "big picture" before I tried to understand the details.
- I listened to a lecture and then thought about it after class.
- I read a book or article and then thought about it afterward.
- I used a variety of media—such as a videos, films, audio recordings, or computers—to assist my learning.
- I went beyond taking notes and wrote in a personal journal.
- I was considering where to attend school and knew I had to actually set foot on each campus before choosing.
- I was shopping for a car and paid more attention to how I felt about test-driving each one than to the sticker prices or mileage estimates.
- I was thinking about going to a movie and carefully read the reviews before choosing one.

Reviewing the list, do you see any patterns in the way you prefer to learn? Briefly describe them.

Directions for completing the Learning Style Inventory

To help you become more aware of learning styles, a psychologist named David Kolb developed the Learning Style Inventory (LSI). Responding to the items in the LSI can help you discover a lot about ways you learn. Following the LSI are suggestions for using the LSI results to promote your success.

The LSI is not a test. There are no right or wrong answers. Your goal is simply to develop a profile of your current learning style. So, take the LSI quickly. You might find it useful to recall a recent time when you learned something new at school, home, or work. However, do not agonize over your responses.

Note that the LSI consists of 12 sentences, each with four different endings. Read each sentence, and then write a 4 next to the ending that best describes the way you currently learn. Then you will continue ranking the other endings with a 3, 2, or 1, representing the ending that least describes you. This is a forced-choice inventory, so you must rank each ending. *Do not leave any endings blank.* Use each number only once for each question.

Following are more specific directions:

1. Read the instructions at the top of page LSI–1. When you understand Example A, you are ready to begin.
2. Before you write on page LSI–1, remove the sheet of paper following page LSI–2.
3. While writing on page LSI–1, *press firmly* so that your answers will show up on page LSI–3.
4. After you complete the 12 items on page LSI–1, go to page LSI–3.

Copyright © 2015 Cengage Learning. All Rights Reserved. May not be scanned, copied or duplicated, or posted to a publicly accessible website, in whole or in part.

Learning Style Inventory

Complete items 1–12 below. Use the following example as a guide:

A. When I learn: __2__ I am happy. __3__ I am fast. __4__ I am logical. __1__ I am careful.

Remember: **4 = Most like you   3 = Second most like you   2 = Third most like you   1 = Least like you**

Do not leave any endings blank. Use each number only once for each question. Before completing the items, remove the sheet of paper following this page. While writing, press firmly.

1. When I learn:	___ I like to deal with my feelings.	___ I like to think about ideas.	___ I like to be doing things.	___ I like to watch and listen.
2. I learn best when:	___ I listen and watch carefully.	___ I rely on logical thinking.	___ I trust my hunches and feelings.	___ I work hard to get things done.
3. When I am learning:	___ I tend to reason things out.	___ I am responsible about things.	___ I am quiet and reserved.	___ I have strong feelings and reactions.
4. I learn by:	___ feeling.	___ doing.	___ watching.	___ thinking.
5. When I learn:	___ I am open to new experiences.	___ I look at all sides of issues.	___ I like to analyze things, break them down into their parts.	___ I like to try things out.
6. When I am learning:	___ I am an observing person.	___ I am an active person.	___ I am an intuitive person.	___ I am a logical person.
7. I learn best from:	___ observation.	___ personal relationships.	___ rational theories.	___ a chance to try out and practice.
8. When I learn:	___ I like to see results from my work.	___ I like ideas and theories.	___ I take my time before acting.	___ I feel personally involved in things.
9. I learn best when:	___ I rely on my observations.	___ I rely on my feelings.	___ I can try things out for myself.	___ I rely on my ideas.
10. When I am learning:	___ I am a reserved person.	___ I am an accepting person.	___ I am a responsible person.	___ I am a rational person.
11. When I learn:	___ I get involved.	___ I like to observe.	___ I evaluate things.	___ I like to be active.
12. I learn best when:	___ I analyze ideas.	___ I am receptive and open-minded.	___ I am careful.	___ I am practical.

Copyright © 2015 Cengage Learning. All Rights Reserved. May not be scanned, copied or duplicated, or posted to a publicly accessible website, in whole or in part.

© Copyright 2007 Experience Based Learning Systems, Inc. Developed by David A. Kolb. All rights reserved. The material found here cannot be replicated, in any format, without written permission from the Hay Group, 116 Huntington Ave., Boston, MA.

Taking the Next Steps

Now that you've finished taking the Learning Style Inventory, you probably have some questions about what it means. You're about to discover some answers! In the following pages, you will find instructions for:

- Scoring your inventory (page LSI-3)

- Plotting your scores on to a Learning Style Graph that literally gives a "big picture" of your learning style (page LSI-5)

- Interpreting your Learning Style Graph by seeing how it relates to four distinct modes, or styles, of learning (page LSI-6)

- Developing all four modes of learning (page LSI-7)

- Balancing your learning preferences (page LSI-8)

Take your time to absorb all this material. Be willing to read through it several times and ask questions.

Your efforts will be rewarded. In addition to discovering more details about *how* you learn, you'll gain a set of strategies for applying this knowledge to your courses. With these strategies, you can use your knowledge of learning styles to actively promote your success in school.

Above all, aim to recover your natural gift for learning—the defining quality of a master student. Rediscover a world where the boundaries between learning and fun, between work and play, all disappear. While immersing yourself in new experiences, blend the sophistication of an adult with the wonder of a child. This path is one that you can travel for the rest of your life.

Copyright © 2015 Cengage Learning. All Rights Reserved. May not be scanned, copied or duplicated, or posted to a publicly accessible website, in whole or in part.

Remove this sheet before completing the Learning Style Inventory.

This page is inserted to ensure that the other writing you do in this book doesn't show through on page LSI-3.

Copyright © 2015 Cengage Learning. All Rights Reserved. May not be scanned, copied or duplicated, or posted to a publicly accessible website, in whole or in part.

Remove this sheet before completing the Learning Style Inventory.

This page is inserted to ensure that the other writing you do in this book doesn't show through on page LSI-3.

Copyright © 2015 Cengage Learning. All Rights Reserved. May not be scanned, copied or duplicated, or posted to a publicly accessible website, in whole or in part.

Scorecard

Brown F   Total _____

Teal W   Total _____

Purple T   Total _____

Orange D   Total _____

Grand Total _____

Now that you have taken the Learning Style Inventory, it's time to fill out the Learning Style Graph (page LSI-5) and interpret your results. To do this, follow these steps.

Scoring Your Inventory

STEP 1 First, add up all of the numbers you gave to the items marked with brown F letters. Then write down that total in the box to the left, next to **"Brown F."** Next, add up all of the numbers for **"Teal W," "Purple T,"** and **"Orange D,"** and also write down those totals in the box to the left.

STEP 2 Add the four totals to arrive at a **Grand Total,** and write down that figure in the box to the left. (*Note: The grand total should equal 120. If you have a different amount, go back and re-add the colored letters; it was probably just an addition error.*) Now remove this page and continue with Step 3 on page LSI-5.

F	**T**	**D**	**W**
W	**T**	**F**	**D**
T	**D**	**W**	**F**
F	**D**	**W**	**T**
F	**W**	**T**	**D**
W	**D**	**F**	**T**
W	**F**	**T**	**D**
D	**T**	**W**	**F**
W	**F**	**D**	**T**
W	**F**	**D**	**T**
F	**W**	**T**	**D**
T	**F**	**W**	**D**

Copyright © 2015 Cengage Learning. All Rights Reserved. May not be scanned, copied or duplicated, or posted to a publicly accessible website, in whole or in part.

**Remove this page after you have completed
Steps 1 and 2 on page LSI-3.
Then continue with Step 3 on page LSI-5.**

Copyright © 2015 Cengage Learning. All Rights Reserved. May not be scanned, copied or duplicated, or posted to a publicly accessible website, in whole or in part.

removethispageremovethispageremovethispage

Learning Style Graph

STEP 3 Remove the sheet of paper that follows this page. Then transfer your totals from Step 2 on page LSI-3 to the lines on the Learning Style Graph below. On the brown (F) line, find the number that corresponds to your **"Brown F"** total from page LSI-3. Then write an X on this number. Do the same for your **"Teal W," "Purple T,"** and **"Orange D"** totals. The graph on this page is for you to keep. The graph on page LSI-7 is for you to turn in to your instructor if required to do so.

STEP 4 Now, pressing firmly, draw four straight lines to connect the four X's, and shade in the area to form a "kite." This is your learning style profile. (For an example, see the illustration below.) Each X that you placed on these lines indicates your preference for a different aspect of learning as described to the right.

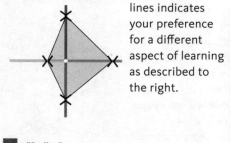

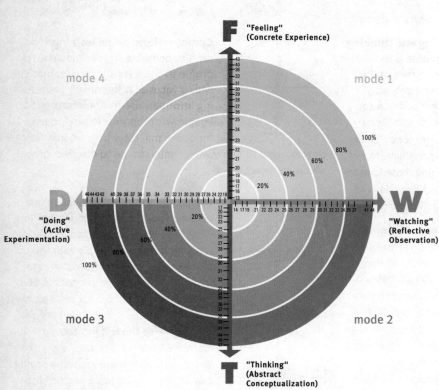

Copyright © 2015 Cengage Learning. All Rights Reserved. May not be scanned, copied or duplicated, or posted to a publicly accessible website, in whole or in part.

F: Feeling
Concrete Experience
The number where you put your X on this line indicates your preference for learning things that have personal meaning. The higher your score on this line, the more you like to learn things that you feel are important and relevant to yourself.

W: Watching
Reflective Observation
Your number on this line indicates how important it is for you to reflect on the things you are learning. If your score is high on this line, you probably find it important to watch others as they learn about an assignment and then report on it to the class. You probably like to plan things out and take the time to make sure that you fully understand a topic.

T: Thinking
Abstract Conceptualization
Your number on this line indicates your preference for learning ideas, facts, and figures. If your score is high on this line, you probably like to absorb many concepts and gather lots of information on a new topic.

D: Doing
Active Experimentation
Your number on this line indicates your preference for applying ideas, using trial and error, and practicing what you learn. If your score is high on this line, you probably enjoy hands-on activities that allow you to test out ideas to see what works.

Interpreting your Learning Style Graph

When you examine your completed Learning Style Graph on page LSI-5, you will notice that your learning style profile (the "kite" that you drew) might be located primarily in one part of the graph. This will give you an idea of your preferred **mode** of learning—the kind of behaviors that feel most comfortable and familiar to you when you are learning something.

Using the descriptions below and the sample graphs, identify your preferred learning mode.

Mode 1 blends feeling and watching. If the majority of your learning style profile is in the upper right-hand corner of the Learning Style Graph, you probably prefer Mode 1 learning. You seek a purpose for new information and a personal connection with the content. You want to know why a course matters and how it challenges or fits in with what you already know. You embrace new ideas that relate directly to your current interests and goals.

Mode 2 blends watching and thinking. If your learning style profile is mostly in the lower right-hand corner of the Learning Style Graph, you probably prefer Mode 2 learning. You are interested in knowing what ideas or techniques are important. You seek a theory to explain events and are interested in what experts have to say. You enjoy learning lots of facts and then arranging these facts in a logical and concise manner. You break a subject down into its key elements or steps and master each one in a systematic way.

Mode 3 blends thinking and doing. If most of your learning style profile is in the lower left-hand corner of the Learning Style Graph, you probably prefer Mode 3 learning. You hunger for an opportunity to try out what you're studying. You get involved with new knowledge by testing it out. You investigate how ideas and techniques work, and you put into practice what you learn. You thrive when you have well-defined tasks, guided practice, and frequent feedback.

Mode 4 blends doing and feeling. If most of your learning style profile is in the upper left-hand corner of the Learning Style Graph, you probably prefer Mode 4 learning. You get excited about going beyond classroom assignments. You like to take what you have practiced and find other uses for it. You seek ways to apply this newly gained skill or information at your workplace or in your personal relationships.

It might be easier for you to remember the modes if you summarize each one as a single question:

> **Mode 1** means asking, *Why* learn this?
> **Mode 2** means asking, *What* is this about?
> **Mode 3** means asking, *How* does this work?
> **Mode 4** means asking, *What if* I tried this in a different setting?

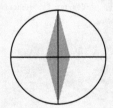

Combinations. Some learning style profiles combine all four modes. The profile to the left reflects a learner who is focused primarily on gathering information—*lots* of information! People with this profile tend to ask for additional facts from an instructor, or they want to know where they can go to discover more about a subject.

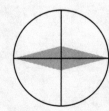

The profile to the left applies to learners who focus more on understanding what they learn and less on gathering lots of information. People with this profile prefer smaller chunks of data with plenty of time to process it. Long lectures can be difficult for these learners.

The profile to the left indicates a learner whose preferences are fairly well balanced. People with this profile can be highly adaptable and tend to excel no matter what the instructor does in the classroom. ■

Copyright © 2015 Cengage Learning. All Rights Reserved. May not be scanned, copied or duplicated, or posted to a publicly accessible website, in whole or in part.

Remove this sheet before completing the Learning Style Graph.

This page is inserted to ensure that the other writing you do in this book does not show through on page LSI-7.

Copyright © 2015 Cengage Learning. All Rights Reserved. May not be scanned, copied or duplicated, or posted to a publicly accessible website, in whole or in part.

Remove this sheet before completing the Learning Style Graph.

This page is inserted to ensure that the other writing you do in this book does not show through on page LSI-7.

Copyright © 2015 Cengage Learning. All Rights Reserved. May not be scanned, copied or duplicated, or posted to a publicly accessible website, in whole or in part.

Developing all four modes of learning

Each mode of learning represents a unique blend of feeling, watching, thinking, and doing. No matter which of these you've tended to prefer, you can develop the ability to use all four modes:

- **To develop Mode 1,** ask questions that help you understand *why* it is important for you to learn about a specific topic. You might also want to form a study group.

- **To develop Mode 2,** ask questions that help you understand *what* the main points and key facts are. Also, learn a new subject in stages. For example, divide a large reading assignment into sections and then read each section carefully before moving on to the next one.

- **To develop Mode 3,** ask questions about *how* a theory relates to daily life. Also allow time to practice what you learn. You can do experiments, conduct interviews, create presentations, find a relevant work or internship experience, or even write a song that summarizes key concepts. Learn through hands-on practice.

- **To develop Mode 4,** ask *what-if* questions about ways to use what you have just learned in several different situations. Also, seek opportunities to demonstrate your understanding. You could coach a classmate about what you have learned, present findings from your research, explain how your project works, or perform your song.

Developing all four modes offers many potential benefits. For example, you can excel in many types of courses and find more opportunities to learn outside the classroom. You can expand your options for declaring a major and choosing a career. You can also work more effectively with people who learn differently from you.

In addition, you'll be able to learn from instructors no matter how they teach. Let go of statements such as "My teachers don't get me" and "The instructor doesn't teach to my learning style." Replace those excuses with attitudes such as "I am responsible for what I learn" and "I will master this subject by using several modes of learning."

The graph on this page is here for you to turn in to your instructor if required to do so.

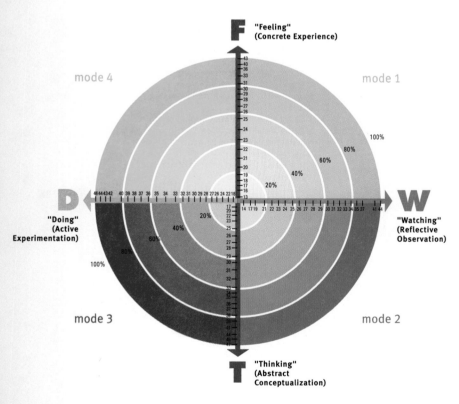

Copyright © 2015 Cengage Learning. All Rights Reserved. May not be scanned, copied or duplicated, or posted to a publicly accessible website, in whole or in part.

Balancing your preferences

The chart below identifies some of the natural talents people have, as well as challenges for people who have a strong preference for any one mode of learning. For example, if most of your "kite" is in Mode 2 of the Learning Style Graph, then look at the lower right-hand corner of the following chart to see whether it gives an accurate description of you.

After reviewing the description of your preferred learning mode, read all of the sections that start with the words "People with other preferred modes." These sections explain what actions you can take to become a more balanced learner.

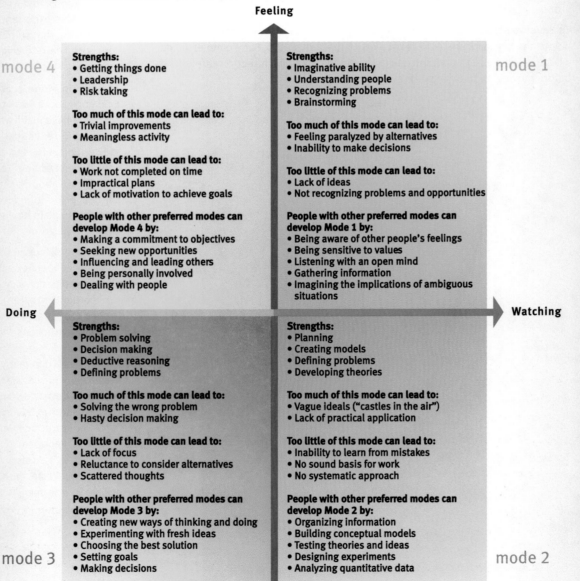

Feeling

mode 4

Strengths:
• Getting things done
• Leadership
• Risk taking

Too much of this mode can lead to:
• Trivial improvements
• Meaningless activity

Too little of this mode can lead to:
• Work not completed on time
• Impractical plans
• Lack of motivation to achieve goals

People with other preferred modes can develop Mode 4 by:
• Making a commitment to objectives
• Seeking new opportunities
• Influencing and leading others
• Being personally involved
• Dealing with people

mode 1

Strengths:
• Imaginative ability
• Understanding people
• Recognizing problems
• Brainstorming

Too much of this mode can lead to:
• Feeling paralyzed by alternatives
• Inability to make decisions

Too little of this mode can lead to:
• Lack of ideas
• Not recognizing problems and opportunities

People with other preferred modes can develop Mode 1 by:
• Being aware of other people's feelings
• Being sensitive to values
• Listening with an open mind
• Gathering information
• Imagining the implications of ambiguous situations

Doing ← → **Watching**

mode 3

Strengths:
• Problem solving
• Decision making
• Deductive reasoning
• Defining problems

Too much of this mode can lead to:
• Solving the wrong problem
• Hasty decision making

Too little of this mode can lead to:
• Lack of focus
• Reluctance to consider alternatives
• Scattered thoughts

People with other preferred modes can develop Mode 3 by:
• Creating new ways of thinking and doing
• Experimenting with fresh ideas
• Choosing the best solution
• Setting goals
• Making decisions

mode 2

Strengths:
• Planning
• Creating models
• Defining problems
• Developing theories

Too much of this mode can lead to:
• Vague ideals ("castles in the air")
• Lack of practical application

Too little of this mode can lead to:
• Inability to learn from mistakes
• No sound basis for work
• No systematic approach

People with other preferred modes can develop Mode 2 by:
• Organizing information
• Building conceptual models
• Testing theories and ideas
• Designing experiments
• Analyzing quantitative data

Thinking

Copyright © 2015 Cengage Learning. All Rights Reserved. May not be scanned, copied or duplicated, or posted to a publicly accessible website, in whole or in part.

USING YOUR LEARNING STYLE PROFILE TO SUCCEED

DEVELOP ALL FOUR MODES OF LEARNING

Each mode of learning highlighted in the Learning Style Inventory represents a unique blend of concrete experience, reflective observation, abstract conceptualization, and active experimentation. You can explore new learning styles simply by adopting new habits related to each of these activities. Consider the following suggestions as places to start. Also remember that any idea about learning styles will make a difference in your life only when it leads to changes in your behavior.

To gain concrete experiences:
- See a live demonstration or performance related to your course content.
- Engage your emotions by reading a novel or seeing a video related to your course.
- Interview an expert in the subject you're learning or a master practitioner of a skill you want to gain.
- Conduct role-plays, exercises, or games based on your courses.
- Conduct an informational interview with someone in your chosen career, or "shadow" that person for a day on the job.
- Look for a part-time job, internship, or volunteer experience that complements what you do in class.
- Deepen your understanding of another culture and extend your foreign language skills by studying abroad.

To become more reflective:
- Keep a personal journal, and write about connections among your courses.
- Form a study group to discuss and debate topics related to your courses.
- Set up a website, blog, e-mail listserv, or online chat room related to your major.
- Create analogies to make sense of concepts; for instance, see whether you can find similarities between career planning and putting together a puzzle.

James Baigrie/Lifesize/Getty Images

- Visit your course instructor during office hours to ask questions.
- During social events with friends and relatives, briefly explain what your courses are about.

To develop abstract thinking:
- Take notes on your reading in outline form; consider using word-processing software with an outlining feature.
- Supplement assigned texts with other books, magazine and newspaper articles, and related websites.
- Attend lectures given by your current instructors and others who teach the same subjects.

Copyright © 2015 Cengage Learning. All Rights Reserved. May not be scanned, copied or duplicated, or posted to a publicly accessible website, in whole or in part.

- Take ideas presented in text or lectures and translate them into visual form—tables, charts, diagrams, and maps.
- Create visuals and use computer software to recreate them with more complex graphics and animation.

To become more active:
- Conduct laboratory experiments or field observations.
- Go to settings where theories are being applied or tested.
- Make predictions based on theories you learn, and then see whether events in your daily life confirm your predictions.
- Try out a new behavior described in a lecture or reading, and observe its consequences in your life.

LOOK FOR EXAMPLES OF THE MODES IN ACTION

To understand the modes of learning, notice when they occur in your daily life. You are a natural learner, and this means that the modes are often at work. You use them when you solve problems, make choices, and experiment with new ideas.

Suppose that your family members ask about your career plans. You've just enrolled for your first semester of classes, and you think it's too early to think about careers. Yet you choose to brainstorm some career options anyway. If nothing else, it might be fun, and you'll have some answers for when people ask you what you're going to do after college. This is an example of Mode 1. You asked, "Why learn about career planning?" and came up with an answer.

During the next meeting of your psychology class, your instructor mentions the career planning center on campus. You visit the center's website and discover its list of services. While you're online, you also register for one of the center's workshops because you want more information about writing a career plan. This illustrates Mode 2: You asked, "What career planning options are available?" and discovered several answers.

In this workshop, you learn about the role that internships and extracurricular activities play in career planning. All of these are ways to test an early career choice and discover whether it appeals to you. You enjoy being with children, so you choose to volunteer at a campus-based child care center. You want to discover how this service-learning experience might help you choose a career. This is Mode 3: You asked, "How can I use what I learned in the workshop?" This led you to working with children.

Your experience at the center leads to a work-study assignment there. On the basis of this new experience, you choose to declare a major in early childhood education. This is an example of Mode 4: You asked, "What if this assignment points to a new direction for my future?" The answer led to a new commitment.

USE THE MODES WHILE CHOOSING COURSES

Remember your learning style profile when you're thinking about which classes to take and how to study for each class. Look for a fit between your preferred mode of learning and your course work.

If you prefer Mode 1, for example, then look for courses that sound interesting and seem worthwhile to you. If you prefer Mode 2, then consider classes that center on lectures, reading, and discussion. If you prefer Mode 3, then choose courses that include demonstrations, lab sessions, role-playing, and others ways to take action. And if you enjoy Mode 4, then look for courses that could apply to many situations in your life—at work, at home, and in your relationships.

You won't always be able to match your courses to your learning styles. View those situations as opportunities to practice becoming a flexible learner. By developing your skills in all four modes, you can excel in many types of courses.

USE THE MODES TO EXPLORE YOUR MAJOR

If you enjoy learning in Mode 1, you probably value creativity and human relationships. When choosing a major, consider the arts, English, psychology, or political science.

If Mode 2 is your preference, then you enjoy gathering information and building theories. A major related to math or science might be ideal for you.

If Mode 3 is your favorite, then you like to diagnose problems, arrive at solutions, and use technology. Again, a major related to health care, engineering, or economics is a logical choice for you.

And if your preference is Mode 4, you probably enjoy taking the initiative, implementing decisions, teaching, managing projects, and moving quickly from planning into action. Consider a major in business or education.

As you prepare to declare a major, remain flexible. Use your knowledge of learning styles to open up possibilities rather than restrict them. Remember that regardless of your mode, you can excel at any job or major; it just may mean developing new skills in other modes.

USE THE MODES OF LEARNING TO EXPLORE YOUR CAREER

Knowing about learning styles becomes especially useful when planning your career.

People who excel at Mode 1 are often skilled at tuning in to the feelings of clients and coworkers. These people can listen with an open mind, tolerate confusion, be sensitive to people's feelings, open up to problems that are difficult to define, and brainstorm a variety of solutions. If you like Mode 1, you may be drawn to a career in counseling, social services, the ministry, or another field that centers on human relationships. You might also enjoy a career in the performing arts.

Copyright © 2015 Cengage Learning. All Rights Reserved. May not be scanned, copied or duplicated, or posted to a publicly accessible website, in whole or in part.

People who prefer Mode 2 like to do research and work with ideas. They are skilled at gathering data, interpreting information, and summarizing—arriving at the big picture. They may excel at careers that center on science, math, technical communications, or planning. Mode 2 learners may also work as college teachers, lawyers, technical writers, or journalists.

People who like Mode 3 are drawn to solving problems, making decisions, and checking on progress toward goals. Careers in medicine, engineering, information technology, or another applied science are often ideal for them.

People who enjoy Mode 4 like to influence and lead others. These people are often described as "doers" and "risk takers." They like to take action and complete projects. Mode 4 learners often excel at managing, negotiating, selling, training, and teaching. They might also work for a government agency.

> **Keep in mind that there is no strict match between certain learning styles and certain careers. Learning is essential to success in all careers.**

Keep in mind that there is no strict match between certain learning styles and certain careers. Learning is essential to success in all careers. Also, any career can attract people with a variety of learning styles. For instance, the health care field is large enough to include people who prefer Mode 3 and become family physicians—*and* people who prefer Mode 2 and become medical researchers.

EXPECT TO ENCOUNTER DIFFERENT STYLES

As higher education and the workplace become more diverse and technology creates a global marketplace, you'll meet people who differ from you in profound ways. Your fellow students and coworkers will behave in ways that express a variety of preferences for perceiving information, processing ideas, and acting on what they learn. Consider these examples:

- A roommate who's continually moving while studying—reciting facts out loud, pacing, and gesturing—probably prefers concrete experience and learning by taking action.

- A coworker who talks continually on the phone about a project may prefer to learn by listening, talking, and forging key relationships.

- A supervisor who excels at abstract conceptualization may want to see detailed project plans and budgets submitted in writing well before a project swings into high gear.

- A study group member who always takes the initiative, manages the discussion, delegates any work involved, and follows up with everyone probably prefers active experimentation.

Differences in learning style can be a stumbling block—or an opportunity. When differences intersect, there is the potential for conflict as well as for creativity. Succeeding with peers often means seeing the classroom and workplace as a laboratory for learning from experience. Resolving conflict and learning from mistakes are all part of the learning cycle.

LOOK FOR SPECIFIC CLUES TO ANOTHER PERSON'S STYLE

You can learn a lot about other people's styles of learning simply by observing them during the workday. Look for clues such these:

Approaches to a task that requires learning. Some people process new information and ideas by sitting quietly and reading or writing. When learning to use a piece of equipment, such as a new computer, they'll read the instruction manual first. Others will skip the manual, unpack all the boxes, and start setting up equipment. And others might ask a more experienced colleague to guide them in person, step by step.

Word choice. Some people like to process information visually. You might hear them say, "I'll look into that" or "Give me the big picture first." Others like to solve problems verbally: "Let's talk though this problem" or "I hear you!" In contrast, some people focus on body sensations ("This product feels great") or action ("Let's run with this idea and see what happens").

Body language. Notice how often coworkers or classmates make eye contact with you and how close they sit or stand next to you. Observe their gestures as well as the volume and tone of their voice.

Content preferences. Notice what subjects coworkers or classmates openly discuss and which topics they avoid. Some people talk freely about their feelings, their families, and even their personal finances. Others choose to remain silent on such topics and stick to work-related matters.

Process preferences. Look for patterns in the way that your coworkers and classmates meet goals. When attending meetings, for example, some of them might stick closely to the agenda and keep an eye on the clock. Other people might prefer to go with the flow, even if it means working an extra hour or scrapping the agenda.

ACCOMMODATE DIFFERING STYLES

Once you've discovered differences in styles, look for ways to accommodate them. As you collaborate on projects with other students or coworkers, keep the following suggestions in mind:

Copyright © 2015 Cengage Learning. All Rights Reserved. May not be scanned, copied or duplicated, or posted to a publicly accessible website, in whole or in part.

Remember that some people want to reflect on the big picture first. When introducing a project plan, you might say, "This process has four major steps." Before explaining the plan in detail, talk about the purpose of the project and the benefits of completing each step.

Allow time for active experimentation and concrete experience. Offer people a chance to try out a new product or process for themselves—to literally get the feel of it.

Allow for abstract conceptualization. When leading a study group or conducting a training session, provide handouts that include plenty of visuals and step-by-step instructions. Visual learners and people who like to think abstractly will appreciate these. Also schedule periods for questions and answers.

When planning a project, encourage people to answer key questions. Remember the four essential questions that guide learning. Answering *Why?* means defining the purpose and desired outcomes of the project. Answering *What?* means assigning major tasks, setting due dates for each task, and generating commitment to action. Answering *How?* means carrying out assigned tasks and meeting regularly to discuss things that are working well and ways to improve the project. And answering *What if?* means discussing what the team has learned from the project and ways to apply that learning to the whole class or larger organization.

When working on teams, look for ways that members can complement one another's strengths. If you're skilled at planning, find someone who excels at doing. Also seek people who can reflect on and interpret the team's experience. Pooling different styles allows you to draw on everyone's strengths.

RESOLVE CONFLICT WITH RESPECT FOR STYLES

When people's styles clash in educational or work settings, you have several options. One is to throw up your hands and resign yourself to personality conflicts. Another option is to recognize differences, accept them, and respect them as complementary ways to meet common goals. Taking that perspective allows you to act constructively. You might do one of the following:

Resolve conflict within yourself. You might have mental pictures of classrooms and workplaces as places where people are all supposed to have the same style. Notice whether you have those pictures, and gently let them go. If you *expect* to find differences in styles, you can more easily respect those differences.

Introduce a conversation about learning styles. Attend a workshop on learning styles. Then bring such training directly to your classroom or office.

Let people take on tasks that fit their learning styles. People gravitate toward the kinds of tasks they've succeeded at in the past, and that's fine. Remember, though, that learning styles are both stable and dynamic. People gravitate toward the kinds of tasks they've succeeded at in the past. People can also broaden their styles by tackling new tasks to reinforce different modes of learning.

Rephrase complaints as requests. "This class is a waste of my time" can be recast as "Please tell me what I'll gain if I participate actively in class." "The instructor talks too fast" can become "What strategies can I use for taking notes when the instructor covers the material rapidly?"

ACCEPT CHANGE—AND OCCASIONAL DISCOMFORT

Seek out chances to develop new modes of learning. If your instructor asks you to form a group to complete an assignment, avoid joining a group where everyone shares your learning style. Work on project teams with people who learn differently than you. Get together with people who both complement and challenge you.

Also look for situations where you can safely practice new skills. If you enjoy reading, for example, look for ways to express what you learn by speaking, such as leading a study group on a textbook chapter.

Discomfort is a natural part of the learning process. Allow yourself to notice any struggle with a task or lack of interest in completing it. Remember that such feelings are temporary and that you are balancing your learning preferences. By choosing to move through discomfort, you consciously expand your ability to learn in new ways. ◼

Copyright © 2015 Cengage Learning. All Rights Reserved. May not be scanned, copied or duplicated, or posted to a publicly accessible website, in whole or in part.

Claim your MULTIPLE INTELLIGENCES

© iStockphoto.com\pavlen

People often think that being smart means the same thing as having a high IQ and that having a high IQ automatically leads to success. However, psychologists are finding that IQ scores do not always predict which students will do well in academic settings—or after they graduate.[2]

Howard Gardner of Harvard University believes that no single measure of intelligence can tell us how smart we are. Instead, Gardner defines intelligence in a flexible way as "the ability to solve problems, or to create products, that are valued within one or more cultural settings." He also identifies several types of intelligence, as described here and in Table 1.1.[3]

People using **verbal/linguistic intelligence** are adept at language skills and learn best by speaking, writing, reading, and listening. They are likely to enjoy activities such as telling stories and doing crossword puzzles.

People who use **mathematical/logical intelligence** are good with numbers, logic, problem solving, patterns, relationships, and categories. They are generally precise and methodical, and are likely to enjoy science.

When people learn visually and by organizing things spatially, they display **visual/spatial intelligence**. They think in images and pictures, and understand best by seeing the subject. They enjoy charts, graphs, maps, mazes, tables, illustrations, art, models, puzzles, and costumes.

People using **bodily/kinesthetic intelligence** prefer physical activity. They enjoy activities such as building things, woodworking, dancing, skiing, sewing, and crafts. They generally are coordinated and athletic, and they would rather participate in games than just watch.

Individuals using **musical/rhythmic intelligence** enjoy musical expression through songs, rhythms, and musical instruments. They are responsive to various kinds of sounds, remember melodies easily, and might enjoy drumming, humming, and whistling.

People using **intrapersonal intelligence** are exceptionally aware of their own feelings and values. They are generally reserved, self-motivated, and intuitive.

Outgoing people show evidence of **interpersonal intelligence**. They do well with cooperative learning and are sensitive to the feelings, intentions, and motivations of others. They often make good leaders.

People using **naturalist intelligence** love the outdoors and recognize details in plants, animals, rocks, clouds, and other natural formations. These people excel in observing fine distinctions among similar items.

Each of us has all of these intelligences to some degree. And each of us can learn to enhance them. Experiment with learning in ways that draw on a variety of intelligences—including those that might be less familiar. When we acknowledge all of our intelligences, we can constantly explore new ways of being smart. ■

Interactive

Exercise 7 Develop your multiple intelligences

Gardner's theory of multiple intelligences complements the discussion of different learning styles in this chapter. The main point is that there are many ways to gain knowledge and acquire new behaviors. You can use Gardner's concepts to explore a range of options for achieving success in school, work, and relationships.

Table 1.1 on the next page summarizes the content of "Claim your multiple intelligences" and suggests ways to apply the main ideas. Instead of merely glancing through this chart, get active. Place a check mark next to any of the "Possible characteristics" that describe you. Also check off the "Possible learning strategies" that you intend to use. Finally, underline or highlight any of the "Possible careers" that spark your interest.

Remember that the chart is *not* an exhaustive list or a formal inventory. Take what you find merely as points of departure. You can invent strategies of your own to cultivate different intelligences.

Copyright © 2015 Cengage Learning. All Rights Reserved. May not be scanned, copied or duplicated, or posted to a publicly accessible website, in whole or in part.

Table 1.1 *Multiple Intelligences*

Type of Intelligence	Possible Characteristics	Possible Learning Strategies	Possible Careers
Verbal/linguistic	☐ You enjoy writing letters, stories, and papers. ☐ You prefer to write directions rather than draw maps. ☐ You take excellent notes from textbooks and lectures. ☐ You enjoy reading, telling stories, and listening to them.	☐ Highlight, underline, and write notes in your textbooks. ☐ Recite new ideas in your own words. ☐ Rewrite and edit your class notes. ☐ Talk to other people often about what you're studying.	Librarian, lawyer, editor, journalist, English teacher, radio or television announcer
Mathematical/logical	☐ You enjoy solving puzzles. ☐ You prefer math or science class to English class. ☐ You want to know how and why things work. ☐ You make careful, step-by-step plans.	☐ Analyze tasks so you can order them in a sequence of steps. ☐ Group concepts into categories, and look for underlying patterns. ☐ Convert text into tables, charts, and graphs. ☐ Look for ways to quantify ideas—to express them in numerical terms.	Accountant, auditor, tax preparer, mathematician, computer programmer, actuary, economist, math or science teacher
Visual/spatial	☐ You draw pictures to give an example or clarify an explanation. ☐ You understand maps and illustrations more readily than text. ☐ You assemble things from illustrated instructions. ☐ You especially enjoy books that have a lot of illustrations.	☐ When taking notes, create concept maps, mind maps, and other visuals. ☐ Code your notes by using different colors to highlight main topics, major points, and key details. ☐ When your attention wanders, focus it by sketching or drawing. ☐ Before you try a new task, visualize yourself doing it well.	Architect, commercial artist, fine artist, graphic designer, photographer, interior decorator, engineer, cartographer
Bodily/kinesthetic	☐ You enjoy physical exercise. ☐ You tend not to sit still for long periods of time. ☐ You enjoy working with your hands. ☐ You use a lot of gestures when talking.	☐ Be active in ways that support concentration; for example, pace as you recite, read while standing up, and create flash cards. ☐ Carry materials with you, and practice studying in several different locations. ☐ Create hands-on activities related to key concepts; for example, create a game based on course content. ☐ Notice the sensations involved with learning something well.	Physical education teacher, athlete, athletic coach, chiropractor, massage therapist, yoga teacher, dancer, choreographer, actor

(Continued)

Copyright © 2015 Cengage Learning. All Rights Reserved. May not be scanned, copied or duplicated, or posted to a publicly accessible website, in whole or in part.

Type of Intelligence	Possible Characteristics	Possible Learning Strategies	Possible Careers
Musical/rhythmic	☐ You often sing in the car or shower. ☐ You easily tap your foot to the beat of a song. ☐ You play a musical instrument. ☐ You feel most engaged and productive when music is playing.	☐ During a study break, play music or dance to restore energy. ☐ Put on background music that enhances your concentration while studying. ☐ Relate key concepts to songs you know. ☐ Write your own songs based on course content.	Professional musician, music teacher, music therapist, choral director, musical instrument sales representative, musical instrument maker, piano tuner
Intrapersonal	☐ You enjoy writing in a journal and being alone with your thoughts. ☐ You think a lot about what you want in the future. ☐ You prefer to work on individual projects rather than group projects. ☐ You take time to think things through before talking or taking action.	☐ Connect course content to your personal values and goals. ☐ Study a topic alone before attending a study group. ☐ Connect readings and lectures to a strong feeling or significant past experience. ☐ Keep a journal that relates your course work to events in your daily life.	Minister, priest, rabbi, professor of philosophy or religion, counseling psychologist, creator of a home-based or small business
Interpersonal	☐ You enjoy group work over working alone. ☐ You have plenty of friends and regularly spend time with them. ☐ You prefer talking and listening to reading or writing. ☐ You thrive in positions of leadership.	☐ Form and conduct study groups early in the term. ☐ Create flash cards, and use them to quiz study partners. ☐ Volunteer to give a speech or lead group presentations on course topics. ☐ Teach the topic you're studying to someone else.	Manager, school administrator, salesperson, teacher, counseling psychologist, arbitrator, police officer, nurse, travel agent, public relations specialist, creator of a midsize to large business
Naturalist	☐ As a child, you enjoyed collecting insects, leaves, or other natural objects. ☐ You enjoy being outdoors. ☐ You find that important insights occur during times you spend in nature. ☐ You read books and magazines on nature-related topics.	☐ During study breaks, take walks outside. ☐ Post pictures of outdoor scenes where you study, and play recordings of outdoor sounds while you read. ☐ Invite classmates to discuss course work while taking a hike or going on a camping trip. ☐ Focus on careers that hold the potential for working outdoors.	Environmental activist, park ranger, recreation supervisor, historian, museum curator, biologist, criminologist, mechanic, woodworker, construction worker, construction contractor or estimator

Copyright © 2015 Cengage Learning. All Rights Reserved. May not be scanned, copied or duplicated, or posted to a publicly accessible website, in whole or in part.

LEARNING BY SEEING, HEARING, AND MOVING:
The VAK system

Another way to approach the topic of learning styles is with a simple and powerful system that focuses on just three ways of perceiving through your senses.

- You perceive by seeing—**visual learning.**
- You also perceive by hearing—**auditory learning.**
- And, you perceive by moving—**kinesthetic learning.**

To recall this system, remember the letters *VAK*, which stand for *visual, auditory*, and *kinesthetic*. The theory is that each of us prefers to learn through one of these senses. And we can enrich our learning with activities that draw on the other channels.

To reflect on your VAK preferences, answer the following questions. Each question has three possible answers. Circle the answer that best describes how you would respond in the stated situation. This is not a formal inventory—just a way to prompt some self-discovery.

Which of the following do you prefer to do when you have problems spelling a word?

1. Look it up in the dictionary.
2. Say the word out loud several times before you write it down.
3. Write out the word with several different spellings and then choose one.

You enjoy courses the most when you get to do which of the following?

1. View slides, overhead displays, videos, and readings with plenty of charts, tables, and illustrations.
2. Ask questions, engage in small-group discussions, and listen to guest speakers.
3. Take field trips, participate in lab sessions, or apply the course content while working as a volunteer or intern.

When giving someone directions on how to drive to a destination, which of these do you prefer to do?

1. Pull out a piece of paper and sketch a map.
2. Give verbal instructions.
3. Say, "I'm driving to a place near there, so just follow me."

When planning an extended vacation to a new destination, which of the following do you prefer to do?

1. Read colorful, illustrated brochures or articles about that place.
2. Talk directly to someone who's been there.
3. Spend a day or two at that destination on a work-related trip before taking a vacation there.

You've made a commitment to learn to play the guitar. What is the first thing you do?

1. Go to a library or music store and find an instruction book with plenty of diagrams and chord charts.
2. Pull out your favorite CDs, listen closely to the guitar solos, and see whether you can play along with them.
3. Buy or borrow a guitar, pluck the strings, and ask someone to show you how to play a few chords.

Copyright © 2015 Cengage Learning. All Rights Reserved. May not be scanned, copied or duplicated, or posted to a publicly accessible website, in whole or in part.

You've saved up enough money to lease a car. Which of the following is the most important factor in your decision when choosing from among several new models?

1. Reading information about the car from sources like *Consumer Reports*.

2. The information you get by talking to people who own the cars you're considering.

3. The overall impression you get by taking each car on a test drive.

You've just bought a new computer system. When setting up the system, what is the first thing you do?

1. Skim through the printed instructions that come with the equipment.

2. Call someone with a similar system and ask her for directions.

3. Assemble the components as best as you can, see whether everything works, and consult the instructions only as a last resort.

You get a scholarship to study abroad next semester, which starts in just three months. You will travel to a country where French is the most widely spoken language. To learn as much French as you can before you depart, you do which of these?

1. Buy a video-based language course that's recorded on a DVD.

2. Set up tutoring sessions with a friend who's fluent in French.

3. Sign up for a short immersion course in an environment in which you speak only French, starting with the first class.

Now take a few minutes to reflect on the meaning of your responses. All of the answers numbered 1 are examples of visual learning. The 2's refer to auditory learning, and the 3's illustrate kinesthetic learning. Finding a consistent pattern in your answers indicates that you prefer learning through one sense channel more than the others. Or you might find that your preferences are fairly balanced.

You'll get suggestions for making learning a rich, multisensory experience. Experiment with these techniques, and create more techniques of your own. Use them to build on your current preferences and develop new options for learning.

TO ENHANCE VISUAL LEARNING:

- Preview reading assignments by looking for elements that are highlighted visually—bold headlines, charts, graphs, illustrations, and photographs.

- When taking notes in class, leave plenty of room to add your own charts, diagrams, tables, and other visuals later.

Juliet White/Digital Vision/Getty Images

- Whenever an instructor writes information on a blackboard or overhead display, copy it exactly in your notes.

- Transfer your handwritten notes to your computer. Use word-processing software that allows you to format your notes in lists, add headings in different fonts, and create visuals in color.

- Before you begin an exam, quickly sketch a diagram on scratch paper. Use this diagram to summarize the key formulas or facts you want to remember.

- During tests, see whether you can visualize pages from your handwritten notes or images from your computer-based notes.

TO ENHANCE AUDITORY LEARNING:

- Reinforce memory of your notes and readings by talking about them. When studying, stop often to recite key points and examples in your own words.

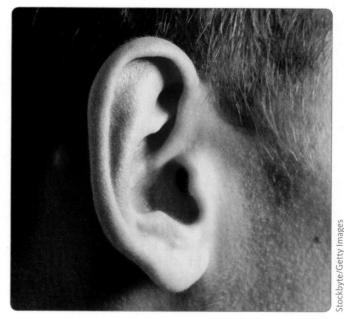

Stockbyte/Getty Images

Copyright © 2015 Cengage Learning. All Rights Reserved. May not be scanned, copied or duplicated, or posted to a publicly accessible website, in whole or in part.

- After reciting several summaries of key points and examples, record your favorite version or write it out.
- Read difficult passages in your textbooks slowly and out loud.
- Join study groups, and create short presentations about course topics.
- Visit your instructors during office hours to ask questions.

TO ENHANCE KINESTHETIC LEARNING:

- Look for ways to translate course content into three-dimensional models that you can build. While studying biology, for example, create a model of a human cell, using different colors of clay.
- Supplement lectures with trips to museums, field observations, lab sessions, tutorials, and other hands-on activities.
- Recite key concepts from your courses while you walk or exercise.
- Intentionally set up situations in which you can learn by trial and error.

- Create a practice test, and write out the answers in the room where you will actually take the exam.

One variation of the VAK system has been called VARK.[4] The *R* describes a preference for learning by reading and writing. People with this preference might benefit from translating charts and diagrams into statements, taking notes in lists, and converting those lists into possible items on a multiple-choice test. ∎

Tara Moore/Riser/Getty Images

Copyright © 2015 Cengage Learning. All Rights Reserved. May not be scanned, copied or duplicated, or posted to a publicly accessible website, in whole or in part.

Interactive

Journal Entry 4
Discovery Statement

Choosing your purpose

Success is a choice—your choice. To *get* what you want, it helps to *know* what you want. That is the purpose of this two-part Journal Entry.

You can begin choosing success by completing this Journal Entry right now. If you choose to do it later, then plan a date, time, and place and then block out the time on your calendar.

Date: _____   Time: _____   Place: _____

Part 1

Select a time and place when you know you will not be disturbed for at least 20 minutes. (The library is a good place to do this exercise.) Relax for two or three minutes, clearing your mind. Next, complete the following sentences—and then keep writing.

When you run out of things to write, stick with it just a bit longer. Be willing to experience a little discomfort. Keep writing. What you discover might be well worth the extra effort.

What I want from my education is . . .

_____

_____

When I complete my education, I want to be able to . . .

_____

_____

I also want . . .

_____

_____

_____

Part 2

After completing Part 1, take a short break. Reward yourself by doing something that you enjoy. Then come back to this Journal Entry.

Now, review the list you just created of things that you want from your education. See whether you can summarize them in one sentence. Start this sentence with "My purpose for being in school is . . . ."

Allow yourself to write many drafts of this mission statement, and review it periodically as you continue your education. With each draft, see whether you can capture the essence of what you want from higher education and from your life. State it in a vivid way—in a short sentence that you can easily memorize, one that sparks your enthusiasm and makes you want to get up in the morning.

You might find it difficult to express your purpose statement in one sentence. If so, write a paragraph or more. Then look for the sentence that seems most charged with energy for you.

Following are some sample purpose statements:

- My purpose for being in school is to gain skills that I can use to contribute to others.

- My purpose for being in school is to live an abundant life that is filled with happiness, health, love, and wealth.

- My purpose for being in school is to enjoy myself by making lasting friendships and following the lead of my interests.

Write at least one draft of your purpose statement.

_____

_____

Copyright © 2015 Cengage Learning. All Rights Reserved. May not be scanned, copied or duplicated, or posted to a publicly accessible website, in whole or in part.

Interactive

Journal Entry 5
Discovery/Intention Statement

Get back to the big picture about learning styles

This chapter introduces many ideas about how people learn—four modes, multiple intelligences, and the VAK system. That's a lot of information! And these are just a few of the available theories.

Remember that there is one "big idea" to take away from all of this material—*metacognition* (pronounced "metta-cog-ni-shun"). *Meta* means "beyond" or "above." *Cognition* refers to everything that goes on inside your brain: perceiving, thinking, and feeling. So, metacognition refers to your ability to stand "above" your current mental activities and observe them. From this larger point of view, you can choose to think and act in new ways.

Metacognition is the heart of the master student process. It's also a major benefit of higher education.

Take a few minutes right now to practice metacognition. Complete the following sentences.

The most important thing that I discovered about myself by doing the learning styles activities in this chapter is . . .

_____

_____

_____

I also discovered that . . .

_____

_____

_____

I discovered that what I would most like to change about the way I learn is . . .

_____

_____

_____

In order to make that change, I intend to . . .

_____

_____

_____

I also intend to . . .

_____

_____

_____

Remember that teachers in your life will come and go. Some are more skilled than others. None of them are perfect. With skill in metacognition, you can see any experience as a chance to learn in ways that work for you. In your personal path toward mastery, you become your own best teacher.

Copyright © 2015 Cengage Learning. All Rights Reserved. May not be scanned, copied or duplicated, or posted to a publicly accessible website, in whole or in part.

Steve Cole/Photodisc/Getty Images

SIX PATHS
to more powerful
THINKING

Thinking is a path to intellectual adventure. Although there are dozens of possible approaches to thinking well, the process boils down to asking and answering questions.

One quality of a master student is the ability to ask questions that lead to deeper learning. Your mind is an obedient servant. It will deliver answers at the same level as your questions. Becoming a critical thinker means being flexible and asking a wide range of questions.

A psychologist named Benjamin Bloom named six levels of thinking. He called them a *taxonomy of educational objectives*—basically, a list of different goals for learning.[5] Each level of thinking calls for asking and answering different kinds of questions.

Level 1: Remembering. At this level of thinking, the key question is *Can I recall the key terms, facts, or events?* To prompt level 1 thinking, an instructor might ask you to do the following:

- List the three parts of the master student process.
- Describe five qualities of a master student.
- Name the master student profiled in Chapter 1 of this book.

To study for a test with level 1 questions, you could create flash cards to review ideas from your readings and class notes. You could also read a book with a set of questions in mind and underline the answers to those questions in the text. Or, you could memorize a list of definitions so that you can recite them exactly. These are just a few examples.

Although remembering is important, this is a relatively low level of learning. No critical or creative thinking is involved. You simply recognize or recall something that you've observed in the past.

Level 2: Understanding. At this level, the main question is *Can I explain this idea in my own words?* Often this means giving examples of an idea based on your own experience. The ability to summarize is also key to this level of thinking. Summarizing helps you to remember and understand.

Suppose that your instructor asks you to do the following:

- Explain the main point of the Power Process: Ideas are tools.
- Write a summary of the steps involved in creating a PowerPoint presentation.
- Compare affirmations with visualizations, stating how they're alike and how they differ.

Other key words in level 2 questions are *discuss, estimate,* and *restate.* All of these are cues to go one step beyond remembering and to show that you truly *comprehend* an idea.

Level 3: Applying. Learning at level 3 means asking: *Can I use this idea to produce a desired result?* That result might include completing a task, meeting a goal, making a decision, or solving a problem.

Some examples of level 3 thinking are listed here:

- Write an affirmation about succeeding in school, based on the guidelines in this text.
- Use the guidelines in this text to write an effective goal for your career.
- Describe an action that you could take to demonstrate a professional work ethic.

Some key words in level 3 questions include *apply, solve, construct, plan, predict,* and *produce.*

Level 4: Analyzing. Questions at this level boil down to this: *Can I divide this idea into parts, groups, or steps?* For example, you could do the following:

- Divide a list of work skills into those that call for creative thinking, critical thinking, collaboration, or communication.
- Organize a list of 30 memory techniques into three different categories.

Copyright © 2015 Cengage Learning. All Rights Reserved. May not be scanned, copied or duplicated, or posted to a publicly accessible website, in whole or in part.

- Take a career goal and then list a series of actions you could take to achieve it by a specific date.

Other key words in level 4 questions are *classify, separate, distinguish*, and *outline*.

Level 5: Evaluating. Learning at level 5 means asking, *Can I rate the truth, usefulness, or quality of this idea—and give reasons for my rating?* This is the level of thinking you would use to do the following:

- Judge the effectiveness of an Intention Statement.
- Recommend a method for taking lecture notes when an instructor talks fast.
- Rank the Power Processes in order of importance to you—from most useful to least useful.

Level 5 involves genuine critical thinking. At this level you agree with an idea, disagree with it, or suspend judgment until you get more information. In addition, you give reasons for your opinion and offer supporting evidence.

Some key words in level 5 questions are *critique, defend*, and *comment*.

Level 6: Creating. To think at this level, ask, *Can I invent something new based on this idea?* For instance, you might do the following:

- Invent your own format for taking lecture notes.
- Prepare a list of topics that you would cover if you were teaching a student success course.

- Imagine that you now have enough money to retire and then write goals you would like to accomplish with your extra time.
- Create a PowerPoint presentation based on ideas found in this chapter. Put the material in your own words, and use visual elements to enhance the points.

Creative thinking often involves analyzing an idea into parts and then combining those parts in a new way. Another source of creativity is taking several ideas and finding an unexpected connection among them. In either case, you are thinking at a very high level. You are going beyond agreement and disagreement to offer something unique—an original contribution of your own.

Questions for creative thinking often start with words such as *adapt, change, collaborate, compose, construct, create, design*, and *develop*. You might also notice phrases such as *What changes would you make . . . ? How could you improve . . . ? Can you think of another way to . . . ? What would happen if . . . ?*

FINDING ANSWERS

In each chapter of this book you will find a Practicing Critical Thinking exercise. As you complete them, you will answer questions at all 6 levels of Bloom's taxonomy. You'll get to solve specific problems and think through the kind of decisions you face in daily life. Approach each exercise as a way to awaken the master thinker inside you. ■

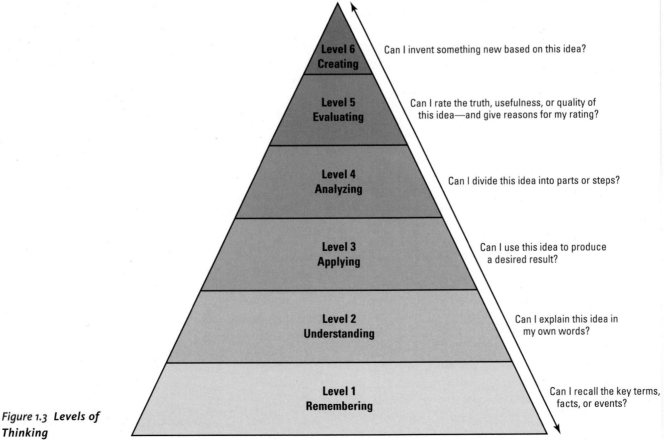

Figure 1.3 Levels of Thinking

Copyright © 2015 Cengage Learning. All Rights Reserved. May not be scanned, copied or duplicated, or posted to a publicly accessible website, in whole or in part.

Practicing Critical Thinking 1

Psychologist Benjamin Bloom described six kinds of thinking:

Level 1: Remembering

Level 2: Understanding

Level 3: Applying

Level 4: Analyzing

Level 5: Evaluating

Level 6: Creating

You can recall any suggestion from this book **(Level 1: Remembering)** and take that idea to a higher level of thinking.

For the purpose of this exercise, take a more detailed look at **Level 2: Understanding.** At this level of thinking, you understand an idea well enough to:

- Explain it in your own words.
- Give examples of the idea.
- Compare it to another idea, stating how the ideas are similar or different.

Suppose that someone asks you to explain the Power Process: Ideas are tools. You could demonstrate your understanding as shown in this example:

This Power Process means that the suggestions in this book are not "right" or "wrong." Instead, they are useful—or not useful—at this point in your life. (**This paragraph explains the Power Process in your own words.**)

For instance, it does not make any sense to pick up a hammer and say that it's right or wrong. A hammer has one main use—to pound nails. If you want to turn a screw or tighten a bolt, you wouldn't use a hammer. You'd use a screwdriver or pliers instead. That doesn't make the hammer "wrong." It just means that the hammer is not useful for turning screws or tightening bolts. (**This paragraph gives examples of the Power Process.**)

All this means is that a suggestion from this book is different than a belief. Beliefs can be right or wrong. You can show that a belief is logical or illogical. You can produce evidence for or against the belief. When it comes to tools, however, logic and evidence are beside the point.

The main question is: Does this tool work for the job I want to do, or does it not work? (**This paragraph compares tools to beliefs and states how they differ.**)

Now it's your turn. Choose another suggestion from this chapter **(Level 1: Remembering)** and think about it at **Level 2: Understanding.** List the suggestion in one sentence as it appears in the book. Follow this sentence with three paragraphs to show that you understand this suggestion. In the first paragraph, restate the suggestion in your own words. In the second paragraph, give at least one example of the idea. Then, in the third paragraph, compare the idea to one that is different.

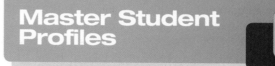

Master Student Profiles

An example of a person who embodies one or more of the master student qualities mentioned in the Introduction to this book is in each chapter of this text as on the next page. As you read about these people and others like them, ask yourself: "How can I apply this?" Look for the timeless qualities in the people you read about. Many of the strategies used by master students from another time or place are tools that you can use today.

The master students in this book demonstrate unusual and effective ways to learn. Remember that these are just 12 examples of master students (one for each chapter).

As you read the Master Student Profiles, also ask questions based on each mode of learning: Why is this person considered a master student? What attitudes or behaviors helped to create her mastery? How can I develop those qualities? What if I could use his example to create positive new results in my own life?

Also reflect on other master students you've read about or know personally. Focus on people who excel at learning. The master student is not a vague or remote ideal. Rather, master students move freely among us.

In fact, there's one living inside your skin.

MASTER STUDENT PROFILE

TERESA AMABILE

(1950–) Professor of business administration, a director of research at Harvard Business School, and author of The Progress Principle: Using Small Wins to Ignite Joy, Engagement, and Creativity at Work

We wanted to look at what makes people happy, motivated, productive, and creative at work. In order to look at that . . . we asked dozens of creative professionals to send us a daily, confidential, electronic diary during the entire course of a creative project they were working on.

So every day Monday through Friday, we sent a diary form via e-mail to all of the people participating in the study, asking them to fill it out at the end of the day. The diary form had some survey questions at the beginning asking them about their emotions and their motivation that day. That's what we call "inner work life." An open-ended question at the end of the diary form asked people to briefly describe one event from the day that stood out in their mind. And we said, it could be anything at all as long as it was relevant to the work or the project.

In all, we had 238 creative professionals in 26 project teams in seven companies keep this diary for us. And all of them were working on projects that required creativity—that is, new ideas that would work. We ended up with nearly 12,000 of these individual daily diary entries, giving us an incredibly rich look at the events these people were experiencing in their lives and in their inner work lives.

So when we put the inner work life data together with separate performance data we'd collected on everyone, we made our first discovery. And that is, when people are feeling most deeply and happily engaged in their work, they're more likely to be creatively productive. We call this the "inner work life effect." . . .

So if inner work life is so important to performance, what drives inner work life? To look at this, we went into those 12,000 diaries and pulled out the very best inner work life days that people were experiencing—those days when they felt happiest and most proud of what they were doing, when they felt most deeply engaged in the work. And we looked at what events were happening on those days.

Teresa Amabile *is a generalist.*
You *can be a generalist by looking for connections between ideas and patterns in behavior.*

That's when we made our second discovery. We call it the Progress Principle. *The number 1 driver of positive inner work life is simply making progress on meaningful work—even if that progress is a small win.* A small win is a step forward in the work that when it happens, it looks so incremental it seems almost trivial. And yet even progress events like that can boost inner work life tremendously. . . .

Keeping a work diary can help you to celebrate the small wins that happen in your work—especially on a day that is so frustrating that it feels like you didn't get anything done on your most important work. You can usually find one thing where you did move forward. If you did, keep track of it. You can celebrate it this way. . . .

You can nurture your own personal growth through your diary. Keeping a diary can help you to work through difficult, even traumatic, events that happened and help you get new perspectives on them.

The other thing that you can do with a diary is to spot patterns in your own reactions and behaviors that can help you to identify your greatest strengths and also the weak spots that you might need to work on.

And it can help you to cultivate patience because it can show you that in the past you have persevered and succeeded on days that might be even worse than whatever you're experiencing today. . . .

Don't forget that small wins can accumulate to big breakthroughs. But unless you occasionally look back at where you've been, it can be hard to see where you're going. ∎

Source: "Teresa Amabile: Track Your Small Wins to Motivate Big Accomplishments," the Behance Team, http://99u.com/videos/7221/Teresa-Amabile-Track-Your-Small-Wins-to-Motivate-Big-Accomplishments.

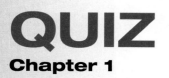

Name: _____

Date: _____

Chapter 1

1. The Power Process: Ideas are tools states that if you want to *use* an idea, you must *believe* in it. True or false? Explain your answer.

   False. If you read about a tool in this book that doesn't sound right, or one that sounds a little goofy, remember that the ideas here are for using, not necessarily for believing. Suspend your judgment. Test the idea for yourself. If it works, use it. If it doesn't, don't use it. (*Power Process: Ideas are tools*, page 32)

2. The First Step technique refers only to telling the truth about your areas for improvement. True or false? Explain your answer.

   False. Although the First Step is all about telling the truth, telling the truth about your areas for improvement is just one part. Taking the First Step involves telling the truth about what is working as well as what isn't, who you are, and what you want. (Explanations may vary.) (*First Step: Truth is a key to mastery*, page 33)

3. The four modes of learning are associated with certain questions. Give the appropriate question for each mode.

   Mode 1: Why? Mode 2: What? Mode 3: How? Mode 4: What if? (*Learning styles: Discovering how you learn*, page 41)

4. List the types of intelligence defined by Howard Gardner.

   Verbal/linguistic intelligence, mathematical/logical intelligence, visual/spatial intelligence, bodily/kinesthetic intelligence, musical/rhythmic intelligence, intrapersonal intelligence, interpersonal intelligence, naturalist intelligence (*Claim your multiple intelligences*, page 47)

5. Describe three learning strategies related to one type of intelligence that you listed.

   (Answers will vary.) Visual/spatial intelligence: charts, maps, graphs, mazes, puzzles (*Claim your multiple intelligences*, page 47)

6. What does the word *kinesthetic* refer to?
   (a) Moving   (b) Hearing
   (c) Seeing   (d) Listening
   (a) Moving (*Learning by seeing, hearing, and moving: The VAK system*, page 50)

7. According to the text, feeling discomfort is a sign that you're failing to correctly apply your knowledge of learning styles. True or false? Explain your answer.

   False. Discomfort is a natural part of the learning process. By choosing to move through discomfort, you consciously expand your ability to learn in new ways. (*Using your learning style profile to succeed*, page 43)

8. List the six levels of thinking described by psychologist Benjamin Bloom.

   1. Remembering (recalling an idea)
   2. Understanding (explaining an idea in your own words and giving examples from your own experience)
   3. Applying (using an idea to produce a desired result)
   4. Analyzing (dividing an idea into parts or steps)
   5. Evaluating (rating the truth, usefulness, or quality of an idea–and giving reasons for your rating)
   6. Creating (inventing something new based on an idea). (*Six paths to more powerful thinking*, page 55)

9. According to the text, useful questions to ask when reading the Master Student profiles in this book include:
   (a) Why is this person considered a master student?
   (b) What attitudes or behaviors helped to create her mastery?
   (c) How can I develop those qualities?
   (d) What if I could use his example to create positive new results in my own life?
   (e) All of the above.
   (e) All of the above. (*Master student profiles*, page 57)

10. Psychologists now define "being smart" as having a high IQ. True or false? Explain your answer.

    False. Psychologists are finding that IQ scores do not always predict which students will do well in academic settings—or after they graduate. (*Claim your multiple intelligences*, page 47)

SKILLS SNAPSHOT
Chapter 1

You'll find a Skills Snapshot at the end of each chapter in this book. Use these exercises to stay aware of your changing attitudes and behaviors—including your progress in developing the qualities of a master student.

Before moving on to a new chapter in this book, take a snapshot of attitudes that can affect your success in school. Clarify your intentions to develop insights into yourself that lead to clear intentions and new behaviors.

Discovery
My score on the Attitude section of the Discovery Wheel was . . .

One of my attitudes that supports my success in school is . . .

One of my attitudes that does not support my success is . . .

Intention
The idea from this chapter that can make the biggest difference in my life right now is . . .

A habit that I can adopt to put this idea into practice is . . .

This habit will be useful in my career if I . . .

Action
The specific new behavior that I will practice is . . .

My cue for doing this behavior is . . .

My reward for following through on this intention will be . . .

INSTRUCTOR TOOLS & TIPS

Chapter 2

TIME

"Dost thou love life, then do not squander time, for that's the stuff life is made of." —Benjamin Franklin

PREVIEW

Chapter 2 addresses one of the great challenges for students—managing their time. Whether they are traditional students attending college right out of high school or returning students attending college for the first time after an absence from formal education, your students each have only 168 hours per week to allocate to their many priorities. Time is an equal opportunity resource: All people, regardless of race, gender, creed, or national origin, have exactly the same number of hours per week. As you help your students choose how to allocate their 168 hours per week, set goals, and overcome procrastination, remind them that planning increases their options. Planning offers them the freedom to act in response to their intentions rather than to their moods. And planning vastly increases the odds of getting what they want.

GUEST SPEAKER

Consider inviting experts from your college or from off-campus who work in fields that emphasize planning, goal setting, or organization. A representative from the counseling department may provide some planning tips and also share information about advisement, scheduling, and personal counseling services.

LECTURE

Suggested lecture topics for this chapter include:

- Planning strategies
- Structure and freedom
- Organizing your space
- Committing to attend class
- Completing projects
- Power Process: Be here now

For specific lecture ideas and key lecture points on text articles, visit the Lecture Ideas section of the Course Manual.

master instructor best practice

❝I think the Time Monitor exercise is one of the most valuable in the book. Until students track their time, most have no idea how they use/waste their time. They just know that they don't have enough of it. This visual really brings home the reality of time. Because time management is so very important, have students do the same exercise of tracking their time toward the end of the semester. Comparing the two should reflect changes the students have made with regard to their time management. There should be a direct correlation between their time management and the success they are having in school, work, and life.❞

—Jo Ella Fields, Oklahoma State University

EXERCISES/ACTIVITIES

1. **Power Process: Be here now (page 62).** This Power Process teaches the skill of focusing attention—a skill essential for taking effective notes in class, maximizing comprehension when reading textbooks, and memorizing content. After students read the article and you review it with them in class, have them stand up and find a partner for this brief "hand mirror" exercise. Facing their partner, students put their hands up, palms facing toward their partner, without touching. In this position, students appear as a mirror image of their partner. Without speaking, for one minute one student is in charge of moving her hands slowly in different directions—up, down, left, right, forward, backward. Her partner focuses his attention and mirrors the movement of her hands with his hands,

master instructor
best practice

big rock planning

This activity helps students build on the ideas they learned in the Time Monitor exercise. Order a text bundle that includes the Master Student Planner. (Ask your sales representative about how to order this special package.) Start the process with a week at a glance by asking students to identify their "A's"—their most time-sensitive activities. Remind students to start their daily plan with a look at the week before it starts. One way to do this is to take seven 3 × 5 cards and write the date and day of the week at the top of each card. After students first list their most time-sensitive activities for the week, adding "B's" and "C's" as their second- and third-level priorities, respectively, planning becomes a less daunting task.

An in-class strategy to illustrate planning and prioritizing is to bring three stones to class: Stone A is roughly the size of a softball, stone B is the size of a golf ball, and stone C is the size of a hazelnut or a marble. Begin by asking for three volunteers. Hand each of the students a stone, and ask students to hold the stones at arm's length, above their heads, for a minute. Ask the student holding the smallest "stone" (stone C—a small foam ball) to let it go so that it hits the student on the head. Then ask, "Did you feel that? Was it painful?" Explain that the three stones are analogous to planning and prioritizing; if you don't accomplish your plan by prioritizing and completing, it can be painful. Then ask the students holding stones A and B how they are feeling about dropping their stones. After they respond, have them put their rocks down without dropping them on their heads. Ask the students who held stones A and B how it felt to be able to put them down. "Even better than B" is a typical response for stone A student. Summarize by making the point that priority equals pleasure (finishing on time) or pain (missing class, turning in assignments late, or failing tests).

—Eldon McMurray, Utah Valley State College

even when they do not move symmetrically. After one minute, they reverse roles for another minute. Afterward, discuss the paradox that it feels both easy and difficult to focus attention for just 60 seconds. It may be beneficial to bring a student forward and demonstrate the activity with him first.

2. **Why? What? How? and What if?** Consider writing these questions on the chalkboard or whiteboard. Post them to your discussion board. Tap into all the different learning styles of your students by asking these questions in class:

   Why? Why does *Becoming a Master Student* cover the topic of planning?

   What? What is planning? Read through the list of articles in this chapter and pick three that look interesting. What about these three articles interests you?

   How? How would you rate your level of success with the ideas covered in this chapter? (How much do you already know about prioritizing your time, setting goals, or avoiding procrastination?)

   What if? What if you start to apply these strategies to your life right now? And what if you don't? Connect to the workplace: What if an employee can't meet deadlines?

3. **The ABC daily to-do list (pages 74–75).** Some students have had prior experience with to-do lists. Their testimonials in class can help convince students who have not yet tried to-do lists to experiment with them. Students can see different perspectives and gain new ideas. For example, a visual learner can gain motivation when another visual learner shares about a visually appealing technique—a unique to-do list pad, use of stickers and colorful markers and pens. The ABC priority aspect is usually a new concept for all students. Learning this technique helps them make better decisions about *what* to do and *when* to do it. Practicing this skill in groups during class helps students get started with to-do lists.

4. **Stop procrastination now (pages 86–87).** Many students report that procrastination is their No. 1 obstacle to success in school, work, and their personal lives. After they have read the antiprocrastination

article and sidebar, divide students into groups of four, and ask them to list situations in which they often procrastinate. Then discuss as a group which of the antiprocrastination strategies might be most appropriate for each situation. Have students create summary charts on poster paper and then present a brief report to the rest of the class.

5. **25 ways to get the most out of now (pages 89–93).** After students have read this article, divide them into groups of four, and ask them to discuss which of the 25 tools they have had success with in the past. Then ask them to discuss five tools that they are interested in trying and to make a verbal commitment to each of their group members. At the beginning of the next class, ask students to report back to their groups to discuss which strategies worked and which did not.

CONVERSATION/SHARING

Workplace Application: The importance of planning at work. Just as time is of the essence for most students, so is it for most employees. Often workers must manage many projects simultaneously while also focusing on quality and efficiency. Many of the topics in Chapter 2 will be useful to students as they transition to the world of work.

- *Goal setting.* Prospective employees are often asked in job interviews, "Where do you see yourself in five years?" Although it is never a good answer to say "In your position", showing the hiring manager that some thought has been given to personal growth and progress will never hurt one's chances. Illustrate for students how they should have a few strong short-term and midterm career goals that lead progressively toward long-term career goals. Remind them career planning is a lifelong process, and goals may change and evolve over time.

- *Daily to-do lists.* Staying organized is essential to success at work. Keeping track of tasks with a daily to-do list adds to workplace efficiency and success. Many workers even keep weekly lists that they review at the end of each day to see what was done and what is left to be finished. There is always such a feeling of accomplishment as each task is checked off as completed.

- *Web-based planning tools.* Technological advances have made time management much easier for workers. Work calendars, e-mail accounts, and task lists can now be synced with cell phones, home personal computers, and tablets. Information is now easily accessed 24/7/365. While this access may be helpful, remind students to understand technology's place and limitations in the world of work.

HOMEWORK

The Time Monitor (pages 65–69). Assign the monitoring step of this exercise the week before you get to this chapter, because the exercise asks students to monitor their activities first so that they will have a detailed picture of how they spend their time. When students complete this exercise *before* they read the chapter, they are motivated to learn strategies to make the most of their 168 hours per week. It is not easy to keep track of oneself for 24 hours a day for a week, so to show students that you know how challenging this exercise really is, share with them that you did it yourself.

Create a lifeline (page 72). Have students tape two sheets of paper side by side to allow for a long lifeline, drawn diagonally from the bottom left-hand corner to the upper right-hand corner. Have them spread the next 10 years across the left-hand page and then 50 years of highlights across the right-hand page. Students could also create a powerful visual through PowerPoint to include images of what they imagine that goal to include.

Master monthly calendar (pages 78–80). Tell students that they cannot control time, but they *can* control the way they respond to it. They cannot control the past, but they *can* learn from it, and they can have an impact on their future by planning the semester. The master monthly calendar is an opportunity for you to work with your students to plan an entire semester. Using the blank monthly calendar in the textbook, have students create their master plan based on the course syllabi from all of their classes. Have them transfer key dates for tests and papers, and ask them to plug in interim deadlines, such as "Write draft of English paper." Some students have success with developing master plans if, during this exercise, they also create a timeline for each of the bigger projects. Encourage students to personalize their schedules and planners, using visual elements such as design, color stickers, markers, and whatever it takes to make this a pleasant tool. If a planner feels cold and impersonal, they are not as likely to use and enjoy it.

EVALUATION

Frequent quizzes ensure that students focus attention during class and keep up with the text reading assignments. In addition, quizzes provide students with opportunities for written reflection regarding new discoveries and intentions. Evaluation instruments also help you identify topics and concepts that students have not yet mastered.

Quiz Ideas for Chapter 2
Ask students to:

- Write a Discovery statement regarding time monitoring/planning.
- Write an Intention statement regarding goal setting.
- Name antiprocrastination tools.
- Describe strategies for getting the most out of now.
- Write a Discovery statement regarding the Power Process: Be here now.

MindTap™

EMBRACE VALUABLE RESOURCES

FOR CHAPTER 2

STUDENT RESOURCES: MINDTAP

- **Engagement Activity: Master Students in Action.** In this video, students hear firsthand from other students about their time management challenges and their strategies for success. The Master Students in Action videos give your students an up-close view of how the strategies in *Becoming a Master Student* have helped their peers overcome obstacles. In special segments, Dave Ellis offers students his best strategies for mastering each chapter's content.

- **Aplia Homework Assignment: The ABC daily to-do list.** In this assignment, students are introduced to the ABC to-do list and use the concept to improve time management skills. By looking at a student's commitments, students are tasked with helping him make the most of his free time by using the ABC daily to-do list to identify the most important and urgent tasks.

- **Reflection Activity. Power Process: Be here now.** Have students watch this short video demonstrating how to put the notion of "be here now" into practice. Or have students create group multimedia PowerPoint presentations based on their understanding of how to "be here now."

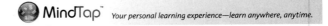 **MindTap™** *Your personal learning experience—learn anywhere, anytime.*

INSTRUCTOR COMPANION SITE

- **Do you have trouble managing your time?** Consider looking at the strategies for instructors who have little time to prepare, and get advice about how to develop and plan your course in the online Course Manual. You can also browse through the sample syllabi provided by other Master Instructors to get ideas for how you might want to reorganize your course for the future.

- **Need some energizing lecture ideas?** Browse through the lecture ideas provided for Chapter 2 in the Course Manual, including the following:

  - **Commit to Coming to Class.** Through a short case study of a student going to a movie, you can show the value of coming to class.

- **Complete It.** Explain to students how sorting and planning can help one become more organized.

- **Looking for test banks?** Customizable, text-specific content quizzes are a great way to test students' knowledge and understanding of the text, and are available for every chapter. Powered by Cognero, the test banks can be exported in an LMS or print-friendly format. You will have no problem accessing the multiple-choice, true/false, completion, and short-answer questions.

Please visit login.cengage.com to log in and access the Instructor Companion Site.

Chapter 2

TIME

Why

Procrastination and lack of planning can quickly undermine your success in school.

How

Take a few minutes to skim this chapter. Find at least three techniques that you intend to use. Make a note to yourself or mark the pages where the strategies that you intend to use are located in the chapter.

What if ...

I could meet my goals with time to spare?

There's an app for that: Using technology for time management Time management activities generally fall into two major categories, no matter which system or set of techniques you use: making lists and using calendars. Today you can choose from dozens of applications for doing both. ■ 85

Make choices about multitasking Multitasking is much harder than it looks. Despite the awe-inspiring complexity of the human brain, research reveals that we are basically wired to do one thing at a time. ■ 64

Stop procrastination now ■ 86

Create a work flow that works ■ 84

What is included ...

BE HERE NOW

Being right here, right now is such a simple idea. It seems obvious. Where else can you be but where you are? When else can you be there but when you are there?

The answer is that you can be somewhere else at any time—in your head. It's common for our thoughts to distract us from where we've chosen to be. Sometimes technology becomes the source of distraction: The arrival of every new text message, Facebook update, or e-mail comes with an attention-grabbing alert. When we let this happen without conscious choice, we lose the benefits of focusing our attention on what's important to us in the present moment.

To "be here now" means to do what you're doing when you're doing it. It means to be where you are when you're there. Students consistently report that focusing attention on the here and now is one of the most powerful tools in this book.

We all have a voice in our head that hardly ever shuts up. If you don't believe it, conduct this experiment: Close your eyes for 10 seconds, and pay attention to what is going on in your head. Please do this right now.

Notice something? Perhaps a voice in your head was saying, "Forget it. I'm in a hurry." Another might have said, "I wonder when 10 seconds is up?" Another could have been saying, "What little voice? I don't hear any little voice."

That's the voice.

This voice can take you anywhere at any time—especially when you are studying. When the voice takes you away, you might appear to be studying, but your brain is somewhere else.

All of us have experienced this voice, as well as the absence of it. When our inner voices are silent, we can experience something that's called "flow": Time no longer seems to exist. We forget worries, aches, pains, reasons, excuses, and justifications. We fully experience the here and now. Life is magic.

Do not expect to be rid of the voice entirely. That is neither possible nor desirable. Inner voices serve a purpose. They enable us to analyze, predict, classify, and understand events out there in the "real" world. The trick is to consciously choose when to be with your inner voice and when to let it go.

Instead of trying to force a stray thought out of your head, simply notice it. Accept it. Tell yourself, "There's that thought again." Then gently return your attention to the task at hand. That thought, or another, will come back. Your mind will drift. Simply notice again where your thoughts take you, and gently bring yourself back to the here and now.

Also remember that planning supports this Power Process. Goals are tools that we create to guide our action in the present. Time management techniques—calendars, lists, and all the rest—have only one purpose. They reveal what's most important for you to focus on right *now*. Ironically, one way to create flow experiences is to plan for them.

The idea behind this Power Process is simple. When you listen to a lecture, listen to a lecture. When you read this book, read this book. And when you choose to daydream, daydream. Do what you're doing when you're doing it. Be where you are when you're there.

Be here now . . . and now . . . and now. ■

Stigur Karlsson/E+/Getty Images

YOU'VE GOT THE TIME

When you say you don't have enough time, you might really be saying that you are not spending the time you do have in the way that you want. This chapter is about ways to solve that problem.

The words *time management* may call forth images of restriction and control. You might visualize a prune-faced Scrooge hunched over your shoulder, stopwatch in hand, telling you what to do every minute. Bad news.

Good news: You do have enough time for the things you want to do. All it takes is thinking about the possibilities and making conscious choices.

Time is an equal opportunity resource. All of us, regardless of gender, race, creed, or national origin, have exactly the same number of hours in a week. No matter how famous we are, no matter how rich or poor, we get 168 hours to spend each week—no more, no less.

Time is an unusual commodity. It cannot be saved. You can't stockpile time like wood for the stove or food for the winter. It can't be seen, heard, touched, tasted, or smelled. You can't sense time directly. Even scientists and philosophers find it hard to describe. Because time is so elusive, it is easy to ignore. That doesn't bother time at all. Time is perfectly content to remain hidden until you are nearly out of it. And when you are out of it, you are out of it.

Time is a nonrenewable resource. If you're out of wood, you can chop some more. If you're out of money, you can earn a little extra. If you're out of love, there is still hope. If you're out of health, it can often be restored. But when you're out of time, that's it. When this minute is gone, it's gone.

Time seems to pass at varying speeds. Sometimes it crawls, and sometimes it's faster than a speeding bullet. On Friday afternoons, classroom clocks can creep. After you've worked a 10-hour day, reading the last few pages of an economics assignment can turn minutes into hours. A year in school can stretch out to an eternity.

At the other end of the spectrum, time flies. There are moments when you are so absorbed in what you're doing that hours disappear like magic.

Everything written about time management can be reduced to three main ideas:

1. Know exactly *what* you want. State your wants as clear, specific goals. And put them in writing.
2. Know *how* to get what you want. Take action to meet your goals. Determine what you'll do *today* to get

what you want in the future. Put those actions in writing as well.
3. Go for balance. When our lives lack this quality, we spend most of our time responding to interruptions, last-minute projects, and emergencies. Life feels like a scramble to just survive. We're so busy achieving someone else's goals that we forget about getting what *we* want.

Sometimes it seems that your friends control your time; your boss controls your time; your teachers or your parents or your kids or somebody else controls your time. Maybe that is not true, though. Approach time as if you are in control.

According to Stephen R. Covey, the purpose of planning is to carve out space in your life for things that are not urgent but are truly important.[1] Examples are exercising regularly, reading, praying or meditating, spending quality time alone or with family members and friends, traveling, and cooking nutritious meals. Each of these contributes directly to our personal goals for the future and to the overall quality of our lives in the present.

Yet when schedules get tight, we often drop important activities. We postpone them for that elusive day when we'll finally "have more time."

Don't wait for that time to come. *Make* the time. Use the exercises in this chapter to let go of being "crazy busy" and align your daily activities with your values. Think of time management as time *investment*. Then spend your most valuable resource in the way you choose. ∎

Make choices about
MULTITASKING

Hand mirroring exercise (focus) 60 sec

"Evidently, studying isn't one of the tasks you perform when you're multitasking."

When we get busy, we get tempted to do several things at the same time. It seems like such a natural solution: Watch TV *and* read a textbook. Talk on the phone *and* outline a paper. Write an e-mail *and* listen to a lecture. These are examples of multitasking.

There's a problem with this strategy: Multitasking is much harder than it looks. Despite the awe-inspiring complexity of the human brain, research reveals that we are basically wired to do one thing at a time.[2]

The solution is an old-fashioned one: Whenever possible, take life one task at a time. Develop a key quality of master students—focused attention—with the following strategies.

UNPLUG FROM TECHNOLOGY

To reduce the temptation of multitasking, turn off distracting devices. Shut off your TV and cell phone. Disconnect from the Internet unless it's required for your planned task. Later, you can take a break to make calls, send texts, check e-mail, and browse the web. When you go online, do so with a clear intention and a time to quit.

CAPTURE FAST-BREAKING IDEAS WITH MINIMAL INTERRUPTION

Your brain is an expert nagger. After you choose to focus on one task, it might issue urgent reminders about 10 more things you need to do. Keep 3 × 5 cards or paper and a

pen handy to write down those reminders. You can take a break later and add them to your to-do list. Your mind can quiet down once it knows that a task has been captured in writing.

HANDLE INTERRUPTIONS WITH CARE

Some breaking events are so urgent that they call for your immediate attention. When this happens, note what you were doing when you were interrupted. For example, write down the number of the page you were reading, or the name of the computer file you were creating. When you return to the task, your notes can help you get up to speed again.

COMMIT TO "SINGLE TASKING"

Today's technology—e-mail, text messages, social media—seems to require multitasking. The key word in the previous sentence is *seems*. Multitasking is actually an option, not a requirement. You can still choose to do one thing at a time with full attention. You might find yourself in a minority. And, you'll enjoy the benefits, including greater effectiveness at whatever you choose to do and lower levels of stress.

Planning helps. Set a goal to keep your daily to-do list short—three items, maximum. Focus on getting these done, one at a time, before tackling other tasks. Even if you fail to achieve this goal, you'll benefit from the increased focus and practice at single tasking.

MULTITASK WITH SKILL   *cooking & studying*

If multitasking seems inevitable in certain situations, then do it as effectively as possible. Pair one activity that requires concentration with another activity that you can do almost automatically. For example, studying for your psychology exam while downloading music is a way to reduce the disadvantages of multitasking. Pretending to listen to your children while watching TV is not.

ALIGN YOUR ACTIVITIES WITH YOUR PASSIONS

Handling routine tasks is a necessary part of daily life. But if you find that your attention frequently wanders throughout the day, ask yourself: "Am I really doing what I want to do? Do my work and my classes connect to my interests?" If the answer is no, then the path beyond multitasking might call for a change in your academic and career plans. Whenever an activity aligns with your passion, the temptation to multitask loses power. ■

powerful!

Exercise 8 The Time Monitor

The purpose of this exercise is to transform time into a knowable and predictable resource. To do this, monitor your time in 15-minute intervals, 24 hours a day, for seven days. Record how much time you spend sleeping, eating, studying, attending lectures, traveling to and from class, working, watching television, listening to music, taking care of the kids, running errands—everything.

If this sounds crazy, hang on for a minute. This exercise is not about keeping track of the rest of your life in 15-minute intervals. It is an opportunity to become conscious of how you spend your time—your life. Use the Time Monitor only for as long as it helps you do that. When you know exactly how you spend your time, you can make choices with open eyes. You can plan to spend more time on the things that are most important to you and less time on the unimportant. Monitoring your time puts you in control of your life. To do this exercise, complete the following steps.

Step 1

Look at Figure 2.1, a sample Time Monitor, on page 66. On Monday, the student got up at 6:45 a.m., showered, and got dressed. He ate breakfast from 7:15 to 7:45. It took him 15 minutes to walk to class (7:45 to 8:00), and he attended classes from 8:00 to 11:00.

List your activities in the same way. When you begin an activity, write it down next to the time you begin. Round off to the nearest 15 minutes. If, for example, you begin eating at 8:06, enter your starting time as 8:00.

Step 2

Fill out *your* Time Monitor. Now it's *your* turn. Using the blank Time Monitor, Figure 2.2, on page 67, choose a day to begin monitoring your time. On that day, start filling out your Time Monitor. Keep it with you all day and use it for one full week. Take a few moments every couple of hours to record what you've done. Or enter a note each time that you change activities.

Step 3

After you've monitored your time for one week, group your activities together into categories. List them in the "Category" column in Figure 2.3 on page 69 which includes the categories "Sleep," "Class," "Study," and "Meals." Think of other categories to add. "Grooming" might include showering, putting on makeup, and getting dressed. "Travel" could include walking, taking the bus, and riding your bike. Other categories might be "Exercise," "Entertainment," "Work," "Television," and "Children." Write in the categories that work for you.

Step 4

List your *estimated* hours for each category of activity. Guess how many hours you *think* you spent on each category of activity. List these hours in the "Estimated" column in Figure 2.3.

Then, list your *actual* hours for each category of activity. Add up the figures from your daily time monitoring. List these hours in the "Actual" column in Figure 2.3. Make sure that the grand total of all categories is 168 hours.

Step 5

Reflect on the results of this exercise. Compare the "Estimated" and "Actual" columns. You might feel disappointed or even angry about where your time goes. Use those feelings as motivation to make different choices. Think about how you would complete these sentences:

- I was surprised at the amount of time I spent on . . .
- I want to spend more time on . . .
- I want to spend less time on . . .

Step 6

Repeat this exercise. Do this exercise as many times as you want. The benefit is developing a constant awareness of your activities. With that awareness, you can make informed choices about how to spend the time of your life.

MONDAY _9_ / _12_		TUESDAY _9_ / _13_	
	Get up		
	Shower		Sleep
7:00	———————	7:00	
7:15	Breakfast	7:15	
7:30	—————	7:30	
7:45	Walk to class	7:45	Shower
8:00	Econ 1	8:00	Dress
8:15		8:15	Eat
8:30		8:30	
8:45		8:45	
9:00		9:00	Art
9:15		9:15	Apprec.
9:30		9:30	Project
9:45		9:45	
10:00	Bio 1	10:00	
10:15		10:15	
10:30		10:30	
10:45		10:45	
11:00		11:00	Data
11:15	Study	11:15	process
11:30		11:30	
11:45		11:45	
12:00		12:00	
12:15	Lunch	12:15	
12:30		12:30	
12:45		12:45	
1:00		1:00	
1:15	Eng. Lit	1:15	Lunch
1:30		1:30	
1:45		1:45	
2:00		2:00	Work
2:15	Coffeehouse	2:15	on book
2:30		2:30	report
2:45		2:45	
3:00		3:00	Art
3:15		3:15	Apprec.
3:30		3:30	
3:45		3:45	
4:00		4:00	
4:15	Study	4:15	
4:30		4:30	
4:45		4:45	
5:00		5:00	Dinner
5:15	Dinner	5:15	
5:30		5:30	
5:45		5:45	
6:00		6:00	Letter to
6:15		6:15	Uncle Jim
6:30	Babysit	6:30	
6:45		6:45	
7:00		7:00	

Figure 2.1 Sample Time Monitor

MONDAY ___/___/___/	TUESDAY ___/___/___/	WEDNESDAY ___/___/___/	THURSDAY___/___/___/
7:00	7:00	7:00	7:00
7:15	7:15	7:15	7:15
7:30	7:30	7:30	7:30
7:45	7:45	7:45	7:45
8:00	8:00	8:00	8:00
8:15	8:15	8:15	8:15
8:30	8:30	8:30	8:30
8:45	8:45	8:45	8:45
9:00	9:00	9:00	9:00
9:15	9:15	9:15	9:15
9:30	9:30	9:30	9:30
9:45	9:45	9:45	9:45
10:00	10:00	10:00	10:00
10:15	10:15	10:15	10:15
10:30	10:30	10:30	10:30
10:45	10:45	10:45	10:45
11:00	11:00	11:00	11:00
11:15	11:15	11:15	11:15
11:30	11:30	11:30	11:30
11:45	11:45	11:45	11:45
12:00	12:00	12:00	12:00
12:15	12:15	12:15	12:15
12:30	12:30	12:30	12:30
12:45	12:45	12:45	12:45
1:00	1:00	1:00	1:00
1:15	1:15	1:15	1:15
1:30	1:30	1:30	1:30
1:45	1:45	1:45	1:45
2:00	2:00	2:00	2:00
2:15	2:15	2:15	2:15
2:30	2:30	2:30	2:30
2:45	2:45	2:45	2:45
3:00	3:00	3:00	3:00
3:15	3:15	3:15	3:15
3:30	3:30	3:30	3:30
3:45	3:45	3:45	3:45
4:00	4:00	4:00	4:00
4:15	4:15	4:15	4:15
4:30	4:30	4:30	4:30
4:45	4:45	4:45	4:45
5:00	5:00	5:00	5:00
5:15	5:15	5:15	5:15
5:30	5:30	5:30	5:30
5:45	5:45	5:45	5:45
6:00	6:00	6:00	6:00
6:15	6:15	6:15	6:15
6:30	6:30	6:30	6:30
6:45	6:45	6:45	6:45
7:00	7:00	7:00	7:00
7:15	7:15	7:15	7:15
7:30	7:30	7:30	7:30
7:45	7:45	7:45	7:45
8:00	8:00	8:00	8:00
8:15	8:15	8:15	8:15
8:30	8:30	8:30	8:30
8:45	8:45	8:45	8:45
9:00	9:00	9:00	9:00
9:15	9:15	9:15	9:15
9:30	9:30	9:30	9:30
9:45	9:45	9:45	9:45
10:00	10:00	10:00	10:00
10:15	10:15	10:15	10:15
10:30	10:30	10:30	10:30
10:45	10:45	10:45	10:45
11:00	11:00	11:00	11:00
11:15	11:15	11:15	11:15
11:30	11:30	11:30	11:30
11:45	11:45	11:45	11:45
12:00	12:00	12:00	12:00

Figure 2.2 Your Time Monitor

FRIDAY ___ / ___ / ___ /	SATURDAY ___ / ___ / ___ /	SUNDAY ___ / ___ / ___ /
7:00	7:00	7:00
7:15	7:15	7:15
7:30	7:30	7:30
7:45	7:45	7:45
8:00	8:00	8:00
8:15	8:15	8:15
8:30	8:30	8:30
8:45	8:45	8:45
9:00	9:00	9:00
9:15	9:15	9:15
9:30	9:30	9:30
9:45	9:45	9:45
10:00	10:00	10:00
10:15	10:15	10:15
10:30	10:30	10:30
10:45	10:45	10:45
11:00	11:00	11:00
11:15	11:15	11:15
11:30	11:30	11:30
11:45	11:45	11:45
12:00	12:00	12:00
12:15	12:15	12:15
12:30	12:30	12:30
12:45	12:45	12:45
1:00	1:00	1:00
1:15	1:15	1:15
1:30	1:30	1:30
1:45	1:45	1:45
2:00	2:00	2:00
2:15	2:15	2:15
2:30	2:30	2:30
2:45	2:45	2:45
3:00	3:00	3:00
3:15	3:15	3:15
3:30	3:30	3:30
3:45	3:45	3:45
4:00	4:00	4:00
4:15	4:15	4:15
4:30	4:30	4:30
4:45	4:45	4:45
5:00	5:00	5:00
5:15	5:15	5:15
5:30	5:30	5:30
5:45	5:45	5:45
6:00	6:00	6:00
6:15	6:15	6:15
6:30	6:30	6:30
6:45	6:45	6:45
7:00	7:00	7:00
7:15	7:15	7:15
7:30	7:30	7:30
7:45	7:45	7:45
8:00	8:00	8:00
8:15	8:15	8:15
8:30	8:30	8:30
8:45	8:45	8:45
9:00	9:00	9:00
9:15	9:15	9:15
9:30	9:30	9:30
9:45	9:45	9:45
10:00	10:00	10:00
10:15	10:15	10:15
10:30	10:30	10:30
10:45	10:45	10:45
11:00	11:00	11:00
11:15	11:15	11:15
11:30	11:30	11:30
11:45	11:45	11:45
12:00	12:00	12:00

Figure 2.2 (Continued)

WEEK OF ___ / ___ / ___ /		
Category	**Estimated Hours**	**Actual Hours**
Sleep		
Class		
Study		
Meals		

Figure 2.3 *Your Estimated and Actual Hours*

Interactive

Journal Entry 6
Discovery/Intention Statement

Discover the impact of technology on your time

Many students find that the Internet becomes a major time drainer. Discover whether this is true for you. For one day, keep track of how much time you spend online. Use a simple system for gathering data. For instance, keep a 3 × 5 card and pen handy. On this card, write down the times when you start using the Internet and when you stop. Another option is to use a web-based time tracker such as SlimTimer (slimtimer.com) or Rescuetime (rescuetime.com).

If possible, include short descriptions of how you spent your online time. For example: *visit Facebook, check e-mail, read the news, do course work,* or *watch videos.* After monitoring your online time, complete the following sentences:

I discovered that the number of minutes I spent online today was . . .

_____

The things that I did online were . . .

_____

_____

Next, think about any changes that you want to make in the amount of time you spend online. For example, you could close your web browser for defined periods each day. Complete the following sentence:

I intend to . . .

_____

_____

Define your VALUES

Values are the things in life that you want for their own sake. They define who you want to be. They also guide your moment-by-moment choices about what to do and what to have.

Values have little meaning unless they change our daily behavior. Our values are truly affirmed in a public way—through behaviors that anyone can observe.

People often say that they live a values-based life—and then act in ways that contradict what they say. They might say that they value contribution and yet avoid doing volunteer work. Students might say that they value education even though they skip classes to party.

One way to take charge of your time and attention is to define your values and then carefully choose your actions. If you discover a mismatch between what you say and what you do, then set a clear intention to use your time differently.

Don't be content with a vague set of ideals. Make your values so clear that they guide you on when to say yes to an activity—and when to say no.

CONSIDER ONE SET OF VALUES

Becoming a Master Student is based on a specific set of values:

- *Focused attention* means "being here now"—fully awake, aware, and present to any task that occupies you in the present moment. People with focused attention can be centered even in the midst of chaos.

- *Self-responsibility* means being the victor rather than the victim. This value is based on the idea that in any circumstance—no matter how difficult—you can still choose how to respond.

- *Integrity* means being someone that people can count on. When you practice integrity, your words and your actions are aligned. People can trust you to keep your agreements.

- *Risk-taking* means being willing to change. People who live by this value are open-minded and courageous. They know that learning calls on us to consider new ideas and experiment with new behaviors—even when we feel fear.

- *Contributing* means being a person who discovers the meaning of life in serving others. People who practice this value gain knowledge and skills so that they can give something back to the world.

If you look carefully, you'll find one or more of these values reflected on every page of this book. For example, the qualities of a master student are a detailed statement of the core values listed here.

TRANSLATE YOUR VALUES INTO VISIBLE BEHAVIORS

1. One way to define your values is to reflect on the qualities of people you appreciate. Describe their behaviors. Then ask yourself what values might serve as the source of those behaviors.

2. You can also define your values by creating your eulogy. This is a detailed statement of how you want to be remembered after you die. After you've put this statement in writing, set goals about what you will *do* to create that legacy. This is not about focusing on death. It's about choosing how to spend your time while you're alive.

Yet another option is to define your values as high-priority activities. In your journal, brainstorm ways to complete this sentence: *It's extremely important that I make time for* . . . Then use your answers to set goals, schedule events, and write daily to-do lists. This strategy translates your values into plans that directly affect the way you manage time.

For example, perhaps it's important for you to make time for staying healthy. Then you can set goals to exercise regularly and manage your weight. In turn, those goals can show up as items on your to-do list and calendar—commitments to go to the gym, take an aerobic class, and include low-fat foods on your grocery list.

You might also place a high value on creating loving relationships. If so, then block out regular times on your calendar for spending time with family members and close friends.

If you value financial security, then set specific goals for increasing your income and reducing your expenses.

In any case, the ultimate time management skill is defining your values and aligning your actions. ■

Setting and Achieving
GOALS

Many people have no goals or have only vague, idealized notions of what they want. They are wonderful, fuzzy, safe thoughts such as "I want to be a good person," "I want to be financially secure," or "I want to be happy."

General outcomes have great potential as achievable goals. When we *keep* these goals in a general form, however, we may become confused about ways to actually achieve them.

Make your goal as real as a finely tuned engine. There is nothing vague or fuzzy about engines. You can see them, feel them, and hear them. You can take them apart and inspect the moving parts.

Goals can be every bit as real and useful. If you really want to meet a goal, then take it apart. Inspect the moving parts—the physical actions that you will take to make the goal happen and fine-tune your life.

There are many useful methods for setting goals. You're about to learn one of them. This method is based on writing goals that relate to several time frames and areas of your life. Experiment, and modify as you see fit.

Write down your goals. Writing down your goals greatly increases your chances of meeting them. Writing exposes undefined terms, unrealistic time frames, and other symptoms of fuzzy thinking. If you've been completing Intention Statements as explained in the Introduction to this book, then you've already had experience writing goals. Both goals and Intention Statements address changes you want to make in your behavior, your values, your circumstances—or all of these.

Write specific goals. State your goals in writing as observable actions or measurable results. Think in detail about how things will be different once your goals are attained. List the changes in what you'll see, feel, touch, taste, hear, be, do, or have.

Suppose that one of your goals is to become a better student by studying harder. You're headed in a powerful direction; now translate that goal into a concrete action, such as "I will study two hours for every hour I'm in class."

Specific goals make clear what actions are needed or what results are expected. Consider these examples:

Vague Goal	Specific Goal
Get a good education.	Graduate with BS degree in engineering, with honors, by 2014.
Get good grades.	Earn a 3.5 grade point average next semester.
Enhance my spiritual life.	Meditate for 15 minutes daily.
Improve my appearance.	Lose 6 pounds during the next 6 months
Get control of my money.	Transfer $100 to my savings account each month.

Write goals in several time frames. To get a comprehensive vision of your future, write down the following:

- **Long-term goals.** Long-term goals represent major targets in your life. These goals can take 5 to 20 years to achieve. In some cases, they will take a lifetime. They can include goals in education, careers, personal relationships, travel, financial security—whatever is important to you. Consider the answers to the following questions as you create your long-term goals: What do you want to accomplish in your life? Do you want your life to make a statement? If so, what is that statement?

- **Midterm goals.** Midterm goals are objectives you can accomplish in one to five years. They include goals such as completing a course of education, paying off a car loan, or achieving a specific career level. These goals usually support your long-term goals.

- **Short-term goals.** Short-term goals are the ones you can accomplish in a year or less. These goals are specific achievements, such as completing a particular course or group of courses, hiking down the Appalachian Trail, or organizing a family reunion. A short-term financial goal would probably include an exact dollar amount. Whatever your short-term goals are, they will require action now or in the near future.

Write goals in several areas of life. People who set goals in only one area of life—such as their career—may find that their personal growth becomes one-sided. They might experience success at work while neglecting their health or relationships with family members and friends.

To avoid this outcome, set goals in a variety of categories. Consider what you want to experience in these areas:

- Education
- Career
- Financial life
- Family life or relationships
- Social life
- Contribution (volunteer activities, community services)
- Spiritual life
- Level of health

Add goals in other areas as they occur to you.

Reflect on your goals. Each week, take a few minutes to think about your goals. You can perform the following spot checks:

- **Check in with your feelings.** Think about how the process of setting your goals felt. Consider the satisfaction you'll gain in attaining your objectives. If you don't feel a significant emotional connection with a written goal, consider letting it go or filing it away to review later.

- **Check for alignment.** Look for connections among your goals. Do your short-term goals align with your midterm goals? Will your midterm goals help you achieve your long-term goals? Look for a fit between all of your goals and your purpose for taking part in higher education as well as your overall purpose in life.

- **Check for obstacles.** All kinds of things can come between you and your goals, such as constraints on time and money. Anticipate obstacles and start looking now for workable solutions.

- **Check for next steps.** Here's a way to link goal setting to time management. Decide on a list of small, achievable steps you can take right away to accomplish each of your

short-term goals. Write these small steps down on a daily to-do list. If you want to accomplish some of these steps by a certain date, enter them in a calendar that you consult daily. Then, over the coming weeks, review your to-do list and calendar. Take note of your progress and celebrate your successes.

Move into action immediately. The idea of making New Year's resolutions is the butt of countless jokes. On January 1, we swear to start exercising regularly. By February 1, we're reaching for the TV remote instead of the jogging shoes.

Don't let your goals suffer such a fate. To increase your odds of success, take immediate action. Decrease the gap between stating a goal and starting to achieve it. If you slip and forget about the goal, you can get back on track at any time by *doing* something about it. Make those jokes about resolutions a part of your past, not a predictor of your future. ■

Interactive

Exercise 9
Create a lifeline

On a large sheet of paper, draw a horizontal line. This line will represent your lifetime. Now add key events in your life to this line, in chronological order. Examples are birth, first day at school, graduation from high school, and enrollment in higher education.

Now extend the lifeline into the future. Write down key events you would like to see occur 1 year, 5 years, and 10 or more years from now. Choose events that align with your core values. Work quickly in the spirit of a brainstorm, bearing in mind that this plan is not a final one.

Afterward, take a few minutes to review your lifeline. Select one key event for the future, and list any actions you could take in the next month to bring yourself closer to that goal. Do the same with the other key events on your lifeline. You now have the rudiments of a comprehensive plan for your life.

Finally, extend your lifeline another 50 years beyond the year when you would reach age 100. Describe in detail what changes in the world you'd like to see as a result of the goals you attained in your lifetime.

Exercise 10 Get real with your goals

One way to make goals effective is to examine them up close. That's what this exercise is about. Using a process of brainstorming and evaluation, you can break a long-term goal into smaller segments until you have taken it completely apart. When you analyze a goal to this level of detail, you're well on the way to meeting it.

For this exercise, you will use a pen, extra paper, and a watch with a second hand. (A digital watch with a built-in stopwatch feature is even better.) Timing is an important part of the brainstorming process, so follow the stated time limits. This entire exercise takes about an hour.

Part 1: Long-term goals

Brainstorm. Begin with an eight-minute brainstorm. Use a separate sheet of paper for this part of the exercise. For eight minutes, write down everything you think you want in your life. Write as fast as you can, and write whatever comes into your head. Leave no thought out. Don't worry about accuracy. The object of a brainstorm is to generate as many ideas as possible.

Evaluate. After you have finished brainstorming, spend the next six minutes looking over your list. Analyze what you wrote. Read the list out loud. If something is missing, add it. Look for common themes or relationships among your goals. Then select three long-term goals that are important to you—goals that will take many years to achieve. Write these goals down.

_____

_____

_____

Before you continue, take a minute to reflect on the process you've used so far. What criteria did you use to select your top three goals?

Part 2: Midterm goals

Brainstorm. Read out loud the three long-term goals you selected in Part 1. Choose one of them. Then brainstorm a list of goals you might achieve in the next one to five years that would lead to the accomplishment of that one long-term goal. These are midterm goals. Spend eight minutes on this brainstorm. Go for quantity.

Evaluate. Analyze your brainstorm of midterm goals. Then select three that you determine to be important in meeting the long-term goal you picked. Allow yourself six minutes for this part of the exercise. Write your selections down.

_____

_____

_____

Again, pause for reflection before going on to the next part of this exercise. Why do you see these three goals as more important than the other midterm goals you generated? Write about your reasons for selecting these three goals.

Part 3: Short-term goals

Brainstorm. Review your list of midterm goals and select one. In another eight-minute brainstorm, generate a list of short-term goals—those you can accomplish in a year or less that will lead to the attainment of that midterm goal. Write down everything that comes to mind. Do not evaluate or judge these ideas yet. For now, the more ideas you write down, the better.

Evaluate. Analyze your list of short-term goals. The most effective brainstorms are conducted by suspending judgment, so you might find some bizarre ideas on your list. That's fine. Now is the time to cross them out. Next, evaluate your remaining short-term goals, and select three that you are willing and able to accomplish. Allow yourself six minutes for this part of the exercise. Then write your selections down.

_____

_____

_____

The more you practice, the more effective you can be at choosing goals that have meaning for you. You can repeat this exercise, employing the other long-term goals you generated or creating new ones.

Deborah Jaffe/Getty Images

THE ABC DAILY TO-DO LIST

One of the most effective ways to stay on track and actually get things done is to use a daily to-do list. While the Time Monitor/Time Plan gives you a general picture of the week, your daily to-do list itemizes specific tasks you want to complete within the next 24 hours.

One advantage of keeping a daily to-do list is that you don't have to remember what to do next. It's on the list. A typical day in the life of a student is full of separate, often unrelated tasks—reading, attending lectures, reviewing notes, working at a job, writing papers, researching special projects, running errands. It's easy to forget an important task on a busy day. When that task is written down, you don't have to rely on your memory.

The following steps present one method for creating and using to-do lists. This method involves ranking each item on your list according to three levels of importance—A, B, or C. Experiment with these steps, modify them as you see fit, and invent new techniques that work for you.

STEP 1 BRAINSTORM TASKS

To get started, list all of the tasks you want to get done tomorrow. Each task will become an item on a to-do list. Don't worry about putting the entries in order or scheduling them yet. Just list everything you want to accomplish on a sheet of paper or planning calendar or in a special notebook. You can also use 3 × 5 cards, writing one task on each card. Cards work well because you can slip them into your pocket or rearrange them, and you never have to copy to-do items from one list to another.

STEP 2 ESTIMATE TIME

For each task you wrote down in Step 1, estimate how long it will take you to complete it. This can be tricky. If you allow too little time, you end up feeling rushed. If you allow too much time, you become less productive. For now, give it your best guess. If you are unsure, overestimate rather than underestimate how long it will take for each task. Overestimating has two benefits: (1) It avoids a schedule that is too tight, missed deadlines, and the resulting

feelings of frustration and failure; and (2) it allows time for the unexpected things that come up every day—the spontaneous to-dos. Now pull out your calendar or Time Monitor/Time Plan. You've probably scheduled some hours for activities such as classes or work. This leaves the unscheduled hours for tackling your to-do lists.

Add up the time needed to complete all your to-do items. Also add up the number of unscheduled hours in your day. Then compare the two totals. The power of this step is that you can spot overload in advance. If you have eight hours' worth of to-do items but only four unscheduled hours, that's a potential problem. To solve it, proceed to Step 3.

STEP 3 RATE EACH TASK BY PRIORITY

To prevent overscheduling, decide which to-do items are the most important, given the time you have available. One suggestion for making this decision comes from the book *How to Get Control of Your Time and Your Life,* by Alan Lakein: Simply label each task A, B, or C.[3]

The A's on your list are those things that are the most critical. They include assignments that are coming due or jobs that need to be done immediately. Also included are activities that lead directly to your short-term goals.

The B's on your list are important, but less so than the A's. B's might someday become A's. For the present, these tasks are not as urgent as A's. They can be postponed, if necessary, for another day.

The C's do not require immediate attention. C priorities include activities such as "shop for a new blender" and "research genealogy on the Internet." C's are often small, easy jobs with no set time line. They too can be postponed.

© ALEXEY GRIGOREV/Shutterstock.com

Step 1: Brainstorm tasks
Step 2: Estimate time
Step 3: Rate each task by priority
Step 4: Cross off tasks
Step 5: Evaluate
Bonus Step: Tinker

Once you've labeled the items on your to-do list, schedule time for all of the A's. The B's and C's can be done randomly during the day when you are in between tasks and are not yet ready to start the next A. Even if you get one or two of your A's done, you'll still be moving toward your goals.

STEP 4 CROSS OFF TASKS

Keep your to-do list with you at all times. Cross off activities when you finish them, and add new ones when you think of them. If you're using 3 × 5 cards, you can toss away or recycle the cards with completed items. Crossing off tasks and releasing cards can be fun—a visible reward for your diligence. This step fosters a sense of accomplishment.

When using the ABC priority method, you might experience an ailment common to students: C fever. Symptoms include the uncontrollable urge to drop that A task and begin crossing C's off your to-do list. If your history paper is due tomorrow, you might feel compelled to vacuum the rug, call your third cousin in Tulsa, and make a trip to the store for shoelaces. The reason C fever is so common is that A tasks are usually more difficult or time-consuming to achieve, with a higher risk of failure.

If you notice symptoms of C fever, ask yourself, "Does this job really need to be done now? Do I really need to alphabetize my CD collection, or might I better use this time to study for tomorrow's data-processing exam?" Use your to-do list to keep yourself on task, working on your A's. But don't panic or berate yourself when you realize that in the last six hours, you have completed nine C's and not a single A. Just calmly return to the A's.

STEP 5 EVALUATE

At the end of the day, evaluate your performance. Look for A priorities you didn't complete. Look for items that repeatedly turn up as B's or C's on your list and never seem to get done. Consider changing them to A's or dropping them altogether. Similarly, you might consider changing an A that didn't get done to a B or C priority.

Be willing to admit mistakes. You might at first rank some items as A's only to realize later that they are actually C's. And some of the C's that lurk at the bottom of your list day after day might really be A's. When you keep a daily to-do list, you can adjust these priorities *before* they become problems.

When you're done evaluating, start on tomorrow's to-do list. That way you can wake up and start getting things done right away.

BONUS STEP TINKER

When it comes to to-do lists, one size does not fit all. Feel free to experiment. Tweak the format of your list so that it works for you.

For example, the ABC system is not the only way to rank items on your to-do list. Some people prefer the 80–20 system. This method is based on the idea that 80 percent of the value of any to-do list comes from only 20 percent of the tasks on that list. So on a to-do list of 10 items, find the 2 that will contribute most to your life today. Complete those tasks without fail.

Another option is to rank items as "yes," "no," or "maybe." Do all of the tasks marked "yes." Delete those marked "no." And put all of the "maybes" on the shelf for later. You can come back to the "maybes" at a future point and rank them as "yes" or "no."

You might find that grouping items by categories such as "Errands" and "Calls" works best. Be creative.

In any case, use your to-do list in close connection with your calendar. On your calendar, note appointments, classes, and other events that take place on a specific date, a specific time, or both. Use your to-do list for items that you can complete between scheduled events. Keeping a separate to-do list means that you don't have to clutter up your calendar with all those reminders.

In addition, consider planning a whole week or even two weeks in advance. Planning in this way can make it easier to put activities in context and see how your daily goals relate to your long-term goals. Weekly planning can also free you from feeling that you have to polish off your whole to-do list in one day. Instead, you can spread tasks out over the whole week.

In any case, make starting your own to-do list an A priority. ■

PLANNING
SETS YOU FREE

Planning sets you free. When you set goals and manage time, your life does not just happen by chance. You are on equal terms with the greatest sculptor, painter, or playwright. You are doing more than creating a work of art: You are designing a life.

Without planning, we simply "dig in." We can actually get less productive and more busy at the same time. Planning replaces this behavior with clearly defined outcomes and action steps.

An effective plan creates options. It is not carved in stone. You can change your plans frequently and still preserve the advantages of planning—choosing your overall direction and taking charge of your life. Even when other people set the goals, you can choose how to achieve them.

Planning is a self-creative venture that lasts for a lifetime. Following are suggestions that flow directly from this point of view.

Schedule for flexibility and fun. Be realistic. Don't set yourself up for failure by telling yourself you can do a four-hour job in two hours. There are only 168 hours in a week. If you schedule 169 hours, you're sunk.

Expect the unexpected. Allow for emergencies by leaving some holes in your schedule—blocks of unplanned time. Consider setting aside time each week marked "flex time" or "open time." Use these hours for spontaneous activities, catching up, or seizing new opportunities.

Include time for errands. The time we spend buying groceries, paying bills, and doing laundry is easy to overlook. These small tasks can destroy a tight schedule and make us feel rushed and stressed all week. Plan for them. Also remember to allow for travel time between locations.

One immediate way to lower your stress level is set *personal* due dates for two or three days before *actual* due dates. If you have a paper to submit on March 15, for example, enter the due date on your calendar as March 13. You now have a two-day buffer to get that writing done.

Also make room for fun. This is important. Brains that are constantly stimulated by new ideas and new challenges need time off to digest them.

© parema/Shutterstock.com

Back up to a bigger picture. When choosing activities for the day or week, take some time to lift your eyes to the horizon. Step back for a few minutes and consider your longer-range goals—what you want to accomplish in the next six months, the next year, the next five years, and beyond.

Ask whether the activities you're about to schedule actually contribute to those goals. If they do, great. If not, ask whether you can delete some items from your calendar or to-do list to make room for goal-related activities. See if you can free up at least one hour each day for doing something you love instead of putting it off to a more "reasonable" or "convenient" time.

Look boldly for things to change. When creating your future, be bold. You can write goals related to money, marriage, career, or anything else. Don't accept the idea that you have to put up with substandard results in a certain area of your life. Staying open-minded about what is possible to achieve can lead to a future you never dreamed was possible.

Look for what's missing—and what to maintain. Goals often arise from a sense of what's missing in our lives. Goal setting is fueled by problems that are not resolved, projects that are incomplete, relationships we want to develop, and careers we still want to pursue.

However, not all planning has to spring from a sense of need. You can set goals to maintain things that you already have, or to keep doing the effective things that you already do. If you exercise vigorously three times each week, you can set a goal to keep exercising. If you already have a loving relationship with your spouse, you can set a goal to nurture that relationship for the rest of your life.

Think even further into the future. To have fun and unleash your creativity, set goals as far in the future as you can. The specific length of time doesn't matter. For some people, long-range planning might mean 10, 20, or even 50 years from now. For others, imagining three years feels right. Do whatever works for you.

Return to the present. Once you've stated your longest-range goals, work backward until you can define a next step to take. Suppose your 30-year goal is to retire and maintain your present standard of living. Ask yourself, "To do that, what financial goals do I need to achieve in 20 years? In 10 years? In a year? In a month? In a week?" Put the answers to these questions in writing. Some people refer to this as "backward planning." It's a way to drill down to details after thinking forward into the future.

To make backward planning more effective, remember the suggestion to schedule for flexibility. Leave some space in your schedule for unplanned events. Give yourself some time to deal with obstacles before they derail from your dreams.

Schedule fixed blocks of time first. When planning your week, start with class time and work time. These time periods are usually determined in advance, so other activities must be scheduled around them. Then schedule essential daily activities such as sleeping and eating. In addition, schedule some time each week for actions that lead directly to one of your written goals.

Set clear starting and stopping times. Tasks often expand to fill the time we allot to them. "It always takes me an hour just to settle into a reading assignment" might become a self-fulfilling prophecy.

As an alternative, schedule a certain amount of time for a reading assignment. Set a timer, and stick to it. Students often find that they can decrease study time by forcing themselves to read faster. They can usually do so without sacrificing comprehension.

A variation of this technique is called *time boxing*. Set aside a specific number of minutes or hours to spend on a certain task. Instead of working on that task until it's done, commit to work on it just for that specific amount of time. Then set a timer, and get to work. In effect, you're placing the task inside a definite "box"—a specific space on your daily calendar.

Feeling rushed or sacrificing quality is not the goal here. The point is to push yourself a little and discover what your time requirements really are.

> *Stay on top of your assignments right from the start. Whenever possible, work ahead. This tactic gives you an edge when the load for a course gets heavier or when big assignments for several courses are due during the same week.*

Plan for changes in your workload. You might find yourself with a lighter load of assignments to complete during the first few days or weeks of any course. Faced with this situation, some students are tempted to let early homework slide. They figure that they'll have plenty of time to catch up later. These students often get a rude surprise when the course shifts into warp speed.

To stay on top of your workload over the entire term, plan for such a change of pace. Stay on top of your assignments right from the start. Whenever possible, work ahead. This tactic gives you an edge when the load for a course gets heavier or when big assignments for several courses are due during the same week.

Involve others when appropriate. Statements such as these often follow a communications breakdown: "I just assumed you were going to pick up the kids from school on Tuesday." "I'm working overtime this week and hoped that you'd take over the cooking for a while." When you schedule a task that depends on another person's involvement, let that person know—the sooner, the better.

Start the day with your Most Important Task. Review your to-do list and calendar first thing each morning. Then visualize the rest of your day as a succession of tasks. For an extra level of clarity, pretend that you have to condense your to-do list to only one top-priority item. This is the thing that you want to complete today *without fail*. Behold your Most Important Task (MIT). Do it as early in the day as possible. Also do your MIT impeccably, with total attention.

Plan in a way that works for you. Even in this high-tech culture, there are many people who prefer to use low-tech tools for planning. This chapter includes paper-and-pencil exercises for students with a more kinesthetic learning style.

Planning that sets you free can be done with any set of tools. What matters above all is clear thinking and specific intentions. You can take any path that gets you there. ◼

Exercise 11 Master monthly calendar

This exercise will give you an opportunity to step back from the details of your daily schedule and get a bigger picture of your life. The more difficult it is for you to plan beyond the current day or week, the greater the benefit of this exercise.

Your basic tool is a one-month calendar. Use it to block out specific times for upcoming events such as study group meetings, due dates for assignments, review periods before tests, and other time-sensitive tasks. To get started, you might want to copy the blank monthly calendars in Figure 2.5 on pages 79–80 onto both sides of a sheet of paper. Or make copies of these pages and tape them together so that you can see several months at a glance.

Be creative. Experiment with a variety of uses for your monthly calendar. For instance, you can note day-to-day changes in your health or moods, list the places you visit while you are on vacation, or circle each day that you practice a new habit. Figure 2.4 shows sample monthly calendars.

Figure 2.4 *Sample Monthly Calendars*

MONDAY	TUESDAY	WEDNESDAY	THURSDAY	FRIDAY	SATURDAY	SUNDAY

Name _____

Month _____

Figure 2.5 Your Monthly Calendar

MONDAY	TUESDAY	WEDNESDAY	THURSDAY	FRIDAY	SATURDAY	SUNDAY

Month _____

Name _____

Figure 2.5 (Continued)

Break it down, get it done:
USING A LONG-TERM PLANNER

> *Planning a day, a week, or a month ahead is a powerful practice. Using a long-term planner— one that displays an entire quarter, semester, or year at a glance—can yield even more benefits.*

With a long-term planner, you can eliminate a lot of unpleasant surprises. Long-term planning allows you to avoid scheduling conflicts—the kind that obligate you to be in two places at the same time three weeks from now. You can also anticipate busy periods, such as finals week, and start preparing for them now. Good-bye, all-night cram sessions. Hello, serenity.

Find a long-term planner, or make your own. Many office supply stores carry academic planners in paper form that cover an entire school year. Computer software for time management offers the same features. You can also be creative and make your own long-term planner. A big roll of newsprint pinned to a bulletin board or taped to a wall will do nicely. You can also search the Internet for a computer application or smartphone app that's designed for planning.

Enter scheduled dates that extend into the future. Use your long-term planner to list commitments that extend beyond the current month. Enter test dates, lab sessions, days that classes will be canceled, and other events that will take place over this term and next term. See Figure 2.6 for an example.

Create a master assignment list. Find the syllabus for each course you're currently taking. Then, in your long-term planner, enter the due dates for all of the assignments in all of your courses. This step can be a powerful reality check.

The purpose of this technique is not to make you feel overwhelmed with all the things you have to do. Rather, its aim is to help you take a First Step toward recognizing the demands on your time. Armed with the truth about how you use your time, you can make more accurate plans.

Include nonacademic events. In addition to tracking academic commitments, you can use your long-term planner to mark significant events in your life outside school. Include birthdays, doctors' appointments, concert dates, credit card payment due dates, and car maintenance schedules.

Use your long-term planner to divide and conquer. For some people, academic life is a series of last-minute crises punctuated by periods of exhaustion. You can avoid that fate. The trick is to break down big assignments and projects into smaller assignments and subprojects, each with their own due date.

When planning to write a paper, for instance, enter the final due date in your long-term planner. Then set individual due dates for each milestone in the writing process—creating an outline, completing your research, finishing a first draft, editing the draft, and preparing the final copy. By meeting these interim due dates, you make steady progress on the assignment throughout the term. That sure beats trying to crank out all those pages at the last minute. Try using the blank long-term planner in Figure 2.7. ■

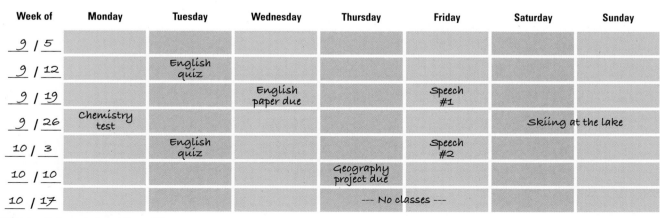

Week of	Monday	Tuesday	Wednesday	Thursday	Friday	Saturday	Sunday
9 / 5							
9 / 12		English quiz					
9 / 19			English paper due		Speech #1		
9 / 26	Chemistry test					Skiing at the lake	
10 / 3		English quiz			Speech #2		
10 / 10				Geography project due			
10 / 17				--- No classes ---			

Figure 2.6 Sample Long-Term Planner

LONG-TERM PLANNER ___ / ___ / ___ to ___ / ___ / ___

Week of	Monday	Tuesday	Wednesday	Thursday	Friday	Saturday	Sunday
___ / ___							
___ / ___							
___ / ___							
___ / ___							
___ / ___							
___ / ___							
___ / ___							
___ / ___							
___ / ___							
___ / ___							
___ / ___							
___ / ___							

Figure 2.7 *Your Long-Term Planner*

LONG-TERM PLANNER ___ / ___ / ___ to ___ / ___ / ___

Week of	Monday	Tuesday	Wednesday	Thursday	Friday	Saturday	Sunday
___ / ___							
___ / ___							
___ / ___							
___ / ___							
___ / ___							
___ / ___							
___ / ___							
___ / ___							
___ / ___							
___ / ___							
___ / ___							
___ / ___							

Figure 2.7 (Continued)

CREATE
a work flow that
WORKS

Ruslan Dashinsky/E+/Getty Images

This chapter offers dozens of strategies for time management. To get the most value from them, weave these strategies into a *work flow*—an organized way of taking projects from start to finish.

The beauty of a work flow is that you can use it for projects at work, school, and home. And once you establish a reliable work flow, you can use it for the rest of your life.

Everyone's work flow is a little different. However, they usually include the following four habits. To aid your memory, each habit starts with the letter C.

1. COLLECT

Use in-baskets to collect:

- Pieces of mail, brochures, handouts from classes, and other printed items

- Notes to yourself—Journal Entries, shopping lists, any ideas that occur to you while you're on the run

- Messages from other people

You will probably use several in-baskets. Start with a physical one—a tray for loose papers. Also create a folder on your computer desktop for e-mail attachments and other digital documents. In addition, think of your e-mail software and the voice mail on your phone as in-baskets.

As you develop the collection habit, welcome feelings of relief. True, all that you're doing is dumping stuff into physical and digital "buckets." The benefit is that you're no longer wondering: *Did I forget something?* The stuff you need to deal with is out of your head and safely collected. This frees up space in your mind to apply the Power Process: Be here now and focus on what you're doing in the present moment.

2. CLARIFY

Next, clarify what each collected item means to you. Pick any item from any of your in-baskets (you can do them in any order). Then make a decision about how to respond to it. You have three basic options:

- *Delete* it. Throw it in the trash or recycling bin.

- *Do* it now. This works well for tasks that you can finish in a minute or two, such as making a quick phone call.

- *Defer* the item—that is, write yourself a reminder to take action at a later time. This reminder can go on your calendar (for scheduled events) or on a to-do list.

Set a goal to empty your in-baskets at least once per week. On your calendar, block off an hour for this purpose at a regular time each week. Friday afternoon and Sunday night are popular choices.

David Allen, author of *Getting Things Done: The Art of Stress-Free Productivity,* describes this activity as a weekly review.[4] This is a time to ask yourself: "What are all my current goals? And what is the *very next action* that I can take to achieve each goal?"

Remember that next actions are specific behaviors. They involve physical movement. For instance, you send an e-mail, run an errand, or walk down the hall to ask someone a question.

With practice, your weekly review can become an enjoyable activity. This is when you will do some of your most important thinking for the next seven days.

3. CLASSIFY

Some of the things that you collect will not require any follow-up action. Even so, you might want to keep them on hand so that you can refer to them later. Examples are insurance policies, owner's manuals, and contact information for your friends and family members.

Set up simple filing systems for these reference materials. Use file folders for pieces of paper. Give each folder a name, and store the folders in alphabetical order. On your computer, create separate folders for each of your current classes and projects. Once a year, go through all of these folders—paper-based and digital—and purge the items that no longer matter to you.

4. COMPLETE

There's one more C, by the way—completing. When you form the habits of collecting, clarifying, and classifying, you get a calendar and to-do list that you can trust. With them in hand, you can make informed, moment-to-moment choices about how to spend the time of your life. And you can actually get things done. Congratulations. ■

There's an app for that:
Using technology for
TIME MANAGEMENT

Time management activities generally fall into two major categories: making lists and using calendars. Today you can choose from dozens of applications for doing both. Many are web-based and synchronize with apps for smart phones and tablets.

A few options are described here. To find more, search the web, using the key words *calendar apps, goal setting apps, time management apps,* and *to-do list managers.*

CALENDAR APPLICATIONS

These tools allow you to keep track of scheduled events and share them with other people if you choose. Some examples are listed here:

- Google Calendar (www.google.com/calendar)
- 30 Boxes (www.30boxes.com)
- Zoho Calendar (www.zoho.com/calendar)

Also check the built-in calendar software that comes with your computer, tablet, or smart phone. It may do everything you want.

LIST MANAGERS

You might wonder why you need sophisticated software just to keep lists of stuff to do. That's a fair question, and it has three answers. First, when a to-do list gets longer than an average grocery list, it gets tough to manage on paper. Second, you'll probably have more than one list to manage—lists of values, goals, to-do items, work-related projects, household projects, and more. And finally, it's convenient to access your lists from any device with an Internet connection.

Many list managers let you add items, delete or cross off items, assign due dates, and send yourself reminders. Here are some options:

- Gubb (www.gubb.net)
- Remember the Milk (www.rememberthemilk.com)
- Todoist (www.todoist.com)

Other list managers offer you access to a community of people who make some of their goals public. You can cheer each other on when progress occurs and suggest strategies. Some of these websites offer a library of action plans based on expert-recommended content. Examples are:

- 43Things (www.43things.com)
- myGoals.com (www.mygoals.com)

Another option is to just create lists with plain text editors that come without all the bells and whistles of word-processing software. Examples are Notepad for Windows and TextEdit for Mac OSX.

Bruno Cullen/Vetta/Getty Images

MORE POSSIBILITIES

You can also use online outliners to manage lists. Just assign each list a major heading and then show or hide any of the items on that list. Possibilities include:

- Workflowy (http://www.workflowy.com)
- Online Outliner (www.online-outliner.com)

Other apps are designed as full-featured time management tools. Check these for starters:

- OmniFocus (www.omnigroup.com/products/omnifocus)
- Nozbe (www.nozbe.com)

WHAT TO CONSIDER BEFORE YOU CHOOSE

You'll be spending a lot of time with your calendar and list manager. Choose carefully and be willing to read reviews and test drive several before making a final choice. Be sure to consider these aspects:

- Speed
- Stability
- Appearance
- Search functions
- Ease of use and syncing
- Ease of customizing
- Voice commands
- Alarms and reminders
- Options for backing up your data
- The developer's track record

Price is not always a major factor. You can spend $50 or more for a time management app or find a freebie that meets your needs perfectly.

Also remember that all of these tools are optional. People lived organized lives long before computers were invented. Even today, there are plenty of people who plan effectively with pencil and paper.

The goal is to actually get stuff done. Keep it simple, make it easy, and do what works. ■

STOP
PROCRASTINATION
NOW

Daniel Grill/JGI/Blend Images/Getty Images

Consider a bold idea: The way to stop procrastinating is to stop procrastinating. Giving up procrastination is actually a simple choice. People just make it complicated.

Sound crazy? Well, test this idea for yourself.

Think of something that you've been putting off. Choose a small, specific task—one that you can complete in five minutes or less. Then do that task today.

Tomorrow, choose another task and do it. Repeat this strategy each day for one week. Notice what happens to your habit of procrastination.

Discover the costs. Find out whether procrastination keeps you from getting what you want. Clearly seeing the side effects of procrastination can help you kick the habit.

Discover your procrastination style. Psychologist Linda Sapadin identifies different styles of procrastination.[5] For example, *dreamers* have big goals that they seldom translate into specific plans. *Worriers* focus on the worst-case scenario and are likely to talk more about problems than about solutions. *Defiers* resist new tasks or promise to do them and then don't follow through. *Overdoers* create extra work for themselves by refusing to delegate tasks and neglecting to set priorities. And *perfectionists* put off tasks for fear of making a mistake.

Awareness of your procrastination style is a key to changing your behavior. If you exhibit the characteristics of an overdoer, for example, then say no to new projects. Also ask for help in completing your current projects.

To discover your procrastination style, observe your behavior. Avoid judgments. Just be a scientist: Record the facts. Write Discovery Statements about specific ways you procrastinate. Follow up with Intention Statements about what to do differently.

Trick yourself into getting started. If you have a 50-page chapter to read, then grab the book and say to yourself, "I'm not really going to read this chapter right now. I'm just going to flip through the pages and scan the headings for 10 minutes." Tricks like these can get you started on a task you've been dreading.

Let feelings follow action. If you put off exercising until you feel energetic, you might wait for months. Instead, get moving now. Then watch your feelings change. After five minutes of brisk walking, you might be in the mood for a 20-minute run. This principle—action generates motivation—can apply to any task that you've put on the back burner.

Choose to work under pressure. Sometimes people thrive under pressure. As one writer puts it, "I don't do my *best* work under deadline. I do my *only* work under deadline." Used selectively, this strategy might also work for you.

Put yourself in control. If you choose to work with a due date staring you right in the face, then schedule a big block of time during the preceding week. Until then, enjoy!

Think ahead. Use a monthly calendar or long-term planner to list due dates for assignments in all your courses. Using these tools, you can anticipate heavy demands on your time and take action to prevent last-minute crunches. Make *Becoming a Master Student* your home base—the first place to turn in taking control of your schedule.

Play with antiprocrastination apps. There are apps for everything these days, including procrastination. Many of these are based on the Pomodoro Technique (www. pomodorotechnique.com). This method is simple—a key benefit for procrastinators: Set a timer for 25 minutes. During that period, get started on just one task that you've been putting off. Then take a five-minute break.

The beauty of this technique is twofold. First, you can do just about anything for 25 minutes—especially when you know a break is coming up. Second, 25 minutes is enough to actually accomplish something.

It might even make you interested in going for another 25 minutes.

Find apps for the Pomodoro Technique by searching the web. Even simpler: Use a kitchen timer or the alarm on your smart phone.

Create goals that draw you forward. A goal that grabs you by the heartstrings is an inspiration to act now. If you're procrastinating, then set some goals that excite you. Then you might wake up one day and discover that procrastination is part of your past. ■

The 7-step antiprocrastination plan

STEP 1 Make it meaningful. **What is important about the task you've been putting off? List all the benefits of completing that task. Look at it in relation to your short-, mid-, or long-term goals. Be specific about the rewards for getting it done, including how you will feel when the task is completed.**

STEP 2 Take it apart. **Break big jobs into a series of small ones you can do in 15 minutes or less. If a long reading assignment intimidates you, divide it into two- or three-page sections. Make a list of the sections, and cross them off as you complete them so you can see your progress. Even the biggest projects can be broken down into a series of small tasks.**

STEP 3 Write an Intention Statement. **If you can't get started on a term paper, you might write, "I intend to write a list of at least 10 possible topics by 9 p.m. I will reward myself with an hour of guilt-free recreational reading." Write your intention on a 3 × 5 card. Carry it with you or post it in your study area, where you can see it often.**

STEP 4 Tell everyone. **Publicly announce your intention to get a task done. Tell a friend that you intend to learn 10 irregular French verbs by Saturday. Tell your spouse, roommate, parents, and children. Include anyone who will ask whether you've completed the assignment or who will suggest ways to get it done. Make the world your support group.**

STEP 5 Find a reward. **Construct rewards to yourself carefully. Be willing to withhold them if you do not complete the task. Don't pick a movie as a reward for studying biology if you plan to go to the movie**

anyway. And when you legitimately reap your reward, notice how it feels.

STEP 6 Settle it now. **Do it now. The minute you notice yourself procrastinating, plunge into the task. Imagine yourself at a cold mountain lake, poised to dive. Gradual immersion would be slow torture. It's often less painful to leap. Then be sure to savor the feeling of having the task behind you.**

STEP 7 Say no. **When you keep pushing a task into a low-priority category, reexamine your purpose for doing that task at all. If you realize that you really don't intend to do something, quit telling yourself that you will. That's procrastinating. Just say no. Then you're not procrastinating. You don't have to carry around the baggage of an undone task.**

Note: **You can use a handy trick to remember these strategies. Tie a key word for each one to a specific day of the week:**

- Link *Make it meaningful* with the word *Monday*.
- Link *Take it apart* with *Tuesday*.
- Link *Write an intention statement* with *Wednesday*.
- Link *Tell everyone* with *Thursday*.
- Link *Find a reward* with *Friday*.
- Link *Settle it now* with *Saturday*.
- Link *Sunday* with *Say no*.

This memory trick offers a reminder: Each day of your life is an opportunity to stop the cycle of procrastination.

Practicing Critical Thinking 2

Psychologist Benjamin Bloom described six kinds of thinking:

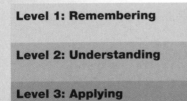

Level 1: Remembering

Level 2: Understanding

Level 3: Applying

Level 4: Analyzing

Level 5: Evaluating

Level 6: Creating

You can recall any suggestion from this book (**Level 1: Remembering**) and take that idea to a higher level of thinking.

For the purpose of this exercise, take a more detailed look at **Level 3: Applying**. Thinking at this level means using an idea to produce a desired result—to complete a task, meet a goal, make a decision, or solve a problem.

For example, one suggestion for overcoming procrastination is to divide a big project into smaller tasks and schedule each task. You could apply this suggestion to writing a paper that's due on November 1 of this year. Make notes on your calendar to:

- Choose a topic for the paper by October 1.
- Finish the first draft by October 15.
- Review the draft with a writing tutor by October 21 (allowing time for the next step).
- Finish the final draft by October 28 (several days before the paper is due).

Creating a step-by-step plan like this one is an example of **Level 3: Applying**. Thinking at this level often means answering questions such as: How will I actually use this idea? What is the very next action I would take? What actions would come next?

Now it's your turn. Choose another suggestion from this chapter (**Level 1: Remembering**) and think about it at **Level 3: Applying**. Summarize the suggestion in one sentence. Then write a bulleted list of actions that you will take to apply the suggestion.

_____

_____

_____

_____

_____

_____

_____

_____

_____

_____

_____

_____

_____

_____

Digital Vision/Getty Images

25 WAYS
to get the most out of
NOW

The following techniques are about getting the most from your coursework. They're listed in four categories:

- **Choosing your time**
- **Choosing your place**
- **Getting focused**
- **Questions that keep you focused**

Don't feel pressured to use all of the techniques or to tackle them in order. As you read, note the suggestions you think will be helpful. Pick one technique to use now. When it becomes a habit, come back to this article and select another one. Repeat this cycle, and enjoy the results as they unfold in your life.

CHOOSING YOUR TIME

Study difficult (or boring) subjects first. If your chemistry problems put you to sleep, get to them first, while you are fresh. We tend to give top priority to what we enjoy studying, yet the courses that we find most difficult often require the most creative energy. Save your favorite subjects for later. If you find yourself avoiding a particular subject, get up an hour earlier to study it before breakfast. With that chore out of the way, the rest of the day can be a breeze.

Continually being late with course assignments indicates a trouble area. Further action is required. Clarify your intentions about the course by writing down your feelings in a journal, talking with an instructor, or asking for help from a friend or counselor. Consistently avoiding study tasks can also be a signal to reexamine your major or course program.

Be aware of your best time of day. Many people learn best in daylight hours. If this is true for you, schedule study time for your most difficult subjects or most difficult people before nightfall.

Unless you grew up on a farm, the idea of being conscious at 5 a.m. might seem ridiculous. Yet many successful businesspeople begin the day at 5 a.m. or earlier. Athletes and yoga practitioners use the early morning too. Some writers complete their best work before 9 a.m.

Others experience the same benefits by staying up late. They flourish after midnight. If you aren't convinced, then experiment. When you're in a time crunch, get up early or stay up late. You might even see a sunrise.

Use waiting time. Five minutes waiting for a subway, 20 minutes waiting for the dentist, 10 minutes in between classes—waiting time adds up fast. Have short study tasks ready to do during these periods, and keep your study materials handy. For example, carry 3 $\times$ 5 cards with facts, formulas, or definitions and pull them out anywhere. A mobile phone with an audio recording app can help you use commuting time to your advantage. Make a recording of yourself reading your notes. Play back the recording as you drive, or listen through headphones as you ride on the bus or subway.

Study two hours for every hour you're in class.
Students in higher education are regularly advised to allow 2 hours of study time for every hour spent in class. If you are taking 15 credit hours, then plan to spend 30 hours a week studying. That adds up to 45 hours each week for school—more than a full-time job. The benefits of thinking in these terms will be apparent at exam time.

This guideline is just that—a guideline, not an absolute rule. Consider what's best for you. If you do the Time Monitor/Time Plan exercise in this chapter, note how many hours you actually spend studying for each hour of class. Then ask how your schedule is working. You might want to allow more study time for some subjects.

Keep in mind that the "two hours for one" rule doesn't distinguish between focused time and unfocused time. In one four-hour block of study time, it's possible to use up two of those hours with phone calls, breaks, daydreaming, and doodling. With study time, quality counts as much as quantity.

Avoid marathon study sessions. With so many hours ahead of you, the temptation is to tell yourself, "Well, it's going to be a long day. No sense rushing into it. Better sharpen about a dozen of these pencils and change the light bulbs." Three 3-hour sessions are usually more productive than one 9-hour session.

If you must study in a large block of time, work on several subjects. Avoid studying similar topics one after the other.

Whenever you study, stop and rest for a few minutes every hour. Give your brain a chance to take a break. Simply moving to a new location might be enough to maintain your focus. When taking breaks fails to restore your energy, it's time to close the books and do something else for a while.

Monitor how much time you spend online. To get an accurate picture of your involvement in social networking and other online activities, use the Time Monitor/Time Plan process in this chapter. Then make conscious choices about how much time you want to spend on these activities. Staying connected is fine. Staying on constant alert for a new text, Twitter stream, or Facebook update distracts you from achieving your goals.

CHOOSING YOUR PLACE

Use a regular study area. Your body and your mind know where you are. Using the same place to study, day after day, helps train your responses. When you arrive at that particular place, you can focus your attention more quickly.

Study where you'll be alert. In bed, your body gets a signal. For most students, that signal is more likely to be "Time to sleep!" than "Time to study!" Just as you train your body to be alert at your desk, you also train it to slow down near your bed. For that reason, don't study where you sleep.

Easy chairs and sofas are also dangerous places to study. Learning requires energy. Give your body a message that energy is needed. Put yourself in a situation that supports this message. For example, some schools offer empty classrooms as places to study. If you want to avoid distractions, look for a room where friends are not likely to find you.

Use a library. Libraries are designed for learning. The lighting is perfect. The noise level is low. A wealth of material is available. Entering a library is a signal to focus the mind and get to work. Many students can get more done in a shorter time frame at the library than anywhere else. Experiment for yourself.

GETTING FOCUSED

Pay attention to your attention. Breaks in concentration are often caused by internal interruptions. Your own thoughts jump in to divert you from your studies. When this happens, notice these thoughts and let them go. Perhaps the thought of getting something else done is distracting you. One option is to handle that other task now and study later. Or you can write yourself a note about it or schedule a specific time to do it.

Agree with living mates about study time. This agreement includes roommates, family, spouses, and children. Make the rules about study time clear, and be sure to follow them yourself. Explicit agreements—even written contracts—work well. One student always wears a colorful hat when he wants to study. When his wife and children see the hat, they respect his wish to be left alone.

Get off the phone. The phone is the ultimate interrupter. People who wouldn't think of distracting you in person might call or text you at the worst times because they can't see that you are studying. You don't have to be a victim of your cell phone. If a simple "I can't talk; I'm studying" doesn't work, use dead silence. It's a conversation killer. Or short-circuit the whole problem: Turn off your phone or silence it.

Learn to say no. Saying no is a time-saver and a valuable life skill for everyone. Some people feel it is rude to refuse a request. But you can say no effectively and courteously. Others want you to succeed as a student. When you tell them that you can't do what they ask because you are busy educating yourself, most people will understand.

Hang a "Do not disturb" sign on your door. Many hotels will give you a free sign, for the advertising. Or you can create a sign yourself. They work. Using signs can relieve you of making a decision about cutting off each interruption—a time-saver in itself.

Get ready the night before. Completing a few simple tasks just before you go to bed can help you get in gear the next day. If you need to make some phone calls first thing in the morning, look up those numbers, write them on 3 × 5 cards, and set them near the phone. If you need to drive to a new location, make a note of the address and put it next to your car keys. If you plan to spend the next afternoon writing a paper, get your materials together: dictionary, notes, outline, paper, pencil, flash drive, laptop—whatever you need. Pack your lunch or put gas in the car. Organize the baby's diaper bag and your briefcase or backpack.

Call ahead. We often think of talking on the telephone as a prime time-waster. Used wisely, though, the telephone can actually help manage time. Before you go shopping, call the store to see whether it carries the items you're looking for. A few seconds on the phone or computer can save hours in wasted trips and wrong turns.

Avoid noise distractions. To promote concentration, avoid studying in front of the television, and turn off the radio. Many students insist that they study better with background noise, and it might be true. Some students report good results with carefully selected and controlled music. For many others, silence is the best form of music to study by.

At times noise levels might be out of your control. A neighbor or roommate might decide to find out how far she can turn up her music before the walls crumble. Meanwhile, your ability to concentrate on the principles of sociology goes down the drain. To avoid this scenario, schedule study sessions during periods when your living environment is usually quiet. If you live in a residence hall, ask whether study rooms are available. Or go somewhere else where it's quiet, such as the library. Some students have even found refuge in quiet coffee shops, self-service laundries, and places of worship.

Setting limits on screen time

Fotosearch/Getty Images

Access to the Internet and wireless communication offers easy ways to procrastinate. We call it "surfing," "texting," "IMing,"—and sometimes "researching" or "working." In his book *Crazy Busy: Overstretched, Overbooked, and About to Snap*, Edward Hallowell coined a word to describe these activities when they're done too often—*screensucking*.

Discover how much time you spend online. People who update their Twitter stream or Facebook page every hour may be sending an unintended message—that they have no life offline.

To get an accurate picture of your involvement in social networking and other online activity, monitor how much time you spend on them for one week. Then make conscious choices about how much time you want to spend online and on the phone. Don't let social networking distract you from meeting personal and academic goals.

Use technology to tame technology. See if you can set your smart phone for "airplane mode." This disables calls and text messages. While using your laptop or desktop computer, consider applications such as Freedom (macfreedom.com), SelfControl (selfcontrolapp.com), and Anti-Social (anti-social.cc). These limit or block Internet access for an amount of time that you determine in advance.

Go offline to send the message that other people matter. It's hard to pay attention to the person who is right in front of you when you're hammering out text messages or updating your Twitter stream. You can also tell when someone else is doing these things and only half listening to you.

An alternative is to close up all your devices and "be here now." When you're eating, stop answering the phone. Notice how the food tastes. When you're with a friend, close up your laptop. Hear every word he says. Rediscover where life actually takes place—in the present moment.

Developing emotional intelligence requires being with people and away from a computer or smart phone. People who break up with a partner through text messaging are not developing that intelligence. True friends know when to go offline and head across campus to resolve a conflict. They know when to go back home and support a family member in crisis. When it counts, your presence is your greatest present.

Manage interruptions. Notice how others misuse your time. Be aware of repeat offenders. Ask yourself whether there are certain friends or relatives who consistently interrupt your study time.

If avoiding the interrupter is impractical, send a clear message. Sometimes others don't realize that they are breaking your concentration. You can give them a gentle, yet firm, reminder: "What you're saying is important. Can we schedule a time to talk about it when I can give you my full attention?" If this strategy doesn't work, there are other ways to make your message more effective.

See whether you can "firewall" yourself for selected study periods each week. Find a place where you can count on being alone and working without interruption.

Sometimes interruptions still happen, though. Create a system for dealing with them. One option is to take an index card and write a quick note about what you're doing the moment an interruption occurs. As soon as possible, return to the card and pick up the task where you left off.

QUESTIONS THAT KEEP YOU FOCUSED

Ask: "What is one task I can accomplish toward achieving my goal?" This technique is helpful when you face a big, imposing job. Pick out one small accomplishment, preferably one you can complete in about 5 minutes; then do it. The satisfaction of getting one thing done can spur you on to get one more thing done. Meanwhile, the job gets smaller.

Ask: "Am I being too hard on myself?" If you are feeling frustrated with a reading assignment, your attention wanders repeatedly, or you've fallen behind on math problems that are due tomorrow, take a minute to listen to the messages you are giving yourself. Are you scolding yourself too harshly? Lighten up. Allow yourself to feel a little foolish, and then get on with the task at hand. Don't add to the problem by berating yourself.

Worrying about the future is another way people beat themselves up: "How will I ever get all this done?" "What if every paper I'm assigned turns out to be this hard?" "If I can't do the simple calculations now, how will I ever pass the final?" Instead of promoting learning, such questions fuel anxiety and waste valuable time.

Labeling and generalizing weaknesses are other ways people are hard on themselves. Being objective and specific in the messages you send yourself will help eliminate this form of self-punishment and will likely generate new possibilities. An alternative to saying "I'm terrible in algebra" is to say, "I don't understand factoring equations." This rewording suggests a plan to improve.

You might be able to lighten the load by discovering how your learning styles affect your behavior. For example, you may have a bias toward concrete experience rather than abstract thinking. If so, after setting a goal, you might want to move directly into action.

In large part, the ability to learn through concrete experience is a valuable trait. After all, action is necessary to achieve goals. At the same time, you might find it helpful to allow extra time to plan. Careful planning can help you avoid unnecessary activity. Instead of using a planner that shows a day at a time, experiment with a calendar that displays a week or month at a glance. The expanded format can help you look further into the future and stay on track as you set out to meet long-term goals.

Ask: "Is this a piano?" Carpenters who construct rough frames for buildings have a saying they use when they bend a nail or accidentally hack a chunk out of a two-by-four: "Well, this ain't no piano." It means that perfection is not necessary. Ask yourself whether what you are doing needs to be perfect. Perhaps you don't have to apply the same standards of grammar to lecture notes that you would apply to a term paper. If you can complete a job 95 percent perfectly in 2 hours and 100 percent perfectly in 4 hours, ask yourself whether the additional 5 percent improvement is worth doubling the amount of time you spend.

Sometimes, though, it *is* a piano. A tiny miscalculation can ruin an entire lab experiment. A misstep in solving a complex math problem can negate hours of work. Computers are notorious for turning little errors into nightmares. Accept lower standards only when appropriate.

A related suggestion is to weed out low-priority tasks. The to-do list for a large project can include dozens of items, not all of which are equally important. Some can be done later, while others can be skipped altogether, if time is short.

Apply this idea when you study. In a long reading assignment, look for pages you can skim or skip. When it's appropriate, read chapter summaries or article abstracts. As you review your notes, look for material that might not be covered on a test, and decide whether you want to study it.

Ask: "Can I do just one more thing?" Ask yourself this question at the end of a long day. Almost always you will have enough energy to do just one more short task. The overall increase in your productivity might surprise you.

Ask: "Can I delegate this?" Instead of slogging through complicated tasks alone, you can draw on the talents and energy of other people. Busy executives know the value of delegating tasks to coworkers. Without delegation, many projects would flounder or die.

You can apply the same principle in your life. Instead of doing all the housework or cooking by yourself, for example, you can assign some of the tasks to family members or roommates. Rather than making a trip to the library to look up a simple fact, you can call and ask a library assistant to research it for you. Instead of driving across town to deliver a package, you can hire a delivery service to do so. All of these tactics can free up extra hours for studying.

It's not practical to delegate certain study tasks, such as writing term papers or completing reading assignments. However, you can still draw on the ideas of others in completing such tasks. For instance, form a writing group to edit and critique papers, brainstorm topics or titles, and develop lists of sources.

If you're absent from a class, find a classmate to summarize the lecture, discussion, and any upcoming assignments. Presidents depend on briefings. You can use the same technique.

Ask: "How did I just waste time?" Notice when time passes and you haven't accomplished what you had planned to do. Take a minute to review your actions and note the specific ways you wasted time. We tend to operate by habit, wasting time in the same ways over and over again. When you are aware of things you do that drain your time, you are more likely to catch yourself in the act next time. Observing one small quirk might save you hours. But keep this in mind: Asking you to notice how you waste time is not intended to make you feel guilty. The point is to increase your skill by getting specific information about how you use time.

Ask: "Could I find the time if I really wanted to?" The way people speak often rules out the option of finding more time. An alternative is to speak about time with more possibility.

The next time you're tempted to say, "I just don't have time," pause for a minute. Question the truth of this statement. Could you find 4 more hours this week for studying? Suppose that someone offered to pay you $10,000 to find those 4 hours. Suppose too that you will get paid only if you don't lose sleep, call in sick for work, or sacrifice anything important to you. Could you find the time if vast sums of money were involved?

Remember that when it comes to school, vast sums of money *are* involved.

Ask: "Am I willing to promise it?" This time-management idea might be the most powerful of all: If you want to find time for a task, promise yourself—and others—that you'll get it done. Unleash one of the key qualities of master students and take responsibility for producing an outcome.

To make this technique work, do more than say that you'll try to keep a promise or that you'll give it your best shot. Take an oath, as you would in court. Give it your word.

One way to accomplish big things in life is to make big promises. There's little reward in promising what's safe or predictable. No athlete promises to place seventh in the Olympic games. Chances are that if you're not making big promises, you're not stretching yourself.

The point of making a promise is not to chain yourself to a rigid schedule or impossible expectations. You can promise to reach goals without unbearable stress. You can keep schedules flexible and carry out your plans with ease, joy, and satisfaction.

At times, though, you might go too far. Some promises may be truly beyond you, and you might break them. However, failing to keep a promise is just that—failing to keep a promise. A broken promise is not the end of the world.

Promises can work magic. When your word is on the line, it's possible to discover reserves of time and energy you didn't know existed. Promises can push you to exceed your expectations. ■

> *This time-management idea might be the most powerful of all: If you want to find time for a task, promise yourself—and others—that you'll get it done.*

BEYOND TIME MANAGEMENT:
Stay focused on what matters

© Falko Matte/Shutterstock.com

Ask some people about managing time, and a dreaded image appears in their minds. They see a person with a 100-item to-do list clutching a calendar chock full of appointments. They imagine a robot who values cold efficiency, compulsively accounts for every minute, and has no time for people.

These stereotypes about time management hold a kernel of truth. Sometimes people fixate so much on time management that they fail to appreciate what they are doing. Time management becomes a burden, a chore, a process that prevents them from actually enjoying the task at hand.

At other times, people who pride themselves on efficiency are merely keeping busy. In their rush to check items off a to-do list, they might be fussing over activities that create little value in the first place.

It might help you to think beyond time management to the larger concept of *planning*. The point of planning is not to load your schedule with obligations. Instead, planning is about getting the important things done and still having time to be human. An effective planner is productive and relaxed at the same time.

FOCUS ON VALUES

View your activities from the perspective of an entire lifetime. Given the finite space between birth and death, determine what matters most to you.

As a way to define your values, write your own obituary. Describe the ways you want to be remembered. List the contributions you intend to make during your lifetime and the kind of person you wish to become. Or simply write your life purpose—a sentence or short paragraph that describes what's most important to you. Keep this handy when scheduling your day and planning your week.

FOCUS ON OUTCOMES

You might feel guilty when you occasionally stray from your schedule and spend two hours napping or watching soap operas. But if you're regularly meeting your goals, there's probably no harm done.

Managing time and getting organized are not ends in themselves. It's possible to be efficient, organized, and miserable. Larger outcomes such as personal satisfaction and effectiveness count more than the means used to achieve them.

Visualizing a desired outcome can be as important as having a detailed action plan. Here's an experiment: Write a list of goals you plan to accomplish over the next six months. Next, create a vivid mental picture of yourself attaining those goals and enjoying the resulting benefits. Visualize this image several times in the next few weeks. Then file the list away, making a note on your calendar to review it in six months. When six months have passed, look over the list and note how many of your goals you have actually accomplished.

DO LESS

Planning is as much about dropping worthless activities as about adding new ones. See whether you can reduce or eliminate activities that contribute little to your values. When you add a new item to your calendar or to-do list, consider dropping a current one.

BUY LESS

Before you purchase an item, estimate how much time it will take to locate, assemble, use, repair, and maintain it. You might be able to free up hours by doing without. If the product comes with a 400-page manual or 20 hours of training, beware. Before rushing to the store to add another possession to your life, see whether you can reuse or adapt something you already own.

SLOW DOWN

Sometimes it's useful to hurry, such as when you're late for a meeting or about to miss a plane. At other times, haste is a choice that serves no real purpose. If you're speeding through the day like a launched missile, consider what would happen if you got to your next destination a few minutes later than planned. Rushing might not be worth the added strain.

Hill Street Studios/Blend Images/Getty Images, © Janaka Dharmasena/Shutterstock.com

FORGET ABOUT TIME

Take time away from time. Schedule downtime—a space in your day where you ignore to-do lists, appointments, and accomplishments. This period is when you're accountable to no one else and have nothing to accomplish. Even a few minutes spent in this way can yield a sense of renewal. One way to manage time is periodically to forget about it.

Experiment with decreasing your overall awareness of time. Leave your watch off for a few hours each day. Spend time in an area that's free of clocks. Notice how often you glance at your watch, and make a conscious effort to do so less often.

Strictly speaking, time cannot be managed. The minutes, hours, days, and years simply march ahead. What we can do is manage ourselves with respect to time. A few basic principles can help us do that as well as a truckload of cold-blooded techniques. ■

HANDLE IT NOW

A long to-do list can result from postponing decisions and procrastinating. An alternative is to handle a task or decision immediately. Answer that letter now. Make that phone call as soon as it occurs to you. Then you don't have to add the task to your calendar or to-do list.

The same idea applies when someone asks you to volunteer for a project and you realize immediately that you don't want to do it. Save time by graciously telling the truth up front. Saying "I'll think about it and get back to you" just postpones the conversation until later, when it might take more time.

REMEMBER PEOPLE

Few people on their deathbeds ever say, "I wish I'd spent more time at the office." They're more likely to say, "I wish I'd spent more time with my family and friends." The pace of daily life can lead us to neglect the people we cherish.

Efficiency is a concept that applies to things—not people. When it comes to maintaining and nurturing relationships, we can often benefit from loosening up our schedules. We can allow extra time for conflict management, spontaneous visits, and free-ranging conversations.

Interactive

Journal Entry 7
Intention Statement

Create a not-to-do list

One of the key skills in time management is choosing what not to do. You can discover this for yourself. Make a list of all your activities during the past 24 hours. (If you did the Time Monitor/Time Plan exercise, then review a day's worth of activity.) Next, review your list and circle any activities that have no relationship to any of your goals. Behold your *not-to-do* list.

Creating a not-to-do list is a simple, useful, and often neglected strategy for building more breathing space into your life. Some items you might want to put on this list are listed here:

- Attending meetings with no clear agenda or end time
- Checking e-mail more than twice per day
- Answering calls from numbers that you don't recognize
- Watching television on weeknights (or any night)
- Carrying a smart phone with you everywhere

Declare your own commitment to simplify your life:

I intend to stop . . .

_____

_____

_____

Michael Didyoung/Retna Ltd./Corbis

MASTER STUDENT PROFILE

SAMPSON DAVIS

(1973–) As a teenager growing up in Newark, New Jersey, Sampson made a pact with two of his friends to "beat the street," attend college, and become a physician.

Medical school was one of the roughest periods of my life. Something unexpected was always threatening to knock me out of the game: family distractions, the results of my first state board exam, the outcome of my initial search for a residency. But through determination, discipline, and dedication, I was able to persevere.

I call them my three D's, and I believe that they are the perfect formula for survival, no matter what you are going through.

Determination is simply fixing your mind on a desired outcome, and I believe it is the first step to a successful end in practically any situation. When I made the pact with George and Rameck at the age of 17, I was desperate to change my life. Going to college and medical school with my friends seemed the best way to make that happen.

But, of course, I had no idea of the challenges awaiting me, and many times over the years I felt like giving up. Trust me, even if you're the most dedicated person, you can get weary when setbacks halt or interfere with your progress. But determination means nothing without the discipline to go through the steps necessary to reach your goal—whether you're trying to lose weight or finish college—and the dedication to stick with it.

When I failed the state board exam, the light in the tunnel disappeared. But I just kept crawling toward my goal. I sought counseling when I needed it, and I found at least one person with whom I could share the range of emotions I was experiencing. If you're going through a difficult time and can't see your way out alone, you

Sampson Davis *is determined.* **You** *can be determined by defining goals that make a huge difference in your life.*

should consider asking for help. I know how difficult that is for most guys. . . . But reaching out to counselors I had come to trust over the years and talking to my roommate Camille helped me unload some of the weight I was carrying. Only then was I able to focus clearly on what I needed to do to change my circumstances.

I'm grateful that I took kung fu lessons as a kid, because the discipline I learned back then really helped me to stay consistent once I started meditating, working out, and studying every single day. . . .

Another important ingredient of perseverance is surrounding yourself with friends who support your endeavor. I can't tell you how much it helped me to have George and Rameck in my life to help me reach my goal. Even though things were awkward between us for a while after I failed the state boards, just knowing they were there and that they expected me to succeed motivated me.

I found motivation wherever I could. One of my college professors once told me that I didn't have what it takes to be a doctor, and I even used that to motivate me. I love being the underdog. I love it when someone expects me to fail. That, like nothing else, can ignite my three D's.

And when success comes, I'm the one who's not surprised. ■

Source: "Sam on Perseverance," from The Pact *by Sampson Davis, George Jenkins, and Rameck Hunt, with Liza Frazier Page. Copyright © 2002 by Three Doctors LLC. Used by permission of Riverhead Books, an imprint of Penguin Group (USA), Inc.*

1. The Power Process: Be here now rules out planning. True or false? Explain your answer.
   False. Remember that planning supports this Power Process. Goals are tools that we create to guide our action in the present. Time management techniques—calendars, lists, and all the rest—have only one purpose. They reveal what's most important for you to focus on right now. (*Power Process: Be here now*, page 62)

2. According to the text, everything written about time management can be reduced to three main ideas. What are they?
   (1) Know exactly what you want. State your wants as clear, specific goals, and put them in writing.
   (2) Know how to get what you want. Take action to meet your goals. Determine what you'll do today to get what you want in the future. Put those actions in writing as well.
   (3) Go for balance. When our lives lack this quality, we spend most of our time responding to interruptions, last-minute projects, and emergencies. Life feels like a scramble just to survive. We're so busy achieving someone else's goals that we forget about getting what we want. (*You've got the time*, page 63)

3. Rewrite the statement "I want to study harder" so that it becomes a specific goal.
   I will study one more hour each night, Monday through Friday, for the next 30 days. After that, I will reflect and evaluate on the impact it has had on my performance in college. (Answers will vary.) (*Setting and achieving goals*, page 71)

4. Define *C fever* as it applies to the ABC priority method.
   (Answers will vary.) When using the ABC priority method, you might experience an ailment common to students: C fever. Symptoms include the uncontrollable urge to drop that A task and begin crossing C's off your to-do list. The reason C fever is so common is that A tasks are usually more difficult or time-consuming to achieve, with a higher risk of failure. (*The ABC daily to-do list*, page 74)

5. You can rank your to-do list items with the ABC priority method. Explain an alternative to this method.
   (Answers will vary.) Some people prefer the 80–20 system. This method is based on the idea that 80 percent of the value of any to-do list comes from only 20 percent of the tasks on that list. So on a to-do list of 10 items, find the two that will contribute most to your life today. Complete these tasks without fail. (*The ABC daily to-do list*, page 74)

6. Define the term *multitasking* and explain one strategy for dealing with it.
   (Answers will vary.) Multitasking can be defined as doing several things at the same time. Examples of multitasking include watching TV and reading a textbook, talking on the phone and outlining a paper, writing an e-mail and listening to a lecture, and so on. Whenever possible, only work on one task at a time in order to develop focused attention. (*Make choices about multitasking*, page 64)

7. Define the term *time boxing*.
   Time boxing can be defined as setting aside a specific number of minutes or hours to spend on a certain task. Instead of working on that task until it's done, commit to work on it just for that specific amount of time. Then set a timer and get to work. In effect, you're placing the task inside a definite "box"—a specific space on your daily calendar. It is one way to overcome resistance to a task, focus your attention, and make a meaningful dent in a large project (*Planning sets you free*, page 76)

8. The text suggests that you do your Most Important Task (MIT):
   (a) During the middle of the day.   (b) As early in the day as possible.
   (c) Right before going to sleep.   (d) At whatever time during the day that you can squeeze it in.
   (b) As early in the day as possible. (*Planning sets you free*, page 76)

9. According to the text, overcoming procrastination is a complex process that can take months or even years. True or false? Explain your answer.
   False. According to the text, ending procrastination is simply a matter of deciding to end it and then acting on that decision. (*Stop procrastination NOW*, page 86)

10. What are at least 3 of the 25 ways to get the most out of now?
    (Answers will vary.) Study difficult (or boring) subjects first; be aware of your best time of day; study 2 hours for every hour you're in class (*25 ways to get the most out of now*, page 89)

 SKILLS SNAPSHOT
Chapter 2

Before moving on to a new chapter in this book, take a snapshot of your current skills in time management. Clarify your intentions to develop more mastery in this area of your life. Then clear a path to taking action.

Discovery
My score on the Time section of the Discovery Wheel was . . .

When it comes to time management, I am skilled at . . .

To get better at time management, I could . . .

A suggestion from this chapter that can help me achieve one of my personal goals is . . .

Intention
A suggestion from this chapter that I will use as long as I'm in school is . . .

A suggestion from this chapter that I will use in my career is . . .

Action
To put the suggestions I just listed into practice, the next actions I will take are . . .

Some possible obstacles to taking those actions are . . .

To overcome these obstacles, I will . . .

INSTRUCTOR TOOLS & TIPS

MEMORY

"The art of true memory is the art of attention." —Samuel Johnson

PREVIEW

A primary objective of student success courses is to foster the fundamental skill of memorizing key information. Simplified, memory is a biological brain change. In one of the most remarkable discoveries about memory and the human brain, neuroscientists at Washington University in St. Louis, using functional MRI technology, point to literal changes in the brain's activity as different learning processes take place.

New learning is accomplished when, within the brain's cognitive neural structure, the student's existing emotional markers match or connect the new information to be learned within the existing brain structure. Understanding the principles of brain-active learning presented in this chapter will help students learn more in less time. It is frustrating when we can't remember something we're certain that we know, especially in a high-stakes situation, such as during a test or at a job interview.

This chapter opens with new information about the brain—how it changes physically by growing more connections between neurons. Help your students improve their memory by learning to "wire" those neural networks into place.

GUEST SPEAKER

Consider inviting a psychology or anatomy colleague as your guest speaker to talk to your students about how the brain works. Your current or former students can also be used as guest speakers. Most students are more receptive to hearing from their peers. Having a student presentation also helps to break up the amount of time spent as the instructor in front of the classroom. For this chapter, ask former students to talk about *Why* Sonia Sotomayor is an example of a master student; *What* qualities Sotomayor has that they would like to emulate; *How* they could obtain and practice these qualities; and *What if,* like Sonia Sotomayor, they fought for what they believed in. Consider videotaping these students as they present the material. A well-stocked library of guest speakers can come in handy when experienced students

master instructor best practice

"I have always loved the 25 memory techniques. . . . In my classes I stress the importance of making all techniques your own. Needless to say, the custom-made memory system is right on target! Throughout the list of techniques, I especially like that each technique has a clear-cut example for the student. It also gives each student choices."

—Maria Parnell, Brevard Community College

are not readily available. This can become a valuable shared resource among other faculty on your campus teaching the course as well. Pool your resources to help make your job's easier.

LECTURE

Consider lecturing about some of the 25 memory techniques you used when you were a student, clarifying how students can use these techniques to maximize their effectiveness in college classes. Provide personal examples of what did and what didn't work for you as a student. For example, you may recall a time when you crammed for an exam, memorizing material, only to forget everything in a week. Students relate to us more readily when they realize that learning is challenging for all of us at times. Another approach is to invite students to ask you for additional information about articles in this chapter.

Workplace Applications: Memory tips for work. Students can use the suggestions found in this chapter to improve memory function in the workplace. Many skills that are important at work like organizing, minimizing distractions, and learning actively are also helpful at

master instructor
best practice

"Here's how I explained Q-Cards (page 112) to a student. I had a frustrated student tell me that, although she had studied and studied, she had failed her exam in biology. We reviewed her study methods: She had created flash cards by putting a question on one side and the answer on the other. Her review questions did not align well with the instructor's test questions, so she was unable to retrieve answers from her memory during the exam. Q-Cards have a question on both sides. Here's the trick: The question on each side of the card contains the answer to the question on the other side. This portable studying device helps students break information into manageable pieces and forces them to use a higher level of thinking. You can promote even further connection with materials by asking students to draw pictures to help them remember concepts. Reviewing these materials consistently before an exam will aid students' recall."

—Eldon McMurray, Utah Valley State College

improving memory. As employees, your students may be called upon in meetings or presentations to share detailed information from memory. Preparation is key. Although employees may not know exactly what to expect at each meeting or presentation, they can review previously shared information, research statistics, and jot down quick notes before the meeting. Encourage them to first relax and know that it is okay to review notes or to ask for permission to gather the requested information as soon as possible.

Good health habits, including both eating well and exercising, improve memory and work performance. An active life outside of work also keeps the brain active and improves memory. Explain to students the importance of work-life balance. Participating in hobbies, spending time with family and friends, and taking care of oneself are all important elements of the successful employee.

For additional lecture ideas, go to Chapter 3 resources in the Course Manual.

EXERCISES/ACTIVITIES

1. **Power Process: Love your problems (page 100).** One of many problem-solving tools in *Becoming a Master Student*, this Power Process helps students explore an alternative to avoiding problems they encounter in college. By embracing a problem, you can diffuse its energy and find a solution. To illustrate this process with an in-class activity, bring a word puzzle or mind game to class. Students who hate these types of puzzles get frustrated. Competitive students become anxious because each wants to be the first to solve it. Allow time for students to try to solve the problem by getting into it. Tell them to relax; enjoy the process; notice their frustration level, competitiveness, and anxiety; and just love the problem. Many students are able to solve the puzzle, individually or in groups. Ask students who enjoy this process to share aloud why they find this process exciting.

2. **The loci system (page 114).** Humor can be an effective memory motivator. Memory techniques that include bizarre, humorous elements stick with us. Demonstrate in class how making up a funny story can help with memorizing word lists. Explain the concept of the loci system, pointing out that because you are all familiar with the classroom, it will serve as the "location" from which to model this technique. But, normally, they would choose a location such as their living room or bedroom, one that they can visualize easily. Start by asking for a show of hands from students who think they can name the first six presidents of the United States. Some students will raise their hands. Then ask how many students think they can remember the presidents in order—that is, if asked for the fifth president, they can recall the fifth president's name. Usually, only one or two students will raise their hands. Write this list on the board for reference:

1. George Washington
2. John Adams
3. Thomas Jefferson
4. James Madison
5. James Monroe
6. John Quincy Adams

Now, position six students around the classroom, each representing one of the presidents. Because location is a key element in the loci system, you can make special note of the placement of students. Then ask each student to make some distinct, unique movement and to state the name of the president he or she represents. For example, the first student standing near the door can wave and say, "I am George Washington." The second student, standing perhaps near the instructor's desk, can jump up and down, saying, "I am John Adams." Then farther to the left, a student standing at the board can shake his head and announce, "I am Thomas Jefferson." Continue with all six students (presidents). Ask these students to repeat this pattern several times. Point out that repetition and recitation help the memory process. Also, the rest of the students in the class hear the "president" students speak (auditory) and watch their motions (visual). This links the order of the presidents with the space order in the room—left to right, near to far. Linking funny gestures and voice patterns can contribute to the strength of the memory process.

Students usually find the process foolishly humorous, which helps them remember it. As you repeat the process, remind students to focus completely on the presidents' names ("Be here now"). Repeat the names, and ask them to join you and talk through the list in unison. The next step is to erase or cover up the words on the board and recite the list again in unison. Next, go up and down the rows, asking students to name the president that goes with a certain number. If a student can't recall the name, ask her to say the list aloud from the beginning. By the time the student gets to the name, she usually can recall it. This usually takes a total of about five minutes. Next, say a number, and ask students to raise their hands if they know the name that goes with that number. Select one student to confirm the name. Continue until it is clear that everyone knows all the names and the number order associated with them.

Point out that if students can memorize six names in five minutes, in order, then they can also memorize important terms for tests fairly quickly if they focus their attention and create a system for memorization. This chapter contains many memorization tools. Most students initially think they can't memorize these names in order, so this exercise boosts confidence in their memory too.

3. **Remembering names (page 119).** This exercise can be used as an opportunity for building relationships. Start students off in groups of four. Have them use tools described in the article to help remember the names of the people in each small group. Then the groups combine to make groups of 8, then 16, then 32, and so on, until everyone in the class can say the first name of every classmate. Talk about how it feels when someone remembers your name and, conversely, how it feels when someone fails to remember your name. Ask students to share stories of times when they failed to remember an important name, and the consequences or embarrassment this may have caused them. Emphasize the importance of this skill in their personal lives and in the workplace as well.

CONVERSATION/SHARING

Divide students into small groups to discuss the topic of memorization in college. Students should share their frustrations with memorization as well as a successful experience they've had remembering something important.

After your students begin to read about memory and learn to activate the connections between neurons, you will have empowered them to connect memory to their learning styles. So they see the connection, be sure to articulate this to your students.

Why?	Why do master students need to have confidence in their ability to remember what they study? Why do master students need these skills in the workplace? Ask students for examples in their own work experiences.
What?	What is memory? Read through the list of articles in this chapter, and pick three that look interesting. What about these three articles interests you?
How?	How can knowing more about how your memory works improve your memory skills? How will this help you in college and in life?
What if?	What if you start to apply these memory techniques to your other classes? And what if you don't? What if employees are unable to demonstrate these skills in the workplace?

HOMEWORK

Remembering your car keys—or anything else (page 113). This exercise helps students practice Learning Styles Mode 3, "How can I use this?" Students are asked to apply the strategies they are learning to a specific, personal memorization situation. An alternative to this assignment would be to ask students to bring in a memorization task from one of their current classes for discussion and analysis in class in groups. As an optional assignment, ask students to research Temple Grandin. As a primarily visual learner diagnosed with autism, Grandin has used her unique visual memory to pave the way for human autistic intervention as well as thoughtful and humane handling of animals.

Get creative (page 115). Students enjoy this creative opportunity to invent their own mnemonic device.

Move from problems to solutions (page 118). Here students discover that they can solve their own problems and that such solutions are usually the most effective.

EVALUATION

Quiz Ideas for Chapter 3
Ask students to:

- Describe four memory techniques from the chapter that work for them and explain how they have used them.
- Describe the tool of setting a trap for your memory.
- Explain the memory process stages and how they can take care of their brain.
- Explain what "love your problems" means.
- Explain why Sonia Sotomayor is considered a master student.

MindTap™ EMBRACE VALUABLE RESOURCES

FOR CHAPTER 3

STUDENT RESOURCES: MINDTAP

- **Learning Outcomes.** Every chapter begins with an engaging video that visually outlines in a mind map format the key learning outcomes for that chapter. Students should find these short introductions not only helpful as chapter organizers, but as valuable note-taking models.

- **Engagement Activity: Master Students in Action.** In this video, Dave Ellis introduces the key memory concepts that students will explore in this chapter.

- **Aplia Homework Assignment: Q-Cards and mnemonic devices.** In this assignment, students

create Q-cards based on given reading assignments and identify the various mnemonic devices that will help them recall important information. By examining a reading they are likely to encounter in future college courses, students are asked to identify what information best belongs on a Q-card.

- **Reflection Activity: A Slice of Monte's Life.** This Slice of Life video, created by student Monte Pope, discusses his need to develop methods of learning very efficiently in order to balance life and work with school.

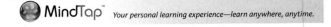

INSTRUCTOR COMPANION SITE

- **Looking for fresh, innovative ways to teach Chapter 3 topics?** Browse through the Best Practices recommendations in the Course Manual to see what other Master Instructors have been successfully doing with their students.

- **Check out the PowerPoint Library for a PowerPoint specifically created for Chapter 3.** This master library of PowerPoint

presentations makes it easy to find the right Power-Point for you! If you're looking for a way to freshen up your lecture, the PowerPoint Library is a great place to start.

Please visit login.cengage.com to log in and access the Instructor Companion Site.

Why

Learning memory techniques can boost your skills at test taking, reading, note taking, and many other tasks.

How

Think of a time when you struggled to remember something that was important. Perhaps you were trying to remember someone's name or recall some key information for a test. Then scan this chapter and find at least three strategies that you will use to prevent this problem in the future.

What if...

I could use my memory to its full potential?

NEW

Your memory and your brain—6 key principles
Sharpening your memory starts with understanding how memory depends on a squishy organ that's inside your head—your brain. Understand these six key things about how you remember and learn. ■ 101

The Memory Jungle ■ 104

TECH

Retool your memory The demands on our attention have accelerated steadily. Yet technology can also be used to increase our mental focus and enhance our memory. ■ 116

What is included ...

© iStockphoto.com/Miroslav Ferkuniak/StudiotOne

POWER PROCESS

LOVE YOUR
PROBLEMS

We all have problems and barriers that block our progress or prevent us from moving into new areas. Often, the way we respond to our problems places limitations on what we can be, do, and have.

Problems often work like barriers. When we bump up against one of our problems, we usually turn away and start walking along a different path. And all of a sudden—bump!—we've struck another barrier. And we turn away again.

As we continue to bump into problems and turn away from them, our lives stay inside the same old boundaries. Inside these boundaries, we are unlikely to have new adventures. We are unlikely to keep learning.

If we respond to problems by loving them instead of resisting them, we can expand the boundaries in which we live our lives.

The word *love* might sound like an overstatement. In this Power Process, the word means to unconditionally accept the fact that your problems exist. The more we deny or resist a problem, the stronger it seems to become. When we accept the fact that we have a problem, we can find effective ways to deal with it.

Suppose one of your barriers is taking a final exam in one of your courses. You fear that you'll forget everything you tried to memorize.

One option for dealing with this barrier is denial. You could walk into the exam room and pretend that you're not afraid. You could tell yourself, "I'm not going to be scared," and then try to force a smile on your face.

A more effective approach is to love your fear. Go into the room, notice how you actually feel, and say to yourself, "I am scared. I notice that my knees are shaking and my mouth feels dry, and I'm having a rush of thoughts about what might happen if I screw up this exam. Yup, I'm scared, and I'm not going to fight it. I'm going to take this exam anyway."

You can apply the same approach to just about any fear—fear of math courses, fear of sounding silly when learning a new language, fear of making mistakes when learning a musical instrument, fear of looking silly when dancing, and much more.

The beauty of this Power Process is that you continue to stay in action—by taking the exam, for example—no matter what you feel. You walk right up to the barrier and then *through* it. You might even find that if you totally accept and experience a barrier, such as fear, it shrinks or disappears. When you relax, you reclaim your natural abilities. You can more easily recall the main points from your notes and readings and maybe even crack a real smile. Even if this does not happen right away, you can still open up to a new experience, apply a strategy for reducing test anxiety, and learn something.

It is impossible to live a life that's free of problems. In fact, problems serve a purpose. They provide opportunities to participate in life. Problems stimulate us and pull us forward.

Seen from this perspective, our goal becomes not to eliminate problems, but to find problems that are worthy of us. The problems worth loving are those that can be solved with the greatest benefits for ourselves and others. Engaging with big problems changes us for the better. Bigger problems give more meaning to our lives.

Loving a problem does not mean *liking* it, by the way. Instead, loving a problem means admitting the truth about it. This helps us take effective action—which can free us of the problem once and for all.

YOUR MEMORY AND YOUR BRAIN—
6 key principles

Sharpening your memory starts with understanding how memory depends on a squishy organ that's inside your head—your brain. Following are six key things to remember about how you remember and learn. They will introduce you to ideas and suggestions that are presented in more detail in the rest of this chapter.

PRINCIPLE 1: SEE MEMORY AS SOMETHING YOU *DO*—NOT SOMETHING YOU HAVE

Once upon a time, people talked about human memory as if it were a closet. You stored individual memories there as you would old shirts and stray socks. Remembering something was a matter of rummaging through all that stuff. If you were lucky, you found what you wanted.

This view of memory creates some problems. For one thing, closets can get crowded. Things too easily disappear. Even with the biggest closet, you eventually run out of space. If you want to pack some new memories in there—well, too bad. There's no room.

Brain researchers shattered this image to bits. Memory is not a closet. It's not a place or a thing. Instead, memory is a *process* that's based in the brain.

On a conscious level, memories appear as distinct and unconnected mental events: words, sensations, images. They can include details from the distant past—the smell of cookies baking in your grandmother's kitchen, or the feel of sunlight warming your face through the window of your first-grade classroom.

On a biological level, each of those memories involves millions of brain cells, or neurons, firing chemical messages to one another. If you could observe these exchanges in real time, you'd see regions of cells all over the brain glowing with electrical charges at speeds that would put a computer to shame.

When a series of brain cells connects several times in a similar pattern, the result is a memory. Psychologist Donald Hebb explains it this way: "Neurons which fire together, wire together."[1]

It means that memories are not really stored. Instead, remembering is a process in which you *encode* information as links between active neurons that fire together. You also *decode*, or reactivate, neurons that wired together in the past.

© iStockphoto.com/sturti

Memory is the probability that certain patterns of brain activity will occur again in the future. In effect, you recreate a memory each time you recall it.

Scientists tell us that the human brain is "plastic." Whenever you efficiently encode and decode, your brain changes physically. You grow more connections between neurons. The more you learn, the greater the number of connections.

For all practical purposes, there's no limit to how many memories your brain can process. Knowing this allows you to step out of your crowded mental closet into a world of infinite possibilities.

PRINCIPLE 2: REMEMBER THAT THE MEMORY PROCESS WORKS IN STAGES

The memory process consists of a series of events. To make the most of your memory, apply an appropriate memory strategy when one of these events takes place:

- *Pay attention to sense experiences.* Memories start as events that we see, hear, feel, touch, or taste. Memory strategies at this stage are about choosing where to focus your attention.

- *"Move" sense experiences to short-term memory.* Sensory memories last for only a few seconds. If you don't want them to disappear, then immediately apply a strategy for moving them into short-term memory, such as reciting the information to yourself several times. Short-term memory is a place where you can "hold" those fleeting sensory memories for up to several minutes.

- *Encode for long-term memory.* If you want to recall information for more than a few minutes, then wire the new neural connections in a more stable way. This calls for a more sophisticated memory strategy—one that allows you to refire the connections for days, weeks, months, or even years into the future.

- *Decode important information on a regular basis.* The more often that you recall information, the more stable the memory becomes. To remember it, retrieve it.

PRINCIPLE 3: SINK DEEPLY INTO SENSE EXPERIENCE

Your brain's contact with the world comes through your five senses. So, anchor your learning in as many senses as possible. For example:

- *Create images.* Draw mind map summaries of your readings and lecture notes. Include visual images. Put main ideas in larger letters and brighter colors.

- *Translate ideas in physical objects.* If one of your career goals is to work from a home office, for example, then create a model of your ideal workspace. Visit an art supplies store to find appropriate materials.

- *Immerse yourself in concrete experiences.* Say that you're in a music appreciation class and learning about jazz. Go to a local jazz club or concert to see and hear a live performance.

PRINCIPLE 4: CHOOSE STRATEGIES FOR ENCODING

Signs of encoding mastery are making choices about *what* to remember and *how* to remember it. This in turn makes it easier for you to decode, or recall, the material at a crucial point in the future—such as during a test.

Say that you're enjoying a lecture in introduction to psychology. It really makes sense. In fact, it's so interesting that you choose to just sit and listen—without taking notes. Two days later, you're studying for a test and wish you'd made a different choice. You remember that the lecture was interesting, but you don't recall much else. In technical terms, your decision to skip note taking was an *encoding error.*

So, you decide to change your behavior and take extensive notes during the next psychology lecture. Your goal is to capture everything the instructor says. This too has mixed results—a case of writer's cramp and 10 pages of dense, confusing scribbles. Oops—another encoding error.

Effective encoding is finding a middle ground between these two extremes. Make moment-to-moment choices about what you want to remember. As you read or listen to a lecture, distinguish between key points, transitions, and minor details. Predict what material is likely to appear on a test. You also stay alert for ideas you can actively apply. These are things you capture in your notes.

Another strategy for effective encoding is to find and create patterns. Your brain is a pattern-making machine. It excels at taking random bits of information and translating them into meaningful wholes. For instance:

- *Use your journal.* Write Discovery and Intention Statements like the ones in this book. Journal Entries prompt you to elaborate on what you hear in class and read in your textbooks. You can create your own writing prompts. For example: "In class today, I discovered that . . ." "In order to overcome my confusion about this topic, I intend to . . ."

- *Send yourself a message.* Imagine that an absent classmate has asked you to send her an e-mail about what happened in class today. Write up a reply and send this e-mail to yourself. You'll actively process your recent learning—and create a summary that you can use to review for tests.

- *Play with ideas.* Copy your notes on to 3 × 5 cards, one fact or idea per card. Then see whether you can arrange them into new patterns—chronological order, order of importance, or main ideas and supporting details.

PRINCIPLE 5: CHOOSE STRATEGIES FOR DECODING

You've probably experienced the "tip of the tongue" phenomenon. You know that the fact or idea that you want to remember is just within reach—so close that you can almost feel it. Even so, the neural connections stop just short of total recall. This is an example of a decoding glitch.

No need to panic. You have many options at this point. These are known as decoding strategies. For example:

- *Relax.* Your mood affects your memory. The information that you want to recall is less likely to appear if you're feeling overly stressed. Taking a long, deep breath and relaxing muscles can work wonders for your body and your brain.

- **Let it go for the moment.** When information is at the tip of your tongue, one natural response is to try hard to remember it. However, this can just create more stress that in turn interferes with decoding. Another option is to stop trying to decode and to do something else for the moment. Don't be surprised if the memory you were seeking suddenly pops into your awareness while you're in the midst of an unrelated activity.

- **Recall something else.** Many encoding strategies are based on association—finding relationships between something you already know and something new that you want to remember. This means that you can often recall information by taking advantage of those associations. Say that you're taking a multiple-choice test and can't remember the answer to a question. Instead of worrying about this, just move on. You might come across a later question on the same topic that triggers the answer to the earlier question. This happens when a key association is activated.

- **Recreate the original context.** Encoding occurs at specific times and places. If a fact or idea eludes you at the moment, then see whether you can recall where you were when you first learned it. Think about what time of day that learning took place and what kind of mood you were in. Sometimes you can decode the information merely by remembering where you wrote the information in your class notes or where on the page you saw it in a book.

PRINCIPLE 6: TAKE CARE OF YOUR BRAIN

Because memory is a brain-based process, it's important to take care of your brain. Starting now, adopt habits to keep your brain lean and fit for life. Consider these research-based suggestions from the Alzheimer's Association.[2]

- **Stay mentally active.** Play challenging games and work crossword puzzles. Seek out museums, theaters, concerts, and other cultural events. Consider learning another language, taking up a musical instrument, traveling to another country, or starting a part-time business. Lifelong learning gives your brain a workout, much like sit-ups condition your abs.

- **Stay socially active.** Having a network of supportive friends can reduce stress levels. In turn, stress management helps to maintain connections between brain cells. Stay socially active by working, volunteering, and joining clubs.

- **Stay physically active.** Physical activity promotes blood flow to the brain. It also reduces the risk of diabetes, cardiovascular disease, and other diseases that can impair brain function. Exercise that includes mental activity—such as learning to dance or doing yoga—offers added benefits.

- **Adopt a brain-healthy diet.** A diet rich in dark-skinned fruits and vegetables boosts your supply of antioxidants—natural chemicals that nourish your brain. Examples of these foods are raisins, blueberries, blackberries, strawberries, raspberries, kale, spinach, brussels sprouts, alfalfa sprouts, and broccoli. Avoid foods that are high in saturated fat and cholesterol, which may increase the risk of Alzheimer's disease.

- **Protect your heart.** In general, what's good for your heart is good for your brain. Protect both organs by eating well, exercising regularly, managing your weight, staying tobacco-free, and getting plenty of sleep. These habits reduce your risk of heart attack, stroke, and other cardiovascular conditions that interfere with blood flow to the brain. ■

Interactive

Journal Entry 8
Discovery/Intention Statement

Reflect on the care and feeding of your brain

Review the list of suggestions for taking care of your brain in "Your memory and your brain—6 key principles." Then complete the following sentences:

I discovered that brain health habits I already practice include . . .

_____

_____

_____

_____

_____

To take even better care of my brain, I intend to adopt a new habit of . . .

_____

_____

_____

_____

_____

THE MEMORY JUNGLE

Think of your memory as a vast, overgrown jungle. This memory jungle is thick with wild plants, exotic shrubs, twisted trees, and creeping vines. It spreads over thousands of square miles—dense, tangled, forbidding.

In the jungle there are animals—millions of them. The animals represent all of the information in your memory. Imagine that every thought, mental picture, or perception you ever had is represented by an animal in this jungle.

Also imagine that the jungle is encompassed on all sides by towering mountains. There is only one entrance to the jungle, a small meadow that is reached by a narrow pass through the mountains.

The memory jungle has two rules: Each thought animal must pass through the meadow at the entrance to the jungle. And once an animal enters the jungle, it never leaves.

Every single event ever perceived by any of your five senses—sight, touch, hearing, smell, or taste—is a thought animal that passed through the meadow and entered the jungle. Some of the thought animals, such as the color of your seventh-grade teacher's favorite sweater, are well hidden. Other thoughts, such as your cell phone number or the position of the reverse gear in your car, are easier to find.

The meadow represents short-term memory. You use this kind of memory when you look up a telephone number and hold it in your memory long enough to make a call. Short-term memory appears to have a limited capacity (the meadow is small) and disappears fast (animals pass through the meadow quickly).

The jungle itself represents long-term memory. This kind of memory allows you to recall information from day to day, week to week, and year to year. Remember that thought animals never leave the long-term memory jungle. The following visualizations can help you recall useful concepts about memory.

VISUALIZATION 1: A WELL-WORN PATH

Imagine what happens as a thought—in this case, we'll call it an elephant—bounds across short-term memory and into the jungle. The elephant leaves a trail of broken twigs and hoof prints that you can follow.

Brain research suggests that thoughts can wear "paths" in the brain.[3] These paths consist of dendrites—string-like fibers that connect brain cells. The more these connections are activated, the easier it is to retrieve (recall) the thought. In other words, the more often the elephant retraces the path, the clearer the path becomes. The more often you recall information and the more often you put the same information into your memory, the easier it is to find.

When you buy a new car, for example, the first few times you try to find reverse, you have to think for a moment. After you have found the reverse gear every day for a week, the path is worn into your memory. After a year, the path is so well worn that when you dream about driving your car backward, you even dream the correct motion for putting the gear in reverse.

VISUALIZATION 2: A HERD OF THOUGHTS

The second picture you can use to your advantage in recalling concepts about memory is the picture of many animals gathering at a clearing—like thoughts gathering at a central location in memory. It is easier to retrieve thoughts that are grouped together, just as it is easier to find a herd of animals than it is to find a single elephant.

Pieces of information are easier to recall if you can associate them with similar information. For example, you can more readily remember a particular player's batting average if you can associate it with other baseball statistics.

VISUALIZATION 3: TURNING YOUR BACK

Imagine releasing the elephant into the jungle, turning your back, and counting to 10. When you turn around, the elephant is gone. This is exactly what happens to most of the information you receive.

Psychological research consistently shows that we start forgetting new material almost as soon as we learn it. The memory loss is steep, with most of it occurring within the first 24 hours.[4] This means that much of the material is not being encoded. It is wandering around, lost in the memory jungle.

The remedy is simple: Review quickly. Do not take your eyes off the thought animal as it crosses the short-term memory meadow. Look at it again (review it) soon after it enters the long-term memory jungle. Wear a path in your memory immediately.

VISUALIZATION 4: DIRECTING THE ANIMAL TRAFFIC

The fourth picture is one you are in. You are standing at the entrance to the short-term memory meadow, directing herds of thought animals as they file through the pass, across the meadow, and into your long-term memory. You are taking an active role in the learning process. You are paying attention. You are doing more than sitting on a rock and watching the animals file past into your brain. You have become part of the process, and in doing so, you have taken control of your memory. ∎

25 MEMORY TECHNIQUES

Experiment with these techniques to develop a flexible, custom-made memory system that fits your style of learning. These techniques are divided into five groups, each of which represents a general principle for improving memory.

Your first task is to escape the short-term memory trap. Capture new information before it disappears from your attention.

Don't stop there. Then you can encode it by *thinking*—playing with information to make it more vivid in your mind. Also encode by *feeling*—by making an emotional connection with ideas and information. And, encode by *moving*—using your body as well as your brain.

In addition, decode by recalling key information on a regular basis. And instead of saying, "I don't remember," say, "It will come to me." The latter statement implies that the information you want is encoded in your brain and that you can retrieve it—just not right now.

Adopt the attitude that you never forget. You might not believe this right now. That's okay. Just be willing to test the idea and see where it leads.

ESCAPE THE SHORT-TERM MEMORY TRAP

1 **Start by understanding the nature of short-term memory.** It's different from the kind of memory you'll need during exam week. For example, most of us can look at an unfamiliar seven-digit phone number once and remember it long enough to dial it. See whether you can recall that number the next day. Short-term memory can fade after a few minutes, and it rarely lasts more than several hours. Come to the rescue with any of the following techniques.

2 **Chunk it.** You already use this technique to dial phone numbers with an area code. For instance, 8006128030 gets chunked into several groups of numbers: 800-612-8030. Chunking works with many other types of information as well. To help you remember the techniques in this article, for instance, they are already chunked into five groups.

3 **Recite and repeat.** When you repeat something out loud, you anchor the concept in two different senses. First, you get the physical sensation in your throat, tongue, and lips when voicing the concept.

Second, you hear it. The combined result is synergistic, just as it is when you create pictures. That is, the effect of using two different senses is greater than the sum of their individual effects.

The "out loud" part is important. Reciting silently in your head can be useful—in the library, for example. Yet it is not as effective as making noise. Your mind can trick itself into thinking it knows something when it doesn't. Your ears are harder to fool.

Don't forget to move your mouth. During a lecture, ask questions. Read key passages from textbooks out loud. Use a louder voice for the main points.

The repetition part is important too. Repetition is a common memory device because it works. Repetition blazes a trail through the pathways of your brain, making the information easier to find. Repeat a concept out loud until you know it; then say it five more times.

Recitation works best when you recite concepts in your own words. For example, if you want to remember that the acceleration of a falling body due to gravity at sea level equals 32 feet per second per second, you might say, "Gravity makes an object accelerate 32 feet per second faster for each second that it's in the air at sea level." Putting a concept into your own words forces you to think about it.

Have some fun with this technique. Recite by writing a song about what you're learning. Sing it in the shower. Or imitate someone. Imagine your textbook being read by Will Ferrell, Madonna, or Johnny Depp.

4 **Review as soon as possible.** A short review within minutes of a class or study session can move material from short-term memory into long-term memory. That quick mini-review—paired with a weekly review of all your class notes—can save you hours of study time when exams roll around.

ENCODE BY THINKING

5 **Be selective.** There's a difference between gaining understanding and drowning in information. During your stay in higher education, you will be exposed to thousands of facts and ideas. No one expects you to memorize all of them. To a large degree, the art of memory is the art of selecting what to remember in the first place.

As you dig into your textbooks and notes, make choices about what is most important to learn. Imagine that you are going to create a test on the material, and consider the questions you would ask.

When reading, look for chapter previews, summaries, and review questions. Pay attention to anything printed in bold type. Also notice visual elements—tables, charts, graphs, and illustrations. They are all clues pointing to what's important. During lectures, notice what the instructor emphasizes. Anything that's presented visually—on the board, in overheads, or with slides—is probably key.

6 **Elaborate with questions.** *Elaboration* means consciously encoding new information. Repetition is one basic way to elaborate. However, current brain research indicates that other types of elaboration are more effective for long-term memory.

One way to elaborate is to ask yourself questions about incoming information: "Does this remind me of something or someone I already know?" "Is this similar to a technique that I already use?" and "Where and when can I use this information?"

When you learned to recognize Italy on a world map, your teacher probably pointed out that the country is shaped like a boot. This is a simple form of elaboration.

The same idea applies to more complex material. When you meet someone new, for example, ask yourself, "Does she remind me of someone else?" Or when reading this book, preview the material using the first page of each chapter.

7 **Organize it.** You remember things better if they have meaning for you. One way to create meaning is to learn from the general to the specific. Before you begin your next reading assignment, skim the passage to locate the main ideas. If you're ever lost, step back and look at the big picture. The details then might make more sense.

You can organize any list of items—even random items—in a meaningful way to make them easier to remember. Although there are probably an infinite number of facts, there are only a finite number of ways to organize them.

One option is to organize any group of items by *category.* You can apply this suggestion to long to-do lists.

For example, write each item on a separate index card. Then create a pile of cards for calls to make, errands to run, and household chores to complete. These will become your working categories.

The same concept applies to the content of your courses. In chemistry, a common example of organizing by category is the periodic table of chemical elements. When reading a novel for a literature course, you can organize your notes in categories such as theme, setting, and plot. Then take any of these categories and divide them into subcategories such as major events and minor events in the story.

Another option is to organize by *chronological order.* Any time that you create a numbered list of ideas, events, or steps, you are organizing by chronological order. To remember the events that led up to the stock market crash of 1929, for instance, create a timeline. List the key events on index cards. Then arrange the cards by the date of each event.

A third option is to organize by *spatial order.* In plain English, this means making a map. When studying for a history exam, for example, you can create a rough map of the major locations where events take place.

Fourth, there's an old standby for organizing lists—putting a list of items in *alphabetical order.* It's simple, and it works.

8 **Create associations.** The data already encoded in your neural networks are arranged according to a scheme that makes sense to you. When you introduce new data, you can remember them more effectively if you associate them with similar or related data.

Think about your favorite courses. They probably relate to subjects that you already know something about. If you have been interested in politics over the last few years, you'll find it easier to remember the facts in a modern history course. Even when you're tackling a new subject, you can build a mental store of basic background information—the raw material for creating associations. Preview reading assignments, and complete those readings before you attend lectures. Before taking upper-level courses, master the prerequisites.

9 **Create pictures.** Draw diagrams. Make cartoons. Use these images to connect facts and illustrate relationships. You can "see" and recall associations within and among abstract concepts more easily when you visualize both the concepts and the associations. The key is to use your imagination. Creating pictures reinforces visual and kinesthetic learning styles.

For example, Boyle's law states that at a constant temperature the volume of a confined ideal gas varies inversely with its pressure. Simply put, cutting the volume in half doubles the pressure. To remember this concept, you might picture someone "doubled over," using a bicycle pump. As she increases the pressure in the pump by decreasing the volume in the pump cylinder, she seems to be getting angrier. By the time she has doubled the pressure (and halved the volume), she is boiling ("Boyle-ing") mad.

Another reason to create pictures is that visual information is associated with a part of the brain that is different from the part that processes verbal information. When you create a picture of a concept, you are anchoring the information in a second part of your brain. Doing so increases your chances of recalling that information.

To visualize abstract relationships effectively, create an action-oriented image, such as the person using the pump. Make the picture vivid too. The person's face could be bright red. And involve all of your senses. Imagine how the cold metal of the pump would feel and how the person would grunt as she struggled with it.

You can also create pictures as you study by using *graphic organizers*. These preformatted charts prompt you to visualize relationships among facts and ideas.

One example is a *topic-point-details* chart. At the top of this chart, write the main topic of a lecture or reading assignment. In the left column, list the main points you want to remember. And in the right column, list key details related to each point. Figure 3.1 is the beginning of a chart based on this article.

You could use a similar chart to prompt critical thinking about an issue. Express that issue as a question, and write it at the top. In the left column, note the opinion about the issue. In the right column, list notable facts, expert opinions, reasons, and examples that support each opinion. Figure 3.2 is about tax cuts as a strategy for stimulating the economy.

TOPIC: 25 Memory Techniques

Point	Details
1. Understand the nature of short-term memory.	Know that information can only be kept in memory for short period unless other techniques are used.
2. Chunk it.	Chunk things into smaller groups to remember them more easily, like phone numbers.
3. Recite and repeat.	Say things out loud, many times.
4. Review as soon as possible.	Reviewing right after learning something new helps move it from short-term to long-term memory.

Figure 3.1 *Topic-Point-Details Chart*

Stimulate the Economy with Tax Cuts?

Opinion	Support
Yes	Savings from tax cuts allow businesses to invest money in new equipment.
	Tax cuts encourage businesses to expand and hire new employees.
No	Years of tax cuts under the Bush administration failed to prevent the mortgage credit crisis.
	Tax cuts create budget deficits.
Maybe	Tax cuts might work in some economic conditions.
	Budget deficits might be only temporary.

Figure 3.2 *Question-Opinion-Support Chart*

Sometimes you'll want to remember the main actions in a story or historical event. Create a time line by drawing a straight line. Place points in order on that line to represent key events. Place earlier events toward the left end of the line and later events toward the right. Figure 3.3 shows the start of a time line of events relating the U.S. war with Iraq.

3/19/03	**3/30/03**	**4/9/03**	**5/1/03**	**5/29/03**
U.S. invades Iraq	Rumsfeld announces location of WMD	Soldiers topple statue of Saddam	Bush declares mission accomplished	Bush: We found WMD

Figure 3.3 *Time Line*

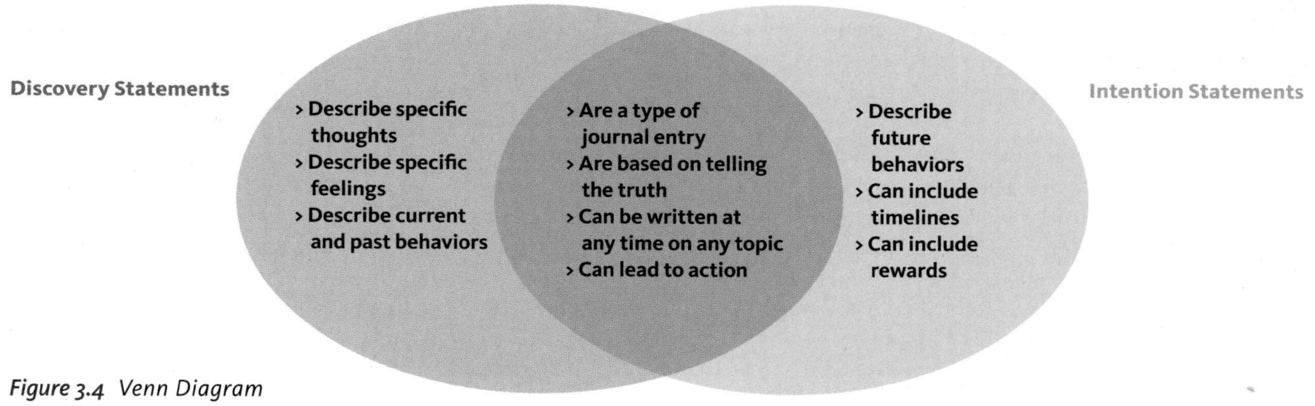

> Describe specific thoughts
> Describe specific feelings
> Describe current and past behaviors

> Are a type of journal entry
> Are based on telling the truth
> Can be written at any time on any topic
> Can lead to action

> Describe future behaviors
> Can include timelines
> Can include rewards

Figure 3.4 Venn Diagram

When you want to compare or contrast two things, play with a Venn diagram. Represent each thing as a circle. Draw the circles so that they overlap. In the overlapping area, list characteristics that the two things share. In the outer parts of each circle, list the unique characteristics of each thing. Figure 3.4 compares the two types of Journal Entries included in this book—Discovery Statements and Intention Statements.

The graphic organizers described here are just a few of the many kinds available. To find more examples, do an Internet search. Have fun, and invent graphic organizers of your own.

10 Restate it. One way to test your understanding and aid your memory at the same time is to put ideas into your own words. For example, you could define decoding simply as the act of recalling information that you learned earlier. Using this technique helps you avoid the trap of memorizing information that you do not understand.

11 Write it down. The technique of writing things down is obvious, yet easy to forget. Writing a note to yourself helps you remember an idea, even if you never look at the note again. Writing notes in the margins of your textbooks can help you remember what you read.

You can extend this technique by writing down an idea not just once, but many times. Let go of the old image of being forced to write "I will not throw paper wads" a hundred times on the chalkboard after school. When you choose to remember something, repetitive writing is a powerful tool.

Writing engages a different kind of memory than speaking. Writing prompts us to be more logical, coherent, and complete. Written reviews reveal gaps in knowledge that oral reviews miss, just as oral reviews reveal gaps that written reviews miss.

Another advantage of written reviews is that they more closely match the way you're asked to remember materials in school. During your academic career, you'll probably take far more written exams than oral exams. Writing can be an effective way to prepare for such tests.

Finally, writing is physical. Your arm, your hand, and your fingers join in. Remember, learning is an active process—you remember what you *do*.

12 Make flash cards. Write a sample test question on one side of a 3 × 5 card, and write the answer to that question on the other side of the card. Use these cards to quiz yourself. Or ask someone else to read the questions, listen to your answers, and compare them to the answers on the card.

You can also use PowerPoint or other presentation software to create flash cards. Add illustrations, color, and other visual effects—a simple and fun way to activate your visual intelligence. A related option is to go online. Do an Internet search with the words *flash, card,* and *online.* You'll find a list of sites that allow you to select from a library of printable flash cards—or create and print your own cards. You can get flash card apps for your smart phone too.

13 Overlearn. One way to fight mental fuzziness is to learn more than you need to know about a subject simply to pass a test. You can pick a subject apart, examine it, add to it, and go over it until it becomes second nature.

This technique is especially effective for problem solving. Do the assigned problems and then do more problems. Find another textbook and work similar problems. Then make up your own problems and solve them. When you pretest yourself in this way, the potential rewards are speed, accuracy, and greater confidence at exam time. Being well prepared can help you prevent test anxiety.

14 Intend to remember. To instantly enhance your memory, form the simple intention to *learn it now* rather than later. The intention to remember can be more powerful than any single memory technique.

You can build on your intention with simple tricks. During a lecture, for example, pretend that you'll be quizzed on the key points at the end of the period. Imagine that you'll get a $5 reward for every correct answer.

Also pay attention to your attention. Each time your mind wanders during class, make a tick mark in the margins of your notes. The act of writing reengages your attention.

If your mind keeps returning to an urgent or incomplete task, then write an Intention Statement about how you will handle it. With your intention safely recorded, return to what's important in the present moment.

ENCODE BY FEELING

15 **Make friends with your amygdala.** This area of your brain lights up with extra neural activity each time you feel a strong emotion. When a topic excites love, laughter, or fear, the amygdala sends a flurry of chemical messages that say, in effect, *This information is important and useful. Don't forget it.*

16 **Relax.** When you're relaxed, you absorb new information quickly and recall it with greater ease and accuracy. Students who can't recall information under the stress of a final exam can often recite the same facts later when they are relaxed.

Relaxing might seem to contradict the idea of active learning, but it doesn't. Being relaxed is not the same as being drowsy, zoned out, or asleep. Relaxation is a state of alertness, free of tension, during which your mind can play with new information, roll it around, create associations with it, and apply many of the other memory techniques. You can be active *and* relaxed.

17 **Use your times of peak energy.** Study your most difficult subjects during the times when your energy peaks. Some people can concentrate more effectively during daylight hours. The early morning hours can be especially productive, even for those who hate to get up with the sun. Observe the peaks and valleys in your energy flow during the day, and adjust study times accordingly. Perhaps you experience surges in memory power during the late afternoon or evening.

18 **Be aware of attitudes.** People who think history is boring tend to have trouble remembering dates and historical events. People who believe math is difficult often have a hard time recalling mathematical equations and formulas. All of us can forget information that contradicts our opinions.

If you think a subject is boring, remind yourself that everything is related to everything else. Look for connections that relate to your own interests.

For example, consider a person who is fanatical about cars. He can rebuild a motor in a weekend and has a good time doing so. From this apparently specialized interest, he can explore a wide realm of knowledge. He can relate the workings of an engine to principles of physics, math, and chemistry. Computerized parts in newer cars

can lead him to the study of data processing. He can research how the automobile industry has changed our cities and helped create suburbs, a topic that relates to urban planning, sociology, business, economics, psychology, and history.

Being aware of your attitudes is not the same as fighting them or struggling to give them up. Just notice your attitudes and be willing to put them on hold.

19 **Relate the material to a personal goal.** You're more likely to remember course material when you relate it to a goal—whether academic, personal, or career—that you feel strongly about. This is one reason why it pays to be specific about what you want. The more goals you have and the more clearly they are defined, the more channels you create for incoming information.

You can use this strategy even when a subject seems boring at first. If you're not naturally interested in a topic, then create interest. Find a study partner in the class—if possible, someone you know and like—or form a study group. Also consider getting to know the instructor personally. When a course creates a bridge to human relationships, you engage the content in a more emotional way.

ENCODE BY MOVING

20 **Sit at full attention, stand up, and move.** Action is a great memory enhancer. Test this theory by studying your assignments with the same energy that you bring to the dance floor or the basketball court.

You can use simple, direct methods to infuse your learning with action. When you sit at your desk, sit up straight. Sit on the edge of your chair as if you were about to spring out of it and sprint across the room.

Also experiment with standing up when you read, write, or recite. It's harder to fall asleep in this position. Some people insist that their brains work better when they stand.

In addition, you can pace back and forth and gesture as you recite material out loud. Use your hands. Go jogging while listening to a recordings of lectures. Get your body moving.

21 **Use it.** Many courses in higher education lean heavily toward abstract thinking. These courses might not offer opportunities to actively experiment with ideas or test them in daily life.

Create those opportunities yourself. For example, your introductory psychology book probably offers some theories about how people remember information. Choose one of those theories, and test it on yourself. See whether it helps you learn.

Your sociology class might include a discussion about how groups of people resolve conflict. See whether you can apply any of those ideas to resolving conflict in your own life right now.

The point behind these examples is the same: To remember an idea, go beyond thinking about it. Make it personal. *Do* something with it.

At the very least, do something to embed new information in two or more of your senses. For example, outlining a chapter allows you to *see* the main points and *write* them, drawing on your sense of touch. You could add another sense by reciting each point out loud as you outline it and recording your speaking with an app on your smart phone. Also, translate the material from an outline to a picture, which allows you to see the ideas in a new way.

RECALL IT

22 **Distribute learning.** As an alternative to marathon study sessions, experiment with several shorter sessions spaced out over time. You might find that you can get far more done in three 2-hour sessions than in one 6-hour session.

For example, when you are preparing for your American history exam, study for an hour or two and then wash the dishes. While you are washing the dishes, part of your mind will be reviewing what you studied. Return to American history for a while, then call a friend. Even when you are deep in conversation, part of your mind will be reviewing history.

You can get more done if you take regular breaks. You can even use the breaks as mini-rewards. After a productive study session, give yourself permission to surf the web, listen to a song, or play 10 minutes of hide-and-seek with your kids.

Distributing your learning is a brain-friendly activity. You cannot absorb new information and ideas during all of your waking hours. If you overload your brain, it will find a way to shut down for a rest—whether you plan for it or not. By taking periodic breaks while studying, you allow information to sink in. During these breaks, your brain is taking the time to rewire itself by growing new connections between cells. Psychologists call this process *consolidation.*[5]

The idea of allowing time for consolidation does have an exception. When you are so engrossed in a textbook that you cannot put it down, when you are consumed by an idea for a term paper and cannot think of anything

To remember something, access it a lot. Test yourself on it. Read it, write it, speak it, listen to it, apply it. Find some way to make contact with the material regularly. Each time you do so, you widen the neural pathway to the material and make it easier to recall the next time.

else—keep going. The master student within you has taken over. Enjoy the ride.

23 **Remember something else.** When you are stuck and can't remember something that you're sure you know, remember something else that is related to it.

If you can't remember your great-aunt's name, remember your great-uncle's name. During an economics exam, if you can't remember anything about the aggregate demand curve, recall what you do know about the aggregate supply curve. If you cannot recall specific facts, remember the example that the instructor used during her lecture. Any piece of information is encoded in the same area of the brain as a similar piece of information. You can unblock your recall by stimulating that area of your memory.

A brainstorm is a good memory jog. If you are stumped when taking a test, start writing down lots of answers to related questions, and—pop!—see whether the answer you need suddenly appears.

24 **Recall it often.** Even information encoded in long-term memory becomes difficult to recall when we don't use it regularly. The pathways to the information become faint with disuse. For example, you can probably remember the names of the courses that you're currently taking. What courses did you take as a freshman in high school?

This example points to a powerful memory technique. To remember something, access it a lot. Test yourself on it. Read it, write it, speak it, listen to it, apply it. Find some way to make contact with the material regularly. Each time you do so, you widen the neural pathway to the material and make it easier to recall the next time.

25 **Teach it.** Another way to make contact with the material is to teach it. Teaching demands mastery. When you explain the function of the pancreas to a fellow student, you discover quickly whether you really understand it yourself. Study groups are especially effective because they put you on stage. The friendly pressure of knowing that you'll teach the group helps focus your attention. ▮

Exercise 12   Use Q-Cards to reinforce memory

One memory strategy you might find useful involves a special kind of flash card. It's called a *Question Card*, or *Q-Card* for short.

To create a standard flash card, you write a question on one side of a 3 × 5 card, and its answer on the other side. Q-Cards have a question on *both* sides. Here's the trick: The question on one side of the card contains the answer to the question on the other side.

The questions you write on Q-Cards can draw on both lower- and higher-order thinking skills. Writing these questions forces you to encode material in different ways. You activate more areas of your brain and burn the concepts even deeper into your memory.

For example, say that you want to remember the subject of the Eighteenth Amendment to the U.S. Constitution—the one that prohibited the sale of alcohol. On one side of a 3 × 5 card, write, *Which amendment prohibited the sale of alcohol?* Turn the card over, and write, *What did the Eighteenth Amendment do?*

To get the most from Q-Cards:

- Add a picture to each side of the card. Doing so helps you learn concepts faster and develop a more visual learning style.

- Read the questions and recite the answers out loud. Two keys to memory are repetition and novelty, so use a different voice whenever you read and recite. Whisper the first time you go through your cards, then shout or sing the next time. Doing this develops an auditory learning style.

- Carry Q-Cards with you, and pull them out during waiting times. To develop a kinesthetic learning style, handle your cards often.

- Create a Q-Card for each new and important concept within 24 hours after attending a class or completing an assignment. This is your *active stack* of cards. Keep answering the questions on these cards until you learn each new concept.

- Review all of the cards for a certain subject on one day each week. For example, on Monday, review all cards from biology; on Tuesday, review all cards from history. These cards make up your *review stacks*.

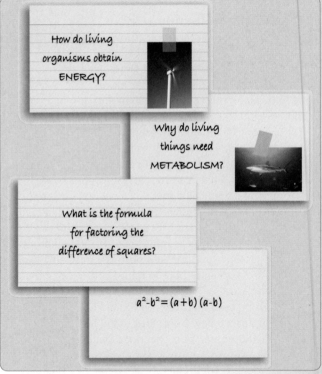

How do living organisms obtain ENERGY?

Why do living things need METABOLISM?

What is the formula for factoring the difference of squares?

$$a^2 - b^2 = (a+b)(a-b)$$

Robert Harding/Photodisc/Getty Images
Stephen Frink/Digital Vision/Getty Images

Get started with Q-Cards right now. One blank represents the front of the card; the other blank represents the back. Start by creating a Q-Card *about* remembering how to use Q-Cards!

© iStockphoto.com/Tatiana Popova

Set a trap for your
MEMORY

When you want to remind yourself to do something, link this activity to another event you know will take place. The key is to "trap" your memory by picking events that are certain to occur.

Say that you're walking to class and suddenly remember that your accounting assignment is due tomorrow. If you wear a ring, then switch it to a finger on the opposite hand. Now you're "trapped." Every time you glance at your hand and notice that you switched the ring, you get a reminder that you were supposed to remember something else. If you empty your pockets every night, put an unusual item in your pocket in the morning to remind yourself to do something before you go to bed. For example, to remember to call your younger sister on her birthday, pick an object that reminds you of her—a photograph, perhaps—and put it in your pocket. When you empty your pocket that evening and find the photo, you're more likely to make the call.

Everyday rituals that you seldom neglect, such as feeding a pet or unlacing your shoes, provide opportunities for setting traps. For example, tie a triple knot in your shoelace as a reminder to set the alarm for your early morning study group meeting.

You can even use imaginary traps. To remember to pay your phone bill, visualize a big, burly bill collector knocking on your front door to talk to you about how much you owe. The next time your arrive at your front door, you'll be glad that you got there before he did. You still have time to make your payment!

Mobile devices work well for setting memory traps. To remind yourself to bring your textbook to class, for example, set an alarm on your cell phone to go off 10 minutes before you leave the house. Visualize yourself picking up the book when the alarm goes off.

Link two activities together, and make the association unusual. ■

Interactive

Exercise 13
Remembering your car keys— or anything else

Pick something you frequently forget. Some people chronically lose their car keys or forget to write down checks in their check register. Others let anniversaries and birthdays slip by.

Pick an item or a task you're prone to forget. Then design a strategy for remembering it. Use any of the techniques from this chapter, research others, or make up your own from scratch. Describe your technique and the results.

In this exercise, as in most of the exercises in this book, a failure is also a success. Don't be concerned with whether your technique will work. Design it, and then find out whether it works. If it doesn't work for you this time, use another method.

MNEMONIC DEVICES

It's pronounced "ne-MON-ik." The word refers to tricks that can increase your ability to recall everything from grocery lists to speeches.

Some entertainers use mnemonic devices to perform "impossible" feats of memory, such as recalling the names of everyone in a large audience after hearing them just once. Using mnemonic devices, speakers can go for hours without looking at their notes.

There is a catch, though. Mnemonic devices have serious limitations. They don't always help you understand material. Mnemonics rely only on rote memorization. And mnemonic devices can be forgotten.

In spite of their limitations, mnemonic devices can be powerful. The trick is to have fun and create devices that are simple enough to learn quickly. There are five main types of mnemonic devices:

| new words | creative sentences | rhymes and songs | the loci system | the peg system |

Make up new words. Acronyms are words created from the initial letters of a series of words. Examples include NASA (**N**ational **A**eronautics and **S**pace **A**dministration) and laser (**l**ight **a**mplification by **st**imulated **e**mission of **r**adiation).

You can make up your own acronyms to recall a series of facts. A common mnemonic acronym is Roy G. Biv, which has helped millions of students remember the colors of the visible spectrum (**r**ed, **o**range, **y**ellow, **g**reen, **b**lue, **i**ndigo, and **v**iolet).

IPMAT helps biology students remember the stages of cell division (**i**nterphase, **p**rophase, **m**etaphase, **a**naphase, and **t**elophase).

OCEAN helps psychology students recall the five major personality factors: **o**pen-mindedness, **c**onscientiousness, **e**xtraversion, **a**greeableness, and **n**euroticism. (You can also use CANOE for this list.)

Use creative sentences. Acrostics are sentences that help you remember a series of letters that stand for something. For example, the first letters of the words in the sentence *Every good boy does fine* (E, G, B, D, and F) are the music notes of the lines of the treble clef staff.

Create rhymes and songs. Madison Avenue advertising executives spend billions of dollars a year on advertisements designed to burn their messages into your memory. The song "It's the Real Thing" was used to market Coca-Cola, despite the soda's artificial ingredients.

Rhymes have been used for centuries to teach basic facts. "*I* before *e*, except after *c*" has helped many a student on spelling tests.

Use the loci system. The word *loci* is the plural of *locus,* a synonym for *place* or *location.* Use the loci system to create visual associations with familiar locations. Unusual associations are the easiest to remember.

The loci system is an old one. Ancient Greek orators used it to remember long speeches, and politicians use it today. For example, if a politician's position were that road taxes must be raised to pay for school equipment, his loci visualizations before a speech might look like the following.

First, as he walks in the door of his house, he imagines a large *porpoise* jumping through a hoop. This reminds him to begin by telling the audience the *purpose* of his speech.

Next, he visualizes his living room floor covered with paving stones, forming a road leading into the kitchen. In the kitchen, he pictures dozens of schoolchildren sitting on the floor because they have no desks.

Now it's the day of the big speech. The politician is nervous. He's perspiring so much that his clothes stick to his body. He stands up to give his speech and his mind goes blank. Then he starts thinking to himself:

I can remember the rooms in my house. Let's see, I'm walking in the front door and—wow!—I see a porpoise. That reminds me to talk about the purpose of my speech. And then there's that road leading to the kitchen. Say, what are all those kids doing there on the floor? Oh, yeah, now I remember—they have no desks! We need to raise taxes on roads to pay for their desks and the other stuff they need in classrooms.

Use the peg system. The peg system is a technique that employs key words that are paired with numbers. Each word forms a "peg" on which you can "hang" mental associations. To use this system effectively, learn the following peg words and their associated numbers well:

bun goes with 1
shoe goes with 2
tree goes with 3
door goes with 4
hive goes with 5
sticks goes with 6
heaven goes with 7
gate goes with 8
wine goes with 9
hen goes with 10

You can use the peg system to remember the Bill of Rights (the first 10 amendments to the U.S. Constitution). For example, amendment number *four* is about protection from unlawful search and seizure. Imagine people knocking at your *door* who are demanding to search your home. This amendment means that you do not have to open your door unless those people have a proper search warrant. ■

National Archives and Records Administration
PhotoSpin

National Archives and Records Administration
PhotoSpin

Interactive

Exercise 14
Get creative

Construct your own mnemonic device for remembering some of the memory techniques in this chapter. Make up a poem, jingle, acronym, or acrostic. Or use another mnemonic system. Describe your mnemonic device.

_____

_____

_____

_____

_____

_____

_____

_____

_____

_____

_____

DrAfter123/Vetta/Getty Images

RETOOL
YOUR MEMORY

Back in the eighteenth century, writer Samuel Johnson noted that the "art of true memory is the art of attention." Johnson focused enough attention on his own work to produce essays, novels, poems, literary criticism, and a two-volume dictionary of the English language.

The demands on our attention have accelerated steadily since Johnson's day. Current technology provides us with ample means to multitask and scatter our concentration.

Yet technology can also be used to increase our mental focus and enhance our memory.

USE MEMORY APPS

Apps such as Anki (http://ankisrs.net/) let you create digital flash cards to use on your smart phone, computer, and tablet. Create or edit a card on one of your devices, and the change will show up on all the others. Other options include Memory Trainer, iCue Memory, Luminosity Brain Trainer, and Mind Games.

STORE IMPORTANT INFORMATION WHERE IT'S JUST ONE CLICK AWAY

Imagine how useful—and fun—it would be to download everything you've ever read or thought and then instantly locate what you want to remember about a particular topic. Websites and computer applications give you a variety of ways to store text and images, organize, search them, and even share them. These applications fall into two major categories.

First are websites for social bookmarking. These allow you to store, tag, share, and search links to specific pages. Examples are Delicious (www.delicious.com), Diigo (www.diigo.com), and Pinboard (http://pinboard.in).

Also check out online notebooks such as Evernote (www.evernote.com), Springpad (http://springpadit.com), and Zoho Notebook (http://notebook.zoho.com). With these, you can "clip" images and text from various web pages, categorize all that content, search it, and add your own notes.

Evernote also allows you to add "offline" content such as digital photos of business cards and receipts. You can search it by using tags and key words.

NAME DIGITAL DOCUMENTS FOR EASY RECALL

No matter where you store documents—on your digital device or online (in the "cloud"), do yourself a favor. Name them so that they're easy to remember.

Avoid generic names such as *agenda.doc* and *notes.doc*. Instead consider adding specific key words that will help you recall what the document contains. For example, include the name of the course and date that the document was created: *biology 2000 12.1.14.doc*. Documents created for work can include the name of a project or coworker.

USE OUTLINING SOFTWARE TO ENCODE INFORMATION

The outlining feature of a word-processing program offers a way to combine several memory techniques in this chapter. Outlining allows you to organize information in a meaningful way. Stating key points in your own words also helps you learn actively.

To create outlined summaries of your textbooks and lecture notes:

- Divide a book chapter or set of handwritten notes into sections.
- Open up a new document in your word-processing program, and list the main points from each section.
- Shift to the outline view of your document, and turn each point into a level-one heading.
- Enter key facts and other details as normal text under the appropriate heading.
- When reviewing for a test, shift your document into outline view so that only the headings are displayed. Scan them as you would scan the headlines in a newspaper.

In the outline view, see whether you can recall the details you included. Then open up the normal text underneath each headline to check the accuracy of your memory.

MAKE CONSCIOUS CHOICES ABOUT WHAT TO REMEMBER

It's true that you can look up just about any fact in seconds with a smart phone and a search engine. Even so, consider the advantages of continuing to memorize the information that matters to your performance at school and at work. For example, coworkers will be impressed if you can deliver a short presentation without notes, recall the main points of a proposal, and instantly match names with faces.

The ultimate memory app is one that's fast, free, and always available—your brain. ■

Practicing Critical Thinking 3

Memory skills connect to several qualities of a master student—being inquisitive, competent, and able to focus attention. Use this exercise as a way to further develop those qualities in yourself.

First, review the six levels of thinking described by Benjamin Bloom:

Level 1: Remembering

Level 2: Understanding

Level 3: Applying

Level 4: Analyzing

Level 5: Evaluating

Level 6: Creating

Now take a more detailed look at **Level 4: Analyzing.** Thinking at this level means dividing an idea into parts, groups, phases, or steps. Test questions that call for analyzing often start with words such as *arrange, categorize, classify, differentiate, distinguish, divide,* or *organize.*

An example is the "memory jungle" described in this chapter. This article explains memory by dividing it into four parts. Each part includes a visualization and related feature about memory. These can all be summarized in a chart:

Visualization 1: A well-worn path	**Memory feature:** Thoughts create "paths" of connected cells in the brain.
Visualization 2: A herd of thoughts	**Memory feature:** Thoughts that are grouped together ("herded") are easier to recall.
Visualization 3: Turning your back	**Memory feature:** We quickly forget ("turn our back") on new material unless we review it.
Visualization 4: Directing the animal traffic	**Memory feature:** You can direct new thoughts ("animals") into your long-term memory by actively using memory techniques.

Creating a chart is one way to analyze an idea. This level of thinking can also involve making lists, drawing maps, and sorting things into groups or categories.

Now it's your turn. Choose another idea from this chapter (**Level 1: Remembering**) and think about it at **Level 4: Analyzing.** Summarize the idea in one sentence. Then draw a two-column chart to show your analysis. In the left column, list the major parts of the idea. In the right column, describe each part in one sentence.

Your summary:

_____

_____

Your chart:

Exercise 15
Move from problems to solutions

Many students find it easy to complain about school and to dwell on problems. This exercise gives you an opportunity to change that habit and respond creatively to any problem you're currently experiencing—whether it be with memorizing or some other aspect of school or life.

The key is to dwell more on solutions than on problems. Do that by inventing as many solutions as possible for any given problem. See whether you can turn a problem into a *project* (a plan of action) or a *promise* to change some aspect of your life. Shifting the emphasis of your conversation from problems to solutions can raise your sense of possibility and unleash the master learner within you.

Describe at least three problems that could interfere with your success as a student. The problems can be related to courses, teachers, personal relationships, finances, or anything else that might get in the way of your success.

My problem is that . . .

_____

_____

My problem is that . . .

_____

_____

My problem is that . . .

_____

_____

Next, brainstorm at least five possible solutions to each of those problems. Ten solutions would be even better. (You can continue brainstorming on a separate piece of paper or on a computer.) You might find it hard to come up with that many ideas. That's okay. Stick with it. Stay in the inquiry, give yourself time, and ask other people for ideas.

I can solve my problem by . . .

_____

_____

I can solve my problem by . . .

_____

_____

I can solve my problem by . . .

_____

_____

Journal Entry 9
Discovery Statement

Revisit your memory skills

Take a minute to reflect on the memory techniques in this chapter. You probably use some of them already without being aware of it. List at least three memory techniques you have used in the past, and describe how you have used them.

_____

_____

_____

_____

_____

_____

_____

_____

_____

_____

_____

_____

_____

_____

_____

_____

_____

REMEMBERING NAMES

New friendships, job contacts, and business relationships all start with remembering names. Here are some suggestions for remembering them.

Recite and repeat in conversation. When you hear a person's name, repeat it. Immediately say it to yourself several times without moving your lips. You can also repeat the name out loud in a way that does not sound forced or artificial: "I'm pleased to meet you, Maria."

Ask the other person to recite and repeat. You can let other people help you remember their names. After you've been introduced to someone, ask that person to spell her name and pronounce it correctly for you. Most people will be flattered by the effort you're making to learn their names.

While you're at it, verify what name people want to be called. "Bob" may actually prefer "Robert."

Visualize. After the conversation, construct a brief visual image of the person. For a memorable image, make it unusual. Imagine the name painted in hot pink fluorescent letters on the person's forehead.

Admit you don't know. Admitting that you can't remember someone's name can actually put people at ease. Most of them will sympathize if you say, "I'm working to remember names better. Yours is right on the tip of my tongue. What is it again?"

Introduce yourself again. Most of the time we assume introductions are one-shot affairs. If we miss a name the first time around, our hopes for remembering it are dashed. Instead of giving up, reintroduce yourself: "We met earlier. I'm Jesse. Please tell me your name again."

Use associations. Link each person you meet with one characteristic that you find interesting or unusual. For example, you could make a mental note: "Vicki Cheng—long, black hair" or "James Washington—horn-rimmed glasses." To reinforce your associations, write them on 3 × 5 cards as soon as you can.

Limit the number of new names you learn at one time. Occasionally, we find ourselves in situations where we're introduced to several people at the same time: "Dad, these are all the people in my Boy Scout troop." "Let's take a tour so you can meet all 32 people in this department."

When meeting a large group of people, concentrate on remembering just two or three names. Free yourself from feeling obligated to remember everyone. Few of the people in mass introductions expect you to remember their names. Another way to avoid memory overload is to limit yourself to learning just first names. Last names can come later.

Ask for photos. In some cases, you might be able to get photos of all the people you meet. For example, a small business where you work might have a brochure with pictures of all the employees. If you're having trouble remembering names the first week of work, ask for individual or group photos, and write in the names if they're not included. You can use these photos as flash cards to drill yourself on names.

Go early. Consider going early to conventions, parties, and classes. Sometimes just a few people show up on time for these occasions. That's fewer names for you to remember. And as more people arrive, you can overhear them being introduced to others—an automatic review for you.

Make it a game. In situations where many people are new to one another, consider pairing up with another person and staging a contest. Challenge each other to remember as many new names as possible. Then choose an award—such as a movie ticket or free meal—for the person who wins.

Use technology. After you meet new people, enter their names as contacts in your e-mail, add them to a database, or enter them into your cell phone. If you get business cards, enter phone numbers, e-mail addresses, and other contact information as well.

Intend to remember. The simple act of focusing your attention at key moments can do wonders for your memory. Test this idea for yourself. The next time you're introduced to someone, direct 100 percent of your attention to hearing that person's name. Do this consistently, and see what happens to your ability to remember names. ■

Tim Sloan/AFP/Getty Images

MASTER STUDENT PROFILE

SONIA SOTOMAYOR

(1954–) Appointed an associate justice of the United States Supreme Court in 2009—the third woman and first Hispanic to serve in that role

When the two big boxes labeled *Encyclopaedia Britannica* arrived, it was Christmas come early. Junior and I sat on the floor surrounded by piles of books like explorers at the base of Everest. Each of the twenty-four volumes was a doorstop, the kind of book you'd expect to see in a library, never in someone's home and certainly not twenty-four of them, including a whole separate book just for the index! As I turned the densely set onionskin pages at random, I found myself wandering the world's geography, pondering molecules like daisy chains, marveling at the physiology of the eye. . . .

There was one more reason, beyond the pleasure of reading, the influence of English, and my Mother's various interventions, that I finally started to thrive at school. Mrs. Reilly, our fifth-grade teacher, unleashed my competitive spirit. She would put up a gold star on the blackboard each time a student did something really well, and I was a sucker for those gold stars! I was determined to collect as many as I could. After the first A's began appearing on my report card, I made a solemn vow that from then on, every report card would have at least one more A than the last one.

A vow on its own wasn't enough; I had to figure out how to make it happen. Study skills were not something that our teachers at Blessed Sacrament had ever addressed explicitly. Obviously, some kids were smarter than others; some kids worked harder than others. But as I also noticed, a handful of kids, the same ones every time, routinely got the top marks. That was the camp I wanted to join. But how did they do it?

Sonia Sotomayor *is willing to be uncomfortable.*

You *can go beyond your comfort zone by taking the initiative to approach people.*

It was then, in Mrs. Reilly's class, under the allure of those gold stars, that I did something very unusual for a child, though it seemed like common sense to me at the time. I decided to approach one of the smartest girls in the class and ask her how to study. Donna Renella looked suprised, maybe even flattered. In any case, she generously divulged her technique: how, while she was reading, she underlined important facts and took notes to condense information into smaller bits that were easier to remember; how, the night before a test, she would reread the relevant chapter. Obvious things once you've learned them, but at the time deriving them on my own would have been like trying to invent the wheel. I'd like to believe that even schools in poor neighborhoods have made some progress in teaching basic study skills, since I was in the fifth grade. But the more critical lesson I learned that day is still one too many kids never figure out: Don't be shy about making a teacher of any willing party who knows what he or she is doing. In retrospect, I can see how important that pattern would become for me: how readily I've sought out mentors, asking guidance from professors or colleagues, and in every friendship soaking up eagerly whatever that friend could teach me. ∎

Source: Sonia Sotomayor, My Beloved World (New York: Alfred A. Knopf, 2013), pp. 70–73.

QUIZ
Chapter 3

Name _____

Date _____

1. Briefly define the word *love* as it is used in the Power Process: Love your problems.
   In the Power Process, the word *love* means to unconditionally accept the fact that your problems exist.
   (*Power Process: Love your problems*, page 100)

2. According to the latest research, memory is which of these?
   (a) A process rather than a thing
   (b) A process that consists of several stages
   (c) Not something you *have*, but something you *do*
   (d) All of the above
   (d) All of the above (*Your memory and your brain—6 key principles*, page 102)

3. In the article about the memory jungle, what is the meadow?
   (a) A place that every animal (thought or perception) must pass through
   (b) A representation for short-term memory
   (c) A representation of the idea that one type of memory has a limited capacity
   (d) All of the above
   (d) All of the above (*The memory jungle*, page 104)

4. Give two examples of ways in which you can organize a long list of items.
   (Answers will vary.) One way of organizing a long list for memorization is by location. An example would be a biology student memorizing the leg muscles from the foot up to the hip. She could organize the muscles by location by grouping the muscles in the foot, those in the calf, those in the knee, and so on. Another way of organizing a list is by continuum. An example would be a student memorizing the types of business organization. He could organize them on a continuum, from the smallest and simplest type (a sole proprietorship) to the largest and most complex (a multinational corporation). (*25 memory techniques*, page 106)

5. Memorization on a deep level can take place if you:
   (a) Repeat the idea.   (b) Repeat the idea.   (c) Repeat the idea.   (d) All of the above
   (d) All of the above (*25 memory techniques*, page 106)

6. The article "25 memory techniques" suggests three ways to encode new memories. What are they?
   Encode by *thinking*—playing with information to make it more vivid in your mind. Also encode by *feeling*—by making an emotional connection with ideas and information. And, encode by *moving*—using your body as well as your brain. (*25 memory techniques*, page 106)

7. Define the term *graphic organizer* and give two examples.
   (Answers will vary.) *Graphic organizer* can be defined as preformatted charts used to prompt the student to visualize relationships among facts and ideas. Examples: topic-point-details chart, Venn diagram. (*25 memory techniques*, page 106)

8. Define *acronym* and give an example of one.
   (Answers will vary.) Acronyms are words created from the initial letters of a series of words. Examples include NASA (**N**ational **A**eronautics and **S**pace **A**dministration) and laser (**l**ight **a**mplification by **s**timulated **e**mission of **r**adiation. (*Mnemonic devices*, page 114)

9. Mnemonic devices are the most efficient ways to memorize facts and ideas. True or false? Explain your answer.
   True. These memory tricks can help you learn information quickly. Therefore, they are efficient. However, they may not be effective for long-term memorization or for understanding. (*Mnemonic devices*, page 114)

10. List three techniques that can be used to remember the names of three specific people you've recently met.
    The student should explain how to use one or more of the remembering names techniques, applying them to the three names chosen. Sample answer: Jerry—I will associate his name with the comedian Jerry Seinfeld. Darwish—I will recite and repeat his name several times to him and others in conversation. Maria—She seems to know all the answers in class, so I will write an intention to remember her name as a way to get to know her better. (*Remembering names*, page 119)

SKILLS SNAPSHOT
Chapter 3

Before moving on to a new chapter in this book, reflect on what you learned and how you will gain value from this chapter. Clarify your intention to adopt a new behavior to promote your success in school and at work.

Discovery
My score on the Memory section of the Discovery Wheel was . . .

Some ideas about memory that I read and already knew about in this chapter include . . .

The most surprising thing about memory that I learned from reading this chapter is . . .

Intention
The idea from this chapter that could make the biggest difference in my life right now is . . .

A habit that I could adopt to put this idea into practice is . . .

A suggestion from this chapter that I will likely use in my career is . . .

Action
The specific new behavior that I will practice is . . .

My cue for doing this behavior is . . .

My reward for following through on this intention will be . . .

INSTRUCTOR TOOLS & TIPS

Chapter **4**

READING

"Reading furnishes our mind only with materials of knowledge; it is thinking that makes what we read ours." —John Locke

PREVIEW

Chapter 4 is the first chapter in the text's academic development section, which includes Chapters 4 through 6. This section of the book employs a time-sensitive critical thinking approach to organize academic learning by considering strategies to employ before, during, and after learning. All three chapters (Chapter 4: Reading, Chapter 5: Notes, and Chapter 6: Tests) follow this approach. This structure makes Chapter 2: Time even more relevant to student success.

Although much of this chapter appears to be simply a review of what students should have learned in elementary or high school, the reality is that many students do not learn the critical reading skills they need to survive and thrive in the academic rigors of college. College reading is more than just the ability to read the words. Critical reading is a complex thinking process and thus is unlike any other "subject" they study in school. The academic literacy training that students receive in this chapter will prove invaluable throughout their academic careers. It is not uncommon for students enrolled in certificate programs or in courses that do not require proficiency in reading college textbooks to face difficulty in comprehending their college materials. Even though students may resist learning this necessary skill, it can directly impact their success in their classes and in the workplace. You may want to point out to students that in their career, they will need to read and respond effectively to interoffice communication (e-mails and memos), communication with clients and outside parties, and professional journals and other publications.

Our motivation, maturity, and life experiences all lead us to value the skills of reading comprehension and reading speed more than we might have as children. Most importantly, you can help your students accelerate their ability to learn new material by helping them activate any prior knowledge to engage with the reading they must do to succeed. Encourage your students to use the information they have learned about the brain in Chapter 3: Memory to enhance their skill at reading.

GUEST SPEAKER

This is a good time to invite a librarian as your guest speaker to talk to students about how they can use the library to research topics for classes. See also a related assignment in the Homework section.

Although the following strategy may take a bit of advance planning and a mobile cart, you may want to gather books from several academic disciplines and take them into the classroom. You can spend time looking at the structure and organization of the textbooks. Ask students to survey the texts, looking for such things as chapter layout and organization, appendices, and details that may differ from other disciplines. These are concepts that might escape students' notice otherwise.

Another possibility is to invite instructors from a variety of disciplines to talk about reading strategies appropriate to their course content. Ask them to come prepared to answer the following questions for your students:

Why?	Why is the reading material in your discipline area unique?
What?	What strategies would work best for tackling the reading material in your discipline area? Suggest that your discipline expert bring a sample passage (as a handout) for students so that they can use this new strategy to read it.
How?	How can students improve their reading comprehension in your discipline area using these strategies?
What if?	What if the students are still having trouble with reading in this discipline? What resources do you suggest (on-campus labs, ancillary textbooks, Web sites, and the like)?

LECTURE

Students may ask, "Why use Muscle Reading? I have been reading since first grade!" Muscle Reading is designed as a balanced literacy approach. It incorporates the three aspects of a metacognitive learning system. This means

master instructor
best practice

" The article "Getting past roadblocks to reading" is one of my favorites. I usually have many students in my online college survival course who are parents. Often, somewhere along the way, they will mention the problems they have with studying because of their kids. I immediately suggest that they read this article, and I have received some really positive feedback from the students who have not only read the article but have successfully used some of the techniques. Many of them have written back to me to thank me for alerting them to this article before it became part of an assigned chapter. Their children have also responded positively to the attention they receive while "helping" Mom or Dad to study!"

—*Diane Beecher, Lake Superior College*

that it presents specific strategies for students to use before, during, and after reading.

Students may also grumble that this approach to reading requires "too much." Lecture on Muscle Reading by walking them through the eight steps for the next chapter, Notes:

- Tell them to *Preview* the chapter by turning the pages, looking at graphs, pictures, article titles, and anything else that stands out for them.

- Next, create an *Outline* by listing the titles of the articles, double-spacing between the article titles. Instruct students to turn each title into a *Question*.

- Then students *Focus* by reading the chapter, highlighting and *Flagging Answers* they discover to their outline list of questions.

- Students *Recite, Review*, and periodically *Review Again* their outline questions and highlighted answers in the book.

This lecture and demonstration will help your students see how the eight-step process can be efficiently streamlined while retaining its effectiveness. For more information, review the sidebar article, "Muscle Reading—a leaner approach," on page 130.

EXERCISES/ACTIVITIES

1. **Power Process: Notice your pictures and let them go (page 124).** Present this Power Process as a problem-solving technique. When students feel

frustrated because reality does not match their expectations, "Notice your pictures and let them go" helps them let go of those expectations and experience what their reality *does* have to offer. In class, have students individually brainstorm "pictures" that interfere with their success in college. Examples include "I'm not smart enough to get a college degree" or "I'll never graduate—I can't stick with anything for four years." Then ask students to select one picture to "let go." Have them write their picture on a piece of paper and fold it up. Take an empty cardboard box into the classroom. Ask the entire class to tear their papers (negative pictures) into shreds and throw them into the box—literally letting them go. Ask students to write briefly about a new, positive picture to replace the negative one they have let go. For some students, this will be a personal exercise, and they may not feel comfortable talking about it with others. Other students may be willing to share with the class their experience of letting their negative picture go.

2. **Muscle Reading (page 125).** Divide your class into three groups: Before, During, and After. Have each group prepare a 10-minute presentation on the steps within their given phase. Each group aims for a memorable lesson that provides examples of their strategies. In conclusion, the three groups come up with a sample test question to help determine how the rest of the class understood their presentation. Give feedback as a class. If students did not understand a presentation, ask them to try to articulate how it might have been made clearer for them. We all understand feedback best when comments are specific and we receive suggestions for future projects.

CONVERSATION/SHARING

Now that your students have practiced using the learning styles in previous chapters, see whether they can generate their own questions before you present yours to the class.

Why?	Why does *Becoming a Master Student* include a chapter on reading?
What?	Read through the list of articles and select three that you believe will enhance your reading skills.
How?	How can you be more successful in college with these additional strategies for successful reading? How can these skills be useful in the workplace?
What if?	What if you apply these reading strategies to your coursework for other classes?

Workplace Application: Reading at work. Workers are often asked to read and comprehend dozens of documents daily, in addition to helping customers, attending meetings, and performing other necessary job duties. All of this can be overwhelming for most people.

Employees can minimize the confusion, while still maintaining efficiency, by following a few simple steps:

1. Avoid the constant onslaught of e-mail and voice messages. It is sometimes difficult not to want to read each e-mail as it hits your inbox, but doing so can curtail an efficient workday. Pick two or three times throughout the day when you will check e-mail and voice messages. Focus on other job duties during the rest of the workday.

2. Create a filing system. It's been said that the easiest way to deal with workplace clutter is to immediately read or handle work documents, or file them to work on later. Encourage students to come up with a system to manage their work that will be meaningful for them.

3. Print online documents to read later. It may not always be feasible or environmentally sound, but students may want to print certain online documents for faster reading and better clarity.

4. Know the importance of information literacy. Inform students that critical thinking and research skills do not end with college. These same skills are utilized daily at work. Knowing how to access, evaluate, and use information is critical. Encourage students to begin cultivating their information literacy skills now and continue to improve them throughout college.

HOMEWORK

Developing information literacy
(pages 141–144). You can tie library research to the workplace. After students have read this article and heard from a librarian (as a guest speaker), give them an assignment to go to the college library to (1) select a potential career to research and (2) narrow topics within the broad career topic. Ask the librarian to discuss library resources that would help in this career research. Librarians can suggest reference books within the library on your campus. Students often rely only on online sources, unfamiliar with books and other sources in the library facility. In addition, you can suggest students research the following site: **http://online.onetcenter.org**. This U.S. Department of Labor site provides attributes and characteristics about hundreds of occupations.

Developing critical thinking strategies throughout the semester will help students master their college-level reading.

Practicing Critical Thinking. One of the strategies suggested for understanding difficult reading material is to read another publication on the same subject. This is one example of critical thinking skills—explaining and assessing alternative views on an issue.

Apply this strategy now. Ask students to find and read a newspaper or magazine article that's relevant to one of their current reading assignments. Have students summarize and compare the viewpoints on the subject presented by both authors. Ask them to list the major questions addressed, along with the answers that are offered, and have them highlight points of disagreement and agreement. Finally, have students consider the methods that the authors use to reach their conclusions and the evidence they present. Have students determine whether one author's viewpoint is more reasonable, given all of the suitable evidence, and then write a paragraph that supports their conclusion.

If you assign this for extra credit or homework, be sure to clarify for your students exactly which materials they should submit. Consider asking them to submit their articles or a bibliography page. If you are trying to encourage students to become familiar with technology, ask them to forward the materials to you in an e-mail attachment or post the materials to your online course management system. You might ask students to create a PowerPoint presentation based on this assignment, allowing you to introduce students to this important presentation tool. Students can find Microsoft tutorials online to help them get started. This provides a comfortable environment for guidance in new technology.

EVALUATION
Frequent quizzes ensure that students face attention during class and keep up with the text reading assignments. In addition, quizzes provide students with opportunities for written reflection regarding new discoveries and intentions. Evaluation instruments also help you identify topics and concepts that students have not yet mastered.

Quiz Ideas for Chapter 4
Ask students to:

- Explain the steps of the Muscle Reading process.
- Describe tools to use when reading tough material.
- List techniques for reading faster.

MindTap™ EMBRACE VALUABLE RESOURCES

FOR CHAPTER 4

STUDENT RESOURCES: MINDTAP

- **Engagement Activity: Master Students in Action.** In this video, students hear firsthand from other students about their reading challenges and their strategies for success. The Master Students in Action videos give your students an up-close view of how the strategies in *Becoming a Master Student* have helped their peers overcome obstacles. In special segments, Dave Ellis offers students his best strategies for Muscle Reading.

- **MindTap Reader.** The MindTap Reader is more than a digital version of a textbook. It is an interactive, learning resource that was built from the ground up to create a digital reading experience based on how students assimilate information in an online environment. The robust functionality of the MindTap Reader allows learners to make notes, highlight text, and even find a definition right from the page.

- **Aplia Homework Assignment: Three phases of muscle reading.** In this assignment, students are introduced to Muscle Reading and must demonstrate an ability to apply the skills associated with each phase of the process. By practicing with a reading they are likely to encounter in future college courses, students are asked to test out and apply the three phases of reading.

MindTap™ *Your personal learning experience—learn anywhere, anytime.*

INSTRUCTOR COMPANION SITE

- **Are students not reading the book?** Look to the online Course Manual for specific suggestions on how to address students who are not reading the textbook. There are other ideas for how to keep students motivated, interested, and engaged in your course.

- **Need some energizing lecture ideas?** Browse through the lecture ideas provided for Chapter 4 in the Course Manual, including the following:

  - **Children Underfoot.** Geared for students who are also parents, this article shares some success tips from other parents about how to get reading completed with children around.

- **Reading Rates.** Explain to students the different categories of reading rates and how to decide which rate works for which type of reading situation.

- **Looking for test banks?** Customizable, text-specific content quizzes are a great way to test students' knowledge and understanding of the text, and are available for every chapter. Powered by Cognero, the test banks can be exported in an LMS or print-friendly format. You will have no problem accessing the multiple-choice, true/false, completion, and short-answer questions.

Please visit login.cengage.com to log in and access the Instructor Companion Site.

Chapter 4

READING

Why

Higher education requires extensive reading of complex material.

TECH **Extending Muscle Reading to Web pages and ebooks** ■ 132

When reading is tough ■ 134

Getting past roadblocks to reading ■ 135

How

Recall a time when you encountered problems with reading, such as finding words you didn't understand or pausing to reread paragraphs more than once. Then identify at least three specific reading skills you want to gain from this chapter.

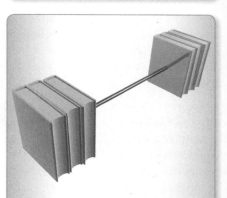

Muscle Reading Effective textbook reading is an active, energy-consuming, sit-on-the-edge-of-your-seat business. That's why this strategy is called Muscle Reading. ■ 125

Developing information literacy ■ 141

What if ...

I could finish my reading with time to spare and easily recall the key points?

What **is included ...**

NOTICE YOUR PICTURES AND **LET THEM GO**

One of the brain's primary jobs is to manufacture images. We use mental pictures to make predictions about the world, and we base much of our behavior on those predictions.

Pictures can sometimes get in our way. Take the student who plans to attend a school he hasn't visited. He chose this school for its strong curriculum and good academic standing, but his brain didn't stop there. In his mind, the campus has historic buildings with ivy-covered walls and tree-lined avenues. The professors, he imagines, will be as articulate as Barack Obama and as entertaining as Conan O'Brien. The cafeteria will be a cozy nook serving everything from delicate quiche to strong coffee. He will gather there with fellow students for hours of stimulating, intellectual conversation. The library will have every book, and the computer lab will boast the newest technology.

The school turns out to be four gray buildings downtown, next to the bus station. The first class he attends is taught by an overweight, balding professor wearing a plaid suit that went out of style sometime during the previous century. The cafeteria is a nondescript hall with machine-dispensed food, and the student's apartment is barely large enough to accommodate his roommate's tuba. This hypothetical student gets depressed. He begins to think about dropping out of school.

It's no wonder that pictures have this kind of power. Your brain is incredibly efficient at processing images. In a matter of seconds, for example, you can recognize a familiar face and "read" it for signs of that person's emotional state. If the emotion is not what you expected, then you could find yourself bracing for conflict. The reason: Reality has failed to match up with one of your precious mental pictures.

The problem with pictures is that they can prevent us from seeing what is really there. That is what happened to the student in this story. His pictures prevented him from noticing that his school is in the heart of a culturally vital city—close to theaters, museums, government offices, clubs, and all kinds of stores. The professor with the weird suit is not only an expert in his field but also a superior teacher. The school cafeteria is skimpy because it can't compete with the variety of inexpensive restaurants in the area.

Our pictures often lead to our being angry or disappointed. We set up expectations of events before they occur. Sometimes we don't even realize that we have these expectations. The next time you discover you are angry, disappointed, or frustrated, look to see which of your pictures aren't being fulfilled.

When you notice that pictures are getting in your way, in the gentlest manner possible let your pictures go. Let them drift away like wisps of smoke picked up by a gentle wind.

This Power Process can be a lifesaver when it comes to reading. Some students enter higher education with pictures about all the reading they'll be required to do before they graduate. They see themselves feeling bored, confused, and worried about keeping up with assignments. If you have such pictures, be willing to let them go. This chapter can help you recreate your whole experience of reading, which is crucial to your success.

Sometimes when we let go of old pictures, it's helpful to replace them with new, positive pictures. These new images can help you take a fresh perspective. Your new pictures might not feel as comfortable and genuine as your old ones. That's okay. Give it time. It's your head, and you're ultimately in charge of the pictures that live there. ■

Philip and Karen Smith/Iconica/Getty Images

MUSCLE READING

Effective textbook reading is an active, energy-consuming, sit-on-the-edge-of-your-seat business. That's why this strategy is called Muscle Reading.

Picture yourself sitting at a desk, a book in your hands. Your eyes are open, and it looks as if you're reading. Suddenly your head jerks up. You blink. You realize your eyes have been scanning the page for 10 minutes, and you can't remember a single thing you have read.

Finally, you get to your books at 8:00 p.m. You begin a reading assignment on something called the *equity method of accounting for common stock investments*. "I am preparing for the future," you tell yourself as you plod through two paragraphs and begin the third.

Suddenly, the clock reads 11:00 p.m. Say good-bye to three hours. Sometimes the only difference between a sleeping pill and a textbook is that the textbook doesn't have a warning on the label about operating heavy machinery.

Contrast this scenario with the image of an active reader, who exhibits the following behaviors:

- Stays alert, poses questions about what she reads, and searches for the answers
- Recognizes levels of information within the text, separating the main points and general principles from supporting details
- Quizzes herself about the material, makes written notes, and lists unanswered questions
- Instantly spots key terms and takes the time to find the definitions of unfamiliar words
- Thinks critically about the ideas in the text and looks for ways to apply them

That sounds like a lot to do. Yet skilled readers routinely accomplish all these things and more—while enjoying the process. Master students engage actively with reading material. They're willing to grapple with even the most challenging texts. They wrestle meaning from each page. They fill the margins with handwritten questions. They underline, highlight, annotate, and nearly rewrite some books to make them their own.

Master students also practice the deepest level of information literacy: They commit to change their lives based on what they read. Of every chapter, they ask, "What's the point? And what's the payoff? How can I use this to live my purpose and achieve my goals?" These students are just as likely to create to-do lists as to take notes on their reading. And when they're done with a useful book, master students share it with others for continuing conversation. Reading becomes a creative act and a tool for building community.

One way to experience this kind of success is to approach reading with a system in mind. An example is Muscle Reading. You can use Muscle Reading to avoid mental minivacations and reduce the number of unscheduled naps during study time, even after a hard day. Muscle Reading is a way to decrease difficulty and struggle by increasing energy and skill. Once you learn this system, you might actually spend less time on your reading and get more out of it.

Boosting your reading skills will promote your success in school. It can also boost your income. According to a report from the National Endowment for the Arts, proficient readers earn more than people with only basic reading skills. In addition, better readers are more likely to work as managers or other professionals.[1]

This is not to say that Muscle Reading will make your job or education a breeze. Muscle Reading might even look like more work at first. That's a normal reaction to have when learning any new skill. Persist with the process. Allow time to develop your new muscles for reading. With time and patience, you'll reap the rewards—understanding more of what you read and remembering more of what you understand. ■

HOW MUSCLE READING WORKS

Muscle Reading is a three-phase technique you can use to extract the ideas and information you want.

- Phase 1 includes steps to take *before* you read.
- Phase 2 includes steps to take *while* you read.
- Phase 3 includes steps to take *after* you read.

Each phase has several steps.

PHASE ONE:

Before you read

Step 1: Preview

Step 2: Outline

Step 3: Question

PHASE TWO:

While you read

Step 4: Focus

Step 5: Flag Answers

PHASE THREE:

After you read

Step 6: Recite

Step 7: Review

Step 8: Review again

To assist your recall of Muscle Reading strategies, memorize three short sentences:

Pry Out Questions.
Focus and Flag Answers.
Recite, Review, and Review again.

These three sentences correspond to the three phases of the Muscle Reading technique. Each sentence is an acrostic. The first letter of each word stands for one of the steps listed above.

To jog your memory, write the first letters of the Muscle Reading acrostic in a margin or at the top of your notes. Then check off the steps you intend to follow.

Take a moment to invent images for each of those sentences.

For *Phase 1*, visualize or feel yourself prying out questions from a text. These questions are ones you want answered based on a brief survey of the assignment. Make a mental picture of yourself scanning the material, spotting a question, and reaching into the text to pry it out. Hear yourself saying, "I've got it. Here's my question."

Then for *Phase 2*, focus on finding answers to your questions. Feel free to underline, highlight, or mark up your text in other ways. Make the answers so obvious that they lift up from the page.

Finally, you enter *Phase 3*. Hear your voice reciting what you have learned. Listen to yourself making a speech or singing a song about the material as you review it.

To jog your memory, write the first letters of the Muscle Reading acrostic in a margin or at the top of your notes. Then check off the steps you intend to follow. Or write the Muscle Reading steps on 3 × 5 cards and then use them for bookmarks.

Muscle Reading might take a little time to learn. At first you might feel it's slowing you down. That's natural when you're gaining a new skill. Mastery comes with time and practice. ■

PHASE 1 BEFORE *you read*

STEP 1 PREVIEW

Before you start reading, preview the entire assignment. You don't have to memorize what you preview to get value from this step. Previewing sets the stage for incoming information by warming up a space in your mental storage area.

If you are starting a new book, look over the table of contents and flip through the text page by page. If you're going to read one chapter, flip through the pages of that chapter. Even if your assignment is merely a few pages in a book, you can benefit from a brief preview of the table of contents.

Read all chapter headings and subheadings. Like the headlines in a newspaper, these are usually printed in large, bold type. Often headings are brief summaries in themselves. For a more thorough preview, read the first few paragraphs and last few paragraphs of a chapter, or the first sentence of each paragraph.

Keep an eye out for summary statements. If the assignment is long or complex, read the summary first. Many textbooks have summaries in the introduction or at the end of each chapter.

When previewing, seek out familiar concepts, facts, or ideas. These items can help increase comprehension by linking new information to previously learned material. Take a few moments to reflect on what you already know about the subject—even if you think you know nothing. This technique prepares your brain to accept new information.

Look for ideas that spark your imagination or curiosity. Inspect drawings, diagrams, charts, tables, graphs, and photographs.

Imagine what kinds of questions will show up on a test. Previewing helps to clarify your purpose for reading. Ask yourself what you will do with this material and how it can relate to your long-term goals. Will you be reading just to get the main points? Key supporting details? Additional details? All of the above? Your answers will guide what you do with each step that follows.

Keep your preview short. If the entire reading assignment will take less than an hour, your preview might take five minutes. Previewing is also a way to get started when an assignment looks too big to handle. It is an easy way to step into the material.

STEP 2 OUTLINE

With complex material, take time to understand the structure of what you are about to read. Outlining actively organizes your thoughts about the assignment and can help make complex information easier to understand.

If your textbook provides chapter outlines, spend some time studying them. When an outline is not provided, sketch a brief one in the margin of your book or at the beginning of your notes, on a separate sheet of paper. Later, as you read and take notes, you can add to your outline.

> *Have fun with this technique. Make the questions playful or creative. You don't need to answer every question that you ask. The purpose of making up questions is to get your brain involved in the assignment. Take your unanswered questions to class, where they can be springboards for class discussion.*

Headings in the text can serve as major and minor entries in your outline. For example, the heading for this article is "Phase 1: Before you read," and the subheadings list the three steps in this phase. When you outline, feel free to rewrite headings so that they are more meaningful to you.

The amount of time you spend on this outlining step will vary. For some assignments, a 10-second mental outline is all you might need. For other assignments (fiction and poetry, for example), you can skip this step altogether.

STEP 3 QUESTION

Before you begin a careful reading, determine what you want from the assignment. Then write down a list of questions, including any questions that resulted from your preview of the materials.

Another useful technique is to turn chapter headings and subheadings into questions. For example, if a heading is "Transference and Suggestion," you can ask yourself, "What are *transference* and *suggestion*? How does *transference* relate to *suggestion*?" Make up a quiz as if you were teaching this subject to your classmates.

If there are no headings, look for key sentences and turn them into questions. These sentences usually show up at the beginnings or ends of paragraphs and sections.

Have fun with this technique. Make the questions playful or creative. You don't need to answer every question that you ask. The purpose of making up questions is to get your brain involved in the assignment. Take your unanswered questions to class, where they can be springboards for class discussion.

Demand your money's worth from your textbook. If you do not understand a concept, write specific questions about it. The more detailed your questions, the more powerful this technique becomes. ■

PHASE 2 WHILE *you read*

STEP 4 FOCUS

You have previewed the reading assignment, organized it in your mind or on paper, and formulated questions. Now you are ready to begin reading.

It's easy to fool yourself about reading. Just having an open book in your hand and moving your eyes across a page doesn't mean that you are reading effectively. Reading takes mental focus.

As you read, be conscious of where you are and what you are doing. When you notice your attention wandering, gently bring it back to the present moment. There are many ways to do this.

To begin, get in a position to stay focused. If you observe chief executive officers, you'll find that some of them wear out the front of their chair first. They're literally on the edge of their seat. Approach your reading assignment in the same way. Sit up. Keep your spine straight. Avoid reading in bed, except for fun.

Avoid marathon reading sessions. Schedule breaks and set a reasonable goal for the entire session. Then reward yourself with an enjoyable activity for 10 or 15 minutes every hour or two.

For difficult reading, set more limited goals. Read for a half-hour and then take a break. Most students find that shorter periods of reading distributed throughout the day and week can be more effective than long sessions.

Visualize the material. Form mental pictures of the concepts as they are presented. If you read that a voucher system can help control cash disbursements, picture a voucher handing out dollar bills. Using visual imagery in this way can help deepen your understanding of the text while allowing information to be transferred into your long-term memory.

Read material out loud, especially if it is complicated. Some of us remember better and understand more quickly when we hear an idea.

Get a "feel" for the subject. For example, let's say you are reading about a microorganism—a paramecium—in your biology text. Imagine what it would feel like to run your finger around the long, cigar-shaped body of the organism. Imagine feeling the large fold of its gullet on one side and the tickle of the hairy little cilia as they wiggle in your hand.

In addition, predict how the author will answer your key questions. Then read to find out if your predictions were accurate.

> It's easy to fool yourself about reading. Just having an open book in your hand and moving your eyes across a page doesn't mean that you are reading effectively. Reading takes mental focus.

STEP 5 FLAG ANSWERS

As you read, seek out the answers to your questions. You are a detective, watching for every clue. When you do find an answer, flag it so that it stands out on the page.

Deface your books. Have fun. Flag answers by highlighting, underlining, writing comments, filling in your outline, or marking up pages in any other way that helps you. Indulge yourself as you never could with your grade school books.

Marking up your books offers other benefits. When you read with a highlighter, pen, or pencil in your hand, you involve your kinesthetic senses of touch and motion. Being physical with your books can help build strong neural pathways in your memory.

You can mark up a text in many ways. For example:

- Place an asterisk (*) or an exclamation point (!) in the margin next to an especially important sentence or term.
- Circle key terms and words to look up later in a dictionary.
- Write short definitions of key terms in the margin.
- Write a *Q* in the margin to highlight possible test questions, passages you don't understand, and questions to ask in class.
- Write personal comments in the margin—points of agreement or disagreement with the author.
- Write mini-indexes in the margin—that is, the numbers of other pages in the book where the same topic is discussed.
- Write summaries in your own words.
- Rewrite chapter titles, headings, and subheadings so that they're more meaningful to you.
- Draw diagrams, pictures, tables, or maps that translate text into visual terms.
- Number each step in a list or series of related points.
- In the margins, write notes about the relationships between elements in your reading. For instance, note connections between an idea and examples of that idea.
- If you infer an answer to a question or come up with another idea of your own, write that down as well.

Avoid marking up a text too soon. Wait until you complete a chapter or section to make sure you know the key points. Then mark up the text. Sometimes, flagging answers after you read each paragraph works best.

Also remember that the purpose of making marks in a text is to call out important concepts or information that you will review later. Flagging key information can save lots of time when you are studying for tests. With this in mind, highlight or underline sparingly—usually less than 10 percent of the text. If you mark up too much on a page, you defeat the purpose: to flag the most important material for review.

Finally, jot down new questions, and note when you don't find the answers you are looking for. Ask these questions in class, or see your instructor personally. Demand that your textbooks give you what you want—answers. ■

Five smart ways to highlight a text

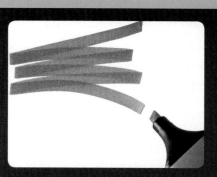

enviromantic/E+/Getty Images

Step 5 in Muscle Reading mentions a popular tool: highlighting. It also presents a danger—the ever-present temptation to highlight too much text. Excessive highlighting leads to wasted time during reviews. Get the most out of all that money you pay for books and the time you spend reading. Highlight in an efficient way that leaves texts readable for years to come and provides you with an easy reviewing method.

Read carefully first. Read an entire chapter or section at least once before you begin highlighting. Don't be in a hurry to mark up your book. Get to know the text first. Make two or three passes through difficult sections before you highlight.

Make choices up front about what to highlight. Perhaps you can accomplish your purposes by highlighting only certain chapters or sections of a text. When you highlight, remember to look for passages that directly answer the questions you posed during Step 3 of Muscle Reading. Within these passages, highlight individual words, phrases, or sentences rather than whole paragraphs. The important thing is to choose an overall strategy before you put highlighter to paper.

Recite first. You might want to apply Step 6 of Muscle Reading before you highlight. Talking about what you read—to yourself or with other people—can help you grasp the essence of a text. Recite first; then go back and highlight. You'll probably highlight more selectively.

Underline, then highlight. Underline key passages lightly in pencil. Then close your text and come back to it later. Assess your underlining. Perhaps you can highlight less than you underlined and still capture the key points.

Use highlighting to monitor your comprehension. Critical thinking plays a role in underlining and highlighting. When highlighting, you're making moment-by-moment decisions about what you want to remember from a text. You're also making inferences about what material might be included on a test.

Take your critical thinking a step further by using highlighting to check your comprehension. Stop reading periodically and look back over the sentences you've highlighted. See whether you are making accurate distinctions between main points and supporting material. Highlighting too much—more than 10 percent of the text—can be a sign that you're not making this distinction and that you don't fully understand what you're reading. Review the rest of this chapter for suggestions that can help.

PHASE 3 AFTER *you read*

STEP 6 RECITE

Talk to yourself about what you've read. Or talk to someone else. When you finish a reading assignment, make a speech about it. When you recite, you practice an important aspect of metacognition—synthesis, or combining individual ideas and facts into a meaningful whole.

One way to get yourself to recite is to look at each underlined point. Note what you marked; then put the book down and start talking out loud. Explain as much as you can about that particular point.

To make this technique more effective, do it in front of a mirror. It might seem silly, but the benefits can be enormous. Reap them at exam time.

A related technique is to stop reading periodically and write a short, free-form summary of what you just read. In one study, this informal "retrieval practice" helped students recall information better than other study techniques.[2]

Classmates are even better than mirrors. Form a group and practice teaching one another what you have read. One of the best ways to learn anything is to teach it to someone else.

In addition, talk about your reading whenever you can. Tell friends and family members what you're learning from your textbooks.

Talking about your reading reinforces a valuable skill—the ability to summarize. To practice this skill, pick one chapter (or one section of one chapter) from any of your textbooks. State the main topic covered in this chapter. Then state the main points that the author makes about this topic.

For example, the main topic up to this point in this chapter is Muscle Reading. The main point about this topic is that Muscle Reading includes three phases—steps to take before you read, while you read, and after you read. For a more detailed summary, you could name each of the steps.

Note: This topic-point method does not work so well when you want to summarize short stories, novels, plays, and other works of fiction. Instead, focus on action. In most stories, the main character confronts a major problem and takes a series of actions to solve it. Describe that problem and talk about the character's key actions—the turning points in the story.

STEP 7 REVIEW

Plan to do your first complete review within 24 hours of reading the material. Sound the trumpets! This point is critical: A review within 24 hours moves information from your short-term memory to your long-term memory.

Review within one day. If you read it on Wednesday, review it on Thursday. During this review, look over your notes and clear up anything you don't understand. Recite some of the main points again.

> *Decades ago, psychologists identified the primacy-recency effect, which suggests that we most easily remember the first and last items in any presentation. Previewing and reviewing your reading can put this theory to work for you.*

Muscle Reading—A leaner approach

Keep in mind that Muscle Reading is an overall approach, not a rigid, step-by-step procedure. Here's a shorter variation that students have found helpful. Practice it with any chapter in this book:

- Preview and question. **Flip through the pages, looking at anything that catches your eye—headings, subheadings, illustrations, photographs. Turn the title of each article into a question. For example, "How Muscle Reading works" can become "How does Muscle Reading work?" List your questions on a separate sheet of paper, or write each question on a 3 × 5 card.**

- Read to answer your questions. **Read each article. Then go back over the text and underline or highlight answers to the appropriate questions on your list.**

- Recite and review. **When you're done with the chapter, close the book. Recite by reading each question—and answering it—out loud. Review the chapter by looking up the answers to your questions. (It's easy—they're already highlighted.) Review again by quizzing yourself one more time with your list of questions.**

This review can be short. You might spend as little as 15 minutes reviewing a difficult two-hour reading assignment. Investing that time now can save you hours later when studying for exams.

STEP 8 REVIEW AGAIN

The final step in Muscle Reading is the weekly or monthly review. This step can be very short—perhaps only four or five minutes per assignment. Simply go over your notes. Read the highlighted parts of your text. Recite one or two of the more complicated points.

The purpose of these reviews is to keep the neural pathways to the information open and to make them more distinct. That way, the information can be easier to recall. You can accomplish these short reviews anytime, anywhere, if you are prepared.

Conduct a five-minute review while you are waiting for a bus, for your socks to dry, or for the water to boil. Three-by-five cards are a handy review tool. Write ideas, formulas, concepts, and facts on cards, and carry them with you. These short review periods can be effortless and fun.

Sometimes longer review periods are appropriate. For example, if you found an assignment difficult, consider rereading it. Start over, as if you had never seen the material before. Sometimes a second reading will provide you with surprising insights.

Decades ago, psychologists identified the primacy-recency effect, which suggests that we most easily remember the first and last items in any presentation.[3] Previewing and reviewing your reading can put this theory to work for you. ◼

Interactive

Journal Entry 10
Discovery/Intention Statement

Experimenting with Muscle Reading

After reading the steps included in Muscle Reading, reflect on your reading skills. Are you a more effective reader than you thought you were? Less effective? Record your observations.

I discovered that I . . .

_____

_____

_____

_____

Many students find that they only do the "read" step with their textbooks. You've just read about the advantages of eight additional steps you should perform. Depending on the text, reading assignment, your available time, and your commitment level to the material, you may discover through practice which additional steps work best for you. Right now, make a commitment to yourself to experiment with all or several of the additional Muscle Reading steps by completing the following Intention Statement.

I intend to use the following Muscle Reading steps for the next 2 weeks in my _____ class:

☐ Preview

☐ Outline

☐ Question

☐ Focus

☐ Flag answers

☐ Recite

☐ Review

☐ Review again

Extending MUSCLE READING TO WEB PAGES AND EBOOKS

© Oleksiy Mark/Shutterstock.com

The techniques suggested in this chapter work for more than printed textbooks. You can still use the three phases of Muscle Reading when accessing a Web page or ebook on a computer, mobile phone, or tablet.

PHASE 1: BEFORE YOU READ

For this phase, the core Muscle Reading techniques are previewing, outlining, and posing questions. These are all about *preparing* to dig into a text. Digital texts offer another level of preparation that allows you to create more readable pages.

To begin, change the appearance of the text. Adjust the size and choose from different fonts. Many ebook readers also allow you to change the color of the text and the amount of contrast between text and background. These settings can be useful when you're reading in a place with dim lighting.

In addition, cut the clutter. Web pages abound with ads, pop-up windows, and animations. Getting rid of all that stuff makes it easier to focus your attention on the core content of the page and avoid time-wasting distractions.

Readability (readability.com) offers extensions and bookmarklets for your Web browser that allow you to do just that. (Bookmarklets are tiny programs that add a specific function to a browser.) Safari and other Web browsers also come with a built-in "reader" mode that does much the same thing as Readability.

PHASE 2: WHILE YOU READ

During this phase, skilled readers focus on finding answers to their questions and flagging them in the text. Ebooks offer features that help with these steps:

- **Access the table of contents.** For a bigger picture of the text, look for a table of contents that lists chapter headings and subheadings. Click on any of these headings to expand the text for that part of the book. Note that charts, illustrations, photos, tables, diagrams, and other visuals might be listed separately in the table of contents.

- **Use navigation tools.** To flip electronic pages, look for *previous* and *next* buttons or arrows on the right and left borders of each page. Many ebooks also offer a "go to page" feature that allows you to key in a specific page number.

- **Search the text.** Look for a search box that allows you to enter key words and find all the places in the text where those words are mentioned.

- **Follow links to definitions and related information.** Many ebook readers will supply a definition of any word in the text. All you need to do is highlight a word and click on it. Also find out if your ebook reader will connect you to Web sites related to the topic of your ebook.

Take Muscle Reading to work

Just think about all the different kinds of documents that you might encounter during the course of a workday: reference manuals, training materials, meeting minutes, brochures, annual reports, job descriptions, and more.

Your purpose for reading any of these is probably to produce a specific outcome—to gain a skill, get a job, or gather information needed to complete a task. Fix that purpose in mind before you dig into a document. Ask yourself: *How can I use this?* Then read to find answers.

You can also turn any text into a to-do list. For example, write a big letter A (for *action*) next to a specific sentence or paragraph. Or draw a small box there and check off the box after taking the appropriate action. The purpose of these strategies is to change your behavior based on what you read.

You can also approach reading as a way to contribute to your coworkers. When you're done with a particularly useful book, pass it on to someone else. Ideas gain power when they're shared.

- *Highlight and annotate.* Ebook readers allow you to select words, sentences, or entire paragraphs and highlight them in a bright color. You can also annotate a book by keying in your own notes tied to specific pages.

  Even with features such as these, you might find that you sometimes prefer the printed version of a book. This is likely to happen when a text includes large illustrations and charts that don't translate well to a small screen. Go to the library or bookstore to see whether you can find those pages in a printed copy of your ebook. Use the print and ebook versions of a text to supplement each other.

PHASE 3: AFTER YOU READ

The final phase of Muscle Reading is about moving information into your long-term memory by reciting and reviewing. These steps call on you to locate the main points in a text and summarize them.

Ebooks can help you create instant summaries. For example, the Amazon Kindle allows you to view all your highlighted passages at once. Another option is to copy these passages and then paste them into a word-processing file. To avoid plagiarism, put these passages within quotation marks and note the source. ■

Interactive

Journal Entry 11
Discovery/Intention Statement

Reflect on your online reading habits

Take a few minutes to reflect on your experience of reading Web pages and ebooks. Suppose that you were able to read a book in three versions—online, print, and ebook. Based on your current experience, do you think that one of these versions would better support your understanding of the content and efficient use of reading time? Would you use different reading strategies for the different versions? Complete the following sentences:

With Web pages and ebooks, I discovered that I read most effectively when I . . .

_____

_____

_____

I read less effectively when I . . .

_____

_____

_____

To get the most from online reading and ebooks in the future, I intend to . . .

_____

_____

_____

When reading is
TOUGH

Graham Bell/Cardinal/Corbis

Sometimes ordinary reading methods are not enough. It's easy to get bogged down in a murky reading assignment. The solution starts with a First Step: When you are confused, tell the truth about it.

Successful readers monitor their understanding of reading material. They do not see confusion as a mistake or a personal shortcoming. Instead, they take it as a cue to change reading strategies and process ideas at a deeper level.

Somehow, students get the idea that reading means opening a book and slogging through the text in a straight line from the first word until the last. Actually, this method can be an ineffective way to read.

Feel free to shake up your routine. Make several passes through tough reading material. During a preview, for example, just scan the text to look for key words and highlighted material.

Then, skim the entire chapter or article again, spending a little more time and taking in more than you did during your preview. Finally, read in more depth, proceeding word by word through some or all of the text. Also consider the following suggestions.

Look for essential words. If you are stuck on a paragraph, mentally cross out all of the adjectives and adverbs, and then read the sentences without them. Find the important words—usually verbs and nouns.

Hold a mini-review. Pause briefly to summarize— either verbally or in writing—what you've read so far. Stop at the end of a paragraph and recite, in your own words, what you have just read. Jot down some notes, or create a short outline or summary.

Read it out loud. Make noise. Read a passage out loud several times, each time using a different inflection and emphasizing a different part of the sentence. Be creative. Imagine that you are the author talking.

Talk to someone who can help. Admit when you are stuck. Then bring questions about reading assignments to classmates and members of your study group. Also make an appointment with your instructor. Most teachers welcome the opportunity to work individually with students. Be specific about your confusion. Point out the paragraph that you found toughest to understand.

Stand up. Changing positions periodically can combat fatigue. Experiment with standing as you read, especially if you get stuck on a tough passage and decide to read it out loud.

Skip around. Jump to the next section or to the end of a tough article or chapter. You might have lost the big picture. Simply seeing the next step, the next main point, or a summary might be all you need to put the details in context. Retrace the steps in a chain of ideas, and look for examples. Absorb facts and ideas in whatever order works for you— which may be different from the author's presentation.

Find a tutor. Many schools provide free tutoring services. If your school does not, other students who have completed the course can assist you.

Use another text. Find a similar text in the library. Sometimes a concept is easier to understand if it is expressed another way. Children's books—especially children's encyclopedias—can provide useful overviews of baffling subjects.

Note where you get stuck. When you feel stuck, stop reading for a moment and diagnose what's happening. At these stop points, mark your place in the margin of the page with a penciled *S* for *Stuck*. A pattern to your marks over several pages might indicate a question you want to answer before going further.

Stop reading. When none of the above suggestions work, do not despair. Admit your confusion and then take a break. Catch a movie, go for a walk, study another subject, or sleep on it. The concepts you've already absorbed might come together at a subconscious level as you move on to other activities. Allow some time for that process. When you return to the reading material, see it with fresh eyes. ■

Getting past ROADBLOCKS TO READING

Henk Badenhorst/Taxi/Getty Images

Even your favorite strategies for reading can fail when you're dealing with bigger issues. Those roadblocks to getting your reading done can come from three major sources:

- Finding enough time to keep up with your reading
- Making choices about what to read once you find the time
- Getting interrupted by other people while you're reading

For solutions to each of these problems, read on.

SCHEDULING TIME FOR READING

Planning dispels panic (*I've got 300 pages to read before tomorrow morning!*) and helps you finish off your entire reading load for a term. Creating a reading plan is relatively simple if you use the following steps.

Step 1. Estimate the total number of pages that you'll read. To arrive at this figure, check the course syllabus for each class that you're taking. Look for lists of reading assignments. Based on what you find, estimate the total number of pages that you'll read for all your classes.

Step 2. Estimate how many pages you can read during one hour. Remember that your reading speed will be different for various materials. It depends on everything from the layout of the pages to the difficulty of the text. To give your estimate some credibility, base it on actual experience. During your first reading assignment in each course, keep track of how many pages you read per hour.

Step 3. Estimate your total number of reading hours. Divide the total number of pages from Step 1 by your pages-per-hour from Step 2. For example, look at this calculation:

600 (total number of pages for all courses this term) ÷ 10 (pages read per hour)
= 60 (total reading hours needed for the term)

The result is the total number of hours you'll need to complete your reading assignments this term. Remember to give yourself some "wiggle room." Allow extra hours for rereading and unplanned events. Consider taking your initial number of projected hours and doubling it. You can always back off from there to an estimate that seems more reasonable.

Step 4. Schedule reading time. Take the total number of hours from Step 3 and divide it by the number of weeks in your current term. That will give you the number of hours to schedule for reading each week.

60 (total reading hours needed for the term) ÷ 16 (weeks in the term)
= 3.75 (hours per week to schedule for reading)

Now, go to your calendar or long-term planner and reflect on it for a few minutes. Look for ways to block out those hours next week.

Step 5. Refine your reading plan. Scheduling your reading takes time. The potential benefits are beyond calculation. With a plan, you can be more confident that you'll actually get your reading done. Even if your estimates are off, you'll still go beyond blind guessing or leaving the whole thing to chance. Your reading matters too much for that.

MAKING CHOICES ABOUT WHAT TO READ

Books about time management often mention the "80–20" principle. According to this principle, 80 percent of the value created by any group derives from only 20 percent of its members. If you have a to-do list of 10 items, for example, you'll get 80 percent of your desired results by doing only 2 items on the list.

The point is not to take these figures literally, but to remember the underlying principle: *Focus on what creates the most value.* Look at your reading in light of the 80–20 principle. For instance:

- In a 10-paragraph article, you might find 80 percent of the crucial facts in the headline and first paragraph. (In fact, journalists are *taught* to write this way.)
- If you have a 50-page assignment, you may find the most important facts and ideas in 10 pages of that total.
- If you're asked to read five books for a course, you may find that most exam questions come from just one of them.

A caution is in order here. The 80–20 principle is not a suggestion to complete only 20 percent of your reading assignments. That choice can undermine your education. To find the most important parts of anything you read, first get familiar with the whole. Only then can you make sound choices about where to focus.

Skilled readers constantly make choices about what to read and what *not* to read. They realize that some texts are more valuable for their purposes than others and that some passages within a single text are more crucial than the rest. When reading, they instantly ask, "What's most important here?"

The answer to this question varies from assignment to assignment, and even from page to page within a single assignment. Pose this question each time that you read, and look for clues to the answers. Pay special attention to the following:

- Any readings that your instructor refers to in class
- Readings that are emphasized in a class syllabus
- Readings that generate the most questions on quizzes and tests
- Parts of a text that directly answer the questions you generated while previewing
- Chapter previews and summaries (usually found at the beginning and end of a chapter or section)

DEALING WITH INTERRUPTIONS

Sometimes the people you live with and care about the most—a friend, roommate, spouse, or child—can become a temporary roadblock to reading. The following strategies can help you stay focused on your reading:

Attend to people first. When you first come home from school, keep your books out of sight. Spend some time with your roommates or family members before you settle in to study. Make small talk and ask them about their day. Give the important people in your life a short period of full, focused attention rather than a longer period of partial attention. Then explain that you have some work to do. Set some ground rules for the amount of time you need to focus on studying. You could be rewarded with extra minutes or hours of quiet time.

Plan for interruptions. It's possible that you'll be interrupted even if you set up guidelines for your study time in advance. If so, schedule the kind of studying that can be interrupted. For instance, you could write out or review flash cards with key terms and definitions. Save the tasks that require sustained attention for more quiet times.

Use "pockets" of time. See whether you can arrange a study time in a quiet place at school before you come home. If you arrive at school 15 minutes earlier and stay 15 minutes later, you can squeeze in an extra half-hour of reading that day. Also look for opportunities to study on campus between classes.

When you can't read everything, read something. Even if you can't absorb an entire chapter while your roommates are blasting music, you can skim a chapter. Or you can just read the introduction and summary. When you can't get it *all* done, get *something* done.

Caution: If you always read this way, your education will be compromised. Supplement this strategy with others from this chapter so that you can get your most important reading done.

Read with children underfoot. It is possible to have both effective study time and quality time with your children. The following suggestions come mostly from students who are also parents. The specific strategies you use will depend on your schedule and the ages of your children.

- *Find a regular playmate for your child.* Some children can pair off with close friends and safely retreat to their rooms for hours of private play. You can check on them occasionally and still get lots of reading done.
- *Create a special space for your child.* Set aside one room or area of your home as a play space. Childproof this space. The goal is to create a place where children can roam freely and play with minimal supervision. Consider allowing your child in this area *only* when you study. Your homework time then becomes your child's reward. If you're cramped for space, just set aside some special toys for your child to play with during your study time.
- *Use television responsibly.* Whenever possible, select educational programs that keep your child's mind active and engaged. Also see whether your child can use headphones while watching television. That way, the house stays quiet while you study.
- *Schedule time to be with your children when you've finished studying.* Let your children in on the plan: "I'll be done reading at 7:30. That gives us a whole hour to play before you go to bed."
- *Ask other adults for help.* Getting help can be as simple as asking your spouse, partner, neighbor, or fellow student to take care of the children while you study. Offer to trade child care with a neighbor: You will take his kids and yours for two hours on Thursday night if he'll take them for two hours on Saturday morning.
- *Find community activities and services.* Ask whether your school provides a day care service. In some cases, these services are available to students at a reduced cost. ∎

Chris Pancewicz/Alamy

READING
FASTER

One way to read faster is to read faster. This idea might sound like double-talk, but it is a serious suggestion. The fact is, you can probably read faster—without any loss in comprehension—simply by making a conscious effort to do so. Your comprehension might even improve.

Experiment with the "just do it" method right now. Read the rest of this article as fast as you can. After you finish, come back and reread the same paragraphs at your usual rate. Note how much you remember from your first sprint through the text. You might be surprised to find out how well you comprehend material even at dramatically increased speeds. Build on that success by experimenting with the following guidelines.

Move your eyes faster. When we read, our eyes leap across the page in short bursts called *saccades* (pronounced "să-käds"). A saccade is also a sharp jerk on the reins of a horse—a violent pull to stop the animal quickly. Our eyes stop like that too, in pauses called *fixations*.

Although we experience the illusion of continuously scanning each line, our eyes actually take in groups of words, usually about three at a time. For most of reading time, our eyes are at a dead stop in those fixations.

Your eyes can move faster if they take in more words with each burst—for example, six instead of three. To practice taking in more words between fixations, find a newspaper with narrow columns. Then read down one column at a time, and fixate only once per line.

In addition, simply make a conscious effort to fixate less. You might feel a little uncomfortable at first. That's normal. Just practice often, for short periods of time.

Notice and release ineffective habits. Our eyes make regressions; that is, they back up and reread words. You can reduce regressions by paying attention to them. Use the handy 3 × 5 card to cover words and lines that you have just read. You can then note how often you stop and move the card back to reread the text. Don't be discouraged if you stop often at first. Being aware of it helps you regress less frequently.

Also notice vocalizing. You are more likely to read faster if you don't read out loud or move your lips. You can also increase your speed if you don't subvocalize—that is, if you don't mentally "hear" the words as you read them. To stop doing it, just be aware of it.

Another habit to release is reading letter by letter. When we first learn to read, we do it one letter at a time. By now you have memorized many words by their shape, so you don't have to focus on the letters at all. Read this example: "Rasrhcers at Cbmrigae Uivnretisy funod taht eprxert raeedrs dno't eevn look at the lteters." You get the point.

Stay flexible. Remember that speed isn't everything. Skillful readers vary their reading rate according to their purpose and the nature of the material. An advanced text in analytic geometry usually calls for a different reading rate than the Sunday comics.

You also can use different reading rates on the same material. For example, you might first sprint through an assignment for the key words and ideas, and then return to the difficult parts for a slower and more thorough reading. ■

Interactive

Exercise 16
Relax

Eyestrain can be the result of continuous stress. Take a break from your reading and use this exercise to release tension.

1. Sit on a chair or lie down, and take a few moments to breathe deeply.

2. Close your eyes, place your palms over them, and visualize a perfect field of black.

3. Continue to be aware of the blackness for two or three minutes while you breathe deeply.

4. Now remove your hands from your eyes, and open your eyes slowly.

5. Relax for a minute more; then continue reading.

Stockbyte

Word power—
EXPANDING
YOUR
VOCABULARY

Having a large vocabulary makes reading more enjoyable and increases the range of materials you can explore. In addition, building your vocabulary gives you more options for self-expression when speaking or writing. With a larger vocabulary, you can think more precisely by making finer distinctions between ideas. And you won't have to stop to search for words at crucial times—such as a job interview.

Strengthen your vocabulary by taking delight in words. Look up unfamiliar terms. Pay special attention to words that arouse your curiosity.

Before the age of the Internet, students used two kinds of printed dictionaries: the desk dictionary and the unabridged dictionary. A desk dictionary is an easy-to-handle abridged dictionary that you can use many times in the course of a day. You can keep this book within easy reach (maybe in your lap) so you can look up unfamiliar words while reading.

In contrast, an unabridged dictionary is large and not made for you to carry around. It provides more complete information about words and definitions not included in your desk dictionary, as well as synonyms, usage notes, and word histories. Look for unabridged dictionaries in libraries and bookstores.

You might prefer using one of several online dictionaries, such as Dictionary.com. Another common option is to search for definitions by using a search engine such as Google.com. If you do this, inspect the results carefully. They can vary in quality and be less useful than the definitions you'd find in a good dictionary or thesaurus.

Construct a word stack. When you come across an unfamiliar word, write it down on a 3 × 5 card. Below the word, copy the sentence in which it was used, along with the page number. You can look up each word immediately, or you can accumulate a stack of these cards and look up the words later. Write the definition of each word on the back of the 3 × 5 card, adding the diacritics—marks that tell you how to pronounce it.

To expand your vocabulary and learn the history behind the words, take your stack of cards to an unabridged dictionary. As you find related words in the dictionary, add them to your stack. These cards become a portable study aid that you can review in your spare moments.

Learn—even when your dictionary is across town. When you are listening to a lecture and hear an unusual word or when you are reading on the bus and encounter a word you don't know, you can still build your word stack. Pull out a 3 × 5 card and write down the word and its sentence. Later, you can look up the definition and write it on the back of the card.

Divide words into parts. Another suggestion for building your vocabulary is to divide an unfamiliar word into syllables and look for familiar parts. This strategy works well if you make it a point to learn common prefixes (beginning syllables) and suffixes (ending syllables). For example, the suffix *-tude* usually refers to a condition or state of being. Knowing this makes it easier to conclude that *habitude* refers to a usual way of doing something and that *similitude* means being similar or having a quality of resemblance.

Infer the meaning of words from their context. You can often deduce the meaning of an unfamiliar word simply by paying attention to its context—the surrounding words, phrases, sentences, paragraphs, or images. Later, you can confirm your deduction by consulting a dictionary.

Practice looking for context clues such as these:

- *Definitions.* A key word might be defined right in the text. Look for phrases such as *defined as* or *in other words*.
- *Examples.* Authors often provide examples to clarify a word meaning. If the word is not explicitly defined, then study the examples. They're often preceded by the phrases *for example, for instance,* or *such as*.
- *Lists.* When a word is listed in a series, pay attention to the other items in the series. They might define the unfamiliar word through association.
- *Comparisons.* You might find a new word surrounded by synonyms—words with a similar meaning. Look for synonyms after words such as *like* and *as*.
- *Contrasts.* A writer might juxtapose a word with its antonym. Look for phrases such as *on the contrary* and *on the other hand*. ∎

MASTERING
THE ENGLISH LANGUAGE

The complexity of English makes it a challenge for people who grew up with another language—and for native speakers of English as well. To get the most benefit from your education, analyze the ways that you speak and write English. Look for patterns that might block your success. Then take steps to increase your mastery.

LEARN TO USE STANDARD ENGLISH WHEN IT COUNTS

Standard English (also called *standard written English*) is the form of the language used by educated speakers and writers. It is the form most likely to be understood by speakers and writers of English, no matter where they live.

Using non-standard English in the classroom or workplace might lead people to doubt your skills, your intentions, or your level of education. Non-standard English comes in many forms, including these:

- *Slang.* These informal expressions often create vivid images. When students talk about "acing" a test or "hanging loose" over spring break, for example, they're using slang.

- *Idioms.* These are colorful expressions with meanings that are not always obvious. For instance, a "fork in the road" does not refer to an eating utensil discarded on a street but rather to a place where a part of the road branches off. Even native speakers of English can find idioms hard to understand.

- *Dialects.* A sentence such as "I bought me a new phone" is common in certain areas of the United States. If you use such an expression in a paper or presentation, however, your audience might form a negative impression of you.

- *Jargon.* Some terms are used mainly by people who work in certain professions. If you talk about "hacking a site" or finding a "workaround," for example, then only students majoring in software engineering might understand you.

Any community of English speakers and writers can reshape the language for its own purposes. People who send text messages are doing that now. So are people who post on Twitter.com, a Web site that limits updates to 140 characters. Even your family, friends, and coworkers might develop expressions that no one else comprehends.

Learning when and how to use non-standard English is part of mastering the language. However, save non-standard expressions for informal conversations with friends. In that context, you can safely try out new words and ask for feedback about how you're using them. If you're not sure whether a particular expression is standard English, then talk to an instructor. And if someone points out that you're using non-standard English, be willing to learn from that experience. You can do this even when the feedback is not given with skill or sensitivity.

BUILD CONFIDENCE

Students who grew up with a language other than English might fall under the category of English as a Second Language (ESL) student, or English Language Learner (ELL). Many ESL/ELL students feel insecure about using English in social settings, including the classroom. Choosing not to speak, however, can delay your mastery of English and isolate you from other students.

As an alternative, make it your intention to speak up in class. List several questions beforehand and plan to ask them. Also schedule a time to meet with your instructors during office hours to discuss any material that you find confusing. These strategies can help you build relationships while developing English skills.

In addition, start a conversation with at least one native speaker of English in each of your classes. For openers, ask about their favorite instructors or ideas for future courses to take.

English is a complex language. Whenever you extend your vocabulary and range of expression, the likelihood of making mistakes increases. The person who wants to master English yet seldom makes mistakes is probably being too careful. Do not look upon mistakes as a sign of weakness. Mistakes can be your best teachers—if you are willing to learn from them.

Remember that the terms *English as a Second Language* and *English Language Learner* describe a difference—not a deficiency. The fact that you've entered a new culture and are mastering another language gives you a broader perspective than people who speak only one language.

And if you currently speak two or more languages, you've already demonstrated your ability to learn.

ANALYZE ERRORS IN USING ENGLISH

To learn from your errors, make a list of those that are most common for you. Next to the error, write a corrected version. For examples, see the chart. Remember that native speakers of English also use this technique—for instance, by making lists of words they frequently misspell.

Errors	Corrections
Sun is bright.	The sun is bright.
He cheerful.	He is cheerful.
I enjoy to play chess.	I enjoy playing chess.
Good gifts received everyone.	Everyone received good gifts.
I knew what would present the teachers.	I knew what the teachers would present.
I like very much burritos.	I like burritos very much.
I want that you stay.	I want you to stay.
Is raining.	It is raining.
My mother, she lives in Iowa.	My mother lives in Iowa.
I gave the paper to she.	I gave the paper to her.
They felt safety in the car.	They felt safe in the car.
He has three car.	He has three cars.
I have helpfuls family members.	I have helpful family members.
She don't know nothing.	She knows nothing.

LEARN BY SPEAKING AND LISTENING

You probably started your English studies by using textbooks. Writing and reading in English are important. Both can help you add to your English vocabulary and master grammar. To gain greater fluency and improve your pronunciation, also make it your goal to *hear* and *speak* standard English.

For example, listen to radio talk shows hosted by educated speakers with a wide audience. Imitate the speaker's pronunciation by repeating phrases and sentences that you hear. During TV shows and personal conversations, notice the facial expressions and gestures that accompany certain English words and phrases.

If you speak English with an accent, do not be concerned. Many people speak clear, accented English. Work on your accent only if you can't be easily understood.

Take advantage of opportunities to read and hear English at the same time. For instance, turn on English subtitles when watching a film on DVD. Also, check your library for audiobooks. Check out the printed book, and follow along as you listen.

USE ONLINE RESOURCES

Some online dictionaries allow you to hear words pronounced. They include Answers.com (**www.answers.com**) and Merriam-Webster Online (**www.m-w.com**).

Other resources include online book sites with a read-aloud feature. An example is Project Gutenberg (**www.gutenberg.org; search on "Audio Books"**). Speaks for Itself (**www.speaksforitself.com**) is a free download that allows you to hear text from Web sites read aloud.

Also, check general Web sites for ESL students. A popular one is Dave's ESL Café (**www.eslcafe.com**), which will lead you to others.

GAIN SKILLS IN NOTE TAKING AND TESTING

When taking notes, remember that you don't have to capture everything that an instructor says. To a large extent, the art of note taking consists of choosing what *not* to record. Listen for key words, main points, and important examples. Remember that instructors will often repeat these things. You'll have more than one chance to pick up on the important material. When you're in doubt, ask for repetition or clarification.

Taking tests is a related challenge. You may find that certain kinds of test questions—such as multiple-choice items—are more common in the United States than in your native country. The suggestions for reading, note-taking, and memorizing in this book can help you master these and many other types of tests.

CREATE A COMMUNITY OF ENGLISH LEARNERS

Learning as part of a community can increase your mastery. For example, when completing a writing assignment in English, get together with other people who are learning the language. Read each other's papers and suggest revisions. Plan on revising your paper a number of times based on feedback from your peers.

You might feel awkward about sharing your writing with other people. Accept that feeling—and then remind yourself of everything you have to gain by learning from a group. In addition to learning English more quickly, you can raise your grades and make new friends.

Native speakers of English might be willing to assist your group. Ask your instructors to suggest someone. This person can benefit from the exchange of ideas and the chance to learn about other cultures.

CELEBRATE YOUR GAINS

Every time you analyze and correct an error in English, you make a small gain. Celebrate those gains. Taken together over time, they add up to major progress in mastering English as a second language. ■

Developing
INFORMATION LITERACY

Masterfile

*Master students find information from appropriate sources, evaluate the information, organize it, and use it to achieve a purpose. The ability to do this in a world where data is literally at your fingertips is called **information literacy**.*

Information literacy is a set of skills that you can use for many purposes. For example, you might want to learn more about a product, a service, a vacation spot, or a potential job. You might want to follow up on something you heard on the radio or saw on TV. Or you might want to develop a topic for a paper or presentation. In each case, success depends on information literacy.

Information literacy happens in a continuous cycle. You ask questions and gather answers. Those answers lead to more questions, which lead to more research. At each stage, you dig deeper. You understand your topic in a more refined way. You ask better questions and find better answers.

To begin, choose your topic with care. A topic that's too broad is hard to cover in a single presentation or paper. A topic that's too narrow won't lead you to many sources of information. The trick is to find a topic that falls in between these extremes.

GET IDEAS FOR A TOPIC

You can use the Web to get some initial ideas for a topic. Go to a search engine such as Google (google.com), Bing (bing.com), or DuckDuckGo (duckduckgo.com). In the search box, enter a key word followed by *research paper topics*—for example, *astronomy research paper topics*.

Another source of topic ideas is Alltop (alltop.com). It lists hundreds of Web sites organized by major topics. You'll find links to the five most recent articles on each site.

If you are writing a paper or preparing a presentation for class, ask your instructor for guidance in choosing your topic. She may have requirements about how many sources—and what kind of sources—to use. Choose a topic to meet those requirements.

DISCOVER QUESTIONS ABOUT YOUR TOPIC

One of the early steps in Muscle Reading involves asking questions. Start with your *main question* about the topic you chose. This is the thing that sparked your curiosity in the first place. Answering it is your purpose for doing research.

Your main question will raise a number of smaller, related questions. These are *supporting questions*. They also call for answers.

DISCOVERING QUESTIONS— AN EXAMPLE

Suppose that you're interested in the economic recession that began during 2008 in the United States. You know that one factor in this recession was the mortgage credit crisis. This occurred when banks loaned large amounts of money to people to buy a house—even if those people had little income and a low credit rating.

Your main question might be: *Leading up to the mortgage credit crisis of 2008, what led banks to lend money to people with a poor credit history?* Your list of supporting questions might include the following:

- What banks were involved in the mortgage credit crisis?
- What is the criteria for a mortgage worthy borrower?
- How do banks discover a person's credit history?
- What are the signs of a poor credit history?

FIND SOURCES

Next, find sources of answers to your questions. Sources include books, articles, Web sites, and people you can interview.

Start with sources that give an overview of your topic. One is an encyclopedia. Through your campus or community library, you might have full access to Encyclopedia Britannica (**www.britannica.com**) and other encyclopedia databases that are not available to the general public. To find out more, make both an online and in-person visit to the library.

Another option is Wikipedia (wikipedia.org). Because the quality of Wikipedia articles varies so much, they are *not* acceptable sources to use for a final paper or presentation. However, many Wikipedia articles mention *other* respected sources.

Google Books (**www.books.google.com**) and Google Scholar (scholar.google.com) offer more ways to find sources. For each site, enter your topic and key words from your questions in the search box. Google Scholar is especially useful for finding peer-reviewed articles in professional journals.

Following are more encyclopedias and search engines to check:

- Dogpile (**www.dogpile.com**)
- Pandia Metasearch (**www.pandia.com/metasearch**)
- Mamma (**www.mamma.com**)

> *One crucial skill for information literacy is using key words. Your choice of key words determines the quality of results that you get from search engines.*

- **http://Bartebly.com**
- **www.Encyclopedia.com**
- **www.Answers.com**
- **www.About.com**

You might find that certain sources appear over and over again in the results that you get from your searches. These are important sources for you to find and read for yourself.

REFINE YOUR TOPIC

A common problem at this point is to discover that your topic is too broad. Fortunately, there are several ways to narrow it down.

One option is Yahoo! Directory (**http://dir.yahoo.com**). What you'll see first is a page with a list of major topics. Click on any of these to find narrower topics (subtopics). Enter some key words in the search box to narrow the topic even more. The DMOZ Open Directory Project (**www.dmoz.org**) and Clusty (**www.clusty.com**) work in a similar way.

REFINE YOUR QUESTIONS

As you skim these sites and the other sources, review the main question and supporting questions that you asked at the beginning of your research. You might choose to drop some of those questions, reword them, or ask new questions based on what you've discovered so far.

REFINE YOUR KEY WORDS

One crucial skill for information literacy is using key words. Your choice of key words determines the quality of results that you get from search engines. For better search results:

Use specific key words. Entering *firefox* or *safari* will give you more focused results than entering *web browser*. *Reading strategies* or *note-taking strategies* will get more specific results than *study strategies*. Do not type in your whole research question as a sentence. The search engine will look for each word and give you a lot of useless results.

Use unique key words. Whenever possible, use proper names. Enter *Beatles* or *Radiohead* rather than *British rock bands*. If you're looking for nearby restaurants, enter *restaurant* and your zip code rather than the name of your city.

Use quotation marks if you're looking for certain words in a certain order. "Audacity of hope" will return a list of pages with that exact phrase.

Search within a site. If you're looking only for articles about college tuition from the *New York Times*, then add *new york times* or *nytimes.com* to the search box.

Remember to think of synonyms. For example, "hypertension" is often called "high blood pressure."

When you're not sure of a key word, add a wild card character. In most search engines, the wild card character is the asterisk (*). If you're looking for the title of a film directed by Clint Eastwood and just can't remember the name, enter *clint eastwood directed* *.

Look for more search options. Many search engines also offer advanced search features and explain how to use them. Look for the word *advanced* or *more* on the site's home page, and click on the link. If in doubt about how to use your library's search engines, ask a librarian for help.

DIG DEEPER INTO THE WEB

When people talk about the Internet, they usually mean the *free Web*—sites that anyone can access through popular search engines. However, this adds up to less than half of all Web sites. Other sites are created by organizations for their employees, partners, or subscribers rather than the general public. Together these make up the *deep Web*.

The deep Web offers several benefits. Here you will find articles written by recognized experts for an audience of scholars. Plus, deep Web sites often have their own search engines, such as:

- H. W. Wilson (**www.hwwilson.com**)
- Highbeam Research (**www.highbeam.com**)
- NewsBank (**www.newsbank.com**)
- Wolters Kluwer UpToDate (**www.uptodate.com**)

To access such sources, go to your school or community library. It will probably have access to a number of deep Web sites.

GET TO KNOW YOUR LIBRARY

Remember that many published materials are available in print as well as online. This is another reason to visit a library. Start by talking to a reference librarian. Tell this person about the questions you want to answer, and ask for good sources of information. Also visit your library's Web site.

Remember that libraries—from the smallest one in your hometown to the Smithsonian in Washington, D.C.—consist of just three basic elements:

- *Catalogs*—databases that list all of the library's accessible sources.
- *Collections*—materials, such as periodicals (magazines, journals, and newspapers), books, pamphlets, ebooks, audiobooks, and materials available from other libraries via interlibrary loan.

- *Computer resources*—online databases that allow you to look at full-text articles from magazines, journals, and newspapers.

TALK TO PEOPLE

Making direct contact with people can offer a welcome relief from hours of solitary research time and give you valuable hands-on involvement. Your initial research will uncover the names of experts on your chosen topic. Consider doing an interview with one of these people—in person, over the phone, or via e-mail.

To get the most from interviews:

- Schedule a specific time for the interview—and a specific place, if you're meeting the expert in person. Agree on the length of the interview in advance and work within that time frame.
- Enter the interview with a short list of questions to ask. Allow time for additional questions that occur to you during the interview.

> *Making direct contact with people can offer a welcome relief from hours of solitary research time and give you valuable hands-on involvement.*

- If you want to record the interview, ask for permission in advance. When talking to people who don't want to be recorded, be prepared to take handwritten notes.
- Ask experts for permission to quote their comments.
- Be courteous before, during, and after the interview; thank the person for taking time to talk with you.
- End the interview at your agreed-on time.
- Follow up on interviews with a thank-you note.
- Be sure to cite your interview as a source for your research.

EVALUATE INFORMATION

Some students assume that anything that's published in print or on the Internet is true. Unfortunately, that's not the case. Some sources of information are more reliable than others, and some published information is misleading or mistaken.

Before evaluating any source of information, make sure that you understand what it says. Use the techniques of Muscle Reading to comprehend an author's message. Then think critically about the information. Be sure to look for the following:

- *Publication date.* If your topic is time-sensitive, then set some guidelines about how current you want your sources to be—for example, that they were published during the last five years.
- *Credibility.* Scan the source for biographical information about the author. Look for educational degrees, training, and work experience that qualify this person to publish on the topic of your research.

- *Bias.* Determine what the Web site or other source is "selling"—the product, service, or point of view it promotes. Political affiliations or funding sources might color the author's point of view. For instance, you can predict that a pamphlet on gun control policies that's printed with funding from the National Rifle Association will promote certain points of view. Round out your research with other sources on the topic.

> *Discover the pleasures of emerging insights and sudden inspiration. You just might get hooked on the adventure of information literacy.*

EVALUATE INTERNET SOURCES WITH EXTRA CARE

Ask the following questions:

Who pays for the site? Carefully check information from an organization that sells advertising. Look for an "About This Site" link—a clue to sources of funding. You want to avoid sources that may pose a conflict of interest.

Who runs the site? Look for a clear description of the person or organization responsible for the content. If the sponsoring person or organization did not create the site's content, then find out who did.

How is the site's content selected? Look for a link that lists members of an editorial board or other qualified reviewers.

Does the site support claims with evidence? Credible sites base their editorial stands on expert opinion and facts from scientific studies. If you find grandiose claims supported only by testimonials, beware. When something sounds too good to be true, it probably is.

Does the site link to other sites? Think critically about these sites as well.

How can readers connect with the site? Look for a way to contact the site's publisher with questions and comments. See whether you can find a physical address, e-mail address, and phone number. Sites that conceal this information might conceal other facts. Also inspect reader comments on the site to see whether a variety of opinions are expressed.

Many Web sites from government agencies and nonprofit organizations have strict and clearly stated editorial policies. These are often good places to start your research.

DISTINGUISH BETWEEN PRIMARY AND SECONDARY SOURCES

In addition, distinguish between primary and secondary sources. *Primary sources* can lead to information treasures. Primary sources are firsthand materials—personal journals, letters, speeches, government documents, scientific experiments, field observations, interviews with recognized experts, archeological digs, artifacts, and original works of art. Primary sources can also include scholarly publications such as the *New England Journal of Medicine*.

Secondary sources summarize, explain, and comment on primary sources. Examples are popular magazines such as *Time* and *Newsweek* and general reference works such as *Encyclopedia Britannica*. Secondary sources are useful places to start your research. Use them to get an overview of your topic. Depending on the assignment, these may be all you need for informal research.

TAKE NOTES AND REFLECT ON THEM

Take careful notes on your sources. Remember to keep a list of all your sources of information and avoid plagiarism. Be prepared to cite your sources in footnotes or endnotes, and a bibliography.

Also make time to digest all the information you gather. Ask yourself:

- Do I have answers to my main question?
- Do I have answers to my supporting questions?
- What are the main ideas from my sources?
- Do I have personal experiences that can help me answer these questions?
- If a television talk show host asked me these questions, how would I answer?
- On what points do my sources agree?
- On what points do my sources disagree?
- Do I have statistics and other facts that I can use to support my ideas?
- What new questions do I have?

The beauty of these questions is that they stimulate *your* thinking. Discover the pleasures of emerging insights and sudden inspiration. You just might get hooked on the adventure of information literacy. ∎

Practicing Critical Thinking 4

By thinking deeply about your reading, you can make an immediate difference in your ability to learn anything.

Recall that psychologist Benjamin Bloom described six levels of thinking:

Level 1: Remembering

Level 2: Understanding

Level 3: Applying

Level 4: Analyzing

Level 5: Evaluating

Level 6: Creating

The purpose of this exercise is to practice thinking at **Level 5: Evaluating.** This means rating the truth, usefulness, or quality of a suggestion—and giving reasons for your rating.

Following is a sample evaluation of Muscle Reading:

The steps of Muscle Reading are useful. Applying all the steps of this method does lead me to actively preview and review as well as read. Doing this consistently would help me stay on top of material throughout the whole term rather than relying on cramming the night before a test. The disadvantage is that eight steps are a lot to remember. For this reason, I prefer the three-step "leaner approach" to Muscle Reading. This approach is easier to remember. Because it only includes three major steps, I am also more likely to use it.

Evaluating often means asking and answering questions such as:

- Does this suggestion make sense? Is it logical and clearly stated?
- What are the possible advantages and disadvantages of this suggestion?
- Could I take steps to apply this suggestion? If so, what are they?
- Could I modify this suggestion to make it more effective? If so, how would I change it?
- Could I replace this suggestion with a different one that is more effective? If so, what is it?

On a test, questions that call for evaluation often begin with words such as *appraise, assess, critique, judge, justify, rank, recommend,* or *support.*

Now it's your turn. Recall any idea from this chapter (**Level 1: Remembering**) and think about it at **Level 5: Evaluating.** Then evaluate your suggestion in three steps:

1. Summarize the suggestion in one sentence.

_____

_____

2. List the questions that you will use to evaluate this suggestion.

_____

_____

_____

3. Write a brief answer to each question.

_____

_____

_____

_____

_____

_____

Courtesy of Matias Manzano

MASTER STUDENT PROFILE

MATIAS MANZANO

(1985–) One of five finalists for Rookie Teacher of the Year in Miami-Dade County, Florida, the fourth largest school district in America

struggled early on with reading. In fourth grade, I scored a 23 percent on a reading proficiency assessment. Many people would have written me off at that young age—a poor, Latino, illegal immigrant who ended up in New York and was destined to fail.

I remember thinking in elementary school that it wasn't fair that the other kids spoke English at home and for that reason, they were better readers than I was. There were times when I would try to read something, and the words would float around the page as if they didn't want to be understood.

I had a teacher in fifth grade, Ms. Leventhaul, who really made me want to improve my reading. She was inspirational. There was something about her demeanor, the way that she carried herself, which was both intimidating and motivational at the same time. She treated me as if she knew that I could achieve greatness.

My brother also challenged me to just read more books. I read at least 20 R. L. Stine *Goosebumps* books in a competition that I had one year with him. We used to have conversations after reading the books. I didn't realize it at the time, but having those conversations allowed me to develop reading skills like making comparisons, identifying main ideas, describing settings, and identifying foreshadowing. By sixth grade, I had scored a 99 percent on the reading assessment.

After high school, I decided to follow in my brother's footsteps and attend Stony Brook University in New York. Money was tight. We would roam around the college, staying with different friends who allowed us to sleep on their floor for the night. I guess I was, in a way, homeless.

Toward the end of my sophomore year, the letter came that our application for legal residence was accepted. I

Matias Manzano *is self-directed.*
You *can be self-directed by focusing your energy on what matters most to you.*

was able to receive financial aid. I no longer had to work 40 hours a week to pay for tuition. I could focus my energy on academics.

The reading skills that I started developing in elementary school became the foundation for my success in college. As a history major and Latin American Caribbean studies minor, I found that my assignments were based on reading scholarly journals and books. My vocabulary improved exponentially. I learned to read entire books in just a few hours.

I can tell you first-hand what the research says is true: The greatest factor impacting the education of our nation's poorest children is the quality of the teacher that they get. All of my students have talents. All of my students have a spark. I joined Teach for America and the staff at Jose De Diego Middle School in Miami because I know that the children living in poverty can achieve at the highest rates.

If I had taken certain tests in Florida when I was in fourth grade, the state would have projected me as a future prison inmate. My apologies to the statisticians who use elementary student achievement scores to predict future prison needs. Soon I will finish my master's degree in educational leadership. I am driven by a desire to be the best and to achieve greatness in all aspects of my life, because I believe that no task is insurmountable. ■

QUIZ
Chapter 4

Name: _____

Date: _____

1. Briefly explain the problem with holding on to mental pictures, as suggested by the Power Process in this chapter.

   Pictures can prevent us from seeing what is really there. Our pictures often lead to our being angry or disappointed. We set up expectations of events before they occur. Sometimes we don't even realize we have these expectations. (*Power Process: Notice your pictures and let them go*, page 124)

2. Name the acrostic that can help you remember the eight steps of Muscle Reading.

   POQ, FFA, RRR = **P**ry **O**ut **Q**uestions, **F**ocus and **F**lag **A**nswers, **R**ecite, **R**eview, and **R**eview again. (*How Muscle Reading works*, page 126)

3. According to the text, Muscle Reading is a step-by-step procedure that cannot be changed. True or false? Explain your answer.

   False. The eight-step process is not an all-or-nothing package. Use it appropriately and choose what steps to apply as you read. (*Muscle Reading—A leaner approach*, page 130)

4. Give three examples of what to look for when previewing a reading assignment.

   Describe at least three of the following: (a) Look over the table of contents. (b) Survey the entire assignment. (c) Keep the preview short. (d) Look for summary statements. (e) Look for familiar concepts, facts, or ideas. (f) Read all chapter headings and subheadings. (g) Inspect drawings, diagrams, charts, tables, graphs, and photographs. (h) Ask yourself what you will do with this material and how it can relate to your long-term goals. (*Phase 1: Before you read*, page 127)

5. Briefly explain how to use headings in a text to create an outline.

   The headings of the text can be used as the major points of an outline, and the subheadings could serve as the subcategories in the outline. (*Phase 1: Before you read*, page 127)

6. In addition to underlining and highlighting, there are other ways to mark up a text. List three possibilities.

   List any three of the following: (a) Use asterisks or exclamation points near important sentences. (b) Circle key terms. (c) Write short definitions of key terms in the margin. (d) Mark possible test questions with a *Q* in the margin. (e) Write personal comments in the margin. (f) Write related page number references in the margin. (g) Write summaries of main points. (h) Rewrite chapter titles, headings, and subheadings. (i) Draw diagrams, pictures, or maps. (j) Number steps in a list or series of related points. (*Phase 2: While you read*, page 128)

7. To get the most benefit from marking a book, underline at least 20 percent of the text. True or false? Explain your answer.

   False. Underlining is generally more effective when only the most important material is flagged. A small portion of underlined text, less than 10 percent, is usually sufficient for review. (*Phase 2: While you read*, page 128)

8. Compare the steps of Muscle Reading with the approach described in "Muscle Reading—A leaner approach." How do these two methods differ?

   (Answers will vary.) The leaner approach is a more structured, simplified approach than Muscle Reading, but both approaches are based on the same ideas and should be equally effective when used appropriately. Whereas Muscle Reading involves steps to take before, during, and after you read, the leaner approach is aimed at the process during reading. (*Muscle Reading—a leaner approach*, pages 125 and 130)

9. Explain at least three strategies you can use when reading is tough.

   Explain at least three of the following: (a) Read it again. (b) Look for essential words. (c) Hold a mini-review. (d) Read it out loud. (e) Talk to your instructor. (f) Stand up. (g) Jump to the next section or the end of the article or chapter. (h) Find a tutor. (i) Use another text. (j) Pretend you understand and then explain it. (k) Ask, "What's going on here?" (l) Stop reading. (*When reading is tough*, page 134)

10. Define the term *information literacy*.

    Information literacy is a set of skills to use whenever you want to answer questions or find information. It involves finding information from appropriate sources, evaluating the information, organizing it, and using it to achieve a purpose. The ability to do this in a world where data is literally at your fingertips is called information literacy. (*Developing information literacy*, page 141)

SKILLS SNAPSHOT
Chapter 4

After studying this chapter, you might want to make some changes in the way you read. First, take a snapshot of your current reading skills. Then set a goal to adopt a habit that will take your reading skills to a new level. Complete the following sentences.

Discovery

My score on the Reading section of the Discovery Wheel was . . .

If someone asked me how well I keep up with my assigned reading, I would say that . . .

To get the most out of a long reading assignment, I start by . . .

When I don't understand something that I've read, I overcome confusion by . . .

Intention

I'll know that I've reached a new level of mastery with reading when . . .

The idea from this chapter that could make the biggest difference in my experience of reading is . . .

Action

The new reading habit that I plan to adopt is . . .

This new habit can help me succeed in the workplace by . . .

At the end of this course, I would like my *Reading* score on the Discovery Wheel to be . . .

INSTRUCTOR TOOLS & TIPS

NOTES

"Rather than try to gauge your note-taking skill by quantity, think in this way: Am I simply doing clerk's work or am I assimilating new knowledge and putting down my own thoughts? To put down your own thoughts you must put down your own words. . . . If the note taken shows signs of having passed through a mind, it is a good test of its relevance and adequacy." —Jacques Barzun and Henry Graff

PREVIEW

Linking Chapters 4, 5, and 6 together is very important because students sometimes tend to compartmentalize these chapters. Introducing note taking as a four-part process asks students to understand the following:

- *Why* it is important to capture the context of *What* they are taking notes on.

- This chapter will help students identify *What* note-taking strategies are effective: observing, recording, and reviewing. Each part of the process is essential and interdependent with the others.

- After students learn new strategies for taking notes, ask them *How* they will apply these techniques to their other courses. Practice is an important element in adopting or adapting effective note-taking techniques. Encourage students to test the new methods over time before they evaluate the effectiveness of a particular method. In class discussions, give students time to interpret the effectiveness of their note taking. Remember to suggest that learning styles have a significant impact on note-taking skill. Visual learners can find note taking more pleasant and effective when they use personalized visual elements like colorful paper, favorite colors in highlighters and pens, or other visual elements that make the notes feel personal and unique.

- Students can also apply *What if* by connecting Chapters 4, 5, and 6 together into a study-skills section for the course.

GUEST SPEAKER

At this point in the term, students should be aware of how they are doing in their classes. It may be a good time to invite guest speakers from academic support services to talk to your students about how to get additional help they may need. Possibilities include the

master instructor best practice

❝*I tell my students, "You are your own best instructor." As an in-class discussion, I ask students to tell me about their favorite recording artist or sports figure. I ask questions such as "Where does she live?" and "How old is he?" Then I switch over to asking students about their professors. I almost always get a blank stare when I ask, "What do you know about your math instructor?" Then I challenge them to brainstorm ideas on how they can learn more about their instructors and how this connectedness will help them in class. Some shy students particularly like the idea of conducting Internet research and reading about their instructors online.*❞

—Eldon McMurray, Utah Valley State College

coordinators of the writing center, tutoring program, or academic success center. Announce the guest speaker to students in advance, and ask students to prepare two or three questions in preparation. For example, they might ask a writing center representative, "In addition to writing classes, how will this service help me in my other classes?" Students can also practice taking Cornell method notes during the guest lecturer's mini-lecture, using their own questions. The questions could be placed in the left-hand column, with the corresponding answers on the right side of the paper. Use these short segments to provide practice sessions. This helps students flex their

master instructor
best practice

❝I share an additional tool for note taking with my students: Use the power of doodling. If you find that you often have drawn circles around every hole on the paper and have added doodles in every open space in your notes, perhaps you need to use your "doodle power" to your advantage. Doodlers often find that they put more effort into their artistic efforts than they do into the content of their notes. Consider using this energy to create notes in the style of a comic strip with stick figures (for speed) and balloons for dialogue. As you invest your energy in depicting the information on paper, you will become more involved in the presentation instead of allowing the doodles to distract you.❞

—*Sam Sink, Wilkes Community College*

note-taking muscles, to better prepare them for longer, more rigorous segments in their college classes.

LECTURE

Many new college students have no idea what they should do when they miss a class. They fail to contact either their instructor or their classmates to find out what handouts, information, and assignments they missed. As a follow-up to the article "What to do when you miss a class" (page 153), consider providing a brief lecture on this topic. It's also a good time to review classroom and campus attendance policies with your students. You might include discussion of topics that may seem obvious to you but can be perplexing to new college students—how to communicate with your college professors (benefits of e-mail, phone calls, or office visits). You might also want to explain to students how to read an office schedule to determine availability of professors or to identify adjunct professors, who may not have a campus office or required office hours.

Workplace Application: Taking notes at work. Remind students that they may be asked to take notes during work meetings and presentations. Even if taking notes is not required, encourage students to do so for their own benefit. Although some workers joke about the tedium of work meetings, meetings are where many important problems are addressed and many decisions are made. Using the textbook suggestions of observing, recording, and reviewing will also work for

note taking at meetings. Students should be reminded of the following:

- *Observe.* There are some things that need to be done before the start of the meeting. Gather all necessary materials, including pens, paper, and important documents to discuss. Review all previous notes. Scan the agenda if it has been handed out early. Arrive at the meeting early so you can get a good seat, one close to the meeting leader and projector. Make notes on who is in attendance.

- *Record.* Come up with a preferred method of recording meeting notes. Students may find that text suggestions such as mind maps and outlines can be adapted to the workplace. It is easy to let the mind wander, but remember that important information is shared in meetings and you should try to be as mentally present as possible. Do not be afraid to add meaningful comments to the conversation and speak up when you need clarification on a topic.

- *Review.* Upon return to the office, review the meetings notes and fill in any holes in information. Consider typing the notes. Notice the follow-up actions discussed, especially ones you are responsible for completing.

EXERCISES/ACTIVITIES

1. **Power Process: I create it all (page 150).** This in-class activity helps bring this process alive. After students have read this process, ask them to recall a recent situation that went well for them at college, work, or home. Give them a few minutes to summarize the situation in their notes. Then ask them to list six ways that they created that successful situation. After they are done, ask for volunteers to share their success and how they created it. Then repeat the exercise, this time identifying a recent situation that did *not* work out well for them. For some students, this part may be much harder to do. Discuss this in class, with students volunteering to share their stories. You may need to give them an example to get the discussion started.

2. **Target class exercise.** Ask your students to select three of their other courses in which they would like to put their advanced note-taking system into practice. By applying the note-taking concepts to their other courses, they start to realize the power of the ideas presented in *Becoming a Master Student*. To give them a head start and to help them understand how setting the stage can contribute to effective note taking, have them prepare for taking notes in class by outlining the textbook reading that the professor's lecture will cover that day.

3. **Getting your money's worth, or "What am I paying for this ticket?"** Set up this demonstration by having a student come up at the beginning of the class and pay you $20 for a front-row seat. If there is no front-row seat available, ask a student to move so that the

paying student can sit there. Do this very seriously, and the irony of the object lesson will catch everyone's attention.

Ask students where they like to sit at a concert that costs $80 or more to attend. Then ask why tickets are so much more expensive for front-row center seats at a concert, at the center court of a professional basketball game, or on the 50-yard line of a football game. All they have to do to get the best seat in class is be on time or come a little early. Sitting in the front requires students to be more diligent and aware, as professors have a front-row seat to observe them as well! But this offers a payback, as professors can often learn the names of students in the front row and relate to their eye contact and the more intimate one-on-one response such a situation offers.

4. **"Be here now" in class.** Ask students to designate the upper right-hand corner of their class note page as their "Be here now" corner. When they catch their mind wandering, they can jot down a note or make a tick mark at the top of the page. They can then bring their attention back to the speaker. Counting tick marks afterward allows students to quantify the number of times their minds wander, and measure progress made in future classes. Practicing this helps them stay focused.

5. **Note-taking tools.** After students have read about the various note-taking strategies, discuss them in class. Divide the class into groups of four, and assign each group one of the new techniques to practice while you give a short lecture. Provide a safety net for this exercise by telling students that you will give them a detailed handout of the lecture at the end of class. This way, they don't have to worry about missing important information while they are trying out a new note-taking tool. After the lecture, the students discuss—with their group and then as a class—what they discovered about using the new strategy, including their initial perceptions of its strengths and weaknesses.

CONVERSATION/SHARING

Ask students to discuss the characteristics that make Richard Blanco a master student, using the list of master student qualities provided in the Introduction. Also ask them to identify *what* traits Blanco has that they feel they do not personally possess. This is followed by further sharing on *how* students can gain these qualities.

This chapter is a good time to facilitate a conversation and sharing about online courses. Some students love them; some hate them. Ask students to share what they have liked and/or disliked about online courses so that those who haven't tried them will have more information before it's time to register for the next term. Ask students their perceptions about the following: time demands of an online class, amount of reading required, expected response time from teachers. Online students can clear up some of these misperceptions by their own examples!

HOMEWORK

Review: The note-taking process flows (page 160). For many students, 24 hours is too long to wait before reviewing and processing their notes into long-term memory. Students can summarize their notes during their review by answering these key questions: *Why* is this idea important? *What* are the details I need to know? *How* will I remember and prepare to be tested on this material? *What if* the test is multiple choice? *What if* the test is an essay format? *How* can I know or anticipate this format in advance of the test?

Revisit your goals. One powerful way to achieve any goal is to periodically assess your progress in meeting it. Provide your students an opportunity to reflect on the materials that have been covered to date. Have students reflect on their goals set earlier in the book and make adjustments to their plan. While discussing this, suggest that your students look back at their Discovery Wheel and review their progress to date. Students will be given a formal post-course Discovery Wheel in Chapter 12.

EVALUATION

Frequent quizzes ensure that students pay attention during class and keep up with the text reading assignments. Moreover, quizzes provide students with opportunities for written reflection regarding new discoveries and intentions. Evaluation instruments also help you identify topics and concepts that students have not yet mastered.

Quiz Ideas for Chapter 5

Ask students to:

- Describe the Cornell note-taking system.
- Describe strategies for taking notes when instructors talk fast.
- Explain what it takes to become an online learner.
- Explain how the Power Process: I create it all can help them be more successful in college.
- List four ways they can be prepared in advance of taking notes.
- Take notes using a particular style, such as Cornell notes, on a brief video you show them.

MindTap™ **EMBRACE VALUABLE RESOURCES**

FOR CHAPTER 5

STUDENT RESOURCES: MINDTAP

- **Learning Outcomes.** Every chapter begins with an engaging video that visually outlines in a mind map format the key learning outcomes for that chapter. Students should find these short introductions not only helpful as chapter organizers, but as valuable note-taking models.

- **Engagement Activity: Master Students in Action.** Students hear firsthand from other students about their note-taking challenges and their strategies for overcoming challenges to note taking.

- **Aplia Homework Assignment: The note-taking process flows. Step one: Observe.** In this

assignment, students are introduced to various strategies that will help them improve their note taking and are asked to respond to questions that test their knowledge of core concepts.

- **Reflection Activity: Learning through Transition.** This Slice of Life video, created by student David Blanchard, discusses making transitions, embracing the unknown, taking risks, and learning through mistakes.

 MindTap™ *Your personal learning experience—learn anywhere, anytime.*

INSTRUCTOR COMPANION SITE

- **Looking for fresh, innovative ways to teach Chapter 5 topics?** Browse through the Best Practices recommendations in the Course Manual to see what other Master Instructors have been successfully doing with their students.

- **Check out the PowerPoint Library for a PowerPoint specifically created for Chapter 5.** This master library of PowerPoint

presentations makes it easy to find the right PowerPoint for you! If you're looking for a way to freshen up your lecture and engage your students with in-class activities, the PowerPoint Library is a great place to start.

Please visit login.cengage.com to log in and access the Instructor Companion Site.

master instructor
best practice

take note

" *I show students an eight-minute segment on polar bears from the PBS series* Nova. *It contains several statistics and Russian names. The videotape is also filled with pictures of "cute little bears." I ask students to take notes on the video. Afterward, I give an open-notes quiz. Between the pictures of bears, the statistics, and the Russian names, many of the students find their notes less*

than adequate. I then introduce mind mapping and the Cornell method of taking notes. The video is presented a second time, and everyone takes notes again, this time using one of the new methods. Students usually see an immediate improvement. This exercise stresses three points:

1. *Preparation and prior exposure to the material improve note taking and comprehension.*
2. *Sometimes the method by which information is given has distracting elements (i.e., cute little bears).*
3. *Note-taking skills can be learned and improved.* "

—Terry Johnson, Lindsey Wilson College

NOTES 5

Why

Note taking helps you remember information and influences how well you do on tests.

TECH

Note taking 2.0 Imagine how useful it would be to have your notes available to you anywhere, any time, from any digital device. Today there are digital tools—many of them free—for doing just that. ■ 170

Turn PowerPoints into powerful notes Some students stop taking notes during a PowerPoint presentation. Find out why this choice can be hazardous to your academic health. ■ 162

How

Recall a recent incident in which you had difficulty taking notes. Perhaps you were listening to an instructor who talked fast, or you got confused and stopped taking notes altogether. Then preview this chapter to find at least three strategies that you can use right away to help you take better notes.

Taking notes while reading
Taking notes on school- or work-related reading requires the same skills that apply to taking notes in class: observing, recording, and reviewing. Use these skills to take notes for review and for research. ■ 164

Record: The note-taking process flows ■ 155

Chapter 5

What if ...

I could take notes that remain informative and useful for weeks, months, or even years to come?

What is included ...

| CREATE
IT ALL

This article describes a powerful tool for times of trouble. In a crisis, "I create it all" can lead the way to solutions. The main point of this Power Process is to treat experiences, events, and circumstances in your life *as if* you created them.

"I create it all" is one of the most unusual and bizarre suggestions in this book. It certainly is not a belief. Use it when it works. Don't when it doesn't.

Keeping that in mind, consider how powerful this Power Process can be. It is really about the difference between two distinct positions in life: being a victim or being responsible.

A victim of circumstances is controlled by outside forces. We've all felt like victims at one time or another. Sometimes we felt helpless.

In contrast, we can take responsibility. Responsibility is "response-ability"—the ability to choose a *response* to any event. You can choose your *response* to any event, even when the event itself is beyond your control.

Many students approach grades from the position of being victims. When the student who sees the world this way gets an F, she reacts probably like this:

"Another F! That teacher couldn't teach her way out of a wet paper bag. She can't teach English for anything. There's no way to take notes in that class. And that textbook—what a bore!"

The problem with this viewpoint is that in looking for excuses, the student is robbing herself of the power to get any grade other than an F. She's giving all of her power to a bad teacher and a boring textbook.

There is another way, called *taking responsibility*. You can recognize that you choose your grades by choosing your actions. Then you are the source, rather than the result, of the grades you get. The student who got an F could react like this:

"Another F! Oh, shoot! Well, hmmm . . . What did I do to create it?"

Now, that's power. By asking, "How did I contribute to this outcome?" you are no longer the victim. This student might continue by saying, "Well, let's see. I didn't review my notes after class. That might have done it." Or "I went out with my friends the night before the test. Well, that probably helped me fulfill some of the requirements for getting an F."

The point is this: When the F is the result of your friends, the book, or the teacher, you probably can't do anything about it. However, if you *chose* the F, you can choose a different grade next time. You are in charge. ▮

Mark Chen/E+/Getty Images

THE NOTE-TAKING
PROCESS FLOWS

One way to understand note taking is to realize that taking notes is just one part of the process. Effective note taking consists of three parts: observing, recording, and reviewing.

First, you *observe* an "event." This can be a statement by an instructor, a lab experiment, a slide show of an artist's works, or a chapter of required reading.

Then you *record* your observations of that event. That is, you "take notes." These can be recorded in a variety of formats—paragraphs, outlines, diagrams, and more.

Finally, you *review* what you have recorded. You memorize, reflect, apply, and rehearse what you're learning. This step lifts ideas off the page and turns them into a working part of your mind.

Each part of the note-taking process is essential, and each depends on the others. Your observations determine what you record. What you record determines what you review. And the quality of your review can determine how effective your next observations will be. If you review your notes on the Sino-Japanese War of 1894, for example, the next day's lecture on the Boxer Rebellion of 1900 will make more sense.

Legible and speedy handwriting is also useful in taking notes. Knowledge of outlining is handy too. A nifty pen, a new notebook, and a laptop computer are all great note-taking devices.

And they're all worthless—unless you participate as an energetic observer *in* class and regularly review your notes *after* class. If you take those two steps, you can turn even the most disorganized chicken scratches into a powerful tool.

This is a well-researched aspect of student success in higher education. Study after study points to the benefits of taking notes. The value is added in two ways. First, you create a set of materials that refreshes your memory and helps you prepare for tests. Second, taking notes prompts you to listen effectively during class. You translate new ideas into your own words and images. You impose a personal and meaningful structure on what you see, read, and hear. You move from passive observer to active participant.[1] It's not that you take notes so that you can learn from them later. Instead, you learn *while* taking notes.

Computer technology takes traditional note taking to a whole new level. You can capture key notes with word-processing, outlining, database, and publishing software. Your notes become living documents that you can search, bookmark, tag, and archive like other digital files.

In short, note-taking is a "brain-friendly" activity. Taking notes leads you to actively encode the material in your own words and images—an effective strategy for moving new information into long-term memory.

Sometimes note taking looks like a passive affair, especially in large lecture classes. One person at the front of the room does most of the talking. Everyone else is seated and silent, taking notes. The lecturer seems to be doing all of the work.

Don't be deceived.

Look more closely. You'll see some students taking notes in a way that radiates energy. They're awake and alert, poised on the edge of their seats. They're writing—a physical activity that expresses mental engagement. These students listen for levels of ideas and information, make choices about what to record, and compile materials to review.

In higher education, you might spend hundreds of hours taking notes. Making them more effective is a direct investment in your success.

Think of your notes as a textbook that *you* create—one that's more current and more in tune with your learning preferences than any textbook you could buy. ■

© iStockphoto.com/Chad McDermott/cmcderm1

Purestock/Getty Images

OBSERVE
THE NOTE-TAKING PROCESS FLOWS

Sherlock Holmes, a fictional master detective and student of the obvious, could track down a villain by observing the fold of his scarf and the mud on his shoes. In real life, a doctor can save a life by observing a mole—one a patient has always had—that undergoes a rapid change.

An accountant can save a client thousands of dollars by observing the details of a spreadsheet. A student can save hours of study time by observing that she gets twice as much done at a particular time of day.

Keen observers see facts and relationships. They know ways to focus their attention on the details and then tap their creative energy to discover patterns.

Observation starts with preparation. Arrive early, and then put your brain in gear by reviewing your notes from the previous class. Scan your reading assignment. Look at the sections you have underlined or highlighted. Review assigned problems and exercises. Note questions you intend to ask.

To further sharpen your classroom observation skills, experiment with the following techniques, and continue to use those that you find most valuable. Many of these strategies can be adapted to the notes you take while reading.

SET THE STAGE

Complete outside assignments. Nothing is more discouraging (or boring) than sitting through a lecture about the relationship of Le Chatelier's principle to the principle of kinetics if you've never heard of Henri Louis Le Chatelier or kinetics. The more familiar you are with a subject, the more easily you can absorb important information during class lectures. Instructors usually assume that students complete assignments, and they construct their lectures accordingly.

Bring the right materials. A good pen does not make you a good observer, but the lack of a pen or notebook can be distracting enough to take the fine edge off your concentration. Make sure you have a pen, pencil, notebook, or any other materials you need. Bring your textbook to class, especially if the lectures relate closely to the text.

If you are consistently unprepared for a class, that might be a message about your intentions concerning the course. Find out if it is. The next time you're in a frantic scramble to

borrow pen and paper 37 seconds before the class begins, notice the cost. Use the borrowed pen and paper to write a Discovery Statement about your lack of preparation. Consider whether you intend to be successful in the course.

Sit front and center. Students who get as close as possible to the front and center of the classroom often do better on tests for several reasons. The closer you sit to the lecturer, the harder it is to fall asleep. The closer you sit to the front, the fewer interesting or distracting classmates are situated between you and the instructor. Material on the board is easier to read from up front. Also, the instructor can see you more easily when you have a question.

Instructors are usually not trained to perform. Some can project their energy to a large audience, but some cannot. A professor who sounds boring from the back of the room might sound more interesting up close.

Sitting up front enables you to become a constructive force in the classroom. By returning the positive energy that an engaged teacher gives out, you can reinforce the teacher's enthusiasm and enhance your experience of the class.

In addition, sound waves from the human voice begin to degrade at a distance of 8 to 12 feet. If you sit more than 15 feet from the speaker, your ability to hear and take effective notes might be compromised. Get close to the source of the sound. Get close to the energy.

Sitting close to the front is a way to commit yourself to getting what you want out of school. One reason students gravitate to the back of the classroom is that they think the instructor is less likely to call on them. Sitting in back can signal a lack of commitment. When you sit up front, you are declaring your willingness to take a risk and participate.

Clarify your intentions. Take a 3 × 5 card to class with you. On that card, write a short Intention Statement about what you plan to get from the class. Describe your intended level of participation or the quality of attention you will bring to the subject. Be specific. If you found your previous class notes to be inadequate, write down what you intend to do to make your notes from this class session more useful.

"BE HERE NOW" IN CLASS

Accept your wandering mind. Focusing your attention is useful when your head soars into the clouds. Don't fight daydreaming, however. When you notice your mind wandering during class, look at it as an opportunity to refocus your attention. If thermodynamics is losing out to beach parties, let go of the beach.

Notice your writing. When you discover yourself slipping into a fantasyland, feel the weight of your pen in your hand. Notice how your notes look. Paying attention to the act of writing can bring you back to the here and now.

You also can use writing in a more direct way to clear your mind of distracting thoughts. Pause for a few seconds and write those thoughts down. If you're distracted by thoughts of errands you need to run after class, list them on a 3 × 5 card and stick it in your pocket. Or simply put a symbol, such as an arrow or asterisk, in your notes to mark the places where your mind started to wander. Once your distractions are out of your mind and safely stored on paper, you can gently return your attention to taking notes.

Be with the instructor. In your mind, put yourself right up front with the instructor. Imagine that you and the instructor are the only ones in the room and that the lecture is a personal conversation between the two of you. Pay attention to the instructor's body language and facial expressions. Look the instructor in the eye.

Remember that the power of this suggestion is immediately reduced by digital distractions—Web surfing, e-mail checking, or text messaging. Taking notes is a way to stay focused. The physical act of taking notes signals your mind to stay in the same room as the instructor.

Notice your environment. When you become aware of yourself daydreaming, bring yourself back to class by paying attention to the temperature in the room, the feel of your chair, or the quality of light coming through the window. Run your hand along the surface of your desk.

Listen to the chalk on the blackboard or the sound of the teacher's voice. Be in that environment. Once your attention is back in the room, you can focus on what's happening in class.

Postpone debate. When you hear something you disagree with, note your disagreement and let it go. Don't allow your internal dialogue to drown out subsequent material. If your disagreement is persistent and strong, make note of it and then move on. Internal debate can

What to do when you miss a class

For most courses, you'll benefit by attending every class session. This allows you to observe and actively participate. If you miss a class, then catch up as quickly as possible. Find additional ways to observe class content.

Clarify policies on missed classes. On the first day of classes, find out about your instructors' policies on absences. See whether you will be allowed to make up assignments, quizzes, and tests. Also inquire about doing extra-credit assignments. If you know in advance that you'll miss some classes, let your instructor know as soon as possible. Create a plan for staying on top of your coursework.

Contact a classmate. Early in the semester, identify a student in each class who seems responsible and dependable. Exchange e-mail addresses and phone numbers. If you know you won't be in class, contact this student ahead of time. When you notice that your classmate is absent, pick up extra copies of handouts, make assignment lists, and offer copies of your notes.

Contact your instructor. If you miss a class, e-mail or call your instructor, or put a note in his mailbox. Ask whether he has another section of the same course that you can attend so you won't miss the lecture information. Also ask about getting handouts you might need before the next class meeting.

Consider technology. If there is a Web site for your class, check it for assignments and handouts you missed. Also, course management software, such as BlackBoard, might allow you to stay in contact with your instructor and fellow students during your absence.

prevent you from absorbing new information. It's okay to absorb information you don't agree with. Just absorb it with the mental tag "My instructor says . . ., and I don't agree with it."

Let go of judgments about lecture styles. Human beings are judgment machines. We evaluate everything, especially other people. If another person's eyebrows are too close together (or too far apart), if she walks a certain way or speaks with an unusual accent, we instantly make up a story about her. We do this so quickly that the process is usually not a conscious one.

Don't let your attitude about an instructor's lecture style, habits, or appearance get in the way of your education. You can decrease the power of your judgments if you pay attention to them and let them go.

You can even let go of judgments about rambling, unorganized lectures. Turn them to your advantage. Take the initiative and organize the material yourself. While taking notes, separate the key points from the examples and supporting evidence. Note the places where you got confused, and make a list of questions to ask.

Participate in class activities. Ask questions. Volunteer for demonstrations. Join in class discussions. Be willing to take a risk or look foolish if that's what it takes for you to learn. Chances are, the question you think is dumb is also on the minds of several of your classmates.

Relate the class to your goals. If you have trouble staying awake in a particular class, write at the top of your notes how that class relates to a specific goal. Identify the reward or payoff for reaching that goal.

Think critically about what you hear. This suggestion might seem contrary to the previously mentioned technique "postpone debate." It's not. You might choose not to think critically about the instructor's ideas during the lecture. That's fine. Do it later, as you review and edit your notes. This is the time to list questions or write down your agreements and disagreements.

WATCH FOR CLUES ABOUT IMPORTANT MATERIAL

Be alert to repetition. When an instructor repeats a phrase or an idea, make a note of it. Repetition is a signal that the instructor thinks the information is important.

Listen for introductory, concluding, and transition words and phrases. Introductory, concluding, and transition words and phrases include phrases such as *the following three factors, in conclusion, the most important consideration, in addition to,* and *on the other hand.* These phrases and others signal relationships, definitions, new subjects, conclusions, cause and effect, and examples. They reveal the structure of the lecture. You can use these phrases to organize your notes.

Watch the board or PowerPoint presentation. If an instructor takes the time to write something down on the board or show a PowerPoint presentation, consider the material to be important. Copy all equations, names, places, dates, statistics, and definitions. If your instructor presents pictures, graphics, or tables, pay special attention. Ask for copies of these, recreate them, or summarize their key points in your notes.

Watch the instructor's eyes. If an instructor glances at her notes and then makes a point, it is probably a signal that the information is especially important. Anything she reads from her notes is a potential test question.

Highlight the obvious clues. Instructors often hint strongly or tell students point-blank that certain information is likely to appear on an exam. Make stars or other special marks in your notes next to this information. Instructors are not trying to hide what's important.

Notice the instructor's interest level. If the instructor is excited about a topic, it is more likely to appear on an exam. Pay attention when she seems more animated than usual. ■

Interactive

Journal Entry 12
Discovery/Intention Statement

Create more value from lectures

Think back on the last few lectures you have attended. How do you currently observe (listen to) lectures? What specific behaviors do you have as you sit and listen? Do you listen more closely in some classes than others? Briefly describe your responses.

I discovered that I . . .

_____

_____

Now create an Intention Statement about any changes you want to make in the way you respond to lectures.

I intend to . . .

_____

_____

_____

RECORD
THE NOTE-TAKING PROCESS FLOWS

The format and structure of your notes are more important than how fast you write or how elegant your handwriting is. The following techniques can improve the effectiveness of your notes.

GENERAL TECHNIQUES FOR NOTE TAKING

Use key words. An easy way to sort the extraneous material from the important points is to take notes using key words. Key words or phrases contain the essence of communication. They include these:

- Concepts, technical terms, names, and numbers
- Linking words, including words that describe action, relationship, and degree (e.g., *most, least,* and *faster*)

Key words evoke images and associations with other words and ideas. They trigger your memory. That characteristic makes them powerful review tools. One key word can initiate the recall of a whole cluster of ideas. A few key words can form a chain from which you can reconstruct an entire lecture.

To see how key words work, take yourself to an imaginary classroom. You are now in the middle of an anatomy lecture. Picture what the room looks like, what it feels like, how it smells. You hear the instructor say:

> *Okay, what happens when we look directly over our heads and see a piano falling out of the sky? How do we take that signal and translate it into the action of getting out of the way? The first thing that happens is that a stimulus is generated in the neurons—receptor neurons—of the eye. Light reflected from the piano reaches our eyes. In other words, we see the piano.*
>
> *The receptor neurons in the eye transmit that sensory signal—the sight of the piano—to the body's nervous system. That's all they can do—pass on information. So we've got a sensory signal coming into the nervous system. But the neurons that initiate movement in our legs are effector neurons. The information from the sensory neurons must be transmitted to effector neurons, or we will get squashed by the piano. There must be some kind of interconnection between receptor and effector neurons. What happens between the two? What is the connection?*

Key words you might note in this example include *stimulus, generated, receptor neurons, transmit, sensory signals, nervous system, effector neurons,* and *connection.* You can reduce the instructor's 163 words to these 12 key words. With a few transitional words, your notes might look like this:

> Stimulus (piano) generated in receptor neurons (eye)
>
> ↓
>
> Sensory signals transmitted by nervous system to effector neurons (legs)
>
> What connects receptor to effector?

Note the last key word of the lecture: *connection.* This word is part of the instructor's question and leads to the next point in the lecture. Be on the lookout for questions like this. They can help you organize your notes and are often clues for test questions.

Use pictures and diagrams. Make relationships visual. Copy all diagrams from the board, and invent your own. A drawing of a piano falling on someone who is looking up, for example, might be used to demonstrate the relationship

of receptor neurons to effector neurons. Label the eyes "receptor" and the feet "effector." This picture implies that the sight of the piano must be translated into a motor response. By connecting the explanation of the process with the unusual picture of the piano falling, you can link the elements of the process together.

Write notes in paragraphs. When it is difficult to follow the organization of a lecture or put information into outline form, create a series of informal paragraphs. These paragraphs should contain few complete sentences. Reserve complete sentences for precise definitions, direct quotations, and important points that the instructor emphasizes by repetition or other signals—such as the phrase "This is an important point."

Copy material from the board and a PowerPoint presentation. Record key formulas, diagrams, and problems that the teacher presents on the board or in a PowerPoint presentation. Copy dates, numbers, names, places, and other facts. You can even use your own signal or code to flag important material.

Use a three-ring binder. Three-ring binders have several advantages over other kinds of notebooks. First, pages can be removed and spread out when you review. This way, you can get the whole picture of a lecture. Second, the three-ring-binder format allows you to insert handouts right into your notes. Third, you can insert your own out-of-class notes in the correct order.

Use only one side of a piece of paper. When you use one side of a page, you can review and organize all your notes by spreading them out side by side. Most students find the benefit well worth the cost of the paper. Perhaps you're concerned about the environmental impact of consuming more paper. If so, you can use the blank side of old notes and use recycled paper.

Use 3 × 5 cards. As an alternative to using notebook paper, use 3 × 5 cards to take lecture notes. Copy each new concept onto a separate 3 × 5 card.

Keep your own thoughts separate. For the most part, avoid making editorial comments in your lecture notes. The danger is that when you return to your notes, you might mistake your own ideas for those of the instructor. If you want to make a comment, clearly label it as your own.

Use an "I'm lost" signal. No matter how attentive and alert you are, you might get lost and confused in a lecture. If it is inappropriate to ask a question, record in your notes that you were lost. Invent your own signal—for example, a circled question mark. When you write down your code for "I'm lost," leave space for the explanation or clarification that you will get later. The space will also be a signal

that you missed something. Later, you can speak to your instructor or ask to see a fellow student's notes.

Label, number, and date all notes. Develop the habit of labeling and dating your notes at the beginning of each class. Number the page too. Sometimes the sequence of material in a lecture is important. Write your name, phone number, and e-mail in each notebook in case you lose it.

Leave blank space. Notes tightly crammed into every corner of the page are hard to read and difficult to use for review. Give your eyes a break by leaving plenty of space. Later, when you review, you can use the blank spaces in your notes to clarify points, write questions, or add other material.

Take notes in different colors. You can use colors as highly visible organizers. For example, you can signal important points with red. Or use one color of ink for notes about the text and another color for lecture notes.

Use graphic signals. The following ideas can be used with any note-taking format:

- Use brackets, parentheses, circles, and squares to group information that belongs together.
- Use stars, arrows, and underlining to indicate important points. Flag the most important points with double stars, double arrows, or double underlines.
- Use arrows and connecting lines to link related groups.
- Use equal signs and greater-than and less-than signs to indicate compared quantities.

To avoid creating confusion with graphic symbols, use them carefully and consistently. Write a master key, or legend, of your symbols in the front of your notebooks; an example is shown here.

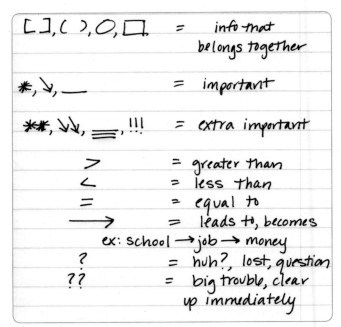

Use recorders effectively. Some students record lectures with audio or digital recorders, but there are persuasive arguments against doing so. When you record a lecture, there is a strong temptation to daydream. After all, you can always listen to the lecture again later on. Unfortunately, if you let the recorder do all of the work, you are skipping a valuable part of the learning process.

There are other potential problems as well. Listening to recorded lectures can take a lot of time—more time than reviewing written notes. Recorders can't answer the questions you didn't ask in class. Also, recording devices malfunction. In fact, the unscientific Hypothesis of Recording Glitches states that the tendency of recorders to malfunction is directly proportional to the importance of the material.

With those warnings in mind, you can use a recorder effectively if you choose. For example, you can use recordings as backups to written notes. Turn the recorder on; then take notes as if it weren't there. Recordings can be especially useful if an instructor speaks fast.

Note: Before you hit the "record" button, check with your instructor. Some prefer not to be recorded.

THE CORNELL METHOD

A note-taking system that has worked for students around the world is the *Cornell method*.[2] Originally developed by Walter Pauk at Cornell University during the 1950s, this approach continues to be taught across the United States and in other countries as well.

The cornerstone of this method is what Pauk calls the *cue column*—a wide margin on the left-hand side of the paper. The cue column is the key to the Cornell method's many benefits. Here's how to use it.

Format your paper. On each sheet of your notepaper, draw a vertical line, top to bottom, about 2 inches from the left edge of the paper. This line creates the cue column—the space to the left of the line. You can also find Web sites that allow you to print out pages in this format. Just do an Internet search using the key words *cornell method pdf*.

Take notes, leaving the cue column blank. As you read an assignment or listen to a lecture, take notes on the right-hand side of the paper. Fill up this column with sentences, paragraphs, outlines, charts, or drawings. Do not write in the cue column. You'll use this space later, as you do the next steps.

Condense your notes in the cue column. Think of the notes you took on the right-hand side of the paper as a set of answers. In the cue column, list potential test questions that correspond to your notes. Write one question for each major term or point.

As an alternative to questions, you can list key words from your notes. Yet another option is to pretend that your notes are a series of articles on different topics. In

the cue column, write a newspaper-style headline for each "article." In any case, be brief. If you cram the cue column full of words, you defeat its purpose—to reduce the number and length of your notes.

Write a summary. Pauk recommends that you reduce your notes even more by writing a brief summary at the bottom of each page. This step offers you another way to engage actively with the material.

CUE COLUMN	NOTES
What are the 3 phases of Muscle Reading?	Phase 1: Before You Read Phase 2: While You Read Phase 3: After You Read
What are the steps in Phase 1?	1. Preview 2. Outline 3. Question
What are the steps in Phase 2?	4. Focus 5. Flag answers
What are the steps in Phase 3?	6. Recite 7. Review 8. Review Again
What's an acronym for Muscle Reading?	Pry Out Questions Focus Flag answers Recite Review Review again
SUMMARY	Muscle Reading includes 3 phases: before, during, and after reading. Each phase includes specific steps. Use the acronym to recall all the steps.

Use the cue column to recite. Cover the right-hand side of your notes with a blank sheet of paper. Leave only the cue column showing. Then look at each item you wrote in the cue column and talk about it. If you wrote questions, answer each question. If you wrote key words, define each word and talk about why it's important. If you wrote headlines in the cue column, explain what each one means and offer supporting details. After reciting, uncover your notes and look for any important points you missed.

MIND MAPPING

Mind mapping, a system developed by Tony Buzan,[3] can be used in conjunction with the Cornell method to take notes. In some circumstances, you might want to use mind maps exclusively.

To understand mind maps, first review the features of traditional note taking. Outlines (explained in the next section) divide major topics into minor topics, which in turn are subdivided further. They organize information in a sequential, linear way.

The traditional outline reflects only a limited range of brain function—a point that is often made in discussions about "left-brain" and "right-brain" activities. People often use the term *right brain* when referring to creative, pattern-making, visual, intuitive brain activity. They use the term *left brain* when talking about orderly, logical, step-by-step characteristics of thought. Writing teacher Gabrielle Rico uses another metaphor. She refers to the left-brain mode as our "sign mind" (concerned with words) and the right-brain mode as our "design mind" (concerned with visuals).[4] A mind map uses both kinds of brain functions. Mind maps can contain lists and sequences and show relationships. They can also provide a picture of a subject. They work on both verbal and nonverbal levels.

One benefit of mind maps is that they quickly, vividly, and accurately show the relationships among ideas. Also, mind mapping helps you think from general to specific. By choosing a main topic, you focus first on the big picture, then zero in on subordinate details. And by using only key words, you can condense a large subject into a small area on a mind map. You can review more quickly by looking at the key words on a mind map than by reading notes word for word.

Give yourself plenty of room. To create a mind map, use blank paper that measures at least 11 by 17 inches. If that's not available, turn regular notebook paper on its side so that you can take notes in a horizontal (instead of vertical) format. If you use a computer in class to take notes, consider software that allows you to create digital mind maps that can include graphics, photos, and URL links.

Determine the main concept of the lecture, article, or chapter. As you listen to a lecture or read, figure out the main concept. Write it in the center of the paper and circle it, underline it, or highlight it with color.

You can also write the concept in large letters. Record concepts related to the main concept on lines that radiate outward from the center. An alternative is to circle or box in these concepts.

Use key words only. Whenever possible, reduce each concept to a single word per line or circle or box in your mind map. Although this reduction might seem awkward at first, it prompts you to summarize and condense ideas to their essence. That means fewer words for you to write now and fewer to review when it's time to prepare for tests. (Using shorthand symbols and abbreviations can help.) Key words are usually nouns and verbs that communicate the bulk of the speaker's ideas. Choose words that are rich in associations and that can help you recreate the lecture.

Create links. A single mind map doesn't have to include all of the ideas in a lecture, book, or article. Instead, you can link mind maps. For example, draw a mind map that sums up the five key points in a chapter, and then make a separate, more detailed mind map for each of those key points. Within each mind map, include references to the other mind maps. This technique helps explain and reinforce the relationships among many ideas. Some students pin several mind maps next to one another on a bulletin board or tape them to a wall. This allows for a dramatic—and effective—look at the big picture.

OUTLINING

A traditional outline shows the relationships among major points and supporting ideas. One benefit of taking notes in the outline format is that doing so can totally occupy your attention. You are recording ideas and also organizing them. This process can be an advantage if the material has been presented in a disorganized way. By playing with variations, you can discover the power of outlining to reveal relationships among ideas. Technically, each word, phrase, or sentence that appears in an outline is called a *heading*. Headings are arranged in different levels:

- In the first, or top, level of headings, note the major topics presented in a lecture or reading assignment.

- In the second level of headings, record the key points that relate to each topic in the first-level headings.

- In the third level of headings, record specific facts and details that support or explain each of your second-level headings. Each additional level of subordinate heading supports the ideas in the previous level of heading.

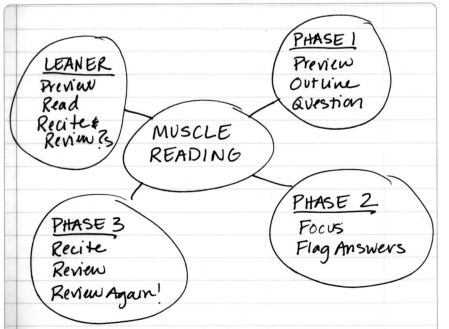

Roman numerals offer one way to illustrate the difference between levels of headings. See the following examples:

First-level heading → I. Muscle Reading includes 3 phases.
Second-level heading → A. Phase 1: Before you read
Third-level heading → 1. Preview
2. Outline
3. Question
B. Phase 2: While you read
1. Focus
2. Flag answers
C. Phase 3: After you read
1. Recite
2. Review
3. Review again

Distinguish levels with indentations only:

Muscle Reading includes 3 phases
Phase 1: Before you read
Preview

Distinguish levels with bullets and dashes:

— Muscle Reading includes 3 phases
• Phase 1: Before you read
- Preview

Distinguish levels by size:

MUSCLE READING INCLUDES 3 PHASES
Phase 1: Before you read
Preview

COMBINING FORMATS

Feel free to use different note-taking systems for different subjects and to combine formats. Do what works for you.

For example, combine mind maps along with the Cornell method. You can modify the Cornell format by dividing your notepaper in half. Reserve one-half for mind maps and the other for linear information such as lists, graphs, and outlines, as well as equations, long explanations, and word-for-word definitions. You can incorporate a mind map into your paragraph-style notes whenever you feel one is appropriate. Minds maps are also useful for summarizing notes taken in the Cornell format.

John Sperry, a teacher at Utah Valley State College, developed a note-taking system that can include all of the formats discussed in this article:

- Fill up a three-ring binder with fresh paper. Open your notebook so that you see two blank pages—one on the left and one on the right. Plan to take notes across this entire two-page spread.

- During class or while reading, write your notes only on the left-hand page. Place a large dash next to each main topic or point. If your instructor skips a step or switches topics unexpectedly, just keep writing.

- Later, use the right-hand page to review and elaborate on the notes that you took earlier. This page is for anything you want. For example, add visuals such as mind maps. Write review questions, headlines, possible test questions, summaries, outlines, mnemonics, or analogies that link new concepts to your current knowledge.

- To keep ideas in sequence, place appropriate numbers on top of the dashes in your notes on the left-hand page. Even if concepts are presented out of order during class, they'll still be numbered correctly in your notes. ■

REVIEW
THE NOTE-TAKING PROCESS FLOWS

Absodels/Getty Images

Think of reviewing as an integral part of note taking rather than an added task. To make new information useful, encode it in a way that connects it to your long-term memory. The key is reviewing.

Review class notes promptly—within 24 hours of taking them. Better yet, review them right after class and once again on the same day. This note-taking technique might be the most powerful one you can use. Use it to save hours of review time later in the term.

Many students are surprised that they can remember the content of a lecture in the minutes and hours after class. They are even more surprised by how well they can read the sloppiest of notes at that time.

Unfortunately, short-term memory deteriorates quickly. The good news is that if you review your notes soon enough, you can move that information from short-term to long-term memory. And you can do it in just a few minutes—often 10 minutes or less.

The sooner you review your notes, the better, especially if the content is difficult. In fact, you can start reviewing during class. When your instructor pauses to set up the overhead display or erase the board, scan your notes. Dot the *i*'s, cross the *t*'s, and write out unclear abbreviations.

Another way to use this technique is to get to your next class as quickly as you can. Then use the four or five minutes before the lecture begins to review the notes you just took in the previous class. If you do not get to your notes immediately after class, you can still benefit by reviewing them later in the day. A review right before you go to sleep can also be valuable.

Think of the day's unreviewed notes as leaky faucets, constantly dripping and losing precious information until you shut them off with a quick review. Remember, it's possible to forget most of the material within 24 hours—unless you review.

Edit your notes. During your first review, fix words that are illegible. Write out abbreviated words that might be unclear to you later. Make sure you can read everything. If you can't read something or don't understand something you *can* read, mark it, and make a note to ask your instructor or another student about it. Check to see that your notes are labeled with the date and class and that the pages are numbered.

Fill in key words in the left-hand column. This task is important if you are to get the full benefit of using the Cornell method. Using the key word principles described earlier in this chapter, go through your notes and write key words or phrases in the left-hand column. These key words will speed up the review process later. As you read your notes, focus on extracting important concepts.

Use your key words as cues to recite. Cover your notes with a blank sheet of paper so that you can see only the key words in the left-hand margin. Take each key word in order, and recite as much as you can about the point. Then uncover your notes and look for any important points you missed.

Conduct short weekly review periods. Once a week, review all of your notes again. These review sessions don't need to take a lot of time. Even a 20-minute weekly review period is valuable. Some students find that a weekend review—say, on Sunday afternoon—helps them stay in continuous touch with the material. Scheduling regular review sessions on your calendar helps develop the habit.

As you review, step back to see the larger picture. In addition to reciting or repeating the material to yourself, ask questions about it: Does this relate to my goals? How does this compare to information I already know, in this field or another? Will I be tested on this material? What will I do with this material? How can I associate it with something that deeply interests me?

Consider typing your notes. Some students type up their handwritten notes on the computer. The argument for doing so is threefold. First, typed notes are easier to read. Second, they take up less space. Third, the process of typing them forces you to review the material.

Another alternative is to bypass handwriting altogether and take notes in class on a laptop. This solution has a potential drawback, though: Computer errors can wipe out your notes files. If you like using this method of taking notes, save your files frequently, and back up your work onto a jump drive, external hard drive, or online backup service.

Create summaries. Mind mapping is an excellent way to summarize large sections of your course notes or reading assignments. Create one map that shows all the main topics you want to remember. Then create another map about each main topic. After drawing your maps, look at your original notes, and fill in anything you missed. This system is fun and quick.

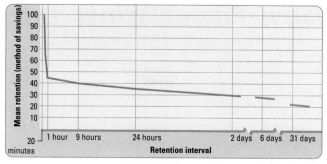

Hermann Ebbinghaus, a psychologist, discovered that most forgetting occurs during the first nine hours after we learn new information—especially during the first hour. Use the strategies in this chapter to prevent forgetting and reverse this "Ebbinghaus curve."

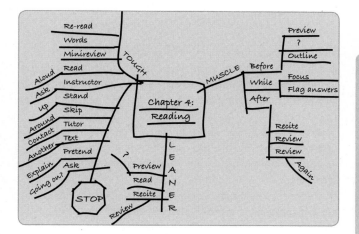

Another option is to create a "cheat sheet." There's only one guideline: Fit all your review notes on a single sheet of paper. Use any note-taking format that you want—mind map, outline, Cornell method, or a combination of all of them. The beauty of this technique is that it forces you to pick out main ideas and key details. There's not enough room for anything else!

If you're feeling adventurous, create your cheat sheet on a single index card. Start with the larger sizes (5 × 7 or 4 × 6) and then work down to a 3 × 5 card.

Some instructors might let you use a summary sheet during an exam. But even if you can't use it, you'll benefit from creating one while you study for the test. Summarizing is a powerful way to review.

While you're reviewing, evaluate your notes. Review sessions are excellent times to look beyond the *content* of your notes and reflect on your note-taking *process*. Remember these common goals of taking notes in the first place:

- *Reduce* course content to its essentials.
- *Organize* the content.
- Demonstrate that you *understand* the content.

If your notes consistently fall short on one of these points, then review this chapter for a strategy that can help. ■

Interactive

Journal Entry 13
Discovery Statement

Reflect on your review habits
Respond to the following statements by selecting "Always," "Often," "Sometimes," "Seldom," or "Never" after each.

I review my notes immediately after class.

_____ Always _____ Often _____ Sometimes

_____ Seldom _____ Never

I conduct weekly reviews of my notes.

_____ Always _____ Often _____ Sometimes

_____ Seldom _____ Never

I make summary sheets of my notes.

_____ Always _____ Often _____ Sometimes

_____ Seldom _____ Never

I edit my notes within 24 hours.

_____ Always _____ Often _____ Sometimes

_____ Seldom _____ Never

Before class, I conduct a brief review of the notes I took in the previous class.

_____ Always _____ Often _____ Sometimes

_____ Seldom _____ Never

Turn PowerPoints into
POWERFUL NOTES

PowerPoint presentations are common. They can also be lethal for students who want to master course content or those who simply want to stay awake.

Some students stop taking notes during a PowerPoint presentation. This choice can be hazardous to your academic health for three major reasons:

- **PowerPoint presentations don't include everything.** Instructors and other speakers use PowerPoint to organize their presentations. Topics covered in the slides make up an outline of what your instructor considers important. Slides are created to flag the main points and signal transitions between points. However, speakers usually add examples and explanations that don't appear on the slides. In addition, slides will not contain any material from class discussion, including any answers that the instructor gives in response to questions.

- **You stop learning.** Taking notes forces you to capture ideas and information in your own words. Also, the act of writing things down helps you remember the material. If you stop writing and let your attention drift, you can quickly get lost.

- **You end up with major gaps in your notes.** When it's time to review your notes, you'll find that material from PowerPoint presentations is missing. This can be a major pain at exam time.

To create value from PowerPoint presentations, take notes on them. Continue to observe, record, and review. See PowerPoint as a way to *guide* rather than to *replace* your own note taking. Even the slickest, smartest presentation is no substitute for your own thinking.

Experiment with the following suggestions. They include ideas about what to do before, during, and after a PowerPoint presentation.

BEFORE THE PRESENTATION

Sometimes instructors make PowerPoint slides available before a lecture. If you have computer access, download these files. Scan the slides, just as you would preview a reading assignment.

Consider printing out the slides and bringing them along to class. (If you own a copy of PowerPoint, then choose the "handouts" option when printing. This will save paper and ink.) You can take notes directly on the pages that you print out. Be sure to add the slide numbers if they are missing.

If you use a laptop computer for taking notes during class, then you might not want to bother with printing. Just open up the PowerPoint file and type your notes in the window that appears at the bottom of each slide.

After class, you can print out the slides in note view. This will show the original slides plus any text that you added.

How Muscle Reading Works	
▸ Phase 1 – Before You Read	
▪ Pry Out Questions	
▸ Phase 2 – While You Read	
▪ Focus and Flag Answers	
▸ Phase 3 – After You Read	
▪ Recite, Review, and Review Again	

DURING THE PRESENTATION

In many cases, PowerPoint slides are presented visually by the instructor *only during class*. The slides are not provided as handouts, and they are not available online for students to print out.

This makes it even more important to take effective notes in class. Capture the main points and key details as you normally would. Use your preferred note-taking strategies.

Be selective in what you write down. Determine what kind of material is on each slide. Stay alert for new topics, main points, and important details. Taking too many notes makes it hard to keep up with a speaker and separate main points from minor details.

In any case, go *beyond* the slides. Record valuable questions and answers that come up during a discussion, even if they are not a planned part of the presentation.

AFTER THE PRESENTATION

If you printed out slides before class and took notes on those pages, then find a way to integrate them with the rest of your notes. For example, add references in your notebook to specific slides. Or create summary notes that include the major topics and points from readings, class meetings, and PowerPoint presentations.

Printouts of slides can make good review tools. Use them as cues to recite. Cover up your notes so that only the main image or words on each slide are visible. See whether you can remember what else appears on the slide, along with the key points from any notes you added.

Also consider editing the presentation. If you have the PowerPoint file on your computer, make another copy of it. Open up this copy, and see whether you can condense the presentation. Cut slides that don't include anything you want to remember. Also rearrange slides so that the order makes more sense to you. Remember that you can open up the original file later if you want to see exactly what your instructor presented. ■

When your instructor talks quickly

Take more time to prepare for class. Familiarity with a subject increases your ability to pick up on key points. If an instructor lectures quickly or is difficult to understand, conduct a preview of the material to be covered.

Be willing to make choices. Focus your attention on key points. Instead of trying to write everything down, choose what you think is important. Occasionally, you will make a less than perfect choice or even neglect an important point. Don't worry. Stay with the lecture, write down key words, and revise your notes immediately after class.

Exchange photocopies of notes with classmates. Your fellow students might write down something you missed. At the same time, your notes might help them. Exchanging photocopies can fill in the gaps.

Leave large empty spaces in your notes. Leave plenty of room for filling in information you missed. Use a symbol that signals you've missed something, so you can remember to come back to it.

See the instructor after class. Take your class notes with you, and show the instructor what you missed.

Use an audio recorder. Recording a lecture gives you a chance to hear it again whenever you choose. Some audio recording software allows you to vary the speed of the recording. With this feature, you can perform magic and actually slow down the instructor's speech.

Before class, take notes on your reading assignment. You can take detailed notes on the text before class. Leave plenty of blank space. Take these notes with you to class, and simply add your lecture notes to them.

Go to the lecture again. Many classes are taught in multiple sections. That gives you the chance to hear a lecture at least twice—once in your regular class and again in another section of the class.

Create abbreviations. Note-taking systems called *shorthand* were specifically designed for getting ideas down fast. Though these systems are dated, you can borrow the general idea. Invent your own shorthand—one- or two-letter abbreviations and symbols for common words and phrases.

A common way to abbreviate is to leave out vowels. For example, *said* becomes *sd, American* becomes *Amrcn.*

The trick is to define abbreviations clearly and use them consistently. When you use an abbreviation such as *comm,* you run the risk of not being able to remember whether you meant *committee, commission, common,* or *commit.* To prevent this problem, write a master key, or legend, that explains all your abbreviations.

Ask questions—even if you're totally lost. Many instructors allow a question session. This is the time to ask about the points you missed.

At times you might feel so lost that you can't even formulate a question. One option is to report this fact to the instructor. She can often guide you to a question. Another option is to ask a related question. Doing so might lead you to the question you really wanted to ask.

Ask the instructor to slow down. This solution is the most obvious. If asking the instructor to slow down doesn't work, ask him to repeat what you missed.

Take this article to work. See fast-talking instructors as people who are training you to take notes during meetings, conferences, and training sessions in the workplace. The ability to think clearly and write concisely under pressure will serve you for a lifetime. ■

Interactive

Exercise 17 Taking notes under pressure

With note taking, the more you practice, the better you become. You can use TV programs and videos to practice listening for key words, writing quickly, focusing your attention, and reviewing. Programs that feature speeches and panel discussions work well for this purpose. So do documentary films.

The next time you watch such a program, use pen and paper to jot down key words and information. If you fall behind, relax. Just leave a space in your notes and return your attention to the program. If a program includes commercial breaks, use them to review and revise your notes.

At the end of the program, spend five minutes reviewing your notes, and create a mind map based on them. Then sum up the main points of the program for a friend.

This exercise will help you develop an ear for key words. Because you can't ask questions or request that speakers slow down, you train yourself to stay totally in the moment.

Don't be discouraged if you miss a lot the first time around. Do this exercise several times, and observe how your mind works.

Another option is to record a program and then take notes. You can stop the recording at any point to review what you've written.

Ask a classmate to do this exercise with you. Compare your notes and look for any points that either of you missed.

TAKING NOTES
WHILE READING

Taking notes on school- or work-related reading requires the same skills that apply to taking notes in class: observing, recording, and reviewing. Use these skills to take notes for review and for research.

REVIEW NOTES

Review notes will look like the notes you take in class. Take review notes when you want more detailed notes than writing in the margin of your text allows. You might want to single out a particularly difficult section of a text and make separate notes. Or make summaries of overlapping lecture and text material. Because you can't underline or make notes in library books, these sources require separate notes too. To take more effective review notes, use the following suggestions.

Set priorities. Single out a particularly difficult section of a text and make separate notes. Or make summaries of overlapping lecture and text material.

Use a variety of formats. Translate text into Cornell notes, mind maps, or outlines. Combine these formats to create your own. Translate diagrams, charts, and other visual elements into words. Then reverse the process by translating straight text into visual elements.

However, don't let the creation of formats get in your way. Even a simple list of key points and examples can become a powerful review tool. Another option is to close your book and just start writing. Write quickly about what you intend to remember from the text, and don't worry about following any format.

Condense a passage to key quotes. Authors embed their essential ideas in key sentences. As you read, continually ask yourself, "What's the point?" Then see whether you can point to a specific sentence on the page to answer your question. Look especially at headings, subheadings, and topic sentences of paragraphs. Write these key sentences word for word in your notes, and put them within quotation marks. Copy as few sentences as you can to still retain the core meaning of the passage.

Condense by paraphrasing. Pretend that you have to summarize a chapter, article, or book on a postcard. Limit yourself to a single paragraph—or a single sentence—and use your own words. This is a great way to test your understanding of the material.

Take a cue from the table of contents. Look at the table of contents in your book. Write each major heading on a piece of paper, or key those headings into a word-processing file on your computer. Include page numbers. Next, see whether you can improve on the table of contents. Substitute your own headings for those that appear in the book. Turn single words or phrases into complete sentences, and use words that are meaningful to you.

Adapt to special cases. The style of your notes can vary according to the nature of the reading material. If you are assigned a short story or poem, for example, then read the entire work once without taking any notes. On your first reading, simply enjoy the piece. When you finish, write down your immediate impressions. Then go over the piece again. Make brief notes on characters, images, symbols, settings, plot, point of view, or other aspects of the work.

Note key concepts in math and science. When you read mathematical, scientific, or other technical materials, copy important formulas or equations. Recreate important diagrams, and draw your own visual representations of concepts. Also write down data that might appear on an exam.

RESEARCH NOTES

Take research notes when preparing to write a paper or deliver a speech. One traditional method of research is to take notes on index cards. You write *one* idea, fact, or quotation per card, along with a note about the source (where you found it). The advantage of limiting each card to one item is that you can easily arrange cards according to the sequence of ideas in your outline. If you change your outline, no problem. Just resort to your cards.

Taking notes on a computer offers the same flexibility as index cards. Just include one idea, fact, or quotation per paragraph, along with the source. Think of each paragraph as a separate "card." When you're ready to create the first draft of your paper or presentation, just move paragraphs around so that they fit your outline.

Include your sources. No matter whether you use cards or a computer, be sure to *include a source for each note that you take.*

Say, for example, that you find a useful quotation from a book. You want to include that quotation in your paper. Copy the quotation word for word onto a card, or key the quotation into a computer file. Along with the quotation, note the book's author, title, date and place of publication, and publisher. You'll need such information later when you create a formal list of your sources—a bibliography or a list of endnotes or footnotes.

For guidelines on what information to record about each type of source, see the sidebar to this article as a place to start. Your instructors might have different preferences, so ask them for guidance as well.

Avoid plagiarism. When people take material from a source and fail to acknowledge that source, they are committing plagiarism. Even when plagiarism is accidental, the consequences can be harsh.

Many cases of plagiarism occur during the process of taking research notes. To prevent this problem, remember that a major goal of taking research notes is to *clearly separate your own words and images from words and images created by someone else.* To meet this goal, develop the following habits:

- If you take a direct quote from one of your sources, then enclose those words in quotation marks, and note information about that source.

- If you take an image (photo, illustration, chart, or diagram) from one of your sources, then note information about that source.

Note this information about your sources

Knowing how to organize and document your sources of information is a key skill for information literacy. Following are checklists of the information to record about various types of sources. Whenever possible, print out or make photocopies of each source. For books, include a copy of the title page and copyright page, both of which are found in the front matter. For magazines and scholarly journals, copy the table of contents.

For each BOOK you consult, record the following:

- Author
- Editor (if listed)
- Translator (if listed)
- Edition number (if listed)
- Full title, including the subtitle
- Name and location of the publisher
- Copyright date
- Specific page numbers for passages that you quote, summarize, or paraphrase

For each ARTICLE you consult, record the following:

- Author
- Editor (if listed)
- Translator (if listed)
- Full title, including the subtitle
- Name of the periodical
- Volume number
- Issue number
- Issue date
- Specific page numbers for passages that you quote, summarize, or paraphrase

For each ONLINE SOURCE you consult, record the following:

- Author
- Editor (if listed)
- Translator (if listed)
- Full title of the page or article, including the subtitle
- Name of the organization that posted the site or published the CD-ROM
- Dates when the page or other document was published and revised
- Date when you accessed the source
- URL for Web pages (the uniform resource locator, or Web site address, which often starts with http://)
- Version number (for CD-ROMs)
- Volume, issue number, and date for online journals

Note: Computer-based sources may not list all the above information. For Web pages, at a minimum record the date you accessed the source and the URL.

For each INTERVIEW you conduct, record the following:

- Name of the person you interviewed
- Professional title of the person you interviewed
- Contact information for the person you interviewed—mailing address, phone number, e-mail address
- Date of the interview

- If you summarize or paraphrase *a specific passage* from one of your sources, then use your own words and note information about that source.

- If your notes include any idea that is closely identified with a particular person, then note information about the source.

- When you include one of your own ideas in your notes, then simply note the source as "me."

If you're taking notes on a computer and using Internet sources, be especially careful to avoid plagiarism. When you copy text or images from a Web site, separate those notes from your own ideas. Use a different font for copied material, or enclose it in quotation marks.

You do *not* need to note a source for these:

- Facts that are considered common knowledge ("The history of the twentieth century includes two world wars").

- Facts that can be easily verified ("The United States Constitution includes a group of amendments known as the Bill of Rights").

> *Many cases of plagiarism occur during the process of taking research notes. To prevent this problem, remember that a major goal of taking research notes is to* clearly separate your own words and images from words and images created by someone else.

- Your own opinion ("Hip-hop artists are the most important poets of our age").

The bottom line: Always present your own work—not materials that have been created or revised by someone else. If you're ever in doubt about what to do, then take the safest course: Cite a source. Give credit where credit is due.

Reflect on your notes. Schedule time to review all the information and ideas that your research has produced. By allowing time for rereading and reflecting on all the notes you've taken, you create the conditions for genuine understanding.

Start by summarizing major points of view on your topic. Note points of agreement and disagreement among your sources.

Also see whether you can find direct answers to the questions that you had when you started researching. These answers could become headings in your paper.

Look for connections in your material, including ideas, facts, and examples that occur in several sources. Also look for connections between your research and your life—ideas that you can verify based on personal experience. ■

Taking notes during meetings

In the workplace, notes matter. During meetings, people are hired, fired, and promoted. Problems are tackled. Negotiations are held. Decisions are made. Your job might depend on what you observe during meetings, what you record, and how you respond.

Consider adding the following topics—the four A's—to your notes on a meeting:

- *Attendance*—Start by observing who shows up. In many organizations, people expect meeting notes to include a list of attendees.

- *Agenda*—One path to more powerful meeting notes is observing the agenda. Think of it as a road map—a way to keep the discussion on track. Skilled planners often put an agenda in writing and distribute it in advance of a meeting. Record this agenda and use it to organize your notes. If there is no formal agenda, then create one in your notes, with separate headings for each major topic being discussed.

- *Agreements*—The purpose of most meetings is to reach an agreement about something—a policy, project, or plan. Record each agreement.

- *Actions*—During meetings, people often commit to take some type of action in the future. Record each follow-up action and who agreed to do it. This last A is especially important. Ask whether any of the points you included in your notes call for follow-up action on *your* part—perhaps a phone call to make, a fact to find, or another task to complete. Highlight such items in your notes. Then add them to your calendar or to-do list and follow through.

Follow-up action is often a make-or-break point for study groups and project teams. One mark of exceptional teams is that people make agreements about what they will do—and then keep those agreements. You can set a powerful example.

VISUALIZE IDEAS
WITH CONCEPT MAPS

Concept mapping, pioneered by Joseph Novak and D. Bob Gowin, is a tool to make major ideas in a book leap off the page.[5] In creating a concept map, you reduce an author's message to its essence—its bare bones. Concept maps can also be used to display the organization of lectures and discussions.

Concepts and links are the building blocks of knowledge. A *concept* is a name for a group of related things or ideas. *Links* are words or phrases that describe the relationship between concepts. Consider the following paragraph:

Muscle Reading consists of three phases. Phase 1 includes tasks to complete before reading. Phase 2 tasks take place during reading. Finally, Phase 3 includes tasks to complete after reading.

In this paragraph, examples of concepts are *Muscle Reading, reading, phases, tasks, Phase 1, Phase 2,* and *Phase 3*. Links include *before, during,* and *after*.

To create a concept map, first list concepts and then arrange them in a meaningful order from general to specific. Then fill in the links between concepts, forming meaningful statements.

Concept mapping promotes critical thinking. It alerts you to missing concepts or faulty links between concepts. Concept mapping mirrors the way that your brain learns—that is, by linking new concepts to concepts that you already know.

In addition, concept mapping is a brain-friendly strategy. Links between concepts can be compared to the links between brain cells that start to form when you encounter new material. A concept map offers a visual reminder of how your brain changes when you learn.

To create a concept map, use the following steps:

1. **List the key concepts in the text.** Aim to express each concept in three words or less. Most concept words are nouns, including terms and proper names. At this point, you can list the concepts in any order.

2. **Rank the concepts so that they flow from general to specific.** On a large sheet of paper, write the main concept at the top of the page. Place the most specific concepts near the bottom. Arrange the rest of the concepts in appropriate positions throughout the middle of the page. Circle each concept.

3. **Draw lines that connect the concepts.** On these connecting lines, add words that describe the relationship between the concepts. Again, limit yourself to the fewest words needed to make an accurate link—three words or less. Linking words are often verbs, verb phrases, or prepositions.

4. **Finally, review your map.** Look for any concepts that are repeated in several places on the map. You can avoid these repetitions by adding more links between concepts. ■

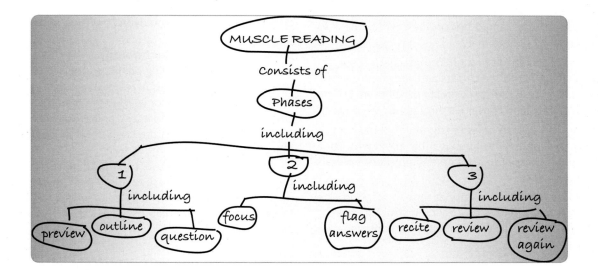

© istockphoto.com/Andrew Rich

Taking effective notes for
ONLINE COURSEWORK

When you are taking an online course, or a course that is heavily supported by online materials, then get ready for new challenges to note taking. You can use a variety of strategies to succeed.

Manage time and tasks carefully. Courses that take place mostly or totally online can become invisible in your weekly academic schedule. This reinforces the temptation to put off dealing with these courses until late in the term.

Avoid this mistake! Consider the real possibility that an online course can take *more* time than a traditional, face-to-face lecture class. Online courses tend to embrace lots of activities—sending and receiving e-mails, joining discussion forums, commenting on blog posts, and more. New content might appear every day.

The biggest obstacle to online learning is procrastination. The solution is to keep up with the course through frequent contact and careful time management.

- Early in the term, create a detailed schedule for online courses. In your calendar, list a due date for each assignment. Break big assignments into smaller steps, and schedule a due date for each step.

- Schedule times in your calendar to complete online course work. Give these scheduled sessions the same priority as regular classroom meetings. At these times, check for online announcements relating to assignments, tests, and other course events. Check for course-related e-mails daily.

- If the class includes discussion forums, check those daily as well. Look for new posts and add your replies. The point of these tools is to create a lively conversation that starts early and continues throughout the term.

- When you receive an online assignment, e-mail any questions immediately. If you want to meet with an instructor in person, request an appointment several days in advance.

- Give online instructors plenty of time to respond. They are not always online. Many online instructors have traditional courses to teach, along with administration and research duties.

- Download or print out online course materials as soon as they're posted on the class Web site. These materials might not be available later in the term.

- If possible, submit online assignments early. Staying ahead of the game will help you avoid an all-nighter at the computer during finals week.

> *Consider the real possibility that an online course can take more time than a traditional, face-to-face lecture class. Online courses tend to embrace lots of activities—sending and receiving e-mails, joining discussion forums, commenting on blog posts, and more.*

If you still struggle with procrastination, remember a basic fact about human psychology. Emotions and behavior can operate independently. In other words, you can still engage with an online course even when you don't *feel* like doing it. Start with a simple task that you can do in five minutes or less. Following through on a small-scale commitment can help you overcome resistance.

Do a trial run with technology. Verify your access to course Web sites, including online tutorials, PowerPoint presentations, readings, quizzes, tests, assignments, bulletin boards, and chat rooms. Ask your instructors for Web site addresses, e-mail addresses, and passwords. Work out any bugs when you start the course and well before that first assignment is due.

If you're planning to use a computer lab on campus, find one that meets course requirements. Remember that on-campus computer labs may not allow you to install all the software needed to access Web sites for your courses or textbooks.

Develop a contingency plan. Murphy's Law of Computer Crashes states that technology tends to break down at the moment of greatest inconvenience. You might not believe this piece of folklore, but it's still wise to prepare for it:

- Find a "technology buddy" in each of your classes—someone who can contact the instructor if you lose Internet access or experience other computer problems.
- Every day, make backup copies of files created for your courses.
- Keep extra printer supplies—paper and toner or ink cartridges—on hand at all times. Don't run out of necessary supplies on the day a paper is due.

Get actively involved with the course. Your online course will include a page that lists homework assignments and test dates. That's only the beginning. Look for ways to engage with the material by submitting questions, completing assignments, and interacting with the instructor and other students. Another way to stay involved is to find out whether your online courses offer apps for smart phones and tablets.

Take notes on course material. You can print out anything that appears on a computer screen. This includes online course materials—articles, books, e-mail messages, chat-room sessions, and more.

The potential problem is that you might skip the note-taking process altogether. ("I can just print out everything!") You would then miss the chance to internalize a new idea by restating it in your own words—a principal benefit of note taking. Result: Material passes from computer to printer without ever intersecting with your brain.

To prevent this problem, take notes in Cornell, mind map, concept map, or outline format. Write Discovery and Intention Statements to capture key insights from the materials and next actions to take. Also talk about what you're learning. Recite key points out loud, and discuss what you find online with other students.

Of course, it's fine to print out online material. If you do, treat your printouts like mini-textbooks, and use reading techniques to extract meaning: Preview and outline them. Pose questions and flag answers in the text. Then review and recite the material that you want to remember.

Another potential problem with online courses is the physical absence of the teacher. In a classroom, you get lots of visual and verbal clues to what kinds of questions will appear on a test. Those clues are often missing from an online course, which means that they could be missing from your notes. Ask your online instructor about what material she considers to be most important.

Set up folders and files for easy reference. Create a separate folder for each class on your computer's hard drive. Give each folder a meaningful name, such as *biology—spring2009*. Place all files related to a course in the appropriate folder. Doing this can save you from one of the main technology-related time wasters: searching for lost files.

Also name individual files with care. Avoid changing extensions that identify different types of files, such as .ppt for PowerPoint presentations or .pdf for files in the Adobe Reader portable document format. Changing extensions might lead to problems when you're looking for files later or sharing them with other users.

Take responsibility. If you register for an online course with no class meetings, you might miss the motivating presence of an instructor and classmates. Instead, manufacture your own motivation. Be clear about what you'll gain by doing well in the course. Relate course content to your major and career goals. Don't wait to be contacted by your classmates and instructor. Initiate that contact on your own.

Ask for help. If you feel confused about anything you're learning online, ask for help right away. This is especially important when you don't see the instructor face-to-face in class. Some students simply drop online courses rather than seek help. E-mail or call the instructor before you make that choice. If the instructor is on campus, you might be able to arrange for a meeting during office hours.

Focus your attention. Some students are used to visiting Web sites while watching television, listening to loud music, or instant messaging. When applied to online learning, these habits can reduce your learning and imperil your grades. To succeed with technology, turn off the television, quit texting and online messaging, and turn down the music. Whenever you go online, stay in charge of your attention.

Ask for feedback. To get the most from online learning, request feedback from your instructor via e-mail. When appropriate, also ask for conferences by phone or in person.

Sharing files offers another source of feedback. For example, Microsoft Word has a Track Changes feature that allows other people to insert comments into your documents and make suggested revisions. These edits are highlighted on the screen. Use such tools to get feedback on your writing from instructors and peers.

Note: Be sure to check with your instructors to see how they want students enrolled in their online courses to address and label their e-mails. Many teachers ask their online students to use a standard format for the subject area so they can quickly recognize e-mails from them.

Contact other students. Make personal contact with at least one other student in each of your classes—especially classes that involve lots of online course work. Create study groups to share notes, quiz each other, critique papers, and do other cooperative learning tasks. This kind of support can help you succeed as an online learner. ■

© Paula kc/Shutterstock.com

NOTE TAKING 2.0

Imagine how useful it would be to have your notes available to you anywhere, any time, from any digital device. Today there are digital tools—many of them free—for doing just that. Gain skills with them now, while you're in school. Then transfer those skills to the workplace for taking notes on seminars, conferences, and training sessions.

START WITH SOFTWARE YOU ALREADY OWN

One option is to create a plain text document for each of your courses and your personal journal. Key your notes into those documents.

Chances are that you already have software for creating plain text documents. Apple computers come loaded with TextEdit, and iPhones offer Notes. Windows users can use NotePad.

The documents you create with such software is called plain text because it's stripped of special formatting. The advantage is that almost any software can read plain text documents, and they consume little memory.

STORE YOUR NOTES IN THE "CLOUD"

To access your documents, store them in DropBox (**www.dropbox.com**), Google Drive (**www.drive.google.com**), or SkyDrive (**www.skydrive.com**), or another Web-based service that backs up documents. Many of them will offer you several gigabytes of online storage for free.

Sign up for the service, create a test document, and then edit it. Check to make sure that the edited version shows up correctly on all your devices.

CONSIDER ONLINE OUTLINERS AND MIND MAPPERS

A growing number of Web sites allow you to create outlines and mind maps. Just sign up for the service and create your first document. It will be available on any device with an Internet connection. And, your notes will remain private unless you choose to share them with specific people. For fun, start with these:

- Workflowy (**https://workflowy.com**) can be used with just a handful of keyboard shortcuts, allowing you to combine simplicity with speed.
- Checkvist (**https://checkvist.com**) offers options for exporting your outlines to other software.
- Online Outliner (**www.online-outliner.com**) is simple and free—no registration required.

- The Outliner of Giants (**www.theoutlinerofgiants.com**) is an ideal choice for creating large scholarly documents that you can export to Microsoft Word.
- Mindmeister (**www.mindmeister.com**) and Mindjet (**www.mindjet.com**) allow you to create mind maps that are stored online for free.
- The Brain (**www.thebrain.com**), though not free, allows you to create multiple mind maps that link to one another, as well as links to Web sites and documents stored on your computer.

CONSIDER DEDICATED NOTE-TAKING SOFTWARE

Many note-taking applications offer features that go beyond plain text editing and online services.

- SimpleNote (**http://simplenote.com**), which comes in free and paid versions, allows you to create text-based notes and store them online.
- Notational Velocity (**www.notational.net**, free and for Mac OSX only) stores text-based notes, searches them with blinding speed, and synchronizes with SimpleNote.
- ResophNotes (**www.resoph.com**) brings the features of Notational Velocity to Windows-based computers.
- Evernote (**www.evernote.com**, free and paid versions) allows you to copy text and images from Web sites and add offline content, such as digital photos of business cards and receipts.
- Springpad (**http://springpad.com**) is an Evernote competitor that is free.
- Microsoft OneNote (**www.office.microsoft.com/en-us/onenote**) also overlaps with Evernote in features and integrates tightly with the Microsoft Office applications.

New tools are always under development. For more options, search the Web with the key words *note-taking software*. ∎

Practicing Critical Thinking 5

Remember that psychologist Benjamin Bloom described six levels of thinking:

Level 1: Remembering

Level 2: Understanding

Level 3: Applying

Level 4: Analyzing

Level 5: Evaluating

Level 6: Creating

The purpose of this exercise is practice thinking at **Level 6: Creating**. This means inventing your own ideas, strategies, suggestions, and techniques.

Test questions that call for creating often begin with words such as *combine, compose, construct, develop, formulate, imagine, invent, produce, revise,* and *synthesize.*

Remember that creating often means taking an existing idea and changing it. You might also take two or more existing ideas and combine them in a unique way.

This chapter presents three major formats for taking notes: the Cornell method, mind mapping, and outlining. These formats can be modified and combined. For example, you could take notes during class with the Cornell method. After class, you could also expand on your notes by capturing some of the main points in mind maps and outlines.

Now it's your turn to create. Based on your experience with this chapter, create a note-taking format of your own. Describe this format briefly here:

_____

_____

_____

_____

_____

Next, create a detailed example or model of your format. Develop your example here.

MASTER STUDENT PROFILE

ZUMA Press, Inc./Alamy

RICHARD BLANCO

(1969–) Richard Blanco, civil engineer, returned to school for an MFA in poetry

On a sunny South Miami morning, Richard Blanco took the podium at a groundbreaking ceremony for his latest project on Sunset Drive. It was spring 2008, and Blanco had directed the renovation of the busy avenue, urbanizing the stretch that serves as the gateway to City Hall.

Next to shovels with yellow ribbons and a mound of rocks and sand, the civil engineer did something few would expect: He read a poem—one he'd written after being inspired by historic pictures inside the municipal center—to the engineers and city officials gathered at the scene.

Less than five years later, he received an invitation to write a poem for a different opening ceremony—this time, Barack Obama's second presidential inauguration.

Blanco, following in the footsteps of Robert Frost and Maya Angelou, is at 44 the youngest person to hold the title of inaugural poet. He's the first one to be Hispanic and also the first to be gay.

"He's been writing nonstop," said his brother Carlos, 51. "He'll stay up until 4 or 5 in the morning."

During the holidays, Carlos Blanco and his two sons visited the poet in Bethel, Maine, the small ski town where Richard Blanco lives with his partner, Mark Neveu.

"Normally when we go up there, we're always together," Carlos Blanco said. "This time, we were on our own, and at night we would get together for dinner. Then he'd go back to his writing."

The poet . . . was born in Madrid after his parents fled Cuba in the late 1960s. Less than two months later, the family moved to New York and then Miami, where Blanco grew up. Though he enjoyed sculpting and painting as a student and dreamed of being an architect, his family had different plans, according to his brother.

"Our parents didn't consider a career in the arts as a real degree," the brother said. "They were always pushing engineering, medicine, all that type of stuff. Richard followed their advice and became a civil engineer."

Blanco received his degree from Florida International University and began working full-time at the Miami engineering firm C3TS/Stantec.

Richard Blanco *is creative.* **You** *can be creative by following your interests, even if they take you in new directions.*

Ramón Castella, the poet's boss at the firm, said he wasn't surprised when a few years later Blanco enrolled again at FIU, this time taking night classes toward a master's degree in creative writing. "Once he started writing and getting into poetry, I realized engineering wasn't what he was all about," Castella said. . . .

In Cuban culture, homosexuality "is not contemplated, and if it is, you keep quiet about it," the brother said.

In 1965, for example, writer Allen Ginsberg was thrown out of Cuba for speaking out against the government's stance against homosexuals. And even as recently as 25 years ago, the Cuban penal code punished those who publicly exhibited homosexual behavior or made homosexual advances.

The poet told the *New York Times* that his latest collection, *Looking for the Gulf Motel,* explores "how I fit between negotiating the world, between being mainstream gay and being Cuban gay."

His career took off in 1997, when he received the Agnes Lynch Starrett Poetry Prize from the University of Pittsburgh Press for his first collection, *City of a Hundred Fires.*

After that, Blanco taught writing at Miami-Dade College and FIU. He later moved to Connecticut to teach at Central Connecticut State University, where he met his life partner. . . .

Between 2003 and 2004, Blanco lectured on poetry at American University and Georgetown University, both in Washington, D.C. In 2005, he published his second book, *Directions to the Beach of the Dead,* which includes a poem, "Sending Palms in a Letter," dedicated to Moustaki.

A few years ago, he and Neveu relocated to the quiet town where he now spends his days writing poems. That's where a call from the White House found him, unprepared—but ready. ■

Source: Melvin Felix, "South Florida engineer becomes Obama's chosen poet," Sun Sentinel, Fort Lauderdale, FL, January 18, 2013, http://articles.sun-sentinel.com/2013-01-18/news/sfl-richard-blanco-20130118_1_civil-engineer-richard-blanco-poem.

QUIZ
Chapter 5

Name _____

Date _____

1. Define the word *responsibility* as it is used in the Power Process: I create it all.

   Responsibility is "response-ability"—the ability to choose a response to any event. You can choose your response to any event, even when the event itself is beyond your control. (*Power Process: I create it all*, page 150)

2. What are the three major parts of effective note taking as explained in this chapter? Summarize each step in one sentence.

   List each of the following and describe in a sentence (answers will vary): (a) Observe—notice spoken or written words. (b) Record—take notes. (c) Review—reread notes frequently. (*The note-taking process flows*, page 151)

3. According to the text, neat handwriting and a knowledge of outlining are the only requirements for effective notes. True or false? Explain your answer.

   False. Neat handwriting and knowing how to outline are useful, but not requirements. (*The note-taking process flows*, page 151)

4. What are some advantages of sitting in the front and center of the classroom?

   (Answers will vary.) (a) The closer you sit to the lecturer, the harder it is to fall asleep. (b) The closer you sit to the front, the fewer interesting or distracting classmates between you and the instructor there are to watch. (c) Material on the board is easier to read from up front. (d) The instructor can see you more easily when you have a question. (e) A professor who sounds boring from the back of the room might sound more interesting if you're closer. (f) Sitting up front is a way to commit yourself to getting what you want out of your education. (g) When you sit in front, you are declaring your willingness to take a risk and participate. (*Observe: The note-taking process flows*, page 152)

5. List the four A's for taking notes at meetings.

   Attendance, agenda, agreements, and actions. (*Taking notes during meetings*, page 166)

6. Instructors sometimes give clues that the material they are presenting is important. List at least three of these clues.

   List at least three of the following: (a) Be alert to repetition. (b) Listen for introductory, concluding, and transition words and phrases. (c) Watch the board or PowerPoint presentation. (d) Watch the instructor's eyes. (e) Highlight the obvious clues. (f) Notice the instructor's interest level. (*Observe: The note-taking process flows*, page 152)

7. Postponing judgment while taking notes means that you have to agree with everything that the instructor says. True or false? Explain your answer.

   False. The purpose of postponing debate is to prevent your internal dialogue about what is being presented from drowning out subsequent material. Thinking critically and postponing debate are not contradictory. Aim to understand the instructor's point before you criticize it. (*Observe: The note-taking process flows*, page 152)

8. Describe the two main types of key words. Then write down at least five key words from this chapter.

   (Answers will vary.) The two main types of key words are (1) Concepts, technical terms, names, and numbers (e.g., *stimulus, generated, receptor neurons, transmit,* and *sensory*); and (2) Linking words, including words that describe action, relationship, and degree (e.g., *most, least, highest, lower,* and *faster*). (*Record: The note-taking process flows*, page 155)

9. Graphic signals include which of the following?
   (a) Brackets and parentheses　　　　(b) Stars and arrows
   (c) Underlining and connecting lines　(d) Equal signs and greater-than and less-than signs
   (e) All of the above

   (e) All of the above (*Record: The note-taking process flows*, page 155)

10. Describe at least three strategies for reviewing notes.

    Describe at least three of the following: (a) Review within 24 hours. (b) Edit your notes. (c) Fill in key words in the left-hand column. (d) Use key words as recitation cues. (e) Conduct short weekly review periods. (f) Type up your notes. (g) Create summaries. (*Review: The note-taking process flows*, page 160)

SKILLS SNAPSHOT
Chapter 5

Take a snapshot of your note-taking skills as they exist today, after reading and doing this chapter. Begin by reflecting on some of your recent experiences with note taking. Then take the next step toward mastery by committing to a specific action in the near future.

Discovery

My score on the Notes section of the Discovery Wheel was . . .

If asked to rate the overall quality of the notes that I've taken in the last week, I would say that . . .

In general, I find my notes to be most useful when they . . .

Intention

I'll know that I've reached a new level of mastery with note taking when . . .

The idea from this chapter that could make the biggest difference in the quality of my notes is . . .

Action

The new note-taking habit that I plan to adopt is . . .

This habit can promote my success at work by . . .

By the time I finish this course, I would like my *Notes* score on the Discovery Wheel to be . . .

INSTRUCTOR TOOLS & TIPS

TESTS

"Keep in mind that neither success nor failure is ever final." —Roger Babson

PREVIEW

Test taking is a high-priority issue for students. Discussing this topic together in class can help students prepare more successfully before tests, while learning to manage anxiety during tests. Point out that Chapter 11 will help them establish better overall health habits, but learning simple breathing techniques or other stress management tools can make a big observable difference in test anxiety. Encourage your students to do a chapter reconnaissance to discover ways to predict test questions or to glean information from a test after it has been returned.

GUEST SPEAKER

Consider inviting faculty members from different departments to talk to your class about their expectations regarding tests. Math and science are particularly problematic subjects for test anxiety. Prompt these faculty members to provide information on the importance of attending class, reading assigned textbook materials, and completing homework assignments. Have students prepare questions to ask them during a question-and-answer session.

Another guest speaker idea is to invite the administrator responsible for student discipline. When students cheat and get caught, they don't talk about it, so students have a misperception that no one's getting caught. The administrator's firsthand discussion of the topic may hit home with students who have considered cheating or have cheated in the past. Learn about your school's policy regarding academic integrity, and consider putting this in your course syllabus.

Another suggestion for a guest speaker is to invite a counselor or staff member from the student health center to talk about test anxiety and relaxation techniques.

LECTURE

What to do when you're stuck. Lecture on what students should do when they are stuck on a test question. Here are some strategies.

- **Read it again.** Eliminate the simplest sources of confusion, such as misreading the question.

master instructor best practice

" *It helps to learn to laugh at ourselves, as the article "Celebrate mistakes" (page 196) discusses. This often helps to take the sting out of actions or circumstances. Years ago I taught my first seminar class with hundreds of students in an auditorium. A strong introvert, I remember my panic as I walked out across that stage, lights glaring. I clutched a glass of water, trying to look casual and composed as I sat on the edge of the desk to speak. Unfortunately, the desk went out from under me, and my water flew across the first three rows of stunned students. I lay flat on my back, laughing and thinking, "It has got to get better from here!" And it did! Students laughed as they helped me to my feet. We got along famously after that; they found me more approachable and fallible. Our students need to see us as master students in progress, learning from our own mistakes and others' mistakes as well.* "

— *Annette McCreedy, Nashville State Community College*

- **Skip the question for now.** Do the ones you are sure of first. This advice is simple—and it works. Tell students to let their subconscious mind work on the answer while they respond to other questions.

- **Look for answers in other test questions.** A term, name, date, or other fact that escapes you might appear in another question on the test. Use other questions to stimulate your memory or to provide a hint or clue.

master instructor
best practice

" *One thing that I tell my students about essay tests is to write as if they were writing to someone who knows absolutely nothing about the subject. In that way, they should include all the basic information that they might not otherwise think of. I also use LIBEC, which stands for legible, introduction, body, example, and conclusion. We talk about these steps and then my students (in groups) write answers to questions I make up from the reading in the chapter. With their group members, they exchange answers and check to see if all the areas were covered. They enjoy working on an essay question with others and then evaluating what others have done.* "

—Barbara Fowler, Longview Community College

- *Treat intuition with care.* In quick-answer questions (multiple choice, true/false), go with your first instinct about which answer is correct. If you think your first answer is wrong because you misread the question, though, do change your answer.

- *Visualize the answer's "location."* Think of the answer to any test question as being recorded someplace in your notes or assigned reading. Close your eyes, take a deep breath, and see whether you can visualize that place—its location on a page in the materials you studied for the test. You might also be able to recall a picture or graph, which often helps the details come flooding back into your mind.

- *Rewrite the question.* See whether you can put a confusing question into your own words. Doing so might release the answer.

- *Free-write.* Just start writing anything at all. On scratch paper or in the margins of your test booklet, record any response to the test question that pops into your head. Instead of just sitting there, stumped, you're doing something—and that can reduce anxiety. Writing might also trigger a mental association that answers the question.

EXERCISES/ACTIVITIES

1. **Power Process: Detach (page 176).** After you have lectured on how to develop and write good essay exam answers, divide students into groups of four, and have them answer the following question: "Fully explain the Power Process: Detach." This provides

them with an opportunity to practice developing an essay answer in a cooperative learning environment. It's also valuable because some students don't fully understand this process without class discussion. Provide students with clear guidelines for a "good" answer. After the groups write their group essay answers, have them pass their papers to another group who then "grades" the essay. Read the highest-scoring answer, and provide your analysis as to the essay's strengths and weaknesses.

2. **Cooperative learning: Studying in groups (pages 182–183).** This article addresses the topic of working together in group study sessions. Divide your class into four groups, assigning each group one of the learning styles. Next, ask students to close their books and write down as many answers to their question (*Why? What? How? What if?*) in relation to test taking as they can in one minute. After a minute, have each group pick their best answer and report about it to the class.

Why?	Why does this chapter appear in *Becoming a Master Student*?
What?	What is included in this chapter?
How?	How can you use this chapter? How can test taking apply to the workplace?
What if?	What if you use the techniques in this chapter to be better prepared for tests?

3. **What to do before the test (pages 179–180).** This article is important to students because so many of them cram at the last minute and therefore have never practiced these strategies. Mind maps are powerful visual review tools that can be effective for students who don't know how to study effectively for tests. Have your students get into groups of four, pick a chapter from *Becoming a Master Student*, and create a mind map of the chapter's content on poster paper, with colored markers. Hang the completed posters on the wall in the classroom, and then have the students review their classmates' work. Having had an opportunity to practice creating mind map summaries in class, they are likely to be more comfortable trying the technique on their own outside class. This activity also allows students to practice the important skill of working in groups.

4. **Ways to predict test questions (page 181).** Divide students into groups and have them practice predicting test questions and answering them for the quizzes that you give in class. Their questions and answers should be based on what they see as the key points you have presented in lectures, activities, and homework, and the key points from the text. They are often surprised at how easy and effective this tool is! If by now you have completed Chapters 1 through 6, you can group students into six groups, asking each group to create 10 questions and answers for their assigned chapter. You can copy all chapter questions and answers to help students review these chapters for the exam.

CONVERSATION/SHARING

As the article "The test isn't over until . . ." (page 195) explains, it is vital for students to find out what questions they missed on a test and to understand why they missed them. Students can use the learning styles questions *(Why? What? How? What if?)* to review their tests. *Why* did I get this question wrong? *What* is the correct answer? *How* should I have studied this material? And they need to understand the consequences: *What if* I do not learn the correct answer for future tests? These four questions are a great foundational structure for this self-analysis. After a quiz or test, divide students into groups and have them share their analyses with each other so that they can all do better on the next evaluation.

Workplace Application: Job interviews as tests. Remind students that they are not necessarily test-free upon graduation. In addition to performance reviews and evaluations, the first foray into a workplace "test" is the job interview. Job interviews are stressful situations for both the job seeker and employer. Both want to make the best first impression while evaluating the other for fit and success. No wonder the thought of a job interview strikes fear in even the most confident professional. This fear can be abated with a little hard work and preparation.

- *Know yourself.* Know what assets you can bring to the organization. What are your greatest strengths? What are your greatest weaknesses? What have you done to address these weaknesses? What are your short- and long-term goals? Answering these questions beforehand will better prepare you.

- *Know the organization.* What does the organization do? Who are the leaders? What position are you applying for, and what qualifications are required?

- *Practice.* Although you can never be sure of the exact questions that an employer will ask, you can be prepared by practicing answers to common questions. Many employers are also now utilizing behavioral interview questions. "Tell me about a time when . . ." Think of a few examples of workplace behavior that you can use to answer these types of questions. You may also want to use the STAR method to answer behavioral interview questions:
  - *S/T: Situation/Task.* Describe a *specific* situation from any relevant event in which you were involved and the *task* that you needed to accomplish. Be sure to give sufficient details.
  - *A: Action.* Describe the *action* you took to address the situation.
  - *R: Result.* What did you accomplish? What did you learn?

- *Pay attention to appearance and presence.* Make sure your clothes are clean, unwrinkled, and in good condition. Make sure your shoes are clean and polished. Keep jewelry, makeup, and perfume to a minimum. Introduce yourself, greet the interviewer(s) by name, and shake hands, if he or she offers to do so. Sit down when invited. Smile, look alert, and answer questions briefly. Thank the interviewer(s) for his or her time. Send a thank you note to all those who interviewed you.

master instructor
best practice

❝*I have always tried to instruct my students to learn something from the tests that they take. This can be an area where the students can gain so much information and yet it is often overlooked. The information in the chart (page 189) is also helpful. This is a great way to say a lot in a small space.*❞

—*Ray Emett, Salt Lake Community College*

HOMEWORK

Journal Entry 14, Explore your feelings about tests (page 178). Having students complete and turn in this Journal Entry regarding how they feel about tests can be helpful to you in understanding the key problem areas for your students before, during, and after a test. Review students' responses to this Journal Entry, and tailor your lectures and activities to address the needs expressed. Possible issues might include test anxiety, procrastination, and past failures.

Journal Entry 15, Notice your excuses and let them go (page 178). Ask students to take a look at how they sabotage their opportunity to "create it all" by making excuses. This self-analysis will help them break the excuses habit by writing their discoveries and intentions about excuses. List common excuses on the board. Ask students, "Which ones have you used?" "Why is this excuse problematic?"

EVALUATION

Giving a quiz that includes multiple-choice, true/false, short-answer, and essay questions will give students an opportunity to practice new skills they've learned in this chapter and provide them with feedback about where they have achieved success in building new skills and where more practice is needed. For example, ask the following quiz question about Master Students Bert and John Jacobs: "Briefly describe the Jacobs' attitude about keeping a positive attitude. Then state whether you agree with it or not, and justify your position."

MindTap™ EMBRACE VALUABLE RESOURCES

FOR CHAPTER 6

STUDENT RESOURCES: MINDTAP

- **Engagement Activity: Master Students in Action.** Students hear firsthand from other students about their test-taking challenges and their strategies for success. The Master Students in Action videos give your students an up-close view of how the strategies in *Becoming a Master Student* have helped their peers overcome obstacles. Dave Ellis also proposes that students think about test taking as a positive opportunity and talks about the value of learning from our mistakes.

- **Aplia Homework Assignment: What to do before the test.** In this assignment, students learn strategies to help them better prepare for a test and

then apply these skills in a test-taking scenario. By examining a sample student scenario, students are asked to help the student identify items that should appear on his pre-test checklist.

- **Reflection Activity: What Kids are Listening to These Days.** This Slice of Life video, created by student Jake Chamberlain, shows how to find unique ways to study while exercising. For example, by listening to audio lectures, you can effectively multitask to accomplish both goals at once.

MindTap™ *Your personal learning experience—learn anywhere, anytime.*

INSTRUCTOR COMPANION SITE

- **Need some energizing lecture ideas?** Browse through the lecture ideas provided for Chapter 6 in the Course Manual, including the following:
  - **IBEC Essay Test Strategy.** Help your students who lack college-level writing skills to succeed in taking essay tests by introducing them to this four-part essay test system.
  - **Comparing Athletic Competitions to Tests.** Draw comparisons between what it takes to excel in athletic competition and on tests, to help students understand the necessary preparations.
- **Unsure of how to assess your own students?** Look at the following articles in the online Course Manual for suggestions on how to implement testing and assessment in your course:
  - Strategies for grading this course
  - Assessment of skills for first-year students

- What is the pre- and post-course assessment
- Creating a pre- and post-course assessment on your campus
- Strategies for working with students who are failing your course
- **Looking for test banks?** Customizable, text-specific content quizzes are a great way to test students' knowledge and understanding of the text, and are available for every chapter. Powered by Cognero, the test banks can be exported in an LMS or print-friendly format. You will have no problem accessing the multiple-choice, true/false, completion, and short-answer questions.

Please visit login.cengage.com to log in and access the Instructor Companion Site.

Chapter 6

TESTS

6

Why

Adopting a few simple techniques can make a major difference in how you feel about tests—and how you perform on them.

Let go of test anxiety ■
188

Getting ready for math tests ■ 190

What to do during the test ■ 184

How

Think about how you want your experience of test taking to change. For example, you might want to walk into every test feeling well rested and thoroughly prepared. Next, preview this chapter to find at least three strategies to accomplish your goal.

Cooperative learning: Studying in groups Study groups can lift your mood on days when you just don't feel like working. If you declare your intention to study with others who are depending on you, your intention gains strength. ■ 182

The high costs of cheating Remember that cheating carries costs. Read about some of the consequences to consider. ■ 187

What if ...

I could let go of anxiety about tests—or anything else?

What is included...

DETACH

This Power Process helps you release the powerful, natural student within you. It is especially useful whenever negative emotions are getting in your way.

Attachments are addictions. When we are attached to something, we think we cannot live without it, just as a drug addict feels he cannot live without drugs. We believe our well-being depends on maintaining our attachments.

We can be attached to just about anything: beliefs, emotions, people, roles, objects. The list is endless.

One person, for example, might be so attached to his car that he takes an accident as a personal attack. Pity the poor unfortunate who backs into this person's car. He might as well have backed into the owner himself.

Another person might be attached to her job. Her identity and sense of well-being depend on it. She could become depressed if she got fired.

When we are attached and things don't go our way, we can feel angry, sad, afraid, or confused.

Suppose you are attached to getting an A on your physics test. You feel as though your success in life depends on getting that A. As the clock ticks away, you work harder on the test, getting more stuck. That voice in your head gets louder: "I must get an A. I *must* get an A. *I must get an A!*"

Now is a time to detach. See whether you can just *observe* what's going on, letting go of all your judgments. When you just observe, you reach a quiet state above and beyond your usual thoughts. This is a place where you can be aware of being aware. It's a tranquil spot, apart from your emotions. From here, you can see yourself objectively, as if you were watching someone else.

That place of detachment might sound far away and hard to reach. You can get there in three ways.

First, pay attention to your thoughts and physical sensations. If you are confused and feeling stuck, tell yourself, "Here I am, confused and stuck." If your palms are sweaty and your stomach is one big knot, admit it.

Second, practice relaxation. Start by simply noticing your breathing. Then breathe more slowly and more deeply. See whether you can breathe the relaxing feeling into your whole body.

Third, practice seeing current events from a broader perspective. In your mind, zoom out to a bigger picture. Ask yourself how much today's test score will matter to you in one week, one month, one year, or one decade from today. You can apply this technique to any challenge in life.

Caution: Giving up an *attachment* to being an A student does not mean giving up *being* an A student. Giving up an attachment to a job doesn't mean giving up the job. When you detach, you get to keep your values and goals. However, you know that you will be okay even if you fail to achieve a goal.

Remember that you are more than your goals. You are more than your thoughts and feelings. These things come and go. Meanwhile, the part of you that can *just observe* is always there and always safe, no matter what happens.

Behind your attachments is a master student. Release that mastery. Detach. ∎

© iStockphoto.com/iSci

THINK BEYOND THE GRADE

On the surface, tests don't look dangerous. Maybe that's why we sometimes treat them as if they were land mines. Suppose a stranger walked up to you on the street and asked, "Does a finite abelian P-group have a basis?" Would you break out in a cold sweat? Would your muscles tense up? Would your breathing become shallow?

Probably not. Even if you had never heard of a finite abelian P-group, you probably would remain coolly detached. However, if you find the same question on a test and you have never heard of a finite abelian P-group, your hands might get clammy.

Grades (A to F) are what we use to give power to tests. And there are lots of misconceptions about what grades are. Grades are not a measure of intelligence or creativity. They are not an indication of our ability to contribute to society. Grades are simply a measure of how well we do on tests.

Some people think that a test score measures what a student has accomplished in a course. This idea is false. A test score is a measure of what a student scored on a test. If you are anxious about a test and blank out, the grade cannot measure what you've learned. The reverse is also true: If you are a lucky guesser, the score won't be an accurate reflection of what you know.

Grades are not a measure of self-worth. Yet we tend to give test scores the power to determine how we feel about ourselves. Common thoughts include "If I fail a test, I am a failure" or "If I do badly on a test, I am a bad person." The truth is that if you do badly on a test, you are a person who did badly on a test. That's all. Carrying around misconceptions about tests and grades can put undue pressure on your performance.

If you experience test anxiety, you might feel that you're a victim of forces outside your control—cruel teachers, obscure textbooks, or trick questions. Another option is to ask: What can *I* do to experience my next test differently? How can I study more effectively? How can I manage test-related stress? When you ask such questions, you start to take back your power.

It is easier to do well on exams if you don't put too much pressure on yourself. Don't give the test some magical power over your own worth as a human being. Academic tests are not a matter of life and death. Scoring low on important tests—standardized tests or medical school, bar exams, CPA exams—usually means only a delay.

Whether the chance of doing poorly is real or exaggerated, worrying about it can become paralyzing. The way to deal with tests is to keep them in perspective. ■

Interactive

Practicing Critical Thinking 6

You might find the Power Process: Detach to be one of the more challenging ideas in this book. Use your thinking skills to unlock the power in this Power Process. One way to demonstrate how to detach is to give an example of it:

> *A son asked his father who was dying from lung cancer how he was feeling.*

> *"Oh, I'm great," said the man with cancer. "Your mom and I have been having a wonderful time just rejoicing in our life together."*

> *"Oh, I'm glad you're doing well," said the man's son. "The prednisone you have been taking must have helped your breathing."*

> *"Well, not exactly. My body is in terrible shape. My breathing has been a struggle these last few days. My body is not working well at all, but I am still great."*

This dying man was painfully aware of his body. He also thought of himself as *more* than his body. Above

all, he celebrated his marriage. He saw the most important fact about himself to be love, not cancer. This man gave his son—who happens to be the author of this book—an unforgettable lesson in detachment.

Now do your own thinking about detachment. Remember the six levels of thinking as described by psychologist Benjamin Bloom.

First, think at **Level 1: Remembering** by reviewing the Power Process: Detach. You might want to underline or highlight key words or sentences.

Next, move up to **Level 2: Understanding**. Imagine that you are going to explain this Power Process to someone who has not read this book. What would you say? Answer this question in a paragraph. Be sure to use your own words rather than quoting the article directly.

In a second paragraph, describe an example of how you practiced detachment in the past—or could practice it in the future.

Journal Entry 14
Discovery Statement

Explore your feelings about tests

Complete the following sentences:

As exam time gets closer, one thing I notice that I do is . . .

_____

_____

When it comes to taking tests, I have trouble . . .

_____

_____

The night before a test, I usually feel . . .

_____

_____

The morning of a test, I usually feel . . .

_____

_____

During a test, I usually feel . . .

_____

_____

After a test, I usually feel . . .

_____

_____

When I learn a test score, I usually feel . . .

_____

_____

Journal Entry 15
Discovery/Intention Statement

Notice your excuses and let them go

Do a timed, four-minute brainstorm of all the reasons, rationalizations, justifications, and excuses you have used to avoid studying. Be creative. Write down your list of excuses.

Now, review your list. Then write a Discovery Statement about patterns that you see in your excuses.

I discovered that I . . .

_____

_____

Next, review your list, pick the excuse that you use the most, and circle it. Write an Intention Statement about what you will do to begin eliminating your favorite excuse. Make this Intention Statement one that you can keep, with a timeline and a reward.

I intend to . . .

_____

_____

_____

_____

_____

_____

_____

_____

_____

_____

_____

_____

_____

_____

"'How To Do Well In School Without Studying' is over there in the fiction section."

Bacall, Aaron/CartoonStock.com

What to do BEFORE THE TEST

Students like to say that they plan to study for a test. There's a big problem with that term: It doesn't always have a clear definition. It might mean "read," "write," or "recite." It could mean all of those things—or something else entirely.

Here's a solution: See each test as a performance. Studying for a test means rehearsing—or even better, *practicing*. Get ready for a test in the same way that an actor gets ready for opening night: Do the same things you'll be asked to do during the performance.

The goal is to define the information you'll want to remember and actively *use* it. Wire it firmly in your long-term memory circuits. Make it easy to retrieve at exam time.

You can prepare for a test in the same way that pilots prepare for a flight—use a checklist. Before taking off, they physically mark off each item they need to check and adjust. A written list helps them to be sure they don't miss anything. Once they are in the air, it's too late.

Taking an exam is like flying a plane. Once the test begins, it's too late to memorize that one equation you forgot to use when practicing problem solving.

Make checklists that include exactly what you'll use to practice for a test. Your checklists will vary because they'll be geared to different subjects. For example, you can list:

- The date and time of the test, along with the name of the course and instructor
- Reading assignments by chapters or page numbers
- Dates of lecture notes
- Types of problems you will need to solve
- Major ideas, definitions, theories, formulas, and equations
- Other skills to master

Remember that a checklist is a to-do list. It contains two things. One is the briefest possible description of *what* items you will use to practice. Second is a description of *how* you will use those items to practice. Here it's important to use active verbs other than *study* or *review*. For example, you can *outline* textbook chapters, *recite* key material based on your lecture notes, and *solve* sample problems.

FIND OR CREATE PRACTICE MATERIALS

Practice tests. Write your own questions based on course material. This is a good activity for study groups. Take your practice test several times before the actual

exam. Type up this "test" so that it looks like the real thing. If possible, take your practice test in the same room where you will take the actual test. Consider testing yourself several times in preparation for an exam, using different practice tests. If this seems like a lot of effort, remember that informal self-testing is a learning strategy that's well supported by research.[1]

Copies of old exams. Copies of previous exams for the class might be available from the instructor, the instructor's department, the library, or the counseling office. Use these as practice tests.

Some cautions: If you rely on old tests exclusively, you might gloss over material the instructor has added since the last test. Also check your school's policy about making past tests available to students. Some schools might not allow it.

Mind map summary sheets. There are several ways to make a mind map as you practice for tests. Start by creating one totally from memory. You might be surprised by how much you already know. After you have gone as far as you can using recall alone, go over your notes and text, and fill in the rest of the map.

Another option is to go through your notes and write down key words as you pick them out. Then, without looking at your notes, create a mind map of everything you can recall about each key word. Go back to your notes and fill in material you left out.

Flash cards. Flash cards are like portable test questions. On one side of 3 × 5 cards, write questions. On the other side, write the answers. It's that simple.

Always carry a pack of flash cards with you, and use them whenever you have a minute to spare. Use flash cards for formulas, definitions, theories, key words from your notes, axioms, dates, foreign language phrases, hypotheses, and sample problems. Create flash cards regularly as the term progresses. Buy an inexpensive card file to keep your flash cards arranged by subject.

You can also create Web-based flash cards to use with your computer, smart phone, or tablet. Options include Quizlet (**www.quizlet.com**), StudyBlue (**www.studyblue.com**), and FlashCardMachine (**www.flashcardmachine.com**).

SCHEDULE YOUR PRACTICE SESSIONS

Many studies support the power of distributed learning.[2] This is opposite of cramming for a test. The goal is to spread (distribute) your learning across a whole term rather than trying to do it in a few marathon sessions.

Schedule specific times in your calendar for practice sessions before a test. Start focusing on key topics at least five days before you'll be tested on them. This allows plenty of time to find the answers to questions and close any gaps in your understanding.

Daily practice. Scan your lecture notes, and then cover them up and recite key points and details. Also practice with textbooks: Before reading a new assignment, scan your notes and the sections you underlined or highlighted in the previous assignment.

Concentrate daily practice on two kinds of material. One is new material from class meetings and your reading. Second is material that involves simple memorization—equations, formulas, dates, definitions. You can start practicing these within seconds after learning. During a lull in class, for example, scan the notes you just took. Immediately after class, scan them again.

Each day that you practice for a test, assess what you have learned and what you still want to learn. See how many items you've covered from your checklist. This helps you evaluate your practice and alerts you to areas that still need attention.

Weekly practice. Practice for each subject at least once a week, allowing about one hour per subject. See if you can do most of the items on your checklist and cover them in more detail than you do in daily practice sessions. For example:

- Look over any summary sheets that you've written and then rewrite them from memory.

- Write answers to review questions in your textbooks.

- Solve problems from your textbooks.

- Recite the points in your notes that you want to remember.

- Rewrite your notes for greater precision and clarity.

Major practice sessions. These can be most helpful during the week before finals or other critical exams. They help you integrate concepts and deepen your understanding of material presented throughout the term.

For major practice sessions, schedule two to five hours at a stretch. Allow for breaks. Remember that the effectiveness of your session begins to drop after an hour or so unless you give yourself a short rest. After a certain point, short breaks every hour might not be enough to refresh you. That's when it's time to quit. Learn your limits by being conscious of the quality of your concentration.

During long sessions, focus on the most difficult subjects when you are the most alert—at the beginning of the session. ■

How to cram (even though you "shouldn't")

Know the limitations of cramming, and be aware of its costs. Cramming won't work if you've neglected all of the reading assignments or if you've skipped most of the lectures and daydreamed through the rest. The more courses you have to cram for, the less effective cramming will be. Also, cramming is not the same as learning: You won't remember what you cram.

If you *are* going to cram, however, then avoid telling yourself that you *should* have studied earlier, you *should* have read the assignments, or you *should* have been more conscientious. All those *shoulds* get you nowhere. Instead, write an Intention Statement about how you will change your study habits. Give yourself permission to be the fallible human being you are. Then make the best of the situation.

Make choices. Pick out a *few* of the most important elements of the course and learn them backward, forward, and upside down. For example, devote most of your attention to the topic sentences, tables, and charts in a long reading assignment.

Make a plan. After you've chosen what elements you want to study, determine how much time to spend on each one.

Recite and recite again. The key to cramming is repetition. Go over your material again and again.

Ways to PREDICT TEST QUESTIONS

Predicting test questions can do more than get you a better grade. It can also keep you focused on the purpose of a course and help you design your learning strategies. Making predictions can be fun too—especially when they turn out to be accurate.

Ask about the nature of the test. Eliminate as much guesswork as possible. Ask your instructor to describe upcoming tests. Do this early in the term so you can be alert for possible test questions throughout the course. Here are some questions to ask:

- What course material will the test cover—readings, lectures, lab sessions, or a combination?
- Will the test be cumulative, or will it cover just the most recent material you've studied?
- Will the test focus on facts and details or major themes and relationships?
- Will the test call on you to solve problems or apply concepts?
- Will you have choices about which questions to answer?
- What types of questions will be on the test—true/false, multiple choice, short answer, essay?

Note: In order to study appropriately for essay tests, find out how much detail the instructor wants in your answers. Ask how much time you'll be allowed for the test and about the length of essay answers (number of pages, blue books, or word limit). Having that information before you begin studying will help you gauge your depth for learning the material.

Put yourself in your instructor's shoes. If you were teaching the course, what kinds of questions would you put on an exam? You can also brainstorm test questions with other students—a great activity for study groups.

Look for possible test questions in your notes and readings. Have a separate section in your notebook labeled "Test questions." Add several questions to this section after every lecture and assignment. You can also create your own code or graphic signal—such as a *T!* in a circle—to flag possible test questions in your notes. Use the same symbol to flag review questions and problems in your textbooks that could appear on a test.

Remember that textbook authors have many ways of pointing you to potential test items. Look for clues in chapter overviews and summaries, headings, lists of key words, and review questions. Some textbooks have related Web sites where you can take practice tests.

Look for clues to possible questions during class. During lectures, you can predict test questions by observing what an instructor says and how he says it. Instructors often give clues. They might repeat important points several times, write them on the board, or return to them in later classes.

Gestures can indicate critical points. For example, your instructor might pause, look at notes, or read passages word for word.

Notice whether your teacher has any strong points of view on certain issues. Questions on those issues are likely to appear on a test. Also pay attention to questions the instructor poses to students, and note questions that other students ask.

When material from reading assignments is covered extensively in class, it is likely to be on a test. For science courses and other courses involving problem solving, work on sample problems using different variables.

Save all quizzes, papers, lab sheets, and graded materials of any kind. Quiz questions have a way of reappearing, in slightly altered form, on final exams. If copies of previous exams and other graded materials are available, use them to predict test questions.

Apply your predictions. To get the most value from your predictions, use them to guide your review sessions.

Remember the obvious. Be on the lookout for these words: *This material will be on the test.* ■

Yellow Dog Productions/Lifesize/Getty Images

Cooperative learning:
STUDYING
IN GROUPS

Study groups can lift your mood on days when you just don't feel like working. If you skip a solo study session, no one else will know. If you declare your intention to study with others who are depending on you, your intention gains strength.

Study groups are especially important if going to school has thrown you into a new culture. Joining a study group with people you already know can help ease the transition.

To multiply the benefits of study groups, seek out people of other backgrounds, cultures, races, and ethnic groups. You can get a new perspective, along with some new friends.

None of us is born with these skills. Use study groups to start expanding your skills at collaboration. The time you invest now can advance your career in the future.

FORM A STUDY GROUP

Choose a focus for your group. Many students assume that the purpose of a study group is to help its members prepare for a test. That's one valid purpose—and there are others.

Through his research on cooperative learning, psychologist Joe Cuseo has identified several kinds of study groups.[3] For instance, members of *test review* groups compare answers and help one another discover sources of errors. *Note-taking* groups focus on comparing and editing notes, often meeting directly after the day's class. Members of *research* groups meet to help one another find, evaluate, and take notes on background materials for papers and presentations. *Reading* groups can be useful for courses in which test questions are based largely on textbooks. Meet with classmates to compare the passages you underlined or highlighted and the notes you made in the margins of your books.

Look for dedicated students. Find people you are comfortable with and who share your academic goals. Look for students who pay attention, participate in class, and actively take notes. Invite them to join your group.

Of course, you can recruit members in other ways. One way is to make an announcement during class. Another option is to post signs asking interested students to contact you. Or pass around a sign-up sheet before class. These methods can reach many people, but they do take

more time to achieve results. And you have less control over who applies to join the group.

Limit groups to four people. Research on cooperative learning indicates that four people are an ideal group size.[4] Larger groups can be unwieldy.

Studying with friends is fine, but if your common interests are pizza and jokes, you might find it hard to focus.

Hold a planning session. Ask two or three people to get together for a snack and talk about group goals, meeting times, and other logistics. You don't have to make an immediate commitment.

As you brainstorm about places to meet, aim for a quiet meeting room with plenty of room to spread out materials. Your campus library probably has study rooms. Campus tutoring services might also have space and other resources for study groups.

Do a trial run. Test the group first by planning a one-time session. If that session works, plan another. After a few successful sessions, you can schedule regular meetings.

CONDUCT YOUR GROUP

Ask your instructor for guidelines on study group activity. Many instructors welcome and encourage study groups. However, they have different ideas about what kinds of collaboration are acceptable. Some activities—such as sharing test items or writing papers from a shared outline—are considered cheating and can have serious consequences. Let your instructor know that you're forming a group, and ask for clear guidelines.

Assign roles. To make the most of your time, ask one member to lead each group meeting. The leader's role is to keep the discussion focused on the agenda and ask for contributions from all members. Assign another person to act as recorder. This person will take notes on the meeting, recording possible test questions, answers, and main points from group discussions. Rotate both of these roles so that every group member takes a turn.

Cycle through learning styles. As you assign roles, think about the learning styles present in your group. Some people excel at raising questions and creating lots of ideas. Others prefer to gather information and think critically. Some like to answer questions and make decisions, whereas others excel at taking action. To create an effective group, match people with their preferred activities. Also change roles periodically. This gives group members a chance to explore new learning styles.

Teach each other. Teaching is a great way to learn something. Turn the material you're studying into a list of topics, and assign a specific topic to each person, who will then teach it to the group. When you're done presenting your topic, ask for questions or comments. Prompt each other to explain ideas more clearly, find gaps in understanding, consider other points of view, and apply concepts to settings outside the classroom.

Test one another. During your meeting, take a practice test created from questions contributed by group members. When you're finished, compare answers. Or turn testing into a game by pretending you're on a television game show. Use sample test questions to quiz one another.

Compare notes. Make sure that all the group's members heard the same thing in class and that you all recorded the important information. Ask others to help explain material in your notes that is confusing to you.

Create wall-size mind maps or concept maps to summarize a textbook or series of lectures. Work on large sheets of butcher paper, or tape together pieces of construction paper. When creating a mind map, assign one branch to each member of the study group. Use a different colored pen or marker for each branch of the mind map.

Monitor effectiveness. On your meeting agenda, include an occasional discussion about your group's effectiveness. Are you meeting consistently? Is the group helping members succeed in class?

Use this time to address any issues that are affecting the group as a whole. If certain members are routinely unprepared for study sessions, brainstorm ways to get them involved. If one person tends to dominate meetings, reel her in by reminding her that everyone's voice needs to be heard.

To resolve conflict among group members, keep the conversation constructive. Focus on solutions. Move from vague complaints ("You're never prepared") to specific requests ("Will you commit to bringing 10 sample test questions next time?"). Asking a "problem" member to lead the next meeting might make an immediate difference.

Ask about extending the focus of your group. If your group is going well, ask members whether they want to discuss problems with transportation, child care, financial aid, and other issues that go beyond class work. Study groups can lead to lasting friendships that support long-term success in school.

Take this article to work. Joining a study group helps you to develop a number of skills for working on teams in the workplace. One of those skills is leading meetings. When it's your turn to lead your study group, keep these ideas in mind as strategies you can also apply at work:

- *Schedule carefully.* Give people plenty of advance notice that you want to meet—at least one week.

- *Set clear starting and stopping times.* Experiment with scheduling less time for a group. If people know that a meeting will only last 60 minutes, they're more likely to show up on time.

- *Set a focused agenda.* At the beginning of each meeting, reach agreement on exactly what you intend to do. Then set a time limit for each agenda item. During the meeting, keep an eye on the clock to make sure that the group stays on schedule.

- *Make sure that necessary materials are available.* If you're planning to take a practice text, for example, make sure that everyone in the group will have a copy.

- *Monitor comprehension.* It's often easy to tell when people in the group are still struggling with a concept. Invite them to keep asking questions until they get clear. Answering those questions can reveal gaps in the group's understanding and suggest new issues to raise in class.

- *End each meeting with a to-do list.* Save the last 10 minutes of each meeting for appointing the next group leader and recorder. Also set a date, time, location, and agenda for your next meeting. If the group came up with questions that no one was able to answer, then assign someone to talk to an instructor about them and share answers with the group. ■

Roy Mehta/Riser/Getty Images

What to do DURING THE TEST

Prepare yourself for the test by arriving early. Being early often leaves time to do a relaxation exercise. While you're waiting for the test to begin and talking with classmates, avoid asking the question "How much did you study for the test?" This question might fuel anxious thoughts that you didn't study enough.

AS YOU BEGIN

Ask the teacher or test administrator whether you can use scratch paper during the test. (If you use a separate sheet of paper without permission, you might appear to be cheating.) If you *do* get permission, use this paper to jot down memory aids, formulas, equations, definitions, facts, or other material you know you'll need and might forget. An alternative is to make quick notes in the margins of the test sheet.

Pay attention to verbal directions given as a test is distributed. Then scan the whole test immediately. Evaluate the importance of each section. Notice how many points each part of the test is worth; then estimate how much time you'll need for each section, using its point value as your guide. For example, don't budget 20 percent of your time for a section that is worth only 10 percent of the points.

Read the directions slowly. Then reread them. It can be agonizing to discover that you lost points on a test merely because you failed to follow the directions. When the directions are confusing, ask to have them clarified.

Now you are ready to begin the test. If necessary, allow yourself a minute or two of "panic" time. Notice any tension you feel, and apply one of the techniques explained in the article "Let Go of Test Anxiety" later in this chapter.

Answer the easiest, shortest questions first. This gives you the experience of success. It also stimulates associations and prepares you for more difficult questions. Pace yourself and watch the time. If you can't think of an answer, move on. Follow your time plan.

If you are unable to determine the answer to a test question, keep an eye out throughout the test for context clues that may remind you of the correct answer or provide you with evidence to eliminate wrong answers.

MULTIPLE-CHOICE QUESTIONS

- *Answer each question in your head first.* Do this step before you look at the possible answers. If you come up with an answer that you're confident is right, look for that answer in the list of choices.

- *Read all possible answers before selecting one.* Sometimes two answers will be similar and only one will be correct.

- *Test each possible answer.* Remember that multiple-choice questions consist of two parts: the stem (an incomplete statement or question at the beginning) and a list of possible answers. Each answer, when combined with the stem, makes a complete statement or question-and-answer pair that is either true or false. When you combine the stem with each possible answer, you are turning each multiple-choice question into a small series of true/false questions. Choose the answer that makes a true statement.

- *Eliminate incorrect answers.* Cross off the answers that are clearly not correct. The answer you cannot eliminate is probably the best choice.

TRUE/FALSE QUESTIONS

- *Read the entire question.* Separate the statement into its grammatical parts—individual clauses and phrases—and then test each part. If any part is false, the entire statement is false.

- *Look for qualifiers.* Qualifiers include words such as *all, most, sometimes,* or *rarely.* Absolute qualifiers such as *always* or *never* generally indicate a false statement.

- *Find the devil in the details.* Double-check each number, fact, and date in a true/false statement. Look for numbers that have been transposed or facts that have been slightly altered. These are signals of a false statement.

- *Watch for negatives.* Look for words such as *not* and *cannot.* Read the sentence without these words and see whether you come up with a true/false statement.

Words to watch for in essay questions

The following words are commonly found in essay test questions. They give you precise directions about what to include in your answer. Get to know these words well. When you see them on a test, underline them. Also look for them in your notes. Locating such key words can help you predict test questions.

- *Analyze:* Break into separate parts and discuss, examine, or interpret each part. Then give your opinion.
- *Compare:* Examine two or more items. Identify similarities and differences.
- *Contrast:* Show differences. Set in opposition.
- *Criticize:* Make judgments about accuracy, quality, or both. Evaluate comparative worth. Criticism often involves analysis.
- *Define:* Explain the exact meaning—usually, a meaning specific to the course or subject. Definitions are usually short.
- *Describe:* Give a detailed account. Make a picture with words. List characteristics, qualities, and parts.
- *Diagram:* Create a drawing, chart, or other visual element. Label and explain key parts.
- *Discuss:* Consider and debate or argue the pros and cons of an issue. Write about any conflict. Compare and contrast.
- *Enumerate:* List the main parts or features in a meaningful order and briefly describe each one.
- *Evaluate:* Make judgments about accuracy, quality, or both (similar to *criticize*).
- *Explain:* Make an idea clear. Show logically how a concept is developed. Give the reasons for an event.
- *Illustrate:* Clarify an idea by giving examples of it. Illustration often involves comparison

and contrast. Read the test directions to see whether the question calls for actually drawing a diagram as well.

- *Interpret:* Explain the meaning of a new idea or event by showing how it relates to more familiar ideas or events. Interpretation can involve evaluation.
- *List:* Write a series of concise statements (similar to *enumerate*).
- *Outline:* List the main topics, points, features, or events, and briefly describe each one. (This does not necessarily mean creating a traditional outline with Roman numerals, numbers, and letters.)
- *Prove:* Support with facts, examples, and quotations from credible sources (especially those presented in class or in the text).
- *Relate:* Show the connections between ideas or events. Provide a larger context for seeing the big picture.
- *State:* Explain precisely and clearly.
- *Summarize:* Give a brief, condensed account. Include main ideas and conclusions. Avoid supporting details, or include only significant details.
- *Trace:* Show the order of events or the progress of a subject or event.

Notice how these words differ. For example, *compare* asks you to do something different from *contrast*. Likewise, *criticize* and *explain* call for different responses.

If any of these terms are still unclear to you, look them up in an unabridged dictionary.

During a test, you might be allowed to ask for an explanation of a key word. Check with instructors for policies.

Then reinsert the negative words and see whether the statement makes more sense. Watch especially for sentences with two negative words. As in math operations, two negatives cancel each other out: *We cannot say that Chekhov never succeeded at short story writing* means the same as *Chekhov succeeded at short story writing.*

COMPUTER-GRADED TESTS

- Make sure that the answer you mark corresponds to the question you are answering.
- Check the test booklet against the answer sheet whenever you switch sections and whenever you come to the top of a column.

- Watch for stray marks on the answer sheet; they can look like answers.
- If you change an answer, be sure to erase the wrong answer thoroughly, removing all pencil marks completely.

OPEN-BOOK TESTS

- Carefully organize your notes, readings, and any other materials you plan to consult when writing answers.
- Write down any formulas you will need on a separate sheet of paper.
- Bookmark the table of contents and index in each of your textbooks. Place sticky notes and stick-on tabs or paper clips on other important pages of books (pages with tables, for instance).
- Create an informal table of contents or index for the notes you took in class.
- Predict which material will be covered on the test, and highlight relevant sections in your readings and notes.

SHORT-ANSWER/FILL-IN-THE-BLANK TESTS

- Concentrate on key words and facts. Be brief.
- Overlearning material can really pay off. When you know a subject backward and forward, you can answer this type of question almost as fast as you can write.

MATCHING TESTS

- Begin by reading through each column, starting with the one with fewer items. Check the number of items in each column to see whether they're equal. If they're not, look for an item in one column that you can match with two or more items in the other column.
- Look for any items with similar wording, and make special note of the differences between these items.
- Match words that are similar grammatically. For example, match verbs with verbs and nouns with nouns.
- When matching individual words with phrases, first read a phrase. Then look for the word that logically completes the phrase.
- Cross out items in each column when you are through with them.

ESSAY QUESTIONS

Managing your time is crucial in answering essay questions. Note how many questions you have to answer, and monitor your progress during the test period. Writing shorter answers and completing all of the questions on an essay test will probably yield a better score than leaving some questions blank.

Find out what an essay question is asking— precisely. If a question asks you to *compare* the ideas of Sigmund Freud and Karl Marx, no matter how eloquently you *explain* them, you are on a one-way trip to No Credit City.

Before you write, make a quick outline. An outline can help speed up the writing of your detailed answer; you're less likely to leave out important facts; and if you don't have time to finish your answer, your outline could win you some points. To use test time efficiently, keep your outline brief. Focus on key words to use in your answer.

Introduce your answer by getting to the point. General statements such as "There are many interesting facets to this difficult question" can cause irritation to teachers grading dozens of tests.

One way to get to the point is to begin your answer with part of the question. Suppose the question is "Discuss how increasing the city police budget might or might not contribute to a decrease in street crime." Your first sentence might be this: "An increase in police expenditures will not have a significant effect on street crime for the following reasons." Your position is clear. You are on your way to an answer.

Then expand your answer with supporting ideas and facts. Start out with the most solid points. Be brief and avoid filler sentences.

Write legibly. Grading essay questions is in large part a subjective process. Sloppy, difficult-to-read handwriting might actually lower your grade.

Write on one side of the paper only. If you write on both sides of the paper, writing may show through and obscure the words on the other side. If necessary, use the blank side to add points you missed. Leave a generous left-hand margin and plenty of space between your answers, in case you want to add points that you missed later on.

Finally, if you have time, review your answers for grammar and spelling errors, clarity, and legibility. ■

THE HIGH COSTS OF CHEATING

Cheating on tests can be a tempting strategy. It offers the chance to get a good grade without having to study.

Instead of studying, we could spend more time watching TV, partying, sleeping, or doing anything that seems like more fun. Another benefit is that we could avoid the risk of doing poorly on a test—which could happen even if we *do* study.

Remember that cheating carries costs. Here are some consequences to consider.

We risk failing the course or getting expelled from college. The consequences for cheating are serious. Cheating can result in failing the assignment, failing the entire course, getting suspended, or getting expelled from college entirely. Documentation of cheating may also prevent you from being accepted to other colleges.

We learn less. Although we might think that some courses offer little or no value, we can create value from any course. If we look deeply enough, we can discover some idea or acquire some skill to prepare us for future courses or a career after graduation.

We lose time and money. Getting an education costs a lot of money. It also calls for years of sustained effort. Cheating sabotages our purchase. We pay full tuition and invest our energy without getting full value for it. We shortchange ourselves and possibly our future coworkers, customers, and clients. Think about it: You probably don't want a surgeon who cheated in medical school to operate on you.

Fear of getting caught promotes stress. When we're fully aware of our emotions about cheating, we might discover intense stress. Even if we're not fully aware of our emotions, we're likely to feel some level of discomfort about getting caught.

Violating our values promotes stress. Even if we don't get caught cheating, we can feel stress about violating our own ethical standards. Stress can compromise our physical health and overall quality of life.

Cheating on tests can make it easier to violate our integrity again. Human beings become comfortable with behaviors that they repeat. Cheating is no exception.

Think about the first time you drove a car. You might have felt excited—even a little frightened. Now driving is probably second nature, and you don't give it much thought. Repeated experience with driving creates familiarity, which lessens the intense feelings you had during your first time at the wheel.

We can experience the same process with almost any behavior. Cheating once will make it easier to cheat again.

And if we become comfortable with compromising our integrity in one area of life, we might find it easier to compromise in other areas.

Cheating lowers our self-concept. Whether or not we are fully aware of it, cheating sends us the message that we are not smart enough or responsible enough to make it on our own. We deny ourselves the celebration and satisfaction of authentic success.

An alternative to cheating is to become a master student. Ways to do this are described on every page of this book. ■

Perils of high-tech cheating

Digital technology offers many blessings, but it also expands the options for cheating during a test. For example, one student tried to read class notes from an iPhone. Another student dictated his class notes into files stored on his iPod and tried to listen to them. At one school, students used cell phones to take photos of test questions. They sent the photos to classmates outside the testing room, who responded by text-messaging the answers.[5]

All of these students were caught. Schools are becoming sophisticated about detecting high-tech cheating. Some install cameras in exam rooms. Others use software that monitors the programs running on students' computers during tests. And some schools simply ban all digital devices during tests.

The bottom line: If you cheat on a test, you are more likely than ever before to get caught.

There's no need to learn the hard way—through painful consequences—about the high costs of high-tech cheating. Using the suggestions in this chapter can help you succeed on tests *and* preserve your academic integrity.

© Chad McDermott/Shutterstock.com

LET GO OF TEST ANXIETY

If you freeze during tests and flub questions when you know the answers, you might be dealing with test anxiety.

To perform gracefully under the pressure of exams, put as much effort into preventing test anxiety as you do into mastering the content of your courses. Think of test taking as the "silent subject" on your schedule, equal in importance to the rest of your courses.

A little tension before a test is fine. That tingly, butterflies-in-the-stomach feeling you get from extra adrenaline can sharpen your awareness and keep you alert. You can enjoy the benefits of a little tension while you stay confident and relaxed.

If you notice that your mind is consumed with worries and fears—that your thoughts are spinning out of control—mentally yell, "Stop!" If you're in a situation that allows it, yell it out loud. This action can allow you to redirect your thoughts.

Once you've broken the cycle of worry or panic, you can use any of the following techniques.

ACCEPT YOUR FEELINGS

Telling someone who's anxious about a test to "just calm down" is like turning up the heat on a pan that's already boiling over: The "solution" simply worsens the problem. If you take such advice to heart, you can end up with two problems. First, there's your worry about the test. Second, there's your worry about the fact that you're worried!

There's a way to deal with both problems at the same time: Simply accept your feelings, whatever they are. Fear and anxiety tend to increase with resistance. The more you try to suppress them, the more intensity the feelings gain.

As an alternative, stop resisting. See anxiety as a cluster of thoughts and body sensations. Watch the thoughts as they pass through your mind. Observe the sensations as they wash over you. Let them arise, peak, and pass away. No feeling lasts forever. The moment you accept fear, you pave the way for its release.

DESCRIBE YOUR THOUGHTS IN WRITING

Certain thoughts tend to increase test anxiety. One way to defuse them is to simply acknowledge them. To get the

Have some FUN!

Contrary to popular belief, finals week does not have to be a drag. In fact, if you have used techniques in this chapter, exam week can be fun. You will have done most of your studying long before finals arrive.

When you are well prepared for tests, you can even use fun as a technique to enhance your performance. The day before a final, go for a run or play a game of basketball. Take in a movie or a concert. A relaxed brain is a more effective brain. If you have studied for a test, your mind will continue to prepare itself even while you're at the movies. Get plenty of rest too. There's no need to cram until 3 a.m. when you have reviewed material throughout the term.

full benefit of this technique, take the time to make a list. Write down what you think and feel about an upcoming test. Capture everything that's on your mind, and don't stop to edit. One study indicates that this technique can relieve anxiety and potentially raise your test score.[6]

DISPUTE YOUR THOUGHTS

You can take the previous technique one step further. Do some critical thinking. Remember that anxiety-creating thoughts about tests often boil down to this statement: *Getting a low grade on a test is a disaster.* Do the math, however: A four-year degree often involves taking about 32 courses (8 courses per year over four years for a full-time student). This means that your final grade on any one course amounts to about only 3 percent of your total grade point average. This is *not* an excuse to avoid studying. It is simply a reason to keep tests in perspective.

PRAISE YOURSELF

Many of us take the first opportunity to belittle ourselves: "Way to go, dummy! You don't even know the answer to the first question on the test." We wouldn't dream of treating a friend this way, yet we do it to ourselves. An alternative is to give yourself some encouragement. Treat yourself as if you were your own best friend. Prepare carefully for each test. Then remind yourself, "I am ready. I can do a great job on this test."

CONSIDER THE WORST

Rather than trying to put a stop to your worrying, consider the very worst thing that could happen. Take your fear to the limit of absurdity. Imagine the catastrophic problems that might occur if you were to fail the test. You might say to yourself, "Well, if I fail this test, I might fail the course, lose my financial aid, and get kicked out of school. Then I won't be able to get a job, so the bank will repossess my car, and I'll start drinking." Keep going until you see the absurdity of your predictions. After you stop chuckling, you can backtrack to discover a reasonable level of concern.

BREATHE

You can calm physical sensations within your body by focusing your attention on your breathing. Concentrate on the air going in and out of your lungs. Experience it as it passes through your nose and mouth. Do this exercise for two to five minutes. If you notice that you are taking short, shallow breaths, begin to take longer and deeper breaths. Imagine your lungs to be a pair of bagpipes. Expand your chest to bring in as much air as possible. Then listen to the plaintive chords as you slowly release the air.

OVER-PREPARE FOR TESTS

Performing artists know that stage fright can temporarily reduce their level of skill. That's why they often over-prepare for a performance. Musicians will rehearse a piece so many times that they can play it without thinking. Actors will go over their parts until they can recite lines in their sleep.

> *Rather than trying to put a stop to your worrying, consider the very worst thing that could happen. Keep going until you see the absurdity of your predictions. After you stop chuckling, you can backtrack to discover a reasonable level of concern.*

As you prepare for tests, you can apply the same principle. Read, recite, and review the content of each course until you know it cold. Then review again. For math courses, work most or all of the problems in your textbook, even problems that are not assigned. The idea is to create a margin of mastery that can survive even the most extreme feelings of anxiety.

CARE FOR YOUR BODY AS MUCH AS YOUR MIND

Being well rested and fed on exam day won't guarantee a higher test score. However, preparing for a test physically as well as mentally can reduce stress. Because sleep deprivation can affect memory, avoid all-nighters as a study strategy. Also moderate your use of mood-altering chemicals, including caffeine and alcohol.

TAKE THIS ARTICLE TO WORK

You are not necessarily done with tests, appraisals, or assessments once you graduate. People in many careers prepare for licensing tests and certification exams. You might even go back to school for another degree. Use the ideas presented to make peace with tests at any stage of your life.

In the workplace, performance reviews offer a test-like situation. These usually take place in a meeting with your direct supervisor at work. Reviews follow various formats, and organizations have their own systems for rating performance. To get the most from these meetings, focus on answering three questions: "What am I doing well? What could I do better? What skills are most important for me to develop right now?"

Also keep this in mind: The same techniques that help you manage test anxiety can also help you approach job interviews with confidence. If you feel nervous before an interview, experiment with disputing your thoughts, praising yourself, accepting the worst possible outcome, and yelling, "Stop!" when stressful thoughts arise. Also apply strategies for relaxing and dealing with emotions. ■

Getting
READY FOR
MATH
TESTS

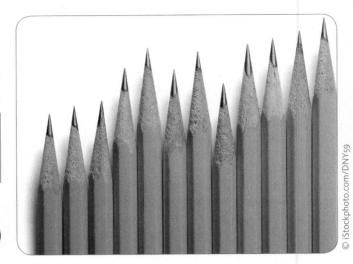

© iStockphoto.com/DNY59

Many students who could succeed in math shy away from the subject. Some had negative experiences in past courses. Others believe that math is only for gifted students.

At some level, however, math is open to all students. There's more to this subject than memorizing formulas and manipulating numbers. Imagination, creativity, and problem-solving skills are important too.

Consider a three-part program for math success. Begin with strategies for overcoming math anxiety. Next, boost your study skills. Finally, let your knowledge shine during tests.

OVERCOME MATH ANXIETY

Many schools offer courses in overcoming math anxiety. Ask your advisor about resources on your campus. Also experiment with the following suggestions.

© Ivanova Natalia/Shutterstock.com

Connect math to life. Think of the benefits of mastering math courses. You'll have more options for choosing a major and a career. Math skills can also put you at ease in everyday situations—calculating the tip for a waiter, balancing your checkbook, working with a spreadsheet on a computer. If you follow baseball statistics, cook, do construction work, or snap pictures with a camera, you'll use math. And speaking the language of math can help you feel at home in a world driven by technology.

Pause occasionally to get an overview of the branch of math that you're studying. What's it all about? What basic problems is it designed to solve? How do people apply this knowledge in daily life? For example, many architects, engineers, and space scientists use calculus daily.

Take a First Step. Math is cumulative. Concepts build upon each other in a certain order. If you struggled with algebra, you may have trouble with trigonometry or calculus.

To ensure that you have an adequate base of knowledge, tell the truth about your current level of knowledge and skill. Before you register for a math course, locate assigned texts for the prerequisite courses. If the material in those books seems new or difficult for you, see the instructor. Ask for suggestions on ways to prepare for the course.

Notice your pictures about math. Sometimes what keeps people from succeeding at math is their mental picture of mathematicians. They see a man dressed in a baggy plaid shirt and brown wingtip shoes. He's got a calculator on his belt and six pencils jammed in his shirt pocket.

These pictures are far from realistic. Succeeding in math won't turn you into a nerd. Actually, you'll be able to enjoy school more, and your friends will still like you.

Mental pictures about math can be funny, but they can have serious effects. If math is seen as a field for white males, then women and people of color are likely to get excluded. Promoting math success for all students helps to overcome racism and sexism.

Change your conversation about math. When students fear math, they often say negative things to themselves about their abilities in this subject. Many times this self-talk includes statements such as *I'll never be fast enough at solving math problems* or *I'm good with words, so I can't be good with numbers.*

Get such statements out in the open, and apply some emergency critical thinking. You'll find two self-defeating assumptions lurking there: *Everybody else is better at math and science than I am* and *Because I don't understand a math concept right now, I'll never understand it.* Both of these statements are illogical.

Replace negative beliefs with logical, realistic statements that affirm your ability to succeed in math: *Any confusion I feel now can be resolved. I learn math without comparing myself to others.* And *I ask whatever questions are needed to aid my understanding.*

Choose your response to stress. Math anxiety is seldom just "in your head." It can also register as sweaty palms, shallow breathing, tightness in the chest, or a mild headache. Instead of trying to ignore these sensations, just notice them without judgment. Over time, simple awareness decreases their power. In addition, use stress management techniques.

No matter what you do, remember to breathe. You can relax in any moment just by making your breath slower and deeper. Practice doing this while you study math. It will come in handy at test time.

BOOST STUDY SKILLS FOR MATH

Choose teachers with care. Whenever possible, find a math teacher whose approach to math matches your learning style. Talk with several teachers until you find one you enjoy.

Another option is to ask around. Maybe your academic advisor can recommend math teachers. Also ask classmates to name their favorite math teachers—and to explain the reasons for their choices.

In some cases, only one teacher will be offering the math course you need. The suggestions that follow can be used to learn from a teacher regardless of his teaching style.

Take math courses back to back. Approach math in the same way that you learn a foreign language. If you take a year off in between Spanish I and Spanish II, you won't gain much fluency. To master a language, you take courses back to back. It works the same way with math, which is a language in itself.

Avoid short courses. Courses that you take during summer school or another shortened term are condensed. You might find yourself doing far more reading and homework each week than you do in longer courses. If you enjoy math, the extra intensity can provide a stimulus to learn. But if math is not your favorite subject, give yourself extra time. Enroll in courses spread out over more calendar days.

Form a study group. During the first week of each math course, organize a study group. Ask each member to bring five problems to group meetings, along with solutions. Also exchange contact information so that you can stay in touch via e-mail, phone, and text messaging.

Make your text top priority. Math courses are often text driven. Budget for math textbooks and buy them as early as possible. Class activities closely follow the book. This fact underscores the importance of completing your reading assignments. Master one concept before going on to the next, and stay current with your reading. Be willing to read slowly and reread sections as needed.

Do homework consistently. Students who succeed in math do their homework daily—from beginning to end, and from the easy problems all the way through the hard problems. If you do homework consistently, you're not likely to be surprised on a test.

When doing homework, use a common process to solve similar problems. There's comfort in rituals, and using familiar steps can help to reduce math anxiety.

Take notes that promote success in math. Though math courses are often text-driven, you might find that the content and organization of your notes makes a big difference as well. Take notes during every class, and organize them by date. Also number the pages of your notes. Create a table of contents or index for them so that you can locate key concepts quickly.

In addition, make separate notes to integrate material from class meetings and reading assignments. Paul Nolting, author of the *Math Study Skills Workbook,* suggests that you create a large table with three columns: Key Words/Rules, Examples, and Explanation.[7] Updating this table weekly is a way to review for tests, uncover questions, and monitor your understanding.

Participate in class. Success in math depends on your active involvement. Attend class regularly. Complete homework assignments *when they're due*—not just before the test. If you're confused, get help right away from an instructor, tutor, or study group. Instructors' office hours, free on-campus tutoring, and classmates are just a few of the resources available to you. Also support class participation with time for homework. Make daily contact with math.

Math tests often involve lists of problems to solve. Ask your instructor about what type of tests to expect. Then prepare for the tests, using strategies from this chapter.

Ask questions fearlessly. It's a cliché, and it's true: In math, there are no dumb questions. Ask whatever questions will aid your understanding. Keep a running list of them, and bring the list to class.

Read actively. To get the most out of your math texts, read with paper and pencil in hand. Work out examples. Copy diagrams, formulas, and equations. Use chapter summaries and introductory outlines to organize your learning. From time to time, stop, close your book, and mentally reconstruct the steps in solving a problem. Before you memorize a formula, understand the basic concepts behind it.

USE TESTS TO SHOW WHAT YOU KNOW

Practice problem solving. To get ready for math tests, work *lots* of problems. Find out whether practice problems or previous tests are on file in the library, in the math department, or with your math teacher.

Isolate the types of problems that you find the most difficult. Practice them more often. Be sure to get help with these kinds of problems *before* exhaustion or frustration sets in.

To prepare for tests, practice working problems fast. Time yourself. This activity is a great one for math study groups.

Approach problem solving with a three-step process, as shown in Figure 6.1. During each step, apply an appropriate strategy.

Practice test taking. In addition to solving problems, create practice tests:

- Print out a set of problems, and set a timer for the same length of time as your testing period.
- Whenever possible, work on these problems in the same room where you will take the actual test.
- Use only the kinds of supporting materials—such as scratch paper or lists of formulas—that will be allowed during the test.
- As you work problems, use deep breathing or another technique to enter a more relaxed state.

To get the most value from practice tests, use them to supplement—not replace—your daily homework.

1: Prepare

- Read each problem two or three times, slowly and out loud whenever possible.

- Consider creating a chart with three columns labeled *What I already know*, *What I want to find out*, and *What connects the two*. The third column is the place to record a formula that can help you solve the problem.

- Determine which arithmetic operations (addition, subtraction, multiplication, division) or formulas you will use to solve the problem.

- See if you can estimate the answer before you compute it.

2: Compute

- Reduce the number of unknowns as much as you can. Consider creating a separate equation to solve each unknown.

- When solving equations, carry out the algebra as far as you can before plugging in the actual numbers.

- Cancel and combine. For example, if the same term appears in both dividend and divisor, they will cancel each other out.

- Remember that it's OK to make several attempts at solving the problem before you find an answer.

3: Check

- Plug your answer back into the original equation or problem and see if it works out correctly.

- Ask yourself if your answer seems likely when compared with your estimate. For example, if you're asked to apply a discount to an item, that item should cost less in your solution.

- Perform opposite operations. If a problem involves multiplication, check your work by division; add, then subtract; factor, then multiply; find the square root, then the square; differentiate, then integrate.

- Keep units of measurement clear. Say that you're calculating the velocity of an object. If you're measuring distance in meters and time in seconds, the final velocity should be in meters per second.

Figure 6.1 Problem-Solving Process for Math Problems

Ask appropriate questions. If you don't understand a test item, ask for clarification. The worst that can happen is that an instructor or proctor will politely decline to answer your question.

Write legibly. Put yourself in the instructor's place. Imagine the prospect of grading stacks of illegible answer sheets. Make your answers easy to read. If you show your work, underline key sections and circle your answer.

Do your best. There are no secrets involved in getting ready for math tests. Master some stress management techniques, do your homework, get answers to your questions, and work sample problems. If you've done those things, you're ready for the test and deserve to do well. If you haven't done all those things, just do the best you can.

Remember that your personal best can vary from test to test, and even from day to day. Even if you don't answer all test questions correctly, you can demonstrate what you *do* know right now.

During the test, notice when solutions come easily. Savor the times when you feel relaxed and confident. If you ever feel math anxiety in the future, these are the times to remember.[8] ■

Exercise 18
Use learning styles for math success

Feel free to modify any of the suggested strategies for mastering math courses so that they work for you. Or invent new techniques of your own.

If you're a visual learner, for example, you might color-code your notes by writing key terms and formulas in red ink. If you like to learn by speaking and listening, consider reading key passages in your textbooks out loud. And if you're a kinesthetic learner, use "manipulatives," such as magnetic boards with letters and numbers, when you study math.

Whatever you choose, commit to using at least one new strategy. Describe what you will do.

_____

_____

_____

_____

_____

_____

_____

_____

_____

Studying across the CURRICULUM

Think for a moment about the range of subjects that you're asked to study in higher education. Schools offer courses in everything from algebra to zoology, and you'll sample a variety of them. The challenge is to shift intellectual gears so that you can succeed in all those different subjects.

Some of the subjects you'll study in higher education share a single purpose—to *propose theories based on observations*. Physics, biology, and chemistry offer theories to explain and predict events in the natural world. Social sciences, such as psychology and sociology, offer theories to predict and explain events in the human world.

Other subjects go beyond theory to *define problems and offer solutions*. Their subjects range from the abstract problems of pure mathematics to the practical problems of engineering and computer science.

Courses in the arts do not propose carefully reasoned theories. Nor do they focus on solving problems. Instead, they *teach through vicarious experience*. When you read a novel, see a play, or watch a film, you view the world through another human being's eyes. Just as you learn from your own experience, you can learn from the experience of others.

To deal with all those differences in subjects, pull out a full toolbox of strategies. When preparing for tests in specific subjects, consider the suggestions in Figure 6.2. Then create more strategies of your own. ■

Subject Area	Strategies for Test Preparation
Humanities: English, literature, public speaking, history, religion, philosophy, fine arts	• Deepen your reading skills by previewing and reviewing each assignment. • Keep a dictionary handy, and create an updated list of new words and their definitions. • Experiment with several different formats for taking notes. • Keep a personal journal in which you practice writing and make connections between the authors and ideas that you're studying. • Take part in class discussions, and welcome chances to speak in front of groups.
Math and natural sciences: algebra, geometry, calculus, chemistry, biology, physics	• Before registering for a course, make sure that you are adequately prepared through prior course work. • In your notes, highlight basic principles—definitions, assumptions, and axioms. • Learn concepts in the sequence presented by your instructor. • If you feel confused, ask a question immediately. • Attend all classes, practice solving problems every day, and check your work carefully. • Translate word problems into images or symbols; translate images and symbols into words. • Balance abstract ideas with concrete experiences, including laboratory sessions and study groups. • Take math courses back to back so you can apply what you learn in one level of a math course immediately to the next level.
Social sciences: sociology, psychology, economics, political science, anthropology, geography	• Pay special attention to theories—statements that are used to explain relationships between observations and predict events. • Expect to encounter complex and contradictory theories, and ask your instructor about ways to resolve disagreements among experts in the field. • Ask your instructor to explain the scientific method and how it is used to arrive at theories in each of the social sciences. • Ask about current issues in the social sciences. • Ask for examples of a theory, and look for them in your daily life.
Foreign languages: learning to speak, read, and write any language that is new to you	• Pay special attention to the "rules"—principles of grammar, noun forms, and verb tenses. For each principle, list correct and incorrect examples. • Spend some time reading, writing, or speaking the language every day. • Welcome the opportunity to practice speaking in class, where you can get immediate feedback. • Start or join a study group in each of your language classes. • Spend time with people who are already skilled in speaking the language. • Travel to a country where the language is widely spoken. • Take your language courses back to back to ensure fluency.

Figure 6.2 Cross-Curriculum Study Strategies

The test isn't over until . . .

Many students believe that a test is over as soon as they turn in the answer sheet. Consider another point of view: You're not done with a test until you know the answer to any question that you missed—and why you missed it.

This point of view offers major benefits. Tests in many courses are cumulative. In other words, the content included on the first test is assumed to be working knowledge for the second test, midterm, or final exam. When you discover what questions you missed and understand the reasons for lost points, you learn something—and you greatly increase your odds of achieving better scores later in the course.

To get the most value from any test, take control of what you do at two critical points: the time immediately following the test and the time when the test is returned to you.

Immediately following the test. After finishing a test, your first thought might be to nap, snack, or go out with friends to celebrate. Restrain those impulses for a short while so that you can reflect on the test. The time you invest now carries the potential to raise your grades in the future.

To begin with, sit down in a quiet place. Take a few minutes to write some Discovery Statements related to your experience of taking the test. Describe how you felt about taking the test, how effective your review strategies were, and whether you accurately predicted the questions that appeared on the test.

Follow up with an Intention Statement or two. State what, if anything, you will do differently to prepare for the next test. The more specific you are, the better.

When the test is returned. When a returned test includes a teacher's comments, view this document as a treasure trove of intellectual gold.

First, make sure that the point totals add up correctly, and double-check for any other errors in grading. Even the best teachers make an occasional mistake.

Next, look at the test items that you missed. Ask these questions:

- On what material did the teacher base test questions—readings, lectures, discussions, or other class activities?
- What types of questions appeared in the test—objective (such as matching items, true/false questions, or multiple choice), short answer, or essay?
- What types of questions did you miss?
- Can you learn anything from the instructor's comments that will help you prepare for the next test?
- What strategies did you use to prepare for this test? What would you do differently to prepare for your next test?

Also see whether you can correct any answers that lost points. To do this, carefully analyze the source of your errors, and find a solution. Consult Figure 6.3 for help. ■

Source of test error	Possible solutions
Study errors—studying material that was not included on the test, or spending too little time on material that *did* appear on the test	• Ask your teacher about specific topics that will be included on a test. • Practice predicting test questions. • Form a study group with class members to create mock tests.
Careless errors, such as skipping or misreading directions	• Read and follow directions more carefully—especially when tests are divided into several sections with different directions. • Set aside time during the next test to proofread your answers.
Concept errors—mistakes made when you do not understand the underlying principles needed to answer a question or solve a problem	• Look for patterns in the questions you missed. • Make sure that you complete all assigned readings, attend all lectures, and show up for laboratory sessions. • Ask your teacher for help with specific questions.
Application errors—mistakes made when you understand underlying principles but fail to apply them correctly	• Rewrite your answers correctly. • When studying, spend more time on solving sample problems. • Predict application questions that will appear in future tests, and practice answering them.
Test mechanics errors—missing more questions in certain parts of the test than others, changing correct answers to incorrect ones at the last minute, leaving items blank, miscopying answers from scratch paper to the answer sheet	• Set time limits for taking each section of a test, and stick to them. • Proofread your test answers carefully. • Look for patterns in the kind of answers you change at the last minute. • Change answers only if you can state a clear and compelling reason to do so.

Figure 6.3 Test Errors and Possible Solutions

Celebrate
MISTAKES

Bluemoon Stock/Brand X Pictures/ Getty Images

The title of this article is no mistake. And it is not a suggestion that you purposely set out to *make* mistakes. Rather, the goal is to shine a light on mistakes so that we can examine them and fix them. Mistakes that are hidden cannot be corrected and are often worth celebrating for the following reasons.

Mistakes are valuable feedback. Mistakes are part of the learning process. In fact, mistakes are often more interesting and more instructive than are successes.

Mistakes demonstrate that we're taking risks. People who play it safe make few mistakes. Making mistakes can be evidence that we're stretching to the limit of our abilities—growing, risking, and learning.

Celebrating mistakes gets them out into the open. When we celebrate a mistake, we remind ourselves that the person who made the mistake is not bad—just human. Everyone makes mistakes. And hiding mistakes takes a lot of energy that could be channeled into correcting errors. This is not a recommendation that you purposely set out to make mistakes. Mistakes are not an end in themselves. Rather, their value lies in what we learn from them. When we make a mistake, we can admit it and correct it.

Mistakes happen only when we're committed to making things work. Imagine a school where teachers usually come to class late. Residence halls are never cleaned, and scholarship checks are always late. The administration is in chronic debt, students seldom pay tuition on time, and no one cares. In this school, the word *mistake* would have little meaning. Mistakes become apparent only when people are committed to quality.

Celebrate mistakes at work. Recall a mistake you made at work and then write about it. In a Discovery Statement, describe what you did to create a result you didn't want ("I discovered that I tend to underestimate the number of hours projects take"). Then write an Intention Statement describing something you can do differently in the future ("I intend to keep track of my actual hours on each project so that I can give more accurate estimates"). Putting your insights and intentions in writing helps you gain perspective and draw powerful lessons from your experience. ∎

F is for feedback

When some students get an F on an assignment, they interpret that letter as a message: "You are a failure." That interpretation is not accurate. Getting an F means only that you failed a test—not that you failed your life.

From now on, imagine that the letter *F* when used as a grade represents another word: *feedback*. An F is an indication that you didn't understand the material well enough. It's a message to do something differently before the next test or assignment. If you interpret F as *failure*, you don't get to change anything. But if you interpret F as *feedback*, you can change your thinking and behavior in ways that promote your success. You can choose a new learning strategy or let go of an excuse about not having the time to study.

Getting prompt and meaningful feedback on your performance is a powerful strategy for learning *anything*. Tests are not the only source of feedback. Make a habit of asking for feedback from your instructors, advisors, classmates, coworkers, friends, family members, and anyone else who knows you. Just determine what you want to improve and ask, "How am I doing?"

NOTABLE *failures*

As you experiment with memory techniques, you may try a few that fail at crucial moments—such as during a test. Just remember that many people before you have failed miserably before succeeding brilliantly. Consider a few examples.

The first time **Jerry Seinfeld** walked onstage at a comedy club as a professional comic, he looked out at the audience and froze.

When **Lucille Ball** began studying to be an actress in 1927, she was told by the head instructor of the John Murray Anderson Drama School, "Try any other profession."

In high school, actor and comic **Robin Williams** was voted "Least Likely to Succeed."

Walt Disney was fired by a newspaper editor because "he lacked imagination and had no good ideas."

R. H. Macy failed seven times before his store in New York City caught on.

Emily Dickinson had only seven poems published in her lifetime.

Decca Records turned down a recording contract with the **Beatles** with an unprophetic evaluation: "We don't like their sound. Groups of guitars are on their way out."

In 1954, Jimmy Denny, manager of the Grand Ole Opry, fired **Elvis Presley** after one performance.

Babe Ruth is famous for his past home run record, but for decades he also held the record for strikeouts. **Mark McGwire** broke that record.

After **Carl Lewis** won the gold medal for the long jump in the 1996 Olympic Games, he was asked to what he attributed his longevity, having competed for almost 20 years. He said, "Remembering that you have both wins and losses along the way. I don't take either one too seriously."

Michael Jordan was cut from his high school basketball team. "I've missed more than 9,000 shots in my career," he later said. "I've lost almost 300 games. Twenty-six times I've been trusted to take the game-winning shot . . . and missed. I've failed over and over and over again in my life. That is why I succeed." ■

Source: Adapted from "But They Did Not Give Up," Division of Educational Studies, Emory University, accessed March 15, 2013, from www.uky.edu/~eushe2/Pajares/ OnFailingG.html.

Interactive

Exercise 19   20 things I like to do

One way to relieve tension is to mentally yell, "Stop!" and substitute a pleasant daydream for the stressful thoughts and emotions you are experiencing.

To create a supply of pleasant images to recall during times of stress, conduct an eight-minute brainstorm about things you like to do. Your goal is to generate at least 20 ideas. Time yourself, and write as fast as you can.

When you have completed your list, study it. Pick out two activities that seem especially pleasant, and elaborate on them by creating a mind map. Write down all of the memories you have about that activity.

You can use these images to calm yourself in stressful situations.

John Rich Photography

MASTER STUDENT PROFILE

BERT AND JOHN JACOBS

Bert Jacobs (1965–) and John Jacobs (1968–), whose job titles are "chief executive optimist" and "chief creative optimist," started their business by selling T-shirts out of the back of a van.

"Life is good" says the T-shirt, the hoodie, the baseball cap, and the onesie, to which one might reasonably respond in these days of doom and gloom, "Really?"

When Bert and John Jacobs launched their self-described optimistic apparel company out of a Boston apartment 15 years ago, we were smack in the middle of the go-go '90s, and those three little words—part lifestyle, part mantra, part last ditch effort by a pair of struggling T-shirt entrepreneurs to make rent money—seemed to mirror the national mood.

Today, not so much. Which oddly enough might make this something of a golden moment for the Life is good company.

"It is generally people who face the greatest adversity who embrace this message the most," says Bert Jacobs, whose company Web site features a section of "inspiring letters that fuel us all to keep spreading good vibes." The letters include testimonials from survivors of a grizzly bear attack, a young amputee, and a soldier stationed in Iraq. "People have a higher sense and appreciation of the simple things when they've been through something difficult. It's our job to see the glass half full."

Life is good doesn't have a demographic, the brothers like to say, but rather a psychographic: the optimists. And while one might imagine that their numbers are dwindling at roughly the same rate as their retirement accounts, some observers suggest otherwise.

That's not to say Life is good is immune to the downturn, but in this company's case it's all relative.

Until last year, the company, whose annual sales top $100 million, had never had a year with less than 30 percent

Bert and John Jacobs *are positive team players.*

You *can detach from negative thoughts and open up to the perspectives of other people.*

growth. In 2008, it grew only 10 percent, a slowdown that Jacobs notes (in apropos parlance) is "not exactly something you bum out about." Especially since the company hasn't spent a dime on advertising.

Life is good was tested once before, not by the company's customers, but its employees. In the days following 9/11, a number of managers approached Bert Jacobs and said that they weren't feeling right about spreading the company's signature tidings. Some had lost friends in the attacks. The news was all about anthrax and terrorism and tips on turning your basement into a bunker. Maybe life wasn't so good, and maybe this was not the message the American people wanted to hear.

But the company forged ahead, launching its first (wildly successful) nationwide fund-raiser. Jacobs calls it the pivotal moment in his business life.

"Our company has this fantastic positive energy, and our brand is capable of bringing people together," he says. "We know there's trauma and violence and hardship. Life is good isn't the land of Willy Wonka. We're not throwing Frisbees all day. We live in the real world. But you can look around you and find good things any time." ■

Source: Joan Anderman, "A Positive Outlook? Apparel Company Says Bad Times Make Its Message More Vital," The Boston Globe, March 17, 2009, www.boston.com/lifestyle/fashion/articles/2009/03/17/a_positive_outlook/?page=1.

QUIZ
Chapter 6

Name _____

Date _____

1. Describe how using the Power Process: Detach differs from giving up.
   Detaching (giving up an attachment to a goal) doesn't mean you give up on the goal. When you detach, you get to keep your values and goals. However, you know you will be okay even if you fail to achieve the goal. (*Power Process: Detach*, page 176)

2. According to the text, test scores measure your accomplishments in a course. True or false? Explain your answer.
   False. Test scores are a measure of how well we do on tests. (*Think beyond the grade*, page 177)

3. The text suggests a problem with the term *study*. Describe that problem and the suggested solution.
   The term *study* doesn't always have a clear definition. It could mean "read," "write," or "recite"—or something else entirely. A solution is to see each test as a performance where you need to rehearse and practice beforehand. Get ready for a test in the same way that an actor gets ready for opening night: Do the very same things you'll be asked to do to during the performance. (*What to do before the test*, page 179)

4. Define the term *study checklist*, and give three examples of what to include on such checklists.
   They are similar to a to-do list or a study plan. List at least three of the following examples of what to include: (Answers will vary.) (a) Reading assignments, listed by page or chapter number (b) Dates of lecture notes (c) Types of problems to be solved (d) Other skills to master (e) A brief description of each item to study (*What to do before the test*, page 179)

5. Study groups can focus on which of the following?
   (a) Comparing and editing class notes
   (b) Doing research to prepare for papers and presentations
   (c) Finding and understanding key passages in assigned readings
   (d) Creating and taking practice tests
   (e) All of the above
   (e) All of the above (*Cooperative learning: Studying in groups*, page 182)

6. When answering multiple-choice questions, the recommended strategy is to read all of the possible answers before answering the question in your head. True or false? Explain your answer.
   False. You should answer the question in your head before looking at the possible answers. If you are confident you are correct in the answer you come up with, you should then look for that answer in the list of choices. (*What to do during the test*, page 184)

7. The presence of absolute qualifiers, such as *always* or *never*, generally indicates a false statement. True or false? Explain your answer.
   True. Because very few things are 100 percent, and you need only to think of one exception to make a statement false, this is generally a trick question. Such qualifiers generally indicate a false statement. (*What to do during the test*, page 184)

8. Describe three techniques for dealing with test anxiety.
   Describe at least three of the following: (a) Accept your feelings, (b) Describe your thoughts in writing, (c) Dispute your thoughts, (d) Praise yourself, (e) Consider the worst, (f) Over-prepare for tests, (g) Care for your body as much as your mind. (*Let go of test anxiety*, page 188)

9. The text offers a three-step process for solving math problems. Name these steps, and list a strategy related to each one.
   (Answers will vary.) First, Prepare. (a) Read each problem. (b) Create a three-column chart: What I know, what I want to find out, and what connects the two. (c) Determine which arithmetic operations or formulas you will use. (d) Estimate the answer before computing it. Second, Compute. (a) Reduce the number of unknowns. (b) Carry out algebraic equations before using actual numbers. (c) Cancel and combine. (d) Remember that it's okay to make several attempts. Third, Check. (a) Plug your answer in to see whether it works out correctly. (b) Compare your answer to your estimate. (c) Perform opposite operations. (d) Keep units of measurement clear. (*Getting ready for math tests*, page 190)

10. According to the text, learning from mistakes is so powerful that we should deliberately set out to *make* mistakes. True or false? Explain your answer.
    False. This textbook does not recommend that you purposely set out to make mistakes. Rather, the value of mistakes lies in what we learn from them. (*Celebrate mistakes*, page 196)

SKILLS SNAPSHOT
Chapter 6

Take your discoveries and intentions about tests to the next level by completing the following sentences.

Discovery
My score on the Tests section of the Discovery Wheel was . . .

One strategy that really helps me with taking tests is . . .

If I feel stressed about a test, I respond by . . .

Intention
The thing that I would most like to change about my experience of tests is . . .

To make this change, I intend to . . .

Action
The specific new behavior that I will practice is . . .

My cue for doing this behavior is . . .

My reward for practicing this habit is . . .

Practicing this habit can add to my career skills by . . .

INSTRUCTOR TOOLS & TIPS

THINKING

"Creativity was in each one of us as a small child. In children it is universal. Among adults it is almost nonexistent. The great question is: What has happened to this enormous and universal human capacity?" —Tillie Olsen

PREVIEW

Critical thinking is an essential skill for success in the classroom and in the workplace. Although critical thinking has already been introduced throughout the book through the Learning Styles Applications, chapter exercises, Journal Entries, and Practicing Critical Thinking exercises, Chapter 7 takes a more in-depth look at how students can practice the strategies presented in Chapters 1 through 6, using higher levels of thinking. At this point, your students will have taken their first tests in their other courses and will have become familiar with the learning strategies presented in the earlier chapters of *Becoming a Master Student*. Now you can help them take the next step toward thinking critically in higher education. The skills they learn in this chapter can be applied immediately to one decision that most of your students must make—choosing a major.

When students ask why they need this chapter, have them complete a chapter reconnaissance of *what* new materials are in this chapter. Together you can discuss *how* these new ideas will help them become better students. Remind your students that, with these techniques, they can open the door of possibility (*What if?*) to solve problems more creatively and make decisions with confidence. Remind students to find the value in their own lives. The key is to plug into these questions: *What* does this material mean to me personally? *How* can I use this information to improve my life?

GUEST SPEAKER

Critical thinking is a priority for many workplace scenarios. A police officer, attorney, or law school professor would be a great guest speaker for this chapter. These guests can provide students with a dramatic reality check that will help you reinforce the importance of critical thinking in the real world. Ask your guests to prepare to talk for approximately 10 minutes on the importance of critical thinking in their jobs.

Another guest speaker idea is to invite a colleague from the department that offers critical and/or creative thinking courses, or logic courses, to talk about classes that students can take to expand on the concepts they learn in this chapter.

LECTURE

Use the following excerpt from Vincent Ryan Ruggiero's *Instructor's Resource Manual to Accompany Becoming a Critical Thinker*, seventh edition, copyright 2012 (reproduced by permission, **www.cengage.com/permissions**) to help you prepare lectures for this chapter:

As a result of the historic neglect of thinking, many people harbor misconceptions about thinking instruction. The following misconceptions are the most damaging:

That thinking can't be taught. A related misconception is that thinking can be taught only to "gifted" people. The basis of both misconceptions is the pessimistic view that intelligence is fixed and therefore cannot be increased. Formal research and the experience of innumerable thinking-skills instructors disprove this notion.

That thinking is taught automatically in certain courses. Some people reason that English courses teach thinking automatically because they deal with the expression of ideas and because expression is intimately connected to thought. Others make similar claims for science because it deals with scientific method, history because it deals with the record of human thought and action, or psychology because it deals with behavior. Research has long made clear that no course content, by itself, can teach thinking; in other words, thinking skills are developed only when students receive direct instruction in them and have frequent opportunities for guided practice.

That thinking skills are necessarily subject specific. According to this view, economists use one set of thinking skills; biologists, another; and anthropologists, yet another—no generic thinking skills exist. Yet close examination of what thinkers do in everyday situations reveals great similarity in their patterns of thought. Moreover, the patterns of error are also remarkably similar. That is why the list of logical fallacies has remained essentially the same since the time of the ancient Greeks. Though different academic disciplines may employ certain patterns of thinking more often and in slightly different ways than others, the fundamental fact is that the human mind created the academic disciplines and is neither defined nor limited by them.

That students learn to think by being exhorted or inspired. Exhortation and inspiration can surely motivate students to learn, but these approaches have little if any teaching force, particularly where skills are involved. No one ever learned to master driving a car or playing the piccolo or dribbling a basketball by hearing a lecture. Similarly, intellectual skills are learned by doing and by receiving guidance and encouragement from knowledgeable people.

EXERCISES/ACTIVITIES

1. **Four ways to solve problems (page 222).** Divide students into groups and have them work through the following problem, using the four-step process in the article. Consider this scenario: A worker has difficulty affording the rising gas prices, making it difficult to get to work and back each day on her salary. Students should define the problem, avoiding preconceived notions. For example, if the problem is that Jane has to drive too far to work, perhaps because of the value of maintaining a good job, the problem may include changing housing rather than jobs. Students should work through steps 1 through 3, creating a plan for solving the problem. Students may consider the following issues to solve this problem: changing jobs, finding alternate modes of travel, and changing housing. This process emphasizes the fact that there can be several valid options to solve the same problem. Have each group make a 90-second summary report to the class about their position on the issue and their justification for that position.

2. **Finding "Aha!"—Creativity fuels critical thinking (page 211).** Ask students to reread this section. Then, describe the following scenario: Adrian is an employee who listens attentively and observes trends in the workplace. He is punctual, dependable, and always "on task." He has a thorough understanding of the dynamics and issues in his job. Adrian is aware of the suggestion box in the employee break room, asking for suggestions to problems in the office, but he chooses not to submit suggestions, preferring to stay "below the radar." Ask students, "Is it possible or advisable for Adrian to *understand* office problems (Bloom's Level 2) without *analyzing* (Level 4), *evaluating* (Level 5), or *creating* (Level 6) solutions?" Now ask how this lack of higher-level Bloom's response can affect Adrian's security and advancement in the workplace. How does an employer view the follow-through phase?

CONVERSATION/SHARING

Begin with a discussion about the media's influence on our lives, using the think-pair-share discussion pattern. Model this process for students first. Discuss products that we buy because of media influence and marketing. Ask the students to think critically about the topic, and then have

master instructor
best practice

❝ *As a warm-up exercise or icebreaker for this chapter, I put my students into groups and give each group an ordinary household object (such as a napkin, candle, coaster, cup). Then I have the groups brainstorm ways to use the objects in a different fashion than the most obviously intended purpose. This helps students embrace different ways of thinking and stretches their minds to see things in new ways.* ❞

—Michelle Martin, TeamUp Consultant

them free-write for a minute about their thoughts on the matter and about the learning styles questions. They need to feel that they can jot down their own ideas without worrying about what you might expect or want them to say. Then have students work in pairs to share their ideas. Cycle through the learning styles questions, and then discuss the topic as a class. More detailed information about this exercise is available on the Instructor Companion Site.

Workplace Application: Decision making for career success. One of the most important decisions a student makes is selecting a career. There is no right career for anyone—we all have interests, skills, and abilities that will be useful in many different professions. Students should explore both their own interests and needs and the world of work to make an informed career decision. One way to do this is through career assessment. Many college career centers offer programs that allow students to take self-assessments to find out their interests, values, and skills. Resources are also available to research educational requirements, wages, and outlook data.

Conducting an information interview in a field of interest may help students clarify career decisions. No amount of online research can compare to actually talking to someone with experience in the field. Have students select one person, in a field that they aspire to, to interview. Interviews can take place in person, over the phone, or via e-mail, but preferably in person. Compile all gathered information into an essay. Consider having students reflect on the information by writing a report or Journal Entry about the experience. Information should include (but is not limited to) the following:

- Title of occupation
- Location of occupation
- Estimated/average occupational salary
- Job description (tasks)
- What types of interests, skills, and work values are necessary to be successful in this field
- What type of education or training is necessary

master instructor
best practice

"WHO SAYS SO?"

Entering first-year students often lack any formal training in the skills of critical thinking. This demonstration aims to provide a model lesson for getting a class to think about five common categories or statements usually lumped together as accepted "truths." Ask students to list on a slip of paper any six statements they take to be true. Then solicit 20 or so random samples of "truths," writing these on the board. Then ask, Who is your authority for the truth of this statement? The following patterns are typically uncovered:

- *I say so—my personal experience is the authority for the truthfulness of the statement.*
- *"They" say so—cultural consensus or common sense is the authority.*
- *Science says so—some aspect of the scientific method is the authority.*
- *"We" say so—some prior established rule is the authority, for example, one dime is worth two nickels.*
- *God says so—a sacred text or tradition is the authority.*

If by chance any category is not represented in this random sample, supply some examples of your own in order to complete the whole pattern. Conclude the lesson by pointing out that we use very different criteria for testing and judging the truth of a statement in each one of the uncovered categories. Thus, it is never wrong to begin the critical thinking process by asking the basic question: Who says so?

— *Carol Lindquist, Borough of Manhattan Community College*

- Work hours and travel
- Working conditions
- Pros and cons of pursuing this career

HOMEWORK

Power Process: Embrace the new (page 202)

Some students feel trapped or stifled when confronted with something that is new. In an ever-changing world, it's never been more important to embrace the new. This article can help students recognize that having an open mind is a key component to both critical and creative thinking. Students can look for a way to get involved in activities that take them outside their own circumstances. Have them describe a time when they took a risk and presented a new idea they'd never thought of before. If they can't think of such a situation, give them a challenging problem and ask them to find a new solution. Consider pairing this process with Exercise 20, Critical thinking scenarios (page 210).

Examining different points of view.

This is an in-class and homework alternative to the Conversation/Sharing activities. Have students read a newspaper article about a current, controversial issue and then answer the first two learning style questions (*Why?* and *What?*) based on the information in the article. Then have them form groups of four to discuss their ideas. Eventually, someone will say that there is not enough information in the article to explore all of the various views on the topic. This provides an opportunity to ask students to continue this project outside the classroom, using campus resources (such as the library and the Internet), to fully answer

the second and third (*What?* and *How?*) learning styles questions. They should also work on the fourth question (*What if?*) at home. At the next class meeting, have the students discuss their findings and draw conclusions.

Selecting classes.

Too often, the hectic process of registering for classes results in a schedule based on convenience rather than critical decision making. Ask students to follow the systematic procedure described in the article "Gaining skill at decision making" (page 221) to decide which classes to take next semester—before the schedule of classes has been published. Emphasize that the section "Use time as an ally" has a flip side. Sometimes acting quickly to make a decision, such as selecting classes, can allow you to select the most desirable teachers and class times—using time as an ally.

Choosing a major.

Invite the director of your career center to be the guest speaker during a class period to talk about the center's services. Then have the students do a follow-up assignment that involves visiting the career center and exploring possible majors. Students should be encouraged to explore the school Web site to find out more about the career center as well. Ask them to write a brief report on what they learned at the center about themselves and about potential careers and/or majors.

EVALUATION

With the skills students have learned about essay test answers in Chapter 6, they are prepared to answer an essay question that requires critical thinking. Ask them to justify their answers to open-ended questions about common mistakes in logic, learning through inquiry, or thinking critically about information on the Internet.

MindTap™ **EMBRACE VALUABLE RESOURCES**

FOR CHAPTER 7

STUDENT RESOURCES: MINDTAP

● **Engagement Activity: Master Students in Action.** In this video, Dave Ellis discusses what it means to be a critical thinker: thinking about what you want and what you want to achieve. He advises students to not be overwhelmed when it seems too hard and to take on problems that are worthy of your efforts.

● **MindTap Reader.** The MindTap Reader is more than a digital version of a textbook. It is an interactive, learning resource that was built from the ground up to create a digital reading experience based on how students assimilate information in an online environment. The robust functionality of the MindTap Reader allows learners to make notes, highlight text, and even find a definition right from the page.

● **Aplia Homework Assignment: Decision making and problem solving.** In this assignment, students learn the four ways to solve problems and apply these techniques in real-world scenarios. Students will examine a student scenario and then define the issue, consider three optional plans, and choose the best plan to address her problem.

● **Reflection Activity: Learning: A Social Experience.** This Slice of Life video, created by student Brad Nelson, discusses the importance of collaborative learning for creative thinking. By finding opportunities to learn all around us, we benefit by expanding our minds so we can create something great.

MindTap™ *Your personal learning experience—learn anywhere, anytime.*

INSTRUCTOR COMPANION SITE

● **Looking for fresh, innovative ways to teach Chapter 7 topics?** Browse through the Best Practices recommendations in the Course Manual to see what other Master Instructors have been successfully doing with their students.

● **Questions about how to incorporate critical thinking into your course?** Look at the following articles in the online Course Manual for suggestions

on how to make critical thinking skills an integral part of your course:

● Strategies for Encouraging More Class Participation from Your Students
● Improving Learning and Problem-Solving Skills
● Using Journaling in Your Course

Please visit login.cengage.com to log in and access the Instructor Companion Site.

Chapter 7

THINKING

Why

The ability to think creatively and critically helps you succeed in any course—and any career.

Don't fool yourself: 15 common mistakes in logic ■ 217

TECH

Think critically about information on the Internet Sources of information on the Internet range from the reputable to the flamboyant. Taking a few simple precautions when you surf the Internet can keep you from crashing onto the rocky shore of misinformation. ■ 220

How

Remember a time in your life when you felt unable to choose among several different solutions to a problem or struggled with making a decision. Then scan this chapter to find useful ideas for decision making, problem solving, and critical thinking.

Ways to create ideas ■ 213

Thinking about your major Weighing the benefits, costs, and outcomes of your choice of major or degree is an intellectual challenge. This is an opportunity to apply your critical-thinking, decision-making, and problem-solving skills. ■ 225

What if...

I could solve problems more creatively and make decisions in every area of life with more confidence?

What is included ...

EMBRACE THE NEW

Heraclitus, the ancient Greek philosopher, said that you can never step into the same river twice. A river is dynamic—ever flowing, ever changing.

The same thing is true of you.

Right now, you are not the same person you were when you started reading this page. Nerve cells in your brain are firing messages and making connections that didn't exist a second ago. There is new breath in your lungs. Old cells in your body have been replaced by new ones.

What's true about your body is also true of your behavior. Think about all the activities that depend on embracing the new: Going to school. Gaining knowledge. Acquiring skills. Succeeding with technology. Making friends. Falling in love.

Both creative thinking and critical thinking call on us to embrace the new. We can think critically about a new idea only if we're willing to *consider* it in the first place. And it's hard to create something original or change our behavior if we insist on sticking with what's already familiar to us. All the game-changing devices in human history—from the wheel to the iPhone—happened only because their inventors were willing to embrace the new.

Embracing the new is more than just a nice idea. It's an essential skill for anyone who wants to survive and thrive in the work world. Your next career might be one that doesn't exist today. Think about job titles—such as *information architect, social media director,* and *content strategist*—that came to life only in the twenty-first century. There are many more opportunities just waiting to be created.

When learning to embrace the new, start with the way you speak. Notice comments such as these:

"That can't possibly be true."

"That idea will never work."

"We tried that last year and failed."

Those statements represent the sound of a closed mind snapping shut. Consider replacing them with:

"What if that *were* true?"

"How could we make that idea work?"

"What could we do differently this time?"

To get the most value from this suggestion, remember that it's about more than being open to ideas. You can embrace the new on many levels: Be willing to think what you've never thought before; to say what you've never said before; to do what you've never done before. This is the essence of learning, and it's the heart of this book.

Also remember that embracing the new does *not* mean trashing the old. Adopting a new attitude does not mean giving up all your current attitudes. Adopting a new habit does not mean changing all your current habits. When you open up to unfamiliar ideas and experiences, you get to keep your core values. You can embrace change and still take a stand for what's important to you.

As you test new ideas and experiment with new strategies, keep those that work and let go of the rest. You might find that your current beliefs and behaviors work well with just a few tweaks and subtle changes. And in any case, you can go into the unknown with a known process—the cycle of discovery, intention, and action.

What's new is often going to stick around anyway. You have two basic options: Resist it. Or embrace it. The former is a recipe for frustration. The latter offers a fresh possibility in every moment. ∎

CRITICAL THINKING: A SURVIVAL SKILL

This flood of appeals leaves us with hundreds of choices about what to buy, where to go, and who to be. It's easy to lose our heads in the crosscurrent of competing ideas—unless we develop skills in critical thinking. When we think critically, we can make choices with open eyes.

Society depends on persuasion. Advertisers want us to spend money on their products. Political candidates want us to "buy" their stands on the issues. Teachers want us to agree that their classes are vital to our success. Parents want us to accept their values. Authors want us to read their books. Broadcasters want us to spend our time in front of the radio or television, consuming their programs and not those of the competition. The business of persuasion has an impact on all of us.

A typical American sees thousands of television commercials each year—and TV is just one medium of communication. Add to that the writers and speakers who enter our lives through radio shows, magazines, books, billboards, brochures, Internet sites, and fund-raising appeals—all with a product, service, cause, or opinion for us to embrace.

This flood of appeals leaves us with hundreds of choices about what to buy, where to go, and who to be. It's easy to lose our heads in the crosscurrent of competing ideas—unless we develop skills in critical thinking. When we think critically, we can make choices with open eyes.

It has been said that human beings are rational creatures. Yet no one is born as an effective thinker. Critical thinking is a learned skill. This is one reason that you study so many subjects in higher education—math, science, history, psychology, literature, and more. A broad base of courses helps you develop as a thinker. You see how people with different viewpoints arrive at conclusions, make decisions, and solve problems. This gives you a foundation for dealing with complex challenges in your career, your relationships, and your community.

Critical thinking frees us from nonsense. Novelist Ernest Hemingway once said that anyone who wants to be a great writer must have a built-in "crap" detector.[1] That inelegant comment points to a basic truth: As critical thinkers, we are constantly on the lookout for thinking that's inaccurate, sloppy, or misleading.

Critical thinking is a skill that will never go out of style. At various times in human history, nonsense has been taken for the truth. For example, people have believed the following:

- Illness results from an imbalance in the four vital fluids: blood, phlegm, water, and bile.
- Racial integration of the armed forces will lead to destruction of soldiers' morale.
- Women are incapable of voting intelligently.
- We will never invent anything smaller than a transistor. (That was before the computer chip.)

The critical thinkers of history arose to challenge shortsighted ideas such as these. These courageous men and women held their peers to higher standards of critical thinking.

Even in mathematics and the hard sciences, the greatest advances take place when people reexamine age-old beliefs. Scientists continually uncover things that contradict everyday certainties. For example, physics presents us with a world where solid objects are made of atoms spinning around in empty space—where matter and energy are two forms of the same substance. At a moment's notice, the world can deviate from the "laws of nature." That is because those "laws" exist in our heads—not in the world.

Critical thinking frees us from self-deception. Critical thinking is a path to freedom from half-truths and deception. You have the right to question everything that you see, hear, and read. Acquiring this ability is a major goal of a college education.

One of the reasons that critical thinking is so challenging—and so rewarding—is that we have a remarkable capacity to fool ourselves. Some of our ill-formed thoughts and half-truths have a source that hits a little close to home. That source is ourselves.

If you take a course in psychology, you might hear about the theory of cognitive dissonance.[2] This is a term for the tension we feel when we encounter a fact that contradicts our deeply-held beliefs. To reduce the discomfort, we might deny the fact or explain it away with deceptive thinking.

For example, consider someone who stakes her identity on the fact that she is a valued employee. During a recession, she gets laid off. On her last day at work, she learns that her refusal to take part in on-the-job training sessions was the major reason that the company let her go. This brute fact contradicts her belief in her value. Her response: "I didn't need that training. I already knew that stuff anyway. Nobody at that company could teach me anything."

A skilled critical thinker would go beyond such self-justifying statements and ask questions instead: "What training sessions did I miss? Could I have learned something from them? Were there any signs that I was about to be laid off, and did I overlook them? What can I do to prevent this from happening again?"

Master students are willing to admit the truth when they discover that their thinking is fuzzy, lazy, based on a false assumption, or dishonest. These students value facts. When a solid fact contradicts a cherished belief, they are willing to change the belief.

More uses of critical thinking.
Clear thinking promotes your success inside and outside the classroom. Any time that you are faced with a choice about what to believe or what to do, your thinking skills come in to play. Consider the following applications:

- *Critical thinking informs reading, writing, speaking, and listening.* These elements are the basis of communication—a process that occupies most of our waking hours.

- *Critical thinking promotes social change.* The institutions in any society—courts, governments, schools, businesses, nonprofit groups—are the products of cultural customs and trends. All social movements—from the American Revolution to the Civil Rights movement—come about through the work of engaged individuals who actively participated in their communities and questioned what was going on around them. As critical thinkers, we strive to understand and influence the institutions in our society.

- *Critical thinking uncovers bias and prejudice.* Working through our preconceived notions is a first step toward communicating with people of other races, ethnic backgrounds, and cultures.

- *Critical thinking reveals long-term consequences.* Crises occur when our thinking fails to keep pace with reality. An example is the world's ecological crisis, which arose when people polluted the earth, air, and water without considering the long-term consequences. Imagine how different our world would

be if our leaders had thought like the first female chief of the Cherokees. Asked about the best advice her elders had given her, she replied, "Look forward. Turn what has been done into a better path. If you are a leader, think about the impact of your decision on seven generations into the future."

Critical thinking as thorough thinking.
For some people, the term *critical thinking* has negative connotations. If you prefer, use *thorough thinking* instead. Both terms point to the same activities: sorting out conflicting claims, weighing the evidence, letting go of personal biases, and arriving at reasonable conclusions. These activities add up to an ongoing conversation—a constant process, not a final product.

We live in a culture that values quick answers and certainty. These concepts are often at odds with effective thinking. Thorough thinking is the ability to examine and reexamine ideas that might seem obvious. This kind of thinking takes time and the willingness to say three subversive words: *I don't know.*

Thorough thinking is also the willingness to change our opinions as we continue to examine a problem. This calls for courage and detachment. Just ask anyone who has given up a cherished point of view in light of new evidence.

Thorough thinking is the basis for much of what you do in school—reading, writing, speaking, listening, note taking, test taking, problem solving, and other forms of decision making. Skilled students have strategies for accomplishing all these tasks. They distinguish between opinion and fact. They ask probing questions and make detailed observations. They uncover assumptions and define their terms. They make assertions carefully, basing them on sound logic and solid evidence. Almost everything that we call *knowledge* is a result of these activities. This means that critical thinking and learning are intimately linked.

Another kind of thorough thinking—planning—has the power to lift the quality of your daily life. When you plan, you are the equal of the greatest sculptor, painter, or playwright. More than creating a work of art, you are designing your life. *Becoming a Master Student* invites you to participate in this form of thinking by choosing your major, planning your career, and setting long-term goals.

Use the suggestions in this chapter to claim the thinking powers that are your birthright. The critical thinker is one aspect of the master student who lives inside you. ■

> *Master students are willing to admit the truth when they discover that their thinking is fuzzy, lazy, based on a false assumption, or dishonest. These students value facts. When a solid fact contradicts a cherished belief, they are willing to change the belief.*

A process for CRITICAL THINKING

Learning to think well matters. The rewards are many, and the stakes are high. Major decisions in life—from choosing a major to choosing a spouse—depend on your skill at thinking.

The Practicing Critical Thinking exercises throughout this book are based on the six types of thinking described by psychologist Benjamin Bloom (see Figure 7.1):[3]

1. Remembering
2. Understanding
3. Applying
4. Analyzing
5. Evaluating
6. Creating

All levels of thinking are useful, and they differ. For example, the lower levels of thinking (1 to 3) give you fewer options than the higher levels (4 to 6). Lower levels of thinking are sometimes about finding one "right" answer to a question. At levels 5 and 6, you can discover several valid answers and create your own solutions. These are signs of mastery in the realms of critical and creative thinking.

Following are strategies that you can use to move freely through all six levels of thinking. The strategies fall into three major categories:

- Check your attitudes
- Check for logic
- Check for evidence

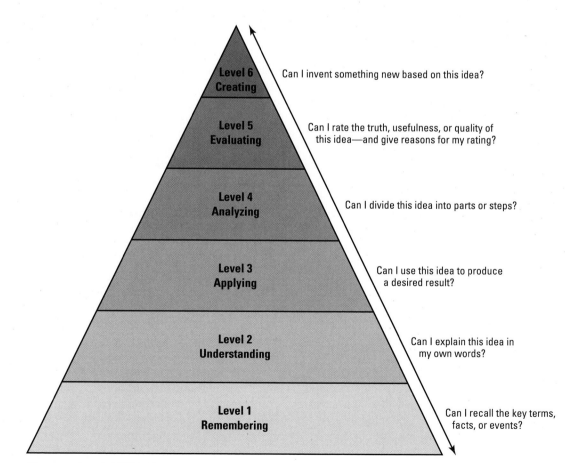

Level 6
Creating — Can I invent something new based on this idea?

Level 5
Evaluating — Can I rate the truth, usefulness, or quality of this idea—and give reasons for my rating?

Level 4
Analyzing — Can I divide this idea into parts or steps?

Level 3
Applying — Can I use this idea to produce a desired result?

Level 2
Understanding — Can I explain this idea in my own words?

Level 1
Remembering — Can I recall the key terms, facts, or events?

Figure 7.1 Levels of Thinking

CHECK YOUR ATTITUDES

Be willing to find various points of view on any issue. Imagine George Bush, Cesar Chavez, and Barack Obama assembled in one room to debate the most desirable way to reshape our government. Picture Madonna, Oprah Winfrey, and Mark Zuckerberg leading a workshop on how to plan your career. When seeking out alternative points of view, let scenes like these unfold in your mind.

Dozens of viewpoints exist on every important issue—reducing crime, ending world hunger, educating our children, and countless other concerns. In fact, few problems have any single, permanent solution. Each generation produces its own answers to critical questions, based on current conditions. Our search for answers is a conversation that spans centuries. On each question, many voices are waiting to be heard. Add yours to the mix.

You can begin by seeking out alternative views with an open mind. When talking to another person, be willing to walk away with a new point of view—even if it's the one you brought to the table, supported with new evidence.

When asking questions, let go of the temptation to settle for just a single answer. Look for at least three. This is especially important when you're *sure* that you have the right answer to a complex question. Once you come up with a new possibility, say to yourself, "Yes, that is one answer. Now what's another?" Using this approach can lead to honest inquiry, creativity, and breakthroughs.

Be prepared: The world is complicated, and critical thinking is a complex business. Some of your answers might contradict others. Resist the temptation to have all of your ideas in a neat, orderly bundle.

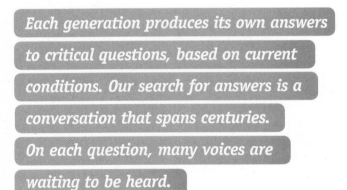

Each generation produces its own answers to critical questions, based on current conditions. Our search for answers is a conversation that spans centuries. On each question, many voices are waiting to be heard.

Practice tolerance. One path to critical thinking is tolerance for a wide range of opinions. Taking a position on important issues is natural. When we stop having an opinion on things, we've probably stopped breathing.

Problems occur when we become so attached to our current viewpoints that we refuse to consider alternatives. Likewise, it can be disastrous when we blindly follow everything any person or group believes without questioning its validity.

Many ideas that are widely accepted in Western cultures—for example, civil liberties for people of color and the right of women to vote—were once considered dangerous. Viewpoints that seem outlandish today might become widely accepted a century, a decade, or even a year from now. Remembering this idea can help us practice tolerance for differing beliefs. Doing this makes room for new ideas that can transform our lives.

Understand before criticizing. Notice that the six levels of thinking build on each other. Before you agree or disagree with an idea, make sure that you *remember* it accurately and truly *understand* it. Polished debaters make a habit of doing this. Often they can sum up their opponents' viewpoint better than anyone else can. This puts them in a much stronger position to *apply, analyze, evaluate,* and *create* ideas.

Effective understanding calls for reading and listening while suspending judgment. Enter another person's world by expressing her viewpoint in your own words. If you're conversing with that person, keep revising your summary until she agrees that you've stated her position accurately. If you're reading an article, write a short summary of it. Then scan the article again, checking to see whether your synopsis is on target.

Watch for hot spots. Many people have mental "hot spots"—topics that provoke strong opinions and feelings. Examples are abortion, homosexuality, gun control, and the death penalty.

To become more skilled at examining various points of view, notice your own particular hot spots. Make a clear intention to accept your feelings about these topics and to continue using critical thinking techniques in relation to them.

One way to cool down our hot spots is to remember that we can change or even give up our current opinions without giving up ourselves. We can remind ourselves that human beings are much more than the sum of their current opinions.

Also be sensitive to other people's hot spots. Demonstrate tolerance and respect before you start discussing highly personal issues.

Be willing to be uncertain. Some of the most profound thinkers have practiced the art of thinking by using a magic sentence: "I'm not sure yet."

It is courageous and unusual to take the time to pause, to look, to examine, to be thoughtful, to consider many points of view—and to be unsure. When a society adopts half-truths in a blind rush for certainty, a willingness to embrace uncertainty can move us forward.

This calls for patience. Remember that the highest levels of thinking call for the highest investments of time and energy. Also, moving from a lower level of thinking to a higher level often requires courage, along with an ability to tolerate discomfort. Give yourself permission to experiment, practice, and learn from mistakes.

CHECK FOR LOGIC

Logic is a branch of philosophy that seeks to distinguish between valid and invalid reasoning. Students of logic look at a series of related sentences to make sure that they are clear, consistent, and coherent.

Learning to think logically offers many benefits: When you think logically, you take your reading, writing, speaking, and listening skills to a higher level. You avoid costly mistakes in decision making. You can join discussions and debates with more confidence, cast your election votes with a clear head, and become a better-informed citizen.

The following suggestions will help you work with the building blocks of logical thinking—terms, assertions, arguments, assumptions.

Define key terms. A *term* is a word or phrase that refers to a clearly defined concept. Terms with several different meanings are ambiguous—fuzzy, vague, and unclear. One common goal of critical thinking is to remove ambiguous terms or define them clearly.

Conflicts of opinion can often be resolved—or at least clarified—when we define our key terms up front. This is especially true with abstract, emotion-laden terms such as *freedom, peace, progress,* or *justice.* Blood has been shed over the meaning of those words. Define them with care.

Your first task is to locate key terms. Skilled writers and speakers often draw attention to them. Even when they don't, you can use clues to spot them:

- Look or listen for words that are new to you.

- Be alert for words or phrases that are frequently repeated—especially in prominent places in a text or in a speech, such as an overview, introduction, summary, or conclusion.

- When reading, check the index for words or phrases that have many page references.

Also see whether the text includes a glossary. And look for words that are printed in *italics* or **boldface.**

As you look for clues, remember that several different words or phrases can stand for the same term. In this chapter, for example, *self-evident truth* and *assumption* are different words that refer to the same concept.

Look for assertions. A speaker or writer's key terms occur in a larger context called an assertion. An *assertion* is a complete sentence that contains one or more key terms. The purpose of an assertion is to define a term or to state relationships between terms. These relationships are the essence of what we mean by the term *knowledge.*

To find a speaker or writer's assertions, listen or look for key sentences. These are sentences that make an important point or state a general conclusion.

Often speakers and writers will give you clues to their key sentences. Speakers will pause to emphasize these sentences or precede them with phrases such as "My point is that . . ." Writers may present key sentences in italics or boldface, or include them in summaries.

Look for arguments. Most of us think of argument as the process of disagreement or conflict. For specialists in logic, this term has a different meaning. For them, an *argument* is a series of related assertions.

There are two major types of reasoning used in building arguments—deductive and inductive.

Deductive reasoning builds arguments by starting with a general assertion and leading to a more specific one. Here's a classic example that you might hear in a beginning philosophy course. It involves Socrates, an ancient Greek philosopher:

- All men are mortal.

- Socrates is a man.

- Therefore, Socrates is mortal.

These three assertions make an argument that Socrates is mortal. Notice that in deductive reasoning, each assertion is like a link in a chain. A weakness or error in any link can break the entire chain.

With *inductive reasoning,* the chain of logic proceeds in the opposite direction—from specific to general. Suppose that you apply for a job and the interviewer says, "We hired two people from your school who did not work out well for us. When we found out where you're taking classes, our management team was concerned."

In this case, the interviewer began with specific examples ("We hired two people from your school"). From there he proceeded to a more general conclusion, which went unstated: *Therefore, students from your school do not make good employees.* This argument is a simple example of inductive reasoning.

As you can see, inductive reasoning can also contain errors. One is the error of *hasty generalization*—coming to a conclusion too quickly. For example, experience with two graduates does not offer enough evidence for judging the abilities of hundreds or even thousands of people who get degrees from your school.

Another possible error is the *false cause.* You will often observe one event that usually happens after another event. However, this does not mean that the first event *caused* the second event. It's true, for example, that children get more dental cavities as they develop a larger vocabulary. However, this does not mean that a large vocabulary causes cavities. Rather, a third factor is involved: children learn more words *and* get more cavities as they get older. Age is the key factor—not vocabulary.

Remember the power of assumptions. Assumptions are beliefs that guide our thinking and behavior. Assumptions can be simple and ordinary. For example, when you drive a car, you assume that other drivers know the meaning of traffic signals and stop signs.

In other cases, assumptions are more complex and have larger effects. Scientists, for instance, assume that events in the world take place in a predictable way. Making this assumption makes it possible to develop the principles of biology, chemistry, and physics.

Despite their power to influence our speaking and action, assumptions are often unstated. People can remain unaware of their most basic and far-reaching assumptions—the very ideas that shape their lives. Heated conflict and hard feelings often result when people argue on the level of opinions and forget that the real conflict lies at the level of their assumptions.

An example is the question about whether the government should fund public works programs that create jobs during a recession. People who argue in favor of such programs assume that creating jobs is an appropriate task for the federal government. In contrast, people who argue against such programs often assume that the government has no business interfering with the free workings of the economy. There's little hope of resolving this conflict of opinion unless we discover the unstated assumptions about the proper role of government.

Look for stated assumptions. Sometimes you will find speakers and writers who are kind enough to state their assumptions directly. A famous example comes from the Declaration of Independence adopted on July 4, 1776, by the 13 colonies that later developed into the United States:

> *We hold these truths to be self-evident, that all men are created equal, that they are endowed by their Creator with certain unalienable Rights, that among these are Life, Liberty and the pursuit of Happiness.—That to secure these rights, Governments are instituted among Men, deriving their just powers from the consent of the governed,—That whenever any Form of Government becomes destructive of these ends, it is the Right of the People to alter or to abolish it, and to institute new Government, laying its foundation on such principles and organizing its powers in such form, as to them shall seem most likely to effect their Safety and Happiness.*

The "self-evident truths" listed in these passages are assumptions:

- All men are created equal.
- Men are born with rights to life, liberty, and happiness.
- Governments exist to secure these rights and deserve to be overthrown if they fail.

This passage points to a key feature of assumptions: They are literally a thinker's starting points. Critical thinkers will produce logical arguments and evidence to support most of their assertions. However, they are willing to take other assertions as "self-evident"—so obvious or fundamental that they do not need to be proved.

Over time, people change their minds about which assumptions are worth accepting. Notice that in their list of assumptions, the men who framed the Declaration of Independence did not assume that women or people of color are "endowed by their Creator with certain unalienable Rights." Later Americans passed amendments to the United States Constitution and a series of laws to widen the scope of the original "self-evident truths."

Look for unstated assumptions. In many cases, assumptions are unstated and offered without evidence. They can sneak up on you in the middle of an argument and take you on a one-way trip to confusion.

In addition, people often hold many assumptions at the same time. And those assumptions might contradict each other. This makes uncovering assumptions a feat worthy of the greatest detective.

You can follow a two-step method for testing the validity of any argument. First, state the assumptions. Second, see whether you can find any exceptions to the assumptions.

Consider this statement: "My mother and father have a good marriage—after all, they're still together after 35 years." Behind this statement is an assumption: *If you've been married a long time, you must have a good relationship.* Yet there are possible exceptions. You might know married couples who have stayed together for decades, even though they are unhappy in the relationship.

Uncovering assumptions and looking for exceptions can help you detect many errors in logic.

CHECK FOR EVIDENCE

In addition to testing arguments with the tools of logic, look carefully at the evidence used to support those arguments. Evidence comes in several forms, including facts, comments from recognized experts in a field, and examples.

To think critically about evidence, ask the following questions:

- Are all or most of the relevant facts presented?
- Are the facts consistent with each other?
- Are facts presented accurately?
- Are enough examples included to make a solid case for the assertion?
- Do the examples truly support the assertion?
- Are the examples typical? That is, could the author or speaker support the assertion with other examples that are similar?
- Is the expert credible—truly knowledgeable about the topic?
- Is the expert biased? For example, is the expert paid to represent the views of a corporation that is promoting a product or service?
- Is the expert quoted accurately?
- If the speaker or writer appeals to your emotions, is this done in a way that is also logical and based on evidence?

Answering these questions takes time and intellectual energy. It's worth it. You'll gain skills in critical thinking that will help you succeed in any class or career that you choose. ■

Exercise 20
Critical thinking scenarios

BUILDING A PORTFOLIO ON A BUDGET

Read the following scenario. Then write about which person in this scenario best demonstrates the attitudes of a master thinker. Give reasons for your choice.

John and Amir are both freshman and enrolled in a student success course. After class, they often walk to the student union for some coffee and conversation. Today they're talking about jobs.

"Our teacher is really big on job hunting," John says. "I get it, but we're only freshman. Isn't it a little early for this topic?"

"Not really," says Amir. "My whole reason for being in school is to get the job I want."

"That makes sense," John replies. "You worked full-time for a few years before coming here to school. You've got more of a career mindset than I do. I'm here straight out of high school."

Amir shrugs his shoulders. "It doesn't matter, man. It's never too early to start finding your place in the work world. It takes time to do that—for some people, years. Better start now."

John takes a moment to think about this before he responds. "Well, okay. So how are *you* doing it?"

"Well, I worked as a Web site designer. I'm still doing that on a freelance basis for 10 to 15 hours per week while I'm in school. In fact, I'm doing some work for nonprofit organizations in order to build a portfolio that I can use after I graduate. I'm discounting my hourly rate, so it's a big win for my clients."

John is stunned. "Man, are you kidding me? Why are you doing that? It doesn't make any sense! If they hire you, they should pay your full rate. You're letting yourself get ripped off."

"I can see why you might think that," Amir replies. "Keep in mind that I set clear limits. I will work up to 40 hours on a project at my discounted rate. After that, my full hourly rate kicks in. My clients know this up front and agree to it. It's right in the contract."

John shakes his head. "Last year I applied for a part-time job at a hardware store. They wanted to pay me at a lower rate while I was in training. After that, I'd get a raise. I couldn't believe they'd try to pull something like that. I just walked out of there and never looked back. My mind is totally made up on this topic: It's a cutthroat world. People always want to take advantage of you. You just can't let them do that."

BIBLIOGRAPHY BLUES

Read the following scenario. Then summarize each person's argument in two or three sentences. Also reread the scenario to find the evidence offered for each argument. Who do you think makes a stronger case? List the reasons for your choice.

Maria enjoys writing. She expected to breeze through the required papers for her classes. Instead, her psychology course has turned into a nightmare.

The professor, Ms. Wright, assigned several research papers, and she's a stickler. She requires students to read at least five articles for each paper. And, she wants those articles to be listed in a bibliography that follows a specific format—the one endorsed by the American Psychological Association (APA).

Maria likes writing the papers. But she finds keeping track of her sources and writing that bibliography to be a real pain. She's meeting with her professor to talk about this.

"Why do we even have to do a bibliography in the first place?" Maria asks. "It takes a lot of time. People can just do a Google search to find the original articles themselves. As long as I mention the title or the author in my paper, isn't that enough?"

Ms. Wright smiles. "You're not the first student to struggle with a bibliography," she says. "But there are good reasons to write one, even though we have the Internet. For one thing, it shows readers that you're careful about documenting your sources. It also shows that you have evidence to back up your ideas. And the ability to write in APA style is a requirement for many jobs in psychology."

"But the whole field of psychology is changing," Maria says. "More and more articles are being published online. They include direct links to their sources. Anything that you want to find is just one click away."

"That's not always true," Ms. Wright says. "Many articles are still published only in print. And you have to pay a fee to access many articles that appear online. That's only fair, and it can also be tough for students to afford."

"This is all going to change," says Maria. "Look at how many newspapers and magazines you can now get online for free. All that content used to cost money. It's only a matter of time—maybe just months—before it's all free. Let's be part of the change. Let's get rid of bibliographies. They're pointless. They're so . . . *twentieth century.*"

WHY BOTHER WITH CAREER PLANNING?

Read the following scenario. Then write a short summary of Richard's argument. Also reflect on his assumptions about career planning. What are they? Are they directly stated, implied, or both? Make a list of Richard's assumptions and also see whether you can list exceptions to any of them.

"I can't believe that we have to write a career plan for our student success class," says Richard. "There's a whole chapter in the textbook about it. What a pointless assignment."

"Why?" asks Ann, his girlfriend.

"Because career planning is pointless. How can you plan a career in today's economy? Just look at the job market. It changes all the time. The manufacturing jobs in this country are all going to China or being taken over by robots. Software companies in America are hiring people in India because they can cut labor costs. And computers are wiping out whole career fields. My mom says she used to call a travel agent to plan her vacation trips. Now she does it all online. Travel agents, bank tellers, tax preparers—jobs like those are all part of the past."

"Whoa!" Ann says. "Slow down. The last time I went into my bank—which was yesterday—there were still tellers. And my dad still hires a guy to do his taxes."

"Okay," Richard says. "Those jobs haven't quite disappeared *yet.* The main point is that planning makes sense only when you can predict events. And when it comes to the economy and jobs, you just can't predict anything. That's why I'm *not* going to plan my career. Any career that I choose now might not even *exist* by the time I graduate. I don't even care so much about getting a specific degree. While I'm in school, I'm just going to take courses I enjoy. I'll figure out the whole career thing after I graduate, when I'm actually in the work force full-time."

Ann frowns. "But isn't that kind of risky? I mean, you're paying a *lot* of money for classes. Are you really okay with leaving your career to chance? You might have a hard time finding a job. Besides, there are still a lot of people who need specific degrees to do the jobs they want. Like lawyers. And doctors. And veterinarians, and medical technicians, and . . ."

Richard raises his hand as if he's in class and says, "Hello, teacher, I'm not interested in *any* of those careers. After I graduate, I'll just get whatever job I can to make money. I'll probably work a lot of different jobs for a few years. That's the only way to find out what you like and what you don't. I just want to be spontaneous and forget about planning."

FINDING "AHA!"—
Creativity fuels critical thinking

This chapter offers you a chance to practice two types of thinking: convergent thinking and divergent thinking.

Convergent thinking involves a narrowing-down process. Out of all the possible solutions to a problem, you choose the one that is the most reasonable. This is the essence of *critical thinking.* Some people see convergent thinking and critical thinking as the same thing.

However, convergent thinking is just one part of critical thinking. Before you choose among viewpoints, generate as many of them as possible. Open up alternatives, and consider all of your options. Define problems in different ways. Keep asking questions and looking for answers.

This opening-up process is called *divergent thinking* or *creative thinking.* Creative thinking provides the basis for convergent thinking. In other words, one path toward having good ideas is to have *lots* of ideas. Then you can pick and choose from among them, combining and refining them as you see fit.

Remember that creative thinking and convergent thinking take place in a continuous cycle. After you've used convergent thinking to narrow down your options, you can return to creative thinking at any time to generate new ones.

Choose when to think creatively. The key is to make conscious choices about what kind of thinking to do in any given moment. Generally speaking, creative thinking is more appropriate in the early stages of planning and problem solving. Feel free to dwell in this domain for a while. If you narrow down your options too soon, you run the risk of missing an exciting solution or of neglecting a novel viewpoint.

Cultivate "aha!" Central to creative thinking is something called the "aha!" experience. Nineteenth-century poet Emily Dickinson described "aha!" this way: "If I feel physically as if the top of my head were taken off, I know that is poetry." "Aha!" is the burst of creative energy heralded by the arrival of a new, original idea. It is the sudden emergence of an unfamiliar pattern, a previously undetected relationship, or an unusual combination of familiar elements. It is an exhilarating experience.

"Aha!" does not always result in a timeless poem or a Nobel Prize. It can be inspired by anything from playing a new riff on a guitar to figuring out why your car's fuel pump doesn't work. A nurse might notice a patient's symptom that everyone else missed. That's an "aha!" An accountant might discover a tax break for a client. That's an "aha!" A teacher might devise a way to reach a difficult student. *Aha!*

Follow through. The flip side of "aha!" is following through. Thinking is both fun and work. It is both effortless and uncomfortable. It's the result of luck and persistence. It involves spontaneity and step-by-step procedures, planning and action, convergent and creative thinking.

Companies that depend on developing new products and services need people who can find "aha!" and do something with it. The necessary skills include the ability to spot assumptions, weigh evidence, separate fact from opinion, organize thoughts, and avoid errors in logic. All these skills involve demanding work. Just as often, they can be energizing and fun. ■

Tangram

A tangram is an ancient Chinese puzzle game that stimulates the play instinct so critical to creative thinking. The cat figure here was created by rearranging seven sections of a square. Hundreds of images can be devised in this manner. Playing with tangrams allows us to see relationships we didn't notice before.

The rules of the game are simple: Use these seven pieces to create something that wasn't there before. Be sure to use all seven. You might start by mixing up the pieces and seeing whether you can put them back together to form a square. Make your own tangram by cutting pieces like these out of poster board. When you come up with a pattern you like, trace around the outside edges of it, and see whether a friend can discover how you did it.

Journal Entry 16
Discovery Statement

Use divergent thinking to brainstorm goals

Candy Chang, an artist and community activist, lived near an abandoned house in New Orleans. She got permission to turn one side of this house into a giant chalkboard and stenciled it with these words printed in big letters: *Before I die, I want to . . .* Anyone who passed by this house could pick up a piece of chalk and complete the sentence in their own way. Some of the answers were:

> *Before I die, I want to sing for millions.*
>
> *Before I die, I want to plant a tree.*
>
> *Before I die, I want to live off the grid.*
>
> *Before I die, I want to be completely myself.*[4]

This Journal Entry invites you to walk by that old house in your imagination and add your contribution. The purpose is not to dwell on death. Instead, it is to think creatively about how you want to be and what you want to do during the rest of your life. To do this, you'll draw on your skills in *divergent thinking*, which refers to opening up options and possibilities. Remember that this is an exercise in pure creativity. For best results, do not stop to censor or edit any of your ideas.

I discovered that before I die, I want to . . .

_____

_____

_____

_____

_____

_____

_____

_____

_____

_____

_____

_____

Journal Entry 17
Intention Statement

Use convergent thinking to plan habits

When applied to goal setting, *convergent thinking* means turning a general idea into a specific plan of action. This kind of thinking is useful in goal setting. Our biggest dreams and desires can easily be forgotten *unless* we turn them into daily habits—physical, visible behaviors.

Say, for example, that before you die, you want to fill your life with loving relationships. That's a wonderful goal. Now turn it into an intention that affects what you do every day. Plan to adopt specific habits that align with your goal.

For more effective planning, take a cue from recent research in psychology and write a list of habits in the form of *implementation intentions*.[5] These intentions follow an "if-then" format. For example:

- *If* I feel angry, *then* I will take three deep breaths before saying anything.
- *If* I am listening to someone, *then* I will wait until they are finished speaking before I begin talking.
- *If* I feel grateful for what someone has done for me, *then* I will express my gratitude directly to that person.

Implementation intentions are useful examples of convergent thinking. They're practical because they link your planned habit to a specific cue that you can remember.

Experiment with convergent thinking now. Review your list of goals from the previous Journal Entry. Then choose one of them and complete the following sentence:

I intend to . . .

_____

_____

Next, create a list of habits to achieve this goal. Write each habit as an implementation intention, using an *If . . . then . . . .* format.

_____

_____

_____

_____

_____

_____

Ways to create IDEAS

Anyone can think creatively. Use the following techniques to generate ideas about anything—whether you're studying math problems, remodeling a house, or writing a best seller.

Conduct a brainstorm. Brainstorming is a technique for creating plans, finding solutions, and discovering new ideas. When you are stuck on a problem, brainstorming can break the logjam. For example, if you run out of money two days before payday every week, you can brainstorm ways to make your money last longer. You can brainstorm ways to pay for your education. You can brainstorm ways to find a job.

The overall purpose of brainstorming is to generate as many solutions as possible. Sometimes the craziest, most outlandish ideas, although unworkable in themselves, can lead to new ways to solve problems. Use the following steps to try out the brainstorming process:

- *Focus on a single problem or issue.* State your focus as a question. Open-ended questions that start with the words *what, how, who, where,* and *when* often make effective focusing questions. For example, "What is my ideal career?" "What is my ideal major?" "How can I raise the quality of relationships?" "What is the single most important change I can make in my life right now?"

- *Relax.* Creativity is enhanced by a state of relaxed alertness. If you are tense or anxious, use relaxation techniques such as slow, deep breathing.

- *Set a quota or goal for the number of solutions you want to generate.* Goals give your subconscious mind something to aim for.

- *Set a time limit.* Use a clock to time it to the minute. Digital sports watches with built-in stopwatches work well. Experiment with various lengths of time. Both short and long brainstorms can be powerful.

- *Allow all answers.* Brainstorming is based on attitudes of permissiveness and patience. Accept every idea. At this stage, there are no wrong answers. If it pops into your head, put it down on paper. Quantity, not quality, is the goal. Avoid making judgments and evaluations during the brainstorming session. If you get stuck, think of an outlandish idea, and write it down. One crazy idea can unleash a flood of other, more workable solutions.

- *Brainstorm with others.* Group brainstorming is a powerful technique. Group brainstorms take on lives of their own. Assign one member of the group to write down solutions. Feed off the ideas of others, and remember to avoid evaluating or judging anyone's ideas during the brainstorm.

After your brainstorming session, evaluate the results. Toss out any truly nutty ideas, but not before you give them a chance.

Also experiment with asking people to brainstorm individually, put their ideas in writing, and then bring their ideas to a larger group. This can lead to an even greater variety of options.

Focus and let go. Focusing and letting go are alternating parts of the same process. Intense focus taps the resources of your conscious mind. Letting go gives your subconscious mind time to work. When you focus for intense periods and then let go for a while, the conscious and subconscious parts of your brain work in harmony.

Focusing attention means being in the here and now. To focus your attention on a project, notice when you pay attention and when your mind starts to wander. And involve all of your senses. For example, if you are having difficulty writing a paper at a computer, practice focusing by listening to the sounds as you type. Notice the feel of the keys as you strike them. When you know the sights, sounds, and sensations you associate with being truly in focus, you'll be able to repeat the experience and return to your paper more easily.

Be willing to recognize conflict, tension, and discomfort in yourself. Notice them and fully accept them rather than fight against them. Look for the specific thoughts and body sensations that make up the discomfort. Allow them to come fully into your awareness, and then let them pass.

You might not be focused all of the time. Periods of inspiration might last only seconds. Be gentle with yourself when you notice that your concentration has lapsed. In fact, that might be a time to let go. *Letting go* means not forcing yourself to be creative. Practice focusing for short periods at first, and then give yourself a break. Play a board game. Go outside and look for shapes in the clouds. Switch to a new location. Take a nap when you are tired. Thomas Edison, the inventor, took frequent naps. Then the lightbulb clicked on.

Cultivate creative serendipity. The word *serendipity* was coined by the English author Horace Walpole from the title of an ancient Persian fairy tale, "The Three Princes of Serendip." The princes had a knack for making lucky discoveries. Serendipity is that knack, and it involves more than luck. It is the ability to see something valuable that you weren't looking for.

History is full of people who make serendipitous discoveries. Country doctor Edward Jenner noticed "by accident" that milkmaids seldom got smallpox. The result was his discovery that mild cases of cowpox immunized them. Penicillin was also discovered by accident. Scottish scientist Alexander Fleming was growing bacteria in a laboratory petri dish. A spore of *Penicillium notatum,* a kind of mold, blew in the window and landed in the dish, killing the bacteria. Fleming isolated the active ingredient. A few years later, during World War II, it saved thousands of lives. Had Fleming not been alert to the possibility, the discovery might never have been made.

Keep your eyes open. You might find a solution to an accounting problem in a Saturday morning cartoon. You might discover a topic for your term paper at the corner convenience store. Multiply your contacts with the world. Resolve to meet new people. Join a study or discussion group. Read. Go to plays, concerts, art shows, lectures, and movies. Watch television programs you normally wouldn't watch.

Also expect discoveries. One secret for success is being prepared to recognize "luck" when you see it.

Keep idea files. We all have ideas. People who treat their ideas with care are often labeled "creative." They not only recognize ideas but also record them and follow up on them.

One way to keep track of ideas is to write them down on 3 × 5 cards. Invent your own categories, and number the cards so you can cross-reference them. For example, if you have an idea about making a new kind of bookshelf, you might file a card under "Remodeling." A second card might also be filed under "Marketable Ideas." On the first card, you can write down your ideas, and on the second, you can write, "See card 321—Remodeling."

Include in your files powerful quotations, random insights, notes on your reading, and useful ideas that you encounter in class. Collect jokes too.

Keep a journal. Journals don't have to be exclusively about your own thoughts and feelings. You can record observations about the world around you, conversations with friends, important or offbeat ideas—anything.

To fuel your creativity, read voraciously, including newspapers, magazines, blogs, and other websites. Explore beyond mainstream journalism. Hundreds of low-circulation specialty magazines and online news journals cover almost any subject you can imagine. Keep letter-size file folders of important documents.

Bookmark Web sites in your browser. Use an online service such as Evernote, Delicious, or Pinboard to save articles that you want to read and refer to later. Create idea files on your computer.

Safeguard your ideas, even if you're pressed for time. Jotting down four or five words is enough to capture the essence of an idea. You can write down one quotation in a minute or two. And if you carry 3 × 5 cards in a pocket or purse, you can record ideas while standing in line or sitting in a waiting room.

Review your files regularly. Some amusing thought that came to you in November might be the perfect solution to a problem in March.

> We all have ideas. People who treat their ideas with care are often labeled "creative." They not only recognize ideas but also record them and follow up on them.

Collect and play with data. Look from all sides at the data you collect. Switch your attention from one aspect to another. Examine each fact and avoid getting stuck on one particular part of a problem. Turn a problem upside down by picking a solution first and then working backward. Ask other people to look at the data. Solicit opinions.

Living with the problem invites a solution. Write down data, possible solutions, or a formulation of the problem on 3 × 5 cards, and carry them with you. Look at them before you go to bed at night. Review them when you are waiting for the bus. Make them part of your life, and think about them frequently.

Look for the obvious solutions or the obvious "truths" about the problem—then toss them out. Ask yourself, "Well, I know X is true, but if X were *not* true, what would happen?" Or ask the reverse: "If that *were* true, what would follow next?"

Put unrelated facts next to each other and invent a relationship between them, even if it seems absurd at first. In *The Act of Creation,* novelist Arthur Koestler says that finding a context in which to combine opposites is the essence of creativity.[6]

Make imaginary pictures with the data. Condense it. Categorize it. Put it in chronological order. Put it in alphabetical order. Put it in random order. Order it from most to least complex. Reverse all of those orders. Look for opposites.

It has been said that there are no new ideas—only new ways to combine old ideas. Creativity is the ability to discover those new combinations.

Create while you sleep. A part of our mind works as we sleep. You've experienced this fact directly if you've ever fallen asleep with a problem on your mind and awakened the next morning with a solution. For some of us, the solution appears in a dream or just before we fall asleep or wake up.

You can experiment with this process. Ask yourself a question as you fall asleep. Keep pencil and paper or a recorder near your bed. The moment you wake up, begin writing or speaking, and see whether an answer to your question emerges.

Many of us have awakened from a dream with a great idea, only to fall asleep again and lose it forever. To capture your ideas, keep a notebook by your bed at all times. Put the notebook where you can find it easily.

There is a story about how Benjamin Franklin used this suggestion. Late in the evenings, as he was becoming drowsy, he would sit in his rocking chair with a rock in his right hand and a metal bucket on the floor beneath the rock. The moment he fell asleep, the rock would fall from his grip into the bottom of the bucket, making a loud noise that awakened him. Having placed a pen and paper nearby, he immediately wrote down what he was thinking. Experience taught him that his thoughts at these moments were often insightful and creative.

Promote creative thinking in groups. Sometimes creative thinking dies in committee. People are afraid to disagree with a forceful leader and instead keep their mouths shut. Or a longstanding group ignores new members with new ideas. The result can be "group think," where no one questions the prevailing opinion. To stimulate creative thinking in groups, try these strategies:

- *Put your opinion on hold.* If you're leading a meeting, ask other people to speak up first. Then look for the potential value in *any* idea. Avoid nonverbal language that signals a negative reaction, such as frowning or rolling your eyes.
- *Rotate group leadership.* Ask group members to take turns. This strategy can work well in groups where people have a wide range of opinions.
- *Divide larger groups into several teams.* People might be more willing to share their ideas in a smaller group.
- *Assign a devil's advocate.* Give one person free permission to poke holes in any proposal.
- *Invite a guest expert.* A fresh perspective from someone outside the group can spark an "aha!"
- *Set up a suggestion box.* Let people submit ideas anonymously, in writing.

Refine ideas and follow through. Many of us ignore the part of the creative process that involves refining ideas and following through. How many great moneymaking schemes have we had that we never pursued? How many good ideas have we had for short stories that we never wrote? How many times have we said to ourselves, "You know, what they ought to do is attach two handles to one of those things, paint it orange, and sell it to police departments. They'd make a fortune." And we never realize that we are "they."

Create on your feet

A popular trend in executive offices is the stand-up desk—a raised working surface at which you stand rather than sit.

Standing has advantages over sitting for long periods. You can stay more alert and creative when you're on your feet. One theory is that our problem-solving ability improves when we stand, due to increased heart rate and blood flow to the brain.

Standing can ease lower-back pain too. Sitting for too long aggravates the spine and its supporting muscles.

Standing while working is a technique with tradition. If you search the Web for stand-up desks, you'll find models based on desks used by Thomas Jefferson, Winston Churchill, and writer Virginia Woolf. Consider setting your desk up on blocks or putting a box on top of your desk so that you can stand while writing, preparing speeches, or studying. Discover how long you can stand comfortably while working and whether this approach works for you.

courtesy of David Ellis

Genius resides in the follow-through—the application of perspiration to inspiration. One powerful tool you can use to follow through is the Discovery and Intention Journal Entry system. First write down your idea in a Discovery Statement, and then write what you intend to do about it in an Intention Statement.

Another way to refine an idea is to simplify it. And if that doesn't work, mess it up. Make it more complex.

Finally, keep a separate file in your ideas folder for your own inspirations. Return to it regularly to see whether there is anything you can use. Today's defunct term paper idea could be next year's A in speech class.

Trust the process. Learn to trust the creative process— even when no answers are in sight. We are often reluctant to look at problems if no immediate solution is at hand. Trust that a solution will show up. Frustration and a feeling of being stuck are often signals that a solution is imminent.

Sometimes solutions break through in a giant *"aha!"* More often they come in a series of little "aha!s." Be aware of what your "aha!s" look, feel, and sound like. This understanding sets the stage for even more flights of creative thinking.

> *Learn to trust the creative process—even when no answers are in sight. We are often reluctant to look at problems if no immediate solution is at hand. Trust that a solution will show up.*

Take these ideas to work. A 2010 article from *Bloomberg Business Week* ("What Chief Executives Really Want") makes the case for creative thinking in the workplace. This article reports the results of a survey: IBM's Institute for Business Value asked 1,500 chief executive officers to name the leadership skill they considered most important. The top answer was creativity.

Every suggestion in this article can help you create ideas for new products, services, and processes on your job. Use creative thinking to thrive in any career you choose. ■

Exercise 21
Explore emotional reactions

Each of us has certain "hot spots"—issues that trigger strong emotional reactions. These topics may include abortion, gay and lesbian rights, capital punishment, and funding for welfare programs. There are many other examples, varying from person to person. Examine your own hot spots by writing a word or short phrase summarizing each issue about which you feel very strongly. Then describe what you typically say or do when each issue comes up in conversation.

After you have completed your list, think about what you can do to become a more effective thinker when you encounter one of these issues. For example, you could breathe deeply and count to five before you offer your own point of view. Or you might preface your opinion with an objective statement such as "There are many valid points of view on this issue. Here's the way I see it, and I'm open to your ideas."

Gary Bate/Digital Vision/Getty Images

Don't fool yourself:
15 COMMON MISTAKES IN LOGIC

Effective reasoning is not just an idle pastime for unemployed philosophers. Learning to think logically offers many benefits: When you think logically, you take your reading, writing, speaking, and listening skills to a higher level.

With more logical thinking, you can avoid costly mistakes in decision making. You can join discussions with more confidence, cast your election votes with a clear head, and become a better-informed citizen. People have even improved their mental health by learning to dispute illogical beliefs.[7]

Students of logic look for valid steps in an *argument*, or a series of statements. The opening statements of the argument are the premises, and the final statement is the conclusion.

Over the last 2,500 years, specialists have listed some classic land mines on the path of coming to conclusions. These common mistakes in thinking are called *fallacies*. The study of fallacies could fill a yearlong course.

Following are 15 examples to get you started. Knowing about them before you string together a bunch of assertions can help you avoid getting fooled.

1 Jumping to conclusions. Jumping to conclusions is the only exercise that some lazy thinkers get. This fallacy involves drawing conclusions without sufficient evidence. Take the bank officer who hears about a student's failing to pay back an education loan. After that, the officer turns down all loan applications from students. This person has formed a rigid opinion on the basis of hearsay. Jumping to conclusions—also called *hasty generalization*—is at work here.

Following are more examples of this fallacy:

- *When I went to Mexico for spring break, I felt sick the whole time. Mexican food makes people sick.*

- *All that Democrats want to do is tax and spend.*

- *All that Republicans want to do is cut taxes.*

- *During a recession, more people go to the movies. People just want to sit in the dark and forget about their money problems.*

Each item in this list includes two statements, and the second statement does not necessarily follow from the first. More evidence is needed to make any possible connection.

2 Attacking the person. The mistake of attacking the person is common at election time. An example is the candidate who claims that her opponent has failed to attend church regularly during the campaign. People who indulge in personal attacks are attempting an intellectual sleight of hand to divert our attention away from the truly relevant issues.

3 Appealing to authority. A professional athlete endorses a brand of breakfast cereal. A famous musician features a soft drink company's product in a rock video. The promotional brochure for an advertising agency lists all of the large companies that have used its services.

In each case, the people involved are trying to win your confidence—and your dollars—by citing authorities. The underlying assumption is usually this: *Famous people and organizations buy our product. Therefore, you should buy it too.* Or: *You should accept this idea merely because someone who's well known says it's true.*

Appealing to authority is usually a substitute for producing real evidence. It invites sloppy thinking. When our only evidence for a viewpoint is an appeal to authority, it's time to think more thoroughly.

4 **Pointing to a false cause.** The fact that one event follows another does not necessarily mean that the two events have a cause-and-effect relationship. All we can actually say is that the events might be correlated. For example, as children's vocabularies improve, they can get more cavities. This does not mean that cavities are the result of an improved vocabulary. Instead, the increase in cavities is due to other factors, such as physical maturation and changes in diet or personal care.

Suppose that you see this newspaper headline: "Student tries to commit suicide after failing to pass bar exam." Seeing this headline, you might conclude that the student's failure to pass the exam lead to a depression that caused his suicide attempt. However, this is simply an assumption that can be stated in the following way: *When two events occur closely together in time, the first event is the cause of the second event.* Perhaps the student's depression was in fact caused by another traumatic event not mentioned in the headline, such as breaking up with a longtime girlfriend.

5 **Thinking in all-or-nothing terms.** Consider these statements: *Doctors are greedy. You can't trust politicians. Students these days are in school just to get high-paying jobs; they lack idealism. Homeless people don't want to work.*

These opinions imply the word *all.* They gloss over individual differences, claiming that all members of a group are exactly alike. They also ignore key facts—for instance, that some doctors volunteer their time at free medical clinics and that many homeless people are children who are too young to work.

All-or-nothing thinking is one of the most common errors in logic. To avoid this fallacy, watch out for words such as *all, everyone, no one, none, always,* and *never.* Statements that include these words often make sweeping claims that require a lot of evidence. See whether words such as *usually, some, many, few,* and *sometimes* lead to more accurate statements. Sometimes the words are implied. For example, the implication in the claim "Doctors are greedy" is that *all* doctors are greedy.

6 **Basing arguments on emotion.** The politician who ends every campaign speech with flag waving and slides of his mother eating apple pie is staking his future on appeals to emotion. So is the candidate who paints a grim scenario of the disaster and ruination that will transpire unless she is elected. Get past the fluff and histrionics to see whether you can uncover any worthwhile ideas.

7 **Using a faulty analogy.** An *analogy* states a similarity between two things or events. Some arguments rest on analogies that hide significant differences. Here is one you're likely to hear during a presidential election: *Running a country is like running a business. Therefore,* *the president should be someone with business experience.* Actually, there are many differences between running a country and running a business. For example, the chief executive of a business can hire people who share her vision and fire people who fail to meet their business objectives. In contrast, the chief executive of a country must work with members of Congress who are elected rather than hired or fired. Also, the purpose of a business depends on making a profit, while the purpose of a government is serving the interests of citizens.

8 **Creating a straw man.** The name of this fallacy comes from the scarecrows traditionally placed in gardens to ward off birds. A scarecrow works because it looks like a man. Likewise, a person can attack ideas that *sound like* his opponent's ideas but are actually absurd. For example, some legislators attacked the Equal Rights Amendment by describing it as a measure to abolish separate bathrooms for men and women. In fact, supporters of this amendment proposed no such thing.

9 **Begging the question.** Speakers and writers beg the question when their colorful language glosses over an idea that is unclear or unproven. Consider this statement: *Support the American tradition of individual liberty, and oppose mandatory seat belt laws!* Anyone who makes such a statement "begs" (fails to answer) a key question: Are laws that require drivers to use seat belts actually a violation of individual liberty?

10 **Confusing fact and opinion.** Facts are statements verified by direct observation or compelling evidence that creates widespread agreement. In recent years, some politicians argued for tax cuts on the grounds that the American economy needed to create more jobs. However, it's not a fact that tax cuts automatically create more jobs. This statement is almost impossible to verify by direct observation, and there's actually evidence against it.

11 **Creating a red herring.** When hunters want to throw a dog off a trail, they can drag a smoked red herring (or some other food with a strong odor) over the ground in the opposite direction. This distracts the dog, who is fooled into following a false trail. Likewise, people can send our thinking on false trails by raising irrelevant issues.

Case in point: At a party you meet someone who is fascinated by the history of World War II and has read many books about Hitler. As this person tells the story of Hitler's rise to power, someone walks up and says, "Why are you talking so much about Hitler? You must be anti-Semitic (prejudiced against Jewish people)." The red herring here is the accusation of prejudice. Merely being interested in the historical events surrounding Hitler is not the same as being anti-Semitic.

12 **Appealing to tradition.** Arguments based on an appeal to tradition take a classic form: *Our current beliefs and behaviors have a long history; therefore, they are correct.* This argument has been used to justify the divine right of kings, feudalism, witch burnings, slavery, child labor, and a host of other traditions that are now rejected in most parts of the world. Appeals to tradition ignore the fact that unsound ideas can survive for centuries before human beings realize that they are being fooled.

13 **Appealing to "the people."** Consider this statement: *Jay-Z sells more albums than Common. Jay-Z must be better.* This is a perfect example of the *ad populum* fallacy. (In Latin, that phrase means "to the people.") The essential error is assuming that popularity, quality, and accuracy are the same.

Appealing to "the people" taps into our universal desire to be liked and to associate with a group of people who agree with us. No wonder this fallacy is also called "jumping on the bandwagon." Following are more examples:

- *Most people exaggerate their experience and qualifications on a résumé. It's just an accepted practice.*
- *Binge drinking is common among college students. It's just part of the experience of higher education.*
- *Same-sex marriages must be immoral. Most Americans think so.*

You can refute such statements by offering a single example: Many Americans once believed that slavery was moral and that people of color should not be allowed to vote. That did not make either belief right.

14 **Distracting from the real issue.** The fallacy of distracting from the real issue occurs when a speaker or writer makes an irrelevant statement and then draws a conclusion based on that statement. For example: *The most recent recession was caused by people who borrowed too much money and bankers who loaned too much money. Therefore, you should never borrow money to go to school.* This argument ignores the fact that a primary source of the recession was loans to finance housing—not loans to finance education. Two separate topics are mentioned, and statements about one do not necessarily apply to the other.

15 **Sliding a slippery slope.** The fallacy of sliding a slippery slope implies that if one undesired event occurs, then other, far more serious events will follow:

- *If we restrict our right to own guns, then all of our rights will soon be taken away.*
- *If people keep downloading music for free, pretty soon they'll demand to get everything online for free.*
- *I notice that more independent bookstores are closing; it's just a matter of time before people stop reading.*

When people slide a slippery slope, they assume that different types of events have a single cause. They also assume that a particular cause will operate indefinitely. In reality, the world is far more complex. Grand predictions about the future often prove to be wrong.

Finding fallacies before they become a fatal flaw (bonus suggestions). Human beings have a long history of fooling themselves. This article presents just a partial list of logical fallacies. You can prevent them and many more by following a few suggestions:

- When outlining a paper or speech, create a two-column chart. In one column, make a list of your main points. In the other column, summarize the evidence for each point. If you have no evidence for a point, a logical fallacy may be lurking in the wings.
- Go back to some of your recent writing—assigned papers, essay tests, journal entries, and anything else you can find. Look for examples of logical fallacies. Note any patterns, such as repetition of one particular fallacy. Write an Intention Statement about avoiding this fallacy.
- Be careful when making claims about people who disagree with you. One attitude of a critical thinker is treating everyone with fairness and respect. ■

kutay tanir/E+/ Getty Images

THINK CRITICALLY
about information on the
INTERNET

Sources of information on the Internet range from the reputable (such as the Library of Congress) to the flamboyant (such as the *National Enquirer*). People are free to post *anything* on the Internet, including outdated facts as well as intentional misinformation.

Newspaper, magazine, and book publishers often employ fact checkers, editors, and lawyers to screen out errors and scrutinize questionable material before publication. Authors of Web pages and other Internet sources might not have these resources or choose to use them.

Taking a few simple precautions when you surf the Internet can keep you from crashing onto the rocky shore of misinformation.

Distinguish between *ideas* and *information*. To think more powerfully about what you find on the Internet, remember the difference between information and ideas. For example, consider the following sentence: *Barack Obama was elected president of the United States in 2008.* That statement provides information about the United States. In contrast, the following sentence states an idea: *When Barack Obama was elected president, the United States entered a new era of politics.*

Information refers to facts that can be verified by independent observers. *Ideas* are interpretations or opinions based on facts. These include statements of opinion and value judgments. Several people with the same information might adopt different ideas based on that information.

People who speak of the Internet as the "information superhighway" often forget to make the distinction between information and ideas. Don't assume that an idea is more current, reasonable, or accurate just because you find it on the Internet. Apply your critical thinking skills to all published material—print and online.

Look for overall quality. Examine the features of a Web site in general. Notice the effectiveness of the text and visuals as a whole. Also note how well the site is organized and whether you can navigate the site's features with ease. Look for the date that crucial information was posted, and determine how often the site is updated.

Next, get an overview of the site's content. Examine several of the site's pages, and look for consistency of facts,

> *People who speak of the Internet as the "information superhighway" often forget to make the distinction between information and ideas. Don't assume that an idea is more current, reasonable, or accurate just because you find it on the Internet.*

quality of information, and competency with grammar and spelling. Are the links within the site easy to navigate?

Also evaluate the site's links to related Web pages. Look for links to pages of reputable organizations. Click on a few of those links. If they lead you to dead ends, it might indicate that the site you're evaluating is not updated often—a clue that it's not a reliable source for late-breaking information.

Look at the source. Find a clear description of the person or organization responsible for the Web site. Many sites include this information in an "About" link.

The domain in the uniform resource locator (URL) for a Web site gives you clues about sources of information and possible bias. For example, distinguish among information from a for-profit commercial enterprise (URL ending in .com); a nonprofit organization (.org); a government agency (.gov); and a school, college, or university (.edu).

If the site asks you to subscribe or become a member, then find out what it does with the personal information that you provide. Look for a way to contact the site's publisher with questions and comments.

Look for documentation. When you encounter an assertion on a Web page or some other Internet resource, note the types and quality of the evidence offered. Look for credible examples, quotations from authorities in the field, documented statistics, or summaries of scientific studies.

Remember that wikis (peer-edited sites) such as Wikipedia do not employ editors to screen out errors or scrutinize questionable material before publication. Do not rely on these sites when researching a paper or presentation. Also, be cautious about citing blogs, which often are not reviewed for accuracy. Such sources may, however, provide you with key words and concepts that help lead you to scholarly research on your topic.

Set an example. In the midst of the Internet's chaotic growth, you can light a path of rationality. Whether you're sending a short e-mail message or building a massive Web site, bring your own critical thinking skills into play. Every word and image that you send down the wires to the Web can display the hallmarks of critical thinking—sound logic, credible evidence, and respect for your audience. ■

© Mike Baldwin. Reproduction rights available from www.CartoonStock.com

GAINING SKILL AT
DECISION MAKING

We make decisions all the time, whether we realize it or not. Even avoiding decisions is a form of decision making. The student who puts off studying for a test until the last minute might really be saying, "I've decided this course is not important." In order to escape such a fate, decide right now to experiment with the following suggestions.

Recognize decisions. Decisions are more than wishes or desires. There's a world of difference between "I wish I could be a better student" and "I will take more powerful notes, read with greater retention, and review my class notes daily." Decisions are specific and lead to focused action. When we decide, we narrow down. We give up actions that are inconsistent with our decision.

Establish priorities. Some decisions are trivial. No matter what the outcome, your life is not affected much. Other decisions can shape your circumstances for years. Devote more time and energy to the decisions with big outcomes.

Base your decisions on a life plan. The benefit of having long-term goals for our lives is that they provide a basis for many of our daily decisions. Being certain about what we want to accomplish this year and this month makes today's choices more clear.

Establish criteria. When making a decision, also define what's most important for you to achieve. When buying a car, for example, your objective could be to save money, get better gas mileage, or maximize comfort. These are the criteria for your decisions. Choose the most important ones.

Balance learning styles in decision making. To make decisions more effectively, balance reflection with action. Take the time to think creatively and generate many options. Then think critically about the possible consequences of each option before choosing one. Remember, however, that thinking is no substitute for experience. Act on your chosen option, and notice what happens. If you're not getting the results that you want, then quickly return to creative thinking to invent new options.

Choose an overall strategy. Every time you make a decision, you choose a strategy—even when you're not

aware of it. Effective decision makers can articulate and choose from among several strategies. For example:

- *Find all of the available options, and choose one deliberately.* Save this strategy for times when you have a relatively small number of options, each of which leads to noticeably different results.

- *Find all of the available options, and choose one randomly.* This strategy can be risky. Save it for times when your options are basically similar and fairness is the main issue.

- *Limit the options, and then choose.* When deciding which search engine to use on the World Wide Web, visit many sites and then narrow the list down to two or three that you choose.

Use time as an ally. Sometimes we face dilemmas—situations in which any course of action leads to undesirable consequences. In such cases, consider putting a decision on hold. Wait it out. Do nothing until the circumstances change, making one alternative clearly preferable to another.

Use intuition. Some decisions seem to make themselves. A solution pops into your mind, and you gain newfound clarity. Using intuition is not the same as forgetting about the decision or refusing to make it. Intuitive decisions usually arrive after you've gathered the relevant facts and faced a problem for some time.

Evaluate your decision. Hindsight is a source of insight. After you act on a decision, observe the consequences over time. Reflect on how well your decision worked and what you might have done differently.

Think *choices*. This final suggestion involves some creative thinking. Consider that the word *decide* derives from the same roots as *suicide* and *homicide*. In the spirit of those words, a decision forever "kills" all other options. That's kind of heavy. Instead, use the word *choice*, and see if it frees up your thinking. When you *choose*, you express a preference for one option over others. However, those options remain live possibilities for the future. Choose for today, knowing that as you gain more wisdom and experience, you can choose again. ■

FOUR WAYS
TO SOLVE PROBLEMS

Think of problem solving as a process with four P's: Define the *problem,* generate *possibilities,* create a *plan,* and *perform* your plan.

1 DEFINE THE PROBLEM

To define a problem effectively, understand what a problem is—a mismatch between what you want and what you have. Problem solving is all about reducing the gap between these two factors.

Tell the truth about what's present in your life right now, without shame or blame. For example: "I often get sleepy while reading my physics assignments, and after closing the book I cannot remember what I just read."

Next, describe in detail what you want. Go for specifics: "I want to remain alert as I read about physics. I also want to accurately summarize each chapter I read."

Remember that when we define a problem in limiting ways, our solutions merely generate new problems. As Albert Einstein said, "The world we have made is a result of the level of thinking we have done thus far. We cannot solve problems at the same level at which we created them."[8]

This idea has many applications for success in school. An example is the student who struggles with note taking. The problem, she thinks, is that her notes are too sketchy. The logical solution, she decides, is to take more notes, and her new goal is to write down almost everything her instructors say. No matter how fast and furiously she writes, she cannot capture all of the instructors' comments.

Consider what happens when this student defines the problem in a new way. After more thought, she decides that her dilemma is not the *quantity* of her notes, but their *quality.* She adopts a new format for taking notes, dividing her notepaper into two columns. In the right-hand column, she writes down only the main points of each lecture. And in the left-hand column, she notes two or three supporting details for each point.

Over time, this student makes the joyous discovery that there are usually just three or four core ideas to remember from each lecture. She originally thought the solution was to take more notes. What really worked was taking notes in a new way.

One simple and powerful strategy for defining problems is simply to put them in writing. When you do this, you might find that potential solutions appear as well.

2 GENERATE POSSIBILITIES

Now put on your creative thinking hat. Open up. Brainstorm as many possible solutions to the problem as you can. At this stage, quantity counts. As you generate possibilities, gather relevant facts. For example, when you're faced with a dilemma about what courses to take next term, get information on class times, locations, and instructors. If you haven't decided which summer job offer to accept, gather information on salary, benefits, and working conditions.

3 CREATE A PLAN

After rereading your problem definition and list of possible solutions, choose the solution that seems most workable. Think about specific actions that will reduce the gap between what you have and what you want. Visualize the steps you will take to make this solution a reality, and arrange them in chronological order. To make your plan even more powerful, put it in writing.

4 PERFORM YOUR PLAN

This step gets you off your chair and out into the world. Now you actually *do* what you have planned.

Ultimately, your skill in solving problems lies in how well you perform your plan. Through the quality of your actions, you become the architect of your own success.

Define the **problem.**	**What** is the problem?
Generate **possibilities.**	**What if** there are several possible solutions?
Create a **plan.**	**How** would this possible solution work?
Perform your plan.	**Why** is one solution more workable than another?

When facing problems, experiment with these four P's, and remember that the order of steps is not absolute. Also remember that any solution has the potential to create new problems. If that happens, cycle through the four P's of problem solving again. ∎

ASKING QUESTIONS—
Learning through inquiry

Thinking is born of questions. Questions wake us up. Questions alert us to hidden assumptions. Questions promote curiosity and create new distinctions. Questions open up options that otherwise go unexplored. Besides, teachers love questions.

There's a saying: "Tell me, and I forget; show me, and I remember; involve me, and I understand." Asking questions is a way to stay involved. One of the main reasons you are in school is to ask questions—a process called *inquiry-based learning*. This process takes you beyond memorizing facts and passing tests. Asking questions turns you into a lifelong learner.

One of the main reasons you are in school is to ask questions. This kind of learning goes beyond memorizing facts and passing tests. Educated people do more than answer questions. They also *ask* questions. They continually search for better questions, including questions that have never been asked before.

Questions have practical power. Asking for directions can shave hours off a trip. Asking a librarian for help can save hours of research time. Asking your academic advisor a question can alter your entire education. Asking people about their career plans can alter *your* career plans.

Asking questions is also a way to improve relationships with friends and coworkers. When you ask a question, you offer a huge gift to people—an opportunity for them to speak their brilliance and for you to listen to their answers.

George Bernard Shaw, the playwright, knew the power of questions. "Some men see things as they are, and say, Why?" he wrote. "I dream of things that never were, and say, Why not?"

Inquiry can take you into uncharted waters. Your questions can call forth possibilities that excite you, confuse you, and even scare you. Such feelings are milestones on the path of learning. They are signs that you're asking questions that matter—the questions that other people forget to ask or fear to ask.

Students often say, "I don't know what to ask." If you have ever been at a loss for questions, here are some ways to discover them. Apply these strategies to any subject you study in school or to any area of your life that you choose to examine.

Ask questions that create possibilities. In Japan, there is a method called *Naikan* that is sometimes used in treating alcoholism. This program is based on asking three questions: "What have I received from others? What have I given to others? And what troubles and difficulties have I caused others?"[9] Taking the time to answer these questions in detail, and with rigorous honesty, can turn someone's life around.

Asking questions is also a way to help people release rigid, unrealistic beliefs: "Everyone should be kind to me." "If I make a mistake, it's terrible." "Children should always do what I say." In her book *Loving What Is*, Byron Katie recommends that you ask four questions about such beliefs: Is it true? Can you absolutely know that it's true? How do you react when you believe that thought? And, who would you be *without* that thought?"[10]

At any moment you can ask a question that opens up a new possibility for someone. Suppose a friend walks up to you and says, "People just never listen to me."

You listen carefully. Then you say, "Let me make sure I understand. Who, specifically, doesn't listen to you? And how do you know they're not listening?"

Another friend comes up to you and says, "I just lost my job to someone who has less experience. That should never happen."

"Wow, that's hard," you say. "I'm sorry you lost your job. Who can help you find another job?"

Then a relative seeks your advice. "My mother-in-law makes me mad," she says.

"You're having a hard time with this person," you say. "What does she say and do when you feel mad at her? And are there times when you *don't* get mad at her?"

These kinds of questions—asked with compassion and a sense of timing—can help people move from complaining about problems to solving them.

Ask questions for critical thinking. In their classic *How to Read a Book,* Mortimer Adler and Charles Van Doren list four different questions to sum up the whole task of thinking critically about any body of ideas:"

- **What is this piece of writing about as a whole?** To answer this question, state the main topic in one sentence. Then list the related subtopics.

- **What is being said in detail, and how?** List the main terms, assertions, and arguments. Also state what problems the writer or speaker is trying to solve.

- **Is it true?** Examine the logic and evidence behind the ideas. Look for missing information, faulty information, and errors in reasoning. Also determine which problems were solved and which remain unsolved.

- **What of it?** After answering the first three questions, prepare to change your thinking or behavior as a result of encountering new ideas.

Discover your own questions. Students sometimes say, "I don't know what questions to ask." Consider the following ways to create questions about any subject you want to study, or about any area of your life that you want to change.

Let your pen start moving. Sometimes you can access a deeper level of knowledge by taking out your pen, putting it on a piece of paper, and writing down questions—even before you know what to write. Don't think. Just watch the pen move across the paper. Notice what appears. The results might be surprising.

Ask about what's missing. Another way to invent useful questions is to notice what's missing from your life and then ask how to supply it. For example, if you want to take better notes, you can write, "What's missing is skill in note taking. How can I gain more skill in taking notes?" If you always feel rushed, you can write, "What's missing is time. How do I create enough time in my day to actually do the things that I say I want to do?"

Pretend to be someone else. Another way to invent questions is first to think of someone you greatly respect. Then pretend you're that person. Ask the questions you think she would ask.

Begin a general question; then brainstorm endings. By starting with a general question and then brainstorming a long list of endings, you can invent a question that you've never asked before. For example:

- What can I do when . . . an instructor calls on me in class and I have no idea what to say? When a teacher doesn't show up for class on time? When I feel overwhelmed with assignments?

- How can I . . . take the kind of courses that I want? Expand my career options? Become much more effective as a student, starting today?

- When do I . . . decide on a major? Transfer to another school? Meet with an instructor to discuss an upcoming term paper?

- What else do I want to know about . . . my academic plan? My career plan? My options for job hunting? My friends? My relatives? My spouse?

- Who can I ask about . . . my career options? My major? My love life? My values and purpose in life?

Ask questions to promote social change. If your friends are laughing at racist jokes, you have a right to ask why. If you're legally registered to vote and denied access to a voting booth, you have a right to ask for an explanation. Asking questions can advance justice.

Ask what else you want to know. Many times you can quickly generate questions by simply asking yourself, *What else do I want to know?* Ask this question immediately after you read a paragraph in a book or listen to someone speak.

Take these ideas to work. When your team or coworkers meet, for example, start by brainstorming answers to key questions: "Why are we doing this project? What would a successful outcome look like? How will we measure our results? What are the next actions to take? Who will take them? By when?"

In any situation, start from the assumption that you are brilliant. Then ask questions to unlock your brilliance. ■

15 questions to try on for size

1. **What is the most important problem in my life to solve right now?**
2. **What am I willing to do to solve this problem?**
3. **How can I benefit from solving this problem?**
4. **Who can I ask for help?**
5. **What are the facts in this situation?**
6. **What are my options in this situation?**
7. **What can I learn from this situation?**
8. **What do I want?**
9. **What am I willing to do to get what I want?**
10. **What will be the consequences of my decision in one week? One month? One year?**
11. **What is the most important thing for me to accomplish today?**
12. **What's the best possible use of my time right now?**
13. **What am I grateful for?**
14. **Who loves me?**
15. **Whom do I love?**

John Lund/Blend Images/Getty Images

Thinking about
YOUR MAJOR

One decision that troubles many students in higher education is the choice of a major or degree program. Weighing the benefits, costs, and outcomes of this choice is an intellectual challenge. This choice is an opportunity to apply your critical-thinking, decision-making, and problem-solving skills. The following suggestions will guide you through this seemingly overwhelming process.

1 DISCOVER OPTIONS

Follow the fun. Perhaps you look forward to attending one of your classes and even like completing the assignments. This is a clue to your choice of major.

See whether you can find lasting patterns in the subjects and extracurricular activities that you've enjoyed over the years. Look for a major that allows you to continue and expand on these experiences.

Also, sit down with a stack of 3 × 5 cards and brainstorm answers to the following questions:

- What do you enjoy doing most with your unscheduled time?
- Imagine that you're at a party and having a fascinating conversation. What is this conversation about?
- What kind of problems do you enjoy solving—those that involve people? Products? Ideas?
- What interests are revealed by your choices of reading material, television shows, and other entertainment?
- What would an ideal day look like for you? Describe where you'd live, who would be with you, and what you'd do throughout the day. Do any of these visions suggest a possible major?

Questions like these can uncover a "fun factor" that energizes you to finish the work of completing a major.

Consider your abilities. In choosing a major, ability counts as much as interest. In addition to considering what you enjoy, think about times and places when you excelled. List the courses that you aced, the work assignments that you mastered, and the hobbies that led to rewards or recognition. Let your choice of a major reflect a discovery of your passions *and* potentials.

Use formal techniques for self-discovery. Explore questionnaires and inventories that are designed to correlate your interests with specific majors. Examples include the Strong Interest Inventory and the Self-Directed Search. Your academic advisor or someone in your school's career planning office can give you more details about these and related inventories. For some fun, take several of them and meet with an advisor to interpret the results. Remember inventories can help you gain self-knowledge, and other people can offer valuable perspectives. However, what you *do* with all this input is entirely up to you.

Link to long-term goals. Your choice of a major can fall into place once you determine what you want in life. Before you choose a major, back up to a bigger picture. List your core values, such as contributing to society, achieving financial security and professional recognition, enjoying good health, or making time for fun. Also write down specific goals that you want to accomplish 5 years, 10 years, or even 50 years from today.

Many students find that the prospect of getting what they want in life justifies all of the time, money, and day-to-day effort invested in going to school. Having a major gives you a powerful incentive for attending classes, taking part in discussions, reading textbooks, writing papers, and completing other assignments. When you see a clear connection between finishing school and creating the life of your dreams, the daily tasks of higher education become charged with meaning.

Ask other people. Key people in your life might have valuable suggestions about your choice of major. Ask for their ideas, and listen with an open mind. At the same time, distance yourself from any pressure to choose a major or career that fails to interest you. If you make a choice based solely on the expectations of other people, you could end up with a major or even a career you don't enjoy.

Gather information. Check your school's catalog or Web site for a list of available majors. Here is a gold mine of information. Take a quick glance, and highlight all the majors that interest you. Then talk to students who have declared them. Also read descriptions of courses required for these majors. Do you get excited about the chance to enroll in them? Pay attention to your "gut feelings."

Also chat with instructors who teach courses in a specific major. Ask for copies of their class syllabi. Go the bookstore and browse the required texts. Based on all this information, write a list of prospective majors. Discuss them with an academic advisor and someone at your school's career-planning center.

Invent a major. When choosing a major, you might not need to limit yourself to those listed in your school catalog. Many schools now have flexible programs that allow for independent study. Through such programs you might be able to combine two existing majors or invent an entirely new one of your own.

Consider a complementary minor. You can add flexibility to your academic program by choosing a minor to complement or contrast with your major. The student who wants to be a minister could opt for a minor in English; all of those courses in composition can help in writing sermons. Or the student with a major in psychology might choose a minor in business administration, with the idea of managing a counseling service some day. An effective choice of a minor can expand your skills and career options.

Think critically about the link between your major and your career. Your career goals might have a significant impact on your choice of major.

You might be able to pursue a rewarding career by choosing among *several* different majors. Even students planning to apply for law school or medical school have flexibility in their choice of majors. In addition, after graduation, many people are employed in jobs with little relationship to their major. And you might choose a career in the future that is unrelated to any currently available major.

② MAKE A TRIAL CHOICE
Pretend that you have to choose a major today. Based on the options for a major that you've already discovered, write down the first three ideas that come to mind. Review the list for a few minutes, and then just choose one.

③ EVALUATE YOUR TRIAL CHOICE
When you've made a trial choice of major, take on the role of a scientist. Treat your choice as a hypothesis, and then design

a series of experiments to evaluate and test it.
For example:

- Schedule office meetings with instructors who teach courses in the major. Ask about required course work and career options in the field.

- Discuss your trial choice with an academic advisor or career counselor.

- Enroll in a course related to your possible major. Remember that introductory courses might not give you a realistic picture of the workloads involved in advanced courses. Also, you might not be able to register for certain courses until you've actually declared a related major.

- Find a volunteer experience, internship, part-time job, or service-learning experience related to the major.

- Interview students who have declared the same major. Ask them in detail about their experiences and suggestions for success.

- Interview people who work in a field related to the major and "shadow" them—that is, spend time with those people during their workday.

- Think about whether you can complete your major given the amount of time and money that you plan to invest in higher education.

- Consider whether declaring this major would require a transfer to another program or even another school.

If your "experiments" confirm your choice of major, celebrate that fact. If they result in choosing a new major, celebrate that outcome as well.

Also remember that higher education represents a safe place to test your choice of major—and to change your mind. As you sort through your options, help is always available from administrators, instructors, advisors, and peers.

④ CHOOSE AGAIN
Keep your choice of a major in perspective. There is probably no single "correct" choice. Your unique collection of skills is likely to provide the basis for majoring in several fields.

Odds are that you'll change your major at least once—and that you'll change careers several times during your life. One benefit of higher education is mobility. You gain the general skills and knowledge that can help you move into a new major or career field at any time.

Viewing a major as a one-time choice that determines your entire future can raise your stress levels. Instead, look at choosing a major as the start of a continuing path that involves discovery, choice, and passionate action. ■

SERVICE-LEARNING:
Turn thinking into
CONTRIBUTION

As part of a service-learning project for a sociology course, students volunteer at a community center for older adults. For another service-learning project, history students interview people in veterans' hospitals about their war experiences. These students plan to share their interview results with a psychiatrist on the hospital staff.

Meanwhile, business students provide free tax-preparation help at a center for low-income people. Students in graphic arts classes create free promotional materials for charities. Other students staff a food cooperative and a community credit union.

These examples of actual projects from the National Service-Learning Clearinghouse demonstrate the working premise of service-learning: Volunteer work and other forms of contributing can become a vehicle for higher education.

Fill yourself up and give it back. *Becoming a Master Student* is about filling yourself up, taking care of yourself, being selfish, and meeting your needs. The techniques and suggestions in these pages focus on ways to get what you want out of school, work, and the rest of your life.

One of the results of all this successful selfishness is the capacity to contribute. This means giving back to your community in ways that enhance the lives of other people.

People who are satisfied with life can share that satisfaction with others. It is hard to contribute to another person's joy until you experience joy yourself. The same is true for love. When people are filled with love, they can more easily contribute love to others. Contributing is what's left to do when your needs are met. It completes the circle of giving and receiving.

Service-learning is a form of contribution that allows you to create ideas for projects and turn those ideas into action. Use the following suggestions to get the most from this process.

> *People who are satisfied with life can share that satisfaction with others. It is hard to contribute to another person's joy until you experience joy yourself. The same is true for love. When people are filled with love, they can more easily contribute love to others. Contributing is what's left to do when your needs are met. It completes the circle of giving and receiving.*

Understand the elements of service-learning. Service-learning generally includes three elements: meaningful community service, a formal academic curriculum, and time for students to reflect on what they learn from service. That reflection can include speeches, journal writing, and research papers.

Service-learning creates a win-win scenario. For one thing, students gain the satisfaction of contributing. They also gain experiences that can guide their career choices and help them develop job skills.

At the same time, service-learning adds to the community a resource with a handsome return on investment. For example, participants in the Learn and Serve America program (administered by the Corporation for National and Community Service) provided community services valued at four times the program cost.[12]

Find service-learning courses. Many schools offer service-learning programs. Look in the index of your school catalog under "service-learning," and search your school's Web site, using those key words. There might be a service-learning office on your campus.

Also turn to national organizations that keep track of service-learning opportunities. One is the Corporation for National and Community Service, a federal government agency (**www.nationalservice.gov**, 202-606-5000). You can also contact the National Service-Learning Clearinghouse (**www.servicelearning.org**, 866-245-7378). These resources can lead you to others, including service-learning programs in your state.

GETTING THE MOST FROM SERVICE-LEARNING

When you design a service-learning project, consider the following suggestions.

Follow your interests. Think of the persistent problems in the world—illiteracy, hunger, obesity, addictions, unemployment, poverty, and more. Which of them generate the strongest feelings in you? Which of them link to your possible career plans and choice of major? The place where passion intersects with planning often creates a useful opportunity for service-learning.

Choose partners carefully. Work with a community organization that has experience with students. Make sure that the organization has liability insurance to cover volunteers.

Learn about the organization. Once you connect with community organization, learn everything you can about it. Find its mission statement and explore its history. Find out what makes this organization unique. If the organization partners with others in the community, learn about those other organizations as well.

Handle logistics. Integrating service-learning into your schedule can call for detailed planning. If your volunteer work takes place off campus, arrange for transportation and allow for travel time.

Include ways to evaluate your project. From your Intention Statements, create action goals and outcome goals. *Action goals* state what you plan to do and how many people you intend to serve; for instance, "We plan to provide 100 hours of literacy tutoring to 10 people in the community." *Outcome goals* describe the actual impact that your project will have: "At the end of our project, 60 percent of the people we tutor will be able to write a résumé and fill out a job application." Build numbers into your goals whenever possible. That makes it easier to evaluate the success of your project.

Build long-term impact into your project. One potential pitfall of service-learning is that the programs are often short-lived. After students pack up and return to campus, programs can die. To avoid this outcome, make sure that other students or community members are willing to step in and take over for you when the semester ends.

Build transferable skills. Review the list of 65 transferable skills on page 354. Use this list as a way to stimulate your thinking. List the specific skills that you're developing through service-learning. Keep this list. It will come in handy when you write a résumé and fill out job applications. And before you plan to do another service-learning project, think about the skills you'd like to develop from that experience.

Make use of mistakes. If your project fails to meet its goals, then turn this result into an opportunity to learn. State—in writing—the obstacles you encountered and possible ways to overcome them. The solutions you offer will be worth gold to the people who follow in your footsteps. Sharing the lessons learned from mistakes is an act of service in itself.

Connect service-learning to critical thinking. Remember that a *service* activity does not necessarily become a *service* attitude. Students can engage in service-learning merely to meet academic requirements and add a line to their résumé. Or students can engage in service-learning as a way to make long-term changes in their beliefs and behavior.

The idea behind service-learning is that community action is a strategy for academic achievement. This is what distinguishes service-learning from other forms of volunteer activity. A service-learning course combines work in the community with activities in the classroom. Contributing to others becomes a powerful and effective way to learn.

Turn to a tool you've used throughout this book—the Discovery and Intention Journal Entry system. Write Discovery Statements about what you gain from service-learning and how you feel about what you're doing. Follow up with Intention Statements about what you'll do differently for your next service-learning experience.

To think critically and creatively about your service-learning project, also ask questions such as these:

- What service did you perform?
- What roles did your service project include, and who filled those roles?
- What knowledge and skills did you bring to this project?
- After being involved in this project, what new knowledge and skills do you want to gain?
- What did you learn from this experience that can make another service-learning project more successful?
- Will this service-learning project affect your choice of a major? If so, how?
- Will this service-learning project affect your career plans? If so, how?

Service-learning provides an opportunity to combine theory and practice, reflection and action, "book learning" and "real-world" experience. Education takes place as we reflect on our experiences and turn them into new insights and intentions. Use service-learning as a way to take your thinking skills to a whole new level. ■

Practicing Critical Thinking 7

Remember that psychologist Benjamin Bloom described six levels of thinking:

Level 1: Remembering

Level 2: Understanding

Level 3: Applying

Level 4: Analyzing

Level 5: Evaluating

Level 6: Creating

For this exercise, you are invited to think at **Level 6: Creating**. What you'll create, however, are not answers, but questions. In fact, a key thinking skill is choosing which questions to ask in the first place. It's also important to state those questions in ways that lead to useful answers.

One eye-opening way to create questions is to write down something you're sure of and then turn it into a question. (You might need to rephrase the question for grammatical sense.) The question that you create can lead to others.

For example, someone might say, "I would never take a philosophy course." This person can write, "I would never take a philosophy course?" This suggests some related questions: "In what ways would taking a philosophy course serve my success in school?" "Could taking a philosophy course help me become a better thinker—and therefore a better speaker and writer?"

Now it's your turn. Write three statements that you accept with certainty. Then rephrase each statement as a question. Finally, write at least two related questions.

Statement 1:

_____

_____

Statement 1 turned into a question:

_____

_____

Related questions:

_____

_____

Statement 2:

_____

_____

Statement 2 turned into a question:

_____

_____

Related questions:

_____

_____

Statement 3:

_____

_____

Statement 3 turned into a question:

_____

_____

Related questions:

_____

_____

MASTER STUDENT
PROFILE

IRSHAD MANJI

Michael Stuparyk/Toronto Star/
ZUMAPRESS/Newscom

(1969–) Controversial journalist, broadcaster, and author of The Trouble with
Islam, *who uses her "Muslim voice of reform, to concerned citizens worldwide"
in an effort to explore faith and community, and the diversity of ideas*

It's to be expected that an author with a book on the verge of publication will lose her cool over a last-minute detail or two. Some might get nervous that their facts won't hold up and run a paranoid, final check. Others might worry about what to wear to their book party. When Irshad Manji's book was about to hit the stands, her concern was a bit different. She feared for her life.

Certain her incendiary book *The Trouble with Islam* would set off outrage in the Muslim community, she called the police, told them she was working on a book that was highly critical of Islam, and asked if they could advise her on safety precautions.

They came to visit her Toronto apartment building several times and suggested she install a state-of-the-art security system, bulletproof windows, and hire a counter-terrorism expert to act as her personal bodyguard.

In her short, plucky book she comes down hard on modern-day Islam, charging that the religion's mainstream has come to be synonymous with literalism. Since the thirteenth century, she said, the faith hasn't encouraged—or tolerated—independent thinking (or as it's known in the faith, *ijtihad*).

The book, which is written like a letter, is both thoughtful and confrontational. In person, Ms. Manji embodied the same conflicting spirit. She was affable and wore a broad smile. Her upbeat, nervous energy rose to the task of filling in every potentially awkward pause. (One of her favorite factoids: "Prophet Mohammed was quite a feminist.")

Her journey scrutinizing Islam started when she was an 8-year-old and taking weekly religious classes at a *madrasa* (religious school) in suburban Vancouver. Her anti-Semitic teacher Mr. Khaki never took her questions seriously; he merely told her to accept everything because it was in the Koran. She wanted to know why she had to study it

Irshad Manji *is courageous.* You *can practice courage by questioning assumptions and creating bold, new ideas.*

in Arabic, which she didn't understand, and was told the answers were "in the Koran."

Her questioning ended up getting her kicked out of school at 14, and she embarked on a 20-year-long private study of the religion. Although she finds the treatment poured on women and foreigners in Islamic nations indefensible, she said that she continues to be a believer because the religion provides her with her values. "And I'm so glad I did because it was then I came to realize that there was this really progressive side of my religion and it was this tradition of critical thinking called *ijtihad*. This is what allows me to stay within the faith."

She calls herself a "Muslim refusenik" because she remains committed to the religion and yet she doesn't accept what's expected of Muslim women. As terrorist acts and suicide bombings refuse to subside, she said it's high time for serious reform within the Islamic faith.

She said many young Muslim supporters are still afraid to come out about their support of her. "Even before 9/11 it was the young Muslims who were emerging out of these audiences and gathering at the side of the stage. They'd walk over and say, 'Irshad, we need voices such as yours to help us open up this religion of ours because if it doesn't open up, we're leaving the mosques.'"

She wants Muslims to start thinking critically about their religion and to start asking more questions. "Most Muslims have never been introduced to the possibility, let alone the virtue, of asking questions about our holy book," she said. "We have never been taught the virtue of interpreting the Koran in different ways." ■

Source: Lauren Mechling, "The Trouble with Writing About Islam," as it appeared in New York Sun,
November 26, 2004. Copyright © 2004. Reprinted with permission of the author.

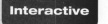

QUIZ
Chapter 7

Name _____

Date _____

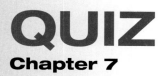

1. According to the Power Process in this chapter, embracing the new means giving up your current values. True or false? Explain your answer.

False. When you open up to unfamiliar ideas and experiences, you get to keep your core values. You can embrace change and still take a stand for what's important to you. (*Power Process: Embrace the new*, page 202)

2. List the three major categories of strategies for critical thinking described in this chapter.

Check your attitudes, check for logic, and check for evidence. (*A process for critical thinking*, page 205)

3. Briefly explain the difference between deductive reasoning and inductive reasoning.

Deductive reasoning starts with a general assertion and leads to a more specific one. With *inductive reasoning*, the chain of logic proceeds in the opposite direction—from specific to general. (*A process for critical thinking*, page 205)

4. Discuss what is meant in this chapter by "aha!"

"Aha!" is the burst of creative energy that comes with the arrival of a new or original idea. (*Finding "aha!"—Creativity fuels creative thinking*, page 211)

5. Briefly describe three strategies for creative thinking.

(Answers will vary.) List and describe three of the following: (a) Conduct a brainstorm; (b) focus and let go; (c) cultivate creative serendipity; (d) keep idea files; (e) collect and play with data; (f) create while you sleep; (g) refine ideas and follow through; (h) trust the process. (*Ways to create ideas*, page 213)

6. List three types of logical fallacies, and give an example of each type.

(Examples will vary.) (a) Jumping to conclusions. (b) Attacking the person. (c) Appealing to authority. (d) Pointing to a false cause. (e) Thinking in all-or-nothing terms. (f) Basing arguments on emotions. (g) Faulty analogy. (h) Creating a straw man. (i) Begging the question. (j) Confusing fact and opinion. (k) Creating a red herring. (l) Appealing to tradition. (m) Appealing to "the people". (n) Distracting from the real issue. (o) Sliding a slippery slope. (*Don't fool yourself: . 15 common mistakes in logic* page 217)

7. Name at least one logical fallacy involved in this statement: "Everyone who's ever visited this school agrees that it's the best in the state."

(Answers will vary.) All or nothing thinking (surely not everyone agrees). (*Don't fool yourself: 15 common mistakes in logic*, page 217).

8. List three questions that you can ask when checking evidence.

Answers will vary, but should include any of the following three: Are all or most of the relevant facts presented? Are the facts consistent with each other? Are facts presented accurately? Are enough examples included to make a solid case for the assertion? Do the examples truly support the assertion? Are the examples typical? Is the expert credible? Is the expert biased? Is the expert quoted accurately? If the speaker or writer appeals to your emotions, is this done in a way that is also logical and based on evidence? (*A process for critical thinking*, page 205)

9. According to the text, the words *choose* and *decide* have the same meaning. True or false? Explain your answer.

False. Using the word *choose* frees up your thinking as it expresses a preference for one thing over another, rather than eliminating other options completely as happens when you "decide." (*Gaining skill at decision making*, page 221)

10. According to the text, information and ideas refer to different things. True or false? Explain your answer.

Information refers to facts that can be verified by independent observers. *Ideas* are interpretations or opinions based on facts. These include statements of opinion and value judgments. Several people with the same information might adopt different ideas based on that information. (*Think critically about information on the Internet*, page 220)

SKILLS SNAPSHOT
Chapter 7

Take a snapshot of your thinking skills as they exist today, after reading and completing the exercises in this chapter. Then take the next step toward mastery by committing to adopt new thinking strategies.

Discovery
My score on the Thinking section of the Discovery Wheel was . . .

When I face a major decision in my life, the way that I usually make that decision is . . .

One of the biggest problems I face right now is . . .

Mastery of critical and creative thinking could help my career by . . .

Intention
By the time I finish this course, I would like my *Thinking* score on the Discovery Wheel to be . . .

I'll know that I've reached a new level of mastery with thinking skills when I am able to . . .

The three suggestions from this chapter that will help me the most in reaching that level of mastery are . . .

Action
To put the suggestions I just listed into practice, the next actions I will take are . . .

Some possible obstacles to taking those actions are . . .

To overcome these obstacles, I will . . .

INSTRUCTOR TOOLS & TIPS

Chapter 8

COMMUNICATING

"You have two ears and one mouth. Remember to use them in more or less that proportion." —Paula Bern

PREVIEW

Communicating effectively is discussed indirectly in many chapters of *Becoming a Master Student*. By taking a closer look at effective communication in this chapter, you can help your students in the related skills of speaking, listening, and writing now that they have the necessary foundations to work toward mastery. This chapter provides an opportunity to discuss conflict resolution, public speaking (including overcoming fear of public speaking), and plagiarism. Communication abilities are essential workplace skills that can be practiced and mastered in the college setting. Use this Annotated Instructor's Edition and other resources available to you to highlight and discuss key concepts in class and to devise assignments that allow students to practice communication skills outside the classroom. And consider this: Developing relationships through effective communication is essential for first-year student success and retention at your college. You can emphasize that these skills are equally important in students' personal lives and in the workplace, making communication a valuable life skill.

GUEST SPEAKER

A librarian or a colleague from the speech/communications department makes a timely guest speaker as a lead-in to the articles on plagiarism and public speaking. Share the related articles with the guest speaker ahead of time so that the speaker's presentation can be focused to complement the text. Let students know who is coming so that they can prepare questions to ask your guest speaker. Ask the guest speaker to discuss the importance of public speaking and communication beyond the classroom.

LECTURE

Appropriate lecture topics for this chapter include active listening and concentration, effective writing, plagiarism, public speaking, and the Power Process: Employ your word. Consider inviting a guest lecturer for one or more of these topics.

Workplace Application: Workplace communication. A team is more than a group of people. It is a collective of individuals who all contribute to the working of the whole, comprising any group of people linked in a common purpose. It is a living, breathing entity made up of individual stories and built through determination, struggle, and hard work. A team is a co-operative unit. A good team makes all the difference to any company. Team building can seem a daunting task at first, but the benefits far outweigh the challenges. One important characteristic of good teams is clear communication. Communication can be defined as the process of creating shared meaning. Effective communication is a constant challenge: we can never be sure the message we send is the message others receive. In successful teams, tasks are explained clearly. The environment is open and welcoming of discussion and feedback. A team that does not feel empowered to speak up will eventually shut down.

Before you can become a part of the work team, you must first be hired! According to the National Association of Colleges and Employers (NACE), interviewers look most for applicants who can communicate well. This is the skill they consistently find lacking in new graduates. Remind students that not all communication is verbal. Employers often focus more on the nonverbal clues like facial expressions and hand gestures when gathering meaning from a prospective employee. Encourage students to practice answering interview questions while looking in a mirror or being videotaped. They can then see how their unconscious mannerisms are portrayed.

EXERCISES/ACTIVITIES

1. **Five ways to say "I" (page 240).** Students who have not taken an interpersonal communications course often do not know how to create "I" statements. Dividing students into groups and having them practice writing and speaking "I" statements can help them understand how to do so and enable them to gauge their effectiveness in communicating.

2. **You deserve compliments (page 249).** This is one of Dave Ellis's favorite class activities. Ask students to pair up with a classmate they have gotten to know during the semester. One will be the speaker; the other, the listener. The speaker says, "What I like about you is . . ." and finishes the sentence with a quality he likes in that person. He continues to repeat this sentence for 45 seconds, each time stating a different quality. If your students get stuck and cannot think of a quality, encourage them to say, "What I like about you is *everything*," over and over again, until they can think of another specific compliment. This keeps the barrage of compliments going. The listener receives the compliments and acknowledges them nonverbally. After 45 seconds, the students switch roles and repeat the exercise. Then have a class discussion about how it felt to *give* and to *receive* compliments. Ask students whether it is more difficult to give or receive compliments.

3. **5 steps to effective complaints (page 251).** Students enjoy this short group activity. Ask your students to recall a recent consumer purchase that disappointed them. Then divide the students into small groups and have them share their experiences, including what happened and how they felt. Have them remain in the groups and review the article for suggestions on how they might be more effective next time. Ask group members to choose one of the examples provided by the group. Instruct them to write a complaint letter to the company.

4. **Mastering public speaking (pages 261–264).** In this activity, students prepare and present a five-minute process speech about their future career plans. This provides them with an opportunity to stand up and speak before the entire class. To lay the groundwork, review the criteria for an effective speech. This practice in a familiar and comfortable environment helps reduce speech anxiety for students who will likely make future presentations in other courses.

5. **Mastering public speaking (pages 261–264).** Participating in class is another excellent way for students to practice speaking in public. Many students experience communication apprehension when they are called on in class or when they must speak before a group. Ask your students to write a Discovery Statement about their memory of this type of situation. Have them describe their physical sensations, the effectiveness of their presentation, feedback from the audience, and so forth. Ask your students to write an Intention Statement concerning how they intend to participate in class in order to experience talking to a group of people. Ask them to be specific about which class they intend to speak in, how they will set up the opportunity to speak (e.g., having questions ready, sitting in front, asking to give a presentation, and so

master instructor
best practice

I assign a PowerPoint project to my College Success students. I lead the class in researching their chosen career through an online career assessment tool and through career research tools. Once students prepare their PowerPoint presentation, each presents a five-minute speech, using the PowerPoint as a visual aid. This assignment can be customized to incorporate current class topics and research tools.

—Annette McCreedy, Nashville State Community College

forth), and how they intend to record their observations of the experience. Tie class participation into the course grade, reminding students that willingness to participate is a valuable skill in the workplace as well as the classroom. Connect this lesson with "Risk being a fool," and you have a practical application of the Power Process in Chapter 10.

CONVERSATION/SHARING

This chapter is certainly one that your students will be energized to discuss. It will be especially easy for them to create schema using their prior knowledge of the subject before learning new information. Spend time focusing on the *What if?* in this chapter. Ask students, *What if* they use the ideas presented in this chapter to help them succeed in the workplace. Ask your students to consider the importance of communication for the major they have chosen (connecting back to Chapter 7) or for their future career choice (looking ahead to Chapter 12).

HOMEWORK

Power Process: Employ your word (page 234). To help illustrate the effectiveness of this Power Process, have students individually think about making two promises, one to themselves and one to a significant person in their lives, and then ask students to write down their promises. This helps demonstrate how to use the ideas in the article. Ask students to answer the following questions concerning their promises: "At which level is this promise?" "What are the possible consequences if I do not keep these promises?" Remind students that the promises they are making are, culturally, the highest level of commitment we make to each other.

Three phases of effective writing (pages 254–258). Are you looking for an assignment that can help your students practice their writing *and* provide them with an opportunity to win a $1,000 scholarship? This is a perfect place to announce the Cengage Learning Scholarship Essay Contest. Host a contest in your classes, select the best essay (that answers the scholarship essay question, posted on the Instructor Companion Site), and submit this winning essay to the national contest. Remind your students that they have the formula for writing a successful essay in their hands!

Academic integrity: Avoid plagiarism (pages 259–260). If students understand how to cite sources properly and feel confident about their ability to do so, many are less likely to "cheat," either intentionally or simply because they don't know how to cite. Explain your college's policy on academic integrity. Consider asking students to go to your college library, find a current controversial topic, and use library reference material to choose a position on their controversial topic. Next, have them find three facts in periodicals or books that directly support their position. Finally, ask them to type their three facts and cite them properly using MLA or APA format. Many students don't know how to find topics in the library, locate reference books, and research a topic using the library's online catalog. Ask a librarian to explain how to do this to your students, as a guest speaker or during a class visit to the library.

Three phases of effective writing (pages 254–258). Convincing your students that writing is as important in the workplace as it is in the classroom is an essential point to drive home. Stress that learning to write well pays many dividends and that writing effectively can help students express themselves. Writing will help them to organize information and adapt their ideas to different audiences. Finally, point out that good writing is a marketable skill. To verify this, have your students look at help-wanted ads in the newspaper or online and determine how many job descriptions call for good writing skills. Have your students look for other transferable skills that they can master in the classroom and utilize in the workplace. Students can write Discovery and Intention Statements after reviewing the help-wanted ads. Ask your students to highlight skills other than writing that will be applicable to their intended career choice.

Master Student Profile: Salman Khan (page 266). Remind students that the Master Student Profiles can be a source of inspiration. You can also use the Master Student Profiles to discuss the topics covered in the article. Ask your students why they think that Salman Khan was selected for the communication chapter. You can assign additional reading or research (another opportunity for students to practice their research and writing) related to this article.

EVALUATION

Frequent quizzes ensure that students focus attention during class and keep up with the text reading assignments. In addition, quizzes provide students with opportunities for written reflection regarding new discoveries and intentions. Evaluation instruments also help you identify topics and concepts that students have not yet mastered.

Quiz Ideas for Chapter 8

Ask students to:

- Describe ways to manage conflict and to give examples of these.

- Share how they would effectively complain in order to get a situation resolved: Present them with an example of a problem between a student and the admissions or records office.

- Provide examples of how to stay safe during online social networking.

- Write Discovery and Intention Statements regarding the Power Process: Employ your word.

MindTap™

EMBRACE VALUABLE RESOURCES

FOR CHAPTER 8

STUDENT RESOURCES: MINDTAP

- **Engagement Activity: Master Students in Action.** Students hear firsthand from other students about their communication challenges and their strategies for success. Students discuss the communication challenges of online courses and Dave Ellis offers up strategies for how to become an effective communicator.

- **Aplia Homework Assignment: Emotional intelligence and managing conflict.** In this assignment, students learn how to develop emotional intelligence and manage conflict. By closely examining

a conflict scenario, students identify what the participants are trying to say and what responses would have been more effective.

- **Reflection Activity: Employ Your Word.** In this video, Ming Tsai talks about the importance of making commitments and keeping promises, specifically about his experiences at his workplace. This is relatable to so many students who are likely to have worked or currently are working in restaurants.

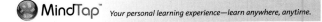 **MindTap™** *Your personal learning experience—learn anywhere, anytime.*

INSTRUCTOR COMPANION SITE

- **Having trouble connecting with your students?** Included in the online Course Manual are many strategies for addressing students, such as how to handle students who resist the class, don't feel they need it, or are plain insulted at having to take the course. Work on improving your communication skills to reach these students.

- **Looking for test banks?** Customizable, text-specific content quizzes are a great way to test students' knowledge and understanding of the text, and are available for every chapter. Powered by Cognero, the test banks can be exported in an LMS or print-friendly format. You will have no problem

accessing the multiple-choice, true/false, completion, and short-answer questions.

- **Check out the PowerPoint Library for a PowerPoint specifically created for Chapter 8.** This master library of PowerPoint presentations makes it easy to find the right PowerPoint for you! If you're looking for a way to freshen up your lecture and engage your students with in-class activities, the PowerPoint Library is a great place to start.

Please visit login.cengage.com to log in and access the Instructor Companion Site.

Chapter 8

COMMUNICATING

Why

Your communication abilities—including your skills in listening, speaking, and writing—are as important to your success as your technical skills.

Choosing to speak ■ 238

Communicating in teams—Getting things done as a group Your experience in higher education will include group projects. Read about some specific communication skills to avoid the pitfalls that take teams down. ■ 243

How

Think of a time when you experienced an emotionally charged conflict with another person. Then scan this chapter for ideas that can help you get your feelings and ideas across more skillfully in similar situations.

TECH

Three phases of effective writing Learn about how to write e-mail that gets results and tips to befriend your word processor. ■ 254

Mastering public speaking Your audiences are like you. The way you plan and present your speech can determine the number of audience members who will stay with you until the end. Polishing your speaking and presentation skills can also help you think on your feet and communicate clearly. You can use these skills in any course, and they'll help you advance in your career as well. ■ 261

What if...

I could consistently create the kind of relationships that I've always wanted?

What is included ...

EMPLOY YOUR
WORD

When you give your word, you are creating—literally. The person you are is, for the most part, a result of the agreements you make. Others know who you are by your words and your commitments. And you can learn who you are by observing which commitments you choose to keep and which ones you choose to avoid.

Relationships are built on agreements. When we break a promise to be faithful to a spouse, to help a friend move to a new apartment, or to pay a bill on time, relationships are strained.

The words we use to make agreements can be placed into six different levels. We can think of each level as one rung on a ladder—the ladder of powerful speaking. As we move up the ladder, our speaking becomes more effective.

The first and lowest rung on the ladder is *obligation*. Words used at this level include *I should, he ought to, someone had better, they need to, I must,* and *I had to.* Speaking this way implies that something other than ourselves is in control of our lives. When we live at the level of obligation, we speak as if we are victims.

The second rung is *possibility*. At this level, we examine new options. We play with new ideas, possible solutions, and alternative courses of action. As we do, we learn that we can make choices that dramatically affect the quality of our lives. We are not the victims of circumstance. Phrases that signal this level include *I might, I could, I'll consider, I hope to,* and *maybe.*

From possibility, we can move up to the third level—*preference*. Here we begin the process of choice. The words *I prefer* signal that we're moving toward one set of possibilities over another, perhaps setting the stage for eventual action.

Above preference is a fourth rung called *passion*. Again, certain words signal this level: *I want to, I'm really excited to,* and *I can't wait to.*

Action comes with the fifth rung—*planning*. When people use phrases such as *I intend to, my goal is to, I plan to,* and *I'll try like mad to,* they're at the level of planning. The Intention Statements you write in this book are examples of planning.

The sixth and highest rung on the ladder is *promising*. This is where the power of your word really comes into play. At this level, it's common to use phrases such as these: *I will, I promise, I am committed,* and *you can count on it.* Promising is where we bridge from possibility and planning to action. Promising brings with it all of the rewards of employing your word. ■

COMMUNICATION—
Keeping the channels
OPEN

© Roberaten/Shutterstock.com

In our daily contact with other people and the mass media, we are exposed to hundreds of messages. Yet the obstacles to receiving those messages accurately are numerous.

For one thing, only a small percentage of communication is verbal. We also send messages with our bodies and with the tone of our voices. Throw in a few other factors, such as a hot room or background noise, and it's a wonder we can communicate at all.

Written communication adds a whole other set of variables. When you speak, you supplement the meaning of your words with the power of body language and voice inflection. When you write, those nonverbal elements are absent. Instead, you depend on your skills at word choice, sentence construction, and punctuation to get your message across. The choices that you make in these areas can help—or hinder—communication.

In communication theory, the term *noise* refers to any factor that distorts meaning. When noise is present, the channels of communication start to close. Noise can be external (a lawn mower outside a classroom) or internal (the emotions of the sender or receiver, such as speech anxiety). To a large extent, skillful communication means reducing noise and keeping channels open.

One powerful technique for doing these crucial things is to separate the roles of sending and receiving. Communication channels get blocked when we try to send and receive messages at the same time. Instead, be aware of when you are the receiver and when you are the sender. If you are receiving (listening or reading), just receive; avoid switching into the sending (speaking or writing) mode. When you are sending, stick with it until you are finished.

Communication works best when each of us has plenty of time to receive what others send *and* the opportunity to send a complete message when it's our turn. Communication is a two-way street. When someone else talks, just listen. Then switch roles so that you can be the sender for a while. Keep this up until you do a reasonably complete job of creating shared meaning. ■

Interactive

Exercise 22
Practice sending or receiving

The purpose of this exercise is to help you slow down the pace of communication and clearly separate the roles of sending and receiving. Begin by applying the following steps to conversations on neutral topics. With some practice, you'll be ready to use this technique in situations that could escalate into an argument.

First, find a partner, and choose a topic for a conversation. Also set a time limit for doing this exercise. Then complete the following steps:

1. Get two 3 × 5 cards. Label one of them *sender*. Label the other *receiver*. Choose one card, and give the other one to your partner.

2. If you chose the *sender* card, then start speaking. If you chose the *receiver* card, then listen to your partner without saying a word.

3. When the sender is done speaking, exchange cards and switch roles. The person who listened in Step 2 now gets to speak. However, *do not exchange cards until the sender in Step 2 declares that she has expressed everything she wants to say.*

4. Keep switching cards and roles until your time is up.

After completing these steps, reflect on the experience. What has this exercise taught you about your current skills as a speaker and listener?

CHOOSING TO LISTEN

Observe a person in a conversation who is not talking. Is he listening? Maybe. Maybe not. Is he focusing on the speaker? Preparing his response? Daydreaming? Effective listening is not easy. It calls for concentration and energy. But it's worth the trouble. People love a good listener. The best salespeople, managers, coworkers, teachers, parents, and friends are the best listeners.

Through skilled listening, you can gain insight into other people and yourself. You can also promote your success in school through more powerful notes, more productive study groups, and better relationships with students and instructors.

To listen well, begin from a clear intention. *Choose* to listen well. Once you've made this choice, you can use the following techniques to be even more effective at listening.

Notice that these suggestions start with nonverbal listening, which involves remaining silent while another person talks. The second set of suggestions is about verbal listening, where you occasionally speak up to fully receive a speaker's message.

NONVERBAL LISTENING

Be quiet. Silence is more than staying quiet while someone is speaking. Allowing several seconds to pass before you begin to talk gives the speaker time to catch her breath and gather her thoughts. She might want to continue. Someone who talks nonstop might fear she will lose the floor if she pauses.

If the message being sent is complete, this short break gives you time to form your response and helps you avoid the biggest barrier to listening—listening with your answer running. If you make up a response before the person is finished, you might miss the end of the message, which is often the main point.

In some circumstances, pausing for several seconds might be inappropriate. Ignore this suggestion completely, as you would in an emergency where immediate action is usually necessary.

Maintain eye contact. Look at the other person while he speaks. Maintaining eye contact demonstrates your attentiveness and helps keep your mind from wandering. Your eyes also let you observe the speaker's body language and behavior. If you avoid eye contact, you can fail to see *and* fail to listen.

This idea is not an absolute. Maintaining eye contact is valued more in some cultures than others. Also, some people learn primarily by hearing; they can listen more effectively by turning off the visual input once in a while.

Display openness. You can display openness through your facial expression and body position. Uncross your arms and legs. Sit up straight. Face the other person, and remove any physical barriers between you, such as a pile of books.

Send acknowledgments. Let the speaker know periodically that you are still there. Words and nonverbal gestures of acknowledgment convey to the speaker that you are interested and that you are receiving his message. These words and gestures include "uh-huh," "okay," "yes," and head nods.

These acknowledgments do not imply your agreement. When people tell you what they don't like about you, your head nod doesn't mean that you agree. It just indicates that you are listening.

Release distractions. Even when your intention is to listen, you might find your mind wandering. Thoughts about what *you* want to say or something you want to do later might claim your attention. There's a simple solution: Notice your wandering mind without judgment. Then bring your attention back to the act of listening.

You can also set up your immediate environment to release distractions. Turn off or silence your cell phone. Stash your laptop and other digital devices. Send the message that your sole intention in the moment is to listen.

Another option is to ask for a quick break so that you can make a written note about what's on your mind. Tell the speaker that you're writing so that you can clear your mind and return to full listening.

Suspend judgments. Listening and agreeing are two different activities. As listeners, our goal is to fully receive another person's message. This does not mean that we're obligated to agree with the message. Once you're confident that you accurately understand a speaker's point of view, you are free to agree or disagree with it. The key to effective listening is understanding *before* evaluating.

VERBAL LISTENING

Choose when to speak. When we listen to another person, we often interrupt with our own stories, opinions, suggestions, and comments. Consider the following dialogue:

"Oh, I'm so excited! I just found out that I've been nominated to be in Who's Who in American Musicians.*"*

"Yeah, that's neat. My Uncle Elmer got into Who's Who in American Veterinarians. *He sure has an interesting job. One time I went along when he was treating a cow, and you'll never believe what happened next. . . ."*

To avoid this kind of one-sided conversation, delay your verbal responses. This does not mean that you remain totally silent while listening. It means that you wait for an *appropriate* moment to respond.

Watch your nonverbal responses too. A look of "Good grief!" from you can deter the other person from finishing his message.

Feed back meaning. Sometimes you can help a speaker clarify her message by paraphrasing it. This does not mean parroting what she says. Instead, briefly summarize. Psychotherapist Carl Rogers referred to this technique as *reflection.*[1]

Feed back what you see as the essence of the person's message: "Let me see whether I understood what you said. . . ." or "What I'm hearing you say is . . . ." Often, the other person will say, "No, that's not what I meant. What I said was . . ."

There will be no doubt when you get it right. The sender will say, "Yeah, that's it," and either continue with another message or stop sending when he knows you understand.

When you feed back meaning, be concise. This is not a time to stop the other person by talking on and on about what you think you heard.

Notice verbal *and* nonverbal messages. You might point out that the speaker's body language seems to convey the exact opposite of what her words do. For example: "I noticed you said you are excited, but you look bored."

Keep in mind that the same nonverbal behavior can have various meanings across cultures. Someone who looks bored might simply be listening in a different way.

Listen for requests and intentions. An effective way to listen to complaints is to look for the request hidden in them. "This class is a waste of my time" can be heard as "Please tell me what I'll gain if I participate actively in class." "The instructor talks too fast" might be asking "What strategies can I use to take notes when the instructor covers material rapidly?"

We can even transform complaints into intentions. Take this complaint: "The parking lot by the dorms is so dark at night that I'm afraid to go to my car." This complaint can result in having a light installed in the parking lot.

Viewing complaints as requests gives us more choices. Rather than responding with defensiveness ("What does he know anyway?"), resignation ("It's always been this way and always will be"), or indifference ("It's not my job"), we can decide whether to grant the request (do what will alleviate the other's difficulty) or help the person translate his own complaint into an action plan.

Allow emotion. In the presence of full listening, some people will share things that they feel deeply about. They might shed a few tears, cry, shake, or sob. If you feel uncomfortable when this happens, see whether you can accept the discomfort for a little while longer. Emotional release can bring relief and trigger unexpected insights.

Ask for more. Full listening with unconditional acceptance is a rare gift. Many people have never experienced it. They are used to being greeted with resistance, so they habitually stop short of saying what they truly think and feel. Help them shed this habit by routinely asking, "Is there anything more you want to say about that?" This question sends the speaker a message that you truly value what she has to say.

Be careful with questions and advice. Questions are directive. They can take conversations in a new direction, which may not be where the speaker wants to go. Ask questions only to clarify the speaker's message. Later, when it's your turn to speak, you can introduce any topic that you want.

Also be cautious about giving advice. Unsolicited advice can be taken as condescending or even insulting. Skilled listeners recognize that people are different, and they do not assume that they know what's best for someone else.

Take care of yourself. People seek good listeners, and there are times when you don't want to listen. You might be distracted with your own concerns. Be honest. Don't pretend to listen. You can say, "What you're telling me is important, but I'm pressed for time right now. Can we set aside another time to talk about this?" It's okay not to listen.

Stay open to the adventure of listening. Receiving what another person has to say is an act of courage. Listening fully—truly opening yourself to the way another person sees the world—means taking risks. Your opinions may be challenged. You may be less certain or less comfortable than you were before.

Along with the risks come rewards. Listening in an unguarded way can take your relationships to a new depth and level of honesty. This kind of listening can open up new possibilities for thinking, feeling, and behaving. And when you practice full listening, other people are more likely to receive when it's your turn to send. ■

Choosing to
SPEAK

Eric Pelaez/Stone+/Getty Images

You have been talking with people for most of your life, and you usually manage to get your messages across. There are times, though, when you don't. Often, these times are emotionally charged.

We all have this problem. Sometimes we feel wonderful or rotten or sad or scared, and we want to express it. Emotions, though, can get in the way of the message. And although you can send almost any message through tears, laughter, fist pounding, or hugging, sometimes words are better. Begin with a sincere intention to reach common ground with your listener. Then experiment with the suggestions that follow.

Replace "you" messages with "I" messages.
It can be difficult to disagree with someone without his becoming angry or your becoming upset. When conflict occurs, we often make statements about the other person, or "you" messages:

"You are rude."
"You make me mad."
"You must be crazy."
"You don't love me anymore."

This kind of communication results in defensiveness. The responses might be similar to these:

"I am not rude."
"I don't care."
"No, *you* are crazy."
"No, *you* don't love *me!*"

"You" messages are hard to listen to. They label, judge, blame, and assume things that may or may not be true. They demand rebuttal. Even praise can sometimes be an ineffective "you" message. "You" messages don't work.

Psychologist Thomas Gordon suggests that when communication is emotionally charged, consider limiting your statements to descriptions about yourself.[2] Replace "you" messages with "I" messages:

"You are rude" might become "I feel upset."
"You make me mad" could be "I feel angry."
"You must be crazy" can be "I don't understand."
"You don't love me anymore" could become "I'm afraid we're drifting apart."

Suppose a friend asks you to pick him up at the airport. You drive 20 miles and wait for the plane. No friend. You decide your friend missed her plane, so you wait three hours for the next flight. No friend. Perplexed and worried, you drive home. The next day, you see your friend downtown.

"What happened?" you ask.
"Oh, I caught an earlier flight."
"You are a rude person," you reply.

Look for and talk about the facts—the observable behavior. Everyone will agree that your friend asked you to pick her up, that she did take an earlier flight, and that you did not receive a call from her. But the idea that she is rude is not a fact—it's a judgment.

She might go on to say, "I called your home, and no one answered. My mom had a stroke and was rushed to Valley View. I caught the earliest flight I could get." Your judgment no longer fits.

When you saw your friend, you might have said, "I waited and waited at the airport. I was worried about you. I didn't get a call. I feel angry and hurt. I don't want to waste my time. Next time, you can call me when your flight arrives, and I'll be happy to pick you up."

"I" messages don't judge, blame, criticize, or insult. They don't invite the other person to counterattack with more of the same. "I" messages are also more accurate. They report our own thoughts and feelings.

At first, "I" messages might feel uncomfortable or seem forced. That's okay. Your skill with using this technique will improve with practice.

Remember that questions are not always questions. You've heard these "questions" before. A parent asks, "Don't you want to look nice?" Translation: "I wish you'd cut your hair, lose the blue jeans, and put on a tie." Or how about this question from a spouse: "Honey, wouldn't you love to go to an exciting hockey game tonight?" Translation: "I've already bought tickets."

We use questions that aren't questions to sneak our opinions and requests into conversations. "Doesn't it upset you?" means "It upsets me," and "Shouldn't we hang the picture over here?" means "I want to hang the picture over here."

Communication improves when we say, "I'm upset" and "Let's hang the picture over here."

Choose your nonverbal messages. How you say something can be more important than what you say. Your tone of voice and gestures add up to a silent message that you send. This message can support, modify, or contradict your words. Your posture, the way you dress, how often you shower, and even the poster hanging on your wall can negate your words before you say them.

Most nonverbal behavior is unconscious. We can learn to be aware of it and choose our nonverbal messages. The key is to be clear about our intention and purpose. When we know what we want to say and are committed to getting it across, our inflections, gestures, and words work together and send a unified message.

Notice barriers to sending messages. Sometimes fear stops us from sending messages. We are afraid of other people's reactions, sometimes justifiably. Being truthful doesn't mean being insensitive to the impact that our messages have on others. Tact is a virtue; letting fear prevent communication is not.

Assumptions can also be used as excuses for not sending messages. "He already knows this," we tell ourselves.

Predictions of failure can be barriers to sending too. "He won't listen," we assure ourselves. That statement might be inaccurate. Perhaps the other person senses that we're angry and listens in a guarded way. Or perhaps he is listening and sending nonverbal messages we don't understand.

Or we might predict, "He'll never do anything about it, even if I tell him." Again, making assumptions can defeat your message before you send it.

It's easy to make excuses for not communicating. If you have fear or some other concern about sending a message, be aware of it. Don't expect the concern to go away. Realize that you can communicate even with your concerns. You can choose to make them part of the message: "I am going to tell you how I feel, but I'm afraid that you will think it's stupid."

Talking to someone when you don't want to could be a matter of educational survival. Sometimes a short talk with an advisor, a teacher, a friend, or a family member can solve a problem that otherwise could jeopardize your education.

Speak candidly. When we brood on negative thoughts and refuse to speak them out loud, we lose perspective. And when we keep joys to ourselves, we diminish our satisfaction. A solution is to share regularly what we think and feel. Psychotherapist Sidney Jourard referred to such openness and honesty as *transparency* and wrote eloquently about how it can heal and deepen relationships.[3]

Sometimes candid speaking can save a life. For example, if you think a friend is addicted to drugs, telling her so in a supportive, nonjudgmental way is a sign of friendship.

Imagine a community in which people freely and lovingly speak their minds—without fear or defensiveness. That can be your community.

This suggestion comes with a couple of caveats. First, there is a big difference between speaking candidly about your problems and griping about them. Gripers usually don't seek solutions. They just want everyone to know how unhappy they are. Instead, talk about problems as a way to start searching for solutions.

Second, avoid bragging. Other people are turned off by constant references to how much money you have, how great your partner is, how numerous your social successes are, or how much status your family enjoys. There is a difference between sharing excitement and being obnoxious.

Offer "feedforward." Giving people feedback about their past performance can be a powerful way to help them learn. Equally useful is "feedforward," which means exploring new options for the future.

Marshall Goldsmith, a management consultant, suggests a way to do this. First, talk about a specific, high-impact behavior that you'd like to change—for example, "I want to be a better listener." Then gather with a small group of trusted friends and ask for suggestions about ways to accomplish your goal. To make this process work, avoid any conversation about what's happened in the past. Focus instead on next actions you intend to take. Also listen to what others suggest without criticizing their ideas.[4]

Speak up! Look for opportunities to practice speaking strategies. Join class discussions, and keep a running list of questions and comments to share. Start conversations about topics that excite you. Ask for information and clarification. Ask for feedback on your skills.

Also speak up when you want support. Consider creating a team of people who help one another succeed. Such a team can develop naturally from a study group that works well. Ask members whether they would be willing to accept and receive support in achieving a wide range of academic and personal goals. Meet regularly to do goal-setting exercises from this book and brainstorm success strategies.

After you have a clear statement of your goals and a plan for achieving them, let family members and friends know. When appropriate, let them know how they can help. You may be surprised at how often people respond to a genuine request for support.

Take these ideas to work. In the workplace, you will regularly meet new coworkers, customers, and clients. One of the most practical communication skills you can develop is the ability to hold one-on-one conversations. The ability to put people at ease through "small talk" makes you valuable to an employer. This is a high-level skill that depends on the ability to listen closely and speak skillfully. Using "I" messages and the other suggestions in this article can help you thrive at work. ∎

Five ways to say "I"

An "I" message can include any or all of the following five elements. Be careful when including the last two elements, though, because they can contain hidden judgments or threats.

Observations. Describe the facts—the indisputable, observable realities. Talk about what you—or anyone else—can see, hear, smell, taste, or touch. Avoid judgments, interpretations, or opinions. Instead of saying, "You're a slob," say, "Last night's lasagna pan was still on the stove this morning."

Feelings. Describe your own feelings. It is easier to listen to "I feel frustrated" than to "You never help me." Stating how you feel about another's actions can be valuable feedback for that person.

Wants. You are far more likely to get what you want if you say what you want. If someone doesn't know what you want, she doesn't have a chance to help you get it. Ask clearly. Avoid demanding or using the word *need*. Most people like to feel helpful, not obligated. Instead of saying, "Do the dishes when it's your turn, or else!" say, "I want to divide the housework fairly."

Thoughts. Communicate your thoughts, and use caution. Beginning your statement with the word "I" doesn't automatically make it an "I" message. "I think you are a slob" is a "you" judgment in disguise. Instead, say, "I'd have more time to study if I didn't have to clean up so often."

Intentions. The last part of an "I" message is a statement about what you intend to do. Have a plan that doesn't depend on the other person. For example, instead of "From now on, we're going to split the dishwashing evenly," you could say, "I intend to do my share of the housework and leave the rest."

Roc Canals Photography/Flickr/Getty Images

Interactive

Exercise 23
Write an "I" message

First, pick something about school that irritates you. Then pretend that you are talking to a person who is associated with this irritation. Write down what you would say to this person as a "you" message.

_____

_____

_____

_____

_____

Now write the same complaint as an "I" message.

_____

_____

_____

_____

_____

_____

Journal Entry 18
Discovery/Intention Statement

Discover communication styles

The concept of *communication styles* can be useful when you want to discover sources of conflict with another person—or when you're in a conversation with someone from a different culture.

Consider the many ways in which people express themselves verbally. These characteristics can reflect an individual's preferred communication style:

- **Extroversion**—talking to others as a way to explore possibilities for taking action.
- **Introversion**—thinking through possibilities alone before talking to others.
- **Dialogue**—engaging in a discussion to hear many points of view before coming to a conclusion or decision.
- **Debate**—arguing for a particular point of view from the outset of a discussion.
- **Openness**—being ready to express personal thoughts and feelings early in a relationship.
- **Reserve**—holding back on self-expression until a deeper friendship develops.
- A **faster pace** of conversation—allowing people to speak quickly and forcefully while filling any gaps in conversation.
- A **slower pace** of conversation—allowing people to speak slowly and quietly while taking time to formulate their thoughts.

These are just a few examples of differences in communication styles. You might be able to think of others.

The point is that people with different communication styles can make negative assumptions about each other. For example, those who prefer fast-paced conversations might assume that people who talk slowly are indecisive. And people who prefer slower-paced conversations might assume that people who talk quickly are pushy and uninterested in anyone else's opinion.

Take this opportunity to think about your preferred communication styles and assumptions. Do they enhance or block your relationships with other people? Think back over the conversations you've had during the past week. Then complete the following sentences:

I discovered that I prefer conversations that allow me to . . .

_____

_____

I discovered that I usually feel uncomfortable in conversations when other people . . .

_____

_____

When people do the things listed in Item 2, I tend to make certain assumptions, such as . . .

_____

_____

As an alternative to making the assumptions listed in Item 3, I intend to . . .

_____

_____

Developing EMOTIONAL INTELLIGENCE

In his book *Working with Emotional Intelligence*, Daniel Goleman defines emotional intelligence as a cluster of traits:

- **Self-awareness**—recognizing your full range of emotions and knowing your strengths and limitations.
- **Self-regulation**—responding skillfully to strong emotions, practicing honesty and integrity, and staying open to new ideas.
- **Motivation**—persisting to achieve goals and meet standards of excellence.
- **Empathy**—sensing other people's emotions and taking an active interest in their concerns.
- **Skill in relationships**—listening fully, speaking persuasively, resolving conflict, and leading people through times of change.

Goleman concludes that "IQ washes out when it comes to predicting who among a talented pool of candidates *within* an intellectually demanding profession will become the strongest leader." At that point, emotional intelligence starts to become more important.[5]

If you're emotionally intelligent, you're probably described as someone with good "people skills." You're aware of your feelings. You act in thoughtful ways, show concern for others, resolve conflict, and make responsible decisions.

Your emotional intelligence skills will serve you in school and in the workplace, especially when you collaborate on project teams. You can deepen your skills with the following strategies.

RECOGNIZE THREE ELEMENTS OF EMOTION

Even the strongest emotion consists of just three elements: physical sensations, thoughts, and action. Usually they happen so fast that you can barely distinguish them. Separating them out is a first step toward emotional intelligence.

Imagine that you suddenly perceive a threat—such as a supervisor who's screaming at you. Immediately your heart starts beating in double-time and your stomach muscles clench (physical sensations). Then thoughts race through your head: *This is a disaster. She hates me. And everyone's watching.* Finally, you take action, which could mean staring at her, yelling back, or running away.

NAME YOUR EMOTIONS

Naming your emotions is a first step to going beyond the "fight or flight" reaction to any emotion. Naming gives you power. The second that you attach a word to an emotion, you start to gain perspective. People with emotional intelligence have a rich vocabulary to describe a wide range of emotions. For examples, do an Internet search with the key words *feeling list*. Read through the lists you find for examples of ways that you can name your feelings in the future.

ACCEPT YOUR EMOTIONS

Another step toward emotional intelligence is accepting your emotions—*all* of them. This can be challenging if you've been taught that some emotions are "good," whereas others are "bad." Experiment with another viewpoint: You do not choose your emotional reactions. However, you can choose what you *do* in response to any emotion.

EXPRESS YOUR EMOTIONS

One possible response to any emotion is expressing it. The key is to speak without blaming others. Use "I" messages to state what you observe, what you feel, and what you intend to do.

RESPOND RATHER THAN REACT

The heart of emotional intelligence is moving from mindless reaction to mindful action. See whether you can introduce an intentional gap between sensations and thoughts on the one hand and your next action on the other hand. To do this more often:

- **Run a "mood meter."** Check in with your moods several times each day. On a 3 × 5 card, note the time of day and your emotional state at that point. Rate your mood on a scale of 1 (relaxed and positive) to 10 (very angry, very sad, or very afraid).
- **Write Discovery Statements.** In your journal, write about situations in daily life that trigger strong emotions. Describe these events—and your usual responses to them—in detail.
- **Write Intention Statements.** After seeing patterns in your emotions, you can consciously choose to behave in new ways. Instead of yelling back at the angry supervisor, for example, make it your intention to simply remain silent and breathe deeply until he finishes. Then say, "I'll wait to respond until we've both had a chance to cool down."

MAKE DECISIONS WITH EMOTIONAL INTELLIGENCE

When considering a possible choice, ask yourself, "How am I likely to feel if I do this?" You can use "gut feelings" to tell when an action might violate your values or hurt someone.

Think of emotions as energy. Anger, sadness, and fear send currents of sensation through your whole body. Ask yourself how you can channel that energy into constructive action. ■

Er Creatives Services Ltd/Iconica /Getty Images

COMMUNICATING IN TEAMS—
Getting things done as a group

Your experience in higher education will include group projects. These projects can be fun and rewarding. They can also fall flat and lead to frustration. To avoid the pitfalls that take teams down, develop some specific skills in communication.

START WITH AN ATTITUDE CHECK

Students come to group projects with a wide range of attitudes. Some people dread working with a team. They get good grades on their own and prefer to study alone. When forced to join a group, they fear getting paired with a dominating leader—or a slacker who does no work and still gets credit.

Those things can happen. And at the same time, group projects are here to stay. In the workplace, collaboration is the norm. Taking a project from a hazy idea to finished product requires the work of people with a variety of specialties and skills. Employers are looking for team players, not solo stars. If you can communicate well in groups, you're more likely to get the job you want and enjoy what you do.

There's a word that describes effective group work— *synergy*, which is short for *synthesized energy*. Master students know about synergy firsthand. Groups of them experience it when they create results that none of them could achieve by working alone.

Your group is more likely to "synergize" when you see that team work presents two distinct issues. One is to produce a *result*, such as a paper or presentation. The second is to find a *process* of working together that leads to this result. Effective teams deal with both of these issues at their first meeting. They also deal with ongoing challenges in communication and take their group projects all the way to an effective conclusion.

MASTER YOUR FIRST MEETING

Following is a list of items to consider as you create the agenda for your first group meeting. For long and complex projects, you might need more than one meeting to get them done.

Introduce yourselves and share key information. Start with housekeeping details. Ask all group members to share their name and contact information—e-mail address,

phone number, and any other details that will help you stay in touch with each other. Also share the times that you're available for group meetings. Make sure that someone captures all this information, puts it in writing, and distributes it to everyone in your group.

Talk about your team experiences. You might get assigned to work with people you've never met before. To learn more about each other, talk about the group work you've done in other courses. Speak openly about what you liked and didn't like. Based on this discussion, create a list of what makes a successful team and ways to prevent any problems you've had with group work in the past.

Define your outcome. According to author Stephen Covey, one habit of successful people is that they begin with the end in mind.[6] In other words, they start a project by describing their desired result.

You can use the same strategy. Pose these questions to your group: How will you know that your group has succeeded? What would a successful outcome look like and sound like? How would you feel when you produced it?

Brainstorm a list of answers, and ask someone in the group to record them. Then combine the best words and phrases into a single sentence that expresses what you agree to produce. Check this sentence against the requirements of your assignment, and get feedback from your instructor.

Choose roles. Groups do their best work when the members agree on the roles that they'll play. For example, the group *leader* sends out the agenda for meetings, starts and ends meetings, monitors the group's overall progress, and keeps the instructor up to date on the group's activity. A *timer* watches the clock to ensure that the group stays on schedule and gets to each item on the agenda. A *recorder* takes notes during meetings and maintains copies of all group-related materials. Beyond these basic roles, add any others that seem useful.

Your instructor might assign people in your group to these roles. If not, ask members to volunteer based on their interests and experience. Also remember that you can rotate roles over the course of your project.

In addition to formal roles, group members take on informal roles based on their learning styles. For instance, some people focus on the group's purpose and ask, "*Why* are we doing this?" Others pose questions such as:

- *What* are we planning to do?
- *How* are we going to get this done?
- *What* if we did this a different way?

Welcome all these questions. They signal that your group is moving through a complete cycle of learning.

Plan tasks and timelines. Once your outcome and roles are clearly defined, create a step-by-step plan to actually get the work done. Answer these questions: In order to produce our outcome, what's the very next action we need to take? What actions will follow that one? Who will take each action? By when?

One handy way to record the results of this discussion is to create a four-column chart:

Action	Assigned to	Due Date	Done

List your planned actions in order, along with a due date and person responsible for each one. When an action is completed, your group leader can check it off in the "Done" column.

Distribute a draft of this chart to your group and revise it until everyone agrees to it. Show the completed chart to your instructor as well and ask for feedback.

A word to the wise about due dates: These are tricky. Students who are new to group work often underestimate the time they'll need to complete tasks. To prevent last-minute stress, start working on your project as soon as it's assigned. Also plan to complete your group project several days before the assigned due date. This leaves your group with a cushion of extra time to deal with surprises and delays.

As you plan tasks and timelines, also ask:

- Which tasks need to be handled by the whole group, and which can be done by individuals?

- Will we need specific applications, such as word-processing, spreadsheet, and presentation software?

- If our final outcome is a paper, who will write the first draft of each section? Who will revise the sections and assemble them into a final copy?

- If our outcome is a group presentation, then what format shall we use? For example, will we divide the presentation into sections and do them individually? What equipment will we need? When will we rehearse as a group before doing our final presentation in class?

Again, check with your instructor as you answer these questions.

Choose when and how to meet. End your first session by scheduling meetings for the rest of your project. Also choose how to stay in contact between meetings. Options include e-mail, text, phone, and Web sites such as Google Drive (**drive.google.com**) that allow groups of people to share documents.

DEAL WITH CHALLENGES

Groups take time to gel. Don't expect yours to function perfectly right away. If conflicts develop between group members, view them as opportunities to develop your communication skills. The following suggestions will help.

Get the most from meeting time. Nothing drains energy from a group more than meetings that crop up at the last minute and waste everyone's time. If you're leading the group, be sure to give plenty of notice before meetings and write up an agenda for each one. Keep it to three items, tops. To focus everyone's thinking, state each agenda item as a question to answer. Instead of listing "project schedule," for example, write: "When is a realistic time for our next meeting?"

When scheduling meetings, also set clear starting and stopping times. Then stick to them.

End each meeting by updating your list of planned actions. Make sure that each action is assigned to a specific person with a clear due date. You'll know that meetings are working when the energy level in the group stays high, and when people have clear commitments to take planned action before the next meeting.

Reign in an overbearing member. A person who dominates the discussion in a meeting can prevent other group members from expressing their ideas. This is a common problem with group brainstorming. To prevent it, ask people to write up their ideas *before* a meeting. Gather these into one document and distribute it several days in advance. Then use this document to begin your discussion.

Resolve conflict. In an effective group, all ideas are welcome. Problems are freely admitted. Any item is open for discussion. Instead of automatically looking for what's wrong with a new idea, group members consider possible ways to use it. Even a proposal that seems outlandish at first might become workable with a few modifications.

Other ways to resolve conflict include:

- ***Allow emotions.*** People can feel angry, hurt, or afraid for reasons that you don't understand. Don't judge them for it. If a group member gets emotional during a meeting, show that you noticed it and invite more details. Say something non-judgmental, such as "You seem upset by what's happening here. Can you tell us what's not working for you?"

- **Listen fully.** When a group member speaks, give that person your complete attention. Don't think about your response while the person is talking; just focus on getting the message. Wait a few seconds after the person finishes speaking. Then invite more: "Thanks for talking. Is there anything more that you want to say?" Conflict can immediately be reduced when people feel that they're being heard.

- **Speak with I-messages.** When emotions run high, avoid criticizing others with statements such as "You're being totally unreasonable." Instead, share what *you* feel and want to do. For example: "I feel worried that we don't have enough information to write a paper. I suggest that we talk to our instructor and ask for more sources to check."

- **Focus on solutions.** When group members disagree, avoid arguments about who is right and who is wrong. Instead, restate the conflict as a question that invites

a solution for everybody, such as, "How can we even out the work load so that no one feels overwhelmed?"

PUT THE FINISHING TOUCHES ON YOUR PROJECT

Many groups come to a halt the moment that they turn in their final project. This deprives the members of the chance to review their group experience, draw lessons from it, and develop continuing relationships. Instead, make it a habit to do the following:

- Send all group members an e-mail thanking them for their work.

- Invite group members to get together socially after the course, if that seems appropriate.

- Keep your own copies of the materials that the group created and turned in to your instructor.

- Write Discovery Statements that describe what worked well in your group and what you'd like to improve.

- Write Intention Statements about what you'll do differently to make your next group project even more effective. ▣

Using technology to collaborate

© Bernhard Lang/Getty Images

When planning group projects, look for tools that allow you to create, edit, and share documents, spreadsheets, drawings, and presentations. Ideally, the technology that you choose will also allow team members to do the following:

- Update files in real time
- Track changes or version history in shared documents

- Share calendars and project-related action lists
- Send instant messages
- Set up video conferences
- Create video and audio recordings of team meetings
- Back up data online (in the "cloud")
- Use mobile devices to access project files

You can find a growing list of applications for these purposes. Their capabilities and prices vary widely, though several are generous with features and also free. Some current options include Google+ Hangouts, AnyMeeting (www.anymeeting.com), Skype (www.skype.com), GoToMeeting (www.gotomeeting.com) and Zoho collaboration applications (www.zoho.com). For more ideas,

do an Internet search with the key words *collaborate online*.

Equally important are "people skills." Whatever technology you use, set up a process to make sure that everyone's voice gets heard during a virtual meeting. People who get silenced will probably tune out.

Also function as a professional whenever you're online. Team members might get to know you mainly through e-mails and instant messages. Consider the impression you're making with your online presence. Avoid slang, idioms, sarcastic humor, and other expressions that can create misunderstanding. A small dose of civility can make a large difference in the quality of your virtual team experience.

© iStockphoto.com /DNY59

Managing CONFLICT

Conflict management is one of the most practical skills you'll ever learn. Here are strategies that can help.

The first five strategies discussed are about dealing with the *content* of a conflict—defining the problem, exploring viewpoints, and discovering solutions. The remaining strategies are about finding a *process* for resolving any conflict, no matter what the content.

To bring these strategies to life, think of ways to use them in managing a conflict that you face right now.

FOCUS ON CONTENT

Back up to common ground. Conflict heightens the differences between people. When this happens, it's easy to forget how much we still agree with each other.

As a first step in managing conflict, back up to common ground. List all of the points on which you are *not* in conflict: "I know that we disagree about how much to spend on a new car, but we do agree that the old one needs to be replaced." Often, such comments put the problem in perspective and pave the way for a solution.

State the problem. Using "I" messages, as explained earlier in this chapter, state the problem. Tell people what you observe, feel, think, want, and intend to do. Allow the other people in a particular conflict to do the same.

Each person might have a different perception of the problem. That's fine. Let the conflict come into clear focus. It's hard to fix something unless people agree on what's broken.

Remember that the way you state the problem largely determines the solution. Defining the problem in a new way can open up a world of possibilities. For example, "I need a new roommate" is a problem statement that dictates one solution. "We could use some agreements about who cleans the apartment" opens up more options, such as resolving a conflict about who will wash the dishes tonight.

State all points of view. If you want to defuse tension or defensiveness, set aside your opinions for a moment. Take the time to understand the other points of view. Sum up those viewpoints in words that the other parties can accept. When people feel that they've been heard, they're often more willing to listen.

Ask for complete communication. In times of conflict, we often say one thing and mean another. So before responding to what the other person says, use active listening. Check to see whether you have correctly received that person's message by saying, "What I'm hearing you say is . . . Did I get it correctly?"

Focus on solutions. After stating the problem, dream up as many solutions as you can. Be outrageous. Don't hold back. Quantity—not quality—is the key. If you get stuck, restate the problem and continue brainstorming.

Next, evaluate the solutions you brainstormed. Discard the unacceptable ones. Talk about which solutions will work and how difficult they will be to implement. You might hit upon a totally new solution.

Choose one solution that is most acceptable to everyone involved, and implement it. Agree on who is going to do what by when. Then keep your agreements.

Finally, evaluate the effectiveness of your solution. If it works, pat yourselves on the back. If not, make changes or implement a new solution.

Focus on the future. Instead of rehashing the past, talk about new possibilities. Think about what you can do to prevent problems in the future. State how you intend to change, and ask others for their contributions to the solution.

FOCUS ON PROCESS

Commit to the relationship. The thorniest conflicts usually arise between people who genuinely care for each other. Begin by affirming your commitment to the other person: "I care about you, and I want this relationship to last. So I'm willing to do whatever it takes to resolve this problem." Also ask the other person for a similar commitment.

Allow strong feelings. Permitting conflict can also mean permitting emotion. Being upset is all right. Feeling angry is often appropriate. Crying is okay. Allowing other people to see the strength of our feelings can help resolve the conflict. This suggestion can be especially useful during times when differences are so extreme that reaching common ground seems impossible.

Expressing the full range of your feelings can transform the conflict. Often what's on the far side of anger is love. When we express and release resentment, we might discover genuine compassion in its place.

Notice your need to be "right." Some people approach conflict as a situation where only one person wins. That person has the "right" point of view. Everyone else loses.

When this happens, step back. See whether you can approach the situation in a neutral way. Define the conflict as a problem to be solved, not as a contest to be won. Explore the possibility that you might be mistaken. There might be more than one acceptable solution. The other person might simply have a different learning style than yours. Let go of being "right," and aim for being effective at resolving conflict instead.

Sometimes this means apologizing. Conflict sometimes arises from our own errors. Others might move quickly to end the conflict when we acknowledge this fact and ask for forgiveness.

Slow down the communication. In times of great conflict, people often talk all at once. Words fly like speeding bullets, and no one listens. Chances for resolving the conflict take a nosedive.

When everyone is talking at once, choose either to listen or to talk—not both at the same time. Just send your message. Or just receive the other person's message. Usually, this technique slows down the pace and allows everyone to become more levelheaded.

To slow down the communication even more, take a break. Depending on the level of conflict, this might mean anything from a few minutes to a few days.

A related suggestion is to do something nonthreatening together. Share an activity with the others involved that's not a source of conflict.

Communicate in writing. What can be difficult to say to another person face-to-face might be effectively communicated in writing. When people in conflict write letters or e-mails to each other, they automatically apply many of the suggestions in this article. Writing is a way to slow down the communication and ensure that only one person at a time is sending a message.

There is a drawback to this tactic, though: It's possible for people to misunderstand what you say in a letter or e-mail. To avoid further problems, make clear what you are *not* saying: "I am saying that I want to be alone for a few days. I am *not* saying that I want you to stay away forever." Saying what you are *not* saying is often useful in face-to-face communication as well.

Before you send your letter or e-mail, put yourself in the shoes of the person who will receive it. Imagine how your comments could be misinterpreted. Then rewrite your note, correcting any wording that might be open to misinterpretation.

© Pete Saloutos/Shutterstock.com

There's another way to get the problem off your chest, especially when strong, negative feelings are involved: Write the nastiest, meanest e-mail response you can imagine, leaving off the address of the recipient so you don't accidentally send it. Let all of your frustration, anger, and venom flow onto the page. Be as mean and blaming as possible. When you have cooled off, see whether there is anything else you want to add.

Then destroy the letter or delete the e-mail. Your writing has served its purpose. Chances are that you've calmed down and are ready to engage in skillful conflict management.

Get an objective viewpoint. With the agreement of everyone involved, set up a video camera, and record a conversation about the conflict. In the midst of a raging argument, when emotions run high, it's almost impossible to see ourselves objectively. Let the camera be your unbiased observer. Another way to get an objective viewpoint is to use a mediator—an objective, unbiased third party. Even an untrained mediator—as long as it's someone who is not a party to the conflict—can do much to decrease tension. Mediators can help everyone get their point of view across. The mediator's role is not to give advice, but to keep the discussion on track and moving toward a solution.

Allow for cultural differences. People respond to conflict in different ways, depending on their cultural background. Some stand close, speak loudly, and make direct eye contact. Other people avert their eyes, mute their voices, and increase physical distance.

When it seems to you that other people are sidestepping or escalating a conflict, consider whether your reaction is based on cultural bias.

Agree to disagree. Sometimes we say all we have to say on an issue. We do all of the problem solving we can do. We get all points of view across. And the conflict still remains, staring us right in the face.

What's left is to recognize that honest disagreement is a fact of life. We can peacefully coexist with other people—and respect them—even though we don't agree on fundamental issues. Conflict can be accepted even when it is not resolved.

See the conflict within you. Sometimes the turmoil we see in the outside world has its source in our own inner world. A cofounder of Alcoholics Anonymous put it this way: "It is a spiritual axiom that every time we are disturbed, no matter what the cause, there is something awry with us."

When we're angry or upset, we can take a minute to look inside. Perhaps we are ready to take offense—waiting to pounce on something the other person said. Perhaps, without realizing it, we did something to create the conflict. Or maybe the other person is simply saying what we don't want to admit is true.

When these things happen, we can shine a light on our own thinking. A simple spot-check might help the conflict disappear—right before our eyes.

Take these ideas to work. If you get into a personal conflict on the job, choose a suggestion from this article and use it. For example, slow down the communication during a conflict by asking people to put their viewpoints in writing. Doing this can immediately lower the tension of conflicts with supervisors, clients, customers, and employees. ■

Interactive

Journal Entry 19
Discovery/Intention Statement

Recreate a relationship

Think about one of your relationships for a few minutes. It can involve a parent, sibling, spouse, child, friend, hairdresser, or anyone else. Write down some things that are not working in the relationship. What bugs you? What do you find irritating or unsatisfying?

I discovered that . . .

_____

_____

_____

_____

Now think for a moment about what you want from this relationship. More attention? Less nagging? More openness, trust, financial security, or freedom? Choose a suggestion from this chapter, and describe how you could use it to make the relationship work.

I intend to . . .

_____

_____

_____

_____

_____

© simonox/Shutterstock.com

FIVE WAYS
to say no . . .
RESPECTFULLY

All your study plans can go down the drain when a friend says, "Time to party!" Sometimes, succeeding in school means replying with a graceful and firm *no*.

Students in higher education tend to have many commitments. Saying no helps you to prevent an overloaded schedule that compromises your health and grade point average. You can use five strategies to say no in a respectful way—gracefully.

Think critically about your assumptions. An inability to say no can spring from the assumption that you'll lose friends if you state what you really want. But consider this: If you cannot say no, then you are not in charge of your time. You've given that right to whoever wants to interrupt you. This is not a friendship based on equality. True friends will respect your wishes.

Plan your refusal. You might find it easier to say no when you don't have to grasp for words. Choose some key words and phrases in advance—for example, "I'd love to, but not today"; "Thanks for asking. I have a huge test tomorrow and want to study"; or "I'd prefer not to do anything tonight; do you want to grab lunch tomorrow instead?"

When you refuse, align your verbal and nonverbal messages. Reinforce your words with a firm voice and a posture that communicates confidence.

Avoid apologies or qualifiers. People give away their power when they couch their no's in phrases such as "I'm sorry, but I just don't know whether I want to" or "Would you get upset if I said no?"

You don't have to apologize for being in charge of your life. It's okay to say no. Give up the need for excuses. Don't assume that you have to explain or defend your response. Saying no for your own reasons is often enough.

Wait for the request. People who worry about saying no often give in to a request before it's actually been made. Wait until you hear a question. "Time to party!" is not a question. Nor is it a call to action. Save your response until you hear a specific request, such as "Would you go to a party with me?"

Remember that one *no* leads to another *yes*. *Yes* and *no* are complementary, not contradictory. Saying no to one activity allows you to say yes to something that's more important right now. Saying no to a movie allows you to say yes to outlining a paper or reading a textbook chapter. You can say an unqualified yes to the next social activity—and enjoy it more—after you've completed some key tasks on your to-do list. ■

You deserve compliments

Some people find it more difficult to accept compliments than criticisms. Here are some hints for handling compliments.

Accept the compliment. People sometimes respond to praise with "Oh, it's really nothing" or "This old thing? I've had it for years." This type of response undermines both you and the person who sent the compliment.

Choose another time to deliver your own compliments. Automatically returning a compliment can appear suspiciously polite and insincere.

Let the compliment stand. "Do you really think so?" questions the integrity of the message. It can also sound as if you're fishing for more compliments.

Accepting compliments is not the same as being conceited. If you're in doubt about how to respond, just smile and say, "Thank you!" This simple response affirms the compliment, along with the person who delivered it.

You are worthy and capable. Allow people to acknowledge that fact.

Exercise 24 VIPs (Very Important Persons)

Step 1

Under the column titled "Name," write the names of at least seven people who have positively influenced your life. They might be relatives, friends, teachers, or perhaps persons you have never met. (Complete each step before moving on.)

Step 2

In the next column, rate your gratitude for this person's influence (from 1 to 5, with 1 being a little grateful and 5 being extremely grateful).

Step 3

In the third column, rate how fully you have communicated your appreciation to this person (again, 1 to 5, with 1 being not communicated and 5 being fully communicated).

Step 4

In the final column, put a U to indicate the persons with whom you have unfinished business (such as an important communication that you have not yet sent).

Name	Grateful (1–5)	Communicated (1–5)	U
1.			
2.			
3.			
4.			
5.			
6.			
7.			

Step 5

Now select two persons with U's beside their names, and write each of them a letter. Express the love, tenderness, and joy you feel toward them. Tell them exactly how they have helped change your life and how glad you are that they did.

Step 6

You also have an impact on others. Write the names of people whose lives you have influenced. Consider sharing with these people why you enjoy being a part of their lives.

_____

_____

_____

_____

_____

_____

Fuse/Getty Images

5 STEPS TO **EFFECTIVE COMPLAINTS**

Sometimes relationship building means making a complaint. Whining, blaming, pouting, screaming, and yelling insults usually don't get results. Consider the following suggestions instead.

1 **Go to the source.** Start with the person who is most directly involved with the problem. When you're in school, that person is usually an instructor. Give this person the first chance to resolve an issue. Instructors usually appreciate feedback, and they can't always read a student's mind to know when a problem occurs.

2 **Present the facts without blaming anyone.** Consider how it might feel to receive complaints like these: "I put a lot of work into this project, but you gave me a C." "Your class is boring." "I just can't trust you."

Your complaint will carry more weight if you document the facts instead. Keep track of names and dates. Note what actions were promised and what results actually occurred.

3 **Learn about other options.** Schools have policies and procedures related to student complaints. Look for them in your school's catalog and Web site. Student government is also a potential resource.

At many schools you can talk to a student or staff ombudsman—someone who is trained to help resolve conflicts between students and instructors.

4 **Ask for commitments.** When you find someone who is willing to solve your problem, get him to say exactly what he is going to do, and when.

5 **Persist.** Assume that others are on your team. Many people are out there to help you. State what you intend to do, and ask for their partnership.

Today many companies shield themselves from complaints with a voicemail maze and lengthy "hold" times. This calls for patience and persistence. It's worth it. Your complaint deserves to be heard. ▪

Criticism is constructive

Although receiving criticism is rarely fun, it is often educational. Here are some ways to get the most value from it.

Avoid finding fault. When your mind is occupied with finding fault in others, you aren't open to hearing constructive comments about yourself.

Take criticism seriously. Some people laugh or joke to cover up their anger or embarrassment at being criticized. A humorous reaction on your part can be mistaken for a lack of concern.

React to criticism with acceptance. Most people don't enjoy pointing out another's faults. Your denial, argument, or joking makes it more difficult for them to give honest feedback. You can disagree with criticism and still accept it calmly.

Keep criticism in perspective. Avoid blowing the criticism out of proportion. The purpose of criticism is to generate positive change and self-improvement. There's no need to overreact to it.

Listen without defensiveness. You can't hear the criticism if you're busy framing your rebuttal.

Staying safe on
SOCIAL NETWORKS

Social networks create value. Web sites such as Facebook, Twitter, Google+, and LinkedIn are known as places to share news, photos, and personal profiles. You can also use such sites to form study groups, promote special events, and make job contacts.

Activity in online communities can also have unexpected consequences. For some students, social networking takes time away from studying and other activities that contribute to long-term goals. Other students get involved in "cyberbullying"—hate speech or threats of violence. And, some students find that embarrassing details from their online profiles come back to haunt them years later—especially when they're looking for a job.

You can use simple strategies to stay in charge of your safety, reputation, and integrity any time you connect with people online.

Post only what you want made public and permanent.

The Internet as a whole is a public medium. This is true of its online communities as well. Avoid oversharing. Post only the kind of information about yourself that you *want* to be made public—forever.

Friends, relatives, university administrators, potential employers, and police officers might be able to access your online profile. Don't post anything that could embarrass you later. (This is a good reason to avoid social networking if you're under the influence of alcohol or other drugs.) Act today to protect the person that you want to be four or five years from now.

Remember that there is no delete key for the Internet. Anything you post online will *stay* online for a long time. And anyone with Internet access can take your words and images and post them on a Web site or distribute them via e-mail to damage your reputation. In the virtual world, you never know who's following you.

To avoid unwanted encounters with members of online communities, also avoid posting the following:

- Your home address
- Your school address
- Your phone number
- Your birth date
- Your screen name for instant messaging
- Your class schedule

> *Don't post anything that could embarrass you later. Act today to protect the person that you want to be four or five years from now.*

- Your financial information, such as bank account numbers, credit card numbers, your social security number, or information about an eBay or PayPal account
- Information about places that you regularly go at certain times of the day
- Information about places you plan to visit in the future
- Provocative pictures or messages with sexual innuendos
- Pictures of yourself at school or at work
- Plans for vacation or out-of-town visits

To further protect your safety, don't add strangers to your list of online friends.

Use similar caution and common sense when joining groups. Signing up for a group with a name like *Binge Drinking Forever* can have consequences for years to come.

Also avoid flirting while you're online. People may not be who they say they are.

Use privacy features. Many online communities offer options for restricting how many people can access your updates and profile. When in doubt, use the most restrictive settings possible. Also consider creating both private and public profiles. For specific instructions, look for a link on each site titled "Help," "Frequently Asked Questions," "Security Features," "Account Settings," or "Privacy Settings." For further protection:

- Review and update your list of followers or friends on a regular basis.
- Find out which third-party applications have permission to access your profile. If you're not familiar with an application or unsure about its privacy policies, revoke its access.
- Protect your profile with a secure password and change it frequently.
- Adjust your profile settings to reduce the number of e-mail notifications and alerts that you get.
- Restrict the number of people that you "friend" or follow. Think twice about connecting with coworkers and supervisors.
- Check the address bar of your browser whenever you use a social networking site. Make sure the site address begins with *https*. The *s* means that the site has built in an extra level of privacy and security.

Monitor your online presence. Use Google or another popular search engine to key in your name. This will reveal what another person—such as a potential employer—might see when he or she goes online to learn about you. If someone else has posted a fake profile in your name, this is one way to find out. Contact your school's information technology department or computer help desk for help in deleting such profiles.

Respect the privacy of others. Post photos of other people only with their permission. Also take care not to reveal confidential or potentially embarrassing information about the people in your network.

"Friend" people with care. You do not have to accept every friend request or "follow" every person who chooses to follow you. Remember that many instructors will not connect with students in social networks, and some schools have policies to discourage this. Networks such as Facebook are by definition social Web sites. The relationship between students and instructors is professional—not social.

Be cautious about meeting community members in person. Because people can give misleading or false information about themselves online, avoid meeting someone you only know online in person. If you do opt for a face-to-face meeting, choose a public place, and bring along a friend you trust.

Report malicious content. If you find online content that you consider offensive or dangerous, report it to site administrators. In many online communities, you can do this anonymously. You can help to prevent online forms of intolerance, prejudice, and discrimination. Set a positive counterexample by posting messages that demonstrate acceptance of diversity.

Remember netiquette. The word *etiquette* refers to common courtesy in interpersonal relationships. Its online equivalent is called *netiquette*—a set of guidelines for using computers, cell phones, or any other form of technology.

Certain kinds of exchanges can send the tone of online communications—including social networking, e-mail messages, and blog postings—into the gutter. To promote a cordial online community, abide by the following guidelines:

- *Respect others' time.* People often turn to the Internet with the hope of saving time—not wasting it. You can accommodate their desires by typing concise messages. Adopt the habit of getting to your point, sticking to it, and getting to the end.

- *Fine-tune the mechanics.* Proofread your message for spelling and grammar—just as you would a printed message. Some e-mail programs have built-in spelling checkers as an optional tool. Give your readers the gift of clarity and precision. Use electronic communications as a chance to hone your writing skills.

- *Avoid typing passages in ALL UPPERCASE LETTERS.* This is the online equivalent of shouting.

- *Design your messages for fast retrieval.* Avoid graphics and attachments that take a long time to download, tying up your recipient's computer.

- *Remember that the message is missing the emotion.* When you communicate online, the people who receive your e-mail will miss out on voice inflection and nonverbal cues that are present in face-to-face communication. Without these cues, words can be easily misinterpreted. Reread your message before sending it to be sure you have clarified what you want to say and how you feel.

- *Avoid writing and then immediately sending e-mails, text messages, and status updates when you feel angry.* Instead, write a rough draft of what you want to say, and let it sit for 24 hours. Then reread and revise your message when you feel calmer. Waiting before you click "Send" is a sign of emotional intelligence.

- *Keep the context in mind.* Whenever you're online for job-related or academic purposes, edit and proofread your updates and posts with special attention. Write with a more formal voice—the same style that you would use for a research paper.

The cornerstone of netiquette is to remember that the recipient on the other end is a human being. Whenever you're at a keyboard or cell phone typing up messages, ask yourself one question: "Would I say this to the person's face?" ■

Text message etiquette— 5 key points

1. **Keep it short.** Limit text messages to about 150 characters. That's two to three sentences. If you go longer, your phone might split the message in two or even drop the last few words. In addition, long texts can be confusing. Send an e-mail or make a phone call instead.

2. **Double-check the outgoing number.** If a message intended for your boyfriend or girlfriend ends up going to your boss, the results can be alarming.

3. **At work and in other public places, set your phone on vibrate.** No one else wants to hear how many text messages you're getting.

4. **Keep the time in mind.** Save 2:00 a.m. text messages for special circumstances and your closest friends. A text can ring at the same volume as a phone call and wake people up.

5. **Reflect on the number of messages you send to each person.** Replacing in-person and phone contact with texting might send a message that the relationship is a low priority.

Three phases of EFFECTIVE WRITING

Effective writing is essential to your success. Papers, presentations, essay tests, e-mail, social networking sites—and even the occasional text message—call for your ability to communicate ideas with force and clarity.

This is another article that you can take to work. The ability to write is in demand. To verify this, scan job postings and notice how many of them call for the skill of writing.

Most new products and services—especially those that involve high budgets—begin with a written proposal. Reports, e-mail messages, web pages, and other documents are essential to the flow of ideas and information.

People without writing skills can only influence people through direct contact. If you can write a persuasive memo, however, your ideas can spread to hundreds of people.

This chapter outlines a three-phase process for writing anything:

1. Getting ready to write
2. Writing a first draft
3. Revising your draft

PHASE 1: GETTING READY TO WRITE

Schedule and list writing tasks. You can divide the ultimate goal—a finished paper—into smaller steps that you can tackle right away. Estimate how long it will take to complete each step. Start with the date your paper is due, and work backward to the present. Say that the due date is December 1, and you have about three months to write the paper. To give yourself a cushion, schedule November 20 as your targeted completion date. Plan what you want to get done by November 1, and then list what you want to get done by October 1.

Choose a topic. It's easy to put off writing if you have a hard time choosing a topic. However, it is almost impossible to make a wrong choice of topic at this stage. You can choose a different topic later if you find the one you've chosen isn't working out.

Using your instructor's guidelines for the paper or speech, write down the list of possible topics that you created earlier. Then choose one. If you can't decide, use scissors to cut your list into single items, put them in a box, and pull one out. To avoid getting stuck on this step, set a precise timeline: "I will choose a topic by 4:00 p.m. on Wednesday."

There's no need to brainstorm topics in isolation. You can harness the energy and the natural creative power of a group to assist you in creating topics for your paper.

Narrow your topic. The most common pitfall is selecting a topic that's too broad. "Harriet Tubman" is not a useful topic for your American history paper because it's too broad. Covering that topic would take hundreds of pages. Instead, consider "Harriet Tubman's activities as a Union spy during the Civil War." Your topic statement can function as a working title.

Write a thesis statement. Clarify what you want to say by summarizing it in one concise sentence. This sentence, called a *thesis statement*, refines your working title. It also helps in making a preliminary outline.

You might write a thesis statement such as "Harriet Tubman's activities with the Underground Railroad led to a relationship with the Union army during the Civil War." A thesis statement that's clear and to the point can make your paper easier to write. Remember, you can always rewrite your thesis statement as you learn more about your topic.

A thesis statement is different from a topic. Like newspaper headlines, a thesis statement makes an assertion or describes an action. It is expressed in a complete sentence including a verb. "Diversity" is a topic. "Cultural diversity is valuable" is a thesis statement.

Consider your purpose. Effective writing flows from a purpose. Discuss the purpose of your assignment with your instructor. Also think about how you'd like your reader or listener to respond after considering your ideas. Do you want your audience to think differently, to feel differently, or to take a certain action?

How you answer these questions greatly affects your writing strategy. If you want someone to think differently, make your writing clear and logical. Support your assertions with evidence. If you want someone to feel differently, consider crafting a story. Write about a character your audience can empathize with, and tell how that character resolves a problem that the audience can relate to. And if your purpose is to move the reader into action, explain exactly what steps to take, and offer solid benefits for doing so.

To clarify your purpose, state it in one sentence, for example, "I will define the term *success* in such a clear and convincing way that I win a scholarship from the publisher of this textbook."

Do initial research. At the initial stage, the objective of your research is not to uncover specific facts about your topic. That comes later. First, you want to gain an overview of the subject. Discover the structure of your topic—its major divisions and branches.

Say that you want to persuade the reader to vote for a certain candidate. You must first learn enough about this person to summarize his background and state his stands on key issues.

Outline. An outline is a kind of map. When you follow a map, you avoid getting lost. Likewise, an outline keeps you from wandering off the topic.

To start an outline, gather a stack of 3 × 5 cards. Brainstorm ideas you want to include in your paper. Write one phrase or sentence per card. Then experiment with the cards. Group them into separate stacks, each stack representing one major category. After that, arrange the stacks in order. Finally, arrange the cards within each stack in a logical order. Rearrange them until you discover an organization that you like. If you write on a computer, consider using the outlining feature of your word-processing software.

PHASE 2: WRITING A FIRST DRAFT

Gather your notes and outline. If you've planned your writing project and completed your research, you've already done much of the hard work. Now you can relax into writing your first draft. To create your draft, gather

☐ Avoid ~~at all costs and at all times the really, really terrible mistake of~~ using ~~way too many~~ unnecessary words, ~~a mistake that some student writers often make when they sit down to write papers for the various courses in which they participate at the fine institutions of higher learning which they are fortunate to attend.~~

© Cengage Learning

your notes and arrange them to follow your outline. Then write about the ideas in your notes. Write in paragraphs, with one idea per paragraph. If you have organized your notes logically, related facts will appear close to one another.

Ease into it. Some people find that it works well to forget the word *writing*. Instead, they ease into the task with activities that help generate ideas. You can free associate, cluster, meditate, daydream, doodle, draw diagrams, visualize the event you want to describe, talk into a voice recorder—anything that gets you started.

Remember that the first draft is not for keeps. You can worry about quality later, when you revise. Your goal at this point is simply to generate lots of material. Later, during phase 3, you can revise and polish it.

Speak it. To get ideas flowing, start talking. Admit your confusion or lack of clear ideas. Then just speak. By putting your thoughts into words, you'll start thinking more clearly. Novelist E. M. Forster said, "'Speak before you think' is creation's motto."[7]

Use free writing. Free writing, a technique championed by writing teacher Peter Elbow, sends a depth probe into your creative mind.[8] There's only one rule in free writing: Write without stopping. Set a time limit—say, 10 minutes—and keep your pencil in motion or your fingers dancing across the keyboard the whole time. Give yourself permission to keep writing. Ignore the urge to stop and rewrite, even if you think what you've written isn't very good. There's no need to worry about spelling, punctuation, or grammar. It's okay if you stray from the initial subject. Just keep writing, and let the ideas flow. Experiment with free writing as soon as your instructor assigns a paper.

Make writing a habit. The word *inspiration* is not in the working vocabulary for many professional writers. Instead of waiting for inspiration to strike, they simply make a habit of writing at a certain time each day. You can use the same strategy. Schedule a block of time to write your first draft. The very act of writing can breed inspiration.

Respect your deep mind. Part of the process of writing takes place outside our awareness. There's nothing mysterious about this process. Many people report that ideas come to them while they're doing something totally unrelated to writing. Often this happens after they've been grappling with a question and have reached a point where they feel stuck. It's like the composer who said, "There I was, sitting and eating a sandwich, and all of a sudden this darn tune pops into my head." You can trust your deep mind. It's writing while you eat, sleep, and brush your teeth.

Get physical. Writing, like jogging or playing tennis, is a physical activity. You can move your body in ways that are in tune with the flow of your ideas. While working on the first draft, take breaks. Go for a walk. Speak or sing your ideas out loud. From time to time, practice relaxation techniques and breathe deeply.

PHASE 3: REVISING YOUR DRAFT

Plan to revise a paper two or three times. Make a clean copy of each revision, and then let the last revised draft sit for at least three or four days.

Schedule time for rewrites before you begin, and schedule at least one day between revisions so that you can let the material sit. On Tuesday night, you might think your writing sings the song of beautiful language. On Wednesday, you will see that those same words, such as

the phrase "sings the song of beautiful language," belong in the trash basket.

Keep in mind the saying "Write in haste; revise at leisure." When you edit and revise, slow down and take a microscope to your work. One guideline is to allow 50 percent of writing time for planning, researching, and writing the first draft. Then give the remaining 50 percent to revising.

While you're in the revising phase, consider making an appointment to see your instructor during office hours. Bring along a current draft of your paper. Be willing to share your thesis and outline. Ask for revision tips. If your school has a writing assistance center, see someone there as well.

One effective way to revise your paper is to read it out loud. The eyes tend to fill in the blanks in our own writing. The combination of voice and ears forces us to pay attention to the details.

Another technique is to ask other people to review your paper. If you do this in class, it's called peer editing. This is never a substitute for your own review, but other people can often see mistakes you miss. Remember, when other people criticize or review your work, they're not attacking you. They're just commenting on your paper. With a little practice, you can actually learn to welcome feedback.

Writing for online readers

Much of your writing may take the form of e-mail messages and text for Web sites. Your readers will be pressed for time and impatient. Do them a favor by getting to the point without taking detours.

Write e-mail that gets results. Be conscious of the amount of e-mail that busy people receive. Send e-mail messages only to the people who need them, and only when necessary.

Start by using a professional e-mail address. Avoid anything that resembles *iliketoparty@yahoo.com*.

Keep the "To" line blank until you've reread and revised your message. That way you'll avoid the main e-mail pitfall—accidentally hitting "Send" too soon. This is especially important for work-related messages and sensitive personal messages.

Next, write an informative subject line. Rather than offering a generic description of your message, include a capsule summary—a complete sentence with the main point of your message.

Write the body of your message in complete, grammatically correct sentences. Highlight important items such as meeting dates and times.

After drafting your message, look at it again to see if you can make it shorter. Overly long e-mails are almost begging to be ignored or trashed.

Use the "Reply to All" feature only when everyone who received a message truly needs to know your response. People will appreciate your help in keeping their incoming messages to a minimum.

Write for Web site readers. Jakob Nielsen, author of *Designing Web Usability: The Practice of Simplicity*, suggests that effectively written web pages have these attributes:

- *Concise*—free of needless words and organized so that the main point of each section and paragraph comes at the beginning.

- *Scannable*—prepared with subheadings and visuals that allow readers to skim and quickly find what they need.

- *Objective*—packed with credible facts and free of "hype," that is, vague or exaggerated claims presented without evidence.[9]

Following these guidelines can assist you in *all* forms of business writing.

When it's your turn to edit someone else's writing, remember two guidelines: First, be positive. Find something that you like about the paper and talk about that. Second, offer a specific suggestion. Begin this statement with words such as: "I think your paper would be even stronger if . . ."

After getting feedback on your draft, revise it while keeping the following suggestions in mind.

Cut. Look for excess baggage. Avoid at all costs and at all times the really, really terrible mistake of using way too many unnecessary words, a mistake that some student writers often make when they sit down to write papers for the various courses in which they participate at the fine institutions of higher learning that they are fortunate enough to attend. (Example: The previous sentence could be edited to "Avoid unnecessary words.")

Approach your rough draft as if it were a chunk of granite from which you will chisel the final product. In the end, much of your first draft will be lying on the floor. What is left will be the clean, clear, polished product. Sometimes the revisions are painful. Sooner or later, every writer invents a phrase that is truly clever but makes no contribution to the purpose of the paper. Grit your teeth and let it go.

> *Approach your rough draft as if it were a chunk of granite from which you will chisel the final product. In the end, much of your first draft will be lying on the floor. What is left will be the clean, clear, polished product. Sometimes the revisions are painful.*

Note: For maximum efficiency, make the larger cuts first—sections, chapters, pages. Then go for the smaller cuts—paragraphs, sentences, phrases, words. Stay within the word limit that your instructor assigns.

Paste. In deleting both larger and smaller passages in your first draft, you've probably removed some of the original transitions and connecting ideas. The next task is to rearrange what's left of your paper or speech so that it flows logically. Look for consistency within paragraphs and for transitions from paragraph to paragraph and section to section.

If all or part of your draft doesn't hang together, reorder your ideas. Imagine yourself with scissors and glue, cutting the paper into scraps—one scrap for each point. Then paste these points down in a new, more logical order.

Fix. Now it's time to look at individual words and phrases. Define any terms that the reader might not know, putting them in plain English whenever you can. Scan your paper for any passages that are written in the language of texting or instant messaging. Rewrite those into full sentences.

In general, rely on vivid nouns and verbs. Using too many adjectives and adverbs weakens your message and adds unnecessary bulk to your writing. Write about the

Befriend your word processor

Today most writing in higher education and the workplace is done with Microsoft Word, a word-processing program. Knowing how to use some common features of "Word" will help you get up to speed with almost any word-processing software.

To get a current list of Word commands, go online to http://office.microsoft.com, find a search box, and enter *keyboard shortcuts microsoft word*. Find out how to open documents, create documents, apply templates, track changes, insert comments, print documents, and save your work. (That last command is the most important one you will ever learn.)

Other companies offer free or low-cost word-processing software with commands and features similar to Word. Examples are Google Docs (drive.google.com) and Zoho Docs (www.zoho.com/docs).

Another option is to use plain text editors. Though they offer fewer features than Word, plain text editors are far less expensive, handle many common writing tasks, and are compatible with most other software. NotePad is a text editor that comes free with the Windows operating system, and TextEdit is bundled with Mac OSX.

In any case, check with your instructors to find out which software and document formats that they will accept.

details, and be specific. Also, use the active rather than the passive verbs.

Instead of writing in the passive voice:
A project was initiated.
You can use the active voice:
The research team began a project.

Instead of writing verbosely:
After making a timely arrival and perspicaciously observing the unfolding events, I emerged totally and gloriously victorious.
You can write to the point, as Julius Caesar did:
I came, I saw, I conquered.

Instead of writing vaguely:
The speaker made effective use of the television medium, asking in no uncertain terms that we change our belief systems.
You can write specifically:
The reformed criminal stared straight into the television camera and shouted, "Take a good look at what you're doing! Will it get you what you really want?"

Prepare. In a sense, any paper is a sales effort. If you hand in a paper that is wearing wrinkled jeans, its hair tangled and unwashed and its shoes untied, your instructor is less likely to buy it. To avoid this situation, format your paper following accepted standards for margin widths, endnotes, title pages, and other details.

Ask your instructor for specific instructions on how to cite the sources used in writing your paper. You can find useful guidelines in the *MLA Handbook for Writers of Research Papers,* a book from the Modern Language Association. Also visit the MLA Web site at **www.mla.org/style**.

If you cut and paste material from a Web page directly into your paper, be sure to place that material in quotation marks and cite the source. And before referencing an e-mail message, verify the sender's identity. Remember that anyone sending e-mail can pretend to be someone else.

Use quality paper for your final version. For an even more professional appearance, bind your paper with a plastic or paper cover.

> *In a sense, any paper is a sales effort. If you hand in a paper that is wearing wrinkled jeans, its hair tangled and unwashed and its shoes untied, your instructor is less likely to buy it.*

Proof. As you ease down the homestretch, read your revised paper one more time. This time, go for the big picture and look for the following:

- A clear thesis statement
- Sentences that introduce your topic, guide the reader through the major sections of your paper, and summarize your conclusions
- Details—such as quotations, examples, and statistics—that support your conclusions
- Lean sentences that have been purged of needless words
- Plenty of action verbs and concrete, specific nouns

Finally, look over your paper with an eye for spelling and grammar mistakes. If you're writing with software that checks for such errors, take advantage of this feature. Also keep in mind that even the best software will miss some mistakes. Computers still cannot replace a skilled human proofreader.

When you're through proofreading, take a minute to savor the result. You've just witnessed something of a miracle—the mind attaining clarity and resolution. That's the "aha!" in writing. ◼

'YOU'VE COPIED ALL THIS OFF THE INTERNET...'

Grizelda/CartoonStock

Academic integrity: AVOID PLAGIARISM

Using another person's words, images, or other original creations without giving proper credit is called plagiarism. *Plagiarism amounts to taking someone else's work and presenting it as your own—the equivalent of cheating on a test.*

Higher education consists of a community of scholars who trust one another to speak and write with integrity. Plagiarism undermines this trust. The consequences of plagiarism can range from a failing grade to expulsion from school.

Plagiarism can be unintentional. Some students don't understand the research process. Sometimes they leave writing until the last minute and don't take the time to organize their sources of information.

Students raised in cultures where identity is based on group membership rather than individual achievement may find it hard to understand how an individual can own creative work. Remember, however, that even accidental plagiarism can lead to penalties.

To avoid plagiarism, ask an instructor where you can find your school's written policy on this issue. Read this document carefully, and ask questions about *anything* you don't understand.

The basic guideline for preventing plagiarism is to cite a source for any fact or idea that is new to you. These include words and images created by another person. The overall goal is to clearly distinguish your own work from the work of others. A secondary goal is to give enough information about your sources so that they are easy for other people to find and use for themselves. There are several ways to ensure that you meet both of these goals consistently.

Know the perils of "paper mills." A big part of the problem is misuse of the Internet. Anyone with a computer can access thousands of Web pages on a given topic. Images and text from those sources are easily copied and pasted into another document. Technology makes it easy to forget that some information is free for the taking—and some is privately owned.

Plagiarism is a now a growth industry. A quick Web search will uncover hundreds of online businesses that sell term papers, essays, and book reports. These businesses are often called "paper mills." Some of them offer to customize their products for an additional fee. Even so, these services are based on plagiarism.

Students who use these services might answer, "When I buy a paper online, it's not plagiarism. I paid for those words, so now they're mine." But in fact, those words were still created by someone else. Plagiarism is more than merely copying words from another source: It's turning in work that you did not produce.

Also remember that plagiarism includes turning in a paper—or portions of a paper—that you have already written for another class. If you want to draw on prior research, talk to your instructor first.

Identify direct quotes. If you use a direct quote from another writer or speaker, put that person's words in quotation marks. If you do research online, you might find yourself copying sentences or paragraphs from a Web page and pasting them directly into your notes. *This is the same as taking direct quotes from your source.* To avoid plagiarism, identify such passages in an obvious way. Besides enclosing them in quotation marks, you could format them in a different font or color.

Paraphrase carefully. Instead of using a direct quote, you might choose to paraphrase an author's words. Paraphrasing means restating the original passage in your own words, usually making it shorter and simpler. Students who copy a passage word for word and then just rearrange or delete a few phrases are running a serious risk of plagiarism. Consider this paragraph:

Higher education also offers you the chance to learn how to learn. In fact, that's the subject of this book. Employers value the person who is a "quick study" when it comes to learning a new job. That makes your ability to learn a marketable skill.

Following is an improper paraphrase of that passage:

With higher education comes the chance to learn how to learn. Employers value the person who is a "quick study" when it comes to learning a new job. Your ability to learn is a marketable skill.

A better paraphrase of the same passage would be this one:

The author notes that when we learn how to learn, we gain a skill that is valued by employers.

Remember to cite a source for paraphrases, just as you do for direct quotes.

When you use the same sequence of ideas as one of your sources—even if you have not paraphrased or directly quoted—cite that source.

Summarize carefully. For some of your notes, you may simply want to summarize your source in a few sentences or paragraphs. To do this effectively:

- Read your source several times for understanding.
- Put your source away; then write a summary in your own words.
- In your summary, include only the author's major points.
- Check your summary against your source for accuracy.

Identify distinctive terms and phrases. Some ideas are closely identified with their individual creators. Students who present such ideas without mentioning the individual are plagiarizing. This is true even if they do not copy words, sentence structure, or overall organization of ideas.

For example, the phrase "seven habits of highly effective people" is closely linked to Stephen Covey, author of several books based on this idea. A student might write a paper titled "Habits of Effective People," using words, sentences, and a list of habits that differ completely from Covey's. However, the originality of this student's thinking could still be called into question. This student would be wise to directly mention Covey in the paper and acknowledge Covey's idea that effectiveness and habits are closely linked.

Note details about each source. Identify the source of any material that you quote, paraphrase, or summarize. For books, details about each source include the author, title, publisher, publication date, location of publisher, and page number. For articles from print sources, record the article title and the name of the magazine or journal as well. If you found the article in an academic or technical journal, also record the volume and number of the publication, and inclusive page numbers for the article as well as the page number for the quote. A librarian can help identify these details.

If your source is a Web page, record as many identifying details as you can find—author, title, sponsoring organization, URL, publication date, and revision date. In addition, list the date that you accessed the page.

Cite your sources as endnotes or footnotes to your paper. Ask your instructor for examples of the format to use.

Submit only your own work. Turning in materials that have been written or revised by someone else puts your education at risk.

Allow time to digest your research. If you view research as a task that you can squeeze into a few hours, then you may end up more confused than enlightened. Instead, allow for time to reread and reflect on the facts you gather. This creates conditions for genuine understanding and original thinking.

In particular, take the time to do these things:

- Read over all your notes without feeling immediate pressure to write.
- Summarize major points of view on your topic, noting points of agreement and disagreement.
- Look for connections in your material—ideas, facts, and examples that occur in several sources.
- Note direct answers to your main and supporting research.
- Revise your thesis statement, based on discoveries from your research.
- Put all your notes away and write informally about what you want to say about your topic.
- Look for connections between your research and your life—ideas that you can verify based on personal experience. ■

Nick Bland/Laurie Smale

MASTERING
public speaking

Some people tune out during a speech. Just think of all the times you have listened to instructors, lecturers, and politicians. Remember all the wonderful daydreams you had during their speeches.

Your audiences are like you. The way you plan and present your speech can determine the number of audience members who will stay with you until the end. Polishing your speaking and presentation skills can also help you think on your feet and communicate clearly. You can use these skills in any course, and they'll help you advance in your career as well.

Creating a presentation is much like writing a paper. Divide the project into three phases:

1. Preparing your presentation
2. Delivering your presentation
3. Reflecting on your presentation

PHASE 1: PREPARING YOUR PRESENTATION

Start from your passions. If your instructor allows you to choose the topic of presentation, then choose one that you find interesting. Imagine that the first words in your presentation will be: "I'm here to talk to you because I feel passionately about . . ." How would you complete the sentence? Turn your answer into your main topic.

Consider a "process speech." In this type of presentation, your purpose is to explain a way to do or make something. Examples are changing a tire, planting asparagus, or preparing a healthy meal in 15 minutes. Choose a short, step-by-step process with a concrete outcome. This makes it easier to organize, practice, and deliver your first presentation.

In the introduction to your process speech, get the audience's attention and establish rapport. State the topic and purpose of your speech. Relate the topic to something that audience members care about. During the body of your speech, explain each step in the process, following a logical order. To conclude, quickly summarize the process, and remind your audience of its usefulness.

Analyze your audience. Developing a speech is similar to writing a paper. Begin by writing out your topic, purpose, and thesis statement. Then carefully analyze your audience by using the strategies in Table 8.1.

If your topic is new to listeners . . .	• Explain why your topic matters to them.
	• Relate the topic to something that listeners already know and care about.
	• Define any terms that listeners might not know.
If listeners already know about your topic . . .	• Acknowledge this fact at the beginning of your speech.
	• Find a narrow aspect of the topic that may be new to listeners.
	• Offer a new perspective on the topic, or connect it to an unfamiliar topic.
If listeners disagree with your thesis . . .	• Tactfully admit your differences of opinion.
	• Reinforce points on which you and your audience agree.
	• Build credibility by explaining your qualifications to speak on your topic.
	• Quote expert figures that agree with your thesis—people whom your audience is likely to admire.
	• Explain that their current viewpoint has costs for them, and that a slight adjustment in their thinking will bring significant benefits.
If listeners may be uninterested in your topic . . .	• Explain how listening to your speech can help them gain something that matters deeply to them.
	• Explain ways to apply your ideas in daily life.

Table 8.1 Tailor Your Topic to Your Audience

Remember that audiences want to know that your presentation relates to their needs and desires. To convince people that you have something worthwhile to say, write down your main point. Then see whether you can complete this sentence: *I'm telling you this because . . .*

Organize your presentation. List 3 to 5 questions that your audience members are likely to ask about your topic. Put those questions in logical order. Organize your presentation so that it directly answers those questions.

Also consider the length of your presentation. As a general guideline, plan on delivering about a hundred words per minute. Remember that you could lose points if your presentation goes over the assigned time limit.

Aim for a lean presentation—enough words to make your point but not so many as to make your audience restless. Leave your listeners wanting more. When you speak, be brief and then be seated.

Speeches are usually organized in three main parts: the introduction, the main body, and the conclusion.

Write the introduction. Rambling speeches with no clear point or organization put audiences to sleep. Solve this problem with your introduction. The following introduction, for example, reveals the thesis and exactly what's coming. It reveals that the speech will have three distinct parts, each in logical order:

> *Dog fighting is a cruel sport. I intend to describe exactly what happens to the animals, tell you who is doing this, and show you how you can stop this inhumane practice.*

Whenever possible, talk about things that hold your interest. Include your personal experiences, and start with a bang. Consider this introduction to a speech on the subject of world hunger:

> *I'm very honored to be here with you today. I intend to talk about malnutrition and starvation. First, I want to outline the extent of these problems; then I will discuss some basic assumptions concerning world hunger; and finally I will propose some solutions.*

You can almost hear the snores from the audience. Following is a rewrite:

> *More people have died from hunger in the past 5 years than have been killed in all of the wars, revolutions, and murders in the past 150 years. Yet there is enough food to go around. I'm honored to be here with you today to discuss solutions to this problem.*

Some members of an audience will begin to drift during any speech, but most people pay attention for at least the first few seconds. Highlight your main points in the beginning sentences of your speech.

A related option is to simply announce the questions you intend to answer. You can number these questions and write them on a flip chart. Or create an overview slide with the list of questions.

People might tell you to start your introduction with a joke. Humor is tricky. You run the risk of falling flat or offending somebody. Save jokes until you have plenty of experience with public speaking and know your audiences well.

Also avoid long, flowery introductions in which you tell people how much you like them, how thrilled you are to

address them, and how humble you feel standing in front of them. If you lay it on too thick, your audience won't believe a word of it.

Draft your introduction, and then come back to it after you've written the rest of your speech. In the process of creating the main body and conclusion, your thoughts about the purpose and main points of your speech might change. You might even want to write the introduction last.

Write the main body. The main body of your speech is the content, which accounts for 70 to 90 percent of most speeches. In the main body, you develop your ideas in much the same way that you develop a written paper. If you raised questions in your introduction, be sure to directly answer them.

Transitions are especially important. Give your audience a signal when you change points. Do so by using meaningful pauses and verbal emphasis as well as transitional phrases: "On the other hand, until the public realizes what is happening to children in these countries . . ." or "The second reason hunger persists is . . ."

In long speeches, recap from time to time. Also preview what's to come. Hold your audience's attention by using facts, descriptions, expert opinions, and statistics.

Write the conclusion. At the end of the speech, summarize your points and draw your conclusion. You started with a bang; now finish with drama. The first and last parts of a speech are the most important. Make it clear to your audience when you've reached the end. Avoid endings such as "This is the end of my speech." A simple standby is "So in conclusion, I want to reiterate three points: First, . . ." When you are finished, stop talking.

Create speaking notes. Some professional speakers recommend writing out your speech in full, and then putting key words or main points on a few 3 × 5 cards. Number the cards so that if you drop them, you can quickly put them in order again. As you finish the information on each card, move it to the back of the pile. Write information clearly and in letters large enough to be seen from a distance.

The disadvantage of the 3 × 5 card system is that it involves card shuffling. Some speakers prefer to use standard outlined notes. Another option is mind mapping. Even an hour-long speech can be mapped on one sheet of paper. You can also use memory techniques to memorize the outline of your speech.

Create supporting visuals. Presentations often include visuals such as PowerPoint slides and posters. With PowerPoint, you can also add video clips from your computer or cell phone. These visuals can reinforce your main points and help your audience understand how your presentation is organized.

Use visuals to *complement* rather than *replace* your speaking. If you use too many visuals—or visuals that are too complex—your audience might focus on them and forget about you. To prevent this:

- Ask your instructor whether it's acceptable to use technology in your presentation.
- Ask yourself whether slides will actually benefit your presentation. If you use PowerPoint simply because you *can*, you run the risk of letting the technology overshadow your message.
- Use fewer slides rather than more. For a 15-minute presentation, 10 slides is enough.
- Use slides to *show* rather than *tell*. Save them for illustrations, photos, charts, and concepts that are hard to express in words. Don't expect your audience to read a lot of text.
- Limit the amount of text on each visual. Stick to key words presented in short sentences or phrases.
- Use a consistent set of plain fonts that are large enough for all audience members to see. Avoid using more than two fonts, and avoid UPPERCASE letters.
- Stick with a simple consistent color scheme. Use dark text on a light background. Keep backgrounds consistent, and avoid colors that compete with each other.

The most popular application for creating presentations is PowerPoint. To learn about it, go online to **http://office.microsoft.com**, find a search box, and enter *keyboard shortcuts powerpoint*. Find out how to open a presentation, create a presentation, apply a template, insert a new slide, add visuals to slides, view a slide show, print a presentation, and save a presentation. (Knowing and using the last command often will save you much time and stage fright.)

Also make backup copies of your presentation. At the very least, attach your PowerPoint file to an e-mail message and send it to yourself.

You might enjoy exploring some of PowerPoint's competitors as well. These include Prezi, Jing, and Animoto as well as Keynote for Mac OSX. Also experiment with Zoho Docs (**www.zoho.com/docs**).

Overcome fear of public speaking. You may not be able to eliminate fear of public speaking entirely, but you can take three steps to reduce and manage it.

First, prepare thoroughly. Research your topic thoroughly. Knowing your topic inside and out can create a baseline of confidence. To make a strong start, memorize the first four sentences that you plan to deliver, and practice them many times. Delivering them flawlessly when you're in front of an audience can build your confidence for the rest of your speech.

Second, accept your physical sensations. You've probably experienced physical sensations that are commonly associated with stage fright: dry mouth, a pounding heart, sweaty hands, muscle jitters, shortness of breath, and a shaky voice. One immediate way to deal with such sensations is to simply notice them. Tell yourself, "Yes,

my hands are clammy. Yes, my stomach is upset. Also, my face feels numb." Trying to deny or ignore such facts can increase your fear. When you fully accept sensations, however, they start to lose power.

Third, focus on content, not delivery. Michael Motley, a professor at the University of California–Davis, distinguishes between two orientations to speaking. People with a *performance orientation* believe that the speaker must captivate the audience by using formal techniques that differ from normal conversation. In contrast, speakers with a *communication orientation* see public speaking simply as an extension of one-to-one conversation. The goal is not to perform but to communicate your ideas to an audience in the same ways that you would explain them to a friend.[10]

Adopting a communication orientation can reduce your fear of public speaking. Instead of thinking about yourself, focus on your message. Your audience is more interested in *what* you have to say than *how* you say it. Forget about giving a "speech." Just give people valuable ideas and information that they can use.

Practice your presentation. The key to successful public speaking is practice. Do this with your "speaker's voice." Your voice sounds different when you talk loudly, and this fact can be unnerving. Get used to it early on.

Several days before you deliver your presentation, start practicing it. If possible, do this in the room where you will actually face your audience. Keep an eye on the time to make sure that you stay within the limit.

Hear what your voice sounds like over a sound system. If you can't practice your speech in the actual room, at least visit the site ahead of time. Also make sure that the materials you will need for your speech, including any audio-visual equipment, will be available when you want them.

Whenever possible, make a recording. Many schools have video recording equipment available for student use. Use it while you practice. Then view the finished recording to evaluate your presentation.

Listen for repeated words and phrases. Examples include *you know, kind of*, and *really*, plus any little *uh's, umm's,* and *ah*'s. To get rid of them, tell yourself that you intend to notice every time they pop up in your daily speech. When you hear them, remind yourself that you don't use those words anymore.

Keep practicing. Avoid speaking word for word, as if you were reading a script. When you know your material well, you can deliver it in a natural way. Practice your presentation until you could deliver it in your sleep. Then run through it a few more times.

PHASE 2: DELIVERING YOUR PRESENTATION

Before you begin, get the audience's attention. If people are still filing into the room or adjusting their seats, they're not ready to listen. When all eyes are on you, then begin.

Dress for the occasion. The clothing you choose to wear on the day of your speech delivers a message that's as loud as your words. Consider how your audience will be dressed, and then choose a wardrobe based on the impression you want to make.

Project your voice. When you speak, talk loudly enough to be heard. Avoid leaning over your notes or the podium.

Maintain eye contact. When you look at people, they become less frightening. Also, remember that it is easier for the audience to listen to someone when that person is looking at them. Find a few friendly faces around the room, and imagine that you are talking to each of these people individually.

Notice your nonverbal communication. Be aware of what your body is telling your audience. Contrived or staged gestures will look dishonest. Be natural. If you don't know what to do with your hands, notice that. Then don't do anything with them.

Notice the time. You can increase the impact of your words by keeping track of the time during your speech. It's better to end early than to run late.

Pause when appropriate. Beginners sometimes feel that they have to fill every moment with the sound of their voice. Release that expectation. Give your listeners a chance to make notes and absorb what you say.

Have fun. Chances are that if you lighten up and enjoy your presentation, so will your listeners.

PHASE 3: REFLECTING ON YOUR PRESENTATION

Many students are tempted to sigh with relief when their presentation is done and put the event behind them. Resist this temptation. If you want to get better at making presentations, then take time to reflect on each performance. Did you finish on time? Did you cover all of the points you intended to cover? Was the audience attentive? Did you handle any nervousness effectively?

Write Journal Entries about what you discovered and intend to do differently for your next presentation. Remember to be as kind to yourself as you would be to someone else after a presentation. In addition to noting areas for improvement, note what you did well. Congratulate yourself on getting up in front of an audience and completing your presentation.

Also welcome feedback from others. Most of us find it difficult to hear criticism about our speaking. Be aware of resisting such criticism, and then let go of your resistance. Listening to feedback will increase your skill. ◼

Making the grade in group presentations

When preparing group presentations, you can use three strategies for making a memorable impression.

Get organized. As soon as you get the assignment, select a group leader and exchange contact information. Schedule specific times and places for planning, researching, writing, and practicing your presentation.

At your first meeting, write a to-do list that includes all of the tasks involved in completing the assignment. Distribute tasks fairly, paying attention to the strengths of individuals in your group. For example, some people excel at brainstorming, whereas others prefer researching.

One powerful way to get started is to define clearly the topic and thesis, or main point, of your presentation. Then support your thesis by looking for the most powerful facts, quotations, and anecdotes you can find.

As you get organized, remember how your presentation will be evaluated. If the instructor doesn't give grading criteria, create your own.

Get coordinated. Get together several times to practice your presentation before it's scheduled to be given in class. Develop smooth, short transitions between individual speakers. Keep track of the time so that you stay within the guidelines for the assignment.

Also practice using visuals such as flip charts, posters, DVDs, videotapes, or slides. To give visuals their full impact, make them appropriate for the room where you will present. Make sure that text is large enough to be seen from the back of the room. For bigger rooms, consider using presentation software or making overhead transparencies.

Get cooperation. Presentations that get top scores take teamwork and planning—not egos. Communicate with group members in an open and sensitive way. Contribute your ideas, and be responsive to the viewpoints of other members. When you cooperate, your group is on the way to an effective presentation.

Practicing Critical Thinking 8

Remember that psychologist Benjamin Bloom described six levels of thinking:

Level 1: Remembering

Level 2: Understanding

Level 3: Applying

Level 4: Analyzing

Level 5: Evaluating

Level 6: Creating

To complete this exercise, you'll experiment with combining levels and taking them in a different sequence.

Level 1: Remembering and Level 2: Understanding
Recall a conflict you are experiencing right now with an important person in your life. (If you cannot think of one, recall a conflict that you experienced in the past.) Describe that conflict.

_____

_____

_____

_____

Level 2: Understanding and Level 5: Evaluating
Now briefly review this chapter for suggestions that could help you resolve this conflict. Choose one suggestion and briefly summarize it in your own words. Also explain why you think it would be useful.

_____

_____

_____

_____

_____

Level 3: Applying and Level 4: Analyzing
Describe how you will use the suggestion that you just described. Include details such as when and where you plan to take action, and what you plan to say. If your plan calls for taking more than one action, then make a list of them.

_____

_____

_____

_____

Level 6: Creating
After reading the chapter and completing this exercise, will you take a new approach to resolving conflict? Briefly explain your answer. Include the reasons for changing—or not changing—your approach.

_____

_____

_____

_____

_____

MASTER STUDENT PROFILE

SALMAN KHAN

(1976—) Founder of one of the most popular education sites on the Web; began by creating amateur videos to help his middle-school cousins with their homework

JIM WILSON/Redux

The current mission of the Khan Academy is to "provide a free world-class education for anyone, anywhere." Yet it began with two people who had no plans of going international—Salman Khan, a hedge fund analyst, and Nadia, his young cousin.

Nadia wanted to get placed in an advanced math track in school, which meant overcoming gaps in her knowledge. In 2004, Khan volunteered to tutor her. The problem was distance: He lived in Boston, and Nadia was in New Orleans.

Their solution was technology. Khan worked with Nadia over the phone and online via Yahoo Doodle. After Nadia's math scores started going up, her brothers Arman and Ali joined in the tutoring sessions.

When scheduling became an issue, Khan turned to instructional videos as an alternate teaching method. "And as soon as I put those first YouTube videos up, something interesting happened," he recalls. "The first was the feedback from my cousins. They told me that they preferred me on YouTube than in person. And once you get over the backhanded nature of that, there was actually something very profound there."

Khan saw no reason to make the videos private, so other people were free to discover them. He got feedback from people around the world—and requests for more videos.

By 2009, Khan was so busy making videos that he decided to quit his job. After living on his savings for nine months, he got a large donation. Funding from Google and Bill and Melinda Gates followed. The Khan Academy—a non-profit educational organization—was fully launched.

Today six million people use Khan Academy resources every month. These include over 4,000 videos on math, science, economics, history, art, and other topics.

Salman Khan *is self-aware.* **You** *can be self-aware by asking for feedback and being willing to accept it.*

Interactive exercises are also available, along with an online "dashboard" that gives students instant scores.

Khan is known for his suggestion to "flip" the classroom. In the traditional model, students listen to lectures during class time, do homework after school, and take occasional tests. Feedback on their work is delayed, and everyone in the class is expected to learn at the same pace.

"Imagine learning to ride a bicycle, and maybe I give you a lecture ahead of time, and I give you that bicycle for two weeks," says Khan. "And then I come back after two weeks, and I say, 'Well, let's see. You're having trouble taking left turns. You can't quite stop. You're an 80 percent bicyclist.' So I put a big C stamp on your forehead and then I say, 'Here's a unicycle.'"

The Khan Academy model reverses this sequence. Students watch video lectures *after* school. During class time, they work problems, take tests, and get immediate feedback from teachers and peers. As a result, they can progress to mastery at their own pace.

"So our model is learn math the way you'd learn anything, like the way you would learn a bicycle," Khan explains. "Stay on that bicycle. Fall off that bicycle. Do it as long as necessary until you have mastery. The traditional model—it penalizes you for experimentation and failure, but it does not expect mastery. We encourage you to experiment. We encourage you to fail. But we do expect mastery." ■

QUIZ
Chapter 8

Name _____

Date _____

1. Name the six rungs on the ladder of powerful speaking from the Power Process: Employ your word.
Obligation, possibility, preference, passion, planning, promising (*Power Process: Employ your word*, page 242)

2. Write one example of a statement on the lowest rung of the ladder of powerful speaking—and another example of a statement on the highest rung.
(Answers will vary.) Lowest rung: "I should feed and walk the dog soon"; highest rung: "You can count on the fact that I will graduate in two years." (*Power Process: Employ your word*, page 242)

3. One strategy for effective communication is to separate the roles of sending and receiving. Briefly explain how to do this.
(Answers will vary.) Communication channels get blocked when we try to send and receive messages at the same time. Instead, be aware of when you are the receiver and when you are the sender. If you are receiving, just receive; avoid switching into the sending mode. When you are sending, stick with it until you are finished. When someone else talks, listen. Then switch roles so that you can be the sender for a while. (*Communication—Keeping the channels open*, page 235)

4. This chapter suggests techniques for nonverbal and verbal listening. Briefly explain the difference between these two approaches to listening, and give one example of each approach.
During nonverbal listening, the listener does not speak and stays focused on what the sender is saying. Examples of nonverbal listening are (list one of the following): maintaining eye contact, displaying openness, sending acknowledgments, releasing distractions, and suspending judgments. During verbal listening, the listener responds to what the sender is saying to indicate that the listener understands what is being communicated. Examples of verbal listening are (list one of the following): feeding back meaning, noticing verbal and nonverbal messages, listening for requests and intentions, allowing emotion, asking for more, being careful with questions and advice, taking care of yourself, and staying open to the adventure of listening. (*Choosing to listen*, page 236)

5. You can listen skillfully to a speaker even when you disagree with that person's viewpoint. True or false? Explain your answer.
True. Listening and agreeing are two different activities. As listeners, our goal is to fully receive another person's message. This does not mean that we're obligated to agree with the message. Once you're confident that you accurately understand a speaker's point of view, you are free to agree or disagree with it. The key to effective listening is understanding before evaluating. (*Choosing to listen*, page 236)

6. Reword the following complaint as a request: "You always interrupt when I talk!"
Possible rewordings include "Before you begin to talk, please let me finish" and "I'd like to finish making my point; please allow me to do that." (*Choosing to speak*, page 238)

7. List the five parts of an "I" message (the five ways to say "I").
(a) Observations, (b) Feelings, (c) Wants, (d) Thoughts, and (e) Intentions. (*Five ways to say "I,"* page 240)

8. Briefly define the term *emotional intelligence*.
Emotional intelligence includes the following components: Self-awareness; Self-regulation; Motivation; Empathy; Skill in relationships. If you're emotionally intelligent, you're probably described as someone with good "people skills." You're aware of your feelings. You act in thoughtful ways, show concern for others, resolve conflict, and make responsible decisions. (*Developing emotional intelligence*, page 242)

9. Define *plagiarism*, and explain ways to avoid it.
Plagiarism is the use of another person's words, pictures, or other original creations without giving proper credit. While taking notes, clearly distinguish between your own ideas and those from others. Be sure to paraphrase and credit paraphrases in the same way you would credit direct quotes. (*Academic integrity: Avoid plagiarism*, page 259)

10. Describe at least three techniques for practicing and delivering a speech.
(a) Practice using your "speaker's voice." (b) Practice in the room in which you will deliver your speech. (c) Make a recording of your speech. (d) Listen for repeated phrases or stumbles. (e) Practice until you can deliver your presentation in a natural way. (f) Dress for the occasion. (g) Project your voice. (h) Maintain eye contact. (i) Notice your nonverbal communication. (j) Notice the time. (k) Pause when appropriate. (l) Have fun. (*Mastering public speaking*, page 261)

⊛ SKILLS SNAPSHOT
Chapter 8

Take a minute to reflect on how you can use this chapter to make a lasting, positive difference in the way that you communicate. First, take a snapshot of your current skills in this area of your life. Then create a clear intention for taking action to develop more mastery.

Discovery
My score on the Communicating section of the Discovery Wheel was . . .

When I feel angry with people, the way I usually express it is . . .

I would describe my current level of emotional intelligence as . . .

Intention
The suggestion from this chapter that can help me most with listening is . . .

The suggestion from this chapter that can help me most with speaking is . . .

The suggestion from this chapter that can help me most with writing is . . .

Using these suggestions can make me more effective in my career by . . .

Action
To take the suggestions that I just listed and put them into practice, the three new habits that I will adopt next are . . .

INSTRUCTOR TOOLS & TIPS

DIVERSITY

"We don't see things as they are, we see things as we are." —Anaïs Nin

PREVIEW

Becoming a Master Student values diversity as a key element to success at school, at work, in our neighborhoods, and in our global community. This chapter focuses specifically on living with diversity and the benefits of learning to understand different customs and relate to different cultures. Communicating sets the stage for discussing diversity and the impact it has on your students' lives. The exercises and activities here and in the additional ancillaries encourage students to work together to build networks of peer support by exchanging ideas across cultures. In this way, students can learn to overcome stereotyping, respect differences, and embrace diversity.

GUEST SPEAKER

Consider inviting a local employer to come to your class and discuss with your students antidiscrimination policies and diversity initiatives as they apply on a corporate level. Alternatively, a representative from your human resources department may be able to provide a similar presentation to your students. If student government coordinates a diversity day, week, or month, seek out the student or faculty leaders of that effort, and ask them to put together a student diversity panel to speak with your class. They can use this opportunity to recruit more volunteers or future organization members to help with their event. A faculty member who teaches cultural anthropology could also present a relevant talk to your students. Or a representative from your accessibility/disabled students program could talk about the rights and issues of people with physical and/or mental challenges. This provides students an opportunity to brainstorm: What is diversity? Whom/what does that include?

LECTURE

The articles "Leadership in a diverse world," "Building relationships across cultures," and "Overcome stereotypes with critical thinking," as well as the Power Process: Choose your conversations, all can provide the basis for a lecture unit on Chapter 9. See additional Lecture Ideas in the Course Manual on the Instructor Companion Site.

master instructor
best practice

"*Diversity is such an important topic in today's world. In order to become a master student, students need to understand and appreciate diversity in order to hopefully, eventually put it to work! However, many instructors (myself included) feel very uncomfortable addressing this delicate subject in the classroom. The inclusion of Chapter 9 in the text has made the task much less daunting. The content focuses on facts, rather than emotions, while the Journal Entries (especially number 21) give the students a chance to think independently and objectively about their own feelings.*"

—*Leigh Smith, Lamar Institute of Technology*

Workplace Application: Understanding the importance of diversity at work. Many people equate diversity with racial differences, but diversity is a much broader concept. Remind students that, just like in the classroom, they will be required to work and interact with people with differing abilities and from various races, genders, sexual orientations, religions, cultures, age groups, and backgrounds. Instead of seeing this as challenging, illustrate the many benefits of working with others who are different. The most important aspect in regards to diversity is respect. The age-old adage from our mothers, "Treat others as you wish to be treated," is just as relevant in the workplace as it once was on the playground. Mutual respect builds productive teams and productive teams foster success. Encourage students to not only recognize the differences among coworkers, but to focus on the values those differences bring to the team. Everyone has something valuable to offer the work group. Productivity and creativity can only increase by the inclusion of various ideas and strengths. Employing different strategies will lead to better creativity and more flexible workplace solutions.

EXERCISES/ACTIVITIES

Joanne Zitik, a diversity consultant for Center Focus, creates diversity exercises for workshops and courses for employees, managers, and executives in organizations. Some of her guidelines for the exercises also apply to the classroom, including these:

- Carefully consider the timing of when you introduce an exercise. For example, be sure to build trust among the students before tackling an exercise that encourages them to delve deeply into and/or reveal things about themselves.

- Make sure that students know that it is all right to "pass" and not participate in an exercise.

- Do not repeat derogatory words and phrases; try to move students away from stereotypes and derogatory language.

- Ask the students to observe confidentiality so that what is said during the exercise is not repeated outside the course.

- Make sure that the exercise is facilitated by a person who has had ample diversity and inclusion training.

1. **Using TV shows or films.** Many popular television series have included at least one episode with a theme of diversity. Watch programs with an eye and ear out for a segment or episode that you might be able to use in your classroom. Or challenge students to find such a program.

    Consider showing the film *The Gods Must Be Crazy* in class. This film illustrates cultural differences and the implications of even a simple act. When a Coke bottle is dropped from an airplane in an African village, havoc ensues, and this tiny cultural intrusion creates ripples in the social fabric of the village.

2. **Diversity circle.** Some diversity trainers use the diversity circle exercise to help workers appreciate diversity and overcome misperceptions. The exercise can be easily adapted for classroom use. Form a group of about 10 students. Arrange your chairs in a circle, and put one additional chair in the center of the circle. A "diverse" group member volunteers to sit in the center chair and become the first "awareness subject." Because all people are diverse in some way (whether by age, gender, ability, or background), everyone is eligible to occupy the center chair.

    The person in the center tells the others how she has felt about being diverse or different and how people have reacted to her diversity. For example, an Inuit described how fellow workers were hesitant to

master instructor
best practice

" *When I start talking about diversity, students tend to focus on very obvious aspects of diversity, such as gender. To help them think more broadly about the many kinds of diversity, I put students into groups of four or five. I ask them, in their groups, to list all the ways that people can be different from one another. I start them off with gender and ethnicity, and give them five minutes to brainstorm other differences. I have the students write these ideas on a flip chart. After they have brainstormed, I ask them to share the responses from their groups. They come up with many ideas and get additional ideas from the other groups—anything from political party preferences to shoe size. This exercise provides the students with a common starting point for the chapter and a much broader sense of what diversity can encompass. "*

—Michelle Martin, TeamUp Consultant

ask him out for a beer because they worried about whether he could handle alcohol.

An equally effective alternative to the procedure just described is to ask each class member to come to the front of the class and describe a significant way in which he or she is different. After each class member has spoken, have the students discuss their observations and interpretations.

CONVERSATION/SHARING

Appreciation for diversity often begins at home. You can increase your students' awareness of the role that family messages play in their own lives and in their perceptions of themselves. Start your class discussion by asking students to talk about the role of diversity in their lives, past and present.

What? What does embracing diversity mean to you?

How? How has diversity played a role in your life?

Why? Why does diversity matter to you? To open a discussion on the impact of diversity, ask your students about discrimination. Have they ever been discriminated against for any reason?

What if? What if you were discriminated against? What if we could wipe out discrimination through education?

master instructor
best practice

❝ *I use an episode from the '90s television sitcom* 3rd Rock from the Sun. *This show was about a family from another planet who came to earth to learn about humans. I use the episode "Dick Like Me." When talking about a topic as sensitive as diversity, be cautious about using humor. I've shown this video to many diverse classes of students, and I have not received any negative feedback about it. For more details about how I use this video in my classroom, go to the Instructor Companion Site.* ❞

—*Dean Mancina, Golden Key College*

master instructor
best practice

❝ *I like to show my class a video, titled* Wealth, Innovation and Diversity, *that is narrated by futurist Joel Barker (published by Star Thrower Productions). Beginning with the Irish potato famine, the video illustrates the vital importance of diversity, casting it in a whole new light. It is diversity that makes human beings strong enough to survive. When we violate the principle of diversity, we pay a price in human suffering every time. When we celebrate diversity, we prosper as a people and as a nation.* ❞

—*Eldon McMurray, Utah Valley State College*

Create groups in class that are varied—in age, gender, ethnicity, ability, and background. Ask each group to discuss how the members celebrate a special event, such as a wedding, in their communities and families. Discussing celebrations is an effective way to gain cultural insight and share positive experiences.

Power Process: Choose your conversations (page 270).
Raise your students' "conversation consciousness" by asking them to reflect on the conversations described in the Power Process. Point out the various options available for the scenario, creating either a positive or a negative experience. Ask students to reflect on their own conversations. These conversations might occur during class meetings or course lectures, in the workplace, at social events, or even while reading or watching television. Students can describe a publication they read regularly (in print or online), pointing out the conversations they have when they read and the insights they gain from this material. Invite your students to write Discovery and Intention Statements highlighting the amount of time they currently spend talking about the past, present, and future, and stating how they intend to change their conversations. A central thesis of *Becoming a Master Student* is that education works when it is value driven. We can choose to engage in value-driven conversations—those that move us toward our goals and affirm our intentions.

Overcome stereotypes with critical thinking (page 279).
To begin a conversation with your students about generalizations and ways to decrease stereotyping, revisit the concepts presented in Chapter 7: Thinking. Then use this article to open up further discussion. The reinforcement will encourage your students to commit to using thinking strategies and to make connections between chapters. This answers the question "*What if* I use the strategies from Chapter 7 and apply them to issues related to diversity?"

Leadership in a diverse world (pages 284–287).
The topic of leadership provides another opportunity for in-class discussion. Ask your students who are leaders (on campus, in the workplace, at their church, at home, in their circle of friends) to share what it's like to be a leader. Then divide the students into small groups and have them discuss the following questions: What are the advantages and disadvantages of being a leader? What are the challenges and perks? Does holding a leadership position help your self-esteem?

HOMEWORK

Dealing with sexism and sexual harassment (pages 282–283).
Most colleges list sexual harassment policies in their student handbooks or post them online. Have your students obtain a copy of your college's policy, and encourage them to find out where to procure related materials provided by your campus and how to use them. After your students have reviewed the college's policy, engage them in a discussion—either in small groups or as a class—about this important issue.

EVALUATION

Ask students to write an essay about the value of diversity. Ask them to write about how to build relationships across cultures. Ask students to describe specific strategies for dealing with sexism and sexual harassment. Tell them to explain how choosing their conversations and community could promote student success.

MindTap™ EMBRACE VALUABLE RESOURCES

FOR CHAPTER 9

STUDENT RESOURCES: MINDTAP

- **Learning Outcomes.** Every chapter begins with an engaging video that visually outlines in a mind map format the key learning outcomes for that chapter. Students should find these short introductions not only helpful as chapter organizers, but as valuable note-taking models.

- **Engagement Activity: Master Students in Action.** Students hear firsthand from other students about their experiences and challenges with diversity. The Master Students in Action videos give your students an up-close view of how the strategies in *Becoming a Master Student* have helped their peers overcome obstacles.

- **Aplia Homework Assignment: Building relationships across cultures.** In this assignment, students explore the value of cross-cultural relationships and think critically in situations that call for cultural sensitivity. By learning from a student scenario, students are able to directly apply the concepts related to cultural sensitivity.

- **Reflection Activity: Learning by Sound.** This Slice of Life video, created by student Tommy Carroll, offers examples of overcoming a major challenge, such as his blindness, to learn in creative ways, as he did when he learned to skateboard by listening.

MindTap™ Your personal learning experience—learn anywhere, anytime.

INSTRUCTOR COMPANION SITE

- **Questions about how to handle the diversity of your own students?** Look to the online Course Manual for various articles detailing strategies for teaching in all kinds of specialized classroom settings, including the following:
  - Racially and Ethnically Diverse Students
  - International and ESL Students
  - Returning Adults
  - Students with Disabilities
  - Lesbian, Gay, Bisexual, and Transgender Students

- **Get your students writing!** Creative writing assignments tailored to get students critically thinking about diversity are available in the Course Manual. Find out more online about this prompt:

- **Teach Critical Thinking with Movies.** Ask students to view the movie *Babe,* which depicts the experience of a young animal navigating cultural discrimination and conflict. Or have students watch *Castaway*—the lead character is forced to reevaluate his notions of time, companionship, food, shelter, and water, on which he relied before he was washed onto a desert island. Ask students to list how he coped with each of these needs on the island, to model the steps of critical problem solving.

Please visit login.cengage.com to log in and access the Instructor Companion Site.

DIVERSITY

Why

You're likely to learn and work with people from many different backgrounds and cultures.

Building relationships across cultures ■ 274

Leadership in a diverse world ■ 284

How

Recall a time when you felt included in a group of people, even though the group was diverse. Next, scan this chapter for ideas that can help you recreate that kind of a supportive environment. Note three strategies that you intend to explore in more detail.

Overcome stereotypes with critical thinking The word *stereotype* originally referred to a method used by printers to produce duplicate pages of text. This usage still rings true. When we stereotype, we gloss over individual differences and assume that every member of a group is a "duplicate." These assumptions are learned, and they can be changed. ■ 279

Diversity is real—and valuable ■ 272

What if...

I could create positive relationships with people from any background or culture?

What is included...

POWER PROCESS

CHOOSE YOUR CONVERSATIONS

Conversations can exist in many forms. One form involves people talking out loud to each other. At other times, the conversation takes place inside our own heads, and we call it *thinking*. We are even having a conversation when we read a magazine or a book, watch television or a movie, or write a letter or a report. These observations have three implications that wind their way through every aspect of our lives.

One implication is that conversations exercise incredible power over what we think, feel, and do. They shape our attitudes, our decisions, our opinions, our emotions, and our actions. If you want clues as to what a person will be like tomorrow, listen to what she's talking about today.

Second, given that conversations are so powerful, it's amazing that few people act on this fact. Most of us swim in a constant sea of conversations, almost none of which we carefully and thoughtfully choose.

The real power of this process lies in a third discovery: We can choose our conversations. Certain conversations create real value for us. They give us fuel for reaching our goals. Other conversations distract us from what we want. They might even create lasting unhappiness and frustration.

Suppose that you meet with an instructor to ask about some guidelines for writing a term paper. She launches into a tirade about your writing skills and lack of preparation for higher education. This presents you with several options. One possibility is to talk about what a jerk the instructor is and give up on the idea of learning to write well. Another option is to refocus the conversation on what you can do to improve your writing skills, such as working with a writing tutor or taking a basic composition class. These two sets of conversations will have vastly different consequences for your success in school.

Also imagine that you're traveling abroad and meet someone who insists that people from North America are rude and greedy. This too presents you with several options. One is to get angry and trade insults. Another option is to choose your conversation by asking, "Is that true? And, how do you know it's true?" When done with patience and sincerity, this might lead to a conversation that reveals the source of misunderstandings.

Another important fact about your conversations is that the people you associate with influence them dramatically. If you want to change your attitude about almost anything—prejudice, politics, religion, humor—choose your conversations by choosing your community. Spend time with people who speak about and live consistently with the attitudes you value. Use conversations to change habits.

Also use conversations to connect with people who differ from you. Explore their ways of seeing the world. Discover what they value and why. Doing this can create new options for your own thinking and behavior.

When we choose our conversations, we discover a tool of unsurpassed power. This tool has the capacity to remake our thoughts—and thus our lives. It's as simple as choosing the next article you read or the next topic you discuss with a friend.

Begin applying this Power Process today. Start choosing your conversations, and watch what happens. ■

© cobalt88/Shutterstock.com

Waking up to DIVERSITY

Learning about diversity is an education in itself. This process can be frightening, frustrating, and even painful. It can also be exciting and enriching.

Consider that the people referred to as "minorities" in the United States are a numerical majority in other parts of the world. To make this idea more real, imagine the human race represented in a single village of just 100 people. If these villagers accurately reflected the Earth's total population, then only 18 would be white, and just 31 would describe themselves as Christian. In addition, 80 would live in substandard housing, 67 would be illiterate, and only 7 would have Internet access.[1]

The diverse cultures of our planet are meeting daily through a growing world economy and a global network of computers. Discussions of diversity often focus on characteristics commonly linked to race—differences in skin tone, facial features, and hair texture. But grouping people according to such differences is arbitrary. We could just as easily classify them on the basis of height, weight, foot size, fingernail length, or a hundred other physical traits.

In this chapter, the word *diversity* refers to differences of any type. From this perspective, diversity can be compared to an iceberg. Only the top of an iceberg is visible; most of it is hidden underwater. Likewise, only a few aspects of diversity are visible, such as obvious differences in physical appearance, language, social and economic background, and behavior. Much remains hidden from our awareness—different ideas about relationships, decision making, and problem solving; different assumptions about the meaning of love and duty, beauty and friendship, justice and injustice; and much more.

This chapter is titled "Diversity" because that term is widely accepted. You might gain more value from thinking about *cultural competence* instead. This term reminds us that even in the most culturally sensitive environment, people can fail at understanding each other and working toward shared goals. *Cultural competence* refers to gaining skills in these areas and actively using those skills in daily life.

You'll learn most by stepping outside your comfort zone and taking risks. Get involved in a study group or campus organization with people from different countries. Keep asking yourself, "What is the next action I could take to live and work more effectively in our global village?" The answers could change your life. ■

> **Diversity can be compared to an iceberg. Only the top of an iceberg is visible; most of it is hidden underwater. Likewise, only a few aspects of diversity are visible.**

Interactive

Journal Entry 20
Discovery Statement

Reflect on the quality of a recent conversation

Review the Power Process: Choose your conversations. Then, describe a conversation you had today. Summarize what was said, and reflect on whether the conversations aligned with your values and goals.

I discovered that . . .

_____

_____

_____

_____

_____

_____

_____

_____

_____

_____

Brand New Images/Lifesize/Getty Images

Diversity is real—and
VALUABLE

This country has a rich tradition of cultural diversity. Many of us come from families who immigrated to the United States or Canada within the last two or three generations. The things we eat, the tools we use, and the words we speak are a cultural tapestry woven by many different peoples.

Think about a common daily routine. A typical American citizen awakens in a bed (an invention from the Near East). After dressing in clothes (possibly designed in Italy), she slices a banana (grown in Honduras) on her bowl (made in China) of cereal, and then brews coffee (shipped from Nicaragua). This scenario presents just a few examples of how the cultures of the world meet in our daily lives.

The word *culture* embraces many kinds of differences. We can speak of the culture of large corporations or the culture of the fine arts. There are the cultures of men and women; heterosexual, homosexual, and bisexual people; and older and younger people. There are the cultures of urban and rural dwellers, the cultures of able-bodied people and people with disabilities, and the cultures of two-parent families and single-parent families. There are cultures defined by differences in standards of living and differences in religion.

Higher education might bring you into the most diverse environment that you will ever encounter. Your fellow students could come from many ethnic groups and countries. In addition, consider faculty members, staff members, alumni, donors, and their families. Think of all the possible differences in their family backgrounds, education, job experiences, religion, marital status, sexual orientation, and political viewpoints. Few institutions in our society can match the level of diversity found on many campuses.

A First Step to living effectively in a diverse world is to remember that many dimensions of culture are alive in you and in the people you meet every day. Once you recognize that such diversity is a fact, you can practice a new level of tolerance and respect for individual differences.

Discrimination is also real. The ability to live with diversity is now more critical than ever. Racism, homophobia, and other forms of discrimination exist in many settings, including higher education. Each year the Federal Bureau of Investigation (FBI) reports hate crimes motivated by biases that relate to race, religion, sexual orientation, ethnicity, and disability.[2] And according to the Anti-Defamation League, college campuses in the United States have become a new "proving ground" for anti-Semitic and racist speakers.[3]

Gay, lesbian, bisexual, and transgendered (GLBT) students have also suffered discrimination and become victims of hate crimes. Tyler Clementi, a freshman at Rutgers University, committed suicide in 2010 after his roommate posted an online video of Clementi having sex with another man. Billy Lucas, a 15-year-old in Indiana, also committed suicide that year after being taunted about being gay. In response, gay activist Dan Savage started "It Gets Better," a YouTube channel that features inspirational videos from people who survived bullying based on their sexual orientation.

Of course, discrimination can be more subtle than bullying. Consider how you would respond to the following situations:

- Members of a sociology class are debating the merits of reforming the state's welfare system. The instructor calls on a student who grew up on a reservation and says, "Tell us: What's the Native American perspective on this issue anyway?" Here the student is being typecast as a spokesperson for her entire ethnic group.

- Students in a mass media communications class are learning to think critically about television programs. They're talking about a situation comedy set in an urban high-rise apartment building with mostly African American residents. "Man, they really whitewashed that show," says one student. "It's mostly about inner-city black people, but they didn't show anybody on welfare, doing drugs, or joining gangs." The student's comment perpetuates common racial stereotypes.

On the first day of the term, students taking English Composition enter a class taught by a professor from Puerto Rico. One of the students asks the professor, "Am I in the right class? Maybe there's been a mistake. I thought this was supposed to be an English class, not a Spanish class." The student assumed that only white people are qualified to teach English courses.

Forrest Toms, of Training Research and Development, defines racism as "prejudice plus power"—the power to define reality, to enshrine one culture as the "correct" set of lenses for viewing the world. The operating assumption is that differences mean deficits. When racism and other forms of intolerance live, we all lose—even if we belong to a group with social and political power. We lose the ability to make friends and to function effectively on teams. We crush human potential. And people without the skills to bridge cultures are already at a disadvantage.

Higher education offers a chance to change this situation. Campuses can become cultural laboratories—places where people of diverse cultures meet in an atmosphere of tolerance. Students who create alliances outside their familiar group memberships are preparing to succeed in both school and work.

Diversity is valuable. Synergy rests on the idea that the whole is more than the sum of its parts. A symphony orchestra consists of many different instruments; when played together, their effect is multiplied many times. A football team has members with different specialties; when their talents are combined, they can win a league championship.

Today we are waking up not only to the *fact* of diversity but also to the *value* of diversity. Biologists tell us that diversity of animal species benefits our ecology. The same idea applies to the human species. Our goal in education can be to see that we are all part of a complex world—that our own culture is different from, not better than, other cultures. Knowing this, we can stop saying, "Ours is the way to work, learn, relate to others, and view the world." Instead, we can say, "Here is the way I have been doing it. I would also like to see your way."

The fact of diversity also presents opportunities in the workplace. Understanding cultural differences will help you to embrace others' viewpoints that lead to profitable solutions. Organizations that are attuned to diversity are more likely to prosper in the global marketplace.

Accepting diversity does not mean ignoring the differences among cultures so that we all become part of an anonymous "melting pot." Instead, we can become more like a mosaic—a piece of art in which each element both maintains its individuality and blends with others to form a harmonious whole.

The more you can embrace diversity, the more friends you can make in school and the better prepared you'll be for the workforce of the twenty-first century. If you plan to pursue a career in health care, for example, you can prepare to work with patients from many ethnic groups. If you choose to start a business, you can prepare to sell to customers from many demographic groups. And if you plan to teach, you can prepare to assist every student who walks into your classroom.

Learning to thrive with diversity is a process of returning to "beginner's mind"—a place where we discover diversity as if for the first time. It is a magical place—a place of new beginnings and fresh options. It takes courage to dwell in beginner's mind—courage to go outside the confines of our own culture and worldview. It can feel uncomfortable at first. Yet there are lasting rewards to be gained.

Even if you've already attended diversity workshops in high school or at work, see whether you can return to beginner's mind. Entering higher education can take your experience of diversity to a whole new level. ◼

Interactive

Exercise 25
Confront the influences of stereotypes

A *stereotype* is an assumption that all members of a group are the same. Stereotypes ignore the differences among people.

To discover how stereotypes can enter your mind, do a short thinking experiment. List the first words that come to mind when you see or hear the following terms. Write quickly and don't stop to think about your responses.

musician . . .

Eskimo . . .

homeless people . . .

mathematicians . . .

football players . . .

computer programmers . . .

Now reflect on your lists. Do you see any evidence of stereotypes? Explain your answer:

_____

_____

_____

_____

_____

John Lund/Blend Images/Getty Images

Building relationships
ACROSS
CULTURES

> *Communicating with people of other cultures is a learned skill—a habit. According to Stephen R. Covey, author of* **The Seven Habits of Highly Effective People,** *a habit is the point at which desire, knowledge, and skill meet.*⁴
> - *Desire is about* **wanting** *to do something.*
> - *Knowledge is* **understanding** *what to do.*
> - *And skill is the* **ability** *to do it.*

Master students merge these qualities in the way that they relate to people of different cultures.

Knowing techniques for communicating across cultures is valuable. And what gives them power is a sincere desire and commitment to create understanding. If you truly value cultural diversity, then you can discover ways to build bridges between people. Use the following suggestions and invent more of your own.

Start with self-discovery. One step to developing diversity skills is to learn about yourself and understand the lenses through which you see the world. One way to do this is to intentionally switch lenses—that is, to consciously perceive familiar events in a new way.

For example, think of a situation in your life that involved an emotionally charged conflict among several people. Now mentally put yourself inside the skin of another person in that conflict. Ask yourself, "How would I view this situation if I were that person?"

You can also learn by asking, "What if I were a person of the opposite gender? Or if I were a member of a different racial or ethnic group? Or if I were older or younger?" Do this exercise consistently, and you'll discover that we live in a world of multiple realities. There are many different ways to interpret any event—and just as many ways to respond, given our individual differences.

Also reflect on how people can have experiences of privilege *and* prejudice. For example, someone might tell you that he's more likely to be promoted at work because he's white and male—*and* that he's been called "white trash" because he lives in a trailer park.

See whether you can recall incidents such as these from your own life. Think of times when you were favored because of your gender, race, or age—and times when you were excluded or ridiculed based on one of those same characteristics. In doing this, you'll discover ways to identify with a wider range of people.

Look for differences between individualist and collectivist cultures. Individualist cultures flourish in the United States, Canada, and Western Europe. If your family has deep roots in one of these areas, you were probably raised to value personal fulfillment and personal success. You received recognition or rewards when you stood out from your peers by earning the highest grades in your class, scoring the most points during a basketball season, or demonstrating another form of individual achievement.

In contrast, collectivist cultures value cooperation over competition. Group progress is more important than individual success. Credit for an achievement is widely shared. If you were raised in such a culture, you probably place a high value on your family and were taught to respect your elders. Collectivist cultures dominate Asia, Africa, and Latin America.

In short, individualist cultures often emphasize "I." Collectivist cultures tend to emphasize "we." Forgetting about the differences between them can strain a friendship or wreck an international business deal.

If you were raised in an individualist culture:

- *Remember that someone from a collectivist culture may place a high value on "saving face."* This idea involves more than simply avoiding embarrassment. This person may *not* want to be singled out from other members of a group, even for a positive achievement. If you have a direct request for this person or want to share something that could be taken as a personal criticism, save it for a private conversation.

- *Respect titles and last names.* Although Americans often like to use first names immediately after meeting someone, in some cultures this practice is acceptable only among family members. Especially in work settings, use last names and job titles during your first meetings. Allow time for informal relationships to develop.

- *Put messages in context.* For members of collectivist cultures, words convey only part of an intended message. Notice gestures and other nonverbal communication as well.

If you were raised in a collectivist culture, you can creatively "reverse" the above list. Keep in mind that direct questions from an American student or coworker are meant not to offend, but only to clarify an idea. Don't be surprised if you are called by a nickname, if no one asks about your family, or if you are rewarded for a personal achievement. In social situations, remember that indirect cues might not get another person's attention. Practice asking clearly and directly for what you want.

Look for common ground. Students in higher education often find that they worry about many of the same things—including tuition bills, the quality of dormitory food, and the shortage of on-campus parking spaces. More important, our fundamental goals as human beings—such as health, physical safety, and economic security—cross culture lines.

The key is to honor the differences among people while remembering what we have in common. Diversity is not just about our differences—it's also about our similarities. On a biological level, less than 1 percent of the human genome accounts for visible characteristics such as skin color. In terms of our genetic blueprint, we are more than 99 percent the same.[5]

Speak and listen with cultural sensitivity. After first speaking with someone from another culture, don't assume that you've been understood or that you fully understand the other person. The same action can have different meanings at different times, even for members of the same culture. Check it out. Verify what you think you have heard. Listen to see whether what you spoke is what the other person received.

If you're speaking with someone who doesn't understand English well, keep the following ideas in mind:

- Speak slowly, distinctly, and patiently.

- To clarify your statement, don't repeat individual words over and over again. Restate your entire message with simple, direct language and short sentences.

- Avoid slang and figures of speech.

- Use gestures to accompany your words.

- English courses for nonnative speakers often emphasize written English, so write down what you're saying. Print your message in capital letters.

- Stay calm, and avoid sending nonverbal messages that you're frustrated.

Look for individuals, not group representatives. Sometimes the way we speak glosses over differences among individuals and reinforces stereotypes. For example, a student worried about her grade in math expresses concern over "all those Asian students who are skewing the class curve." Or a white music major assumes that her black classmate knows a lot about jazz or hip-hop music. We can avoid such errors by seeing people as individuals—not spokespersons for an entire group.

Find a translator, mediator, or model. People who move with ease in two or more cultures can help us greatly. Diane de Anda, a professor at the University of California, Los Angeles, speaks of three kinds of people who can communicate across cultures. She calls them *translators, mediators,* and *models.*[6]

A *translator* is someone who is truly bicultural—a person who relates naturally to both people in a mainstream culture and people from a contrasting culture. This person can share her own experiences in overcoming discrimination, learning another language or dialect, and coping with stress.

Mediators are people who belong to the dominant or mainstream culture. Unlike translators, they might not be bicultural. However, mediators value diversity and are committed to cultural understanding. Often they are teachers, counselors, tutors, mentors, or social workers.

Models are members of a culture who are positive examples. Models include students from any racial or cultural group who participate in class and demonstrate effective study habits. Models can also include entertainers, athletes, and community leaders.

Your school might have people who serve these functions, even if they're not labeled translators, mediators, or models. Some schools have mentor or "bridge" programs that pair new students with teachers of the same race or culture. Ask your student counseling service about such programs.

Develop support systems. Many students find that their social adjustment affects their academic performance. Students with strong support systems—such as families, friends, churches, self-help groups, and mentors—are using a powerful strategy for success in school. As an exercise, list the support systems that you rely on right now. Also list new support systems you could develop.

Support systems can help you bridge culture gaps. With a strong base of support in your own group, you can feel more confident in meeting people outside that group.

Be willing to accept feedback. Members of another culture might let you know that some of your words or actions had a meaning other than what you intended. For example, perhaps a comment that seems harmless to you is offensive to them. And they may tell you directly about it.

Avoid responding to such feedback with comments such as "Don't get me wrong," "You're taking this way too seriously," or "You're too sensitive." Instead, listen without resistance. Open yourself to what others have to say. Remember to distinguish between the *intention* of your behavior and its actual *impact* on other people. Then take the feedback you receive and ask yourself how you can use it to communicate more effectively in the future.

You can also interpret such feedback positively—a sign that others believe you can change and that they see the possibility of a better relationship with you.

If you are new at responding to diversity, expect to make some mistakes along the way. As long as you approach people in a spirit of tolerance, your words and actions can always be changed.

Speak up against discrimination. You might find yourself in the presence of someone who tells a racist joke, makes a homophobic comment, or utters an ethnic slur. When this happens, you have a right to state what you observe, share what you think, and communicate how you feel. Depending on the circumstance, you might say:

- "That's a stereotype, and we don't have to fall for it."

- "Other people are going to take offense at that. Let's tell jokes that don't put people down."

- "I realize that you don't mean to offend anybody, but I feel hurt and angry by what you just said."

- "I know that an African American person told you that story, but I still think it's racist and creates an atmosphere that I don't want to be in."

This kind of speaking may be the most difficult communicating you ever do. However, if you *don't* do it, you give the impression that you agree with biased speech.

In response to your candid comments, many people will apologize and express their willingness to change. Even if they don't, you can still know that you practiced integrity by aligning your words with your values.

Change the institution. None of us lives in isolation. We all live in systems, and these systems do not always tolerate diversity. As a student, you might see people of color ignored in class. You might see people of a certain ethnic group passed over in job hiring or underrepresented in school organizations. And you might see gay and lesbian students ridiculed or even threatened with violence. One way to stop these actions is to point them out.

You can speak more effectively about what you believe by making some key distinctions. Remember the following:

- *Stereotypes* are errors in thinking—inaccurate ideas about members of another culture.

- *Prejudice* refers to positive or negative feelings about others, which are often based on stereotypes.

- *Discrimination* takes places when stereotypes or prejudice gets expressed in policies and laws that undermine equal opportunities for all cultures.

Federal civil rights laws, as well as the written policies of most schools, ban racial and ethnic discrimination. If your school receives federal aid, it must set up procedures that protect students against such discrimination.

Prevent cyberbullying

Cyberbullying means using digital technology to harass, humiliate, or intimidate. It can take many forms, such as those listed here:

- An e-mail or text message with a hostile or threatening tone

- Rumors about you that are posted on your Facebook page or other social networking profile

- Getting deleted from a "friend list" as a deliberate attempt to upset you

- An online profile that's created by someone who pretends to be you

- Any of the above that happens on a repeated basis

Don't put up with cyberbullying in any form. Start by ignoring the harassment or getting offline for a while. If that's not enough, block the perpetrators by changing the privacy settings on your e-mail and text-messaging software. You can also change the username, password, and e-mail address used for your profiles on social networking Web sites.

If you discover a fake online profile about you, then contact the company that runs the Web site and tell them to take it down. To find out how, go to the home page and look for a "Help" link. Click it and then look for a search box. Key in *safety tips, abuse,* or similar keywords.

Also keep an eye on your stress level. If cyberbullying makes it hard for you to carry out your daily activities, that's a definite sign to get professional help. Talk to your academic advisor and a counselor at the campus health service. This is a problem that can be solved.

Throughout recent history, students have fueled social change. Student action helped to shift Americans' attitudes toward segregated universities, the Vietnam War, the military draft, and the invasion of Iraq. When it comes to ending discrimination, you are in an environment where you can make a difference. Run for student government. Write for school publications.

Speak at rallies. Express your viewpoint. This is training for citizenship in a multicultural world.

Take these ideas to work. The term *cultural competence* is starting to replace *diversity skills*. The reason is simple: It's one thing to create a workplace that includes people of various cultural backgrounds. It's another thing to create a workplace where all those people feel welcome. There are many things that you can do to help your organization achieve this goal.

During job interviews, be prepared to give evidence of your cultural competence. Talk about cooperative learning projects with diverse members—and how you involved everyone on the team.

If you travel to other countries for work, also learn to expect differences in behavior. Most of us unconsciously judge others by a single set of cultural standards— our own. That can lead to communication breakdown. Consider some examples:

- A man in Costa Rica works for a company that's based in the United States and has offices around the world. He turns down a promotion that would take his family to California. This choice mystifies the company's executives. Yet the man has grandparents who are in ill health, and leaving them behind would be taboo in his country.

- A Caucasian woman from Ohio travels to Mexico City on business. She shows up promptly for a 9:00 a.m. meeting and finds that it starts 30 minutes late and goes an hour beyond its scheduled ending time. She's entered a culture with a flexible sense of time.

- An American executive schedules a meeting over dinner with people from his company's office in Italy. As soon as the group orders food, the executive launches into a discussion of his agenda items. He notices that his coworkers from Italy seem unusually silent and wonders whether they feel offended. He forgets that they come from a culture where people phase in to business discussions slowly—only after building a relationship through "small talk."

To prevent misunderstandings, remember that culture touches every aspect of human behavior, ranging from the ways that people greet each other to the ways they resolve conflict. Expecting differences up-front helps you keep an open mind.

> *Throughout recent history, students have fueled social change. Student action helped to shift Americans' attitudes toward segregated universities, the Vietnam War, the military draft, and the invasion of Iraq. When it comes to ending discrimination, you are in an environment where you can make a difference.*

Exercise 26   Becoming a culture learner

To learn about other cultures in depth, actively move through the cycle of learning. This exercise, which has three parts, illustrates one way to apply the cycle of learning. Use additional paper as needed to complete each part.

Step 1: Concrete experience

Think of a specific way to interact with people from a culture different from your own. For example, attend a meeting for a campus group that you normally would not attend. Or sit in a campus cafeteria with a new group of people.

Describe what you will do to create your experience of a different culture.

_____

_____

_____

_____

Step 2: Reflective observation

Describe the experience you had while doing Step 1 of this exercise. Be sure to separate your observations—what you saw, heard, or did—from your interpretations. In addition, see whether you can think of other ways to interpret each of your observations.

Use Table 9.1 as a guide for how you can complete this step of the exercise.

Table 9.1 Reflective Observation

Observation	Your Initial Interpretation	Other Possible Interpretations
For 30 minutes, starting at noon on Tuesday, I sat alone in the northeast section of the cafeteria in our student union. During this time, all of the conversations I overheard were conducted in Spanish.	I sat alone because the Spanish-speaking students did not want to talk to me. They are unfriendly.	The Spanish-speaking students are actually friendly. They were just not sure how to start a conversation with me. Perhaps they thought I wanted to eat alone or study. Also, I could have taken the initiative to start a conversation.

Step 3: Abstract conceptualization

Next, see whether you can refine your initial interpretations and develop them into some informed conclusions about your experience in Step 1. Do some research about other cultures, looking specifically for information that can help you understand your experience. (Your instructor and a librarian can suggest ways to find such information.) Whenever possible, speak directly to people of various cultures. Share your observations from Step 1, and ask for *their* interpretations.

Reflect on the information you gather. Does it reinforce any of the interpretations you listed in Step 2? Does it call for a change in your thinking? Summarize your conclusions.

_____

_____

_____

_____

OVERCOME STEREOTYPES
WITH CRITICAL THINKING

Consider assertions such as these: "College students like to drink heavily," "People who speak English as a second language are hard to understand," and "Americans who criticize the president are unpatriotic."

These assertions are examples of stereotyping—generalizing about a group of people based on the behavior of isolated group members. The word *stereotype* originally referred to a method used by printers to produce duplicate pages of text. This usage still rings true. When we stereotype, we gloss over individual differences and assume that every member of a group is a "duplicate." These assumptions are learned, and they can be changed.

Stereotypes infiltrate every dimension of human individuality. People are stereotyped on the basis of their race, ethnic group, religion, political affiliation, geographic location, birthplace, accent, job, economic status, age, gender, sexual orientation, IQ, height, hair color, or hobbies.

Stereotypes have many possible sources: fear of the unknown, uncritical thinking, and negative encounters between individual members of different groups. Whatever their cause, stereotypes abound. In themselves, generalizations are neither good nor bad. In fact, they are essential. Mentally sorting people, events, and objects into groups allows us to make sense of the world.

But when we consciously or unconsciously make generalizations that rigidly divide the people of the world into "us" versus "them," we create stereotypes and put on the blinders of prejudice.

You can take several steps to free yourself from stereotypes.

Look for errors in thinking. Some of the most common errors in thinking are the following:

- *Selective perception.* Stereotypes can literally change the way we see the world. If we assume that homeless people are lazy, for instance, we tend to notice only the examples that support our opinion. Stories about homeless people who are too young or too ill to work will probably escape our attention.

- *Self-fulfilling prophecy.* When we interact with people based on stereotypes, we set them up in ways that confirm our thinking. For example, when people of color were denied access to higher education based on stereotypes about their intelligence, they were deprived of opportunities to demonstrate their intellectual gifts.

- *Self-justification.* Stereotypes can allow people to assume the role of victim and to avoid taking responsibility for their own lives. An unemployed white male might believe that affirmative action programs are making it impossible for him to get a job—even as he overlooks his own lack of experience or qualifications.

Create categories in a more flexible way. Stereotyping has been described as a case of "hardening of the categories." Avoid this problem by making your categories broader. Instead of seeing people based on their skin color, you could look at them on the basis of their heredity (people of all races share most of the same genes). Or you could make your categories narrower. Instead of talking about "religious extremists," look for subgroups among the people who adopt a certain religion. Distinguish between groups that advocate violence and those that shun it.

Test your generalizations about people through action. You can test your generalizations by actually meeting people of other cultures. It's easy to believe almost anything about certain groups of people as long as we never deal directly with individuals. Inaccurate pictures tend to die when people from different cultures study together, work together, and live together. Consider joining a school or community organization that will put you in contact with people of other cultures. Your rewards will include a more global perspective and an ability to thrive in a multicultural world.

Be willing to see your own stereotypes. One belief about yourself that you can shed is *I have no pictures about people from other cultures.* Even people with the best of intentions can harbor subtle biases. Admitting this possibility allows you to look inward even more deeply for stereotypes.

Every time we notice an inaccurate picture buried in our mind and let it go, we take a personal step toward embracing diversity. ■

Students with disabilities:

KNOW YOUR RIGHTS

Andersen Ross/Blend Images/Getty Images

Even the most well-intentioned instructors can forget about assisting people with disabilities. One reason is that disabilities vary so much. For example, some disabilities are visible. Other disabilities—such as hyperactivity disorders and learning disabilities—are invisible. Some disabilities are permanent. Others—such as a broken leg from last weekend's ski trip—are temporary.

At one time, students with disabilities faced a restricted set of choices in school. New technologies, such as computers and calculators operated with voice commands, changed that. Students with disabilities can now choose from almost any course or major offered in higher education.

To protect your rights when dealing with any kind of disability, speak up. Ask for what you want. Listen actively when people respond. Also use the following strategies.

LEARN ABOUT LAWS THAT APPLY TO YOU

Equal opportunity for people with disabilities is the law. In the United States, both the Civil Rights Act of 1964 and the Rehabilitation Act of 1973 offer legal protection. The Americans with Disabilities Act of 1990 extends earlier legislation.

These laws give you the right to ask for academic adjustments based on your needs. Some examples are listed here:

- Arranging for priority registration
- Reducing a course load
- Substituting one course for another
- Providing note takers, recording devices, and sign language interpreters
- Equipping school computers with screen-reading, voice-recognition, or other adaptive software or hardware
- Installing a teletypewriter/telephone device for the deaf (TTY/TDD) in your dorm room if telephones are provided there

In making an adjustment, your school is *not* obligated to change the essential requirements for a course. For example, you can ask for extra testing time. However, your instructor is not required to change the content of the test.

LEARN ABOUT SERVICES AT YOUR SCHOOL

Visit the disability services office at your school. Ask about the adjustments listed here and other options, such as these:

- Permits that allow you to park a car closer to classrooms
- Lecture transcriptions
- Textbook-reading services
- Assistants for laboratory courses in science
- Shuttle buses for transportation between classes
- Closed captioning for instructional television programs
- Interpreters for the hearing impaired
- Books and other course materials in Braille or on audio

The student health center may also offer certain services to people with disabilities. In addition, the Job Accommodation Network offers help in placing employees with learning or physical disabilities. For more information, call (800) 526-7234, or go online to **askjan.org**.

ASK FOR AN ADJUSTMENT

You do not have to reveal that you have a disability. If you want an adjustment or choose to use disability services, however, then you will need to disclose the facts about your condition.

You will probably be asked to document that you have a disability and that you need an adjustment. This documentation might include a written evaluation from a physician, psychologist, or other professional who has worked with you.

To get the adjustment that you want, be prepared to describe the challenges that your disability has created in the past. Help instructors and administrators understand how your education has been affected. Also describe possible solutions, and be as specific as possible.

Ask for adjustments and services as early as possible. These will not be provided automatically. In higher education, you are expected to advocate for yourself.

USE TECHNOLOGY TO YOUR ADVANTAGE

If you have a disability, then gain as many computer skills as possible. Also set up your computer to promote your success. For example, find out how to do the following:

- Enlarge the cursor and adjust its blink rate.
- Enlarge all fonts and icons.
- Zoom in on all or a portion of the screen image.
- Adjust the screen display to remove all color and render images in black and white or gray scale.
- Use voice recognition, rather than the keyboard, for menu options.
- Turn on text-to-speech capabilities so that a computer-generated voice reads menu options, alerts, and Web pages out loud.
- Choose a keyboard layout that's more convenient for typing with one hand or finger.

To access such features in the Windows operating system, select the Windows Control Panel or use the Accessibility Wizard. In Mac OS X, click on the Apple menu in the upper-left corner of the screen and select "System Preferences." In the System Preferences pane, click "Universal Access."

SPEAK ASSERTIVELY

Tell instructors when it's appropriate to consider your disability. If you use a wheelchair, for example, ask for appropriate transportation on field trips. If you have a visual disability, request that instructors speak as they write on the chalkboard. Also ask them to use high-contrast colors and to write legibly.

PLAN AHEAD

Meet with your counselor or advisor to design an educational plan—one that takes your disability into account. A key part of this plan is choosing instructors. Ask for recommendations before registering for classes. Interview prospective instructors, and ask to sit in on their classes. Express an interest in the class; ask to see a course outline; and discuss any adjustments that could help you complete the course.

USE EMPOWERING WORDS

Changing just a few words can make the difference between asking for what you want and apologizing for it. When people refer to disabilities, you might hear words such as *special treatment, accommodation,* and *adaptation.* Experiment with using the terms *adjustment* and *alternative* instead. The difference between these two groups of terms involves equality. Asking for an adjustment in an assignment or for an alternative assignment is asking for the right to produce equal work—not for special treatment that waters down the assignment.

ASK FOR APPROPRIATE TREATMENT

Many instructors will be eager to help you. In fact, at times they might go overboard. For example, a student who has trouble writing by hand might ask to complete in-class writing assignments on a computer. "Okay," the teacher might reply, "and take a little extra time. For you, there's no rush."

For some students this is a welcome response. Others, who have no need for an extended timeline, can reply, "Thank you for thinking of me. I'd prefer to finish the assignment in the time frame allotted for the rest of the class."

FOLLOW UP WHEN NECESSARY

If the academic adjustment that you requested is not working, let your school know right away. Talk to the person who helped set up the adjustment. Remember that schools usually have grievance procedures for resolving conflicts about the services you're receiving.

Almost every school has a person who monitors compliance with disability laws. This person is often called the Section 504 coordinator, ADA coordinator, or disability services coordinator. If you think a school is discriminating against you because of your disability, this is the person to contact. You can also file a complaint against the school with the Office for Civil Rights. For more information, do an Internet search with the key words *contact OCR,* or call (800) 421-3481.

TAKE CARE OF YOURSELF

Many students with chronic illnesses or disabilities find that rest breaks are essential. If this is true for you, write such breaks into your daily or weekly plan.

A related suggestion is to treat yourself with respect. If your health changes in a way that you don't like, avoid berating yourself. Focus on finding an effective medical treatment or other solution.

It's important to accept compliments and periodically review your accomplishments in school. Fill yourself with affirmation. As you educate yourself, you are attaining mastery. ■

DEALING WITH
sexism and sexual
HARASSMENT

Sexism and sexual harassment are real. Incidents that are illegal or violate organizational policies occur throughout the year at schools and in workplaces.

Until the early nineteenth century, women in the United States were banned from attending colleges and universities. Today, women make up the majority of first-year students in higher education, yet they still encounter bias based on gender. Although men also can be subjects of sexism and sexual harassment, women are more likely to experience this form of discrimination.

Bias based on gender can take many forms. For example, instructors might gloss over the contributions of women. Students in philosophy class might never hear of a woman named Hypatia, an ancient Greek philosopher and mathematician. Those majoring in computer science might never learn about Rear Admiral Grace Murray Hopper, who pioneered the development of a computer language named COBOL. And your art history textbook might not mention the Mexican painter Frida Kahlo or the American painter Georgia O'Keeffe.

Even the most well-intentioned people might behave in ways that hurt or discount women. Sexism is a factor in these situations:

- Instructors use only masculine pronouns—*he, his,* and *him*—to refer to both men and women.

- Career counselors hint that careers in mathematics and science are not appropriate for women.

- Students pay more attention to feedback from a male teacher than from a female teacher.

- Women are not called on in class; their comments are ignored; or they are overly praised for answering the simplest questions.

- People assume that middle-aged women who return to school have too many family commitments to study adequately or do well in their classes.

Many kinds of behavior—both verbal and physical—can be categorized as sexual harassment. This kind of discrimination involves unwelcome sexual conduct. Examples of such conduct in a school setting include the following:

- Sexual advances

- Any other unwanted touch

- Displaying or distributing sexually explicit materials

- Sexual gestures or jokes

- Pressure for sexual favors

- Spreading rumors about someone's sexual activity or rating someone's sexual performance

Sexual Harassment: It's Not Academic, a pamphlet from the U.S. Department of Education, quotes a woman who experienced sexual harassment in higher education: "The financial officer made it clear that I could get the money I needed if I slept with him."[7] That's an example of *quid pro quo harassment.* This legal term applies when students believe that an educational decision depends on submitting to unwelcome sexual conduct. *Hostile environment harassment* takes place when such incidents are severe, persistent, or pervasive.

The feminist movement has raised awareness about all forms of harassment. We can now respond to such incidents in the places we live, work, and go to school. Specific strategies follow.

Point out sexist language and behavior. When you see examples of sexism, point them out. Your message can be more effective if you avoid personal attacks. Focus on simply stating what you observe and how you feel about it.

Indicate the specific statements and behaviors that you consider sexist. To help others understand sexism, you might rephrase a sexist comment so that it targets another group, such as Jews or African Americans. People sometimes spot anti-Semitism or racism more readily than sexism.

Keep in mind that men can also be subjected to sexism, ranging from antagonistic humor to exclusion from jobs that have traditionally been done by women.

Observe your own language and behavior. Looking for sexist behavior in others is a good first step in dealing with it. Detecting it in yourself can be just as powerful. Write a Discovery Statement about specific comments that could be interpreted as sexist. Then notice whether you say any of these things. Also, ask people you know to point out occasions when you use similar statements. Follow up with an Intention Statement that describes how you plan to change your speaking or behavior.

You can also write Discovery Statements about the current level of intimacy (physical and verbal) in any of your relationships at home, work, or school. Be sure that any increase in the level of intimacy is mutually agreed upon.

Encourage support for women. Through networks, women can work to overcome the effects of sexism. Strategies include study groups for women, women's job networks, and professional organizations, such as the Association for Women in Communications. Other examples are counseling services and health centers for women, family planning agencies, and rape prevention centers.

If your school does not have the women's networks you want, you can help form them. Help set up a one-day or one-week conference on women's issues. Create a discussion or reading group for the women in your class, department, residence hall, union, or neighborhood.

Take action. If you are sexually harassed, take action. Title IX of the Education Amendments of 1972 prohibits sexual harassment and other forms of sex discrimination. The law also requires schools to have grievance procedures in place for dealing with such discrimination. If you believe that you've been sexually harassed, report the incident to a school official. This person can be a teacher, administrator, or campus security officer. Check to see whether your school has someone specially designated to handle your complaint, such as an affirmative action officer or Title IX coordinator.

You can also file a complaint with the Office for Civil Rights (OCR), a federal agency that makes sure schools and workplaces comply with Title IX. In your complaint, include your name, address, and daytime phone number, along with the date of the incident and a description of it. Do this within 180 days of the incident. You can contact the OCR at (800) 421-3481. Or do an Internet search with the key words *contact OCR*.

Your community might offer more resources to protect against sexual discrimination. Examples are public interest law firms, legal aid societies, and unions that employ lawyers to represent students. ■

8 strategies for nonsexist communication

Following are tools you can use to speak and write in ways that are gender fair—without twisting yourself into verbal knots.

1. Use gender-neutral terms. Instead of writing *policeman* or *chairman*, for example, use *police officer* or *chairperson*. In many cases there's no need to identify the gender or marital status of a person. This allows us to dispose of expressions such as *female driver* and *lady doctor*.

2. Use examples that include both men and women. Good writing thrives on examples and illustrations. As you search for details to support the main points in your paper, include the stories and accomplishments of women as well as men.

3. Alternate pronoun gender. In an attempt to be gender fair, some writers make a point of mentioning both sexes whenever they refer to gender. Another method is to alternate the gender of pronouns throughout your writing. Still another option is to alternate male and female pronouns—the strategy used in this book. This allows you to avoid using awkward wording such as "He/she should open his/her book."

4. Switch to plural. Because plural pronouns in English are not gender specific, a sentence such as *The*

writer has many tools at her disposal becomes *Writers have many tools at their disposal.*

5. Consider the "singular their." An example is *Somebody left their laptop here*. Technically, this is not grammatically correct: The subject and pronoun do not agree in number (*Somebody* is singular; *their* is plural.) The correct versions are *Somebody left* his *laptop here* and *Somebody left* her *laptop here*. However, language use changes over time, and the "singular their" is winning acceptance. Ask your instructors if they accept it.

6. Avoid words that imply sexist stereotypes. Included here are terms such as *tomboy, sissy, office boy, advertising man, man-eater, mama's boy, old lady,* and *powder puff*.

7. Use parallel names. When referring to men and women, use first and last names consistently. Within the same paper, for instance, avoid the phrase *President Barack Obama and his wife*. Instead, write the First Lady's full name: *Michelle Obama*.

8. Visualize a world of gender equality. Our writing is a direct reflection of the way we perceive the world. As we make a habit of recognizing women in roles of leadership, our writing can reflect this shift in viewpoint. That's a powerful step toward gender-fair writing.

Jeff Hunter/Getty Images

LEADERSHIP IN A DIVERSE WORLD

Many people mistakenly think that the only people who are leaders are those with formal titles such as supervisor or manager. In fact, though, some leaders have no such titles. Some have never supervised others. Like Mahatma Gandhi, some people change the face of the world without ever reaching a formal leadership position.

At some point in our lives, all of us will be called to a leadership role. While many of us will never become so well known, we all have the capacity to make significant changes in the world around us. Through our actions and words we constantly influence what happens in our classrooms, offices, communities, and families. We are all leaders, even if sometimes we are unaware of that fact.

Yet no one is born knowing how to lead. We acquire the skills over time. Begin now, while you are in higher education. Campuses offer continual opportunities to gain leadership skills. Volunteer for clubs, organizations, and student government. Look for opportunities to tutor or to become a peer advisor or mentor. No matter what you do, take on big projects—those that are worthy of your time and talents.

The U.S. Census Bureau predicts that the groups once classified as minorities—Hispanics, African Americans, East Asians, and South Asians—will become the majority by the year 2042. For Americans under age 18, this shift will take place in 2023.[8] Translation: Your supervisors and coworkers could be people whose life experiences and views of the world differ greatly from yours.

We live in a world where Barack Obama, a man with ancestors from Kenya and Kansas, became president of the United States; where Bobby Jindal, the son of immigrants from India, became governor of Louisiana; and where Oprah Winfrey, an African American woman, could propel a book to the best seller list simply by recommending it on her television show. These people set examples of diversity in leadership that many others will follow.

Although many of us will never become so well known, we all have the capacity to make significant changes in the world around us. Through our actions and words, we constantly influence what happens in our classrooms, offices, communities, and families. We are all leaders, even if sometimes we are unconscious of that fact.

To become a more effective leader, understand the many ways you naturally influence others. This kind of self-awareness—and the ability to harness that influence

for positive goals—are qualities of master students. Also prepare to apply your leadership skills in a multicultural world.

The following strategies can help you have a positive impact on your relationships with your friends and family members. Also use them when you join study groups and project teams in the workplace.

OWN YOUR LEADERSHIP

Let go of the reluctance that many of us feel toward assuming leadership. It's impossible to escape leadership. Every time you speak, you lead others in some small or large way. Every time you take action, you lead others through your example. Every time you ask someone to do something, you are in essence leading that person. Leadership becomes more effective when it is consciously applied.

BE COURAGEOUS

Leadership is a courageous act. Leaders often are not appreciated or even liked. They are not always comfortable or confident. They can feel isolated—cut off from their colleagues. This isolation can sometimes lead to self-doubt and even fear. Before you take on a leadership role, be aware that you might experience such feelings. Also remember that none of these feelings has to stop you from leading. Courage is the ability to feel your feelings—whatever they are—and still take action.

ALLOW HUGE MISTAKES

The more important and influential you are, the more likely it is that your mistakes will have huge consequences. The chief financial officer for a large company can make a mistake that costs thousands or even millions of dollars. A physician's error could cost a life. As commander-in-chief of the armed forces, the president of a country can make a decision that costs thousands of lives. At the same time, these people are in a position to make huge changes for the better—to save thousands of dollars or lives through their power, skill, and influence.

People in leadership positions can become paralyzed and ineffective if they fear making a mistake. It's necessary for them to act even when information is incomplete or when they know a catastrophic mistake is a possible outcome.

TAKE ON BIG PROJECTS

Leaders make promises. And effective leaders make big promises. These words—*I will do it* and *You can count on me*—distinguish a leader.

Look around your world to see what needs to be done, and then take it on. Consider taking on the biggest project you can think of—ending world hunger, eliminating nuclear weapons, wiping out poverty, promoting universal literacy. Think about how you'd spend your life if you knew that you could make a difference regarding these overwhelming problems. Then take the actions you considered. See what a difference they can make for you and for others.

Tackle projects that stretch you to your limits—projects that are worthy of your time and talents.

TAKE ON SMALL PROJECTS

Great leaders, including those with the grandest vision, can still focus on details when they choose. If they commit to a goal that will take 50 years to achieve, they divide that goal into a related series of smaller projects. In turn, those projects get translated into action steps that people can start doing today. Leaders recognize that long journeys begin with small, carefully planned steps.

> *Leadership is the art of helping others lift their eyes to the horizon—keeping them in touch with the ultimate value and purpose of a project. Keeping the vision alive helps spirits soar.*

PROVIDE FEEDBACK

An effective leader is a mirror to others. Share what you see. Talk with others about what they are doing effectively—and what they are doing ineffectively.

Keep in mind that people might not enjoy your feedback. Some would probably rather not hear it at all. Two things can help. One is to let people know up front that if they sign on to work with you, they can expect feedback. Also give your feedback with skill. Back up any criticisms with specific observations and facts. And when people complete a task with exceptional skill, point that out too.

PAINT A VISION

Help others see the big picture—the ultimate purpose of a project. Speak a lot about the end result and the potential value of what you're doing.

There's a biblical saying: "Without vision, the people perish." Long-term goals usually involve many intermediate steps. Unless we're reminded of the purpose for those day-to-day actions, our work can feel like a grind. Leadership is the art of helping others lift their eyes to the horizon—keeping them in touch with the ultimate value and purpose of a project. Keeping the vision alive helps spirits soar.

MODEL YOUR VALUES

"Be the change you want to see" is a useful motto for leaders. Perhaps you want to see integrity, focused attention, and productivity in the people around you. Begin by modeling these qualities yourself. It's easy to excite others about a goal when you are enthusiastic about it yourself. Having fun while being productive is contagious. If you bring these qualities to a project, others might follow suit.

MAKE REQUESTS— LOTS OF THEM

An effective leader is a request machine. Making requests—both large and small—is an act of respect. When we ask a lot from others, we demonstrate our respect for them and our confidence in their abilities.

At first, some people might get angry when we make requests of them. Over time, however, many will see that requests are compliments and opportunities to expand their skills. Ask a lot from others, and they might appreciate you because of it.

FOLLOW UP

What we don't inspect, people don't respect. When other people agree to do a job for you, follow up to see how it is going. You can do so in a way that communicates your respect and interest—not your fear that the project might flounder. When you display a genuine interest in other people and their work, they are more likely to view you as a partner in achieving a shared goal.

FOCUS ON SOLUTIONS

Sometimes projects do not go as planned. Big mistakes occur. If this happens, focus on the project and the mistakes—not the personal faults of your colleagues. People do not make mistakes on purpose. If they did, we would call them "on-purposes," not mistakes. Most people will join you in solving a problem if your focus is on solving a problem, not on what they did wrong.

ACKNOWLEDGE OTHERS

Express genuine appreciation for the energy and creativity that others have put into their work. Take the time to be interested in what others have done and to care about the results they have accomplished. Thank and acknowledge them with your eyes, your words, and the tone of your voice.

SHARE CREDIT

As a leader, constantly give away the praise and acknowledgment that you receive. When you're congratulated for your performance, pass the praise on to others. Share the credit with the group.

When you're a leader, the results you achieve depend on the efforts of many others. Acknowledging that fact often is more than telling the truth—it's essential if you want to continue to count on the support of others in the future.

DELEGATE

Ask a coworker or classmate to take on a job that you'd like to see done. Ask the same of your family or friends. Delegate tasks to the mayor of your town, the governor of your state, and the leaders of your country.

Take on projects that are important to you. Then find people who can lead the effort. You can do this even when you have no formal role as a leader.

We often see delegation as a tool that's available only to those above us in the chain of command. Actually, delegating up or across an organization can be just as effective. Consider delegating a project to your boss. That is, ask him to take on a job that you'd like to see accomplished. It might be a job that you cannot do, given your position in the company.

BALANCE STYLES

Think for a moment about your own learning style. To lead effectively, assess your strengths, and look for people who can complement them. If you excel at gathering information and setting goals, for example, then recruit people who like to make decisions and take action. Also enlist people who think creatively and generate different points of view.

Leaders on leadership

Leadership has a harder job to do than just choose sides. It must bring sides together.
–Jesse Jackson

You take people as far as they would like to go, not as far as you would like them to go.
–Jeannette Rankin

The brand of leadership we propose has a simple base of MBWA (Management By Wandering Around). To "wander," with customers, vendors, and our own people, is to be in touch with the first vibrations of the new.
–Tom Peters and Nancy Austin

The only real training for leadership is leadership.
–Antony Jay

Uncertainty will always be part of the taking-charge process.
–John J. Gabarro

Some leaders are born women.
–Slogan, United Nations International Women's Day Conference

Leadership cannot really be taught. It can only be learned.
–Harold Green

I start with the premise that the function of leadership is to produce more leaders, not more followers.
–Ralph Nader

Look for different styles in the people who work with you. Remember that learning results from a balance between reflection, action, abstract thinking, and concrete experience. The people you lead will combine these characteristics in infinite variety. Welcome that variety, and accommodate it.

You can defuse and prevent many conflicts simply by acknowledging differences in style. Doing so opens up more options than blaming the differences on "politics" or "personality problems."

> *Leadership is an acquired skill. No one is born knowing how to make requests, give feedback, create budgets, do long-range planning, or delegate tasks. We learn these things over time.*

LISTEN

As a leader, be aware of what other people are thinking, feeling, and wanting. Listen fully to their concerns and joys. Before you criticize their views or make personal judgments, take the time to understand what's going on inside them. This is not merely a personal favor to the people you work with. The more you know about your coworkers or classmates, the more effectively you can lead them.

COMMUNICATE ASSERTIVELY— NOT AGGRESSIVELY OR PASSIVELY

Aggressive communication is ineffective. People who act aggressively are domineering. They often get what they want by putting down other people or using strong-arm methods. When aggressive people win, other people lose.

Assertive communication is asking directly and confidently for what you want *and* showing respect for others at the same time. This is one sign of an effective leader. Assertive people are committed to win-win solutions.

Some of us don't act assertively out of fear that we will appear aggressive. This is *passive* communication— neither assertive nor aggressive—that gets us nowhere. By remaining quiet and submissive, we allow others to infringe on our rights. When others run our lives, we fail to have the lives we want.

PRACTICE

Leadership is an acquired skill. No one is born knowing how to make requests, give feedback, create budgets, do long-range planning, or delegate tasks. We learn these things over time, with practice, by seeing what works and what doesn't.

As a process of constant learning, leadership calls for all of the skills of master students. Look for areas in which you can make a difference, and experiment with these strategies. Right now there's something worth doing that calls for your leadership. Take action, and others will join you. ■

Journal Entry 21
Discovery/Intention Statement

Removing barriers to communication

Effective leaders act as a mirror to others. They talk with others about what they are doing effectively—*and* what they are doing ineffectively.

People might not enjoy your feedback. Some would probably rather not hear it at all. Two things can help. One is to let people know up front that if they work with you, they can expect feedback. Also, give your feedback with skill.

Whenever you serve as a leader, examine your relationships. Then complete the following statements:

I discovered that I am not communicating about . . .

_____

_____

with . . .

_____

I discovered that I am not communicating about . . .

_____

_____

with . . .

_____

I discovered that I am not communicating about . . .

_____

_____

with . . .

_____

Now choose one idea from this chapter that can open communication with these people in these areas. Describe how you will use this idea.

I intend to . . .

_____

_____

_____

_____

_____

Practicing Critical Thinking 9

Remember that psychologist Benjamin Bloom described six levels of thinking:

Level 1: Remembering

Level 2: Understanding

Level 3: Applying

Level 4: Analyzing

Level 5: Evaluating

Level 6: Creating

To complete this exercise, you'll experiment with combining levels and taking them in a different sequence.

Level 1: Remembering and Level 2: Understanding

Recall an example of discrimination or sexual harassment that you've personally experienced or witnessed. If you cannot come up with an example from your own life, then describe one that you remember from a book, television program, video, or film. Briefly describe this event.

_____

_____

_____

_____

Level 5: Evaluating

List two or three of the most valuable suggestions you gained from this chapter for overcoming discrimination or sexual harassment. Explain why you think these suggestions are valuable.

_____

_____

_____

_____

Level 3: Applying and Level 4: Analyzing

Describe the actions you could take to use these suggestions that you just listed.

_____

_____

_____

_____

Level 6: Creating

Has reading this chapter and completing this exercise changed the way you will communicate with people from other cultures? If so, explain what you will do differently in the future. If not, give reasons for continuing your current behavior.

_____

_____

_____

_____

MASTER STUDENT PROFILE

David Levenson/Getty Images
Entertainment/Getty Images

CHIMAMANDA ADICHIE

(1977–) Born in Nigeria, earned graduate degrees from Johns Hopkins and Yale, and authored novels Purple Hibiscus *and* Half of a Yellow Sun

When Chimamanda Adichie left her native Nigeria to attend college in the United States, her first roommate was American. She was surprised that Adichie spoke English so well.

Adichie told her that the official language of Nigeria is English.

Her roommate asked to listen to some of Adichie's "tribal music."

Adichie pulled out a tape of Mariah Carey songs.

The roommate also assumed that Adichie did not know how to use a stove.

In reality, Adichie's father was a professor at the University of Nigeria, and her mother worked there as an administrator. Their family could afford live-in, domestic help. Chinua Achebe—one of Africa's most famous writers—had once lived in their house.

During a TED Talk in 2009, Adichie recalled this conversation. "My roommate had a single story of Africa: a single story of catastrophe. In this single story there was no possibility of Africans being similar to her in any way, no possibility of feelings more complex than pity, no possibility of a connection as human equals."

Adichie also recalled that she learned to read before age 5, devouring British and American children's books. By age 7, she was writing stories with crayon illustrations. Her characters were white. They ate apples. They enjoyed playing in the snow and talking about the weather, especially when the sun finally emerged from cloudy skies.

Yet she was living in Nigeria, a land of constant sun and no snow. She ate mangoes, not apples. And her friends never discussed the weather.

To Adichie, this conflict between life from literature demonstrates the danger of a single story.

Chimamanda Adichie *is able to suspend judgment.*
You *can suspend judgment by looking for more than a single way of describing any event.*

Things changed when she discovered books from African writers such as Achebe and Camara Laye: "I realized that people like me, girls with skin the color of chocolate, whose kinky hair could not form ponytails, could also exist in literature." She learned that books can tell more than one story, and that any event can be described from more than one viewpoint.

This is a theme that Adichie explores in much of her writing. Her novel *Half of a Yellow Sun*, for example, is told from the perspective of three characters: a teenage Nigerian boy, a rich young Nigerian woman, and a white man from England.

"Generalizations are always reductive, I think, because they shrink you from a whole to a mere part," Adichie says. "I am Nigerian, feminist, Black, Igbo [an ethnic group in southeastern Nigeria], and more, but when I am categorized as one, it makes it almost impossible to be seen as all of the others, and I find this limiting."

Adichie says that storytelling and power are closely linked. When anyone can tell a single story about us and make it the *only* story, that person dominates us.

This is why novelists and other storytellers are so important in our multinational world. They can tell many stories about any person or place. They open our eyes to complexity and diversity. And in embracing those varied stories, Adichie says, "we regain a kind of paradise." ■

QUIZ
Chapter 9

Name _____

Date _____

1. The Power Process: Choose your conversations describes several forms of conversation and then lists three implications. List those implications.

   Conversations exercise incredible power over what we think, feel, and do. Given that conversations are so powerful, it's amazing that few people act on this fact. We can choose our conversations. (*Power Process: Choose your conversations*, page 270)

2. Give two examples of differences between individualist and collectivist cultures.

   Individualist cultures value personal fulfillment and personal success and emphasize "I" over "we." Collectivist cultures value cooperation over competition and believe that group progress is more important than individual success. (*Building relationships across cultures*, page 274)

3. Briefly describe three strategies for building relationships across cultures.

   List and discuss three of the following (answers will vary): (a) Start with self-discovery. (b) Learn about other cultures. (c) Look for differences between individualist and collectivist cultures. (d) Reach out. (e) Look for common ground. (f) Speak and listen with cultural sensitivity. (g) Look for individuals, not group representatives. (h) Find a mediator, translator, or model. (i) Develop support systems. (j) Be willing to accept feedback. (k) Speak up against discrimination. (l) Change the institution. (*Building relationships across cultures*, page 274)

4. Explain the differences among *stereotypes*, *prejudice*, and *discrimination*.

   Stereotypes are inaccurate ideas about members of another culture. Prejudice refers to positive or negative feelings about others, often based on stereotypes. Discrimination occurs when stereotypes or prejudice is expressed in policies and laws that undermine equal opportunities for all cultures. (*Building relationships across cultures*, page 274)

5. Define the terms *translator*, *mediator*, and *model* as explained in this chapter.

   A *translator* is truly bicultural and relates skillfully to both people in a mainstream culture and people from a contrasting culture. *Mediators* belong to the dominant or mainstream culture. Though perhaps not bicultural, mediators value diversity and are committed to cultural understanding. *Models* are positive examples of members of a culture. Models may include entertainers, athletes, and community leaders. (*Building relationships across cultures*, page 274)

6. The text suggests looking for individuals rather than group representatives. Explain this suggestion in your own words.

   We should consider and think about people as individuals, not of a certain ethnicity or group. This helps us avoid seeing all members of certain groups in a stereotypical way. (*Building relationships across cultures*, page 274)

7. Describe an error in thinking that helps to create stereotypes.

   Answers will vary but should include one of the following: *Self-justification* helps people avoid responsibility, seeing themselves as victims rather than responsible for their own circumstances. *Selective perception* can change the way we see the world and we tend to notice only the examples that support our opinion. *Self-fulfilling prophecy* is when we set people up in ways that confirm our thinking. (*Overcome stereotypes with critical thinking*, page 279)

8. Briefly explain the difference between *quid pro quo harassment* and *hostile environment harassment*.

   Quid pro quo harassment occurs when students believe that an educational decision depends on their submitting to unwelcome sexual conduct, whereas *hostile environment harassment* takes place when such incidents are severe, persistent, or pervasive (*Dealing with sexism and sexual harassment*, page 282)

9. Rewrite the following sentence so that it is gender neutral: "Any writer can benefit from honing his skill at observing people."

   (Answers will vary.) One possibility is switching to the plural: "Writers can benefit from honing their skills at observing people." (*Strategies for nonsexist communication*, page 283)

10. According to the text, few of us get the chance to be leaders. True or false? Explain your answer.

    False. We all have the capacity to make significant changes in the world around us. Almost all of us encounter situations in which we can function as leaders. (*Leadership in a diverse world*, page 284)

⊛ SKILLS SNAPSHOT
Chapter 9

Now that you've reflected on the ideas in this chapter and experimented with some new strategies, reflect on your current skills at living with diversity. Then create a specific intention to act with more mastery in this area of your life.

Discovery

My score on the Diversity section of the Discovery Wheel was . . .

If I talk to people who express racial and ethnic stereotypes, I respond by . . .

When I meet someone whose culture differs in a major way from mine, my first reaction is often to . . .

Intention

I'll know that I've reached a new level of mastery with diversity when I am able to . . .

To reach this level of mastery, I intend to . . .

I intend to apply my new skills to my career by . . .

Action

In thinking about diversity, the most important new habit that I can adopt right now is . . .

My cue for remembering to practice this habit is . . .

INSTRUCTOR TOOLS & TIPS

MONEY

"There are people who have money and people who are rich." —Coco Chanel

PREVIEW

Money—or rather the lack of money—is the most common reason students give for withdrawing from college. This important issue has been covered in all editions of *Becoming a Master Student*, but with tuition increases on the rise in most states, the need for first-year college students to develop a mature financial literacy is crucial to their college survival. Understanding the economic aspects of completing a degree is more essential now than ever. The articles in this chapter help students explore ways to manage money during tough times and relate their learning style to how they spend their money. This chapter also challenges students to think about what money means to them and how they can use money to achieve their goals without letting money use them. Spend time explaining the concept of credit scores to your students. For many, this is a new concept. Encourage students to share their success stories as well as financial challenges as you cover this chapter.

GUEST SPEAKER

Invite the Financial Aid Director from your campus to talk to students about financial aid opportunities, deadlines, and forms they need to fill out. You may discover that your students have more questions for this guest speaker than for any of the others! Discussing money in class can raise student awareness and provide opportunity to model critical thinking.

LECTURE

There are three absolute financial disasters awaiting unsuspecting college students that can be avoided—avoiding late fees, keeping a current account register, and protecting yourself from identity theft.

Avoid late fees. Prioritizing spending with a simple budget can help students avoid paying late fees. Discuss the importance of paying credit card bills on time. Point out that after just one late payment, some credit card companies boost interest rates beyond 31 percent and charge late fees of nearly $40. And some credit card

master instructor best practice

five-year plan of action

"*I have students start researching jobs in their field of study. We then will go to specific Web sites that advertise jobs, looking at the descriptions, education required, and so on. I then ask them if they think the curriculum of their major will give them the required background to be able to apply for a particular job. This gives them the opportunity to review our curriculum, and they can decide the course of action needed to pursue various jobs in their field of choice. We then discuss the issue of debt and financing the debt. We look at realtor.com and review costs of living expenses and compare the cost of living in two or three different locations. When they compare jobs and salaries, they should have a complete understanding of how job salaries differ, based on multiple variables, including the cost of living from one city to another. We utilize Kiplinger.com as a supplemental Web site for additional materials, like worksheets. Students submit a research paper and PowerPoint presentation based on their findings.*"

—Donald W. Becker, Delaware State University

master instructor
best practice

"Periods of economic difficulty provide an opportunity to talk to your classes about prospering in spite of hardship. For example, I provide examples of people in our country's history who made their fortunes in difficult times. Changes in the economic climate call for critical thinking skills. We must change our patterns as circumstances change. We discuss the differences between needs and wants, as well as how to find "hidden money" in our budgets. We look at scenarios where there are many possible solutions, and we discuss the stages of decision making found in Chapter 7. We discuss the fact that students often delay purchasing textbooks, waiting for financial aid checks. We look at ways to save for next semester's textbooks this semester, asking students to recall the problems they face when they do not purchase their textbooks in a timely manner. Half the battle of financial security is advance planning."

—Annette McCreedy, Nashville State Community College

companies raise rates if you miss a deadline on another card, even if you have a spotless record with them. Suggest that students pay scheduled bills automatically if possible. Setting up a separate account so that their set bills will be paid automatically from their bank account saves students the hassle of writing monthly checks and worrying about mail delays; it also protects them from costly missed deadlines. Illustrate for students the benefit of paying more than the minimum on credit.

Keep a current account register. Maintaining an up-to-date account register can be the difference between graduating and dropping out. Barry Oats, a former collegiate football player, suggests a trick he learned from legendary football coach Lavell Edwards that can help any student. Simply play your money like a weekly football game.

First, make a financial "game plan" for the week by predicting your income and expenses. On Thursday night, do a "half-time check" to make sure your income tops your expenses. Finally, on Sunday afternoon reconcile your accounts by matching your receipts with your game plan. If you have cash left over after accounting for all your spending, you win! If you don't have leftover cash,

analyze what happened to throw you off your financial game. All coaches and players know the impact of reviewing what went right . . . and what went wrong.

EXERCISES/ACTIVITIES

1. **Education by the hour (page 312).** Consider having your students complete this exercise during class. When all the students have computed their actual direct and indirect costs of attending one class meeting, have them write the figure anonymously on a 3×5 card and put the cards on the chalk/whiteboard tray in order from lowest to highest. Then point out that the amount on the card is also the amount that students throw away each time they miss a class meeting during the term. Bring $100 in $1 bills and select a card with an amount that is close to $100 without going over it. Dramatically pull the hundred bills out of your pocket and count out the total on the 3×5 card, tossing the $1 bills onto a table one by one. Then pick up the wad of cash and throw it into the classroom trash can as a graphic illustration of how money is lost every time a class meeting is skipped. Without fail, you'll likely hear students gasp! Of course, the money loss is just one aspect of missing class, but students will get the point. Ask them each to retrieve their card and put it where they will see it frequently and be reminded of the cost of missing classes.

   Preparation note: Although students are doing their calculations and filling out their cards, sneak over to the trash can and line it with another trash bag to protect the dollar bills you'll throw in it later! Don't worry about forgetting to retrieve your cash—the students' eyes won't leave the trash can until you pull out the liner with the cash! (*Note:* This activity is adapted from a similar presentation by Dave Ellis when he was teaching instructors how to illustrate the articles in *Becoming a Master Student*.)

2. **Take charge of your credit (pages 308–310).** A month before you get to Chapter 10, tell students to keep all credit card offers they receive in the mail. Have them bring the offers to class on a specific day. Divide the class into groups, and ask them to analyze the offers in terms of the promotional interest rate, regular interest rate, credit limits, annual fees, and penalties for late payments. Students who did not receive any offers can borrow some from students who received several daily! Then ask the students if any of the offers in their group provide a better deal than the rate, limit, fees, and penalties on the credit card(s) they currently use. Most students won't know these facts about their current credit card(s). This is a good lead-in to a homework assignment to investigate their credit cards. Remind students to shred these offers when you finish this exercise.

3. **Master Student Profile: Sara Blakely (page 316).** After students have read this inspirational story, divide them into groups, and ask them to brainstorm a money-making product or service idea. Then brainstorm

five steps that would be necessary to bring this idea to fruition and five marketing ideas that would help promote the product or service. Ask each group to make a two-minute summary report to the rest of the class.

CONVERSATION/SHARING

Power Process: Risk being a fool (page 294). Begin the discussion of this Power Process by asking students, "What percentage of the shots you never take in a basketball game will you miss?" (Zero percent is the answer.) Then follow up with this question: "Will you ever win a game?" The answer, of course, is no. This example helps students connect to this Power Process by thinking about the risks they are taking—or not taking. Then we cycle through the learning styles reasoning model.

Why?　Why is "Risk being a fool" a Power Process that applies to you? If not, why not?

What?　What do you have to understand in order to practice "Risk being a fool"?

How?　How can you transfer the power out of this process and into your life as a student?

What if?　What if you apply "Risk being a fool" in your other classes? Or what if you don't?

Workplace Application: Working while in school. For many students attending college is a full time job in itself. Others find it necessary to explore employment opportunities while taking classes. There are many benefits to working while in school. School and work can be managed successfully with good time-management and organizational skills. Encourage students to visit the campus job placement or career services office for information on job postings and on-campus interviews. Online resources such as Indeed and Monster can also be helpful with a job search.

Networking is a skill students need to become comfortable with as early as possible in their college career. Statistics show that although online and newspaper job advertisements are somewhat useful, the most successfully job search method is networking. Students can begin to successfully cultivate their network as soon as they enroll in school. Remind them that their network is made of people they know through school, work, church, or community affiliations. Networking can be a rewarding, lifelong activity that should always be part of professional development. Encourage students to approach networking as more than just a request for a job; they will want to build meaningful relationships with others.

Students may also be eligible to work on campus through the Federal Work-Study Program. Students can visit the campus financial aid office for information on eligibility and requirements. The Federal Work-Study Program allows eligible students to gain valuable work experience while obtaining needed funds for school. Many students prefer work-study positions for the convenience and opportunity to further connect with the campus community. Successful work-study students have even been offered full-time positions with the college upon graduation.

HOMEWORK

The ultimate question. This is a good time to use an "ultimate question" activity to encourage students to read this chapter and engage in a critical thinking approach to exploring the ideas and learning how they can manage money. Many students waste money by not keeping track of their spending. For some students, this is simply due to a lack of skills. In contrast, knowing what financial resources they have at any given moment is characteristic of master students. Begin this chapter by having your students ask themselves the "ultimate question": *What do I not know about money that I need to know?*" Then encourage your students to learn *how* they can acquire this knowledge. Ask them to predict: *What if* they were to apply these new skills to their course work—and in the workplace. Have your students review the list of articles included in the chapter and put an "X" by the topics they do know and a check mark by the items they don't know or are unsure of. As they go through the list, they can also rate their knowledge of the topic or their confidence in their skills, using a scale of 1 to 10 (with 10 being very knowledgeable or confident). Then they can do a chapter reconnaissance by touching each page of the chapter. When this approach is finished, your students will have created an active framework in their mind for the financial literacy information in this chapter.

The Money Monitor/Money Plan (pages 296–300). Tell your students that this is similar to the Time Monitor in Chapter 2. The first step in managing their money is to see objectively how much money they have and how they spend it. If they think back to the invaluable knowledge they obtained from the Time Monitor, they will be willing to spend the time to complete this admittedly lengthy task for the awareness it will provide them.

As students examine the findings of this exercise, remind them that simple changes can make a big difference. Start by examining small possibilities: making coffee at home in the mornings, changing to energy-saving lightbulbs, cutting down on their driving, or just slowing down to conserve fuel when driving. See whether your local electric company provides hints for cutting down energy usage in the home. Ask students to make a note in their planners to examine their financial progress in a month or more.

EVALUATION

Ask students to describe ways of making more money while in college. Have them write specific Intention Statements about protecting their money online. Ask them how they intend to spend less money and to discuss one or more money-management strategies that are especially useful during tough economic times. Ask students how they can take charge of their credit cards.

MindTap™ **EMBRACE VALUABLE RESOURCES**

FOR CHAPTER 10

STUDENT RESOURCES: MINDTAP

- **Engagement Activity: Master Students in Action Video.** Students hear firsthand from other students about their experiences and challenges with managing money. The Master Students in Action videos give your students an up-close view of how the strategies in *Becoming a Master Student* have helped their peers overcome obstacles. In special segments, Dave Ellis offers students his best strategies for mastering each chapter's content.

- **This book is worth $1,000.** Are your students struggling to pay for school? Suggest that they enter Cengage Learning's College Success Scholarship Essay Contest to win one of three $1,000 awards. All they have to do to enter is to write an essay answering the question "How Do You Define Success?" This essay should not exceed 750 words. Find out more information at **www.cengage.com**.

- **Aplia Homework Assignment: Money Monitor/Money Plan.** In this assignment, students learn how to use a money monitor to improve their decision making in matters of personal finance. Students are tasked with calculating a sample student's expenses and how they relate to his income.

- **Reflection Activity: Keep on Peeling.** This Slice of Life video, created by student and animator Sean Kai Rafferty, uses peeling an orange in a spiral as a metaphor for the importance of perseverance and loving what you do.

MindTap™ *Your personal learning experience—learn anywhere, anytime.*

INSTRUCTOR COMPANION SITE

- **Looking for test banks?** Customizable, text-specific content quizzes are a great way to test students' knowledge and understanding of the text, and are available for every chapter. Powered by Cognero, the test banks can be exported in an LMS or print-friendly format. You will have no problem accessing the multiple-choice, true/false, completion, and short-answer questions.

- **Looking for fresh, innovative ways to teach Chapter 10 topics?** Browse through the Best Practices recommendations in the Course Manual to see what other Master Instructors have been successfully doing with their students.

  Please visit login.cengage.com to log in and access the Instructor Companion Site.

master instructor
best practice

"I find that many of our students have no experience with budgeting. They get money from their parents when they overspend, or work extra hours when they get in serious debt. Many will not buy textbooks because money is tight. This is a big, big problem on our large urban campus. Students get into debt and then work 30 or more hours per week to pay it down or for general living expenses. Because of this extra workload their grades suffer and they lose financial aid and the cycle starts all over again. ... I like that the exercise makes students realize where (and on what) they're spending money each month. They often complain that they have no money for books or school-related expenses, not realizing that they've spent money on designer clothing and accessories, electronic gadgets, eating out, trips, and so on."

—*Letitia Thomas, University at Buffalo*

MONEY

10

Why

Money can stop being a barrier to getting what you want from school—and from your life.

How

Scan this chapter with an eye for strategies that could help you increase your income, decrease your expenses, or both. Note three money strategies that you'd like to use right away.

What if...

I could adopt habits that would free me from money worries for the rest of my life?

TECH

Use tools to tame your money ■ 313

Education pays off—and you can pay for it Education is one of the few things you can buy that will last a lifetime. It can't rust, corrode, break down, or wear out. It can't be stolen, burned, repossessed, or destroyed. Once you have a degree, no one can take it away. ■ 312

Managing money during tough times If the economy tanks, we can benefit by telling the truth about it. It's one thing to have an unpaid balance on a credit card or wipe out a savings account and still believe that we are in charge of our money. ■ 306

What is included ...

RISK BEING A FOOL

A master student has the courage to take risks. And taking risks means being willing to fail sometimes—even being willing to be a fool. This idea can work for you because you already are a fool.

Don't be upset. All of us are fools at one time or another. There are no exceptions. If you doubt it, think back to that stupid thing you did just a few days ago. You know the one. Yes . . . *that* one. It was embarrassing, and you tried to hide it. You pretended you weren't a fool. This happens to everyone.

We are all fallible human beings. Most of us, however, spend too much time and energy trying to hide our foolhood. No one is really tricked by this—not even ourselves. It's okay to look ridiculous while dancing. It's all right to sound silly when singing to your kids. Sometimes it's okay to be absurd. It comes with taking risks.

This Power Process comes with a warning label: Taking risks does *not* mean escaping responsibility for our actions. "Risk being a fool" is not a suggestion to get drunk at a party and make a fool of yourself. It is not a suggestion to fool around or do things badly. Mediocrity is not the goal.

The point is that mastery in most activities calls for the willingness to do something new, to fail, to make corrections, to fail again, and so on.

Take money, for example. This chapter asks you to consider an outrageous idea—that you can end money worries. If you share this idea with your friends, they might think you've fallen for some get-rich-quick scheme. Someone might even call you a fool. If you're okay with those reactions, then nobody's criticism will stop you. You're free to explore any idea and even make a few mistakes. In the process, you could learn something that changes your whole experience of money.

"Risk being a fool" means that foolishness—along with courage, cowardice, grace, and clumsiness— is a human characteristic. We all share it. You might as well risk being a fool because you already are one, and nothing in the world can change that. Why not enjoy it once in a while?

There's one sure-fire way to avoid any risk of being a fool, and that's to avoid life. The writer who never finishes a book will never have to worry about getting negative reviews. The center fielder who sits out every game is safe from making any errors. And the comedian who never performs in front of an audience is certain to avoid telling jokes that fall flat. The possibility of succeeding at any venture increases when we're comfortable with making mistakes—that is, with the risk of being a fool. ▆

The end of
MONEY
WORRIES

> *Most money problems result from spending more than is available. It's that simple, even though we often do everything we can to make the problem much more complicated.*

The solution also is simple: *Don't spend more than you have.* If you are spending more than you have, then increase your income, decrease your spending, or do both. This idea has never won a Nobel Prize in Economics, but you won't go broke applying it to your life.

Money produces more unnecessary conflict and worry than almost anything else. And it doesn't seem to matter how much money a person has. People who earn $10,000 a year never have enough. People who earn $100,000 a year might also say that they never have enough.

Let's say they earned $1 million a year. Then they'd have enough, right? Not necessarily. Money worries can upset people no matter how much they have, especially when the economy dips into recession.

Money management may be based on a simple idea, but there is a big incentive for us to make it seem more complicated and scarier than it really is. If we don't understand money, then we don't have to be responsible for it. After all, if you don't know how to change a flat tire, then you don't have to be the one responsible for fixing it.

"I can't afford it" is a common reason that students give for dropping out of school. Actually, "I don't know how to pay for it" or "I don't think it's worth it" are probably more accurate ways to state the problem.

Using the strategies in this chapter could help you create financial peace of mind. That's a bold statement—perhaps even an outrageous one. But what if it's true? Approach this idea as a possibility. Then experiment with it, using your own life as the laboratory.

This chapter can benefit you even during a recession. Although the state of the overall economy matters as well, your financial fate depends far more on the small choices you make every day about spending and earning money.

The strategies you're about to learn are not complicated. In fact, they're not even new. The strategies are all based on the cycle of discovery, intention, and action that you've already practiced with the Journal Entries in this book. With these strategies—and the abilities to add and subtract—you have everything you need to manage your money.

There are three main steps in money management:
- First, tell the truth about how much money you have and how much you spend (discovery).
- Second, commit to spend less than you have (intention).
- Finally, apply the suggestions for earning more money, spending less money, or both (action).

If you do these three things consistently, you can eventually say goodbye to most money worries. For example, the single habit of paying off your entire credit card balance each month might be enough to transform your financial life.

This chapter about money does not tell you how to become a millionaire, though you can certainly adopt that as a goal if you choose. Instead, the following pages reveal what many millionaires know—ways to control money instead of letting money control you. ∎

This book is worth $1,000

Cengage Learning is proud to present three students each year with a $1,000 scholarship for tuition reimbursement. Any post-secondary school in the United States and Canada can nominate one student for the scholarship. To be considered, write an essay that answers the question "How do you define success?"

Exercise 27
The Money Monitor/Money Plan

Many of us find it easy to lose track of money. It likes to escape when no one is looking. And usually, no one *is* looking. That's why the simple act of noticing the details about money can be so useful—even if this is the only idea from the chapter that you ever apply.

Use this exercise as a chance to discover how money flows into and out of your life. The goal is to record all the money you receive and spend over the course of one month. This sounds like a big task, but it's simpler than you might think. Besides, there's a big payoff for this action. With increased awareness of income and expenses, you can make choices about money that will change your life. Here's how to begin.

Step 1. Tear out Figure 10.2, the Money Monitor/Money Plan form on page 299.

Make photocopies of this form to use each month. The form helps you do two things. One is to get a big picture of the money that flows in and out of your life. The other is to plan specific and immediate changes in how you earn and spend money.

Step 2. Keep track of your income and expenses.

Use your creativity to figure out how you want to carry out this step. The goal is to create a record of exactly how much you earn and spend each month. Use any method that works for you. And keep it simple. Following are some options:

- **Save all receipts and file them.** Every time you buy something, ask for a receipt. Then stick it in your wallet, purse, or pocket. When you get home, make notes about the purchase on the receipt. Then file the receipts in a folder labeled with the current month and year (for example, January 2014). Every time you get a paycheck during that month, also save the stub and add it to the folder. If you do not get a receipt or record of payment, then create one of your own. Detailed receipts will help you later on when you file taxes, categorize expenses (such as food and entertainment), and check your purchases against credit card statements.

- **Use money apps for your smartphone.** If you always carry a smartphone, then you have a device for recording income and expenses. To find current apps for this purpose, do an Internet search with the key words *money trackers Android* or *money trackers iOS*.

- **Use personal finance software.** Learn to use Quicken or a similar product that allows you to record income and expenses on your computer and to sort them into categories.

- **Use online banking services.** If you have a checking account that offers online services, take advantage of the records that the bank is already keeping for you. Every time you write a check, use a debit card, or make a deposit, the transaction will show up online. You can use a computer to log in to your account and view these transactions at any time. Some bank Web sites even allow you to set up categories for your income and expenses and tag transactions with one of these categories. If you're unclear about how to use online banking, go in to your bank and ask for help.

- **Experiment with several of the provided options.** Settle into one that feels most comfortable to you. Or create a method of your own. Anything will work, as long as you end each month with an *exact and accurate* record of your income and expenses.

Step 3. On the last day of the month, fill out your Money Monitor/Money Plan.

Pull out a blank Money Monitor/Money Plan from Figure 10.2. Label it with the current month and year. Fill out this form, using the records of your income and expenses for the month.

Notice that the far left column of the Money Monitor/Money Plan includes categories of income and expenses. (You can use the blank rows for categories of income and expenses that are not already included.) Write your total for each category in the middle column.

For example, if you spent $300 at the grocery store this month, write that amount in the middle column next to *Groceries*. If you work a part-time job and received two paychecks for the month, write the total in the middle column next to *Employment*. See Figure 10.1, the sample Money Monitor/Money Plan on the next page for more examples.

Remember to split expenses when necessary. For example, you might write one check each month to pay the balance due on your credit card. The purchases listed on your credit card bill might fall into several categories. Total up your expenses in each category, and list them separately.

Suppose that you used your credit card to buy music online, purchase a sweater, pay for three restaurant meals, and buy two tanks of gas for your car. Write the online music expense next to *Entertainment*. Write the amount you paid for the sweater next to *Clothes*. Write the total you spent at the restaurants next to *Eating Out*. Finally, write the total for your gas stops next to *Gas*.

Now look at the column on the far right of the Money Monitor/Money Plan. This column is where the magic happens. Review each category of income and expense. If you plan to reduce your spending in a certain category during the next month, write a minus sign (−) in the far right column. If you plan a spending increase in any category next month, write a plus sign (+) in the far right column. If you think that a category of income or expense will remain the same next month, leave the column blank.

Look again at Figure 10.1, the sample Money Monitor/Money Plan on page 298. This student plans to reduce her spending for eating out and entertainment (which for her includes movies and DVD rentals). She plans to increase the total she spends on groceries. She figures that even so, she'll save money by cooking more food at home and eating out less.

Step 4. After you've filled out your first Money Monitor/Money Plan, take a moment to congratulate yourself.

You have actively collected and analyzed the data needed to take charge of your financial life. No matter how the numbers add up, you are now in conscious control of your money. Repeat this exercise every month. It will keep you on a steady path to financial freedom.

No budgeting required

Notice one more thing about the Money Monitor/Money Plan: It does not require you to create a budget. Budgets—like diets—often fail. Many people cringe at the mere mention of the word *budget*. To them it is associated with scarcity, drudgery, and guilt. The idea of creating a budget conjures up images of a penny-pinching Ebenezer Scrooge shaking a bony, wrinkled finger at them and screaming, "You spent too much, you loser!"

That's not the idea behind the Money Monitor/Money Plan. In fact, there is no budget worksheet for you to complete each month. And no one is pointing a finger at you. Instead of budgeting, you simply write a plus sign or a minus sign next to each expense or income category that you *freely choose* to increase or decrease next month. There's no extra paperwork, no shame, and no blame.

Sample Money Monitor/Money Plan

Income	This Month	Next Month	Expenses	This Month	Next Month
Employment	500		Books and Supplies		
Grants	100		Car Maintenance		
Interest from Savings			Car Payment		
Loans	300		Clothes		
Scholarships	100		Deposits into Savings Account		
			Eating Out	50	–
			Entertainment	50	–
			Gas	100	
			Groceries	300	+
			Insurance (Car, Life, Health, Home)		
			Laundry	20	
			Phone	55	
			Rent/Mortgage Payment	400	
			Tuition and Fees		
			Utilities	50	
Total Income	1000		Total Expenses	1025	–

Figure 10.1 Sample Money Monitor/Money Plan

Money Monitor/Money Plan
Month_____ Year____

Income	This Month	Next Month	Expenses	This Month	Next Month
Employment			Books and Supplies		
Grants			Car Maintenance		
Interest from Savings			Car Payment		
Loan			Clothes		
Scholarships			Deposits into Savings Account		
			Eating Out		
			Entertainment		
			Gas		
			Groceries		
			Insurance (Car, Life, Health, Home)		
			Laundry		
			Phone		
			Rent/Mortgage Payment		
			Tuition and Fees		
			Utilities		
Total Income			Total Expenses		

Figure 10.2 Money Monitor/Money Plan

Money Monitor/Money Plan
Month_____ Year____

Income	This Month	Next Month	Expenses	This Month	Next Month
Employment			Books and Supplies		
Grants			Car Maintenance		
Interest from Savings			Car Payment		
Loan			Clothes		
Scholarships			Deposits into Savings Account		
			Eating Out		
			Entertainment		
			Gas		
			Groceries		
			Insurance (Car, Life, Health, Home)		
			Laundry		
			Phone		
			Rent/Mortgage Payment		
			Tuition and Fees		
			Utilities		
Total Income			Total Expenses		

Figure 10.2 (Continued)

Journal Entry 22
Discovery/Intention Statement

Reflect on your Money Monitor/Money Plan

Now that you've experimented with the Money Monitor/Money Plan process, reflect on what you're learning. To start creating a new future with money, complete the following statements:

After monitoring my income and expenses for one month, I was surprised to discover that . . .

_____

_____

_____

_____

When it comes to money, I am skilled at . . .

_____

_____

_____

_____

When it comes to money, I am *not* so skilled at . . .

_____

_____

_____

_____

I could increase my income by . . .

_____

_____

_____

_____

I could spend less money on . . .

_____

_____

_____

_____

After thinking about the most powerful step I can take right now to improve my finances, I intend to . . .

_____

_____

_____

_____

MAKE MORE MONEY

For many people, finding a way to increase income is the most appealing way to fix a money problem. This approach is reasonable, but it has a potential problem: When their income increases, many people continue to spend more than they make. This means that money problems persist even at higher incomes. To avoid this problem, manage your expenses, no matter how much money you make.

If you do succeed at controlling your expenses over the long term, then increasing your income is definitely a way to build wealth. Among the ways to make more money are to focus on your education, consider financial aid, work while you're in school, and do your best at every job.

Focus on your education. You can use your education to develop knowledge, experience, and skills that create income for the rest of your life. According to the U.S. Department of Commerce, people with a bachelor's degree can expect to earn an average of $1 million more during their lifetime than people with a high school diploma.[1] In addition, people with a bachelor's degree are less likely to be unemployed.[2]

Once you graduate and land a job in your chosen field, continue your education. Look for ways to gain additional skills or certifications that lead to higher earnings and more fulfilling work assignments.

Consider financial aid. Student grants and loans can play a major role in your college success by freeing you up from having to work full-time or even part-time. Many students erroneously assume they don't qualify for educational grants or low-interest student loans. Visit the financial aid office at your school to discover your options.

Increase your income while you're in school. If you work while you're in school, you earn more than money. You gain experience, establish references, interact with a variety of people, and make contact with people who might hire you in the future. Also, regular income in any amount can make a difference in your monthly cash flow.

Many students work full-time or part-time jobs. Work and school don't have to conflict, especially if you plan your week carefully and ask for your employer's support.

On most campuses, the financial aid office employs a person whose job it is to help students find work while they're in school. See that person. Some jobs are just made for students. Serving or delivering food may not be glamorous, but the tips can really add up. Other jobs, such as working the reference desk at the campus library or monitoring the front desk in a dorm, offer quiet times that are ideal for studying.

If you're already working, consider finding a job with a higher salary or hourly rate and flexible hours. Ask someone in the financial aid office about jobs that can be done from home with an Internet connection. A growing number of companies hire people who work online to handle their customer service, and many consultants work this way.

Another option is to start your own business. Consider a service you could offer—anything from lawn mowing to computer consulting. Students can boost their income in many other ways, such as running errands, giving guitar lessons, tutoring, designing Web sites, walking pets, detailing cars, and house sitting. Charge reasonable rates, provide impeccable service, and ask your clients for referrals.

See whether you can find a job related to your chosen career. Even an entry-level job in your field can provide valuable experience. Once you've been in such a job for a while, find out how to get promoted.

Do your best at every job. Once you get a job, make it your intention to excel as an employee. A positive work experience can pay off for years by leading to other jobs, recommendations, and contacts.

Make yourself indispensable. Look for ways to excel at your job by building relationships, becoming a rock-star collaborator, and consistently delivering results. Whenever possible, exceed your work-related goals. These are strategies for making more money and increasing job security.

To maximize your earning power, also keep honing your job-hunting skills. The career planning office at your school can help.

Finally, keep things in perspective. If your job is lucrative and rewarding, great. If not, remember that almost any job can support you in becoming a master student and reaching your educational goals.

Give yourself a raise before you start work.

Effective salary discussion can make a huge difference to your financial well-being. Consider the long-term impact of making just an extra $1,000 per year. Over the next decade, that's an extra $10,000 dollars in pretax income, even if you get no other raises.

It's possible to discuss salary too early in the interview process. Let the interviewer bring up this topic. In many cases, an ideal time to talk about salary is when the interviewer is ready to offer you a job. This often takes place during a second or even third interview. At this point the employer might be willing to part with some more money.

Many interviewers use a standard negotiating strategy: They come to the interview with a salary range in mind. Then they offer a starting salary at the lower end of that range.

This strategy holds an important message for you: Salaries are sometimes flexible. You do not have to accept the first salary offer.

When you finally get down to money, be prepared. Begin by knowing the income that you want. First, figure out how much money you need to maintain your desired standard of living. Then add some margin for comfort. If you're working a job that's comparable to the one you're applying for, consider adding 10 percent to your current salary. As you do this, take into account the value of any benefits the employer provides. Also consider stating a desired salary range at first rather than a fixed figure.

Find out the salary range for the job you want. This information might be available online. Start with America's Career InfoNet at **www.careerinfonet.org** and click on Occupation Information. Also go to your favorite Internet search engine, and key in the term *salary ranges*.

Other sources of salary information are friends who work in your field and notes from your information interviews. Another option is the obvious one—directly asking interviewers what salary range they have in mind.

Once you know that range, aim higher rather than lower. Name a figure toward the upper end, and see how the interviewer responds. Starting high gives you some room to negotiate. See whether you can get a raise now rather than later.

Salary negotiation gives you an opening to ask about benefits. Depending on the company and the job involved, these might include health insurance, life insurance, disability plans, use of a company car, reimbursement for travel expenses, retirement plans, and tuition reimbursement. ■

Free fun

Sometimes it seems that the only way to have fun is to spend money. Not true. Search out free entertainment on campus and in your community. Beyond this, your imagination is the only limit. Some suggestions are listed here. If you think they're silly or boring, create better ideas of your own.

Browse a bookstore.

Volunteer at a child care center.

Draw.

Exercise.

Find other people who share your hobby, and start a club.

Give a massage.

Do yoga with a friend.

Play Frisbee golf.

Make dinner for your date.

Picnic in the park.

Take a long walk.

Ride your bike.

Listen to music that you already own but haven't heard for a while.

Take a candlelight bath.

Play board games.

Have an egg toss.

Test-drive new cars.

Donate blood.

Make yourself breakfast in bed.

SPEND LESS MONEY

Controlling your expenses is something you can do right away. Use ideas from the following list, and invent more of your own.

Look to big-ticket items. When you look for places to cut expenses, start with the items that cost the most. Choices about where to live, for example, can save you thousands of dollars. Sometimes a place a little farther from campus, or a smaller house or apartment, will be much less expensive. You can also keep your housing costs down by finding a roommate. Offer to do repairs or maintenance in exchange for reduced rent. Pay your rent on time, and treat property with respect.

Another high-ticket item is a car. Take the cost of buying or leasing and then add expenses for parking, insurance, repairs, gas, maintenance, and tires. You might find that it makes more sense to walk, bike, use public transportation, ride a campus shuttle, and call for an occasional taxi ride. Or carpool. Find friends with a car, and chip in for gas.

Track your expenses to discover the main drains on your finances. Then focus on one or two areas where you can reduce spending while continuing to pay your fixed monthly bills such as rent and tuition.

Look to small-ticket items. Reducing or eliminating the money you spend on low-cost purchases can make the difference between saving money or going into debt. For example, $3 spent at the coffee shop every day adds up to $1,095 over a year. That kind of spending can give anyone the jitters.

Do comparison shopping. Prices vary dramatically. Shop around, wait for off-season sales, and use coupons. Check out secondhand stores, thrift stores, and garage sales. Before plunking down the full retail price for a new item, consider whether you could buy it used. You can find "pre-owned" clothes, CDs, furniture, sports equipment, audio equipment, and computer hardware in retail stores and on the Internet.

Also go online to find Web sites that will compare prices for you. Examples include Yahoo! Shopping (**http://shopping.yahoo.com**) and Google Product Search (**www.google.com/prdhp**).

Ask for student discounts. Movie theaters, restaurants, bars, shopping centers, and other businesses sometimes discount prices for students. Also see if your college bookstore sells software at reduced rates. In addition, ask your bank whether you can open a student checking and savings account with online banking. The fees and minimum required amounts could be lower. Go online to check your balances weekly so that you avoid overdraft fees.

Be aware of quality. The cheapest product is not always the least expensive over the long run. Sometimes, a slightly more expensive item is the best buy because it will last longer. Remember, there is no correlation between the value of something and the amount of money spent to advertise it. Carefully inspect things you are considering to buy to see whether they are well made.

Save money on eating and drinking. This single suggestion could significantly lower your expenses. Instead of hitting a restaurant or bar, head to the grocery store. In addition, clip food coupons. Sign up for a shopper's discount card.

Cooking for yourself doesn't need to take much time if you do a little menu planning. Create a list of your five favorite home-cooked meals. Learn how to prepare them. Then keep ingredients for these meals always on hand. To reduce grocery bills, buy these ingredients in bulk.

If you live in a dorm, review the different meal plans you can buy. Some schools offer meal plans for students who live off campus. These plans might be cheaper than eating in restaurants while you're on campus.

More deals are online. Find coupons at Web sites such as Groupon (**groupon.com**) and Living Social (**livingsocial.com**).

Lower your phone bills. If you use a cell phone, pull out a copy of your latest bill. Review how many minutes you used last month. Perhaps you could get by with a less expensive phone, fewer minutes, fewer text messages, and a cheaper plan.

Do an Internet search on *cell phone plan comparison,* and see whether you could save money by switching providers. Also consider a family calling plan, which might cost less than a separate plan for each person. In addition, consider whether you need a home phone (a land line) *and* a cell phone. Dropping the home phone could save you money right away.

Keep an eye on Web-based options for turning your voice into a digital signal that travels over the Internet. This technology is called Voice over Internet Protocol (VoIP), and Skype (**www.skype.com**) is just one example of it. Using VoIP can be cheaper than making international phone calls.

Go "green." To conserve energy and save money on utility bills, turn out the lights when you leave a room. Keep windows and doors closed in winter. In summer, keep windows open early in the day to invite lots of cool air into your living space. Then close up the apartment or house to keep it cool during the hotter hours of the day. Leave air-conditioning set at 72 degrees or above. In cool weather, dress warmly and keep the house at 68 degrees or less. In hot weather, take shorter, cooler showers.

Unplug any electric appliances that are not in use. Appliances like microwaves, audio systems, and cell phone chargers use energy when plugged in even when they're not in use. Also, plug computer equipment into power strips that you can turn off while you sleep.

Explore budget plans for monthly payments that fluctuate, such as those for heating your home. These plans average your yearly expenses so you pay the same amount each month.

Pay cash. To avoid interest charges, deal in cash. If you don't have the cash, don't buy. Buying on credit makes it more difficult to monitor spending. You can easily bust next month's money plan with this month's credit card purchases.

Postpone purchases. If you plan to buy something, leave your checkbook or credit card at home when you first go shopping. Look at all the possibilities. Then go home and make your decision when you don't feel pressured. When you are ready to buy, wait a week, even if the salesperson pressures you. What seems like a necessity today may not even cross your mind the day after tomorrow.

Notice what you spend on "fun." Blowing your money on fun is fun. It is also a fast way to blow your savings. When you spend money on entertainment, ask yourself what the benefits will be and whether you could get the same benefits for less money. You can read magazines for free at the library, for example. Most libraries also loan CDs and DVDs for free.

Use the envelope system. After reviewing your monthly income and expenses, put a certain amount of cash each week in an envelope labeled *Entertainment/Eating Out*. When the envelope is empty, stop spending money on these items for the rest of the week. If you use online banking, see whether you can create separate accounts for various spending categories. Then deposit a fixed amount of money into each of those accounts. This is an electronic version of the envelope system.

Don't compete with big spenders. When you watch other people spend their money, remember that you don't know the whole story. Some students have parents with deep pockets. Others head to Mexico every year for spring break but finance the trips with high-interest credit cards. If you find yourself feeling pressured to spend money so that you can keep up with other people, stop to think about how much it will cost over the long run. Maybe it's time to shop around for some new friends.

Use the money you save to prepare for emergencies and reduce debt. If you apply strategies such as those listed here, you might see your savings account swell nicely. Congratulate yourself. Then choose what to do with the extra money. To protect yourself during tough times, create an emergency fund. Then reduce your debt by paying more than the minimum on credit card bills and loan payments.

Spend less, and feel the power. Cutting your spending might be challenging at first. Give it time. Spending less is not about sacrificing pleasure. It's about something that money can't buy—the satisfaction of choosing exactly where your money goes and building a secure financial future. Every dollar that you save on a frivolous expense is a dollar you can invest in something that truly matters to you. ∎

Interactive

Exercise 28
Show me the money

See whether you can use *Becoming a Master Student* to create a financial gain that is many times more than the cost of the book. Scan the entire text, and look for suggestions that could help you save money or increase income in significant ways; for example:

- Use suggestions for career planning and job hunting to find your next job more quickly—and start earning money sooner.
- Use suggestions for résumé writing and job interviewing to get a higher paying job.
- Use suggestions from this chapter to reduce your monthly expenses and fatten up your savings account.

Write down your ideas for creating more money from your experience of this book.

_____

_____

_____

_____

© zimmytws/Shutterstock.com

Managing money
DURING
TOUGH TIMES

A short-term crisis in the overall economy can reduce your income and increase your expenses. So can the decision to go back to school.

The biggest factor in your long-term financial well-being, though, is your daily behavior. Habits that help you survive during tough times will also help you prosper after you graduate and when the economy rebounds.

If the economy tanks, we can benefit by telling the truth about it and ourselves. It's one thing to condemn the dishonesty of mortgage bankers and hedge fund managers. It's another thing to have an unpaid credit card or wipe out a savings account and still believe that we are in charge of our money.

The first step to changing such behaviors is simply to admit that they don't work. Taking informed action is a way to cut through financial confusion and move beyond fear. Start by collecting the details about what you're spending and earning right now.

With that knowledge, you can choose your next strategy from among the following.

SPEND LESS AND SAVE MORE

The less you spend, the more money you'll have on hand. Use that money to pay your monthly bills, pay off your credit cards, and create an emergency fund to use in case you lose your job or a source of financial aid.

Author Suze Orman recommends three actions to show that you can reduce spending at any time: (1) Do not spend money for one day; (2) do not use your credit card for one week; and (3) do not eat out for one month. Success with any of these strategies can open up your mind to other possibilities for spending less and saving more.[3]

MAKE SURE THAT YOUR SAVINGS ARE PROTECTED

The Federal Deposit Insurance Corporation (FDIC) backs individual saving accounts. The National Credit Union Administration (NCUA) offers similar protection for credit union members. If your savings are protected by these programs, every penny you deposit is safe. Check your statements to find out, or go online to **www.fdic.gov/edie/index.html**.

PAY OFF YOUR CREDIT CARDS

If you have more than one credit card with an outstanding balance, then find out which one has the highest interest rate. Put as much money as you can toward paying off that balance while making the minimum payment on the other cards. Repeat this process until all unpaid balances are erased.

INVEST ONLY AFTER SAVING

The stock market is only for money that you can afford to lose. Before you speculate, first save enough money to live on for at least six months in case you're unemployed. Then consider what you'll need over the next five years to finish your schooling and handle other major expenses. Save for these expenses before taking any risks with your money.

DO STELLAR WORK AT YOUR CURRENT JOB

The threat of layoffs increases during a recession. However, companies will hesitate to shed their star employees. If you're working right now, then think about ways to become indispensable. Gain skills and experience that will make you more valuable to your employer.

No matter what job you have, be as productive as possible. Look for ways to boost sales, increase quality, or accomplish tasks in less time. Ask yourself every day how you can create extra value by solving a problem, reducing costs, improving service, or attracting new clients or customers.

THINK ABOUT YOUR NEXT JOB

Create a career plan that describes the next job you want, the skills that you'll develop to get it, and the next steps you'll take to gain those skills. Stay informed about the latest developments in your field. Find people who are already working in this area, and contact them for information interviews.

You might want to start an active job hunt now, even if you have a job. Find time to build your network, go to job-related conferences, and stay on top of current job openings in your field.

Remember that even during a recession, the state of the economy at large does not determine your individual prospects for finding a job. When people say, "There are no jobs," maybe what they really mean is "My current job hunting method is not working." There's a world of difference between those statements. The first one kills options. The second one *creates* options. Go to your school's career planning office to learn new strategies for job hunting.

RESEARCH UNEMPLOYMENT BENEFITS

Unemployment benefits have limits and may not replace your lost wages. However, they can cushion the blow of losing a job while you put other strategies in place. To learn about the benefits offered in your state, go online to **www.servicelocator.org**. Click "Unemployment Benefits." Then enter your state.

GET HEALTH INSURANCE

A sudden illness or lengthy hospital stay can drain your savings. Health insurance can pick up all or most of the costs instead. If possible, get health insurance through your school or employer. Another option is private health insurance. This can be cheaper than extending an employer's policy if you lose your job. To find coverage, go online to the Web site of the National Association of Health Underwriters (**www.nahu.org**) and **www.ehealthinsurance.com**.

GET HELP THAT YOU CAN TRUST

Avoid debt consolidators that offer schemes to wipe out your debt. What they don't tell you is that their fees are high, and that using them can lower your credit rating. Turn instead to the National Foundation for Credit Counseling (**www.nfcc.org**). Find a credit counselor that is accredited by this organization. Work with someone who is open about fees and willing to work with all your creditors. Don't pay any fees up front, before you actually get help.

PUT YOUR PLAN IN WRITING

List the specific ways that you will reduce spending and increase income. If you have a family, consider posting this list for everyone to see. The act of putting your plan in writing can help you feel in control of your money. Review your plan regularly to make sure that it's working and that everyone who's affected is on board.

COPE WITH STRESS IN POSITIVE WAYS

When times get tough, some people are tempted to reduce stress with unhealthy behaviors like smoking, drinking, and overeating. Find better ways to cope. Exercise, meditation, and a sound sleep can do wonders.

Social support is one of the best stress busters. If you're unemployed or worried about money, connect with family members and friends often. Turn healthy habits such as exercising and preparing healthy meals into social affairs.

CHOOSE YOUR MONEY CONVERSATIONS

When the economy tanks, the news is filled with gloomy reports and dire predictions. Remember that reports are constantly competing for your attention. Sometimes they use gloom-and-doom headlines to boost their ratings.

Keep financial news in perspective. Recessions can be painful. And they eventually end. The mortgage credit crisis in recent years was due to speculation, not to a lack of innovation. Our economy will continue to reward people who create valuable new products and services.

To manage stress, limit how much attention you pay to fear-based articles and programs. You can do this even while staying informed about news. Avoid conversations that focus on problems. Instead, talk about ways to take charge of your money and open up job prospects. Even when the economy takes a nosedive, there is always at least one more thing you can do to manage stress and get on a firmer financial footing.

Talk about what gives your life meaning beyond spending money. Eating at home instead of going out can bring your family closer together and save you money weekly, monthly, and annually. Avoiding loud bars and making time for quiet conversation can deepen your friendships. Finding free sources of entertainment can lead you to unexpected sources of pleasure. Letting go of an expensive vacation can allow you to pay down your debts and find time for a fun hobby. Keeping your old car for another year might allow you to invest in extra skills training.

When tough times happen, use them as a chance to embrace the truth about your money life rather than resist it. Live from conscious choice rather than unconscious habit. Learning to live within your means is a skill that can bring financial peace of mind for the rest of your life. ■

© iStockphoto.com/Laurent davoust /daboost

TAKE CHARGE
of your
CREDIT

A credit card is compact and convenient. That piece of plastic seems to promise peace of mind. Low on cash this month? Just whip out your credit card, slide it across the counter, and relax. Your worries are over—that is, until you get the bill. Credit cards often come with a hefty interest rate—sometimes as high as 30 percent.

A good credit rating will serve you for a lifetime. With this asset, you'll be able to borrow money any time you need it. A poor credit rating, however, can keep you from getting a car or a house in the future. You might also have to pay higher insurance rates, and you could even be turned down for a job.

To take charge of your credit, borrow money only when truly necessary. If you do borrow, make all of your payments, and make them on time. This is especially important for managing credit cards and student loans.

A 2009 report by Sallie Mae, a student loan corporation, revealed that the average credit card debt among undergraduate students is $3,173.[4] However, many students are carrying higher amounts of debt with costs that can soar over time.

Use the following strategies to take control of your credit cards.

Balance the benefits with the real costs. Credit cards do offer potential benefits, of course. Having one means that you don't have to carry around a checkbook or large amounts of cash, and they're pretty handy in emergencies. Getting a card is one way to establish a credit record. Some cards offer rewards, such as frequent flier miles and car rental discounts.

Used unwisely, however, credit cards can create a debt that takes decades to repay. Here's an example published by the Federal Trade Commission. Suppose that you make a $1,500 purchase with a credit card with a 19 percent interest rate. Also suppose that you pay only the minimum balance on that card every month. It will take you 106 months to pay off this purchase, and you will pay $889 in interest. This will be true even if you never use the card again and pay no late fees.[5]

Credit card debt can seriously delay other goals—paying off student loans, financing a new car, buying a home, or saving for retirement.

Pay off the balance each month. An unpaid credit card balance is a sure sign that you are spending more money than you have. To avoid this outcome, keep track of how much you spend with credit cards each month. Pay off the card balance each month, on time, and avoid finance or late charges.

If you do accumulate a large credit card balance, go to your bank and ask about ways to get a loan with a lower interest rate. Use this loan to pay off your credit cards. Then promise yourself never to accumulate credit card debt again.

Scrutinize credit card offers. Finding a card with a lower interest rate can make a dramatic difference. Suppose that you have an $8,000 balance on a card with a 16 percent APR. Your interest charges would be $1,280 per year. If you have the same balance on a card with a 4.9 percent APR, your annual interest charges would be $392. It pays to shop around.[6]

However, look carefully at credit card offers. Low rates might be temporary. After a few months, they could double or even triple. Also look for annual fees, late fees, and other charges buried in the fine print.

Be especially wary of credit card offers made to students. Remember that the companies who willingly dispense cards on campus are not there to offer an educational service. They are in business to make money by charging you interest.

Avoid cash advances. Due to their high interest rates and fees, credit cards are not a great source of spare cash. Even when you get cash advances on these cards from an ATM, it's still borrowed money. As an alternative, get a debit card tied to a checking account, and use that card when you need cash on the go.

Check statements against your records. File your credit card receipts each month. When you get the bill for each card, check it against your receipts for accuracy. Mistakes in billing are rare, but they can happen. In addition, checking your statement reveals the interest rate and fees that are being applied to your account.

Credit card companies can change the terms of your agreement with little or no warning. Check bills carefully for any changes in late fees, service charges, and credit limits. When you get letters about changes in your credit card policies, read them carefully. Cancel cards from companies that routinely raise fees.

Use just one credit card. To simplify your financial life and take charge of your credit, consider using only one card. Choose one with no annual fee and the lowest interest rate. Consider the bottom line, and be selective. If you do have more than one credit card, pay off the one with the highest interest rate first. Then consider cancelling that card.

Get a copy of your credit report. A credit report is a record of your payment history and other credit-related items. You are entitled to get a free copy each year. Go to your bank and ask someone there how to do this. You can also request a copy of your credit report online at **https://www.annualcreditreport.com**. This site was created by three nationwide consumer credit–reporting companies—Equifax, Experian, and TransUnion. Check your report carefully for errors or accounts that you did not open. Do this now, before you're in financial trouble.

Protect your credit score. Whenever you apply for a loan, the first thing a lender will do is check your credit score. The higher your score, the more money you can borrow at lower interest rates. To protect your credit score:

- Pay all your bills on time.
- Hold on to credit cards that you've had for a while.
- Avoid applying for new credit cards.
- Pay off your credit card balance every month—especially for the cards that you've had the longest.
- If you can't pay off the entire balance, then pay as much as you can above the minimum monthly payment.
- Never charge more than your limit.
- Avoid using a credit card as a source of cash.
- Avoid any actions that could lead a credit card company to reduce your credit limit.

> *A college degree is one of the best investments you can make. But you don't have to go broke to get that education. You can make that investment with the lowest debt possible.*

MANAGE STUDENT LOANS

A college degree is one of the best investments you can make. But you don't have to go broke to get that education. You can make that investment with the lowest debt possible.

Choose schools with costs in mind. If you decide to transfer to another school, you can save thousands of dollars the moment you sign your application for admission. In addition to choosing schools on the basis of reputation, consider how much they cost and the financial aid packages that they offer.

Avoid debt when possible. The surest way to manage debt is to avoid it altogether. If you do take out loans, borrow only the amount that you cannot get from other sources—scholarships, grants, employment, gifts from relatives, and personal savings. Predict what your income will be when the first loan payments are due and whether you'll make enough money to manage continuing payments.

Also set a target date for graduation, and stick to it. The fewer years you go to school, the lower your debt.

Shop carefully for loans. Go to the financial aid office and ask whether you can get a Stafford loan. These are fixed-rate, low-interest loans from the federal government. If you qualify for a subsidized Stafford loan, the government pays the interest due while you're in school. Unsubsidized Stafford loans do not offer this benefit, but they are still one of the cheapest student loans you can get. Remember that *anyone* can apply for a Stafford loan. Take full advantage of this program before you look into other loans. For more information on the loans that are available to you, visit **www.studentaid.ed.gov**.

If your parents are helping to pay for your education, they can apply for a PLUS loan. There is no income limit, and parents can borrow up to the total cost of their children's education. With these loans, your parents—not you—are the borrowers. A new option allows borrowers to defer repayment until after you graduate.

If at all possible, avoid loans from privately owned companies. These companies often charge higher interest rates and impose terms that are less favorable to students. Unfortunately, there are loan companies that prey on students. To avoid them, calculate the total amount of interest that you'll be charged over the life of a loan. You can do this with online tools such as SallieMae's Student Loan Repayment Calculator (**http://smartoption.salliemae.com/Entry.aspx**).

While you're shopping around, ask about options for repaying your loans. Lenders might allow you to extend the payments over a longer period or adjust the amount of your monthly payment based on your income.

Some lenders will forgive part of a student loan if you agree to take a certain type of job for a few years—for example, teaching in a public school in a low-income neighborhood or working as a nurse in a rural community.

Repay your loans. If you take out student loans, find out exactly when the first payment is due on each of them. Make all your payments, and make them on time. Don't assume that you can wait to start repayment until you find a job. Any bill payments that you miss will hammer your credit score.

Also ask your financial aid office about whether you can consolidate your loans. This means that you lump them all together and owe just one payment every month. Loan consolidation makes it easier to stay on top of your payments and protect your credit score. ◼

Common credit terms

Annual fee—a yearly charge for using a credit card, sometimes called a *membership fee* or *participation fee*.

Annual percentage rate (APR)—the interest that you owe on unpaid balances in your account. The APR equals the periodic rate times the number of billing periods in a year.

Balance due—the remaining amount of money that you owe a credit card company or other lender.

Balance transfer—the process of moving an unpaid debt from one lender to another lender.

Bankruptcy—a legal process that allows borrowers to declare their inability to pay their debts. People who declare bankruptcy transfer all their assets to a court-appointed trustee and create a plan to repay some or all of their borrowed money. Bankruptcy protects people from harassment by their creditors and lowers their credit scores.

Credit score—a three-digit number that reflects your history of repaying borrowed money and paying other bills on time (also called a *FICO score*—an acronym for the Fair Isaac Corporation, which was the first company to create credit ratings). This number ranges from 300 to 850. The higher the number, the better your credit rating.

Default—state of a loan when the borrower fails to make required payments or otherwise violates the terms of the agreement. Default may prompt the creditor to turn the loan over to a collection agency, which can severely harm the borrower's credit score.

Finance charge—the total fee for using a credit card, which includes the interest rate, periodic rate, and other fees. Finance charges for cash advances and balance transfers can be different from finance charges for unpaid balances.

Grace period—for a credit card user who pays off the entire balance due, a period of time when no interest is charged on a purchase. When there is no grace period, finance charges apply immediately to a purchase.

Interest rate—an annual fee that borrowers pay to use someone else's money, normally a percentage of the balance due.

Minimum payment—the amount you must pay to keep from defaulting on an account; usually 2 percent of the unpaid balance due.

Payment due date—the day that a lender must receive your payment—*not* the postmarked date or the date you make a payment online. Check your statements carefully, as credit card companies sometimes change the due dates.

Periodic rate—an interest rate based on a certain period of time, such as a day or a month.

Journal Entry 23
Intention Statement

Create a new experience of money

You can create a new experience of money now. This is true even if you are in debt and living in a dorm on a diet of macaroni. If you're not convinced, then read on.

Remember that when it comes to money, you can declare two different types of intention. Either can lead to profound changes in your personal finances.

One is an intention to create new **outcomes**. Here are some examples:

- Saving $2,000 to buy a new computer by December 31 of this year
- Saving $5,000 for a car down payment by January 1, 2015
- Saving $10,000 for a house down payment by July 1, 2020

Second is an intention to create new **habits** related to money. These intentions are not tied to a particular outcome such as having a specific amount of money in hand by a certain date. Instead, habits are things that you intend to do on a daily, weekly, or monthly basis.

Some examples of habits related to money are listed here:

- Saving 5 percent of every paycheck received and depositing that in a savings account to use for emergency expenses.
- Reducing restaurant expenses by splitting meals and skipping desserts.
- Reducing entertainment expenses by streaming movies with a computer rather than going to a theater.

Outcome goals can involve large amounts of money and often depend on your having a certain level of income.

In contrast, habits can involve any amount of money, and they are not tied to any income level. You can set a goal to save 5 percent of every paycheck, whether that amount is $5, $50, or $500. Such habits might produce only modest results in the near future. When sustained over decades, however, they can make a major difference in your net worth.

Write at least three intentions. Clearly label each one as an outcome or habit. If your intention is to create a new habit, then be sure to describe an observable behavior.

I intend to . . .

_____

_____

I intend to . . .

_____

_____

I intend to . . .

_____

_____

If you get into trouble . . .

You might face obstacles to meeting your financial goals. Money problems are common. Solve them in ways that protect you for the future.

Get specific data. Gather all your receipts and bank account statements for the past several months. Determine the exact amount of money that flowed into your life during that period and the amount that flowed out. See if you can spot the exact points when you got into trouble with money.

Be honest with creditors. Determine the amount that you are sure you can repay each month, and ask the creditor whether that would work for your case.

Go for credit counseling. Most cities have agencies with professional advisors who can help straighten out your financial problems.

Change your spending patterns. If you have a history of overspending (or underearning), change *is* possible. This chapter is full of suggestions.

Keep your money secure. To prevent other security breaches when managing money, regularly monitor online bank accounts. Use Web sites with an address (URL) that begins with *https://* rather than *http://*. The extra *s* stands for *secure*, meaning that any data you send will be encrypted.

EDUCATION PAYS OFF—
AND YOU CAN PAY FOR IT

Education is one of the few things you can buy that will last a lifetime. It can't rust, corrode, break down, or wear out. It can't be stolen, burned, repossessed, or destroyed. Once you have a degree, no one can take it away. That makes your education a safer investment than real estate, gold, oil, diamonds, or stocks.

Higher levels of education are associated with the following:[7]

- Greater likelihood of being employed
- Greater likelihood of having health insurance
- Higher income
- Higher job satisfaction
- Higher tax revenues for governments, which fund libraries, schools, parks, and other public goods
- Lower dependence on income support services, such as food stamps
- Higher involvement in volunteer activities

In short, education is a good deal for you and for society. It's worth investing in it periodically to update your skills, reach your goals, and get more of what you want in life.

Millions of dollars are waiting for people who take part in higher education. The funds flow to students who know how to find them.

There are many ways to pay for school. The kind of help you get depends on your financial need. In general, *financial need* equals the cost of your schooling minus what you can reasonably be expected to pay.

A financial aid package includes three major types of assistance:

- Money you do not pay back (grants and scholarships)
- Money you *do* pay back (loans)
- Work-study programs

Many students who get financial aid receive a package that includes all of the listed elements.

To find out more, visit your school's financial aid office on a regular basis. Also go online. Start with Student Aid on the Web at **http://studentaid.ed.gov**. ∎

Interactive

Exercise 29 Education by the hour

Diamond Sky Images/Digital Vision /Getty Images

Determine exactly what it costs you to go to school. Fill in the blanks, using totals for a semester, quarter, or whatever term system your school uses.

Note: Include only the costs that relate directly to going to school. For example, under "Transportation," list only the amount that you pay for gas to drive back and forth to school—not the total amount you spend on gas for a semester.

Tuition	$_____
Books	$_____
Fees	$_____
Transportation	$_____
Clothing	$_____
Food	$_____
Housing	$_____
Entertainment	$_____
Other expenses (such as insurance, medical costs, and child care)	$_____
Subtotal	$_____
Salary you could earn per term if you weren't in school	$_____
Total (A)	$_____

Now figure out how many classes you attend in one term. This is the number of your scheduled class periods per week multiplied by the number of weeks in your school term. Put that figure here:

Total (B) $_____

Divide the **Total (B)** into the **Total (A)**, and put that amount here:

$_____

This is what it costs you to go to one class one time.

Now, describe your responses to discovering this figure. Also list anything you will do differently as a result of knowing the hourly cost of your education.

© Christos Georghiou/Shutterstock.com

USE TOOLS
to tame your money

You can use technology to track the details of your money life and gain more financial peace of mind. The following tools—both digital and paper-based—offer ways to begin.

LEARN SPREADSHEET SOFTWARE

With spreadsheet programs such as Microsoft's Excel, you can enter data into a chart with rows and columns and then apply various formulas.

You can use Excel to create budgets, income reports, expense records, and investment projections. Many organizations use spreadsheets to track their finances. Master this software now and you'll have a marketable skill to add to your résumé.

To get a current list of Excel commands, go online to **www.office.microsoft.com**, find a search box, and enter *keyboard shortcuts Excel*. Find out how to apply templates, enter data into a spreadsheet, sort that data, apply formulas, print a spreadsheet, and save your spreadsheets.

Other companies offer free or low-cost spreadsheet software with commands and features similar to Excel. An example is Zoho Docs (**www.zoho.com/docs**).

EXPLORE OTHER APPLICATIONS

Most Web-based applications allow you to download transactions from your checking and savings accounts, sort those transactions into categories, create budgets and projections, and keep other financial records. Examples are Buxfer (**www.buxfer.com**) and Mint (**www.mint.com**). Note that there's a monthly fee for some of these services.

Instead of going online, you might prefer to download an application to your computer, smartphone, or tablet. For example, Mint also comes in a desktop version. Other popular applications include Microsoft Money and Quicken.

ORGANIZE YOUR MONEY FILES

You probably use notebooks and folders to organize your coursework. Treat your money information with the same level of care. Doing this will help you pay bills on time and promote financial peace of mind.

You can use a paper-based filing system or create money-related folders on a computer. Start with the following folders and then change them to meet your individual needs:

- *Bank statements* for your checking and savings accounts
- *Bills* due this month (check this folder once per week)
- *Financial aid*—copies of your applications; records of scholarships, grants, and work-study income; records of loan repayments; notes on your conversations with people in the financial aid office
- *Insurance*—copies of life, health, car, and renter's policies
- *Major purchases*—receipts and warranties related to major expenses, such as appliances and cars
- *School*—copies of transcripts and other records of courses completed, credits earned, and grades received
- *Taxes*—W2 forms, paycheck stubs, and copies of tax returns

You'll probably have some money documents—such as records of bills paid and receipts for smaller purchases—that don't fit into any of the above categories. File these documents in folders labeled by month and year. The Internal Revenue Service recommends that you keep these records for seven years.

PROTECT YOUR MONEY

Guard your private information, including social security number and bank account numbers. People who steal this information might be able to access your money and even pretend to *be* you (something that's called *identity theft*):

- Give your private information only to people and organizations you trust, such as a tax preparer, accountant, or employer that you know personally.
- Delete any e-mails or text messages that ask you for private information.
- Share private information online only via a secure Web site from an organization that you trust.
- Use strong passwords for financial Web sites and change those passwords at least once per year.
- Shred any paper-based financial records that are more than seven years old.
- Check your credit card and bank account statements to make sure that they include only purchases that *you* made.
- If you check your statements and see purchases that you did *not* make, call your bank immediately. In case of major theft, notify the police. ■

YOUR MONEY
AND YOUR VALUES

Want a clue to your values? Look at the way you handle money.

You might not think about values when you pull out a credit card or put cash on the counter. Even so, your values are at work.

For example, the amount you spend on fast food shows how much you value convenience. The amount you spend on clothes shows how much you value appearance. And the amount you spend on tuition shows how much you value education.

Think of any value as having two aspects. One is invisible, and the other is visible.

The *invisible* aspect is a belief about what matters most in life. You can define this belief by naming something you want and asking, "*Why* do I want that?" Keep asking until you reach a point where the question no longer makes sense. At that point, you'll bump into one of your values.

Suppose that you want to start dating. Why do you want that? Perhaps you want to find someone who will really listen to you and also share his deepest feelings. Why do you want *that*? Perhaps because you want to love and be loved. If someone asks why you want *that*, you might say, "I want that because . . . well, I just want it." At that point, the *why?* question no longer applies. To you, love is an end in itself. You desire love simply for its own sake. Love is one of your values.

The *visible* aspect of any value is a behavior. If you value love, you will take action to meet new people. You'll develop close friendships. You'll look for a spouse or life partner and build a long-term relationship. These behaviors are visible signs that you value love.

We experience peace of mind when our behaviors align with our values. However, this is not always the case. If you ever suspect that there's a conflict between your values and your behavior, then look at your money life for clues.

For example, someone says that he values health. After monitoring his expenses, he discovers that he spent $200 last month on fast food. He's discovered a clear source of conflict. He can resolve that conflict by redefining his values or changing his behavior. We sometimes work to buy more things that we have no

time to enjoy . . . because we work so much. This can be a vicious cycle.

Sometimes we live values that are not our own. Values creep into our lives due to peer pressure or advertising. Movies, TV, and magazines pump us full of images about the value of owning more *stuff*—bigger houses, bigger cars, better clothes. All that stuff costs a lot of money. The process of acquiring it can drive us into debt—and into jobs that pay well but deny our values.

Money gives us plenty of opportunities for critical thinking. For example, think about the wisdom of choosing to spend money on the latest video game or digital gadget rather than a textbook or other resource needed for your education. Games and gadgets can deliver many hours of entertainment before they break down. Compare that to the value of doing well in a course, graduating with better grades, and acquiring skills that increase your earning power for the rest of your career.

One way to align your behaviors with your beliefs is to ask one question whenever you spend money: *Is this expense consistent with my values?* Over time, this question can lead to daily changes in your behavior that make a big difference in your peace of mind.

Keeping track of your income and expenses allows you to make choices about money with your eyes open. It's all about handling money on purpose and living with integrity. With the financial facts at hand, you can spend and earn money in ways that demonstrate your values. ■

Practicing Critical Thinking 10

Remember that psychologist Benjamin Bloom described six levels of thinking:

Level 1: Remembering

Level 2: Understanding

Level 3: Applying

Level 4: Analyzing

Level 5: Evaluating

Level 6: Creating

Suppose that a friend says to you, "I want to get the most value from the money and time I invest in higher education. Can you give me a list of the most important things to do?"

For the purpose of this exercise, focus on **Level 5: Evaluating**. Reflect on what you've experienced so far in higher education. Then, as a creative challenge, see if you can give your friend a *short* list—three to five items. Limit yourself to the success strategies that you think are most useful. List your suggestions, along with reasons why you think they are valuable.

Suggestion 1:

_____

Reasons for Suggestion 1:

_____

_____

_____

Suggestion 2:

_____

Reasons for Suggestion 2:

_____

_____

_____

Suggestion 3:

_____

Reasons for Suggestion 3:

_____

_____

_____

Suggestion 4:

_____

Reasons for Suggestion 4:

_____

_____

_____

Suggestion 5:

_____

Reasons for Suggestion 5:

_____

_____

_____

Moses Robinson/WireImage /Getty Images

MASTER STUDENT PROFILE

SARA BLAKELY

(1971–) Founder of Spanx, a hosiery company, turned $5,000 in savings; into a business worth a billion dollars

For me, I feel like money just makes you more of who you already were. It just holds a magnifying glass up to the person that you are.

I don't subscribe at all to money as the root of all evil. I think money is a wonderful thing. And it's great to share, and it's fun to spend, and it's fun to make. I've always had a very positive outlook about what money can do.

I had always thought I would be a lawyer, growing up. And so I took the LSAT (Law School Admission Test). I basically failed it. And I remember at that moment it being this life-changing moment that sent me on a different course.

And the way I initially handled it was try again. I took the course. I tried it again. And then when it didn't go as I planned, I asked myself a lot of questions: What is life trying to tell me? Do I have a different path? Maybe I'm supposed to be open to something else. And that's what set me on the journey that ended up creating Spanx.

I think what surprised me the most with the Spanx journey is the emotional impact that this brand and these products have had on women's lives. I just didn't expect that. I was looking for no panty lines and a smooth look in white pants. And women literally are incredibly emotionally impacted and moved by our brand. And that's an amazing feeling.

The things that I'm most proud of achieving are achieving this level of success that is beyond my wildest dreams and doing it in a way that I feel like I can still look

Sara Blakely *is willing to change.*

You *can be willing to change by seeing failure as a chance to choose a new path in life.*

myself in the mirror and feel really good about how I got here. My Oprah moment—getting the call from her. My first chance to sell my second product on QVC and selling over 8,000 in six minutes and realizing I'm not a one-hit wonder. And then launching internationally, building a team. There were different moments where it just started feeling like I was so proud of different stages of the Spanx journey. . . .

So some examples of how I've been paying it forward is that at Spanx we have a Leg Up program where we highlight a female entreprenuer that's just starting out like I was. And we put her in our catalog that goes out to over a million subscribers. We don't gain anything from doing it other than hoping that she gets that big step forward in the beginning part of her business.

In the next decade I see Spanx going worldwide—everywhere. No butt left behind! It's going to be all over the world, and it's going to become an aspirational brand that transcends categories. We're already transcending age. We're now into men's [clothing]. There are so many things we can improve upon or make better, and that's the true inspiration behind the brand Spanx. ∎

Source: "Spanx's Sara Blakely Turns $5,000 into a Billion," Forbes.com, http://video.forbes.com/fvn/billionaires-2012/sara-blakely-spanx-billionaire/.

QUIZ
Chapter 10

Name _____

Date _____

1. The Power Process: Risk being a fool suggests that sometimes you should take action without considering the consequences. True or false? Explain your answer.

   False. Risk being a fool does not mean escaping responsibility or avoiding consequences. It simply means we should be open to taking risks, making mistakes, making corrections, and trying again. (*Power Process: Risk being a fool*, page 294)

2. Summarize the three main steps in money management, as explained in this chapter.

   (Answers will vary.) The three main steps in money management can be summarized by (1) telling the truth about how much money you have and how you spend it (discovery); (2) committing to spending less than you have (intention); and (3) applying the suggestions for earning more money, spending less money, or both (action). (*The end of money worries*, page 295)

3. Describe a strategy for increasing your income while you are in school.

   (Answers will vary.) Consider financial aid—by applying for financial aid, you can free yourself from having to work full-time or even part-time. Never assume you do not qualify for any type of financial aid. (*Make more money*, page 302)

4. List three ways to decrease your expenses while you are in school.

   (Answers will vary.) List any three of the following (answers will vary): (a) Look to big-ticket items. (b) Look to small-ticket items. (c) Ask for student discounts. (d) Do comparison shopping. (e) Be aware of quality. (f) Save money on eating and drinking. (*Spend less money*, page 304)

5. According to the text, what is the biggest factor in your long-term financial well-being?
   (a) The state of the overall economy
   (b) The interest rates on your credit cards
   (c) The federal deficit
   (d) Your daily behavior
   (e) None of the above
   (d) Your daily behavior (*Managing money during tough times*, page 306)

6. What are three ways that you can avoid getting into financial trouble when you use credit cards?

   List any three of the following (answers may vary): (a) Pay off the balance each month. (b) Scrutinize credit card offers. (c) Avoid cash advances. (d) Check statements against your records. (e) Use just one credit card. (f) Get a copy of your credit report. (g) Protect your credit score. (*Take charge of your credit*, page 308)

7. Privately owned companies generally offer better student loans than the federal government. True or false? Explain your answer.

   False. Privately owned companies often charge higher interest rates and impose terms that are less favorable to students. (*Take charge of your credit*, page 308).

8. List three sources of money to help students pay for their education.

   Three sources of money include: grants and scholarships, loans, and work-study programs. (*Education pays off—and you can pay for it*, page 312)

9. List three strategies you can use to prevent identity theft.

   Answers will vary: (a) Give your private information only to people and organizations you trust, such as a tax preparer, accountant, or employer that you know personally. (b) Delete any e-mails or text messages that ask you for private information. (c) Share private information online only via a secure Web site from an organization that you trust. (d) Use strong passwords for financial Web sites and change those passwords at least once per year. (e) Shred any paper-based financial records that are more than seven years old. (f) Check your credit card and bank account statements to make sure that they include only purchases that *you* made. (g) If you check your statements and see purchases that you did *not* make, call your bank immediately. In case of major theft, notify the police. (*Use tools to tame your money*, page 313)

10. What is a question that you can ask to align your expenses with your values?

    Is this expense consistent with my values? (*Your money and your values*, page 314)

SKILLS SNAPSHOT
Chapter 10

Now that you've reflected on the ideas in this chapter and experimented with some new strategies, reflect on your money skills. Then think about the most powerful action you could take in the near future to gain more financial mastery.

Discovery
My score on the Money section of the Discovery Wheel was . . .

Right now my main sources of income are . . .

My three biggest expenses each month are . . .

Intention
I plan to graduate by (month and year) . . .

I plan to pay for my education next year by . . .

Mastery with money will enhance my career by . . .

Action
To reach that level of mastery, the most important habit I can adopt is . . .

My cue for remembering to practice this habit is . . .

My reward for practicing this habit will be . . .

INSTRUCTOR TOOLS & TIPS

HEALTH

"To be somebody you must last." —*Ruth Gordon*

PREVIEW

Staying healthy while pursuing higher education is an important skill all students need to master. Juggling work, college courses, and family responsibilities can be quite stressful. It is essential that first-year students start their education on the right foot, with strategies for maintaining their "machine." This chapter provides resources for beginning conversations about such topics as eating well, exercising, personal safety, self-esteem, alcohol abuse, and addiction. Don't hesitate to seek an opinion—from your campus health center or a community outreach program—when you need an expert's voice to support the text.

Some of you may feel uncertain *how* to begin discussing serious health issues in your classroom. Don't feel you must have all the answers. Share your own personal health journey with your students if you feel comfortable doing so. It often helps students to hear that we, as teachers and mentors, face challenges as well. The secret is being open to growing and improving our behaviors and beliefs. Healthy living is often an informed, proactive process. One way to begin this process is to have students revisit the answers they filled in on their Discovery Wheel. Using the Discovery and Intention Journal Entry system, a discussion about stress can begin with *what* factors are causing your students to feel stress, and this can lead to asking *why* these issues might be considered stressful. As a class, you can brainstorm possible *what if* scenarios to reduce students' stress. Then have your students write Intention Statements about steps they can take the next time they are experiencing high levels of stress.

GUEST SPEAKER

Invite a guest speaker from the student wellness or health center for this portion of the class. If your school offers health and wellness classes, consider inviting a faculty member from this department. You could even contact your county health department as a resource. Often, students will pay more attention to a visiting professional. Ask your presenter to discuss the importance of health and the relationship of health to learning. Be sure to allow time for a question-and-answer period.

Another idea is to ask whether a local chapter of Alcoholics Anonymous or Narcotics Anonymous can provide a guest speaker or, better yet, a panel of speakers. Although these programs emphasize anonymity, some participants, as part of their program of recovery, choose to share their story as a way of educating others. These individuals can have a powerful impact on your students.

Healthy Living: Making the right choices

Difficulties encountered by college students don't always originate during freshman year. Problems may begin during high school. They may occur at home. But college is a different environment, and students may be distracted. Whether it's about living arrangements, time management, or new friends, students have many choices to make. Drinking, sexually transmitted diseases, and psychological problems may create unsafe and unhealthy conditions.

LECTURE

Workplace Application. Managing stress in the workplace. Stress is anything that places a demand on us physically, mentally, or emotionally. Stress is a factor in everyone's life. All stress isn't bad. *Eustress* is the good type, whereas *distress* is the more difficult to manage. Despite this, stress can help us foster change, focus on work responsibilities, and inspire creativity and efficiency. Job stress is a common and costly problem in the American workplace, leaving few workers untouched. Sources of work stress vary widely, from dealing with conflict and tension among coworkers to being vigilant in dangerous work environments. Employees can better manage stress by following a few simple tips:

● ***Focus only on what you can control.*** You cannot control others' work and behavior, but you can control your work performance and attitude. Try to remain positive, even in the face of difficult or tension-filled situations. This will allow you to feel empowered to do your best.

master instructor
best practice

stress management plan

"I have students do this project to help them understand how to cope with stress.

1. *Research several possible stress-management strategies.*
   - *Explore stress-management strategies.*
   - *Try to explore an area that you would be interested in incorporating into your life. This may include physical exercise, journaling, music therapy, or humor therapy.*
   - *Choose one strategy that you would consider using on a regular basis, and complete item 2 below.*

2. *Write a two- to three-page essay or create a PowerPoint presentation in which you:*
   - *Describe the stress-management strategy. Give some background. For example, if you choose yoga, give some history of yoga and how people have used this as effective stress reduction.*
   - *Then relate that strategy to your personal life, and discuss how you plan to incorporate the stress-management plan into your lifestyle.*
   - *Include photos or clip art in work."*

—Annette McCreedy, Nashville State Community College

- *Maintain healthy habits.* Get a good night's sleep. Eat a healthy, balanced breakfast. Listen to music. Take an alternate route to work. Do anything that mentally prepares you to have a great day.

- *Maintain good work habits—plan your work and work your plan.* Plan your workday. Take your allotted breaks, maybe even taking a short walk. Cut big projects into smaller, manageable tasks.

- *Maintain good habits away from work.* If at all possible, leave work at work. Build positive relationships with friends, family, coworkers and others who may provide support in stressful times. Exercise, participate in a sport, or engage in a fun activity.

EXERCISES/ACTIVITIES

Master Student Profile: Randy Pausch (page 348). After students read the inspirational story about Randy Pausch, ask them to think about how their childhood dreams can be connected to their career goals. Remind students that they can view "The Last Lecture" by Randy Pausch online in its entirety.

CONVERSATION/SHARING

Power Process: Surrender (page 320). Use the following example to open a discussion about this Power Process with your students:

Sally and Jane leave work on Friday at the same time. Both are caught in rush-hour traffic. Sally frets, honks her horn, and changes lanes as frequently as possible, with the hope of saving time. She curses the light when it changes to red, gets aggravated at cars that don't start moving fast enough when the light changes to green, frantically listens to the traffic reports on the radio, agonizes about all the things she's missing at home, worries because she is getting very low on gas, and arrives home at 6:09 p.m. with a headache. Jane surrenders. Rather than fighting and resisting the traffic, she accepts it and flows with it. She listens to her favorite radio station, plans her activities for the weekend, thinks of a better way for taking purchase orders at work, sees a new Chinese restaurant she wants to try, notices the trees and plants telling her that spring is here, repeats her affirmations about self-improvement, anticipates the warm greeting she will receive from her family, and arrives home at 6:09 p.m. with a smile.

HOMEWORK

Choose to sleep (page 325). College students frequently complain that they have trouble getting a good night's sleep. For a homework assignment, have them do online research for solutions to sleep disorders and bring an interesting article to class. Have them share these articles in small groups, and then discuss the body's need for rest and how sleep deprivation can affect their schoolwork.

Alcohol, tobacco, and drugs: The truth (page 340). Some college students are trying to enhance their focus, memory, and brain performance by taking controlled medications that are prescribed

master instructor
best practice

"When change is requested of students, they often unconsciously say, "I can't. ..." I ask my students to take a closer look at times when they say these statements and begin to replace the "I can't" with "I won't."

Have your students make a list of those "I can't" statements. From this list, have them select one and restate the sentence with "won't" instead of "can't." Then, ask students to describe any distinction between these two statements. Generally students will say that the "I won't" statement implies some choice in the matter, and the experience changes from being one of victimization to taking some responsibility.

The last step is to have students replace the "I won't" with "I don't know how." Again, I ask students to describe any distinction between this statement and the "I won't" statement. Students often experience a weight off their shoulders or realize they were operating under a false expectation such as "I should know this." Students at this point can write a Discovery and Intention Statement about their experience.

Chapter 11 provides students with an opportunity to practice taking more responsibility for their thoughts (intrapersonal communications) and to use the steps in critical thinking.

I have students list some of their negative thinking. They often say things like "I'll never get as much sleep as suggested" or "I'll never reduce my anxiety before test taking."

I ask students to rewrite their sentences to look like this: "I thought I would never get enough sleep" or "I thought I would never reduce my anxiety before test taking."

I have students rewrite these statements over and over again, emphasizing the word "thought." At some point, students will smile and say, "Oh I get it, I just 'thought' I would never get enough sleep," or "I see it now; I 'thought' I would never reduce my anxiety before test taking."

We often turn our thoughts into reality or a belief without going through the steps in critical thinking. This is related to a self-fulfilling prophecy, or self-efficacy, described in the article "Developing a strong self-image" in Chapter 11 and the Power Process: I create it all in Chapter 5.

—*Fred Kester, Yavapai College*

for other purposes. These drugs include Ritalin, Adderall, and Provigil. Assign students to research the intended medical purposes of these drugs as well as the precautions and side effects associated with them.

EVALUATION

Frequent quizzes ensure that students focus attention during class and keep up with the text reading assignments. In addition, quizzes provide students with opportunities for written reflection regarding new discoveries and intentions. Evaluation instruments also help you identify topics and concepts that students have not yet mastered. Consider the use of evaluation tools

that require synthesis and application of chapter principles rather than memorization.

Quiz Ideas for Chapter 11
Ask students to:

- Describe strategies to find more time to exercise.
- Write Discovery and Intention Statements about ways to develop self-esteem.
- Describe tools for dealing with emotional pain.
- Identify several strategies that can be used to quit smoking.
- List three new strategies for improving their diet.

MindTap™ | **EMBRACE VALUABLE RESOURCES**

FOR CHAPTER 11

STUDENT RESOURCES: MINDTAP

- **Learning Outcomes.** Every chapter begins with an engaging video that visually outlines in a mind map format the key learning outcomes for that chapter. Students should find these short introductions not only helpful as chapter organizers, but as valuable note-taking models.

- **Engagement Activity: Master Students in Action.** Students hear firsthand from other students about their experiences and challenges with diversity. The Master Students in Action videos give your students an up-close view of how the strategies in *Becoming a Master Student* have helped their peers overcome obstacles.

- **Aplia Homework Assignment: Choose exercise, and choose your fuel.** In this assignment, students learn how to plan a healthy lifestyle by examining what makes up a healthy diet, and how sleep can affect classroom performance.

- **Reflection Activity: Balance.** This Slice of Life video, created by student Malia Lavin, discusses the importance of finding and embracing a balanced lifestyle as the best way to successfully learn.

MindTap™ *Your personal learning experience—learn anywhere, anytime.*

INSTRUCTOR COMPANION SITE

- **Need some energizing lecture ideas?** Browse through the lecture ideas provided for Chapter 11 in the Course Manual, including the following:
  - **Addiction.** Facts and statistics about a variety of wellness issues can help students make choices.
  - **Burnout.** Discuss with your students the warning signs of burnout and prevention techniques.

- **Looking for fresh, innovative ways to teach Chapter 11 topics?** Browse through the Best Practices recommendations in the Course Manual to see what other Master Instructors have been successfully doing with their students.

Please visit login.cengage.com to log in and access the Instructor Companion Site.

master instructor
best practice

" *The college years are the time for many students to experiment with sexual behaviors. Many know that they need to practice abstinence to be totally safe, or, if sexually active, to practice safer sex. However, many students do not know what behaviors are considered risky or what skills are involved in practicing safer sex. So I teach not only the fact that condoms may prevent the transmission of HIV but also specific skills in condom usage. My primary objectives are for students to learn effective communication skills in negotiating the use of a condom with their partners as well as learning the skills needed to stay safe during sexual activities. I use explicit language; I incorporate humor and frank discussion, as well as a demonstration on how to use a condom. This is one topic where you will find the entire class will "be here now." "*

—*Deborah Warfield, Seminole Community College*

HEALTH 11

Why

Succeeding in higher education calls for a baseline of physical and emotional well-being.

How

Think about the main health concern that you're experiencing right now. Then preview this chapter for ideas that can help you resolve this concern. Note the strategies that you want to learn about, along with the pages where you can read more about them.

What if...

I could meet the demands of daily life with energy and optimism to spare?

NEW

Choose freedom from distress ■ 324

Choose to stay safe

Although schools make every effort to promote student safety, you can always benefit from knowing how to protect yourself. ■ 334

Asking for help ■ 331

Choose your fuel ■ 322

Choose to exercise ■ 323

What is included ...

SURRENDER

Life can be magnificent and satisfying. It can also be devastating. Sometimes there is too much pain or confusion. Problems can be too big and too numerous. Life can bring us to our knees in a pitiful, helpless, and hopeless state. A broken relationship, a sudden diagnosis of cancer, a dependence on drugs, or a stress-filled job can leave us feeling overwhelmed—powerless.

In these troubling situations, the first thing we can do is to admit that we don't have the resources to handle the problem. No matter how hard we try and no matter what skills we bring to bear, some problems remain out of our control. When this is the case, we can tell the truth: "It's too big and too mean. I can't handle it." In that moment, we take a step toward greater health.

Desperately struggling to control a problem can easily result in the problem controlling us. Surrender is letting go of being the master in order to avoid becoming the slave.

Many traditions make note of this idea. Western religions speak of surrendering to God. Hindus say surrender to the Self. Members of Alcoholics Anonymous talk about turning their lives over to a Higher Power. Agnostics might suggest surrendering to their intellect, their intuition, or their conscience.

In any case, surrender means being receptive. Once we admit that we're at the end of our rope, we open ourselves up to help. We learn that we don't have to go it alone. We find out that other people have faced similar problems and survived. We give up our old habits of thinking and behaving as if we have to be in control of everything. We stop acting as general manager of the universe. We surrender. And that creates a space for something new in our lives.

Surrender is not "giving up." It is not a suggestion to quit and do nothing about your problems. Giving up is fatalistic and accomplishes nothing. You have many skills and resources. Use them. You can apply all of your energy to handling a situation and still surrender at the same time. You can surrender to weight gain even as you step up your exercise program. You can surrender to a toothache even as you go to the dentist. You can surrender to the past while adopting new habits for a healthy future.

Surrender includes doing whatever you can in a positive, trusting spirit. Let go, keep going, and know when a source of help lies beyond you.

© Hannamariah/Shutterstock.com

Wake up to HEALTH

Some people see health as just a matter of common sense. These people might see little value in reading a health chapter. After all, they already know how to take care of themselves.

Yet *knowing* and *doing* are two different things. Health information does not always translate into healthy habits.

We expect to experience health challenges as we age. Even youth, though, is no guarantee of good health. Over the last 3 decades, obesity among young adults has tripled. Twenty-nine percent of young men smoke. And 70 percent of deaths among adults ages 18 to 29 result from unintentional injuries, accidents, homicide, and suicide.[1]

As a student, your success in school is directly tied to your health. Anxiety, depression, sleep difficulties, and stress have been associated with lower academic performance among undergraduate students.[2]

Any health habit that undermines your success in school can also undermine your success in later life. Few students need another lecture about the health risks of drug dependence, unprotected sex, sleep deprivation, and a high-calorie diet. You already know about that. What students might forget, however, is that employers value a strong work ethic. This implies showing up for work, staying alert, and tackling tasks with energy. Poor health can undermine these qualities and hurt our chances for getting a job, keeping a job, and earning more money.

On the other hand, we can adopt habits that sustain our well-being. One study found that people lengthened their lives an average of 14 years by adopting just four habits: staying tobacco-free, eating more fruits and vegetables, exercising regularly, and drinking alcohol in moderation if at all.[3]

Health also hinges on a habit of exercising some tissue that lies between your ears—the organ called your brain. One path to greater health starts not with new food or a new form of exercise, but with new ideas.

Consider the power of beliefs. Some of them create barriers to higher levels of health: "Your health is programmed by your heredity." "Some people are just low on energy." "Healthy food doesn't taste very good." "Over the long run, people just don't change their

© Olena Pivnenko/Shutterstock.com

habits." Be willing to test these ideas and change them when it serves you.

People often misunderstand what the word *health* means. Remember that this word is similar in origin to *whole, hale, hardy,* and even *holy.* Implied in these words are qualities that most of us associate with healthy people: alertness, vitality, vigor, resilience. Healthy people meet the demands of daily life with energy to spare. Illness or stress might slow them down for a while, but then they bounce back. They know how to relax, create loving relationships, and find satisfaction in their work.

To open up your inquiry into health—and to open up new possibilities for your life—consider three ideas.

First, health is a continuum. On one end of that continuum is a death that comes too early. On the other end is a long life filled with satisfying work and fulfilling relationships. Many of us exist between those extremes at a point we might call average. Most of the time we're not sick. And most of the time we're not truly thriving either.

Second, health changes. Health is not a fixed state. In fact, health fluctuates from year to year, day to day, and moment to moment. Those changes can occur largely by chance. Or they can occur more often by choice, as we take conscious control of our thinking and behavior.

Third, even when faced with health challenges, we have choices. We can choose attitudes and habits that promote a higher quality of life. For example, people with diabetes can often manage the disease by exercising more and changing their diet.

Health is one of those rich, multilayered concepts that we can never define completely. In the end, your definition of *health* comes from your own experience. The proof lies not on these pages but in your life—in the level of health that you create, starting now.

You have choices. You can remain unaware of habits that have major consequences for your health. Or you can become aware of current habits (discovery), choose new habits (intention), and take appropriate action.

Health is a choice you make every moment, with each thought and behavior. Wake up to this possibility by experimenting with the suggestions in this chapter. ■

© joyfull/Shutterstock.com

Choose your
FUEL

Food is your primary fuel for body and mind. And even though you've been eating all your life, entering higher education is bound to change the way that you fuel yourself.

There have been hundreds of books written about nutrition. One says don't drink milk. Another says the calcium provided by milk is an essential nutrient we need daily. Although such debate seems confusing, take comfort. There is actually wide agreement about how to fuel yourself for health.

The Department of Agriculture (USDA) and the Department of Health and Human Services (HHS) issue updates dietary guidelines every five years. Here you will find safe and scientifically-based suggestions for consuming fewer calories, staying physically active, and maintaining a healthy weight. These are important strategies to reduce your risk of chronic disease and to stay healthy. To find the latest guidelines, go online to your favorite search engine and use the key words *USDA dietary guidelines*.

Certain guidelines remain consistent from year to year. Examples include:

- Emphasize fruits, vegetables, whole grains, and fat-free or low-fat milk and milk products.
- Include lean meats, poultry, fish, beans, eggs, and nuts.
- Choose foods that are low in saturated fats, trans fats, cholesterol, salt (sodium), and added sugars.

Michael Pollan, a writer for the *New York Times Magazine,* spent several years sorting out the scientific literature on nutrition.[4] He boiled the key guidelines down to seven words in three sentences:

- *Eat food.* In other words, choose whole, fresh foods over processed products with a lot of ingredients.
- *Not too much.* If you want to manage your weight, then control how much you eat. Notice portion sizes. Pass on snacks, seconds, and desserts—or indulge just occasionally.
- *Mostly plants.* Fruits, vegetables, and grains are loaded with chemicals that help to prevent disease. Plant-based foods, on the whole, are also lower in calories than foods from animals (meat and dairy products).

Finally, forget diets. *How* you eat can matter more than *what* you eat. If you want to eat less, then eat slowly. Savor each bite. Stop when you're satisfied instead of when you feel full. Use meal times as a chance to relax, reduce stress, and connect with people. ■

Prevent and treat eating disorders

Eating disorders affect many students. These disorders involve serious disturbances in eating behavior. Examples are overeating or extreme reduction of food intake, as well as irrational concern about body shape or weight. Women are much more likely to develop these disorders than are men, though cases are on the rise among males.

Bulimia involves cycles of excessive eating and forced purges. A person with this disorder might gorge on a pizza, doughnuts, and ice cream and then force herself to vomit. Or she might compensate for overeating with excessive use of laxatives, enemas, or diuretics.

Anorexia nervosa is a potentially fatal illness marked by self-starvation. People with anorexia may practice extended fasting or eat only one kind of food for weeks at a time.

These disorders are not due to a failure of willpower. They are real illnesses in which harmful patterns of eating take on a life of their own.

Eating disorders can lead to many complications, including life-threatening heart conditions and kidney failure. Many people with eating disorders also struggle with depression, substance abuse, and anxiety. They need immediate treatment to stabilize their health. This is usually followed by continuing medical care, counseling, and medication to promote a full recovery.

If you're worried you might have an eating disorder, visit a doctor, campus health service, or local public health clinic. If you see signs of an eating disorder in someone else, express your concern by stating the facts about what you observe and asking if that person has ever thought about getting help with his or her relationship to food.

For more information, contact the National Eating Disorders Association at 1-800-931-2237 or online at www.nationaleatingdisorders.org.

CHOOSE TO EXERCISE

joyfull/Shutterstock.com

Our bodies need to be exercised. The world ran on muscle power back in the era when we had to hunt down a woolly mammoth every few weeks and drag it back to the cave. Now we can grab a burger at a drive-up window. Today we need to make a special effort to exercise.

Exercise promotes weight control and reduces the symptoms of depression. It also helps to prevent heart attack, diabetes, and several forms of cancer.[5] Exercise also refreshes your body and your mind. If you're stuck on a math problem or blocked on writing a paper, take an exercise break. Chances are that you'll come back with a fresh perspective and some new ideas.

If you get moving, you'll create lean muscles, a strong heart, and an alert brain. If the word *exercise* turns you off, think *physical activity* instead. Here are some things you can do:

Stay active throughout the day. Park a little farther from work or school. Do your heart a favor by walking some extra blocks. Take the stairs instead of riding elevators. For an extra workout, climb two stairs at a time.

An hour of daily activity is ideal, but do whatever you can. Some activity is better than none.

No matter what you do, ease into it. For example, start by walking briskly for at least 15 minutes every day. Increase that time gradually, and add a little jogging.

There's some evidence that sitting a lot during the day promotes obesity—even if you exercise regularly.[6] So, make it a point to move more throughout the day. For example, stand up when you take a phone call. If you sit at the computer for long periods of time, get up and walk around the room a couple of time each hour. During long car trips, stop regularly to stretch your legs.

Adapt to your campus environment. Look for exercise facilities on campus. Search for classes in aerobics, swimming, volleyball, basketball, golf, tennis, and other sports. Intramural sports are another option. School can be a great place to get in shape.

Do what you enjoy. Stay active with aerobic activities that you enjoy. You might like martial arts, kickboxing, yoga, ballroom dance classes, stage combat classes, or mountain climbing. Check your school catalog for such courses.

Vary your routine. Find several activities that you like to do, and rotate them throughout the year. Your main form of activity during winter might be ballroom dancing, riding an exercise bike, or skiing. In summer, you could switch to outdoor sports. Whenever possible, choose weight-bearing activities such as walking, running, or stair climbing.

Get active early. Work out first thing in the morning. Then it's done for the day. Make it part of your daily routine, just like brushing your teeth.

Exercise with other people. Making exercise a social affair can add a fun factor and raise your level of commitment.

Join a gym without fear. Many health clubs welcome people who are just starting to get in shape.

Look for gradual results. If your goal is to lose weight, be patient. Because 1 pound equals 3,500 calories, you might feel tempted to reduce weight loss to a simple formula: *Let's see . . . if I burn away just 100 calories each day through exercise, I should lose 1 pound every 35 days.*

Actually, the relationship between exercise and weight loss is complex. Many factors—including individual differences in metabolism and the type of exercise you do—affect the amount of weight you actually lose.[7]

When you step on the bathroom scale, look for small changes over time rather than sudden, dramatic losses. Gradual weight loss is more healthy, anyway—and easier to sustain over the long term.

Weight loss is just one potential benefit of exercise. Choosing to exercise can lift your mood, increase your stamina, strengthen your bones, stabilize your joints, and help prevent heart disease. It can also reduce your risk of high blood pressure, diabetes, and several forms of cancer. If you do resistance training—such as weight machines or elastic-band workouts—you'll strengthen your muscles as well. For a complete fitness program, add stretching exercises to enjoy increased flexibility.[8]

Before beginning any vigorous exercise program, consult a health care professional. This is critical if you are overweight, over age 60, in poor condition, or a heavy smoker, or if you have a history of health problems. ■

CHOOSE FREEDOM FROM DISTRESS

Stress is not always harmful. It can result from pleasant experiences as well as unpleasant ones. Both excitement and fear produce rapid heart rates, increased adrenaline flow, and muscle contractions.

Stress—at appropriate times and appropriate levels—is normal and useful. It can sharpen our awareness and boost our energy just when we need it the most.

When stress persists or becomes excessive, it turns into *distress*. This is a mental and physical state that interferes with your memory, ability to learn, sleep patterns, and resistance to illness.

Chances are that your stress level is too high if you consistently experience any of the following: headache, chest pain, increased heart rate, shortness of breath, muscle aches, indigestion, fatigue, and insomnia.[9]

Managing stress starts with taking it apart. Stress—no matter how intense—has only two main elements: physical *sensations* such as shallow breathing and muscle tension, and negative *thoughts*, including predictions of failure.

All stress management techniques target one or both of these elements. The good news is that even if you can't always control the *sources* of stress, you can choose your *response* to them. Finding even one technique that works can bring immediate relief from stress.

The following techniques can help you deal with any type of stress in any situation, from test anxiety to stage fright.

© iStockphoto.com/AlbanyPictures

ACCEPT PHYSICAL SENSATIONS

Make contact with the present moment.
If you feel anxious, see whether you can focus your attention on a specific sight, sound, or other sensation that's happening in the present moment. Examine the details of a painting. Study the branches on a tree. Observe the face of your watch right down to the tiny scratches in the glass.

When you're in class, take a few seconds to listen to the sounds of squeaking chairs, the scratching of pencils, the muted coughs. Touch the surface of your desk and notice the texture. Focus all of your attention on one point—anything other than the flow of thoughts through your head.

Scan your body. Simple awareness is an effective response to unpleasant physical sensations. Discover this for yourself by bringing awareness to each area of your body. To begin, sit comfortably and close your eyes. Focus your attention on the muscles in your feet, and notice if they are relaxed. Tell the muscles in your feet that they can relax. Move up to your ankles, and repeat the procedure.

Next, go to your calves and thighs and buttocks, telling each group of muscles to relax. Do the same for your lower back, diaphragm, chest, upper arms, lower arms, fingers, upper back, shoulders, neck, jaw, face, and scalp.

Describe sensations. Trying to deny or ignore physical sensations is a strategy that often backfires. Instead, describe your physical experience of stress in detail. Put your description in writing, tell someone about it, or do both. This is a way of opening up to the experience. When you completely experience the physical sensations related to stress, you might find that they subside or lose a little of their power.

View sensations as something to accept— rather than problems to solve. Consider typical responses to problems. If a car has a flat tire, that's a problem. The solution is to repair or replace the tire. If a bathroom faucet drips, that's a problem. The solution is to repair or replace part of the faucet.

This problem-solution approach often works well when applied to events outside ourselves. It does not work so well, however, when applied to events inside us. When we define anger, sadness, fear, or any emotion as a problem, we tend to search for a solution. However, emotions respond differently than flat tires and drippy faucets.

Typical attempts to "solve" unpleasant emotions include eating, drinking, watching TV, or surfing the Internet. These are actually attempts to resist the emotions and try to make them go away. For a short time, this strategy might work. Over the long term, however, our efforts to repair or replace emotions often have the opposite effect: The emotions persist or even get stronger. Our solutions actually become part of the problem.

An alternative to problem solving is acceptance. We can stop seeing unpleasant physical sensations as problems. This attitude frees us from having to search for solutions (which often fail anyway). Acceptance means just letting our feelings be—releasing any resistance to how we feel in the moment. This approach is a wise one, since what we resist usually persists.

Even the most unpleasant physical sensations fade sooner or later. The next time you are feeling distress, simply let sensations wash over you and then pass away.

Choose to sleep

A lack of rest can decrease your immunity to illness and impair your performance in school. You still might be tempted to cut back drastically on your sleep once in a while for an all-night study session. Instead, remember that cutting back on sleep is a choice you can avoid.

If you have trouble falling asleep, experiment with the following suggestions:

- **Exercise daily.** For many people, regular exercise promotes sounder sleep. However, finish exercising several hours before you want to go to sleep.
- **Avoid naps during the daytime.**
- **Monitor your caffeine intake,** especially in the afternoon and evening.
- **Avoid using alcohol to feel sleepy.** Drinking alcohol late in the evening can disrupt your sleep during the night.
- **Develop a sleep ritual**—a regular sequence of calming activities that end your day. You might take a warm bath and do some light reading. Turn off the TV and computer at least one hour before you go to bed.
- **Use your bed for sleeping.** Avoid studying in bed.
- **Keep your sleeping room cool.**
- **Keep a regular schedule** for going to sleep and waking up.
- **Sleep in the same place each night.** When you're there, your body gets the message: "It's time to go to sleep."
- **Practice relaxation techniques while lying in bed.** A simple one is to count your breaths and release distracting thoughts as they arise.
- **Make tomorrow's to-do list before you go to sleep** so you won't lie there worrying that tomorrow you'll forget about something you need to do.
- **Get up and study** or do something else until you're tired.
- **See a doctor** if sleeplessness persists.

CHANGE YOUR THINKING

Dispute thoughts. Martin Seligman, author of *Learned Optimism,* states that the key difference between optimists and pessimists is *explanatory style*—the way that they explain events. Pessimists might describe the transition to higher education in ways that are:

- *Permanent:* "I'll never be able to handle college-level classes."

- *Pervasive:* "Whenever I get involved in a new situation, I always make a lot of mistakes."

- *Personal:* "I'm just no good at making transitions."

In contrast, optimists tend to make statements that can be described as:

- *Temporary:* "I'm feeling anxious about starting school, and that's normal at first."

- *Specific:* "This transition may be hard for me, but on the whole I can learn to handle change well."

- *External:* "My circumstances have changed a lot, so it's natural to find that I have a lot of new feelings."

The key point is that over time you can learn to change your explanatory style. Doing this can make a difference in your stress level. Notice when you talk about difficult events in terms that are permanent, pervasive, or personal. Then write Intentions Statements about speaking in ways that are more temporary, specific, and external.

Meditate. Meditation can provide a deeper form of rest than sleep. This ancient practice is now being actively researched and prescribed as a treatment for stress-related conditions such as chronic pain.

To practice meditation, you do not have to give up your current beliefs or adopt any new ones. Meditation is a practice—not a dogma.

There are many different definitions of meditation. As a starting point, think of it as a state of inner stillness. Ordinarily our minds are occupied 24 hours a day with a stream of images and words. With unpleasant mental states, such as stress, our minds tend to race, manufacturing distressing thoughts at rapid-fire speed.

Meditation reverses this process. While meditating, you focus your attention on a single object such as the sensation of your own breathing. Instead of thinking, you simply notice your thoughts and then let them go. Eventually, your thinking slows down. You may find that your stream of thinking comes to a complete stop, even as you remain alert and aware. People variously describe this state as inner peace, wisdom, serenity, enlightenment, bliss, the present moment, or the "peace that passes all understanding." Ultimately the words don't matter. The experience does.

Many churches, synagogues, and mosques teach forms of meditation. You can also find courses in meditation through medical clinics, YMCAs, and other community organizations.

Use guided imagery. Relax completely, and take a quick fantasy trip. Close your eyes, free your body of tension, and imagine yourself in a beautiful, peaceful, natural setting. Create as much of the scene as you can. Be specific. Use all of your senses.

For example, you might imagine yourself at a beach. Hear the surf rolling in and the seagulls calling to each other. Feel the sun on your face and the hot sand between your toes. Smell the sea breeze. Taste the salty mist from the surf. Notice the ships on the horizon and the rolling sand dunes. Use all of your senses to create a vivid imaginary trip.

Find a place that works for you, and practice getting there. When you become proficient, you can return to it quickly for trips that might last only a few seconds. With practice, you can use this technique even while you are taking a test.

TAKE CONSTRUCTIVE ACTION

Take care of your body. Your thoughts and emotions can get scrambled if you go too long feeling hungry or tired. Follow the suggestions in this chapter for eating, exercise, and sleep.

Vigorous exercise is especially powerful. Performing aerobic exercise is one technique to reduce stress. Exercise regularly during the days you review for a test. See what effect it has on your ability to focus your attention, relax, and see the world with fresh eyes.

Do some kind of exercise that will get your heart beating at twice your normal rate and keep it beating at that rate for 15 or 20 minutes. Aerobic exercise includes rapid walking, jogging, swimming, bicycling, basketball, and anything else that elevates your heart rate and keeps it elevated.

Share what you're thinking and feeling. Revealing your inner world with a family member or friend is a powerful way to gain perspective. The simple act of describing a problem can sometimes reveal a solution or give you a fresh perspective.

Stay engaged with daily activities. A related strategy is to do something—*anything* that's constructive, even if it's not a solution to a specific problem. For example, mop the kitchen floor. Clean out your dresser drawers. Iron your shirts. This sounds silly, but it works.

The basic principle is that you can separate emotions from actions. It is appropriate to feel miserable when you do. It's normal to cry and express your feelings. It is also possible to go to class, study, work, eat, and feel miserable at the same time. Unless you have a diagnosable problem with anxiety or depression, you can continue your normal activities until the misery passes.

Japanese psychiatrist Morita Masatake, a contemporary of Sigmund Freud, based his whole approach to treatment on this insight: We can face our emotional pain directly and still take constructive action. One of Masatake's favorite suggestions for people who felt depressed was that they tend a garden.[10]

Plan your day and focus on one task at a time.

It's easy to feel stressed if you dwell on how much you have to accomplish this year, this term, this month, or even this week. One solution is effective planning.

Remember that an effective plan for the day does two things. First, it clarifies what you're choosing *not* to do today. (Tasks that you plan to do in the future are listed on your calendar or to-do list.) Second, an effective plan reduces your day to a series of concrete tasks—such as making phone calls, going to classes, running errands, or reading chapters—that you can do one at a time.

If you feel overwhelmed, just find the highest-priority task on your to-do list. Do it with total attention until it's done. Then go back to your list for the next high-priority task. Do *it* with total attention. Savor the feeling of mastery and control that comes with crossing each task off your list.

Solve problems.

Although you can't "fix" a bad feeling in the same way that you can fix a machine, you can choose to change a situation associated with that feeling. There might be a problem that needs a solution. You can use the experience of stress as motivation to solve that problem.

Sometimes an intense feeling of sadness, anger, or fear is related to a specific situation in your life. Describe the problem. Then brainstorm solutions and choose one to implement. Reducing your course load, cutting back on hours at work, getting more financial aid, delegating a task, or taking some other concrete action might solve the problem and help you feel better.

Find alternatives to chemicals.

When faced with stress, some people turn to relief in the form of a pill, a drink, or a drug in some other form. Chemicals such as caffeine and alcohol can change the way you feel. They also come with costs that go beyond money. For example, drinking alcohol can relax you and interfere with your attention and memory. Caffeine or energy drinks might make you feel more confident in the short term. Watch what happens, though, when you start to come down from a caffeine-induced high. You might feel even more irritable than you did before drinking that double espresso.

All moral lectures aside, chemicals that you take without a prescription are often ineffective ways to manage anxiety. Use other techniques to calm your nerves instead, such as a taking a hot bath, getting a massage, going for a walk, or spending time with a close friend. Find healthy solutions that provide long-term benefits.

> *Although you can't "fix" a bad feeling in the same way that you can fix a machine, you can choose to change a situation associated with that feeling.*

Reach out for help.

Remember a basic guideline about *when* to seek help: whenever problems with your thinking, moods, or behavior consistently interfere with your ability to sleep, eat, go to class, work, or sustain positive relationships.

You can get help at the student health center on campus. This is not just a service for treating colds, allergies, and flu symptoms. Counselors expect to help students deal with adjustment to campus, changes in mood, academic problems, and drug abuse and dependence.

Students with anxiety disorders, clinical depression, bipolar disorder, and other diagnoses might get referred to a professional outside the student health center. The referral process can take time, so seek help right away. Your tuition helps to pay for these services. It's smart to use them now.

You can find resources to promote emotional health even if your campus doesn't offer counseling services. Start with a personal physician—one person who can coordinate all of your health care. (For suggestions, go to your school's health center.) A personal physician can refer you to another health professional if it seems appropriate.

These two suggestions can also work after you graduate. Managing stress is a skill to use for the rest of your life. ■

Interactive

Journal Entry 24
Discovery/Intention Statement

Choose your stress management strategies

Carefully monitoring your stress and planning to manage it can make a difference in your success in school and at work. Take a few minutes now to gain more awareness of this aspect of your health and clarify your intentions.

To begin, think about the chronic stressors in your life. These are people, circumstances, and events that are consistently linked to the physical and mental experience of distress. Some common stressors for students are test taking, failing a class, dealing with credit card debt, and ending a long-term romantic relationship. Complete the following sentence:

I discovered that the main sources of distress in my life are . . .

_____

_____

Next, think about your strategies for coping with distress. There are students who rely on drinking and other drug use for this purpose. Others watch TV or play video games for hours. Some students turn to close friends for a listening ear or seek relief in vigorous daily exercise. For a moment, set aside any self-judgments and make a list of your top three strategies for managing stress, no matter what they are.

I discovered that I usually manage stress by . . .

_____

I also . . .

_____

In addition, I . . .

_____

Now, think about how well each of these strategies works for you in managing stress *and* maintaining your overall health. Rate each strategy on a scale of 1 to 5, with 5 being most effective. Write this rating next to each strategy, and circle the number.

Finally, think about whether you want to make any changes in the way you manage stress. If your current strategies are effective—fine. Your intention might be to simply continue them. Another option is to choose some new stress management strategies and turn them into habits. Complete the following sentences:

To more effectively manage stress, I intend to . . .

_____

I also will . . .

_____

In addition, I will . . .

_____

Masterfile

DEVELOPING A STRONG SELF-IMAGE

> The challenge of higher education often puts our self-image at risk. The rigors of class work, financial pressures, and new social settings can test our ability to adapt and change. Your **self-image** is the way you see yourself. It includes beliefs and feelings about your potential to succeed.

Self-image can erode in ways that are imperceptible to us. Over time, we can gradually buy into a reduced sense of our own possibilities. These views make it less likely that we'll take risks, and set and achieve goals.

Self-image is related to what psychologists call *self-efficacy*. This field of research is closely associated with psychologist Albert Bandura of Stanford University.¹¹

Efficacy refers to the ability to produce a desired effect. *Self-efficacy* refers to your belief in your ability to determine the outcomes of events—especially outcomes that are strongly influenced by your own behavior.

A strong self-image allows you to tackle problems with confidence, set long-term goals, and see difficult tasks as creative challenges rather than potential disasters. With a strong self-image, you believe that your action counts. You see yourself as someone who can make a positive difference in the world.

No one has to live with a poor self-image. Your self-image is flexible. It changes over time, and you can influence it with the following strategies.

SET UP SITUATIONS IN WHICH YOU CAN WIN

Start by planning scenarios in which you can succeed. Bandura calls these "mastery situations." For example, set yourself up for success by breaking a big project down into small, doable tasks. Then tackle and complete the first task. This accomplishment can help you move on to the next task with higher self-efficacy. Success breeds more success.

SET GOALS WITH CARE

If you want to boost your self-image, be picky about your goals. According to the research, goals that you find easy to meet will not make much of a difference in the way

you see yourself. Instead, set goals that call on you to overcome obstacles, make persistent effort, and even fail occasionally.

At the same time, it's important to avoid situations in which you are *often* likely to fail. Setting goals that you have little chance of meeting can undermine your self-image. Ideal goals are both challenging *and* achievable.

ADOPT A MODEL

In self-efficacy research, the word *model* has a special definition. This term refers to someone who is similar to you in key ways and who succeeds in the kinds of situations in which you want to succeed. To find a model, gather with people who share your interests. Look for people with whom you have a lot in common—and who have mastered the skills that you want to acquire. Besides demonstrating strategies and techniques for you to use, these people hold out a real possibility of success for you.

CHANGE THE CONVERSATION ABOUT YOURSELF

Monitor what you say and think about yourself. Remember that your self-talk might be so habitual that you don't even notice it. Whether or not you are fully aware of these thoughts, they can make or break your sense of self-image.

Pay close attention. Notice when you speak or think negatively about yourself. Telling the truth about your weaknesses is one thing. Consistently underrating yourself is another. In the conversation about yourself, go for balance. Tell the truth about the times you set a goal and missed it. Also take the time to write and speak about the goals you meet and what works well in your life.

People with a strong self-image attribute their failures to skills that they currently lack—and that they can acquire in the future. This approach chooses not to look on failures as permanent, personal defects. Rather than saying, "I just don't have what it takes to become a skilled test taker," say, "I can adopt techniques to help me remember key facts even when I feel stressed."

INTERPRET STRESS IN A NEW WAY

Achieving your goals might place you right in the middle of situations in which you feel stress. You might find yourself meeting new people, leading a meeting, speaking in public, or doing something else that you've never done before. That can feel scary.

Remember that stress comes in two forms—thoughts and physical sensations. Thoughts can include mental pictures of yourself making mistakes or being publicly humiliated. They also can be statements such as "This is the worst possible thing that could happen to me." Sensations can include shortness of breath, dry mouth, knots in the stomach, tingling feelings, headaches, and other forms of discomfort.

The way you interpret stress as you become aware of it can·make a big difference in your self-image.

During moments when you want to do well, you might rely on a stream of personal impressions to judge your performance. In those moments, see whether you can focus your attention. Rather than attaching negative interpretations to your experience of stress, simply notice your thoughts and sensations. Release them instead of dwelling on them or trying to resist them. As you observe yourself over time, you might find that the physical sensations associated with your sense of stress and your sense of excitement are largely the same. Instead of viewing these sensations as signs of impending doom when they are caused by stress, see them as a boost of energy and enthusiasm that you can channel into performing well.

COMPARE YOURSELF TO YOURSELF

Our own failures are often more dramatic to us than the failures of others. Our own successes are often more invisible to us. When we're unsure of ourselves, we can look in any direction and see people who seem more competent and more confident than we do. When we start the comparison game, we open the door to self-doubt.

There is a way to play the comparison game and win: Instead of comparing yourself with others, compare yourself to yourself. Measure success in terms of self-improvement rather than in terms of triumphs over others. Take time to note any progress you've made toward your goals over time. Write Discovery Statements about that progress. Celebrate your success in any area of life, no matter how small that success might seem.

SURROUND YOURSELF WITH SUPPORT

Seek out people who share your values and support your goals. This might mean going beyond your family. If you are the first student in your family to attend college, for example, your family might support you and still not understand your experiences. Find additional support by joining a study group, getting to know instructors, meeting with your advisor, and getting involved in a campus organization.

When you find supportive people, be willing to receive their encouragement. Instead of deflecting compliments ("It was nothing"), fully receive the positive things that others say about you ("Thank you"). Also, take public credit for your successes. "Well, I was just lucky" can change to "I worked hard to achieve that goal." ■

© iStockphoto.com/Rtimages

ASKING FOR
HELP

The world responds to people who ask. If you're not consistently getting what you want in life, then consider the power of asking for help.

"Ask and you shall receive" is a gem of wisdom from many spiritual traditions. Yet acting on this simple idea can be challenging.

Some people see asking for help as a sign of weakness. Actually, it's a sign of strength. Focus on the potential rewards. When you're willing to receive and others are willing to give, resources become available.

Remember that asking for help pays someone a compliment. It means that you value what people have to offer. Many will be happy to respond. The key is asking with skill.

ASK WITH CLARITY

Before asking for help, think about your request. Take time to prepare, and consider putting it in writing before you ask in person.

The way you ask has a great influence on the answers you get. For example, "I need help with money" is a big statement. People might not know how to respond. Be more specific: "Do you know any sources of financial aid that I might have missed?" Or "My expenses exceed my income by $200 each month. I don't want to work more hours while I'm in school. How can I fill the gap?"

ASK WITH SINCERITY

People can tell when a request comes straight from your heart. Although clarity is important, remember that you're asking for help—not making a speech. Keep it simple and direct. Just tell the truth about your current situation, what you want, and the gap between the two. It's okay to be less than perfect.

ASK WIDELY

Consider the variety of people who can offer help. They include parents, friends, classmates, coworkers, mentors, and sponsors. People such as counselors, advisors, and librarians are *paid* to help you.

Also be willing to ask for help with tough issues in any area of life—sex, health, money, career decisions, and more. If you consistently ask for help only in one area, you limit your potential.

To get the most value from this suggestion, direct your request to an appropriate person. For example, you wouldn't ask your instructors for advice about sex. However, you can share any concern with a professional counselor.

ASK WITH AN OPEN MIND

When you ask for help, see whether you can truly open up. If an idea seems strange or unworkable, put your objections on hold for the moment. If you feel threatened or defensive, just notice the feeling. Then return to listening. Discomfort can be a sign that you're about to make a valuable discovery. If people only confirm what you already think and feel, you miss the chance to learn.

ASK WITH RESPONSIBILITY

If you want people to offer help, then avoid statements such as "You know that suggestion you gave me last time? Wow, that really bombed!"

When you act on an idea and it doesn't work, the reason may have nothing to do with the other person. Perhaps you misunderstood or forgot a key point. Ask again for clarity. In any case, the choice about what to do—and the responsibility for the consequences—is still yours.

ASK WITH AN OPENING FOR MORE IDEAS

Approaching people with a specific, limited request can work wonders. So can asking in a way that takes the conversation to a new place. You can do this with creative questions: "Do you have any other ideas for me?" "Would it help if I approached this problem from a different angle?" "Could I be asking a better question?"

ASK AGAIN

People who make a living by selling things know the power of a repeated request. Some people habitually respond to a first request with "no." They might not get to "yes" until the second or third request.

Some cultures place a value on competition, success, and "making it on your own." In this environment, asking for help is not always valued. Sometimes people say no because they're surprised or not sure how to respond. Give them more time and another chance to come around. ■

Journal Entry 25
Discovery/Intention Statement

Reflect on your experience with asking for help

Note: This Journal Entry could arouse some strong and unpleasant emotions. Plan to do it at a time when your overall stress level is low and you feel emotionally supported. Also, you might want to keep your responses confidential. If so, then do your writing on separate paper or create a private document on your computer.

Think back to a time in your life when you experienced so much stress that you felt overwhelmed and doubted your ability to cope. Perhaps this was a time after the death of a family member or close friend. Maybe you were dealing with the end of a marriage or other romantic relationship. Or perhaps it was a different situation entirely.

In any case, describe what happened at this point in your life.

I discovered that I felt overwhelmed when . . .

_____

_____

_____

Next, reflect on the strategies you used to cope with this stressful event in your life. Did they include asking another person for help? If so, describe the nature of the support that you received, and how you requested it. Perhaps you made an appointment at the campus health service and saw a physician, therapist, or other trained professional. Maybe you called a close friend and talked on the phone until you felt better and gained more clarity about how to respond to the stressful situation.

Describe any source of formal or informal support and how you requested that help.

I discovered that the help I received was . . .

_____

_____

_____

In order to get this help, what I did was . . .

_____

_____

Now suppose that you could go back in time and relive this experience of asking for help. Would you do anything differently? For example, you might choose to ask for help sooner than you did, or turn to a different source of help. Complete the following sentence:

I discovered that in asking for help at this time of my life, it would have been wise for me to . . .

_____

_____

Finally, turn your discoveries into an effective plan. Clarify what you will do to effectively ask for help in the future.

I intend to . . .

_____

_____

SUICIDE
IS NO SOLUTION

While preparing for and entering higher education, people typically face major changes. The stress they feel can lead to depression and anxiety. Both are risk factors for suicide—the second leading cause of death on college campuses.[12]

To prevent suicide, start by recognizing danger signals:

- **Talking about suicide.** People who attempt suicide often talk about it first. They might say, "I just don't want to live anymore." Or "I want you to know that no matter what happens, I've always loved you." Or "Tomorrow night at 7:30 I'm going to end it all with a gun."

- **Planning for it.** People planning suicide will sometimes put their affairs in order. They might close bank accounts, give away or sell precious possessions, or make or update a will. They might even develop specific plans on how to kill themselves.

- **Having a history of previous attempts.** The American Foundation for Suicide Prevention estimates that up to 50 percent of the people who kill themselves have attempted suicide at least once before.[13]

- **Dwelling on problems.** Expressing extreme helplessness or hopelessness about solving problems can indicate that someone might be considering suicide.

- **Feeling depressed.** Although not everyone who is depressed attempts suicide, almost everyone who attempts suicide feels depressed.

TAKE PROMPT ACTION

Most often, suicide can be prevented. If you suspect that someone you know is considering suicide, do whatever it takes to ensure the person's safety. Let this person know that you will persist until you are certain that she's safe. Any of the following actions can help:

- **Take it seriously.** Taking suicidal comments seriously is especially important when you hear them from young adults. Suicide threats are more common in this age group and might be dismissed as normal. Err on the side of being too careful rather than negligent.

- **Listen fully.** Encourage the person at risk to express thoughts and feelings appropriately. If he claims that he doesn't want to talk, be inviting, be assertive, and be persistent. Be totally committed to listening.

- **Speak powerfully.** Let the person at risk know that you care. Trying to talk someone out of suicide or minimizing problems is generally useless. Acknowledge that problems are serious and that they can be solved. Point out that suicide is a permanent solution to a temporary problem—and that help is available.

- **Get professional help.** Suggest that the person see a mental health professional. If she resists help, offer to schedule the appointment for her and to take her to it. If this fails, get others involved, including the depressed person's family or school personnel.

- **Remove access to firearms.** Most suicides are attempted with guns. Get rid of any guns that might be around. Also remove all drugs and razors.

- **Ask the person to sign a "no-suicide contract."** Get a promise, in writing, that the person will not hurt himself before speaking to you. A written promise can provide the "excuse" he needs not to take action.

- **Handle the event as an emergency.** If a situation becomes a crisis, do not leave the person alone. Call a crisis hotline, 911, or a social service agency. If necessary, take the person to the nearest hospital emergency room, clinic, or police station.

- **Follow up.** Someone in danger of attempting suicide might resist further help even if your first intervention succeeds. Ask the person whether she's keeping counseling appointments and taking prescribed medication. Help this person apply strategies for solving problems. Stay in touch.

> Trying to talk someone out of suicide or minimizing problems is generally useless. Acknowledge that problems are serious and that they can be solved. Point out that suicide is a permanent solution to a temporary problem.

TAKE CARE OF YOURSELF

If you ever begin to think about committing suicide, remember that you can apply any of these suggestions to yourself. For example, look for warning signs and take them seriously. Seek out someone you trust. Tell this person how you feel. If necessary, make an appointment to see a counselor, and ask someone to accompany you. When you're at risk, you deserve the same compassion that you'd willingly extend to another person.

*Find out more from the American Foundation for Suicide Prevention at 1-800-273-8255 or **www.afsp.org**. Another excellent resource is the It Gets Better Project at **www.itgetsbetter.org**.* ▪

CHOOSE
TO STAY SAFE

Although schools make every effort to promote student safety, you can always benefit from knowing how to protect yourself.

TAKE GENERAL PRECAUTIONS

Three simple actions can significantly increase your personal safety. One is to always lock doors when you're away from home. If you live in a dorm, follow the policies for keeping the front doors secure. Don't let an unauthorized person walk in behind you. If you commute to school or have a car on campus, keep your car doors locked.

The second action is to avoid walking alone, especially at night. Many schools offer shuttle buses to central campus locations. Use them. As a backup, carry enough spare cash for a taxi ride.

Third, be prepared for a crisis. Ask your instructors about what to do in classroom emergencies. Look for emergency phones along the campus routes that you normally walk. You can always use your cell phone to call 911 for help.

Also, be willing to make that call when you see other people in unsafe situations. For example, you might be at a party with a friend who drinks too much and collapses. In this situation, some underage students might hesitate to call for help. They fear getting charged with illegal alcohol possession. Don't make this mistake. Every minute that you delay calling 911 puts your friend at further risk.

PREVENT SEXUAL ASSAULT

You need to know how to prevent sexual assault while you're on campus. This problem could be more common at your school than you think. People often hesitate to report rape for many reasons, such as fear, embarrassment, and concerns that others won't believe them.

Both women and men can take steps to prevent rape from occurring in the first place:

- Get together with a group of people for a tour of the campus. Make a special note of danger spots, such as unlighted paths and unguarded buildings. Keep in mind that rape can occur during daylight and in well-lit places.

- Ask whether your school has escort services for people taking evening classes. These might include personal escorts, car escorts, or both. If you do take an evening class, ask whether there are security officers on duty before and after the class.

- Take a course or seminar on self-defense and rape prevention. To find these courses, check with your student counseling service, community education center, or local library.

If you are raped, get medical care right away. Go to the nearest rape crisis center, hospital, student health service, or police station. Also arrange for follow-up counseling. It's your decision whether to report the crime. Filing a report does not mean that you have to press charges. And if you do choose to press charges later, having a report on file can help your case. ■

Observe thyself

You are an expert on your body. You are more likely to notice changes before anyone else does. Pay attention to these changes. They are often your first clue about the need for medical treatment or intervention. Watch for signs such as the following:

- Weight loss of more than 10 pounds in 10 weeks with no apparent cause
- A sore, scab, or ulcer that does not heal in three weeks
- A skin blemish or mole that bleeds; itches; or changes size, shape, or color
- Persistent or severe headaches
- Sudden vomiting that is not preceded by nausea
- Fainting spells
- Double vision
- Blood that is coughed up or vomited
- Black and tarry bowel movements
- Rectal bleeding
- Pink, red, or unusually cloudy urine
- Discomfort or difficulty when urinating or during sexual intercourse
- Lumps or thickening in a breast
- Vaginal bleeding between menstrual periods or after menopause

If you are experiencing any of these symptoms, get help from your doctor or campus health service—*before* a minor illness or injury leads to more-serious problems.

© iStockphoto.com /Sherwin McGehee

Choose sexual health:
PREVENT DISEASE

People with a sexually transmitted disease (STD) might feel no symptoms for years and not even discover that they are infected. Know how to protect yourself.

STDs can result from vaginal sex, oral sex, anal sex, or any other way that people contact semen, vaginal secretions, and blood. Without treatment, some of these diseases can lead to blindness, infertility, cancer, heart disease, or even death.[14]

There are at least 25 kinds of STDs. Common examples are chlamydia, gonorrhea, and syphilis. Sexual contact can also spread the human papillomavirus (HPV, the most common cause of cervical cancer) and the human immunodeficiency virus (HIV, the virus that causes AIDS).

Most STDs can be cured if treated early. (Herpes and AIDS are important exceptions.) Prevention is better. Some guidelines for prevention follow.

Abstain from sex. Abstain from sex, or have sex exclusively with one person who is free of disease and has no other sex partners. These are the only ways to be absolutely safe from STDs.

Talk to your partner. Before you have sex with someone, talk about the risk of STDs. If you are infected, tell your partner.

Use condoms. Male condoms are thin membranes stretched over the penis prior to intercourse. Condoms prevent semen from entering the vagina. For the most protection, use latex condoms—not ones made of lambskin or polyurethane. Use a condom every time you have sex, and for any type of sex.

Condoms are not guaranteed to work all of the time. They can break, leak, or slip off. In addition, condoms cannot protect you from STDs that are spread by contact with herpes sores or warts.

Talk to your doctor before using condoms, lubricants, spermicides, and other products that contain nonoxynol-9. This chemical can irritate a woman's vagina and cervix and can actually increase the risk of STDs.

Stay sober. People are more likely to have unsafe sex when drunk or high.

Do not share needles. Sharing needles or other paraphernalia with other drug users can spread STDs.

Take action soon after you have sex. Urinate soon after you have sex. Wash your genitals with soap and water.

Get vaccinated. Vaccines are available to prevent hepatitis B and HPV infection. See your doctor.

Get screened for STDs. The only way to find out whether you're infected is to be tested by a health care professional. If you have sex with more than one person, get screened for STDs at least once each year. Do this even if you have no symptoms. Remember that many schools offer free STD screening.

The more people you have sex with, the greater your risk of STDs. You are at risk even if you have sex only once with one person who is infected.

The U.S. Centers for Disease Control and Prevention recommends chlamydia screening for all sexually active women under age 26. Women age 25 and older should be screened if they have a new sex partner or multiple sex partners.[15]

Recognize the symptoms of STDs. Symptoms include swollen glands with fever and aching; itching around the vagina; vaginal discharge; pain during sex or when urinating; sore throat following oral sex; anal pain after anal sex; sores, blisters, scabs, or warts on the genitals, anus, tongue, or throat; rashes on the palms of your hands or soles of your feet; dark urine; loose and light-colored stools; and unexplained fatigue, weight loss, and night sweats.

Get treated right away. If you think you have an STD, go to your doctor, campus health service, or local public health clinic. Early treatment might prevent serious health problems. To avoid infecting other people, abstain from sex until you are treated and cured. ■

Choose sexual health:
PREVENT UNWANTED PREGNANCY

You and your partner can avoid unwanted pregnancy. There are many options. But choosing among them can be a challenge. Think about whether you want to have children someday, the number of sexual partners you have, your comfort with using a birth control method, possible side effects, and your overall health.

Even birth control methods that are usually effective can fail when used incorrectly. To prevent pregnancy, make sure you understand your chosen method. Then use it *every* time you have sex. Start with these listed ideas. Also talk to your doctor.

Abstinence. Abstinence is choosing *not* to have sex—vaginal, oral, or anal. You might feel pressured to change your mind about this choice. However, many people exist happily without having sex. Abstinence, when practiced without exception, is the only sure way to prevent pregnancy and sexually transmitted diseases (STDs).

Natural family planning. Natural family planning is based on abstaining from sex when a woman is most fertile (likely to become pregnant). It is sometimes called the "rhythm method." For women with a regular menstrual cycle, this fertile time is about nine days each month. It includes the days right before and after ovulation. There are no side effects with natural family planning. However, it is difficult to know for sure when a woman is ovulating. Before you consider natural family planning, talk to a qualified instructor.

Barrier methods. Several methods of birth control create barriers that prevent sperm from reaching a woman's egg. One is the sponge. This is a soft disk made of polyurethane that

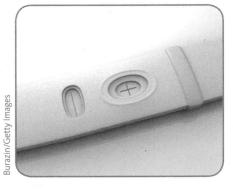

Burazin/Getty Images

contains nonoxynol-9—a spermicide (chemical that kills sperm). To use a sponge, a woman runs it under water and then places it inside her vagina to cover the cervix (the opening to the womb). If you choose to use the sponge, ask your doctor for instructions on when to remove it after you have intercourse. Keep in mind that nonoxynol-9 can irritate tissue in the vagina and anus with frequent use, making it easier for STDs to enter the body. Some women are sensitive to nonoxynol-9, so the sponge is not an option for them.

Other barrier methods include the diaphragm, cervical cap (FemCap), and cervical shield (Lea's Shield). These are cups made out of silicone or latex. The woman fills them with a spermicide and then places them inside her vagina to cover the cervix before having sex. The diaphragm and cervical cap come in various sizes, meaning that a woman has to see her doctor to get fitted for one. The cervical shield comes in only one size. Again, ask a doctor about when to remove these devices.

Male condoms, another type of barrier, are wrapped over an erect penis before sex. For better protection, use them with a spermicide. Also, use a new condom every time you have sex. The male latex condom is the only form of birth control known to protect against STDs.

If you use male condoms, keep some precautions in mind. Do not use them with oil-based lubricants such as petroleum jelly, lotions, baby oil, or massage oils. All of these can cause condoms to break. Instead, use lubricated condoms or add a water-based lubricant, such as K-Y Jelly. Remember that "natural" condoms—condoms made from lambskin—do not prevent STDs. Also, storing condoms in a warm place—such as a car or wallet—can weaken them and lead to breakage.

Female condoms are made of polyurethane. They are lubricated and placed inside the woman's vagina. Carefully follow the instructions about when to insert the female condom. Use a new condom each time you have sex. Do not use a female condom and a male condom at the same time.

Spermicides come in several forms: tablets, suppositories, cream, film, gel, and foam. They work best with a barrier method, such as a condom, cervical cap, or diaphragm. Note that some spermicides include nonoxynol-9, which can irritate tissue in the vagina and anus and make it easier for STDs to enter the body. Also, vaginal yeast infections can make spermicides less effective.

Hormonal methods. There are several hormonal methods for preventing pregnancy. These methods work by preventing ovulation, fertilization, or implantation of a fertilized egg.

An oral contraceptive—the *Pill*—is a synthetic hormone that "tells" a woman's body not to produce eggs. Many kinds are available. Talk to your doctor to make an informed choice. You might be advised to avoid the Pill if you are older than 35 and smoke, if you've had blood clots, or if you've had cancer. Antibiotics can interfere with the Pill, so ask your doctor about other methods of birth control when you're taking this medication.

Women can choose from several methods that release hormones to stop ovulation. These include a skin patch (Ortho Evra), an injection (Depo-Provera), and a vaginal ring (NuvaRing). Again, ask your doctor about possible side effects and for specific instructions on how to use these methods.

Implants. Some devices for preventing pregnancy are placed inside a woman's body and left there for several years. These devices release a hormone that prevents sperm from reaching an egg. They can also prevent a fertilized egg from implanting in the lining of the uterus. The rod (Implanon) goes under the skin of the upper arm. Intrauterine devices (IUDs) go inside a woman's uterus. They include the copper IUD (ParaGard) and the hormonal IUD (Mirena).

Talk to your doctor about how implants are inserted, how long they stay inside you, and which option would be most effective for you.

Emergency contraceptives. When women have vaginal sex without using birth control, or when they use birth control that fails, they can take "morning-after" pills. These pills are taken in two doses, 12 hours apart. The pills release hormones that stop ovulation or stop sperm from fertilizing an egg. This method works best when the pills are taken within 72 hours after sex.

Permanent methods. Some birth control methods are only for people who do not want to have children, or want to stop having children. One method is surgical sterilization.

For women this means cutting, tying, or sealing the fallopian tubes (where eggs travel to get implanted in the uterus). Men get a vasectomy, which prevents sperm from going to the penis. Remember that sperm can stay in a man's body for about three months after surgery. Use another form of birth control during this time.

Women can also be sterilized without surgery. The doctor inserts an implant (Essure) that causes scar tissue to form in the fallopian tubes. Until the scarring appears—usually in about three months—another form of birth control is needed.

> *Be sure you know how to use your chosen method of birth control. A doctor might assume that you already have this knowledge. If you don't, ask questions freely. Remember that some methods require practice and special techniques.*

Where to get birth control. You can buy condoms, sponges, and spermicides over the counter at a store. Other birth control devices—including morning-after pills for women under age 18—require a prescription.

Note: **Withdrawal does not work.** Withdrawal happens when a man takes his penis out of the woman's vagina before he has an orgasm. Don't rely on this method for birth control. It requires extraordinary self-control. In addition, men can release some sperm before they have an orgasm. This can lead to pregnancy. If the man has an STD, the withdrawal method can pass the disease on to the woman as well.

Evaluate birth control methods. Be sure you know how to use your chosen method of birth control. A doctor might assume that you already have this knowledge. If you don't, ask questions freely. Remember that some methods require practice and special techniques. For example, male condoms have an inside and outside surface, and they work best when there's a little space left at the tip for fluid.

Table 11.1 summarizes the effectiveness of various birth control methods and possible side effects. However, effectiveness rates can only be estimated. The estimates depend on many factors—for example, the health of the people using them, their number of sex partners, and how often they have sex. *Remember that a method can work only if used consistently and correctly.* ■

Method	Failure Rate (the number of pregnancies expected per 100 women)	Some Side Effects and Risks
Sterilization surgery for women	Less than 1	Pain Bleeding Complications from surgery Ectopic (tubal) pregnancy
Sterilization implant for women (Essure)	Less than 1	Pain Ectopic (tubal) pregnancy
Sterilization surgery for men	Less than 1	Pain Bleeding Complications from surgery
Implantable rod (Implanon)	Less than 1 Might not work as well for women who are overweight or obese	Acne Weight gain Ovarian cysts Mood changes Depression Hair loss Headache Upset stomach Dizziness Sore breasts Changes in period Lower interest in sex
Intrauterine device (ParaGard, Mirena)	Less than 1	Cramps Bleeding between periods Pelvic inflammatory disease Infertility Tear or hole in the uterus
Shot/Injection (Depo-Provera)	Less than 1	Bleeding between periods Weight gain Sore breasts Headaches Bone loss with long-term use
Oral Contraceptives (combination pill, or "the pill")	5 Being overweight may increase the chance of getting pregnant while using the pill.	Dizziness Upset stomach Changes in your period Changes in mood Weight gain High blood pressure Blood clots Heart attack Stroke New vision problems
Oral contraceptives (continuous/extended use, or "no-period pill")	5 Being overweight may increase the chance of getting pregnant while using the pill.	Same as combination pill Spotting or bleeding between periods Hard to know whether pregnant

Table 11.1 *Birth Control Methods*

(continues)

Method	Failure Rate (the number of pregnancies expected per 100 women)	Some Side Effects and Risks
Oral contraceptives (progestin-only pill, or "mini-pill")	5 Being overweight may increase the chance of getting pregnant while using the pill.	Spotting or bleeding between periods Weight gain Sore breasts
Skin patch (Ortho Evra)	5 It may not work as well in women weighing more than 198 pounds.	Similar to side effects for the combination pill Greater exposure to estrogen than with other methods
Vaginal ring (NuvaRing)	5	Similar to side effects for the combination pill Swelling of the vagina Irritation Vaginal discharge
Male condom	11–16	Allergic reactions
Diaphragm with spermicide	15	Irritation Allergic reactions Urinary tract infection Toxic shock if left in too long
Sponge with spermicide (Today Sponge)	16–32	Irritation Allergic reactions Hard time taking it out Toxic shock if left in too long
Female condom	20	Irritation Allergic reactions
Natural family planning (rhythm method)	25	None
Spermicide alone	30 It works best if used along with a barrier method, such as a condom.	Irritation Allergic reactions Urinary tract infection
Emergency contraception ("morning-after pill," "Plan B One-Step," "Next Choice")	1 pregnancy It must be used within 72 hours of having unprotected sex. It should not be used as regular birth control, but only in emergencies.	Upset stomach Vomiting Lower stomach pain Fatigue Headache and dizziness Irregular bleeding Breast tenderness

Source: U.S. Department of Health and Human Services, Office on Women's Health, "Birth Control Methods: Frequently Asked Questions," November 21, 2011, accessed February 17, 2013, from www.womenshealth.gov/publications/our-publications/fact-sheet/birth-control-methods.pdf.

Alcohol, tobacco, and drugs:
THE TRUTH

The truth is that getting high can be fun. In our culture, and especially in our media, getting high has become synonymous with having a good time. Even if you don't smoke, drink, or use other drugs, you are certain to come in contact with people who do.

For centuries, human beings have devised ways to change their feelings and thoughts by altering their body chemistry. The Chinese were using marijuana 5,000 years ago. Herodotus, the ancient Greek historian, wrote about a group of people in eastern Europe who threw marijuana on hot stones and inhaled the vapors. More recently, during the American Civil War, customers could buy opium and morphine at neighborhood stores.[16]

Today we are still a drug-using society. Of course, some of those uses are therapeutic and lawful, including taking drugs as prescribed by a doctor or psychiatrist. The

In addition to the payoffs, there are costs. For some people, the cost is much greater than the payoff. Even if drug use doesn't make you broke, it can make you crazy. This is not necessarily the kind of crazy where you dress up like Napoleon. Rather, it is the kind where you care about little else except finding more drugs—friends, school, work, and family be damned.

Substance abuse is only part of the picture. People can also relate to food, gambling, money, sex, and even work in compulsive ways.

Some people will stop abusing a substance or activity when the consequences get serious enough. Other people don't stop. They continue their self-defeating behaviors, no matter the consequences for themselves, their friends, or their families. At that point, the problem goes beyond abuse. It's addiction.

© VR Photos/Shutterstock.com
© Givaga/Shutterstock.com
© iStockphoto.com/Sergey Mostovoy

problem comes when we turn to drugs as *the* solution to any problem. Are you uncomfortable? Often the first response is "Take something."

We live in times when reaching for instant comfort via chemicals is not only condoned but encouraged. If you're bored, tense, or anxious, you can drink a can of beer, down a glass of wine, or light up a cigarette. If you want to enhance your memory, take a "smart drug," which includes prescription stimulants and caffeine. And these are only the legal options. If you're willing to take risks, you can pick from a large selection of illegal drugs on the street. And if that seems too risky, you can abuse prescription drugs.

There is a big payoff in using alcohol, tobacco, caffeine, cocaine, heroin, or other drugs—or people wouldn't do it. The payoff can be direct, such as relaxation, self-confidence, comfort, excitement, or the ability to pull an all-nighter. At times, the payoff is avoiding rejection or defying authority.

With addiction, the costs can include overdose, infection, and lowered immunity to disease. These can be fatal. Long-term heavy drinking, for example, damages every organ system in the human body. And about 440,000 Americans die annually from the effects of cigarette smoking, including secondhand smoke.[17]

Lectures about the reasons for avoiding alcohol and drug abuse and addiction can be pointless. We don't take care of our bodies because someone says we should. We might take care of ourselves when we see that the costs of using a substance outweigh the benefits.

Acknowledging that alcohol, tobacco, and other drugs can be fun infuriates a lot of people. Remember that this acknowledgment is *not* the same as condoning drug use. The point is this: People are more likely to abstain when they're convinced that using these substances leads to more pain than pleasure over the long run. You choose. It's your body. ■

Exercise 30
Addiction: How do I know?

People who have problems with drugs and alcohol can hide this fact from themselves and from others. It is also hard to admit that a friend or loved one might have a problem. The purpose of this exercise is to give you an objective way to look at your relationship with drugs or alcohol. There are signals that indicate when drug or alcohol use has become abusive or even addictive. This exercise can also help you determine if a friend might be addicted.

Answer the following questions quickly and honestly with yes, no, or n/a (not applicable). If you are concerned about someone else, rephrase each question using that person's name.

_____ Are you uncomfortable discussing drug abuse or addiction?

_____ Are you worried about your own drug or alcohol use?

_____ Are any of your friends worried about your drug or alcohol use?

_____ Have you ever hidden from a friend, spouse, employer, or coworker the fact that you were drinking? (Pretended you were sober? Covered up alcohol breath?)

_____ Do you sometimes use alcohol or drugs to escape lows rather than to produce highs?

_____ Have you ever gotten angry when confronted about your use?

_____ Do you brag about how much you consume? ("I drank her under the table.")

_____ Do you think about or do drugs when you are alone?

_____ Do you store up alcohol, other drugs, cigarettes, or caffeine (in coffee or soft drinks) to be sure you won't run out?

_____ Does having a party almost always include alcohol or drugs?

_____ Do you try to control your drinking so that it won't be a problem? ("I drink only on weekends now." "I never drink before 5:00 p.m." "I drink only beer.")

_____ Do you often explain to other people why you are drinking? ("It's my birthday." "It's my friend's birthday." "It's Veterans Day." "It sure is a hot day.")

_____ Have you changed friends to accommodate your drinking or drug use? ("She's okay, but she isn't excited about getting high.")

_____ Has your behavior changed in the last several months? (Grades down? Lack of interest in a hobby? Change of values or of what you think is moral?)

_____ Do you routinely drink or use drugs to relieve tension? ("What a day! I need a drink.")

_____ Do you have medical problems (stomach trouble, malnutrition, liver problems, anemia) that could be related to drinking or drugs?

_____ Have you ever decided to quit drugs or alcohol and then changed your mind?

_____ Have you had any fights, accidents, or similar incidents related to drinking or drugs in the last year?

_____ Has your drinking or drug use ever caused a problem at home?

_____ Do you envy people who go overboard with alcohol or drugs?

_____ Have you justified drinking or using other drugs by telling yourself you can quit at any time?

_____ Have you ever been in trouble with the police after or while you were drinking?

_____ Have you ever missed school or work because you had a hangover?

_____ Have you ever had a blackout (a period you can't remember) during or after drinking?

_____ Do you wish that people would mind their own business when it comes to your use of alcohol or drugs?

_____ Is the cost of alcohol or other drugs taxing your budget or resulting in financial stress?

_____ Do you need increasing amounts of the drug to produce the desired effect?

_____ When you stop taking the drug, do you experience withdrawal?

_____ Do you spend a great deal of time obtaining and using alcohol or other drugs?

_____ Have you used alcohol or another drug when it was physically dangerous to do so (such as when driving a car or working with machines)?

_____ Have you been arrested or had other legal problems resulting from the use of a substance?

If you answered yes to any of the above questions, then talk with a professional. This does not necessarily mean that you are addicted. It does point out that alcohol or other drugs are adversely affecting your life. Talk to someone with training in recovery from chemical dependency. Do not rely on the opinion of anyone who lacks such training.

If you filled out this questionnaire about another person and you answered yes two or more times, then your friend might need help. You probably can't provide that help alone. Seek out a counselor or a support group such as Al-Anon. Call the local Alcoholics Anonymous chapter to find out about an Al-Anon meeting near you.

Some facts . . .

The National Institute on Alcohol Abuse and Alcoholism reports the following annual consequences of excessive and underage drinking by college students in Table 11.2.[18] For more information, go online to www.collegedrinkingprevention.gov.

Table 11.2 Annual Consequences of Excessive and Underage Drinking by College Students

Death	1,825 college students between the ages of 18 and 24 die from alcohol-related unintentional injuries, including motor vehicle crashes.
Injury	599,000 students between the ages of 18 and 24 are unintentionally injured under the influence of alcohol.
Assault	696,000 students between the ages of 18 and 24 are assaulted by another student who has been drinking.
Sexual Abuse	97,000 students between the ages of 18 and 24 are victims of alcohol-related sexual assault or date rape.
Unsafe Sex	400,000 students between the ages of 18 and 24 had unprotected sex.
	More than 100,000 students between the ages of 18 and 24 report having been too intoxicated to know if they consented to having sex.
Academic Problems	About 25 percent of college students report academic consequences of their drinking, including missing class, falling behind, doing poorly on exams or papers, and receiving lower grades overall.
Health Problems/ Suicide Attempts	More than 150,000 students develop an alcohol-related health problem, and between 1.2 and 1.5 percent of students indicate that they tried to commit suicide within the past year due to drinking or drug use.
Drunk Driving	3,360,000 students between the ages of 18 and 24 drive under the influence of alcohol.
Vandalism	About 11 percent of college student drinkers report that they have damaged property while under the influence of alcohol.
Property Damage	More than 25 percent of administrators from schools with relatively low drinking levels and over 50 percent from schools with high drinking levels say their campuses have a "moderate" or "major" problem with alcohol-related property damage.
Police Involvement	About 5 percent of four-year college students are involved with the police or campus security as a result of their drinking, and 110,000 students between the ages of 18 and 24 are arrested for an alcohol-related violation such as public drunkenness or driving under the influence.
Alcohol Abuse and Dependence	31 percent of college students met criteria for a diagnosis of alcohol abuse and 6 percent for a diagnosis of alcohol dependence in the past 12 months, according to questionnaire-based self-reports about their drinking.

Photodisc/Fotosearch

FROM *dependence to* RECOVERY

The technical term for drug addiction is *drug dependence*. This disease is defined by the following:

- **Loss of control**—continued substance use or activity in spite of adverse consequences.

- **Pattern of relapse**—vowing to quit or limit the activity or substance use and continually failing to do so.

- **Tolerance**—the need to take increasing amounts of a substance to produce the desired effect.

- **Withdrawal**—signs and symptoms of physical and mental discomfort or illness when the substance is taken away.[19]

This list can help you determine whether dependence is a barrier for you right now. Addiction can apply to anything from cocaine use to compulsive gambling.

If you have a problem with dependence in any form, get help. Consider the following suggestions.

Use responsibly. Show people that you can have a good time without alcohol or other drugs. If you do choose to drink, consume alcohol with food. Pace yourself. Take time between drinks.

Avoid promotions that encourage excess drinking. "Ladies Drink Free" nights are especially dangerous. Women are affected more quickly by alcohol, making them targets for rape. Also stay out of games that encourage people to guzzle. And avoid people who make fun of you for choosing not to drink.

Pay attention. Whenever you use alcohol or another drug, do so with awareness. Then pay attention to the consequences. Act with deliberate decision rather than out of habit or under pressure from others.

Look at the costs. There is always a tradeoff to dependence. Drinking six beers might result in a temporary high, and you will probably remember that feeling. You might feel terrible the morning after consuming six

beers, but some people find it easier to forget *that* pain. Stay aware of how dependence makes you feel.

Before going out to a restaurant or bar, set a limit for the number of drinks you will consume. If you consistently break this promise to yourself and experience negative consequences afterward, then you have a problem.

Admit the problem. People with active dependencies are a varied group—rich and poor, young and old, successful and unsuccessful. Often these people do have one thing in common: They are masters of denial. They deny that they are unhappy. They deny that they have hurt anyone. They are convinced that they can quit any time they want. They sometimes become so adept at hiding the problem from themselves that they die.

Take responsibility for recovery. Nobody plans to become an addict. If you have pneumonia, you seek treatment and recover without guilt or shame. Approach drug dependence in the same way. You can take responsibility for your recovery without blame, shame, or guilt.

Get help. People cannot treat dependence on their own. Behaviors tied to dependence are often symptoms of an illness that needs treatment.

Two broad options exist for getting help. One is the growing self-help movement. The other is formal treatment. People recovering from addiction often combine the two.

Many self-help groups are modeled after Alcoholics Anonymous (AA). AA is made up of recovering alcoholics and addicts. These people understand the problems of abuse firsthand, and they follow a systematic, 12-step approach to living without it. AA is one of the oldest and most successful self-help programs in the world. Chapters of AA welcome people from all walks of life, and you don't have to be an alcoholic to attend most meetings. Programs based on AA principles exist for many other forms of dependence as well.

Some people feel uncomfortable with the AA approach. They can use other options, including private therapy and group therapy. Also investigate organizations such as Women for Sobriety, the Secular Organizations for Sobriety, and Rational Recovery. Use whatever works for you.

Treatment programs are available in almost every community. They might be residential (you live there for weeks or months at a time) or outpatient (you visit several hours a day). Find out where these treatment centers are located by calling a doctor, a mental health professional, or a local hospital. If you don't have insurance, it is usually possible to arrange some other payment program. Cost is no reason to avoid treatment.

Get help for a friend or family member. You might know someone whose behavior meets the criteria for dependence. If so, you have every right to express your concern to that person. Wait until the person is clearheaded. Then mention specific incidents. For example: "Last night you drank five beers when we were at my apartment, and then you wanted to drive home. When I offered to call a cab for you instead, you refused." Also be prepared to offer a source of help, such as the phone number of a local treatment center. ■

Succeed in quitting smoking

There is no magic formula for becoming tobacco-free. However, you can take steps to succeed sooner rather than later. The American Cancer Society suggests the following.[20]

Make a firm choice to quit. All plans for quitting depend on this step. If you're not ready to quit yet, then admit it. Take another look at how smoking affects your health, finances, and relationships.

Set a date. Choose a "quit day" within the next month. That's close enough for a sense of urgency—and time to prepare. Consider a date with special meaning, such as a birthday or anniversary. Let friends and family members know about the big day.

Get personal support. Involve other people. Sign up for a quit smoking class. Attend Nicotine Anonymous or a similar group.

Consider medication. Medication can double your chances of quitting successfully.[21] Options include bupropion hydrochloride (Zyban) and varenicline (Chantix), as well as the nicotine patch, gum, nasal spray, inhaler, and lozenge.

Prepare the environment. Right before your quit day, get rid of all cigarettes and ashtrays at home and at work. Stock up on oral substitutes such as sugarless gum, candy, and low-fat snacks.

Deal with cravings for cigarettes. Distract yourself with exercise or another physical activity. Breathe deeply. Tell yourself that you can wait just a little while longer until the craving passes. Even the strongest urges to smoke will pass. Avoid alcohol use, which can increase cravings.

Learn from relapses. If you break down and light up a cigarette, don't judge yourself. Quitting often requires several attempts. Think back over your past plans for quitting and how to improve on them. Every relapse contains a lesson about how to succeed next time.

To find more strategies for quitting nicotine, go online to www.cancer.org and enter the key words quit smoking in the search box.

WARNING: ADVERTISING
CAN BE DANGEROUS TO YOUR HEALTH

The average American is exposed to hundreds of advertising messages per day. Unless you are stranded on a desert island, you are affected by advertising.

Advertising serves a useful function. It helps us make choices about how we spend our money. We can choose among thousands of companies that provide goods and services. Advertising makes us aware of the options.

Advertising also plays on our emotions. And some ads are dangerously manipulative.

Consider how advertising can affect your health. Advertising alcohol, tobacco, pain relievers, and other health-related products is a big business. Much of the revenue earned by newspapers, magazines, radio, television, and Web sites comes from ads for these products. This means that advertisers are a major source of information about health and illness.

Advertising influences our food choices. The least nutritious foods often bring in the most advertising money. So, advertisers portray the primary staples of our diet as sugary breakfast cereals, candy bars, and soft drinks.

Ads for alcohol glorify drinking. Advertisers imply that daily drinking is the norm. Pleasant experiences are enhanced by drinking. Holidays naturally include alcohol. Parties are a flop without it. Relationships are more romantic over cocktails. Everybody drinks.

Advertising also targets our emotional health. The message behind many ads is *Buying our product will make you okay*. This message is used to sell clothes, makeup, and hair products to make us look okay; drugs, alcohol, and food to make us feel okay; perfumes, toothpaste, and deodorants to make us smell okay. According to many ads,

buying the right product is essential to having the right relationships in our lives.

A related problem concerns images of women. Ads give us the impression that women love to spend hours discussing floor wax, deodorants, tampons, and laundry detergent—and that they think constantly about losing weight and looking sexy. In some ads, women handle everything from kitchen to bedroom to boardroom—true superwomen.

Images such as these are demeaning to women and damaging to men. Women lose when they allow their self-image to be influenced by ads. Men lose when they expect real-life women to look and act like the women on television.

Advertising creates illusions. The next time you're in a crowd, notice how few people look like those in ads.

Advertising often excludes people of color. If our perceptions were based solely on advertising, we would be hard-pressed to know that our society is racially and ethnically diverse. See how many examples of cultural stereotypes you can find in the ads you encounter this week.

Use advertising as a continual opportunity to develop the qualities of a critical thinker. Don't assume that every claim is accurate. Whenever an advertised product or service could affect your health, do your own research. Ask: What's the main message, and what's the evidence for it?

Stay aware of how a multibillion-dollar industry affects your health. ■

Practicing Critical Thinking 11

This exercise involves thinking at higher levels—analyzing, evaluating, and creating. To get the most value from this thinking, practice the master student qualities of honesty and courage.

Note: You may want to keep your responses to this exercise confidential.

To begin, **analyze** your current level of health in more detail by completing the following sentences. If a statement does not apply to you, then skip it.

Eating

What I know about the way I eat is . . .

_____

_____

What I would most like to change about my diet is . . .

_____

_____

My eating habits lead me to be . . .

_____

_____

Exercise

The way I usually exercise is . . .

_____

_____

The last time I did 20 minutes or more of aerobic exercise was . . .

_____

_____

As a result of my physical conditioning, I feel . . .

_____

_____

And I look . . .

_____

_____

_____

It would be easier for me to work out regularly if I . . .

_____

_____

The most important benefit I can get from exercising more is . . .

_____

_____

Substances

My history of cigarette smoking is . . .

_____

_____

An objective observer would say that my use of alcohol is . . .

_____

_____

In the last seven days, the number of alcoholic drinks I have had is . . .

_____

_____

I would describe my use of coffee, colas, and other caffeinated drinks as . . .

_____

_____

I have used the following illegal drugs in the past week:

_____

_____

When it comes to drugs, what I am sometimes concerned about is . . .

_____

_____

I take the following prescription drugs:

_____

_____

Emotional Health and Relationships

Someone who knows me fairly well would describe my emotional health as . . .

_____

_____

If I am upset or worried about something, I can talk about it with . . .

_____

_____

The last time that I felt too upset to work, study, or go to classes was . . .

_____

_____

I would describe the overall quality of my relationships as . . .

_____

_____

Sleep

The number of hours I sleep each night is . . .

_____

_____

On weekends I normally sleep . . .

_____

_____

I have trouble sleeping when . . .

_____

_____

Last night I . . .

_____

_____

The quality of my sleep is usually . . .

_____

_____

Next, take a few minutes to review and **evaluate** your responses. Based on what you just wrote, what is the one aspect of your health that you are most concerned about right now? Explain why you think it is most important.

_____

_____

_____

Finally, experiment with the idea that your health is something that you **create** over the long term. Write a goal that addresses the concern you just listed—one that would make a big and positive difference in the quality of your life over the next year. Also list the actions you will take to achieve this goal. In your list, include people that you would contact and school services that you would use.

_____

_____

_____

MASTER STUDENT PROFILE

RANDY PAUSCH

(1960–2008) Pausch was a professor at Carnegie Mellon University, who, shortly after being diagnosed with pancreatic cancer, gave a "last lecture"—a reflection on his personal and professional journey—that became a hit on YouTube (this lecture was later adapted into a book of the same title). He devoted the remaining nine months of his life to creating a legacy.

It's a thrill to fulfill your own childhood dreams, but as you get older, you may find that enabling the dreams of others is even more fun.

When I was teaching at the University of Virginia in 1993, a 22-year-old artist-turned-computer-graphics-wiz named Tommy Burnett wanted a job on my research team. After we talked about his life and goals, he suddenly said, "Oh, and I have always had this childhood dream."

Anyone who uses "childhood" and "dream" in the same sentence usually gets my attention.

"And what is your dream, Tommy?" I asked.

"I want to work on the next *Star Wars* film," he said.

Remember, this was in 1993. The last Star Wars movie had been made in 1983, and there were no concrete plans to make any more. I explained this. "That's a tough dream to have because it'll be hard to see it through," I told him. "Word is that they're finished making *Star Wars* films."

"No," he said, "they're going to make more, and when they do, I'm going to work on them. That's my plan."

Tommy was 6 years old when the first Star Wars film came out in 1977. "Other kids wanted to be Hans Solo," he told me. "Not me. I wanted to be the guy who made the special effects—the space ships, the planets, the robots."

He told me that, as a boy, he read the most technical *Star Wars* articles he could find. He had all the books that explained how the models were built, and how the special effects were achieved. . . . I figured Tommy's big dream would never happen, but it might serve him well somehow. I could use a dreamer like that. I knew from my NFL desires that even if he didn't

Randy Pausch *was energetic.*

You *can build energy with effective habits for eating, sleeping, and managing stress.*

achieve his, they could serve him well, so I asked him to join our research team. . . .

When I moved to Carnegie Mellon, every member of my team from the University of Virginia came with me—everyone except Tommy. He couldn't make the move. Why? Because he had been hired by producer/director George Lucas' company, Industrial Light & Magic. And it's worth noting that they didn't hire him for his dream; they hired him for his skills. In his time with our research group, he had become an outstanding programmer in the Python language, which as luck would have it, was the language of choice in their shop. Luck is indeed where preparation meets opportunity.

It's not hard to guess where this story is going. Three new *Star Wars* films would be made—in 1999, 2002, and 2005—and Tommy ended up working on all of them.

On *Star Wars Episode II: Attack of the Clones,* Tommy was a lead technical director. There was an incredible fifteen-minute battle scene on a rocky red planet, pitting clones against droids, and Tommy was the guy who planned it all out. He and his team used photos of the Utah desert to create a virtual landscape for the battle. Talk about cool jobs. Tommy had one that let him spend each day on another planet. ■

Source: From the book The Last Lecture by Randy Pausch with Jeffrey Zaslow, pp. 117–119. Copyright © 2008 Randy Pausch. Reprinted by permission of Hyperion. All rights reserved.

ABCNEWS.COM

1. How does the Power Process: Surrender differ from giving up?
   Surrender is not "giving up." Surrender includes doing whatever you can in a positive, trusting spirit. Let go, keep going, and know when a source of help lies beyond you. (*Power Process: Surrender*, page 320)

2. List Michael Pollan's guidelines for nutrition.
   Eat food. Not too much. Mostly plants. (*Choose your fuel*, page 322)

3. List two ways you can build more physical activity into your day, outside of a scheduled time for exercise.
   (Answers will vary): (a) Stay active throughout the day. (b) Adapt to your campus environment. (c) Do what you enjoy. (d) Vary your routine. (e) Get active early. (f) Exercise with other people. (g) Join a gym without fear. (h) Look for gradual results. (*Choose to exercise*, page 323)

4. List the two main elements of stress. Then describe one strategy for managing each element.
   Stress has two main elements: physical *sensations* such as shallow breathing and muscle tension, and negative *thoughts*, including predictions of failure. Strategies will vary. (*Choose freedom from distress*, page 324)

5. According to the text, the best way to deal with physical sensations of stress is to ignore them. True or false? Explain your answer.
   Trying to deny or ignore physical sensations is a strategy that often backfires. Instead, describe your physical experience of stress. Put your description in writing, tell someone about it, or do both. When you completely experience the physical sensations related to stress, you might find that they subside or lose a little of their power. (*Choose freedom from distress*, page 324)

6. The suggested guidelines for asking for help include these:
   (a) Ask with clarity.
   (b) Ask with sincerity.
   (c) Ask widely.
   (d) Ask with an open mind.
   (e) All of the above
   (e) All of the above (*Asking for help*, page 331)

7. Name three behaviors that signal a danger of suicide.
   Answers include any three of the following: talking about suicide, planning for it, having a history of previous attempts, dwelling on problems, and feeling depressed. (*Suicide is no solution*, page 333)

8. Key signs of dependence include the following:
   (a) Loss of control
   (b) A pattern of relapse
   (c) Tolerance
   (d) Withdrawal
   (e) All of the above
   (e) All of the above (*From dependence to recovery*, page 343).

9. One of the suggestions for dealing with addiction is "Pay attention." This implies that it's okay to use drugs, as long as you do so with full awareness. True or false? Explain your answer.
   False. The suggestion to "Pay attention" refers to being aware of the consequences of behavior under the influence of drugs. Respond to that awareness with deliberate decision rather than out of habit or under pressure from others. (*From dependence to recovery*, page 343)

10. The only option for long-term recovery from dependence is treatment based on the steps of Alcoholics Anonymous. True or false? Explain your answer.
    False. Many recovery groups are based on the AA system, but there are many other systems, such as private therapy. People should explore different systems and pursue the one that works best for them. (*From dependence to recovery*, page 343)

SKILLS SNAPSHOT
Chapter 11

Now that you've reflected on the ideas in this chapter and experimented with some new strategies, reflect on your current skills in maintaining health. Also think about ways to develop more mastery in this area of your life.

Discovery

My score on the Health section of the Discovery Wheel was . . .

To monitor my current level of health, I look for specific changes in . . .

After reading and doing this chapter, my top three health concerns are . . .

Intention

In order to respond to the health concerns I just listed, I intend to . . .

I also intend to . . .

I will use these behaviors to enhance my performance at work by . . .

Action

At the end of this course, I would like my *Health* score on the Discovery Wheel to be . . .

The most important health habit that I can adopt right now is . . .

My cue for remembering to practice this habit is . . .

Chapter

12

NEXT STEPS

"Live as if you were to die tomorrow. Learn as if you were to live forever." —*Gandhi*

PREVIEW

As this student success course comes to an end, it's time to celebrate accomplishments and prepare to take the next step. Use your class sessions at the end of the semester to help students understand that time spent in school is a stepping-stone to the future. Revisit goals set earlier in the term to help guide students from "School is something I have to do for now" to "School is the first step toward achieving the goals I have set for my life." When students choose life missions that direct and energize their efforts both in and out of class, you and your students can celebrate this true sign of success—yours and theirs.

GUEST SPEAKER

A local employer who looks to your institution to find workers is an appropriate choice for a guest speaker for this chapter. Another possibility is to invite a career counselor who specializes in helping students prepare to apply for jobs, interview, and enter the workplace. Now is also the time to ask your current students to consider coming back next term to be your guest speakers on the first day of class. Your new students will be very interested in meeting your former students. They can be an inspiration to new students who are not fully committed to continuing in your class. You might want to consider filming current students as you ask them to share their experiences and personal growth. These testimonials will make a powerful impact on incoming students next semester.

LECTURE

Appropriate lecture topics for this chapter include the following:

- What students can do next term to keep the tools learned in this course fresh in their minds
- The connection between the skills learned in this course and the skills employers are looking for
- Putting together an effective résumé
- Interviewing successfully for a job
- Skills for starting a new job

master instructor
best practice

❝As you hurry to complete the term, you may need to carefully select significant exercises so you do not rush the critical semester closing. This should be a time to reflect on growth and look forward to new endeavors. You may want to emphasize the importance of personal, academic, and workplace goals as you transition. As you examine students' progress throughout the semester, you and your students will especially want to see the results of Exercise 37: "The Discovery Wheel—Coming full circle" (pages 376–379). The Discovery Wheel provides visual evidence of growth and development, and the results warrant discussion and recognition in class discussion.**❞**

—*Annette McCreedy, Nashville State Community College*

Workplace Application: Informational interview. Students may find conducting an informational interview helpful as they plan their career. The term *informational interview*, coined by best-selling career development author Richard N. Bolles in *What Color is Your Parachute?*, is an informal meeting where students can gather career information and advice from someone working in a field to which they aspire. Although the purpose of the interview is not to obtain employment, students will get practice in the valuable art of networking and tapping into the "hidden job market" (researchers estimate between 60 and 80 percent of all available jobs are never posted on job boards and other job search formats, hence the term "hidden").

Students select one person to interview. The interview should preferably take place in person but can be conducted over the phone or via e-mail at the convenience of the person being interviewed. Students can find interview subjects through friends, family, instructors, or alumni and advancement offices at the college. Students should prepare before the interview by researching the occupation and drafting a list of questions to ask the person being interviewed. Although this is a formal meeting and not a job interview, encourage your students to remain polite and professional, and to thank the person for their time. Some topics for discussion include these:

- Title of occupation
- Location of occupation
- Estimated/average occupational salary
- Job description (tasks)
- What types of interests, skills, education, training, and work values are necessary to be successful in this field
- Work hours and travel
- Working conditions
- Pros and cons of pursuing this career

Have students reflect on this assignment by writing a Journal Entry analyzing their experience or sharing their results in class.

EXERCISES/ACTIVITIES

1. **The Discovery Wheel—Coming full circle (pages 376–379).** Begin this in-class assignment by having your students complete the Discovery Wheel in this final chapter. Ask them to compare the scores they have just given themselves with the scores from the Discovery Wheel they completed in Chapter 1. Then have students subtract their first Discovery Wheel scores from their second Discovery Wheel scores. This difference can be very insightful. It represents the change in the students' self-confidence. Many students see dramatic improvements. This comparison is a powerful tool—the Discovery Wheel reveals the truth about students to themselves.

   Some students also like to divide the first Discovery Wheel scores by the second Discovery Wheel scores and note the percentage change. They describe the result as a percentage increase in their academic awareness.

   Note: Occasionally, you will have a student whose scores go down. This is an important example of the power of telling the truth and how the truth can change. Sometimes, students' scores are lower now that they are more aware of the meanings and significance of topics and questions. The results of the Discovery Wheel in the beginning of the term may have been slightly skewed by lack of understanding and/or reflection.

master instructor
best practice

" *I try to make sure all my students know what a degree plan is, how to file one, and how to follow one. Remind students that college is a long progression of acquiring knowledge and learning how to use that knowledge, but it is also a chance to explore life and take risks. Learning from the mistakes of others shows real maturity. Invite students to remember another time in life when they began a project, followed the appropriate sequence, and completed the project successfully. Examples can be anything from baking a cake to teaching swimming lessons.*

The chapter might also remind students that a successful semester in college isn't necessarily a 4.0 grade point average. In college, being successful means growing, learning, and evolving into a better person. Invite students to challenge themselves in nontraditional ways. "

—Joseph Fly, South Plains College

2. **Power Process: Persist (page 352).** As this class nears its completion, it's exciting for students to reflect on their educational and career goals one last time before exiting the course. Once they learn to use the tools and strategies presented in *Becoming a Master Student*, many students raise their level of expectation to include additional educational and career achievements. They now know the work required of them to pursue goals they would never have considered before. In class, ask them to brainstorm individually a list of their hopes, dreams, and goals. Have them answer the following questions: What do you want to be? What do you want to do? What do you want to get there? Then ask the students to sit in a large circle. Ask them to change the *want*'s to *be*'s. Ask them to look at their revised statements and read them silently to themselves. Seeing this change on paper will make students feel as if the future is happening in the present!

CONVERSATION/SHARING

The culminating chapter of *Becoming a Master Student* focuses on the transfer of knowledge that is best displayed by Mode 4 learners who ask *What if?* Your students will have practiced using the metacognitive map for a whole semester. Now you can challenge them to think of questions related to Chapter 12 and Mode 4. *What if* they apply the skills they learned in this course to all of their future courses? *What if* they apply these skills in the workplace? *What if* they select one major and then want to change majors because they have changed career goals? This is a great way to introduce a discussion about transferable skills. As a class, list some of these transferable skills on the board. Ask specifically: "*How* are these skills related to the workplace?" Ask students to share examples in their own lives.

Encourage your students to look ahead to the following semester and make a commitment to review the chapters of this textbook, one per week, to keep the concepts and strategies fresh in their mind. As part of the final week's assignment, have students reread the textbook's Introduction: The Master Student, which will make even more sense to them now that they have read the entire book. This assignment demonstrates the benefits of a later, second reading of the text. Ask students to engage in a group conversation about what they discovered on rereading the Introduction.

HOMEWORK

Exercise 32: Do something you can't (page 359).
In this powerful exercise, students face their fears and take a risk. Then they write about what they discovered.

Create your own course. This unique activity will challenge students to create their own student success course and identify what they see as the key elements of such a class. This is not only a powerful, creative homework assignment for them, but it can also provide the instructor with valuable feedback about what to keep in the course next term and what to change. You might want to share these results with other student success teachers on your campus. You may find it helpful to debrief at the end of the semester. You may also wish to develop your own course evaluation tool to gather student feedback. Sharing experiences and feedback with other instructors can provide direction and clarity for future semesters.

Have students create portfolios. Your first-year student success course is a perfect place for students to begin collecting their work in a way that reflects their academic development and accomplishments. Encourage students to personalize their portfolios and help them reflect on their growth over time. A portfolio is a work in progress. Each student's portfolio will be unique and different from all others at the conclusion of the course. Consider having a sharing day and an end-of-semester celebration at the end of your course so that students can review and reflect on one another's portfolios.

Help students to create a personal profile. Personal profiles help to catalog your students' background, education, employment, activities, hobbies, and college skills. The profile can be used as a resource for learning more about your students. A sample personal profile form is available for downloading and distributing to your students from the Instructor Companion Site. Consider customizing the profile to your liking and to your campus. Consider allowing students to omit sensitive items if they prefer not to answer them (especially if you are requiring that they submit the profile for a grade).

Review goal-setting exercises. *Becoming a Master Student* provides students with many opportunities for setting goals. Beginning with Exercise 10: Get real with your goals (page 73), students can begin to plan long-term goals, mid-term goals, and short-term goals. Periodically, they are encouraged to revisit these goals and make updates. Filing this material in a portfolio enables them to easily measure their growth and note their changes throughout their semester and college experience. Have your students assess the skills that they come to college with, and work with your students to plan for accomplishments throughout their college experience and their future in the workplace.

Help students prepare for the future. As students assess their majors and career interests, they can use their portfolios to keep track of their education plans, lists of courses they need to complete in order to graduate, and other program requirements. Suggest that students also consider what types of materials may be relevant to share with prospective employers. For example, if a student writes for a publication on your campus, he can add his published articles to his portfolio and share them during an interview. If a student participates in campus organizations or service-learning projects, she can add photographs and materials documenting her activities to her portfolio.

Even if students do not have previous work experience, encourage them to focus on student accomplishments, extracurricular activities, offices held, and skills which can transfer to the workplace. Remind students to refer to their multiple intelligences from Chapter 1 for personal strengths that can be an advantage on the job.

EVALUATION

Here are some ideas for final exam questions for your course:

1. Which Master Student Profile in the text inspired you the most, and why?
2. What were the three most valuable textbook articles that you read in this course? How did they change the way you are as a student?
3. If you were to write a top ten list of reasons why students entering college should take this course their first semester, what would be your top five reasons?
4. Name the five most important skills you learned in this course, and explain how you will ensure that you use—and do not lose—these skills as you continue your college experience after this course ends.

MindTap™

EMBRACE VALUABLE RESOURCES

FOR CHAPTER 12

STUDENT RESOURCES: MINDTAP

- **Engagement Activity: Master Students in Action.** In this inspiring video, Dave Ellis discusses the importance of writing down a list of the things you want to achieve in the future. Students then hear firsthand from other students about what their dreams and next steps are.

- **Aplia Homework Assignment: Jump-start your education with transferable skills.** In this assignment, students learn how to discover and name the transferable skills that will help them to excel in school and life. By examining a sample

student's accomplishments, students practice identifying transferable skills that can be listed in résumés or job applications.

- **Reflection Activity: Peel of the Day.** This Slice of Life video, created by student Addie Ratcliff, discusses themes such as being willing to fail, turning failure into success, being adaptable and open to changes in plans, and finding creative solutions to challenges.

 **MindTap™** *Your personal learning experience—learn anywhere, anytime.*

INSTRUCTOR COMPANION SITE

- **What are your next steps?** Look to the online Course Manual to discover ways to evaluate the success of your course and how you can play a role in student retention with these articles:
  - Creating evaluations of your course
  - Start now: Evaluate today's class
  - The role of faculty in retaining students on campus

- **Looking for fresh, innovative ways to teach Chapter 12 topics?** Browse through the Best Practices recommendations in the Course Manual to see what other Master Instructors have been successfully doing with their students.

Please visit login.cengage.com to log in and access the Instructor Companion Site.

master instructor
best practice

master student hall of fame powerpoint

Students select a Master Student, or pick one whom they identify with, research that Master Student, create a PowerPoint, and present it at one of our last classes of the semester. I scaffold student success on the PowerPoint project, by teaching them to create a planning schedule for larger projects to prevent procrastination. I have those who are experienced PowerPoint creators raise their hands so that the students who will need extra help can go to a fellow classmate or sit by them while we're working on it. I bring in an IT instructor as a guest speaker to teach them advanced skills, like adding video or speech, or to answer questions that they need help with. We do Internet research for tips on a quality PowerPoint and the students present at least one tip each to the class. As students present, we give positive and constructive feedback for their future PowerPoint assignments in other classes. It is a very motivating and inspirational time because of the people they are telling us about who overcame obstacles to achieve success and because for many it is their very first PowerPoint and they're thrilled to achieve it.

—Dana Dildine, Eastern New Mexico University

Chapter 12

NEXT STEPS

Why

You can use the techniques introduced in this book to set a course to graduation and lifelong learning.

How

Visualize yourself at a commencement ceremony, walking up to the front of the room and receiving the diploma for your degree. Also imagine what you'd most like to do during the year after you graduate. Preview this chapter for strategies that can help you turn these visions into realities.

What if...

I could gain any skill or master any subject I wanted—at any point in my life?

What is included...

NEW

Taking the road to graduation ■ 360

NEW

Discover the hidden job market ■ 370

Persist on the path of mastery ■ 373

TECH

Tools for lifelong learning
Learning can happen anywhere, anytime—both inside and outside the classroom and long after you graduate. ■ 375

PERSIST

Most students enter school with the desire to graduate. Ask them what it takes to succeed and you'll get a lot of great ideas. What students sometimes forget is the power of persistence—doing the gritty and unglamorous things that really work, day after day.

This is how habits pay off. For instance, exercising for better health is a great idea. And exercising is bound to fail if you only go to the gym once. Networking is highly recommended for finding a job. And it's pointless if you stop after talking to one person. These are just a couple of examples. The point is that the power of any strategy or habit emerges only when you persist.

Research indicates that it takes about 10,000 hours of deliberate practice for athletes, musicians, and other performers to win international competitions.[1] Look into the biographies of Master Students profiled in this book and you'll find many examples of deliberate practice—a fancy term for persistence.

One such example is Abraham Lincoln, who failed in business in 1831 and 1833. He was also defeated while running for elected seats in 1832, 1838, 1840, 1843, 1855, 1856, and 1858. In 1860, Lincoln was elected president of the United States.

More recently, the manuscripts for the Harry Potter books were rejected by multiple editors. Author J. K. Rowling persisted until she eventually found a publisher. She went on to sell 450 million books.

In 2006, a young student named Stefani Germanotta signed a deal with Def Jam Records. In three months, the company decided that her style was not a good fit and cancelled the contract. After that, Germanotta spent a couple years playing in small clubs, making little money, and crafting her performance skills. People noticed. Finally there was another record deal and a new name for her act: Lady Gaga.

The willingness to persist unleashes many qualities of a master student—competence, courage, self-direction, and more. To make this Power Process work, remember four things.

First, persistence is not about positive thinking or mental cheerleading. Persistence works better when you tell the truth about your current abilities. Accepting who you are—with all your strengths and weaknesses—makes it easier to take setbacks in stride, learn from mistakes, and move back into action.

Second, persistence is not about blind determination. If a strategy fails to produce the results that you want, then feel free to give it up and choose a new one. Keep your eyes on the prize—your goal—and stay flexible about ways to achieve it. If plan A fizzles out, then move on to plan B or C.

Third, persistence is not about going it alone. In life, there are no solos. We are social creatures and find strength in community. One key to persistence is finding people who have already achieved what you want. Seek out these people. Spend time with them. Ask them for guidance. They are living reminders that getting what you want is possible—if you persist.

Finally, persistence calls on you to give up the constant desire for instant gratification. This can be tough to remember when we see advertisements for drugs that promise quick relief; when we see self-help books telling us that we can turn our lives around in a few weeks, a few days, or even a few hours; when we see movies about people who overcome tremendous obstacles in 90 minutes.

Master students harness their critical thinking skills to cut through all the hype. They know that they are in the game for the long haul and that there are no quick fixes. They know that getting a degree is like training for a marathon. They remember that every class attended and every assignment completed is one small win on the way to a big victory.

Becoming a Master Student is about getting what you ultimately want. There's nothing mysterious about the process of doing this: Discover the outcomes that you want to achieve. Make it your intention to do what it takes to produce those outcomes. Then act on your intentions.

And persist.

JUMP-START
your education with
TRANSFERABLE
SKILLS

When meeting with an academic advisor, you may be tempted to say, "I've just been taking general education and liberal arts courses. I don't have any marketable skills." Think again.

Few words are as widely misunderstood as *skill.* Defining it carefully can have an immediate and positive impact on your career planning. One dictionary defines *skill* as "the ability to do something well, usually gained by training or experience."

Work-content skills **are acquired through formal schooling, on-the-job training, or both.** For instance, the ability to repair fiber-optic cables or do brain surgery are considered work-content skills.

However, *transferable skills* **are skills that we develop through experiences both inside and outside the classroom.** These are abilities that help people thrive in any job—no matter what work-content skills they have. You start developing these skills even before you take your first job.

Perhaps you've heard someone described this way: "She's really smart and knows what she's doing, but she's got lousy people skills." People skills—such as *listening* and *negotiating*—are prime examples of transferable skills.

SUCCEED IN MANY SITUATIONS

Transferable skills are often invisible to us. The problem begins when we assume that a given skill can be used in only one context, such as being in school or working at a particular job. Thinking in this way places an artificial limit on our possibilities.

As an alternative, think about the things you routinely do to succeed in school. Analyze your activities to isolate specific skills. Then brainstorm a list of jobs where you could use the same skills.

Consider the task of writing a research paper. This calls for the following skills:

- **Planning**, including setting goals for completing your outline, first draft, second draft, and final draft
- **Managing time** to meet your writing goals
- **Interviewing** people who know a lot about the topic of your paper
- **Researching** using the Internet and campus library to discover key facts and ideas to include in your paper
- **Writing** to present those facts and ideas in an original way
- **Editing** your drafts for clarity and correctness

Now consider the kinds of jobs that draw on these skills.

For example, you could transfer your skill at writing papers to a possible career in journalism, technical writing, or advertising copywriting.

You could use your editing skills to work in the field of publishing as a magazine or book editor.

Interviewing and research skills could help you enter the field of market research. And the abilities to plan, manage time, and meet deadlines will help you succeed in all the jobs mentioned so far.

Use the same kind of analysis to think about transferring skills from one job to another. Say that you work part-time as an administrative assistant at a computer dealer that sells a variety of hardware and software. You take phone calls from potential customers, help current customers solve problems using their computers, and attend meetings where your coworkers plan ways to market new products. You are developing skills at *selling, serving customers,* and *working on teams.* These skills could help you land a job as a sales representative for a computer manufacturer or software developer.

The basic idea is to take a cue from the word *transferable*. Almost any skill you use to succeed in one situation can *transfer* to success in another situation.

The concept of transferable skills creates a powerful link between higher education and the work world. Skills are the core elements of any job. While taking any course, list the specific skills you are developing and how you can transfer them to the work world. Almost everything you do in school can be applied to your career—if you consistently pursue this line of thought.

ASK FOUR QUESTIONS

To experiment further with this concept of transferable skills, ask and answer four questions.

***Why* identify my transferable skills?** Getting past the "I-don't-have-any-skills" syndrome means that you can approach job hunting with more confidence. As you uncover these hidden assets, your list of qualifications will grow as if by magic. You won't be padding your résumé. You'll simply be using action words to tell the full truth about what you can do.

Identifying your transferable skills takes a little time. And the payoffs are numerous. A complete and accurate list of transferable skills can help you land jobs that involve more responsibility, more variety, more freedom to structure your time, and more money. Careers can be made—or broken—by the skills that allow you to define your job, manage your workload, and get along with people.

Transferable skills help you thrive in the midst of constant change. Technology will continue to develop. Ongoing discoveries in many fields could render current knowledge obsolete. Jobs that exist today may disappear in a few years, only to be replaced by entirely new ones.

In the economy of the twenty-first century, you can't always count on job security. What you *can* count on is "skills security"—abilities that you can carry from one career to another or acquire as needed.

***What* are my transferable skills?** Discover your transferable skills by reflecting on key experiences. Recall a time when you performed at the peak of your ability, overcame obstacles, won an award, gained a high grade, or met a significant goal. List the skills you used to create those successes.

For a more complete picture of your transferable skills, describe the object of your action. Say that one of the skills on your list is *organizing*. This could refer to organizing ideas, organizing people, or organizing objects in a room. Specify the kind of organizing that you like to do.

***How* do I perform these skills?** You can bring your transferable skills into even sharper focus by adding adverbs—words that describe *how* you take action. You might say that you edit *accurately* or learn *quickly*.

65 transferrable skills

There are literally hundreds of transferable skills. To learn more, check out O*Net OnLine, a Web site from the federal government at www.onetonline.org. There you'll find tools for discovering your skills and matching them to specific occupations. Additional information on careers and job hunting is available through CareerOneStop (www.careeronestop.org).

As you read through the following list of transferable skills, notice how many of them are addressed in this book. Underline or highlight those that are most essential to the career that you want.

SELF-DISCOVERY AND SELF-MANAGEMENT SKILLS

1. Assessing your current knowledge and skills
2. Seeking out opportunities to acquire new knowledge and skills
3. Choosing and applying learning strategies
4. Showing flexibility by adopting new attitudes and behaviors

TIME MANAGEMENT SKILLS

5. Scheduling due dates for project outcomes
6. Scheduling time for goal-related tasks
7. Choosing technology and applying it to goal-related tasks
8. Choosing materials and facilities needed to meet goals
9. Designing other processes, procedures, or systems to meet goals
10. Working independently to meet goals
11. Planning projects for teams
12. Managing multiple projects at the same time
13. Monitoring progress toward goals
14. Persisting in order to meet goals
15. Delivering projects and outcomes on schedule

READING SKILLS

16. Reading for key ideas and major themes
17. Reading for detail
18. Reading to synthesize ideas and information from several sources
19. Reading to discover strategies for solving problems or meeting goals
20. Reading to understand and follow instructions

continued

NOTE-TAKING SKILLS

21. Taking notes on material presented verbally, in print, or online
22. Creating pictures, graphs, and other visuals to summarize and clarify information
23. Organizing information and ideas in digital and paper-based forms
24. Researching by finding information online or in the library
25. Gathering data through field research or working with primary sources

TEST-TAKING AND RELATED SKILLS

26. Assessing personal performance at school or at work
27. Using test results and other assessments to improve performance
28. Working cooperatively in study groups and project teams
29. Managing stress
30. Applying scientific findings and methods to solve problems
31. Using mathematics to do basic computations and solve problems

THINKING SKILLS

32. Thinking to create new ideas, products, or services
33. Thinking to evaluate ideas, products, or services
34. Evaluating material presented verbally, in print, or online
35. Thinking of ways to improve products, services, or programs
36. Choosing appropriate strategies for making decisions
37. Choosing ethical behaviors

38. Stating problems accurately
39. Diagnosing the sources of problems
40. Generating possible solutions to problems
41. Weighing benefits and costs of potential solutions
42. Choosing and implementing solutions
43. Interpreting information needed for problem solving or decision making

COMMUNICATION SKILLS

44. Assigning and delegating tasks
45. Coaching
46. Consulting
47. Counseling
48. Editing publications
49. Giving people feedback about the quality of their performance
50. Interpreting and responding to nonverbal messages
51. Interviewing people
52. Leading meetings
53. Leading project teams
54. Listening fully (without judgment or distraction)
55. Preventing conflicts (defusing a tense situation)
56. Resolving conflicts
57. Responding to complaints
58. Speaking to diverse audiences
59. Writing
60. Editing

MONEY SKILLS

61. Monitoring income and expenses
62. Raising funds
63. Decreasing expenses
64. Estimating costs
65. Preparing budgets

In summary, you can use a three-column chart to list your transferable skills. For example:

Verb	Object	Adverb
Organizing	Records	Effectively
Serving	Customers	Courteously
Coordinating	Special events	Efficiently

Add a specific example of each transferable skill to your skills list, and you're well on the way to an engaging résumé and a winning job interview.

What if I could expand my transferable skills?

In addition to thinking about the skills you already have, consider the skills you'd like to acquire. Describe them in detail. List experiences that can help you develop them. Let your list of transferable skills grow and develop as you do. ◼

Interactive

Journal Entry 26
Use the "five Cs" to develop transferable skills

This Journal Entry offers an additional way to recognize your transferable skills and develop more of them.

According to the AMA 2010 Critical Skills Survey conducted by the American Management Association, employers are now looking for people with four categories of transferable skills. Conveniently, each category starts with the letter C. They include:

- **Creative thinking.** Companies value people who can create ideas for new products and services and turn those ideas into reality.
- **Critical thinking.** People with this skill can state questions precisely, consider a variety of possible answers, and test them for logic and evidence. Critical thinkers excel at making decisions and solving problems.
- **Communication.** No matter where you work, you'll benefit from excellence at speaking, listening, writing, and reading. This means knowing your purpose for communicating and finding ways to achieve that purpose with a variety of audiences.
- **Collaboration.** Projects get done by teams. If you can work with a diverse group of people, set goals and achieve them, you'll have another skill that employers value.

There's also a fifth C that you can develop by using this book:

- **Character.** Even though it's not on the AMA's original list, you'll find that this factor is just as important. Character takes transferable skills and embeds them in a larger context. While the four Cs are about what you *do*, character is about who you *are*. This C refers to master student qualities such as a positive attitude, commitment, flexibility, willingness to learn, and trustworthiness. When employers talk about a "professional work ethic," they're referring to character.

You can use the master student process—the cycle of discovery, intention, and action—to turn the five Cs into practical tools for personal development.

Part One: Discovery

To begin, take about 15 minutes to assess your current level of mastery in each of the five Cs. Do this honestly while suspending self-judgment. Your goal is to be objective about your strengths and areas to improve. Describe yourself the way a neutral observer would.

Score yourself on a scale of 1 to 5 for each C, with 5 being the highest score. Also explain why you chose each rating. You might find that it helps to think of recent examples of assignments and projects that you completed for school, for work, or both.

Reasons for Choosing this Score
Critical thinking score
Creative thinking score
Communication score
Collaboration score
Character score
Expertise score

Part Two: Intention

When you're ready, flip through the pages of this book. Scan for specific suggestions that will help you develop the five Cs. Writing on separate paper, summarize each suggestion in one sentence and note the page numbers where you can find more details about them. Plan to spend about 30 minutes doing this.

Next, scan the list that you just created. It's time to set priorities. Narrow down your list to the top five suggestions that you intend to use—one suggestion for each C. Complete the following sentences:

To develop my skill in creative thinking, I intend to . . .

_____

_____

To develop my skill in critical thinking, I intend to . . .

_____

_____

To develop my skill in communication, I intend to . . .

_____

_____

To develop my skill in collaboration, I intend to . . .

_____

_____

To develop my character, I intend to . . .

_____

_____

Part Three: Action

Finally, list specific actions you will take to follow through on the intentions that you just created. Make these actions specific enough to include on a to-do list or enter in your calendar.

_____

_____

_____

_____

_____

_____

_____

_____

_____

_____

_____

_____

_____

_____

_____

_____

Exercise 31

Recognize your skills

This exercise about discovering your skills includes three steps. Before you begin, gather at least a hundred 3 × 5 cards and a pen or pencil. Or open up a computer file and use any software that allows you to create lists. Allow about one hour to complete the exercise.

Step 1: List recent activities

Recall your activities during the past week or month. Write down as many of these activities as you can. Include work-related activities, school activities, and hobbies. Spend at least 10 minutes on this step.

Step 2: List rewards and recognitions

Next, list any rewards you've received, or other recognition of your achievements, during the past year. Examples include scholarship awards, athletic awards, or recognitions for volunteer work. Allow at least 10 minutes for this step as well.

Step 3: List work-content skills

Now review the two lists you just created. Then take another 10 minutes to list any specialized areas of knowledge needed to do those activities, win those awards, and receive those recognitions. These areas of knowledge indicate your *work-content skills*. For example, tutoring a French class requires a working knowledge of that language. List all of your skills that fall into this category, labeling each one as "work-content."

Step 4: List transferable skills

Go over your list of activities one more time. Spend 10 minutes looking for examples of *transferable skills*—those that can be applied to a variety of situations. For instance, giving a speech or working as a salesperson in a computer store requires the ability to persuade people. Tuning a car means that you can attend to details and troubleshoot. List all your skills that fall into this category. Label each one as "transferable."

Step 5: Review and plan

You now have a detailed picture of your skills. Review all the lists you created in the previous steps. See whether you can add any new items that occur to you. Plan to update your lists of work-content and transferable skills at least once each year. These lists will come in handy for writing your résumé, preparing for job interviews, and doing other career-planning tasks.

Exercise 32
Do something you can't

Few significant accomplishments result from people sticking to the familiar. You can accomplish much more than you think you can. Doing something you can't involves taking risks.

Part 1

Select something that you have never done before, that you don't know how to do, that you are fearful of doing, or that you think you probably can't do. Describe what you have chosen.

Perhaps you've never learned to play an instrument, or you've never run a marathon. Be smart. Don't pick something that will hurt you physically, such as flying from a third-floor window.

_____

_____

Part 2

Do it. Of course, this is easier to say than to do. This exercise is not about easy. It is about discovering capabilities that stretch your self-image.

To accomplish something that is bigger than your self-perceived abilities, use any of the tools you have gained from this book. Develop a plan. Divide and conquer. Stay focused. Use outside resources. Let go of self-destructive thoughts.

Summarize the tools you will use.

_____

_____

_____

_____

_____

Part 3

Write about the results of this exercise.

_____

_____

_____

_____

_____

TAKING
THE ROAD TO
GRADUATION

Alex Slobodkin/E+/Getty Images

People go to school with many different definitions of success. For most students, that definition includes getting a degree. Every chapter in *Becoming a Master Student* offers a set of strategies that you can use for this purpose. Following are some additional suggestions for persisting to the day you graduate.

DISCOVER WHAT YOUR ACADEMIC GOALS MEAN FOR TODAY

One key to persistence is knowing exactly what you want from your education. Some students enter higher education with only a vague idea of their goals. These students can find it easy to disengage from school and let other activities take over.

This is where the master student process can make the difference between staying in school and dropping out. As you plan your week, write a Discovery Statement to complete these sentences:

- *What I most want from school is . . .*
- *What I also want is . . .*
- *To get what I want from school, the main goals for me to achieve this term are . . .*

This writing will give you the big picture of your priorities. Now zoom in for a close-up view. Create Intention Statements by completing the following sentences at least once each month:

- *To achieve my main goal for this term, the things that I intend to accomplish this month are . . .*
- *To meet my goals for this month, the things I intend to do this week are . . .*

Your answers to the last sentence will be tasks that you can add to a daily to-do list or enter in your calendar.

Persistence depends on planning. Goals become real only when they dictate what we do in the present moment. Take the goal of graduation and ask yourself: What does that goal mean for *today*?

CONNECT WITH SERVICES

After you finish this course, you never have to feel that you're alone and unsupported. A whole catalog of student services awaits you. Any of them can help you succeed in school, and many of them are free.

Name a problem that you're facing right now—financial problems, the need for child care, conflict with a teacher, or anything else that seems like an obstacle to getting your degree. Chances are that a school service can help you solve that problem.

Start with academic advising. You've already been encouraged to visit with your academic advisor. If you want to graduate on time, then be sure to *stay* in contact with this person until you graduate. Your academic advisor is there to help you adapt to the culture of higher education, choose a major, and select the courses needed to complete your degree.

Schedule a meeting with your advisor early during your first term. Then meet with this person at least once per term as long as you're in school. Prepare carefully for each meeting by writing down your questions and listing courses you're interested in taking.

Following are examples of other student services that your college may offer:

- Child care
- Fitness and athletic centers
- Computer labs and help desks
- Counseling services
- Career planning services
- Financial aid
- Legal aid services
- Security and safety services
- Special needs and disability services
- Student health clinics
- Tutoring
- Student organizations and extracurricular activities

Check your school Web site for the specific options available to you. Also remember that you can connect with many services online as well as in person.

The key is to seek services the moment when you need help. Do this right away, before a small problem grows into a barrier to getting your degree.

CONNECT WITH PEOPLE

School can be a frightening place for new students. Older students, people from different backgrounds and cultures, commuter students, and people with disabilities can feel excluded. Some people attend classes for months and still feel they're standing on the outside, looking in.

Students who overcome isolation increase their chances of staying in school and getting to graduation. Begin by planning to meet people. Write an Intention Statement promising to meet three new people each week. Name specific people, and describe how you intend to meet them. For example, introduce yourself to classmates. Get to class early and break the ice by discussing the previous assignment, or stay late and talk about the lecture.

Your instructors are people, too! Meet with your instructors outside of class. You will discover human beings who want you to succeed. Students who persist to graduation tend to develop long-term relationships with instructors who act as mentors, advisors, and coaches. These instructors can assist you by writing letters of recommendation and becoming part of your job-hunting network.

LIGHT THE PATH WITH LOTS OF REWARDS

One key to persistence is filling the long road to graduation with lots of small "wins." These are rewards that you enjoy on a regular basis—even on days when money is tight, the kids are crabby, or a schedule crammed with work and classes leaves you feeling exhausted.

According to Teresa Amabile and Steven Kramer, authors of *The Progress Principle: Using Small Wins to Ignite Joy, Engagement, and Creativity at Work*, the single most important source of motivation is making daily progress on meaningful work.[2] This idea applies to students. Keep a record of your academic successes, no matter how small. Take one minute each day to notice something that you've done well—a perfect score on a pop quiz, a well-written essay, a presentation where you connect with your audience, or anything else that you feel good about.

Whenever you successfully complete a task that brings you closer to graduation, pause to reflect on and remember it. Also tell someone—a family member or friend—about it. Accept compliments from others, and from yourself.

Notice that this suggestion differs from the typical problem-solving approach, where you look for something that's wrong and find ways to fix it. To apply the progress principle, you look for something that's right and find ways to celebrate it.

In your journal, also write Discovery Statements in response to these questions:

- What was it about getting a degree that originally excited you?
- When have you felt enthusiastic about going to school?
- When have you felt proud of the work you're doing in school?
- What parts of going to school do you find motivating and fun?

Staying in touch with your original reasons for going to school can rekindle your enthusiasm for persisting to graduation.

FIND THE TIME AND THE MONEY

Make careful choices about balancing school with work. If you're a full-time student, think of this commitment as on par with a 40-hour-per-week job. (If you study two hours for every hour that you spend in class, you might even spend *more* than 40 hours per week on school.) This places obvious limits on the number of hours per week that you can work.

Also create a complete plan for funding your education. Get to know the staff at your school's financial aid office. Meet with them regularly to discuss work-study programs, grants, loans, scholarships, and other financial resources. Make sure that you know how you're going to fund each term from now until the day you graduate.

REVISIT YOUR STRATEGIES

Becoming a Master Student comes with a guarantee. The strategies explained in this book are guaranteed to work—except when they don't. A technique that works in one class with one instructor might fail in another class with a different instructor. When that happens, it's time to modify the technique or find a new one.

Here is where your skills in creative and critical thinking come into play. Taking the road to graduation is about consistently asking two questions: *What kind of results am I getting right now in my academic life? And, what can I do differently to get better results?*

One way to answer these questions is to learn from the people around you. When you meet excellent students, observe them. Isolate specific things they do and say to promote their mastery. Then adopt one of these behaviors and see if it works for you. Also look for self-defeating habits you see in other students and draw lessons from them on what to avoid.

In addition, observe yourself during the times you're "on" as a student—times when learning is effortless and joyful. Notice the attitudes and actions that create such moments of success. These are more clues to your next steps on the road to graduation. ■

Journal Entry 27
Discovery/Intention Statement

Whom are you bringing with you?

As you persist on your path to graduation, remember that there are people who stand behind you and services that exist to help you succeed. Take some time now to discover the details about this intricate network of support that's available whenever you ask for help.

Discovery Statement

Reflect on all the people who helped you get this far in your educational journey. These people might include valued teachers, family members, fellow students, and friends. Think of those who helped you at a crucial point in your schooling and encouraged you to continue your education. These are the people who stand with you as you work to succeed in school. List their names.

I discovered that the people who've made a special contribution to my education so far include . . .

_____

_____

_____

_____

_____

Intention Statement

Next, create an intention to use campus services. Examples include academic advising, counseling, tutoring, and services from the housing, financial aid, and health offices at your school. For ideas, see your school catalog and Web site. List specific services that interest you.

To support my success in school, I intend to . . .

_____

_____

_____

_____

_____

Action Statement

Finally, prepare to follow up with people on both of the lists that you've just created. List contact information (name, address, phone number, Web site address, and e-mail address) for the people included in your Discovery Statement. Plan to thank them for supporting you. Keep them updated on how you're doing in school. Also list contact information for the services included in your Intention Statement, and schedule a time to see someone from each office.

Exercise 33
Make a trial choice of major

Step 1: Discover options

Look at your school's catalog or Web site for a list of majors. Make a photocopy of that list or print it out. Spend at least five minutes reading through all the majors that your school offers.

Step 2: Make a trial choice

Next, cross out all of the majors that you already know are not right for you. You will probably eliminate well over half the list. Scan the remaining majors. Next to the ones that definitely interest you, write "yes." Next to majors that you're willing to consider and are still unsure about, write "maybe."

Now, focus on your "yes" choices. See whether you can narrow them down to three majors. List those here:

_____

_____

_____

Finally, put an asterisk next to the major that interests you most right now. *This is your trial choice of major.*

Step 3: Evaluate your trial choice

Congratulations on making your choice! Now take a few minutes to reflect on it. Does it align with your interests, skills, and career plans? Set a goal to test your choice of major with out-of-classroom experience. Examples are internships, field experiences, study abroad programs, and work-study assignments. Note that this experience might confirm your trial choice—or lead to a new choice of major.

Exercise 34
Begin your academic plan

An academic plan is a road map for getting the most out of your education. This document is a list of all the courses you plan to take and *when* you plan to take each one. (At some schools, it is called a *degree plan* instead.)

After you made a trial choice of your major, use the following chart to create a rough draft of your academic plan:

- In the first column, list the name of each course you plan to take.
- Use a second column to write the number of credits for each course.
- In the third column, note the term you plan to take each course (e.g., *Spring 2016*). Be sure to check your college catalog for course prerequisites or corequisites.

Course	Credits	Term

Now check your rough academic plan to see that it fulfills these criteria:

- Gives you the total number of credits you need to graduate
- Meets your school's requirements for general education
- Meets the requirements for your major, your minor, or both

After completing this exercise, reach out to your instructors, academic advisor, and counselor for help in creating a more formal academic plan. Be sure to update that plan at least once each term to reflect any changes in your declared major and course schedule.

TRANSFERRING
to a new school

West Rock/Taxi/Getty Images

If you ever choose to change schools, you won't be alone. The New York Times *reports that about 60 percent of students graduating from college attend more than one school.*[3]

The way that you choose a new school will have a major impact on your education. This is true whether you're transferring from a community or technical college to a four-year school or you're choosing a graduate school.

Even if you don't plan to go through the process of choosing schools again, you can use the following ideas to evaluate your current school.

KNOW KEY TERMS

As you begin researching schools, take a few minutes to review some key terms.

Articulation agreements are official documents that spell out the course equivalents that a school accepts.

An *associate of arts (AA)* or *associate of science (AS)* is the degree title conferred by many two-year colleges. Having a degree from a two-year college can make it easier to change schools than transferring without a degree.

Course equivalents are courses you've already taken that another school will accept as meeting its requirements for graduation.

Prerequisites are courses or skills that a school requires students to complete or have before they enter or graduate.

GATHER INFORMATION

To research schools, start with publications. These include print sources, such as school catalogs, and school Web sites. Next, contact people—academic advisors, counselors, other school staff members, and current or former students from the schools you're considering. Contact the advisor at the new school to find out what the acceptance and graduation requirements are.

Use your research to dig up key facts such as these about each school you're considering:

- Location
- Number of students
- Class sizes
- Possibilities for contact with instructors outside class
- Percentage of full-time faculty members
- Admissions criteria
- Availability of degrees that interest you
- Tuition and fees
- Housing plans
- Financial aid programs
- Religious affiliation
- Diversity of students and staff
- Course requirements
- Retention rates (how many students come back to school after their freshman year)

To learn the most about a school, go beyond the first statistics you see. For example, a statement that "30 percent of our students are persons of color" doesn't tell you much about the numbers of people from specific ethnic or racial groups.

Also, you could transfer to a school that advertises student–instructor ratios of 15 to 1 and then find yourself in classes with 100 people. Remember that any statement about average class size is just that—an average. To gain more details, ask how often you can expect to enroll in smaller classes, especially during your final terms.

Take trips to the two or three schools that interest you most. Ask for a campus tour and a chance to sit in on classes.

In addition, gather facts about your current academic profile. Include your grades, courses completed, degrees attained, and grade point average (GPA). Standardized test scores are important. They include your scores on the Scholastic Assessment Test (SAT), American College Test (ACT), Graduate Record Examinations (GRE), and any advanced placement (AP) tests you've taken.

CHOOSE YOUR NEW SCHOOL

As you sort through all this information, remember that your impressions of a school will go beyond a dry list of facts. Also pay attention to your instincts and intuitions—your "gut feelings" of attraction to one school or hesitation about another. These impressions can be important to your choice. Allow time for such feelings to emerge.

You can also benefit from putting your choice of schools in a bigger context. Consider the purposes, values, and long-term goals you've generated by doing the exercises and Journal Entries in this book. Consider which school is most likely to support the body of discoveries and intentions that you've created.

Your prior experience in higher education gives you strengths. Acknowledge them, even as you begin at your new school.

As you choose your new school, consider the needs and wishes of your family members and friends. Ask for their guidance and support. If you involve them in the decision, they'll have more stake in your success.

At some point, you'll just choose a school. Remember that there is no one "right" choice. You could probably thrive at many schools—perhaps even at your current one. Use the suggestions in this book to practice self-responsibility. Take charge of your education no matter which school you attend.

SUCCEED AT YOUR NEW SCHOOL

Be willing to begin again. Some students approach a transfer with a "been there, done that" attitude. Having enrolled in higher education before, they assume that they don't need the orientation, advising, or other student services available at their new school.

Consider an alternative. Because your tuition and fees cover all these services, you might as well take advantage of them. By doing so, you could uncover opportunities that you missed while researching schools. At the very least, you'll meet people who will support your transition.

Your prior experience in higher education gives you strengths. Acknowledge them, even as you begin again at your new school. While celebrating your past accomplishments, you can explore new paths to student success.

Connect to people. At your new school, you'll be in classes with people who have already developed social networks. To avoid feeling left out, seek out chances to meet people. Join study groups, check out extracurricular activities, and consider volunteering for student organizations. Making social connections can ease your transition to a new academic environment.

Check credits. If you plan to transfer, meet with an advisor at your new school as soon as possible. Talk about how the credits that you've already earned will transfer to that school. This can save you a lot of tuition money. Find out whether you can get credit for prior learning in the workplace or military service. If you have results from College Level Examination Programs (CLEPs) or certification from massive open online courses (MOOCs), ask about credit for those as well.

No two schools offer the same sets of courses, so determining credits is often a matter of interpretation. In some cases, you might be able to persuade a registrar or the admissions office to accept some of your previous courses. Keep a folder of syllabuses from your courses for this purpose. Ask your academic advisor for help. Taking care of these details can help you graduate from your new school on time, with the education that you want. ■

START CREATING YOUR
CAREER

Many people approach career planning as if they were panning for gold. They keep sifting through the dirt, clearing dust, and throwing out rocks. They hope to strike it rich and discover the perfect career.

Instead of seeing a career as something you discover, you can see it as something you choose. You don't *find* the right career. You *commit* to it.

There's a big difference between these two approaches. Thinking that there's only one "correct" choice for your career can lead to a lot of anxiety: "Did I choose the right one?" "What if I made a mistake?"

Viewing your career as your creation helps you relax. Instead of anguishing over finding the right career, you can stay open to possibilities. Choose one career today, knowing that you can choose again later.

Career planning involves continuous exploration. There are dozens of effective paths to take. Begin now with the following ideas.

REMEMBER THAT YOU HAVE A WORLD OF CHOICES

Our society offers a limitless array of careers. You no longer have to confine yourself to a handful of traditional categories, such as business, education, government, or manufacturing. People are constantly creating new products and services to meet emerging demands. The number of job titles is expanding so rapidly that we can barely keep track of them.

In addition, people are constantly creating new goods and services to meet emerging needs. For instance, there are people who work as *ritual consultants*, helping people plan weddings, anniversaries, graduations, and other ceremonies. *Space planners* help individuals and organizations arrange furniture and equipment efficiently. *Auto brokers* visit dealers, shop around, and buy a car for you. *Professional organizers* will walk into your home or office and advise you on managing time and paperwork. *Pet psychologists* will help you raise a happy and healthy animal. And *life coaches* will assist you in setting and achieving goals relating to your career or anything else.

The global marketplace creates even more options for you. Through Internet connections and communication satellites that bounce phone calls across the planet, you can exchange messages with almost anyone, anywhere. Your customers or clients could be located in Colorado or China, Pennsylvania, or Panama. Your skills in thinking globally and communicating with a diverse world could help you create a new product or service for a new market—and perhaps a career that does not even exist today.

CONSIDER THREE FACTORS WHEN DEVELOPING CAREER SKILLS

Enjoying your work is important: If you enjoy what you do, you're more likely to excel at it. In a competitive job market, you can also benefit by considering two other factors as well.

One is your level of skill. For example, someone can enjoy playing the guitar and never do it well enough to make a living as a musician. It pays to get honest feedback on how well you've mastered the skills that you bring to your career.

The other factor is market demand. If your passion is teaching philosophy, for instance, you might have to wait for years for a job opening.

Keep looking for connections between your passion, skills, and market demand. Also remember that there's probably more than one career that can give you a satisfying experience of work.

USE CAREER-PLANNING SERVICES TO EXPLORE YOUR OPTIONS

Visit the career-planning office on campus. The counselors can help you explore possibilities as you seek your niche in the work world. Take career-planning workshops and go to career fairs.

Also ask about assessments that can help you discover more about your skills and identify jobs that call for those skills. These have several names, including *interest assessments, vocational aptitude tests,* or *skill inventories.* Some examples follow:

- *Campbell™ Interest and Skill Survey,* a well-known assessment that includes several hundred multiple-choice items. This assessment links to specific information about 60 possible careers.

- *Keirsey™ Temperament Sorter*, based on the Myers-Briggs Type Indicator®, a prominent personality assessment. Use the Keirsey results as a basis for taking more career-focused assessments.

- *Career Liftoff Interest Inventory (CLII)*, a 240-item assessment linked to a set of codes for classifying job interests.

- *Career Maze*, an online assessment that aims to provide an 82-item list of your personal characteristics and ways to connect them with specific jobs.

These can be useful resources for discovering your work-related preferences and planning your career. Although assessments cannot offer the final word on what kind of work is best for you, they can yield ideas that might not occur to you—and suggest useful ways to follow up.

Remember that what you do with the results is always a personal choice. No assessment can dictate your career direction or substitute for your gut instincts. If the result of an assessment seems wildly off base to you, then it probably is. Take what seems most valuable from each assessment and leave the rest.

TEST YOUR CAREER CHOICE— AND BE WILLING TO CHANGE

Once you have a career choice, translate it into workplace experience. For example:

- Contact people who are actually doing the job you're researching, and ask them a lot of questions about what it's like (an *information interview*).

- Choose an internship or volunteer position in a field that interests you.

- Get a part-time or summer job in your career field.

If you find that you enjoy such experiences, you've probably made a wise career choice. And the people you meet are possible sources of recommendations, referrals, and employment in the future.

If you did *not* enjoy your experiences, celebrate what you learned about yourself. Now you're free to refine your initial career choice or go in a new direction.

Career planning is not a once-and-for-all proposition. Rather, career plans are made to be changed and refined as you gain new information about yourself and the world.

Expect to learn a lot. Although getting a degree gives you an edge in the job market, it is not a one-way ticket to the career of your dreams. You might find yourself taking an entry-level position and working your way up as you gain technical skills, people skills, and experience.

Remember that you can approach *any* position in a way that takes you one step closer to your career goals. Do your best at every job, and stay flexible. Career planning never ends, and the process is the same, whether you're choosing your first career or your fifth.[4] ∎

Another option: Don't plan your career

When they hear the term *career plan*, some people envision a long document that lists goals with due dates and action steps. This is one type of career plan, and it can be useful for people with careers in stable industries. However, there are few of those left anymore.

In the spirit of the Power Process: Ideas are tools, consider another approach: Don't plan your career—at least in the conventional way. In an economy that's constantly shedding jobs and adding new ones, you can gain stability with an alternative approach to managing your career.

Choose your direction rather than your destination. Instead of listing specific jobs that you'd like to have in the years to come, get in touch with your values. Determine what matters to you most about working. Ask yourself these questions:

- Do you want to work primarily with people? Ideas? Specific products or materials?

- Do you want to manage people—or answer only to yourself and a handful of clients?

- What's the one thing that you do best—and enjoy doing—that creates value for people?

Put your answers in writing and revise them at least once each year. The result can be a stable and flexible direction for your career, no matter what happens to the economy.

Take one new step in that direction. Determine the very next action you will take to move in your chosen direction. Create an intention that you can act on immediately. If you want to become self-employed, for instance, then contact one person who started a successful business and ask for an information interview.

Reflect on what you learned—and choose your next step. Write Discovery Statements about the results of acting on your intention. What did you learn? In light of those lessons, what is the *next* step you'll take to move in your desired career direction?

The key is to take frequent action and reflect on the results. This process of determining your values and aligning your actions can teach you much about the work world—and open up opportunities that you might have never planned.

Journal Entry 28
Intention Statement

Plan a career by naming names

Experiment with career planning, starting now. See your response to this Journal Entry as a statement of a career direction rather than a detailed career plan. Also remember that a key part of career planning is changing your direction as you learn more about your skills, your interests, and the job market.

Of course, there are many possible ways to capture your career-related discoveries and intentions. For now, experiment with career planning by "naming names."

Note: To prepare for this writing, you might want to review a list of careers and related job titles such as the *Occupational Outlook Handbook* (http://bls.gov/ooh).

Name your skills

List the skills that you've enjoyed using in school and in past work or volunteer experiences.

_____

_____

_____

_____

_____

Name your job

Now, list the kinds of jobs that draw on the skills you just listed. What are those jobs called?

_____

_____

_____

_____

_____

Name your company

Perhaps you know of some businesses or non-profit organizations that you'd like to work for. List them.

If you prefer to be self-employed or start your own business instead, then name the products or services that you'd like to sell. Also list some possible names for your business.

_____

_____

_____

_____

_____

Name the people in your network

Finally, begin listing the names of people in your network. Include *anyone* who could help you find a job that interests you. Possibilities include former employers, your current employer, roommates, classmates, teachers, friends, relatives, people in your school's career planning office, and people who've graduated from your school and are now working in jobs similar to those you listed previously.

_____

_____

_____

_____

Finally, plan to meet with three people in your network for an information interview.

I will contact . . .

1. _____

2. _____

3. _____

START CREATING YOUR RÉSUMÉ

You can gain a lot from writing a résumé now, even if you don't plan to apply for a job in the near future. Start *building* your résumé now and update it each term that you're in school. Use this document as a plan for choosing the skills that you'd like to develop and describing them to potential employers.

There are many formats for résumés. The career planning center at your school can give you samples. Following are suggestions for writing a persuasive résumé—no matter what format you choose.

Focus on what you can do for an employer. Ask yourself: *From an employer's perspective, what kind of person would make an ideal candidate for this job?* Then write your résumé to answer this question directly.

If you include an objective in your résumé, avoid self-centered phrases such as "a job in the software industry where I can develop my sales skills." Instead, state your objective as "a sales position for a software company that wants to continually generate new customers and exceed its revenue goals."

Highlight your accomplishments. The body of a résumé usually includes a section titled *Experience.* Here is where you give a few relevant details about your past jobs, listed in chronological order starting with your most recent position.

This is where many résumé writers go off track. To avoid common mistakes, remember to focus the body of your résumé on what you *accomplished*—not just on what you *did*.

Whenever possible, use phrases that start with an active verb: "*supervised* three people," "*generated* leads for sales calls," "*wrote* speeches and *edited* annual reports," "*designed* a process that reduced production expenses by 20 percent."

Active verbs refer directly to your skills. Make them relevant to the job you're seeking, and be prepared to discuss them in more detail during a job interview.

The same focus on accomplishment applies to the *Education* section of your résumé. List any degree that you attained beyond high school. Also mention honors and awards. If you have a decent grade point average, include it.

If you are currently enrolled in classes, note that as well. Include your planned degree and date of graduation.

Keep it short and skimmable. Write one page. Period. A longer résumé sends a message that the writer has trouble communicating the big picture of her work life.

Besides, the people who screen your résumé are pressed for time. They'll spend only a few seconds scanning it. For this reason, avoid writing in full sentences and paragraphs. Bulleted lists work better. If you're applying for a specific position, be sure to include key words from the job listing.

A résumé has only one purpose—to get a job interview. Include just enough detail to make a potential employer say, "This person sounds interesting. Let's meet him in person so that we can find out more."

Cut the fluff. Avoid boilerplate language—stock wording or vague phrases such as "proven success in a high-stress environment," "highly motivated self-starter," or "a demonstrated capacity for strategic thinking." These can eliminate you from the hiring process and send your résumé straight to the trash.

Get feedback. Plan to write many drafts of your résumé. Ask friends and family members if your résumé is persuasive and easy to understand. Also ask them to check for grammar and spelling errors.

In addition, get feedback from people at your school's career-planning center. Revise your résumé based on their comments. Then revise some more.

Fine-tune your cover letter. Address your letter to a specific person. Make sure to use this person's correct title and mailing address. Also tailor each letter you write to the specific company and position you are applying for. Sending a "stock letter" implies that you don't really care about the job.

In your first sentence, address the person who can hire you and grab that person's attention. Make a statement that appeals directly to her self-interest.

Finally, refer the reader to your résumé. Mention that you'll call at a specific point to follow up. Then make good on your promise. ■

© Santiago Cornejo/Shutterstock.com

DISCOVER
the hidden
JOB MARKET

One of the most useful job skills you can ever develop is the ability to discover job openings *before* they are advertised. In fact, many openings exist even though they are never posted. This is the hidden job market.

Conventional job hunting is passive. It relies on sending out résumés and waiting for responses. Instead, get active and tap the hidden job market. The following suggestions will get you started.

THINK LIKE AN EMPLOYER

Imagine yourself working as the hiring manager for a small business or head of human resources for a larger company. Your organization has a job opening, and your task is to fill it as soon as possible. You have the following options:

1. Hiring someone you know—a current or former employee or intern—with appropriate qualifications
2. Hiring someone who is *recommended* by a current or former employee or intern
3. Asking other members of your professional network to recommend a person for the job
4. Hiring someone else who has already contacted you and demonstrated that he or she has the appropriate qualifications
5. Contracting with an employment agency to screen potential applicants
6. Running blind ads in newspapers or posting openings online—and preparing for the dreaded onslaught of résumés

If you're like most people in charge of hiring, you'll choose from options 1 through 4 whenever possible. That makes sense: You'd prefer to hire someone you know well or have met. This is probably safer than risking your luck on a total stranger.

Unfortunately, many job hunters rely primarily on options 5 and 6. The traditional job-hunting method proceeds in *exactly the opposite direction* that employers use. No wonder people get frustrated.

To prevent this disconnection, think like an employer. Determine the specific job that you want and then get to know people. Do research to find organizations that interest you. Find out who does the hiring at those organizations, and contact those people directly.

DISCOVER YOUR NETWORK

You already have a network. The key is to discover it and develop it.

Begin by listing contacts—any person who can help you find a job. Contacts can include roommates, classmates, teachers, friends, relatives, and their friends. Also list former employers and current employers.

In addition, go to your school's alumni office and see if you can get contact information for past graduates— especially people who are working in your career field. This is a rich source of contacts that many students ignore.

Start your contact list now. List each person's name, phone number, and e-mail address. Use word-processing, database, or contact-management software, or an app on your smart phone.

CONTACT PEOPLE IN YOUR NETWORK

Next, send a short e-mail to a person on your list— someone who's doing the kind of work that you'd love to do. Invite that person to coffee or lunch. If that's not feasible, then ask for a time to talk together on the phone. Explain that you'd like to have a 20-minute conversation to learn more about what the job entails. In other words, you're asking for an *information interview* rather than a job interview.

EXPAND YOUR NETWORK

Also tap the power of the Internet. Get the name of the person that you'd like to meet, and key it into your favorite search engine. Scan the search results to find out whether this person has a Web site, blog, or both. Also look for their presence on social networks such as Facebook, Twitter, and LinkedIn. With this information, you can do many things to connect. For example:

- Comment on a blog post that the person wrote.
- Join Twitter and post an update about this person or "retweet" one of their updates.
- Create your own Web site, add a blog, and write a post about this person.
- Send a short e-mail—or handwritten note—that expresses your appreciation for the work the person does.

In any case, do not ask anything of people at this stage. Your goal is simply to show up on their personal "radar." Over time, they might initiate a contact with you. When this happens, celebrate. You're tapping the hidden job market. ■

Develop
INTERVIEWING SKILLS

Job interviews are times for an employer to size up applicants. The reverse is also true: Interviews offer *you* a chance to size up potential employers. Careful preparation and follow-up can help you get the job that you want.

It's never too early to develop interviewing skills. Begin now with the following strategies, even if you're not actively seeking a job.

BEFORE YOU GO TO AN INTERVIEW

Prepare for common questions. Many interviewers have the following five questions on their mind, even if they don't ask them directly:

- How did you find out about us?
- Will we be comfortable working with you?
- How can you help us?
- Will you learn this job quickly?
- What makes you different from other people applying for this job?

Write out brief answers to those questions. Also describe your skills and give specific examples of how you used them to create positive results.

Next, summarize the main points you want to make on a single sheet of paper. Then practice delivering them verbally to the point where you barely refer to the sheet. Your goal is to sound prepared without delivering canned answers. This is something that you can start doing now, even if you're not actively looking for a job.

When you *do* start job hunting, learn everything you can about each organization that interests you. Start by searching the Internet. Then head to your campus and public libraries. Tell a reference librarian that you're researching specific companies in preparation for a job interview, and ask for good sources of information.

DURING THE INTERVIEW

Plan to arrive early for your interview. While you're waiting, observe the workplace. Notice what people are saying and doing. See whether you can "read" the company culture by making informal observations.

Just before the interview begins, remind yourself that you have one goal—to get the *next* interview.

The top candidates for a job often talk to several people in a company.

When you meet the interviewer, do three things right away: smile, make eye contact, and give a firm handshake. Nonverbal communication creates a lasting impression.

Stay aware of how much you talk during the interview. Avoid answers that are too brief or too long. Respond to each question for a minute or two. If you have more to say, end your answer by saying, "Those are the basics. I can add more if you want."

Save questions about benefits, salary, and vacation days for the second interview. When you get to that point, you know that the employer is interested in you. You might have leverage to negotiate.

Be sure to find out the next step in the hiring process and when it will take place. Also ask interviewers for their business cards and how they want you to follow up. Some people are fine with a phone call, or e-mail. Others prefer a good, old-fashioned letter.

If you're truly interested in the job and feel comfortable with the interviewer, ask one more question: "Do you have any concerns about hiring me?" Listen carefully to the reply. Then respond to each concern in a polite way.

AFTER THE INTERVIEW

Now comes follow-up. This step can give you the edge that leads to a job offer.

Write thank-you notes to the people who interviewed you. Do this within two business days after the interview. If you talked to several people at the same company, then write a different note to each one.

If you get turned down for the job after your interview, don't take it personally. Every interview is a source of feedback about what works—and what doesn't work—in contacting employers. Use that feedback to interview more effectively next time.

Also remember that each person you talked to is now a member of your network. This is true even if you do not get a job offer. Follow up by asking interviewers to keep you in mind for future job openings. Using this approach, you gain from every interview, no matter what the outcome. ■

Interactive

Exercise 35
Craft the story of you

Job interviewers are like most of us: They enjoy a good story. That's what they really want when they say things like *Tell me a little about yourself*. Instead of responding with a verbal version of your résumé, craft a story that's both true and compelling—one that the interviewer will immediately want to share with colleagues.

You can take a cue from storytelling experts—Hollywood screenwriters. Many films are based on a three-act structure:

Act I is about a *complication* (problem) faced by the main character.

Act II is about the *challenges* that character faces in dealing with the complication.

Act III is about *closure*—how the character resolved the complication by changing herself, her circumstances, or both.

For this exercise, take a significant event from your work experience and write a story about it. Keep it short—three paragraphs. Devote one paragraph to each "act" of your story. Remember that your overall goal is to narrate true events in a memorable way.

Start with an interesting complication. For instance, you might write about one of these occurrences:

- You worked on a project team with people who wouldn't talk to each other.

- You were assigned to train a coworker that no one wanted to work with.

- You faced a sudden funding shortfall for your nonprofit organization and had only one month to raise the money you needed.

Then describe the challenges that followed and how you solved them. Here's an example:

> *I was the manager on duty at a coffee shop. We usually got extremely busy during the morning rush hour—from 8 a.m. to 9 a.m.—when many of our customers stopped by on their way to work. On one morning, the line stretched almost out the door. (Complication)*

> *A customer stepped up to the counter and ordered a large espresso drink that was complicated to make—a skim, extra hot, half-decaffeinated latté with extra whipped cream. My coworker, who was making the drinks, forgot the "extra hot" part. The customer took her latté, shouted that it was "frigid" and called us incompetent. Then she stormed over to a table, sat down, and sulked. (Challenge)*

> *I gave her a few minutes to cool down. Then I went over and apologized that we'd made a mistake with her drink and offered to make another one for free. I'd seen her come in the store before, so I also asked what it would take for her to become a regular customer. It turned out that she had restaurant experience, and she answered my question with some great ideas for making our service more efficient. The next time she came in, she saw that we'd acted on several of her suggestions. After that, she stopped by the shop every day. (Closure)*

Now write your story. Then practice telling it in a way that sounds natural and unscripted.

_____

_____

_____

_____

_____

_____

_____

PERSIST
on the path of
MASTERY

You are on the edge of a universe so miraculous and full of wonder that your imagination, even at its most creative moment, cannot encompass it. Paths are open to lead you to worlds beyond your wildest dreams.

If this sounds like a pitch for the latest recreational drug, it might be. That "drug" is enthusiasm. It is automatically generated by your body when you are learning, planning, taking risks, achieving goals, and discovering new worlds inside and outside your skin. This is a path of mastery that you can travel for the rest of your life.

Consider the possibility that you can create the life of your dreams. Your responses to any of the ideas, exercises, and Journal Entries in this book can lead you to think new thoughts, say new things, and do what you never believed you could do. If you're willing to master new ways to learn, the possibilities are endless.

The key is to continue the cycle of discovery, intention, and action that's included in every chapter of this book. In other words, persist with the master student process.

If you used this book fully—if you actively participated in reading the content, writing the Journal Entries, doing the exercises, practicing critical thinking, and putting the suggestions to work—you have had quite a journey.

Recall some high points of that journey. The first half of this book is about the nuts and bolts of education—the business of acquiring knowledge. All of this activity prepares you for another goal of education—generating new knowledge. Meeting this goal leads you to the topics in the second half of this book: thinking for yourself, enhancing your communication skills, and creating a unique place for yourself in the world. All are steps on the path of becoming a master student.

Now what? What's your next step? Start with the following answers. Then create more of your own.

Keep a journal. Psychotherapist Ira Progoff based his Intensive Journal System on the idea that regular journaling can be a path to life-changing insights.[5] To begin journaling, consider buying a bound notebook in which to record your private reflections and dreams for the future. Get a notebook that will be worthy of your personal discoveries and intentions. Or keep an electronic journal on your computer.

Write or type in your journal daily. Record what you are learning about yourself and the world.

Write about your hopes, wishes, and goals. Keep a record of significant events. Consider using the format of Discovery Statements and Intention Statements that you learned in this book.

Take a workshop. Schooling doesn't have to stop at graduation, and it doesn't have to take place on a campus. In most cities, a variety of organizations sponsor ongoing workshops covering topics from cosmetology to cosmology.

Take workshops to learn skills, understand the world, and discover yourself. You can be trained in cardiopulmonary resuscitation (CPR), attend a lecture on developing nations, or take a course on assertiveness training.

Take an unrelated class. Sign up for a class that is totally unrelated to your major. If you are studying economics, take a physics course. If you are planning to be a doctor, take an accounting course. Take a course that will help you develop new computer skills and expand your possibilities for online learning.

Becoming a Master Student **373**

You can discover a lot about yourself and your intended future when you step out of old patterns. In addition to formal courses offered at your school, check out local community education courses. They offer a low-cost alternative that poses no threat to your grade point average.

Travel. See the world. Visit new neighborhoods. Travel to other countries. Explore. Find out what it looks like inside buildings that you normally have no reason to enter, museums that you never found interesting before, cities that are out of the way, forests and mountains that lie beyond your old boundaries, and far-off places that require planning and saving to reach.

Get counseling. Solving emotional problems is not the only reason to visit a counselor, therapist, or psychologist. These people are excellent resources for personal growth. You can use counseling to look at and talk about yourself in ways that might be uncomfortable for anyone except a trained professional. Counseling offers a chance to focus exclusively on yourself—something that is usually not possible in normal social settings.

Form a support group. Just as a well-organized study group can promote your success in school, an organized support group can help you reach goals in other areas of your life.

Today, people in support groups help one another lose weight, stay sober, cope with chronic illness, recover from emotional trauma, and overcome drug addiction.

Groups can also brainstorm possibilities for job hunting, career planning, parenting, solving problems in relationships, promoting spiritual growth—strategies for reaching almost any goal you choose.

Find a mentor—or become one. Seek coaching from experienced people whom you respect and admire. Use them as role models. If they are willing, ask them to be sounding boards for your plans and ideas. Many people are flattered to be asked.

You can also become a mentor. If you want to perfect your skills as a master student, teach them to someone else. Offer to coach another student in study skills in exchange for child care, free lunches, or something else you value. A mentor relationship can bridge the boundaries of age, race, and culture.

Make a habit of asking powerful questions. You can also mentor yourself. The key is asking questions that stretch your thinking. Powerful questions invite more than one answer. They start from the assumption that you can choose your response to any circumstance, no matter how challenging. And, they invite action.

As you pose questions, take a cue from the key words at the beginning of this chapter. For example, ask: *Why* am I in school? *What* new outcomes in life do I want? *How* can I produce that outcome? *What if* I could be relaxed and productive as I achieve my goals?

Consider further education and training. Your career plan might call for continuing education, additional certifications, or an advanced degree. Remember that the strategies in this book can help you gain new knowledge and skills at any point in your life.

Redo this book. If you didn't get everything you wanted from this book, it's not too late. You can read part of it or all of it again at any time.

Also redo portions of the book that you found valuable. Redo the quizzes to test your ability to recall certain information. Redo the exercises that were particularly effective for you. They can work again. Many of the exercises in this book can produce a different result after a few months. You are changing, and your responses change too.

You can also redo any of the Journal Entries in this book. Use them as a springboard for creating a journal that you keep for the rest of your life.

As you redo this book or any part of it, reconsider techniques that you skimmed over or skipped before. They might work for you now. Modify the suggestions, or add new ones. Redoing this book can refresh and fine-tune your study habits.

Another way to redo this book is to retake your student success course. People who do this often say that the second time is much different from the first. They pick up ideas and techniques that they missed the first time around and gain deeper insight into things they already know. ■

> *If you didn't get everything you wanted from this book, it's not too late. You can read part of it or all of it again at any time.*

Katie Edwards/Ikon Images/Getty Images

TOOLS FOR LIFELONG LEARNING

Learning can happen anywhere, anytime—both inside and outside the classroom and long after you graduate. In addition to taking courses for credit at your school, consider the following strategies.

START WITH THESE ONLINE RESOURCES

Begin by doing an Internet search on any topic that interests you. To get ideas, go online to Alltop (**alltop.com**), a site that links to articles and blog posts from many popular Web sites. Also look for Web sites related to your courses, including blogs by your instructors and the authors of your textbooks.

Some Web sites are devoted to lifelong learning. Examples are:

- eduFire (**www.edufire.com**)
- MindTools.com (**www.mindtools.com**)
- Learn Out Loud (**www.learnoutloud.com**)
- About.com (**www.about.com**)
- Open Culture (**www.openculture.com**) curates a growing collection of free ebooks, audio books, films, videos, and online courses. Look for more options at Coursera (**www.coursera.org**) and OpenCourseWare Consortium (**www.ocwconsortium.org**).

For additional ways to learn online, do a Internet search using key words such as *online education, virtual education, instructional Web sites*, and *distance learning*. If you're an iTunes user, also check the offerings from iTunesU. Make the Internet your classroom.

EXPLORE MOOCS

As you explore these resources, you'll find links to massive online open courses (MOOCs) offered by major universities. Some of these offer digital "badges" to certify that you've mastered course content. This kind of credential demonstrates your initiative and can give you an edge in a competitive job market, even before you get your degree.

STAY ON TOP OF THE NEWS

You might find dozens of Web sites that you want to check on a regular basis. News readers (also called *RSS readers*) make this easier to do. Applications such as FeedDemon, Net-NewsWire, and NetVibes will check your favorite Web sites for hourly or daily updates. This new content is displayed as a list of headlines. Skim them and choose what to read in more detail, just as you would do with the articles in a traditional newspaper.

READ BOOKS

Long before the Internet, there were books. They aren't going away any time soon. Whether in print or digital form, books still offer a way to explore topics in more depth and detail than online sources can deliver.

MEET PEOPLE

Conversation still offers one of the richest, most natural, and most powerful ways to learn. Start now by meeting with fellow students and instructors outside of class. You might develop friendships that last a lifetime.

Informal classes and workshops offer another way to meet people interested in learning something. Check your local library's calendar for upcoming events that will take place on campus and in your larger community. ■

Interactive

Exercise 36

This book shouts, "Use me!"

Becoming a Master Student is designed to be used for years. The success strategies presented here are not likely to become habits overnight. There are more suggestions than can be put into action immediately. Some of what is discussed might not apply to your life right now, but it might be just what you could use in a few months.

Plan to keep this book and use it again. Imagine that your book has a mouth. (Visualize the mouth.) Also imagine that it has arms and legs. (Visualize them.)

Now picture your book sitting on a shelf or table that you see every day. Imagine a time when you are having trouble in school and struggling to be successful as a student. Visualize your book jumping up and down, shouting, "Use me! Read me! I might have the solution to your problem, and I know I can help you solve it."

This is a memory technique to remind you to use a resource. Sometimes when you are stuck, all you need is a small push or a list of possible actions. At those times, hear your book shout, "Use me!"

Exercise 37

The Discovery Wheel—Coming full circle

This book doesn't work. It is worthless. Only you can work. Only you can make a difference and use this book to become a more effective student.

The purpose of this book is to give you the opportunity to change your behavior. The fact that something seems like a good idea doesn't necessarily mean that you will put it into practice. This exercise gives you a chance to see what behaviors you have changed on your journey toward becoming a master student.

Answer each question quickly and honestly. Record your results on the Discovery Wheel in Figure 12.1. If you completed an earlier Discovery Wheel in Chapter 1 of this book, then compare the two sets of scores.

The scores on this Discovery Wheel indicate your current strengths and weaknesses on your path toward becoming a master student. The last Journal Entry in this chapter provides an opportunity to write about how you intend to change. As you complete this self-evaluation, keep in mind that your commitment to change allows you to become a master student. *Your scores might be lower here than on your earlier Discovery Wheel.* That's okay. Lower scores might result from increased self-awareness and honesty, as well as other valuable assets.

Note: The online version of this exercise does not include number ratings, so the results will be formatted differently from those described here. If you did your previous Discovery Wheel online, do it online again. This will help you compare your two sets of responses more accurately.

5 points	This statement is always or almost always true of me.
4 points	This statement is often true of me.
3 points	This statement is true of me about half the time.
2 points	This statement is seldom true of me.
1 point	This statement is never or almost never true of me.

① Attitude

_____ I enjoy learning.

_____ I understand and apply the concept of multiple intelligences.

_____ I connect my courses to my purpose for being in school.

_____ I make a habit of assessing my personal strengths and areas for improvement.

_____ I am satisfied with how I am progressing toward achieving my goals.

_____ I use my knowledge of learning styles to support my success in school.

_____ I am willing to consider any idea that can help me succeed in school.

_____ I regularly remind myself of the benefits I intend to get from my education.

_____ **Total Score: Attitude**

② Time

_____ I set long-term goals and periodically review them.

_____ I set short-term goals to support my long-term goals.

_____ I write a plan for each day and each week.

_____ I assign priorities to what I choose to do each day.

_____ I plan review time so I don't have to cram before tests.

_____ I plan regular recreation time.

_____ I adjust my study time to meet the demands of individual courses.

_____ I have adequate time each day to accomplish what I plan.

_____ **Total Score: Time**

③ Memory

_____ I am confident of my ability to remember.

_____ I can remember people's names.

_____ At the end of a lecture, I can summarize what was presented.

_____ I apply techniques that enhance my memory skills.

_____ I can recall information when I'm under pressure.

_____ I remember important information clearly and easily.

_____ I can jog my memory when I have difficulty recalling.

_____ I can relate new information to what I've already learned.

_____ **Total Score: Memory**

④ Reading

_____ I preview and review reading assignments.

_____ When reading, I ask myself questions about the material.

_____ I underline or highlight important passages when reading.

_____ When I read textbooks, I am alert and awake.

_____ I relate what I read to my life.

_____ I select a reading strategy to fit the type of material I'm reading.

_____ I take effective notes when I read.

_____ When I don't understand what I'm reading, I note my questions and find answers.

_____ **Total Score: Reading**

⑤ Notes

_____ When I am in class, I focus my attention.

_____ I take notes in class.

_____ I am aware of various methods for taking notes and choose those that work best for me.

_____ I distinguish important material and note key phrases in a lecture.

_____ I copy down material that the instructor writes on the board or overhead display.

_____ I can put important concepts into my own words.

_____ My notes are valuable for review.

_____ I review class notes within 24 hours.

_____ **Total Score: Notes**

⑥ Tests

_____ I use techniques to manage stress related to exams.

_____ I manage my time during exams and am able to complete them.

_____ I am able to predict test questions.

_____ I adapt my test-taking strategy to the kind of test I'm taking.

_____ I understand what essay questions ask and can answer them completely and accurately.

_____ I start reviewing for tests at the beginning of the term.

_____ I continue reviewing for tests throughout the term.

_____ My sense of personal worth is independent of my test scores.

_____ **Total Score: Tests**

7 Thinking

_____ I have flashes of insight and think of solutions to problems at unusual times.

_____ I use brainstorming to generate solutions to a variety of problems.

_____ When I get stuck on a creative project, I use specific methods to get unstuck.

_____ I learn by thinking about ways to contribute to the lives of other people.

_____ I am willing to consider different points of view and alternative solutions.

_____ I can detect common errors in logic.

_____ I construct viewpoints by drawing on information and ideas from many sources.

_____ As I share my viewpoints with others, I am open to their feedback.

_____ **Total Score: Thinking**

8 Communicating

_____ I am honest with others about who I am, what I feel, and what I want.

_____ Other people tell me that I am a good listener.

_____ I can communicate my upset and anger without blaming others.

_____ I can make friends and create valuable relationships in a new setting.

_____ I am open to being with people I don't especially like in order to learn from them.

_____ I can effectively plan and research a large writing assignment.

_____ I create first drafts without criticizing my writing, then edit later for clarity, accuracy, and coherence.

_____ I know ways to prepare and deliver effective speeches.

_____ **Total Score: Communicating**

9 Diversity

_____ I build rewarding relationships with people from diverse backgrounds.

_____ I use critical thinking to overcome stereotypes.

_____ I point out examples of discrimination and sexual harassment and effectively respond to them.

_____ I am constantly learning ways to thrive with diversity.

_____ I can effectively resolve conflict with people from other cultures.

_____ My writing and speaking are free of sexist expressions.

_____ I take diversity into account when assuming a leadership role.

_____ I respond effectively to changing demographics in my country and community.

_____ **Total Score: Diversity**

10 Money

_____ I am in control of my personal finances.

_____ I can access a variety of resources to finance my education.

_____ I am confident that I will have enough money to complete my education.

_____ I take on debts carefully and repay them on time.

_____ I have long-range financial goals and a plan to meet them.

_____ I make regular deposits to a savings account.

_____ I pay off the balance on credit card accounts each month.

_____ I can have fun without spending money.

_____ **Total Score: Money**

11 Health

_____ I have enough energy to study and work—and still enjoy other areas of my life.

_____ If the situation calls for it, I have enough reserve energy to put in a long day.

_____ The way I eat supports my long-term health.

_____ The way I eat is independent of my feelings of self-worth.

_____ I exercise regularly to maintain a healthful weight.

_____ My emotional health supports my ability to learn.

_____ I notice changes in my physical condition and respond effectively.

_____ I am in control of any alcohol or other drugs I put into my body.

_____ **Total Score: Health**

12 Purpose

_____ I see learning as a lifelong process.

_____ I relate school to what I plan to do for the rest of my life.

_____ I see problems and tough choices as opportunities for learning and personal growth.

_____ I use technology in a way that enriches my life and supports my success.

_____ I am developing skills that will be useful in the workplace.

_____ I take responsibility for the quality of my education—and my life.

_____ I live by a set of values that translates into daily actions.

_____ I am willing to accept challenges even when I'm not sure how to meet them.

_____ **Total Score: Purpose**

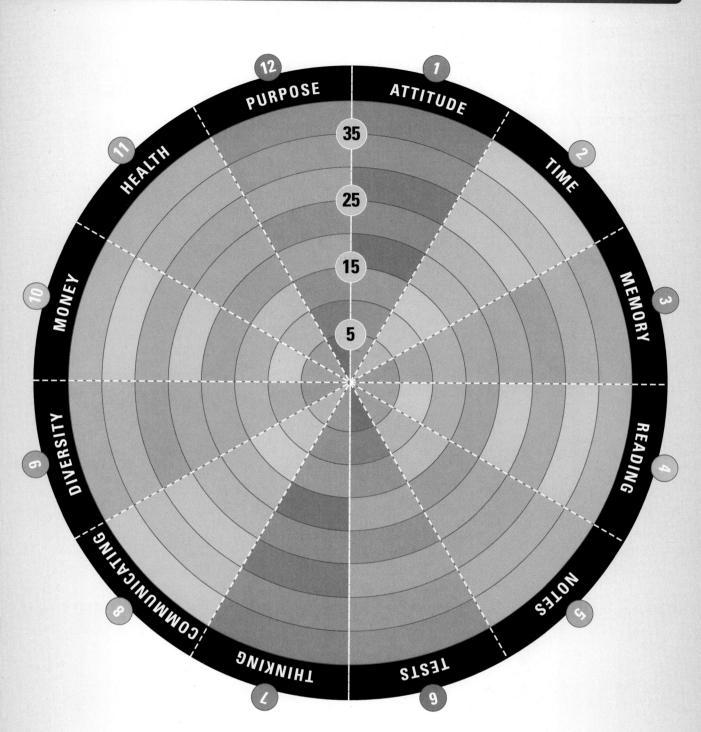

Figure 12.1 Your Discovery Wheel

Filling in your Discovery Wheel

Using the total score from each category, shade in each corresponding wedge of the Discovery Wheel in Figure 12.1. Use different colors, if you want. For example, you could use green to denote areas you want to work on. When you have finished, complete the Skills Snapshot on the next page.

SKILLS SNAPSHOT

Discovery Wheel

Revisiting your Discovery Wheels

The purpose of this exercise is to (1) review both of the Discovery Wheels you completed in this book, (2) summarize your insights from doing them, and (3) declare how you will use these insights to promote your continued success in school.

Again, a lower score on the second Discovery Wheel does not necessarily indicate decreased personal effectiveness. Instead, the lower score could result from increased honesty and greater self-awareness.

Enter your Discovery Wheel scores from both chapters.

	Chapter 1	This Chapter
Attitude		
Time		
Memory		
Reading		
Notes		
Tests		
Thinking		
Communicating		
Diversity		
Money		
Health		
Purpose		

Comparing the Discovery Wheel in this chapter with the Discovery Wheel in Chapter 1, I discovered that I . . .

In the next six months, I intend to review the following articles from this book for additional suggestions I could use:

Journal Entry 29
Discovery/Intention Statement

Celebrate your gains, clarify your intentions

This Journal Entry invites you to step back from your daily routine and reflect on what you've gained from your student success course. If you've fully participated with this book, then you've made discoveries and created intentions that can make a huge difference in the continuing quality of your life. Don't let this work go to waste. Capture the high points of your learning now, before they fade into distant memories.

There are at least two major reasons for doing a Journal Entry such as this one. The first is to celebrate your progress. Believe it or not, success is something that's easy to overlook. Our shortcomings and failures have a magnetic pull on our attention. Many students find it easy to focus on what's *not* working in their lives rather than what *is* working. Do yourself a favor by taking the time to shift your attention and choose a new conversation. Noticing any evidence of progress, no matter how small, can be tremendously motivating.

Second, you can turn your mistakes into your most powerful teachers. Every mistake has a lesson to offer us *if* we take the time to find it.

Set aside about one hour to complete the following sentences. This could be one of the most productive hours that you spend this term.

In preparation, you might find that it helps to quickly page through this book and glance over your responses to previous Journal Entries and exercises. When you're done, immediately begin writing.

Discovery
In reflecting on my experience with this course, I discovered that my biggest gain was . . .

_____

_____

The most useful thing I learned was . . .

_____

_____

The smartest decision I made was . . .

_____

_____

The biggest risk I took was . . .

_____

_____

My biggest surprise was . . .

_____

_____

The biggest compliment that I received was . . .

_____

_____

The biggest compliment that I gave was . . .

_____

_____

If I could repeat this course, the most important thing I would do differently is . . .

_____

_____

Intention

After reviewing my Discovery Statements, the goal that I would be most excited to achieve this year is . . .

_____

_____

Another goal that excites me is . . .

_____

_____

The people that I am most committed to loving are . . .

_____

_____

Action

As I reflect on my intention to complete my degree, the most important new habit I will adopt is . . .

_____

_____

Another important habit that I will develop is . . .

_____

_____

Three reasons to celebrate mistakes

Celebration gets mistakes out into the open. This is the opposite of covering up mistakes or blaming others for them. Hiding mistakes takes a lot of energy—energy that could be channeled into correcting errors.

Celebration includes everyone. Celebrating mistakes reminds us that the exclusive club named the Perfect Performance Society has no members. All of us make mistakes. When we notice them, we can work together more effectively.

Celebration cuts the problem down to size. On top of the mistake itself, there is often a layer of stress or desperation about making *the* mistake in the first place. When we celebrate mistakes, we strip away that layer of concern. With our regret behind us, we can get down to the business of learning from mistakes and using them to change our behavior.

Practicing Critical Thinking 12

Remember that psychologist Benjamin Bloom described six levels of thinking:

Level 1: Remembering

Level 2: Understanding

Level 3: Applying

Level 4: Analyzing

Level 5: Evaluating

Level 6: Creating

Now reflect on your experience of *Becoming a Master Student* by combining the levels and taking them in a different sequence.

Level 1: Remembering and Level 2: Understanding

Consider your experience with this book and your student success class. Which of your attitudes and habits have changed as a result of this experience?

_____

_____

_____

_____

Level 5: Evaluating

List three suggestions from this book that you've already applied. Rate each suggestion for its effectiveness on a scale of 1 to 5 (1 is least effective, and 5 is most effective). Describe your reasons for each rating.

_____

_____

_____

_____

_____

Level 3: Applying and Level 4: Analyzing

Next, list three suggestions from this book that you would like to apply but have not yet acted upon. Describe the actions you will take to implement these suggestions.

_____

_____

_____

_____

Level 6: Creating

Consider this statement: "You are on the edge of a universe so miraculous and full of wonder that your imagination at its most creative moment cannot encompass it. Paths are open to lead you to worlds beyond your wildest dreams." If you adopted this statement as a working principle, what new values would you adopt? What new goals would you set?

_____

_____

_____

MASTER STUDENT PROFILE

LALITA BOOTH

Once homeless, now a student at the University of Central Florida (UCF), and accepted to Harvard University Business School

Sitting in front of a classroom of LEAD Scholars, Lalita Booth looks like any other junior. The brown-eyed, freckle-faced student blends in with her peers in the University of Central Florida (UCF) leadership development program in every way.

That is, until she opens her mouth.

"You're looking at the face of a child abuse survivor, a perpetual runaway, a high school dropout," she says, as idle chitchat turns to complete silence.

"I was a teenage mother, a homeless parent, and a former welfare recipient."

Lalita's parents divorced when she was young; by age 12 she was a runaway pro—asking for permission to go somewhere and then simply not returning for a few days or a few weeks. . . .

She became proficient in "couch surfing" at friends' homes. When there was no couch to crash on, the teen would take her nightly refuge behind the closest dumpster and rest in the park during the day.

Furthering her quest to be a grownup, at 17 she married her long-time buddy and fellow high school dropout, Quinn. Three months later, she found out she was pregnant with her son, Kieren. What normally would be a joyful time was instead a stressful one while the new couple struggled in a prison of deep poverty. The miserable situation began to take its toll, and after just two and a half years of marriage, Quinn was ready to call it quits.

With her new boyfriend, Carl, and her most precious cargo, Kieren, in tow, Booth fled to Boulder, Colorado. Kieren lived with his paternal grandparents for seven months while Lalita and Carl attempted to get back on their feet.

Being in Colorado proved to be fruitful for the 21-year-old Lalita. It started with an interesting job opportunity

Lalita Booth *is willing to work.* **You** *can work effectively by setting goals that align with your dreams.*

as an enrolled agent—an expert in U.S. taxation who can represent taxpayers before the Internal Revenue Service. Lalita could acquire the license without further schooling. Better yet, it would boost her income to $32,000. She buckled down and read all 4,000 pages of the study guide, and, thanks to her nearly photographic memory, she aced the test.

But once again, she was in the wrong place at the wrong time. Carl's brother in Orlando was very ill, and he needed to move to Florida.

The only way to ensure her independence was to do something that frightened her to the very core—go back to school. . . .

And soon after, she enrolled at Seminole Community College. . . .

In May 2005, Lalita was selected to attend the Salzburg Global Seminar, where she brainstormed ways to solve global problems with a group of international students. The thought-provoking trip led to her mission: to help others escape the choke hold of poverty.

Back in the states, Booth's world became even more dream-like when she won the Jack Kent Cooke Foundation Scholarship.

Lalita Booth strongly believes, and for good reason, that "things that are worth achieving are absolutely unreasonable." She advises, "Set unreasonable goals, and chase them unreasonably." ■

Source: Adapted from Sarah Sekula, "Escape Artist," Pegasus, July/August 2008, UCF Alumni Life, 20–26. Reprinted with permission.

Seminole State College of Florida

QUIZ
Chapter 12

Name _____

Date _____

1. According to the Power Process in this chapter, the ability to persist calls for giving up the constant desire for instant gratification. True or false? Explain your answer.

   True. Master students harness their critical thinking skills to cut through all the hype. They know that they are in the game for the long haul, and that there are no quick fixes. They know that getting a degree is like training for a marathon. They remember that every class attended and every assignment completed is one small win on the way to a big victory. (*Power Process: Persist*, page 352)

2. Explain how work-content skills and transferable skills differ.

   (Answers will vary.) A work-content skill is an ability gained by training or experience. It involves a specialized body of knowledge needed to do a specific kind of work. An example is the ability to repair fiber-optic cable. A transferable skill is an ability developed without formal training that helps people thrive in any job. Examples include listening and negotiating. (*Jump-start your education with transferable skills*, page 353)

3. List two examples of work-content skills.

   (Answers will vary.) Work-content skills include the ability to repair fiber-optic cables and perform brain surgery. (*Jump-start your education with transferable skills*, page 353)

4. List five examples of transferable skills.

   (Answers will vary.) Transferrable skills include planning projects for teams, persisting in order to meet goals, choosing and applying learning strategies, reading for detail, and managing stress (*65 transferable skills*, page 354)

5. List three examples of transferable skills related to reading.

   (a) Reading for key ideas and major themes. (b) Reading for detail. (c) Reading to synthesize ideas and information from several sources. (d) Reading to discover strategies for solving problems or meeting goals. (e) Reading to understand and follow instructions. (*65 transferable skills*, page 354)

6. Give three examples of ways to test your career choice.

   (Answers will vary.) Three ways to test a career choice are to interview people who are actually doing the job, obtain an internship or volunteer position in that field, and get a part-time or summer job in that field. For example, a person considering a career as a veterinarian might interview and ask questions of a working veterinarian, seek out a volunteer or internship position at a local animal care shelter, and get a part-time job at a veterinarian's office for the summer. (*Start creating your career*, page 366)

7. According to the text, the best résumé is one that gives the full details about your background and experience, even if it is longer than one page. True or false? Explain your answer.

   False. Write one page. Period. A longer résumé sends a message that the writer has trouble communicating the big picture of her work life. (*Start creating your résumé*, page 369)

8. Define the term *hidden job market*. Then list three strategies you can use to access it.

   One of the most useful job skills you can ever develop is the ability to discover job openings *before* they are advertised. In fact, many openings exist even though they are *never* posted. This is the hidden job market. (*Discover the hidden job market*, page 370)

9. List five common questions that job interviewers have in their mind, even if they don't ask them directly.

   How did you find out about us? Will we be comfortable working with you? How can you help us? Will you learn this job quickly? What makes you different from other people applying for this job? (*Develop interviewing skills*, page 371)

10. List at least three ways in which you can persist on the path of mastery after completing this book.

    (Answers will vary): (a) Keep a journal. (b) Take a workshop. (c) Take an unrelated class. (d) Travel. (e) Get counseling. (f) Form a support group. (g) Find a mentor—or become one. (h) Make a habit of asking powerful questions. (i) Consider further education and training. (j) Redo this book. (*Persist on the path of mastery*, page 373)

SKILLS SNAPSHOT
Chapter 12

If you fully participated with this chapter, then you've got a lot of ideas about staying on the path of mastery that you began with this book and with this course. Now take a few minutes to clarify your intentions about continuing on this path.

Discovery
My score on the Purpose section on the Discovery Wheel was . . .

What I want most from my education is . . .

What I want most from any career is . . .

Intention
The most important work-content skills that I intend to develop are . . .

The most important transferable skills that I intend to develop are . . .

I intend to use these skills to succeed in the workplace by . . .

Action
The very next thing that I will do to develop the work-content skills I just listed is . . .

The very next thing that I will do to develop the transferable skills I just listed is . . .

The Master Guide to
Becoming a Master Student

It is impossible to summarize every strategy from *Becoming a Master Student* in two pages. However, it is possible to summarize the process that inspired all those strategies. You can use the master student process to create your own strategies for success in any area of life:

- **Discovery**. Tell the truth about your current thoughts, feelings, behaviors, and circumstances. Record the specifics in writing. Be honest, and release self-judgment.
- **Intention**. Based on your discoveries, commit to make specific changes in your behavior. As with discoveries, put your intentions in writing.
- **Action**. Translate your intentions into real changes in behavior. Successful people are those who consistently produce the results that they want. The secret is sustained action.

This process is a cycle. First, you write Discovery Statements about where you are now. Next, you write Intention Statements about where you want to be and the specific steps you will take to get there. Follow up with action—the sooner, the better.

A **master student** is someone who uses this cycle so often and so well that it becomes second nature. **Mastery** is a level of skill that goes beyond technique, and beyond explanation.

About success

Success means setting and achieving goals.

A **goal** is any outcome or result that you desire. Goals lead to changes in what you *have* (such as more money or higher grades), in what you *do* (such as gaining a new skill), or both.

A **strategy** is any action that you take in order to achieve a goal. Strategies might also be called *habits, tools, tips, techniques, methods, processes, procedures, skills,* or *suggestions.*

Becoming a Master Student is a catalog of success strategies. You can use these strategies to achieve any goal, including goals related to your success in school.

A **value** is something that you desire for its own sake—something you'd like to *be.* For example, you might want to be happy, healthy, and loving. Values shape your goals and strategies.

The Power Processes

Students consistently find that certain strategies presented in this book are especially useful in achieving their goals. These "super strategies" are called *Power Processes* and include the following:

Discover what you want. To more consistently get the results that you desire, carefully define your values and goals.

Ideas are tools. Rather than looking for what's wrong with a new idea, see whether you can find something in it that's potentially valuable.

Be here now. To do anything more effectively, give it your full attention.

Love your problems. To solve a problem, move beyond denial and resistance to acceptance and action.

Notice your pictures and let them go. To release frustration and take effective action, be willing to release rigid beliefs about the way things "ought" to be.

I create it all. When you experience a problem, ask whether it results from any of your own beliefs or behaviors.

Detach. Discover a source of serenity that does not depend on achieving any goal.

Embrace the new. Be willing to think what you've never thought before, to say what you've never said before, and to do what you've never done before.

Employ your word. Speak about your possibilities, preferences, passions, plans, and promises as a way to direct your behavior.

Choose your conversations. Conversations exercise incredible power over what we think, feel, and do; choose them with care.

Risk being a fool. Remember that mastery calls for the courage to do something new, fail, make corrections, and fail again before succeeding.

Surrender. Recognize when you've reached your limits, and ask for help.

Persist. Success is often about doing the gritty and unglamorous things that really work, day after day.

Making the transition to higher education

Use the Discovery-Intention-Action cycle to:

- Connect to resources—campus clubs and organizations, and school and community services.
- Meet with your academic advisor.
- Attend every class and participate actively.
- Take the initiative to meet new people.
- Share your feelings with friends, family members, and a counselor.

Learning styles

Move through a complete cycle of learning by asking:

- **Why?** Your answer to this question helps you discover a reason for learning (Mode 1).
- **What?** Your answer to this question helps you gather relevant information (Mode 2).
- **How?** Your answer to this question helps you experiment with ways to apply what you're learning (Mode 3).
- **What if?** Your answer to this question helps you integrate new knowledge and skills into your day-to-day life (Mode 4).

Time

Use the Discovery-Intention-Action cycle to:

- Monitor your activities, and use the data you collect to make informed choices about how to spend your time.
- Use a monthly or yearly calendar to anticipate heavy demands on your time.
- Restate your wants as goals—specific outcomes with clear due dates.
- List the actions you'll take to achieve your goals on your to-do list and calendar.
- Overcome procrastination, accept feelings of discomfort about a task, and then move into action.

Memory

Use the Discovery-Intention-Action cycle to:

- Organize new material so that it is easier to remember.
- Change studying from a passive affair to an active process that involves all your senses.
- Engage your emotions, take advantage of your peak energy periods, and elaborate on new information.
- Review important ideas and information on a regular basis and recall them whenever you want.
- Experiment with a variety of memory strategies, including mnemonics.

Reading

Use the Discovery-Intention-Action cycle to:

- Experiment with Muscle Reading, a process that includes previewing a text, reading to answer specific questions, and reviewing the answers.
- Monitor your understanding of a text and get past confusion.
- Adjust reading speed to your purpose and the nature of the material.
- Expand your vocabulary.
- Develop information literacy—the ability to find information in appropriate sources, evaluate the information, and use it to achieve a purpose.
- Stay on top of your reading load in the midst of a busy life.

Notes

Use the Discovery-Intention-Action cycle to:

- Get the most value from note taking by carefully observing what happens in class, recording the material that matters, and reviewing what you record.
- Experiment with variety of note-taking formats, such as the Cornell method, mind maps, outlines, and concept maps.
- Take effective notes on reading material.
- Continue taking effective notes even when you feel confused.
- Take effective notes for online coursework.

Tests

Use the Discovery-Intention-Action cycle to:

- Predict test questions.
- Review important material several times before a test.
- Create study groups that promote your success.
- Manage your time effectively during a test and respond to questions in a variety of formats, such as multiple choice, true-false, and essay questions.
- Learn from tests after they are scored and returned to you.
- Manage test-related anxiety.

Thinking

Use the Discovery-Intention-Action cycle to:

- Think flexibly by moving freely through all the levels of Bloom's taxonomy (remembering, understanding, applying, analyzing, evaluating, and creating).
- Detect logical fallacies.
- Uncover assumptions.
- Make decisions in a way that balances creative and critical thinking.
- Define problems, create possible solutions, implement solutions, and evaluate them.
- Ask questions that deepen your thinking.
- Gain life-changing lessons from service-learning experiences.

Communicating

Use the Discovery-Intention-Action cycle to:

- Improve your ability to listen fully while another person speaks respond in ways that deepen your relationship.
- Speak honestly about your thoughts and feelings without judging or blaming other people.
- Develop an emotional intelligence that makes you an effective team member.
- Manage conflict in a way that respects the views of all people involved.
- Plan your writing to meet a specific purpose, complete a quick first draft, and allow plenty of time for revision.
- Create presentations that are organized, memorable, and designed for your audience.

Diversity

Use the Discovery-Intention-Action cycle to:

- Understand how culture shapes our thoughts, feelings, and behaviors.
- Recognize how you differ from people from other cultures.
- Respond to those differences with respect and the ability to find common ground.
- Overcome stereotypes and prevent sexism.
- Take leadership roles in a diverse world.

Money

Use the Discovery-Intention-Action cycle to:

- Monitor how much money you earn and spend each month.
- Live within your means by increasing income.
- Live within your means by decreasing expenses.
- Use credit cards with caution.
- Borrow as little money as possible and select loans carefully.

Health

Use the Discovery-Intention-Action cycle to take a fearless look at your health-related habits, including those that relate to:

- Eating
- Exercise
- Drug use
- Personal relationships
- Sleep
- Stress management

Next steps

Use the Discovery-Intention-Action cycle to:

- Develop work-content skills and transferable skills.
- Connect with people and services that can help you persist in school through graduation.
- Translate academic goals into daily tasks and celebrate when you complete them.
- Begin career planning now and return to this activity throughout your working years.
- Test your choice of a career through internships and other work experiences.
- Tap the hidden job market through a network of friends, relatives, coworkers, and fellow students.
- Begin writing a résumé that is easy to scan and documents specific accomplishments in your education and work experience.
- Prepare for job interviews by practicing your answers to the common questions.
- Enhance your personal growth with tools such as continuing education, counseling, life coaching, mentoring, and support groups.

Endnotes

INTRODUCTION

1. Excerpts from *Creating Your Future*. Copyright © 1998 by David B. Ellis. Adapted by permission of Houghton Mifflin Company. All rights reserved.

2. A. H. Maslow, *The Farther Reaches of Human Nature* (New York: Viking Compass, 1972), 41–52.

3. "Education Pays . . . ," U.S. Department of Labor, Bureau of Labor Statistics, January 28, 2013, accessed March 6, 2013, from www.bls.gov/emp/ep_chart_001.htm.

4. "Away from Reprimands, Toward Self-Regulation," Association for Supervision and Curriculum Development, June 13, 2012, accessed March 6, 2013, from http://inservice.ascd.org/whole-child/away-from-reprimands-toward-self-regulation/.

5. "U.S. Census Bureau Facts for Feature: Back to School: 2009-2010," Reuters, August 17, 2009, accessed March 6, 2013, from www.reuters.com/article/2009/08/17/idUS139193+17-Aug-2009+PRN20090817.

6. Brad Isaac, "Jerry Seinfeld's Productivity Secret," Lifehacker, July 24, 2007, accessed March 6, 2013, from http://lifehacker.com/software/motivation/jerry-seinfelds-productivity-secret-281626.php.

7. Charles Duhigg, *The Power of Habit: Why We Do What We Do in Life and Business* (New York: Random House, 2012), 276–286.

CHAPTER 1

1. David A. Kolb, *Experiential Learning: Experience as the Source of Learning and Development* (Englewood Cliffs, NJ: Prentice-Hall, 1984).

2. Douglas A. Bernstein, Louis A. Penner, Alison Clarke-Stewart, and Edward J. Roy, *Psychology* (Boston: Houghton Mifflin, 2006), 368–369.

3. Howard Gardner, *Frames of Mind: The Theory of Multiple Intelligences* (New York: Basic Books, 1993).

4. Neil Fleming, "VARK: A Guide to Learning Styles," 2012, accessed March 6, 2013, from www.vark-learn.com/.

5. L. W. Anderson and D. R. Krathwohl, *A Taxonomy For Learning, Teaching, and Assessing: A Revision Of Bloom's Taxonomy of Educational Objectives* (New York: Addison Wesley Longman, 2001).

CHAPTER 2

1. Stephen R. Covey, *The Seven Habits of Highly Effective People: Restoring the Character Ethic* (New York: Simon & Schuster, 1990), 150–154.

2. Mei-Ching Lien, Eric Ruthruff, and James C. Johnston, "Attentional Limitations in Doing Two Tasks at Once: The Search for Exceptions," *Current Directions in Psychological Science* 15, no. 2 (2005): 89–93.

3. Alan Lakein, *How to Get Control of Your Time and Your Life* (New York: New American Library, 1973; reissue 1996).

4. David Allen, *Getting Things Done: The Art of Stress-Free Productivity* (New York: Penguin, 2001), 46–47.

5. Linda Sapadin, with Jack Maguire, *It's About Time! The Six Styles of Procrastination and How to Overcome Them* (New York: Penguin, 1997).

CHAPTER 3

1. Donald Hebb, quoted in D. J. Siegel, "Memory: An Overview," *Journal of the American Academy of Child and Adolescent Psychiatry* 40, no. 9 (2001): 997–1011.

2. "Brain Health," 2010, Alzheimer's Association, 2013, accessed March 6, 2013, from www.alz.org/we_can_help_brain_health_maintain_your_brain.asp.

3. Siegel, "Memory: An Overview."

4. Daniel L. Schacter, *The Seven Sins of Memory: How the Mind Forgets and Remembers* (Boston: Houghton Mifflin, 2001), 13–15.

5. Siegel, "Memory: An Overview."

CHAPTER 4

1. "To Read or Not to Read: A Question of National Consequence," National Endowment for the Arts, November 7, 2007, accessed March 6, 2013, from www.nea.gov/research/ToRead_ExecSum.pdf.

2. Jeffrey D. Karpicke and Janell R. Blunt, "Retrieval Practice Produces More Learning than Elaborative Studying with Concept Mapping," *Science* 20 (January 2011), accessed March 6, 2013, from www.sciencemag.org/content/331/6018/772.abstract.

3. O. Pineño and R. R. Miller, "Primacy and Recency Effects in Extinction and Latent Inhibition: A Selective Review with Implications for Models of Learning," *Behavioural Processes* 69 (2005): 223–235.

CHAPTER 5

1. Gayle A. Brazeau, "Handouts in the Classroom: Is Note Taking a Lost Skill?" *American Journal of Pharmaceutical Education* 70, no. 2 (April 15, 2006): 38.

2. Walter Pauk and Ross J. Q. Owens, *How to Study in College*, 10th ed. (Boston: Cengage Learning, 2011).

3. Tony Buzan, *Use Both Sides of Your Brain* (New York: Dutton, 1991).

4. Gabrielle Rico, *Writing the Natural Way* (New York: Penguin, 2000).

5. Joseph Novak and D. Bob Gowin, *Learning How to Learn* (New York: Cambridge University Press, 1984).

CHAPTER 6

1. Annie Murphy Paul, "Highlighting Is a Waste of Time: The Best and Worst Learning Techniques," *Time*, January 9, 2013, accessed March 6, 2013, from http://ideas.time.com/2013/01/09/highlighting-is-a-waste-of-time-the-best-and-worst-learning-techniques/.

2. Paul, "Highlighting Is a Waste of Time."

3. Joe Cuseo, "Academic-Support Strategies for Promoting Student Retention and Achievement during the First Year of College," University of Ulster Office of Student Transition and Retention, accessed September 4, 2003, from www.ulster.ac.uk/star/resources/acdemic_support_strat_first_years.pdf.

4. Cuseo, "Academic-Support Strategies."

5. Jonathan D. Glater, "Colleges Chase as Cheats Shift to Higher Tech," *New York Times*, May 18, 2006, accessed March 6, 2013, from www.nytimes.com/2006/05/18/education/18cheating.html.

6. Gerardo Ramirez and Sian L. Beilock, "Writing About Testing Worries Boosts Exam Performance in the Classroom," *Science* 331 (January 14, 2011): 211–213.

7. Paul D. Nolting, *Math Study Skills Workbook* (Boston: Cengage Learning, 2012), 57.

8. This article incorporates detailed suggestions from reviewer Frank Baker.

CHAPTER 7

1. Robert Manning, "Hemingway in Cuba," *The Atlantic* 216, no. 2, August 1965, 101–108.

2. Leon Festinger, *A Theory of Cognitive Dissonance* (Palo Alto, CA: Stanford University Press, 1957).

3. L. W. Anderson and D. R. Krathwohl, *A Taxonomy For Learning, Teaching, and Assessing: A Revision Of Bloom's Taxonomy of Educational Objectives* (New York: Addison Wesley Longman, 2001).

4. Candy Chang, "Before I die I want to . . . .," TED Talks, November 2012, accessed March 19, 2013, from www.ted.com/talks/candy_chang_before_i_die_i_want_to.html.

5. Peter M. Gollwitzer, "Implementation Intentions," accessed March 19, 2013, from http://dccps.nci.nih.gov/brp/constructs/implementation_intentions/goal_intent_attain.pdf.

6. Arthur Koestler, *The Act of Creation* (New York: Dell, 1964), 35.

7. Martin E. P. Seligman, *Authentic Happiness: Using the New Positive Psychology to Realize Your Potential for Lasting Fulfillment* (New York: Simon and Schuster, 2002).

8. Quoted in Alice Calaprice, ed., *The Expanded Quotable Einstein* (Princeton, NJ: Princeton University Press, 2000).

9. David K. Reynolds, *A Handbook for Constructive Living* (New York: William Morrow, 1995), 36.

10. Byron Katie, *Loving What Is: Four Questions That Can Change Your Life* (New York: Harmony Books, 2002).

11. Mortimer Adler and Charles Van Doren, *How to Read a Book: The Classic Guide to Intelligent Reading* (New York: Simon and Schuster, 1972), 164–165.

12. Center for Human Resources, *National Evaluation of Learn and Serve America*, July 1999, accessed February 5, 2011, from www.cpn.org/topics/youth/k12/pdfs/Learn_and_Serve1999.pdf.

CHAPTER 8

1. Lawrence M. Brammer and Everett L. Shostrom, *Therapeutic Psychology: Fundamentals of Actualization Counseling and Psychotherapy* (Englewood Cliffs, NJ: Prentice-Hall, 1968), 194–203.

2. Thomas Gordon, *Parent Effectiveness Training: The Tested New Way to Raise Responsible Children* (New York: New American Library, 1975), 114–159.

3. Sidney Jourard, *The Transparent Self* (New York: Van Nostrand, 1971).

4. Marshall Goldsmith, "Try Feedforward Instead of Feedback," 2002, accessed March 19, 2013, from www.marshallgoldsmithlibrary.com/cim/articles_display.php?aid=110.

5. Daniel Goleman, *Emotional Intelligence: Why It Can Matter More Than IQ* (New York: Bantam, 1995), xiv–xv.

6. Stephen Covey, The Seven Habits of Highly Effective People: Power Lessons in Personal Change (New York: Fireside, 1989), 95–144.

7. Quoted in Richard Saul Wurman, Loring Leifer, and David Sume, *Information Anxiety #2* (Indianapolis, IN: QUE, 2001), 116.

8. Peter Elbow, *Writing with Power: Techniques for Mastering the Writing Process* (New York: Oxford University Press, 1981), 13–19.

9. Jakob Nielsen, "How Users Read on the Web," October 1, 1997, accessed March 19, 2013, from www.nngroup.com/articles/how-users-read-on-the-web/.

10. M. T. Motley, *Overcoming Your Fear of Public Speaking: A Proven Method* (New York: Houghton Mifflin, 1998).

CHAPTER 9

1. Family Care Foundation, "If the World Were a Village of 100 People," 2011, accessed March 19, 2013, from www.familycare.org/news/if_the_world.htm.

2. Federal Bureau of Investigation, " Hate Crime Statistics 2011," December 10, 2012, accessed March 19, 2013, from www.fbi.gov/about-us/cjis/ucr/hate-crime/2011/hate-crime.

3. Anti-Defamation League, "Challenges on Campus," 2013, accessed March 19, 2013, from www.adl.org/education-outreach/campus-affairs/c/challenges-on-campus.html.

4. Stephen R. Covey, *The Seven Habits of Highly Effective People: Restoring the Character Ethic* (New York: Simon & Schuster, 1989), 47.

5. Maia Szalavitz, "Race and the Genome," Howzfard University Human Genome Center, March 2, 2001, accessed March 19, 2013, from www.genomecenter.howard.edu/article.htm.

6. Diane de Anda, *Bicultural Socialization: Factors Affecting the Minority Experience* (Washington, DC: National Association of Social Workers, 1984).

7. Office for Civil Rights, *Sexual Harassment: It's Not Academic*, U.S. Department of Education, 2008, accessed March 14, 2011, from www2.ed.gov/about/offices/list/ocr/docs/ocrshpam.html.

8. U.S. Census Bureau, "An Older and More Diverse Nation by Midcentury," August 14, 2008, accessed March 19, 2013, from www.census.gov/newsroom/rejleases/archives/population/cb08-123.html.

CHAPTER 10

1. Tiffany Julian, "Work-Life Earnings by Field of Degree and Occupation for People with a Bachelor's Degree: 2011," U. S. Department of Commerce, October 2012, accessed March 19, 2013, from www.census.gov/prod/2012pubs/acsbr11-04.pdf.

2. "Education Pays," U. S. Department of Labor, January 28, 2013, accessed March 19, 2013, from www.bls.gov/emp/ep_chart_001.htm.

3. Suze Orman, *Suze Orman's 2009 Action Plan: Keeping Your Money Safe & Sound* (New York: Spiegel & Grau, 2009), 125.

4. "Study Finds Rising Number of College Students Using Credit cards for Tuition," Sallie Mae, April 13, 2009, accessed March 15, 2011, from https://www.salliemae.com/about/news_info/newsreleases/.

5. "Paying Down Credit Card Debt," Federal Trade Commission, August 2012, accessed March 19, 2013, from https://www.consumer.ftc.gov/articles/0333-paying-down-credit-card-debt.

6. "Be debt savvy with credit cards," Sallie Mae, accessed March 19, 2013, from https://www.collegeanswer.com/manage-your-money/managing-credit/credit-cards/choosing-a-credit-card-wisely.aspx.

7. "Education Pays 2010," College Board, accessed March 19, 2013, from http://trends.collegeboard.org/education_pays.

CHAPTER 11

1. Centers for Disease Control and Prevention, "Health Habits of Adults Aged 18–29 Highlighted in Report on Nation's Health," February 18, 2009, accessed March 19, 2013, from, www.cdc.gov/media/pressrel/2009/r090218.htm.

2. American College Health Association, "National College Health Assessment: Undergraduate Students—Reference Group Data Report," Spring 2012, accessed March 19, 2013, from www.acha-ncha.org/docs/ACHA-NCHA-II_UNDERGRAD_ReferenceGroup_DataReport_Spring2012.pdf.

3. Kay-Tee Khaw, Nicholas Wareham, Sheila Bingham, Ailsa Welch, Robert Luben, and Nicholas Day, "Combined Impact of Health Behaviours and Mortality in Men and Women: The EPIC-Norfolk Prospective Population Study," *PLoS Medicine* 5, no. 1 (2008), accessed March 19, 2013, from www.plosmedicine.org/article/info:doi/10.1371/journal.pmed.0050012.

4. Michael Pollan, "Unhappy Meals," *New York Times*, January 28, 2007, accessed March 19, 2013, from www.nytimes.com/2007/01/28/magazine/28nutritionism.t.html.

5. Harvard Medical School, "HEALTHbeat: 20 No-Sweat Ways to Get More Exercise," e-mail newsletter from Harvard Health Publications, October 14, 2008.

6. Ken Smith, "Science Scolds Us: 'Don't Just Sit There!'" PBS, March 14, 2013, accessed March 19, 2013, from www.nextavenue.org/article/2012-12/science-scolds-us-dont-just-sit-there.

7. Jane Brody, "Exercise = Weight Loss, Except When It Doesn't," *New York Times*, September 12, 2006, accessed March 19, 2013, from www.nytimes.com/2006/09/12/health/nutrition/12brody.html.

8. Harvard Medical School, "HEALTHbeat Extra: The Secret to Better Health—Exercise," e-mail newsletter from Harvard Health Publications, January 27, 2009.

9. "Stress symptoms: Effects on your body, feelings and behavior," Mayo Clinic, February 19, 2011, accessed March 19, 2013, from www.mayoclinic.com/health/stress-symptoms/SR00008_D.

10. David Reynolds, *A Handbook for Constructive Living* (New York: Morrow, 1995), 98.

11. Albert Bandura, "Self-Efficacy," in V. S. Ramachaudran, ed., *Encyclopedia of Human Behavior*, vol. 4 (New York: Academic Press, 1994), 71–81.

12. M. Schaffer, E.L. Jeglic, and B. Stanley, "The Relationship between Suicidal Behavior, Ideation, and Binge Drinking among College Students," *Archives of Suicide Research* 12 (2008): 124–132.

13. American Foundation for Suicide Prevention, "Risk Factors for Suicide" (2010), accessed March 19, 2013, from www.afsp.org/content/search?SearchText=risk+factors+for+suicide.

14. Minnesota Department of Health, "Sexually Transmitted Disease Facts" (2009), accessed March 19, 2013, from www.health.state.mn.us/divs/idepc/dtopics/stds/stdfactssummary.html#complications.

15. Centers for Disease Control and Prevention, "Trends in Reportable Sexually Transmitted Diseases in the United States, 2007" (2009), accessed March 19, 2013, from www.cdc.gov/nchhstp/newsroom/docs/STDTrendsFactSheet.pdf.

16. Andrew Weil and Winifred Rosen, *From Chocolate to Morphine: Everything You Need to Know About Mind-Altering Drugs* (Boston: Houghton Mifflin, 1993), 45.

17. U.S. Centers for Disease Control and Prevention, "Tobacco-Related Mortality," March 9, 2011, accessed March 19, 2013, from www.cdc.gov/tobacco/data_statistics/fact_sheets/health_effects/tobacco_related_mortality/.

18. "A Snapshot of Annual High-Risk College Drinking Consequences," National Institute on Alcohol Abuse and Alcoholism, July 1, 2010, accessed March 19, 2013, from www.collegedrinkingprevention.gov/StatsSummaries/snapshot.aspx.

19. American Psychological Association, *Diagnostic and Statistical Manual of Psychoactive Substance Abuse Disorders* (Washington, DC: American Psychological Association, 1994).

20. American Cancer Society, "Guide to Quitting Smoking" January 17, 2013, accessed March 19, 2013, from www.cancer.org/healthy/stayawayfromtobacco/guidetoquittingsmoking/.

21. American Cancer Society, "Guide to Quitting Smoking."

CHAPTER 12

1. K. Anders Ericsson, et al., "The Making of an Expert," *Harvard Business Review*, July-August 2007, accessed March 19, 2013, from www.uvm.edu/~pdodds/files/papers/others/everything/ericsson2007a.pdf.

2. Teresa Amabile and Steven Kramer, *The Progress Principle: Using Small Wins to Ignite Joy, Engagement and Creativity* (Boston: Harvard Business Review Press, 2011).

3. Kate Zernike, "College, My Way," *New York Times*, April 23, 2006, accessed March 19, 2013, from www.nytimes.com/2006/04/23/education/edlife/zernike.html.

4. Adapted from Dave Ellis, Stan Lankowitz, Ed Stupka, and Doug Toft, *Career Planning*, 3rd ed. Copyright © 2003 by Houghton Mifflin Company.

5. Ira Progoff, *At a Journal Workshop* (New York: Dialogue House, 1975).

Additional Reading

BOOKS

Allen, David. *Getting Things Done: The Art of Stress-Free Productivity.* New York: Penguin, 2001.

Belsky, Scott. *Making Ideas Happen: Overcoming the Obstacles Between Vision and Reality.* New York: Portfolio, 2010.

Bolles, Richard N. *What Color Is Your Parachute? A Practical Manual for Job-Hunters and Career-Changers.* Berkeley, CA: Ten Speed, updated annually.

Bronson, Po. *What Should I Do with My Life? The True Story of People Who Answered the Ultimate Question.* New York: Random House, 2003.

Colvin, George. *Talent Is Overrated: What Really Separates World-Class Performers from Everybody Else.* New York: Portfolio, 2008.

Coplin, Bill. *10 Things Employers Want You to Learn in College: The Know-How You Need to Succeed.* Berkeley, CA: Ten Speed, 2004.

Covey, Stephen R. *The Seven Habits of Highly Effective People: Powerful Lessons in Personal Change.* New York: Simon & Schuster, 1989.

Cushman, Kathleen. *First in the Family: Advice About College From First-Generation Students.* Providence, RI: Next Generation Press, 2006.

Davis, Deborah. *The Adult Learner's Companion,* 2nd ed. Boston: Cengage, 2012.

Downing, Skip. *On Course: Strategies for Creating Success in College and in Life,* 7th ed. Boston: Cengage, 2014.

Friedman, Thomas. *The World Is Flat 3.0: A Brief History of the Twenty-First Century.* New York: Picador, 2007.

Glie, Jocelyn K. *Manage Your Day-to-Day: Build Your Routine, Find Your Focus, and Sharpen Your Creative Mind.* Amazon Publishing, 2013.

Godin, Seth. *Linchpin: Are You Indispensable?* New York: Portfolio, 2010.

Godin, Seth. *Purple Cow: Transform Your Business by Being Remarkable.* New York: Portfolio, 2009.

Greene, Susan D., and Melanie C. L. Martel. *The Ultimate Job Hunter's Guidebook.* Boston: Cengage, 2012.

Hoffman, Reid and Ben Casnocha. *The Start-up of You: Adapt to the Future, Invest in Yourself, and Transform Your Career.* New York: Crown Business, 2012.

Levy, Frank, and Richard J. Murnane. *The New Division of Labor: How Computers Are Creating the Next Job Market.* Princeton, NJ: Princeton University Press, 2004.

Light, Richard J. *Making the Most of College: Students Speak Their Minds.* Cambridge, MA: Harvard University Press, 2001.

Newport, Cal. *How to Win at College.* New York: Random House, 2005.

Newport, Cal. *So Good They Can't Ignore You: Why Skills Trump Passion in the Quest for Work That You Love.* New York: Business Plus, 2012.

Nolting, Paul D. *Math Study Skills Workbook,* 4th ed. Boston: Cengage, 2012.

Orman, Suze. *2009 Action Plan: Keeping Your Money Safe & Sound.* New York: Spiegel & Grau, 2009.

Peddy, Shirley, Ph.D. *The Art of Mentoring: Lead, Follow and Get Out of the Way.* Houston, TX: Bullion Books, 2001.

Robinson, Adam. *What Smart Students Know: Maximum Grades, Optimum Learning, Minimum Time.* New York: Crown, 1993.

Sethi, Ramit. *I Will Teach You To Be Rich.* New York: Workman, 2009

Toft, Doug, ed. *Master Student Guide to Academic Success.* Boston: Cengage, 2005.

Trapani, Gina. *Lifehacker: 88 Tech Tricks to Turbocharge Your Day.* Indianapolis, IN: Wiley, 2007.

U.S. Department of Education. *Funding Education Beyond High School: The Guide to Federal Student Aid.* Published yearly, http://studentaid.ed.gov/students/publications/student_guide/index.html.

Watkins, Ryan, and Michael Corry. *E-learning Companion: A Student's Guide to Online Success,* Third Edition. Boston: Cengage, 2011.

Wurman, Richard Saul. *Information Anxiety 2.* Indianapolis: QUE, 2001.

WEBSITES

99U
99u.com
Strategies for taking creative projects from planning to completion

Art of Non-Conformity Blog
chrisguillebeau.com
Strategies for personal development, life planning, and becoming an entrepreneur

Brain Pickings
brainpickings.org
Connecting art, philosophy, science, and technology—an Internet-powered engine for cross-disciplinary learning and creative thinking

Brazen Careerist
brazencareerist.com/
Articles, online courses, and other resources for students in higher education and young professionals

GTD Times
gtdtimes.com
A community of people interested in Getting Things Done®, centered on the work of David Allen, author of Getting Things Done: The Art of Stress-Free Productivity

I Will Teach You To Be Rich
iwillteachyoutoberich.com
Guidance from author and speaker Ramit Sethi on job hunting on taking charge of your money and finding your dream job, geared to recent graduates

JobHuntersBible.com
jobhuntersbible.com
A rich set of online resources from Richard Bolles, author of the best-seller What Color Is Your Parachute? A Practical Manual for Job-Hunters and Career-Changers *and* The Job-Hunters' Survival Guide: How to Find Hope and Rewarding Work, Even When "There Are No Jobs"

Lifehacker
lifehacker.com
Tips and tricks for success at school, work and at home, geared to people interested in technology

Open Culture
openculture.com
Links to free ebooks, audiobooks, videos, and courses for lifelong learning

Study Hacks
calnewport.com/blog
Unconventional ideas for succeeding in school and planning your life from Cal Newport, author of How to Win at College *and* So Good They Can't Ignore You: Why Skills Trump Passion in the Quest for Work You Love

Zen Habits
zenhabits.net
Strategies for transforming your life by living simply, slowing down, and making small but significant changes in your daily behaviors

Index